Praise for *Contested*

"Magolda, Baxter Magolda, and Carducci have curated an impressive volume, assembling an impressive collection of leading voices to grapple with how student affairs scholars and practitioners can and should promote growth, learning, and development for all students as they navigate environments marked by various forms of oppression and marginalization. In addition to tackling everything from how to support students managing trauma to student affairs' larger role as an agent of social justice, this text is a primer on how to engage in complex, sometimes contentious, discourse around difficult issues. So much can be learned from how the authors affirm, challenge, and push each other and our field to have the hard conversations necessary to move colleges and universities forward. We don't always agree, and there isn't always a clear-cut 'right' or 'wrong,' but the editors and contributors of this text show us how authentic, thoughtful, critical engagement can lead to action and progress toward real solutions to persistent challenges facing the academy." —*Kimberly A. Griffin*, *Associate Professor, University of Maryland; Editor,* Journal of Diversity in Higher Education

"A cross between professional development resource and inspirational essays, *Contested Issues in Troubled Times* artfully draws readers into a series of carefully crafted conversations about contentious issues in higher education, invites personal reflection, and then encourages courageous action. This book promises to help student affairs educators channel their potential to put professional philosophy, commitments, research, and competencies to work to become agents for cultivating and sustaining inclusive learning environments." —*Jillian Kinzie*, *Assistant Director, Center for Postsecondary Research, Indiana University Bloomington*

"In this new companion to the original *Contested Issues*, a new generation of scholars challenges the usefulness and authenticity of many of the habits that we have lazily and superficially adopted. They rightly question best practices and position the profession of student affairs to focus on changing systems and structures to increase equity for marginalized students." —*Anna Ortiz*, *Professor of Educational Leadership, Long Beach State University*

"Just as the original, *Contested Issues in Student Affairs,* this companion volume, *Contested Issues in Troubled Times*, will become a go-to book for student affairs graduate courses and professional development opportunities on campus. Magolda, Baxter Magolda, and Carducci have assembled a timely book that engages the most difficult and important issues facing student affairs professionals today—and likely into the future. The array of contributors—representing faculty members and professional staff at all stages of careers—lends to the usefulness of this volume through the presentation of diverse and challenging perspectives." —*Robert D. Reason*, *Professor, Student Affairs and Higher Education, Iowa State University*

"*Contested Issues in Troubled Times* invites readers to engage some of the most perplexing issues confronting college and university educators in the twenty-first century. As the essayists wrestle with provocative questions that defy simplistic solutions, they model productive dialogue and offer a rich constellation of perspectives for the reader to consider. *Contested Issues* urges those of us invested in the student affairs profession to think beyond traditional field assumptions and strategies as we construct novel and nuanced practices that will help us move from troubled times toward a promising future." —*Alyssa Rockenbach*, *Professor of Higher Education, North Carolina State University*

"*Contested Issues in Troubled Times* offers fresh perspectives on the role of student affairs educators and practitioners in engaging in the difficult but crucial work of promoting inclusive environments on college campuses. Importantly, it does so in a way that does not hide—and indeed celebrates—the diversity of viewpoints shared among colleagues. This book will undoubtedly serve as a valuable springboard for rich discussions in the classroom and in the student affairs profession." —*Linda J. Sax*, *Professor of Higher Education and Organizational Change; Graduate School of Education & Information Studies; University of California, Los Angeles*

"In an era where overt oppression, righteous indignation, and name-calling are on the rise, an important skill for student affairs educators to practice is engaging about difficult issues productively. The contributors of this book model this kind of dialogue in thoughtful ways. Stemming from their previous innovative *Contested Issues in Student Affairs* volume, this companion book by Peter M. Magolda, Marcia B. Baxter Magolda, and Rozana Carducci adds a unique perspective on the important goal of building coalitions across differences." —*Stephen John Quaye*, *Past President, ACPA–College Student Educators International; Associate Professor, Miami University*

CONTESTED ISSUES IN TROUBLED TIMES

CONTESTED ISSUES IN TROUBLED TIMES

Student Affairs Dialogues on Equity, Civility, and Safety

Edited by

PETER M. MAGOLDA,
MARCIA B. BAXTER MAGOLDA,
and
ROZANA CARDUCCI

Foreword by
LORI D. PATTON

STERLING, VIRGINIA

Published by Stylus Publishing, LLC.
22883 Quicksilver Drive
Sterling, Virginia 20166-2019

Library of Congress Cataloging-in-Publication Data
Names: Magolda, Peter Mark, editor. | Baxter Magolda, Marcia B.,
    1956-editor. | Carducci, Rozana, editor.
Title: Contested issues in troubled times : student affairs dialogues on
    equity, civility, and safety / [edited by] Peter M. Magolda, Marcia Baxter
    Magolda, & Rozana Carducci.
Description: First edition. | Sterling, Virginia : Stylus Publishing, [2019] |
    Includes bibliographic references.
Identifiers: LCCN 2018031035 (print) | LCCN 2019002475 (ebook)
    | ISBN 9781620368022 (Library networkable e-edition) | ISBN
    9781620368039 (Consumer e-edition) | ISBN 9781620368008
    (cloth : alk. paper) | ISBN 9781620368015 (pbk. : alk. paper) | ISBN
    9781620368022 (library networkable ebk.) | ISBN 9781620368039
    (ebk.)
Subjects: LCSH: Student affairs services--United States. | Educational
    equalization--United States. | Minorities--Education (Higher)--United
    States.
Classification: LCC LB2342.92 (ebook) | LCC LB2342.92 .C674 2019
    (print) | DDC 378.1/97--dc23
LC record available at https://lccn.loc.gov/2018031035

13-digit ISBN: 978-1-62036-800-8 (cloth)
13-digit ISBN: 978-1-62036-801-5 (paperback)
13-digit ISBN: 978-1-62036-802-2 (library networkable e-edition)
13-digit ISBN: 978-1-62036-803-9 (consumer e-edition)

Printed in the United States of America

All first editions printed on acid-free paper
that meets the American National Standards Institute
Z39-48 Standard.

Bulk Purchases
Quantity discounts are available for use in workshops and
for staff development.
Call 1-800-232-0223

First Edition, 2019

Dedicated in memory of Marjorie A. Baxter, who was always open to a new perspective, and Bernardo Carducci, a wonderful dad who welcomed opportunities to dialogue across difference.

Peter M. Magolda was the driving force behind this volume as well as the prior companion volume titled Contested Issues in Student Affairs: Diverse Perspectives and Respectful Dialogue. *His love of cultural anthropology guided his interest in the complexity and nuances of multiple perspectives, particularly those less visible or audible. As an educator, he constantly asked students to entertain the questions "Whose interests are being served?" and "Whose interests are being overlooked?" Those questions stood at the base of his scholarship, which aimed to illuminate the inner workings of subcultures, rituals, ethnographic research, and higher education practices. He gravitated toward contested issues in student affairs and beyond, constantly pursuing a deeper understanding of those whose experiences and perspectives differed from his. This volume reflects Peter's commitment to emphasize contested issues in student affairs and higher education, to bring diverse perspectives from multiple professionals into dialogue, to learn from others, and to model for educators how to productively engage difficult dialogues. We hope this commitment is realized through readers' use of this volume to constructively explore the complex issues we face.*

CONTENTS

PART TWO
Cultivating Inclusive Learning Environments: Equity, Civility, and Safety

PART THREE
Cultivating Professional Capacities to Foster Inclusive Learning Environments

PART FOUR
Epilogue

FOREWORD

I love the field of student affairs, yet it has not always loved me back.
As a highly involved undergraduate, one would think my pathway into student affairs was certain. However, like many colleagues, I did not know student affairs was a field during my college days. I didn't learn otherwise until I was working full-time outside higher education. How is it that a highly involved, Black, undergraduate woman like me fell through the cracks initially? I was an honors student; a senator and director of public relations for student government on separate occasions; and a member and vice president of Delta Sigma Theta Sorority, Inc., which had consistently been recognized as organization of the year with a strong reputation for service both on and off campus. I knew many of the student life staff on a first-name basis, lived on campus, and was even voted homecoming queen. My undergraduate résumé read like the quintessential future student affairs professional. Yet, I graduated with no clue about the field I would pursue first as a graduate student at Bowling Green State University and later at Indiana University.

While a seeming surprise, the fact that I wasn't "tapped" for the field isn't necessarily earthshattering. I don't blame any person or entity. Sh*t happens. However, it is my opinion that this particular type of sh*t reflects the daily operation of college campuses and our field. I am fully aware that campus inequities fueled at the nexus of racism, sexism, capitalism, and hetero cispatriarchy regularly work in sync and in such a way to normalize the invisibility I, and others like me, experience. Such invisibility is wholly possible even in a field like student affairs, one that prides itself on acknowledging and addressing equity, diversity, and inclusion on college campuses and within the profession itself.

Ladson-Billings aptly referenced education as a "nice" field.[1] As someone who spent the greater portion of my career in student affairs, I have often borrowed this language to argue that student affairs, as a subfield, is particularly nice. Student affairs educators value holistic student development and consistently work to create educational environments that promote student well-being and success. The values we espouse are important and continue to guide the field, but only to the extent that we avoid unpacking uncomfortable questions. When we discuss *student development*, what do we really mean and whose interests are served? Whose well-being is centered in our work and at whose expense? What does *success* really mean and are some students able to access these definitions more readily than others? How do our responses to these questions shift when we use critical lenses that excavate power relations, reveal White supremacist structures, and name realities that might otherwise be left in the margins?

Contested Issues in Troubled Times: Student Affairs Dialogues on Equity, Civility, and Safety is a resource that has the capacity to bridge the gap between who we say we are as student affairs educators, who we actually are, and who we hope to become. The contributors effectively grapple with issues plaguing our campuses and influencing our roles as professionals. The questions to which contributors respond not only raise awareness of critical and contested issues but also prompt readers to do the difficult work of considering how the field both fuels and works to disrupt them.

Contested Issues in Troubled Times forces us to directly reckon with the ideas of equity, civility, and safety. In essence, the book prompts us to consider notions of equity as we work in campus environments dripping with inequities in nearly every functional area comprising the field. Civility also requires us to consider how those fighting for justice on campus are often situated as the problem, rather than raisers of consciousness to whom we should be attuned. Safety, the most vital need of our students, is under attack and perhaps an unrealistic expectation, particularly for those living through multiple forms of vulnerability.

These observations and many more salient considerations should be central to our positionalities as student affairs educators. I am thrilled about the potential of *Contested Issues in Troubled Times* to introduce and promote critical dialogue about who we are and what we should be doing in service to students. Although dialogue is an important step, I also see the promise of *Contested Issues in Troubled Times* in igniting action in a way that requires us to put ourselves on the line rather than allowing students to make sacrifices while we take the credit. I also hope the book pushes us beyond simply being "nice" toward acting as accomplices and advocates who genuinely fight for institutional change. Perhaps most important, I look forward to *Contested Issues in Troubled Times* inspiring readers to approach their work with critical love that is concerned with not only catching those who fall through the cracks but also concerted efforts to repair the cracks and remove the circumstances that cause the cracks; critical love that is centered on humanity and loving communities that have consistently been treated as disposable; and critical love rooted in solidarity and action to ensure that equity, civility, and safety become a reality in higher education, rather than ideals to which we simply aspire.

Lori D. Patton
Professor
Indiana University

Note

1. Ladson-Billings, G. (1998). Just what is critical race theory and what's it doing in a nice field like education? *International Journal of Qualitative Studies in Education, 11(1),* 7–24.

PREFACE

Peter M. Magolda, Marcia B. Baxter Magolda,
and Rozana Carducci

ow do graduate preparation program faculty prepare future student affairs educators to address the complexities of higher education? What kinds of continuing education opportunities do divisions of student affairs offer in the interest of optimizing student learning and staff success? In 2011 we contributed as coeditors and/or authors to *Contested Issues in Student Affairs: Diverse Perspectives and Respectful Dialogue,* a collection of essays by faculty, administrators, and graduate students that offered diverse responses to these complex professional questions. The contested issues examined in the original book are as relevant today as they were in 2011. Student affairs practice continues to be complicated by competing values, structural inequalities, and polarizing discourses. With the aim of continuing to foster productive dialogue on complex issues framing the work of student affairs educators, we offer this companion book, *Contested Issues in Troubled Times: Student Affairs Dialogues on Equity, Civility, and Safety.* In this new volume, we invited a new set of contributors to explore new questions which foreground issues of equity, civility, and safety—themes dominating higher education headlines and campus conversations.

The overarching question that *Contested Issues in Troubled Times* attempts to answer is: How can student affairs educators create an equitable climate conducive to learning in a dynamic environment fraught with complexity and a sociopolitical context characterized by escalating intolerance, incivility, and overt discrimination? The book includes 24 contemporary, critical, and contentious questions (e.g., How do student affairs educators navigate the tension between the First Amendment right to free speech and the expression of ideas that create a hostile campus climate?). Primary and response essayists in each chapter introduce diverse ideological and political conceptualizations of these 24 questions. Writing in the style of op-ed commentaries, authors are not seeking to offer readers absolute truths and definitive solutions to these persistent and messy issues. Rather, contributors are role modeling productive dialogue across differences, illustrating the possibilities and promise of acknowledging multiple approaches to addressing contentious issues, articulating a persuasive argument anchored in professional judgment, listening attentively to others for points of connection as well as divergence, and drawing on new ways of thinking to foster safe and inclusive campuses. In the interest of extending the dialogue beyond the pages of the text, readers are invited to contemplate and share their reactions to the essays by posting comments on book-sponsored social media venues.

Political Contexts Shaping Dialogues Across Difference

The need to address inequities and facilitate learning-centered civil discourse to ensure safe campuses has never been greater. In 2018, Giridharadas[1] noted threats to this goal:

> In a moment when America faces great big questions about who we are and what we wish to become, we are turning into a society so perpetually offended by one another that we are less and less capable of actually arguing about our future. And citizens who cannot argue are begging to be ruled.

These troubling dynamics are unmistakably present in American higher education. Quests to ameliorate inequities and injustices in the academy (e.g., victimization of transgender and gender-nonconforming students) have spawned multiple and competing visions for higher education. Often we base these visions on our life experiences, which influence what we see, how we interpret, and how we act. Subsequent contentious and polarizing rhetoric often "offends" rather than educates the other, which is a threat to democracy—a bedrock foundation of American higher education.

Few opportunities on campuses exist for individuals to pose and thoughtfully listen to and critique others' arguments about politically charged issues such as institutional racism, sexual assault, White privilege, gender discrimination, guns on campus, and freedom of speech, decreasing the probability of collaborative problem-solving and establishing equitable and safe campuses. Our goal is to explicitly discuss issues of *equity, civility,* and *safety* in the interest of opening up, rather than shutting down conversations. As the contributors to this volume have done, we encourage student affairs educators to engage in civil dialogue across difference with the intention of changing conditions that perpetuate discrimination within and beyond college campuses and creating inclusive campus climates conducive to learning.

Several contributors raise questions and share diverse interpretations of *civility* (particularly from the perspective of those groups that have been historically marginalized). For some, calls for civility are coded demands that oppressed individuals and groups remain silent or express their outrage respectfully when confronting those in power who unconsciously or knowingly perpetuate discrimination and create dangerous communities.[2] Protest cannot and should not always be quiet; there are times when demands for change must be bold and loud to call attention to injustice and imagine a new reality. However, within the context of higher education institutions broadly and the student affairs profession specifically, conversations centered on the complex and controversial issues of equity and safety could benefit from greater civility. The vision of civility[3] that frames this book encourages deep and meaningful dialogue about differences. Rather than ending tough conversations by acknowledging trivial points of agreement and/or politely "agreeing to disagree," our vision of civility demands that individuals must engage in the "hard work of staying present even with those with whom they have deep-rooted and fierce disagreements."[4] Contributors to *Contested Issues in Troubled Times* role model the promise and practice of engaging in civil dialogues across difference, articulating diverse approaches to addressing 24 contested issues in student affairs. On some points the authors agree, highlighting points of convergence and shared reasoning. On other matters, contributors respectfully disagree, drawing upon different identities, values and principles, professional knowledge, and/or evidence to support their arguments. Sometimes the differences of perspective are moderate; in other cases, the contrasts are starker. In all cases, however, the dialogues are civil, respectfully engaging with the ideas of those with whom they are in community.

When framing our vision of respectful dialogue across difference, we also felt it was important to acknowledge that civility is a political act, necessitating that individuals negotiate interpersonal and institutional power while "claiming and caring for one's identity, needs, and beliefs without degrading someone else's in the process."[5] Accordingly, choosing to engage in authentic dialogue about differences requires participants to take risks that can have real consequences for one's well-being and professional success. To help readers understand and negotiate the political dimensions of participating in efforts to discuss and address contested issues of equity, civility, and safety, contributors to this volume share their personal stories of and/or strategies for navigating the politics of this work. We thank them for their candor and productive insight.

As noted earlier, although the premise for this book is similar to *Contested Issues in Student Affairs* (i.e., the student affairs profession and institutions of higher education benefit from meaningful dialogue on complex issues that shape the learning environment), contributors to this volume were asked to consider 24 new contentious questions framing the work of contemporary student affairs educators. New tensions and challenges have gained prominence in the last eight years, capturing the attention of students, campus administrators, and the media. While free speech controversies and student demands for racial justice and gender inclusive campuses are not new, the political context within which student affairs professionals practice has shifted dramatically in recent years. The emergence of the #BlackLivesMatter and #MeToo movements, the adoption and subsequent repeal of the Deferred Action for Childhood Arrivals (DACA) immigration policy, legislative mandates regarding campus carry and transgender rights, and physical clashes over the presence of White supremacist speakers on campus have altered the higher education landscape and placed student affairs educators at the center of many contentious campus conversations. *Contested Issues in Troubled Times* is situated within these turbulent times and perpetually shifting political contexts. The 24 questions posed in this book are far from settled, with new campus policy, legislative actions, and legal precedent established daily. Indeed, since the inception of this book project in May 2017, DACA has undergone a series of legal challenges, leaving both students and student affairs professionals in limbo. Although we cannot know what the future holds for DACA recipients, the contested question of how campuses should support undocumented students in an era of political uncertainty and open hostility is a prime example of the need for student affairs educators to cultivate the capacity to engage in tough conversations characterized by diverse ideological principles and priorities.

Book Format

The 24 contested questions featured in this book are organized into 4 parts. Part One serves as the introduction. In this preface we establish the context for the book's purpose and the climate in which it evolved. The essays in Part One set the stage for the volume by exploring the challenges inherent in fostering equitable learning environments in student affairs and the complexity of dialoging across difference. Part Two: Cultivating Inclusive Learning Environments: Equity, Civility, and Safety, raises questions and tensions in multiple arenas that affect learning environments. These essays include campus racial climate, social class, political activism, the definition of *student success*, and the tension between free speech and creating hostile environments. They also address the role of campus sexual violence and trauma in student learning. Multiple essays address creating equitable learning environments for students with marginalized identities; given the current political climate, specific attention is focused on students from historically underrepresented racial and ethnic groups, transgender students, and undocumented students. Considering the current sociopolitical climate, the last essay addresses tensions among legislative action, institutional roles, and public policy advocacy. How can or should student affairs educators respond when legislative mandates conflict with personal values? Part Three: Cultivating Professional Capacities to Foster Inclusive Learning Environments shifts focus. In this section, contributors reflect on the professional skills, knowledge, and/or dispositions needed to thrive and facilitate systemic change in contemporary higher education organizations. This section includes multiple essays that examine diverse professional development contexts, including graduate preparation programs and professional organization engagement. What are the possibilities for addressing racism in student affairs graduate preparation classrooms? What support is needed to help graduate students navigate the tensions inherent in their dual roles as students and professional staff? What types of professional development opportunities are essential for cultivating the capacity to make good decisions when faced with the unknown? These are questions nearly all student affairs educators will confront at one point or another in their careers, and these essays provide a foundation for productive dialogue across different perspectives. Additional essays explore research, assessment, and the conceptualization of a personal learning design approach in developing professional capacities to foster equitable learning environments. Essays also address managing personal and professional identities via social media and the nature of self-care for professionals in complex work settings. The essays in Part Three illustrate the political nature of student affairs work and offer insights on navigating these tensions with integrity. Part Four: Epilogue, examines the promise and potential for student affairs educators to create equitable learning environments. In this final chapter, the essayists issue calls to action, encouraging student affairs educators to exhibit the moral courage needed to critically examine routine practices that (un)knowingly perpetuate inequity and enact the foundational values and principles upon which the student affairs profession was founded.

Structurally, each chapter begins with a question posed in the title and includes 2 essays: a 4,000-word primary essay written by authors selected for their expertise that offers an in-depth examination of the focal question and a 2,000-word response essay written by another student affairs educator with expertise in the topic. The primary essays situate the focal issues historically in the professional literature, present background information and context, define key terms, summarize the diverse ideological and theoretical approaches to responding to the question, make explicit the author's perspectives about the question, and discuss political implications. The shorter response essays critique the primary essays, note areas of agreement, introduce and discuss relevant issues not addressed in the primary essay, make explicit the author's perspectives about the question, and discuss the political dimensions of the central argument. Each essay concludes with discussion questions that guide readers in further considering the issue at hand. The questions may be used to spark individual reflection or provide a framework for group dialogue.

The book's focal themes and structure are intended to initiate a sustained conversation within the student affairs profession that allows educators to converse with each other about contentious issues respectfully regardless of ideology. We intentionally focus on difficult dialogues across difference with an emphasis on talking with, not at, one another. This dialogic process is modeled in the coupling of primary and response essays. As noted, individuals were invited to contribute to this volume based on their professional expertise. We attempted to identify authors who would bring unique and informed perspectives to the focal questions.

Although the book aims to role model the process of engaging in conversation with those we disagree, we did not intentionally recruit authors with diametrically opposed views on the selected topics. For example, when choosing authors for Chapter 10, "What Role Should Student Affairs Educators Play in Supporting Undocumented Students in the Current Political Climate?" we did not seek a student affairs professional who opposes institutional support for undocumented students. Rather, we attempted to select student affairs educators who were knowledgeable about the topic of undocumented college students but would likely approach the complex issue from different perspectives, offering diverse interpretations of key considerations and possible actions.

Readers of this book will certainly encounter situations in which they must navigate fierce disagreements in fundamental values and principles; however, it is more common for student affairs educators to enter into dialogue with colleagues who share commitments to broad professional goals (e.g., creating safe campuses) but differ with respect to preferred approaches for achieving shared aims (e.g., programming, policy, advocacy). The goal of this book is not to help student affairs educators hold their own in bombastic ideological and policy arguments like those that dominate 24-hour cable news networks.

The book models dialogue (instead of debate) in order to illustrate for educators the kind of learning partnerships[6] that promote complex thinking about difficult issues. Respecting one another's thoughts and perspectives and sharing authority to make sense of complex issues is essential to address the contentious issues contained in these pages. We include essays in the introduction that specifically detail dialogic processes.

Finally, it is also important to note that we intentionally selected contributors from a range of professional roles, including graduate students and early career professionals, midlevel and senior administrators, graduate preparation faculty, and staff of national professional development and nonprofit organizations. In addition to professional roles, we also attended to representation of diverse social identities (e.g., race and ethnicity, gender identity) and institutional type (e.g., community college, small liberal arts institutions). While we recognize that attempts to include diverse perspectives will inevitably fall short on one or more dimensions, contributors to this volume represent an impressive range of personal and professional wisdom and we are confident readers will find their insights to be thought-provoking.

Using This Book as a Guide for Professional Development

Contested Issues in Troubled Times was developed with multiple audiences in mind: graduate students and faculty in student affairs professional preparation programs, new professionals and their midcareer supervisors, senior student affairs officers, and the staff of national student affairs organizations. Although these groups represent diverse institutional roles and contexts, they share a commitment to cultivating the student affairs profession's capacity for establishing civil, equitable, and safe higher education institutions. As mentioned previously, our hope is that this book serves as both a call to action and resource for engaging in dialogues across difference that lead to systemic change. For this aim to be realized, readers must not only wrestle with the 24 contentious questions featured in this book but also practice the dialogic process that serves as the book's central premise and structural framework. In the following sections we offer suggestions for using the book to guide individual and collective professional development efforts, including both face-to-face and virtual learning opportunities.

Engaging in Virtual Dialogues

The book's social media companion resources (see "Find Us Online," p. xxxi) offer opportunities for readers to exchange perspectives with educators around the world. We encourage individuals to read and discuss individual essays, which transcend most functional areas, in staff development meetings and discussions and post their perspectives in this book's blog.

We encourage readers to post comments to the accompanying social media sites commenting on and critiquing the essays and responses. Too often dialogue is limited to people in close geographic proximity. The social media sites provide unique and multiple opportunities to engage in dialogue with professionals in multiple preparation programs, multiple student affairs divisions at diverse institutions, and contexts around the world. It encourages dialogue across disciplines; functional roles; and moral, political, and ideological perspectives. These sites invite professionals, who share an interest in a particular contested issue, to join a sustained conversation about how to navigate the complexities of those issues in various contexts. These online forums also provide emerging and veteran educators with opportunities to share information about their professional career paths.

Graduate Preparation Programs

As was the case with the original volume, *Contested Issues in Student Affairs*, faculty and graduate students in student affairs professional preparation programs will likely find *Contested Issues in Troubled Times* a valuable resource given the nature and scope of questions examined across the 24 chapters. Faculty members teaching a diverse array of courses (e.g., foundations; capstone; research and assessment; practica; seminars that address diversity, equity, and marginalization) may find the book useful with respect to introducing professional themes that transcend functional areas (e.g., public policy, student success, racial justice). Beyond assigning the text as required reading, course assignments designed to foster individual and collective reflection can be framed around the discussion questions posed at the end of each chapter. In addition to individual journaling and/or virtual discussions on course discussion boards, faculty may want to consider inviting students to engage in dialogue with student affairs educators beyond their local contexts via the book's virtual resources or other social media platforms. Additionally, graduate students may be challenged to identify contentious questions not discussed in the book and asked to address these issues via essays and/or presentations that enact the dialogic processes illustrated throughout *Contested Issues in Troubled Times*.

For faculty, the book may also hold value beyond engagement within graduate preparation classrooms. Several chapters speak directly to faculty, challenging them to reconsider conventional approaches to graduate education and higher education research. For example, the essayists in chapter 18 engage in dialogue about addressing discrimination and bias in the graduate classroom. In chapter 19, the essayists wrestle with the question: What is the value of student affairs research as it relates to issues of equity, civility, and safety? In the interest of critically examining and disrupting taken-for-granted assumptions and practices that perpetuate inequitable and unsafe learning environments, why not suspend the typical monthly faculty meeting agenda and instead participate in an authentic dialogue with colleagues framed by a shared reading of one or more of this book's chapters? Graduate preparation faculty may also find the book's framework and content a useful guide for initiating productive dialogues with campus partners (e.g., assistantship/practicum supervisors) who play a critical role in professional preparation yet may approach this work with different values, priorities, and expectations.

Similarly, graduate students wrestling with specific challenges in their assistantship or practica settings (e.g., supporting students who have experienced trauma) as well as those navigating broader professional dilemmas (e.g., balancing their dual roles as graduate students and professional staff) will benefit from individual reflection and collective dialogue on the contested issues examined in this book. In addition to campus-based peer reading groups or conversations with supervisors framed by the discussion questions of a specific chapter, graduate students may benefit from engaging with the book's social media resources and participating in a virtual dialogue with others who are grappling with similar questions.

Supervision and Professional Development

The dialogic principles and processes as well as specific contentious questions featured in *Contested Issues in Troubled Times* may also serve as a valuable framework for supervision conversations and professional development programming. For example, graduate students/new professionals and their supervisors may find it useful to regularly set aside time during one-on-one meetings to discuss the complex issues examined in the book (e.g., best practices for supporting transgender students, equitable approaches to assessment, integrating personal and professional identities in digital spaces). Framing these conversations as dialogues across difference and utilizing the chapter discussion questions to structure the conversations will facilitate the establishment of learning partnerships in which all participants contribute and benefit.

Student affairs educators charged with designing and facilitating professional development programming at the unit, division, or national association level may also find *Contested Issues in Troubled Times* a useful framework and resource. In addition to the facilitation of in-person and virtual reading groups that focus on one or more of the book's chapters, the book's content provides curricula for a diverse array of professional development initiatives, including workshops, panel discussions, webinars, conference sessions, and so on. For example, a divisional professional development committee could design a monthly professional development series framed by *Contested Issues in Troubled Times*. In the first session, participants could be introduced to the principles and practice of dialogues across difference (chapter 2). Subsequent monthly sessions could focus on one of the featured questions (e.g., ethical approaches to public policy advocacy, self-care in turbulent times, the influence of social class on student learning), providing participants with a chance to enact the principles of meaningful dialogue, identifying points of consensus and disagreement with a focus on deepening their collective understanding and enhancing their capacity to foster equitable, civil, and safe campus communities. Near the end of the series, participants could be organized into teams, tasked with identifying contentious issues most salient to their own campus and developing plans for initiating campus dialogues across diverse stakeholders. A professional development series such as this would not only expand the participants' commitment to engaging in meaningful dialogue across difference but also likely facilitate organizational transformation.

Finally, many of the contested issues examined in *Contested Issues in Troubled Times* closely align with *American College Personnel Association (ACPA)/NASPA Professional Competency Areas for Student Affairs Educators*,[7] including: social justice and inclusion, student learning and development, technology, and personal and ethical foundations. Student affairs educators seeking to advance their professional competence could use the competency rubrics[8] to identify professional learning outcomes of interest and then select relevant chapters from *Contested Issues in Troubled Times* to serve as the foundation of their professional development curricula. For example, a student affairs educator seeking to develop their technology digital identity and citizenship competence (specifically achievement of the intermediate outcome, "proactively cultivate a digital identity presence and reputation that models appropriate online behavior and constructive engagement with others in virtual communities"[9]) could draw on the essays and resources featured in chapter 22 as the foundation for a personalized professional development plan. In addition to reflecting on discussion questions posed at the end of the chapter, the professional might also outline goals for discussing this topic with their supervisor, engaging in virtual dialogue with others exploring this issue on the book's social media platforms, and participating in relevant professional development opportunities sponsored by regional and national professional associations (e.g., webinars or conference sessions sponsored by the NASPA Technology Knowledge Community).

Although we developed this book with multiple target audiences in mind and hope readers will find this volume a valuable professional development resource, ultimately its potential to serve as a guide for individual as well as organizational reflection, action, and transformation is a function of the reader's willingness to engage in the messy, uncomfortable, and risky work of dialogue across difference. Collaborating with peers near and far to enact the professional development strategies described in this section will likely increase both one's comfort and skill in facilitating conversations on contested issues within the student affairs profession.

Conclusion

The book's overarching goal is for readers to consider the following questions: What is your level of understanding of these moral, ideological, and political issues that student affairs educators regularly encounter? What is your personal responsibility in addressing these issues? What are the rationales behind your decisions? What are the theoretical options you might choose and why? How do your responses compare with those of colleagues?

While the book is situated in a particular moment in history, processes of civil dialogue transcend this particular moment; readers can draw upon the dialogic lessons of the book to address contested issues not featured in this volume. Because higher education is about learning, it is important that difficult dialogues about contested issues be framed not in terms of the abstract ideals but in terms of the concrete goal of creating a challenging and enriching educational experience for the entire campus community. We suspect some of these issues and arguments advanced in this text will make readers uncomfortable. Our hope is that readers will individually and collectively work through the discomfort and engage in actions focused on fostering safe, equitable, and civil learning environments.

Editors' Note

Many contributors use the pronouns they/their/them when referring to an individual to reflect multiple identities. We retain authors' varied usages to honor author preferences.

Notes

1. Giridharadas, A. (2018). What woke America and great America can learn from each other. *Huffpost.* Retrieved from https://www.huffingtonpost.com/entry/opinion-giridharadas-outrage-america_us_5aaa93b6e4b073bd82929695

2. Smith, N. (2017). When civility really means silence. *Huffpost.* Retrieved from https://www.huffingtonpost.com/nadine-smith/when-civility-really-mean_b_9632602.html

3. What is civility. (2018). *Institute for Civility in Government.* Retrieved from https://www.instituteforcivility.org/who-we-are/what-is-civility/

4. Ibid., para. 1.

5. Spath, T., & Dahnke, C. (2018). *Institute for Civility in Government.* Retrieved from https://www.instituteforcivility.org/who-we-are/what-is-civility/

6. Baxter Magolda, M. B. (2004). Learning partnerships model: A framework for promoting self-authorship. In M. B. Baxter Magolda and P. King, Eds., *Learning partnerships: Theory and models of practice to educate for self-authorship* (pp. 37–62). Sterling, VA: Stylus.

7. ACPA & NASPA. (2015). *Professional competency areas for student affairs educators.* Washington DC: Authors. Retrieved from https://www.naspa.org/images/uploads/main/ACPA_NASPA_Professional_Competencies_FINAL.pdf

8. ACPA & NASPA. (2016). *ACPA & NASPA professional competencies rubrics.* Washington DC: Authors. Retrieved from https://www.naspa.org/images/uploads/main/ACPA_NASPA_Professional_Competency_Rubrics_Full.pdf

9. Ibid., p. 33.

ACKNOWLEDGMENTS

We have been fortunate to live and work in higher education communities as undergraduates, graduate students, student affairs educators, and faculty members. We have encountered a seemingly endless number of contested issues in these communities and are thankful for the students, practitioners, policymakers, researchers, supervisors, mentors, and friends who have offered us keen insights about how to think differently and more complexly about these matters. We are forever grateful for the learning environments that modeled respectful dialogue among diverse perspectives and the opportunities to continue to question existing practice.

In 2011, Stylus Publishing published *Contested Issues in Student Affairs: Diverse Perspectives and Respectful Dialogue,* a collection of essays about complex questions in higher education and student affairs. Our goal as coeditors and contributors was to illuminate multiple perspectives on these issues and foster respectful dialogue among readers. More than 50 higher education professionals contributed to the book, providing us with new insights and modeling productive dialogue. We continue to learn from conversations with those who have read the book as well as from contributions to the *Contested Issues* blog (https://contestedissues.wordpress.com). Although none of the original contested issues could be or have been resolved, we continue to learn in community with those who explore them. Our appreciation of these insights coupled with a desire to explore a new set of complex and compelling questions prompted us to coedit *Contested Issues in Troubled Times: Student Affairs Dialogues on Equity, Civility, and Safety.*

In this book, we again invited more than 50 colleagues—many of whom have profoundly influenced higher education and us—to share insights about a series of critical issues facing the academy in general and student affairs in particular. We selected an entirely new slate of issues and contributors to further extend dialogues. Contributors include graduate students, a university president, chief student affairs officers, academic affairs professionals, numerous new and midcareer professionals, faculty, and independent consultants. These educators have worked in public and private higher education—both large and small institutions, including traditional four-year degree granting colleges as well as community colleges. Although their areas of expertise are too numerous to mention, suffice to say they are sufficiently sensible and modest to recognize that there are no simple solutions to these complex problems and that their "solutions" are thought-provoking, helpful, and imperfect. We sincerely appreciate the contributors' honesty and willingness to act as public intellectuals and submit their ideas for public consumption and scrutiny, for the betterment of higher education.

We are grateful to Nick Rathbone who conceptualized and is implementing the social media plan that augments this book. We met Nick through a Skype call with a graduate class in which he was enrolled. His expertise in social media has been invaluable in finding new ways to extend dialogues into broader contexts.

John von Knorring, the president of Stylus, encouraged us to develop this new book and has been highly supportive of creating meaningful dialogues through the online components of this book. He acted as a constant, creative, and candid counsel, offering superb suggestions for the book and website content and organization. We especially appreciate John's commitment to publishing an affordable book that prioritizes the needs of readers.

All these individuals' labors have helped us immensely and have enhanced the quality both of this book and of our lives. For this we are thankful.

COMPANION SOCIAL MEDIA OPPORTUNITIES

Nick Rathbone

Readers are invited to share their reflections on the chapters and interact with colleagues beyond campus through participation in the book's online, moderated Wordpress blog.

You can find links to all of our online communities here. We look forward to sharing news and starting conversations with you!

Find Us Online

Facebook:
/ContestedIssues

Twitter:
@ContestedIssues

LinkedIn:
Contested Issues in Student Affairs
bit.ly/CITTLI

WordPress Blog:
Contested Issues in Troubled Times
bit.ly/CITTblog

Use the #ContestedIssues and #TroubledTimes hashtags to find others discussing contested issues online!

PART ONE

Introduction

1

Why Is It So Hard for the Student Affairs Profession to Foster Inclusive Environments for Learning?

Bonding and Bridging for Community and Democracy

Penny Rue

Colleges and universities have been engaged in questioning and shaping society for generations. Social progress is developed, studied, and ignited on college campuses. And while there are numerous sectors across the higher education landscape, with widely differing scopes, missions, and constituents, they share the aspiration to make the world a better place.

The role of fostering inclusion within higher education has historically fallen to student affairs professionals, viewed less as an intellectual task and more as personal adjustment. In the 1960s, efforts toward inclusion focused on access to higher education by non-Whites, and these efforts led us to focus on the quality of the experience of inclusion in subsequent decades. Offices with a mission to support students from diverse backgrounds emerged in leading edge institutions in the 1960s and are still being formed today. As I began my professional career in 1977, diversity training focused on individual prejudice reduction. Subsequent decades brought efforts to foster positive interactions among racial groups.[1] For over two decades, research has been conducted on implicit bias[2] to help increase our understanding of how deep-seated racial and ethnic biases can be. Lagging far behind are dedicated initiatives to help majority students understand their stake in learning with and from diverse others.

As I write these words, the experiment that is American democracy is undergoing significant stress and challenge, as truth is undermined and voting rights are eroded. While these words from the Declaration of Independence, "that all men are created equal, that they are endowed by their Creator with certain unalienable rights" have always been aspirational, as a nation we have made deliberate, if uneven, progress toward a more just society. Currently, that progress toward equity is under assault through the rise of White nationalism—and higher education's role in that advancement is being questioned.

In 2017, Pew Research discovered that a majority of Republicans and Republican-leaning independents (58%) said that colleges and universities have a negative effect on the country, up from 45% the previous year.[3] Analysts attribute this rise to concern about cultural elitism bred on campuses and a chilly climate for conservative viewpoints. Silencing of speakers and demand for safe spaces are cited as reasons for the decline in confidence.[4] The very purpose of higher education and its relationship to democracy is under debate, reduced by many Americans to simply getting a job.[5]

Why Does Inclusive Excellence Matter?

A series of papers commissioned by the American Association of Colleges & Universities in 2005 made a compelling case for the value of inclusive excellence, countering the often unstated belief that inclusion and excellence are mutually exclusive. Diverse learning environments lead to a broader collection of thoughts, ideas, and opinions held by students and are more likely to expose them to a wider array of perspectives. Research shows that "when students encounter novel ideas and new social situations, they are pressed to abandon automated scripts and think in more active ways."[6] Researchers particularly note the power of interracial friendships in enhancing self-confidence, motivation, educational aspirations, cultural awareness, and commitment to racial equity.[7] Student affairs educators play an essential role in fostering such friendships.

Inclusive excellence is neither universally embraced as an educational outcome nor simple to achieve. College students arrive with limited experience with diversity. Existing structures built to support marginalized students were created in a less complex world. Now universities must also meet the needs of transgender students, Muslim students, Dreamers, students with disabilities, and those who live in the intersections among identities. Social and political forces press upon universities, calling into question the very curricular and cocurricular initiatives designed to foster inclusion. This essay explores these forces and considers what universities can do to bring about change and progress.

Guess Who's Coming to College

Every year colleges and universities are recreated as roughly a quarter of our student population turns over. Those of us who work with traditional-aged students welcome 18-year-olds and want them to interact fluidly with diverse others as soon as they step onto our campuses. How prepared are they for that challenge?

In a 2017 study of over 40 years of racial segregation in southern schools, researchers found that Black student contact with Whites has fallen steadily since 1980, and White student contact with Black students is disproportionately low.[8] The Supreme Court decision in the University of Michigan case that argued for the ability to consider race as a factor in admissions recognized that the majority of students came from racially homogeneous high schools and residential communities.[9]

Students from fairly homogeneous school environments have had scant opportunity to learn about America's history of segregation and discrimination. Reports by the Southern Poverty Law Center[10] find that the civil rights movement receives little attention in high schools. The further the state is from the South, the weaker the civil rights history curriculum, with some notable exceptions, including California and New York. Henry Louis Gates notes that the history of the Jim Crow laws that maintained segregation after the end of the American Civil War isn't taught, and he wonders how today's students can be expected to understand the importance of *Brown v. Board of Education*, the March on Washington, or the Civil Rights Act of 1964 absent that context.[11]

Julie Park conducted a qualitative study that explored students' high school experiences and found they lacked meaningful engagement around issues of diversity, thus doing little to prepare students for such interactions in college. She identified that many students lack exposure to diverse others in high school, that teachers there do little to foster such interactions, and that high school students are less developmentally equipped to manage the complexity of race and identity issues.[12] This limited experience makes students ill-prepared to contribute positively to the campus racial climate.

According to a 2014 MTV poll,[13] 91% of millennials believe in equality and 89% believe everyone should be treated equally. Likewise, 84% say their families taught them to treat everyone the same, no matter their race, and 89% believe everyone should be treated as equals. Yet, only 37% of respondents (30% of Whites and 46% of minorities) say they were raised in families that talk about race. And although they believe their generation is more progressive than previous generations, they do not believe that racial preferences are fair and believe that focusing on race prevents society from becoming color-blind. It is safe to say that students arrive on our campuses with little preparation for engaging with and learning from diverse others.

Today's students are coming to college from an increasingly politically polarized environment. The Pew Research Center notes that from 1994 to 2004, the spread and overlap on ideals from consistently conservative to consistently liberal remained virtually the same, with considerable overlap on many issues between Republicans and Democrats. In the past decade, however, these groups' attitudes have moved right and left, now showing virtually no overlap.[14]

For the first time in surveys dating from 1992, majorities in both parties express not just unfavorable but *very* unfavorable views of the other party. And today, sizable shares of both Democrats and Republicans say the other party stirs feelings of not just frustration, but fear and anger. More than half of Democrats (55%) say the Republican Party makes them afraid, while 49% of Republicans say the same about the Democratic Party.[15]

Students are coming to college, then, from a largely homogeneous educational system, with little understanding of our racial history or of root causes of systemic inequality and from families who likely hold stridently negative views of those with political differences. What could go wrong?

The Identity Development Journey

Developmental theorists and student affairs educators alike have long recognized college as a place where identity is solidly established. Students naturally navigate to niches where their identity is affirmed, where they are mirrored and have voice. Despite our best intentions that college be the optimal time for learning from diverse others, the individual identity search often takes precedence. Until I know who I am, difference is threatening. Most colleges are admirably equipped to foster the identity development of majority students, to help them find a niche, defend a position, develop a skill, follow their interests, branch out to the unknown, fall in love, find a mentor, and develop passions—all of which help individuals figure out who they are and what they stand for.

For underrepresented students, it's a different story. They are likely one of a handful of students of color in the residence hall, and faculty role models are hard to find. They may be asked regularly to speak for their race in the classroom. Frequently assumed to be an athlete or a product of affirmative action, their very right to be in college is questioned.

Critics lament the self-segregation of identity centers on campus, believing that they undermine the opportunities for cross-racial interactions that lead to greater open-mindedness. Yet for students trying to establish their identity, they are a lifeline. Scholars cite their effectiveness in creating buffers against acts of bias and providing coaching on how to tap into informal networks, navigate to leadership roles, and address stereotypes when confronted with them.[16]

Torres and colleagues ask the question, "Why should higher education be concerned with the identity development of diverse students?" They write,

> the desire to intentionally influence positive learning and development requires those working in higher education to understand the conflicts students must resolve to develop their sense of self and in turn how we can assist them in resolving those conflicts.[17]

Since the 1970s numerous theorists have posited models that capture the added task required to develop a strong sense of identity as a member of a nondominant population. Cross's theory of nigrescence[18] and Helms' people of color model[19] were early portrayals of these theoretical approaches. Though the lived experience cannot be captured within any model, many scholars followed this foundational work to illuminate nuanced identity development experiences for a diverse array of subpopulations and intersecting identities. In healthy development, over time we can achieve a secure inner sense of self and appreciate both the positive and negative aspects of our own culture and other cultures. Allies are made, and cross-racial interactions become fluid and natural, with other aspects of identity—student as poet, daughter, athlete, scientist—becoming integrated with racial, ethnic, and gender identity. Fostering this development is the natural and critical work of student affairs educators.

This work is an essential pillar of the student affairs profession; it is for good reason that most of our graduate preparation programs and our professional competencies[20] focus on student learning and development. I find the work of Robert Putnam on different forms of social capital—bonding and bridging—to be relevant here.[21] Bonding refers to social networks between homogenous groups. Bonding can be valuable for oppressed and marginalized people to come together in groups and networks and support their collective needs. Bridging occurs across groups who share and exchange information, ideas, and innovations and can help create more inclusive environments through cooperative and collaborative initiatives.

What Is the Role of the Faculty in Shaping an Inclusive Learning Environment?

Faculty and classrooms are increasingly playing an important role in fostering an educationally powerful inclusive environment—or in creating a hostile one. In addition to empirical research on classroom interactions, experience with bias response demonstrates that faculty are differentially able to create an inclusive and welcoming classroom environment. Students all too frequently name experiences of tokenism (being expected to speak for all people who share their racial or ethnic background) or microaggressions (subtle forms of being told they are different or marginal within the classroom).

In the early 1990s Rendon focused on the influence of academic validation on student success,[22] and Hurtado and colleagues have extended this work through the Diverse Learning Environments survey. They found that,

> while there are direct and indirect effects of discrimination and bias on students' sense of belonging, validating experiences help to offset these experiences: students who reported validating experiences were also less likely to report experiences of discrimination and bias, and the direct effect of discrimination and bias on sense of belonging was diminished after accounting for validating experiences.[23]

Student affairs educators also have very real power to affirm and validate students and negate the effects of negative interactions.

Greg Walton and colleagues' work offers an additional approach to improving student success for underrepresented students. By adopting a student-centered perspective, they looked beyond improving their own delivery of academic content to reduce disparate outcomes and instead considered ways to disrupt beliefs and worries that prevent students from taking full advantage of learning opportunities. They found that stealthy psychological interventions could make a positive difference in student success. If new students were introduced to the ways in which upperclassmen had struggled, stumbled, and yet prevailed, they were able to stay motivated when encountering difficulties of their own. When marginalized students used to negative stereotypes worried that negative feedback was a result of faculty bias, they were encouraged to see critical feedback as a sign of their teacher's high standards and their ability to reach them, fostering trust between student and teacher.[24] These scholars have gone on to form the College Transition Collaborative to extend this work.

It should be noted that faculty diversity lags behind student diversity on most campuses. Across the nation, in the fall of 2013, of all full-time faculty at degree-granting postsecondary institutions, 43% were White males, 35% were White females, 3% were Black males, 3% were Black females,

2% were Hispanic males, 2% were Hispanic females, 6% were Asian/Pacific Islander males, and 4% were Asian/Pacific Islander females.[25] This lack of faculty diversity means that role models are lacking for students of color and that majority students have few opportunities to respect faculty of color as experts and authorities.

Faculty also establish the curriculum, and many campuses periodically review the general education requirements in the face of both a changing population and a changing society. Student demands for greater relevance, as well as the desire to ensure that majority students encounter the work of diverse scholars and authors, have propelled many such initiatives. Threats to the classical canon, and therefore to the very worth of a discipline, can be met with fierce opposition and charges of political correctness. The study of race, class, and gender can be seen as the province only of those directly affected, once again creating a gulf of understanding for majority students who may never rigorously encounter the works or experiences of those who do not look like them.

Social Media Rules

Perspectives differ on whether the current status of diversity and inclusion efforts is fundamentally different from those of an earlier age. Students today are sometimes described as postracial, yet this attitude has not come from meaningful engagement in understanding prejudice and discrimination, but in the vague sense that "we should all get along." One thing that *has* changed is the role of social media. Ninety percent of young adults use social media, and those with a college education are even more likely than their noncollege peers to engage in such sites.[26]

More and more, we curate what we see and who we hear. We follow who we like on Instagram, Twitter, and Facebook, and we receive targeted ads based upon what we already follow. The mainstream news media has segmented itself to reflect predominant strains of civic life, and there are more slanted channels on both the left and the right. Social scientists analyzing Facebook use identified that users sought information that strengthened their preferred narratives and rejected information that undermined it. When deliberately false information was introduced into these echo chambers, it was absorbed and viewed as credible as long as it conformed to the primary narrative.[27] Mihailidis found that peer content drives both news consumption and political expression. Traditional media outlets were seldom consulted unless they arose in a Google search, while Facebook and Twitter were the primary outlets for news consumption.[28] In these ways, stereotypes and bias are promoted and confirmed, further driving wedges within our society.

Despite its ubiquity in students' lives, the online environment is not always a positive one. Anonymous sites in particular can be harsh, and civility has been eroded on many social media sites. Cyberbullying has been documented for high school and college students alike. Twenge notes that girls in particular are subject to and perpetrators of cyberbullying.[29] Researchers have found that students who differ in some way, such as race, ethnicity, sexual orientation, religion, or appearance, are more vulnerable to being victimized in cyberspace.[30] What *The Chronicle of Higher Education* calls "the Internet outrage machine"[31] has been known to rain down on not only faculty and administrators but also students who speak out on issues of discrimination. A Yale student who was videotaped shouting at her residential college master was pilloried on the Internet, and her safety was threatened.

It should be noted that online platforms also offer opportunities to join and form affirming communities and to unite with individuals who share a passion or identity, no matter where they are. Students increasingly connect online with others who share their commitments, and students share strategies for improving their campus climates in this way.

I'm Not Listening, You're Not Listening!

The prevalence of echo chambers, where we are prone to hear only that which we agree with, deepens the challenge of communication with and across difference in a meaningful way. Students come to us with little experience in empathic listening or with listening for understanding when another's viewpoint is alien. When students believe that it is a grave interpersonal risk to disagree with others, further retreat into their own digital cocoon is likely.

That echo chamber is being extended to the campus commons as well. Freedom of expression, long a cherished principle within American society and especially higher education, is under assault. Speakers considered to be offensive are disinvited, shouted down, or shut down. I am sympathetic to the concern, raised by some student activists, that to provide a platform to an offensive speaker is to create a psychologically unsafe environment on campus, yet these approaches make meaningful communication less likely, further deepening the challenge of creating true understanding. Within these heightened tensions, the desire for a psychologically safe space is ridiculed rather than understood as an expression of trauma. A college should be a place where a wide variety of viewpoints are professed and critiqued. To quote Clark Kerr, the president of the University of California, Berkeley, when the student free speech movement was born, "the University is not engaged in making ideas safe for students. It is engaged in making students safe for ideas."[32]

How Can Bridging Be Fostered?

Proponents of identity-based safe spaces also advocate for meaningful opportunities to dialogue across difference. Some of the most promising strategies for bridging divides of identity and ideology employ organized approaches to dialogue and can be fostered by students, faculty, and staff alike. Tienda discusses the cognitive structures that prefer homogeneity and are activated to distinguish friend from foe. Due to these hard-wired structures, "merely bringing together a socially, economically, demographically, and ideologically diverse group of students reproduces group boundaries."[33] To activate what she calls coalition-building systems and foster inclusion, "it is necessary for members of different groups to interact in ways that challenge preexisting stereotypes about others."[34] Higher education has developed and employed several strategies to accomplish this goal.

Sustained Dialogue

In the early 2000s students at the University of Virginia (UVA) brought to campus Sustained Dialogue, a program developed by Harold Saunders from lessons learned through international peace negotiations. UVA is noted for its tradition of student self-governance, and Sustained Dialogue was a program ideally suited to flourish in that environment. In it, students form moderated peer-led weekly discussion groups designed to delve into controversial topics in a spirit of openness and respect for differing viewpoints. The Sustained Dialogue Institute defines *dialogue* as "listening deeply enough to be changed by what you learn."[35] Now on 44 campuses and in myriad communities, research has demonstrated its effectiveness. In a study of postgraduate participants, researchers found that Sustained Dialogue shaped major life decisions and helped develop skills used at work and home.[36] The Sustained Dialogue Campus Network surveys group members pre- and postparticipation and finds a much greater tendency to discuss across difference and to examine their own attitudes postparticipation.[37] My own experience as a member of a faculty-staff dialogue group was profound. We were able to put aside differences in status as well as identities to learn deeply from one another's experiences.

Deliberative Dialogue

Deliberative Dialogue is another structured approach to teaching the skills required for deep communication across difference, with a goal to increase the civic participation and citizen engagement needed to preserve a robust democracy. Researchers investigated whether the model provided by the Kettering Foundation's National Issues Forum (NIF) could be adapted to the college classroom to foster true civic engagement, given the existing political alienation of young people. The NIF model brings together citizens with diverse viewpoints and experiences to discuss difficult issues with the help of an issue guide, an overview of a public problem, and three or four possible approaches to the problem, along with the potential costs, consequences, and tradeoffs that would likely result from following any of the approaches. Researchers found that while students arrive at college distrustful of group decision-making, they "can be taught to imagine and to implement a new kind of politics through deliberation."[38] Perhaps more importantly, a longitudinal follow-up of their participants and a matched sample found that, while both cohorts disliked the degree of political polarization, program participants were more involved in the political process and more likely to believe that their education prepared them for such involvement. They also cited the usefulness in other life arenas of the skills taught, making them better listeners, invested in understanding those with whom they disagree, and appreciative of alternative viewpoints.[39]

Intergroup Dialogue

Perhaps the most structured and well-researched form of dialogue across difference is Intergroup Dialogue,[40] often but not exclusively a curricular approach that brings together an equal number of participants from two groups who are divided by historically strained relationships or conflict. At the University of California, San Diego we employed Intergroup Dialogue as a cocurricular strategy to develop sustainable relationships between pro-Palestine and pro-Israel students. The three broad goals of Intergroup Dialogue are to develop intergroup understanding, foster positive intergroup relationships, and foster intergroup collaboration for personal and social responsibility toward greater social justice.[41] This method employs active and engaged learning, structured interaction, and facilitated learning environments for maximum impact. Because the dialogue is sustained across a full term and benefits from skilled moderation, deeper impacts can occur than those found in briefer initiatives. A nine-university collaborative study found consistent positive effects across intergroup understanding, relationships, collaboration, and engagement.[42]

Who's Coming Next?

By the time this volume is in print, the generation that will follow Millennials to college will be on our doorsteps. Variously called Gen Z, iGen, or the Homeland generation, we know that they differ from Millennials in meaningful ways, although members on the cusps of two generations are more alike than different. Twenge has just published *iGen: Why Today's Super-Connected Kids Are Growing Up Less Rebellious, More Tolerant, Less Happy—and Completely Unprepared for Adulthood.*[43] Her concerns for the mental health of these young people are worth noting, but she also captures some trends toward inclusion and acceptance. In addition, she highlights their reliance on smartphones to mediate all of their communication and their low-risk approach to face-to-face communication, both real challenges to inclusive learning environments. Turkle, in her books *Alone Together*[44] and *Reclaiming Conversation,* also identified that these digital natives literally do not know what it is like to engage in face-to-face interactions, which she calls "the most human—and humanizing—thing we do."[45] It is clear that colleges and universities will have much work to do to realize the benefits of real dialogue for the next generation of collegians, and sustained academic and cocurricular partnerships will be most effective in achieving this outcome.

Am I Ready to Lead This Conversation?

One of the challenges for student affairs educators in providing leadership on campuses to foster a more equitable campus climate is the fact that we are products of the same culture and climate that have created inequities. Our profession has made sustained progress in attracting more diverse and inclusive members to join, lead, and teach the field, yet we are reflective of societal biases and prejudices.

As someone who provides leadership for staff development and training around social and racial justice issues, I observe that we vary widely in the ability to engage critically in these issues. Some staff are products of graduate preparation programs that have given them the tools of critical analysis, and others are not. Majority colleagues are often afraid of saying the wrong thing and being called racist, a potentially career-ending label. Colleagues of color are tired of being asked to do the heavy lifting to educate White colleagues about the realities of race in America. Responsible leadership in student affairs mandates sustained efforts at prejudice reduction and antiracist professional development.

While the challenges are real, there is no better place to do this work than on a college campus, the place in our society most likely to be made up of diverse individuals, full of open minds, and characterized by the spirit of inquiry. Student affairs educators can be catalysts for this work, armed with our knowledge of how students grow and develop and capable of creating learning environments in a variety of settings. The imperative is clear: We must answer the charge of creating inclusive learning environments. Our students deserve it, and our democracy demands it. We must elevate our collective ability to confront racism and advance social justice in order to meet this goal, and we will have to partner with faculty and students to do so. Such work, however, is life-giving and affirming. It has the capacity to restore our souls and give us hope for the future.

Discussion Questions

1. Given the increasingly polarized and digital nature of our society, how best can colleges and universities increase our capacity to have rich and meaningful conversations across our differences?
2. Given the centrality of the identity development process and the added layers for members of underrepresented groups, how can their journey best be supported?
3. How can majority students best be helped to understand the stake they have in knowing how to live and work in a diverse environment with cultural humility?

Notes

1. National Coalition Building Institute. (2017, September 10). Retrieved from http://ncbi.org/; Anti-Defamation League. (2017, September 10). Retrieved from https://www.adl.org/who-we-are/our-organization/signature-programs/a-world-of-difference-institute

2. Project Implicit. (2017, September 10). Retrieved from https://implicit.harvard.edu/implicit/aboutus.html

3. Pew Research Center. (2017, July 10). *Sharp partisan divisions in views of national institutions.* Retrieved from http://www.people-press.org/2017/07/10/sharp-partisan-divisions-in-views-of-national-institutions/

4. Bump, P. (2017, July 17). The new culture war targeting American universities appears to be working. *The Washington Post.* Retrieved from https://www.washingtonpost.com/news/politics/wp/2017/07/10/the-new-culture-war-targeting-american-universities-appears-to-be-working/?utm_term=.3214141f415c; Gomez, L. (2017, July 17). More Republicans say colleges hurt America. Blame safe spaces? Retrieved from http://www.sandiegouniontribune.com/opinion/the-conversation/sd-republicans-think-colleges-are-bad-20170710-htmlstory.html

5. Hora, Matthew T. (2018). Beyond the skills gap: How the vocationalist framing of higher education undermines student, employer, and societal interests. *Liberal Education, 104*(2), 20–27. Washington DC: Association of American Colleges & Universities.

6. Milem, J. F., Chang, M. J., & Antonio, A. L. (2005). *Making diversity work on campus: A research-based perspective.* Washington DC: Association of American Colleges & Universities, p. 8

    7. Ibid., p. 9

    8. Frankenberg, E., Hawley, G. S, Ee, J., & Orfield, G. (2017). *The civic rights project.* Retrieved from https://www.civilrightsproject.ucla.edu/research/k-12-education/integration-and-diversity/southern-schools-brown-83-report

    9. Gurin, P., Dey, E., Gurin, G., & Hurtado, S. (2004). The educational value of diversity. In P. Gurin, J. Lehman, & E. Lewis (Eds.), *Defending diversity: Affirmative action at the University of Michigan* (pp. 97–188). Ann Arbor, MI: University of Michigan Press.

    10. Southern Poverty Law Center. (2011). *Report of the Teaching Tolerance Program, Montgomery, Alabama.* Retrieved from http://www.tolerance.org/sites/default/files/general/Teaching_the_Movement.pdf

    11. Southern Poverty Law Center. (2014). *Report of the Teaching Tolerance Program, Montgomery, Alabama.* Retrieved from http://www.tolerance.org/sites/default/files/general/Teaching%20the%20Movement%202014_final_web_0.pdf

    12. Park, J. J., & Chang, S. H. (2015). Understanding students' precollege experiences with racial diversity: The high school as microcosm. *Journal of College Student Development, 56*(4), 349–363.

    13. Bouie, J. (2014, May 16). Why do millennials not understand racism? *Slate.* Retrieved from http://www.slate.com/articles/news_and_politics/politics/2014/05/millennials_racism_and_mtv_poll_young_people_are_confused_about_bias_prejudice.html

    14. Pew Research Center. (2014, June 12). *United States—Political polarization in the American public.* Retrieved from http://www.people-press.org/2014/06/12/political-polarization-in-the-american-public/

    15. Ibid.

    16. Harper, S. (2015). Black male college achievers and resistant responses to racist stereotypes at predominantly White colleges and universities. *Harvard Educational Review, 85*(4), 646–674; Park, J. (2011). Why is it so challenging for collegians and student affairs educators to talk about race? In P. M. Magolda & M. B. Baxter Magolda (Eds.), *Contested issues in higher education: Diverse perspective and respectful dialogue* (pp. 225–235). Sterling, VA: Stylus; Patton, L. D. (2006). The voice of reason: A qualitative examination of Black student perceptions of Black cultural centers. *Journal of College Student Development, 47*(6), 628–646.

    17. Torres, V., Howard-Hamilton, M. F., & Cooper, D. L. (2004). *Identity development of diverse populations: Implications for teaching and administration in higher education.* Association for the Study of Higher Education (ASHE). San Francisco, CA: Jossey-Bass, Wiley Periodicals, p. 14.

    18. Cross, W. E., Jr. (1995). The psychology of nigrescence: Revising the Cross model. In J. G. Ponterotto, J. M. Casas, L. A. Suzuki, & C. M. Alexander (Eds.), *Handbook of multicultural counseling* (pp. 93–122). Thousand Oaks, CA: Sage.

    19. Helms, J. E. (1993). Introduction: Review of racial identity terminology. In J. E. Helms (Ed.), *Black and White identity: Theory, research, and practice* (pp. 3–8). Westport, CT: Praeger.

20. ACPA & NASPA. (2015). *Professional competency areas for student affairs educators*. Retrieved from https://www.naspa.org/images/uploads/main/ACPA_NASPA_Professional_Competencies_.pdf

21. Putnam, R. (2007). E Pluribus Unum: Diversity and community in the twenty-first century—The 2006 Johan Skytte Prize Lecture. *Scandinavian Political Studies, 30*(2), 137–174.

22. Rendon, L. (1994). Validating culturally diverse students: Toward a new model of learning and student development. *Innovative Higher Education, 31*(2), 161–183.

23. Hurtado, S., Ruiz-Alvarado, A., & Guillermo-Wann, C. (2015). The mediating effect of faculty and staff validation on the relationship of discrimination/bias to students' sense of belonging. *Journal Committed to Social Change on Race and Ethnicity, 1*(1), 60–80, pp. 73–74.

24. Walton, G. M., & Cohen, G. L. (2013). Addressing achievement gaps with psychological interventions. *Phi Delta Kappa: Kappan*, February, 62–65.

25. National Center for Education Statistics. (2017, September 9) *Race/ethnicity of college faculty*. Retrieved from https://nces.ed.gov/fastfacts/display.asp?id=61

26. Duggan, M., & Smith, A. (2017). The political environment on social media. Washington DC: Pew Research Center. Retrieved from http://www.pewinternet.org/2016/10/25/political-content-on-social-media/

27. Quattrociocchi, W., Scala A., & Sunstein, C. (2016). *Echo chambers on Facebook*. Retrieved from https://ssrn.com/abstract=2795110

28. Mihailidis, P. (2014). The civic–social media disconnect: Exploring perceptions of social media for engagement in the daily life of college students. *Information, Communication, & Society, 17*(9), 1059–1071.

29. Twenge, J. M. (2017, September). Have smartphones destroyed a generation? *The Atlantic*. Retrieved from https://www.theatlantic.com/magazine/archive/2017/09/has-the-smartphone-destroyed-a-generation/534198/

30. Baldasare, A., Bauman, S., Goldman, L., & Robie, A. (2012). Cyberbullying? Voices of college students. In L. A. Wankel & C. Wankel (Eds.), *Cutting-edge technologies in higher education: Vol. 5, Misbehavior online in higher education* (pp. 127–155). New York, NY: Emerald Group.

31. McMurtrie, B. (2017, June 26). What colleges can do when the Internet outrage machine comes to campus. *Chronicle of Higher Education*. Retrieved from http://www.chronicle.com/article/What-Colleges-Can-Do-When-the/240445

32. Kerr, C. (2017, September 10). Former UC President Clark Kerr, a national leader in higher education, dies at 92. *UC Berkeley News*. Retrieved from http://www.berkeley.edu/news/media/releases/2003/12/02_kerr.shtml

33. Tienda, M. (2013). Diversity ≠ inclusion: Promoting integration in higher education. *Educational Researcher, 42*(9), 471.

34. Ibid.

35. Sustained Dialogue Institute. (2017, September). *Transform campus relationships*. Retrieved from http://sustaineddialogue.org/

36. Diaz, A., & Perrault, R. (2010, Fall). Sustained dialogue and civic life: Post-college impacts. *Michigan Journal of Community Service Learning*. Retrieved from http://www.sdcampusnetwork.org/ht/a/GetDocumentAction/i/112057-26-17

37. Sustained Dialogue Institute. (2017, September). Retrieved from http://sustaineddialogue.org/our-impact/

38. McMillan, J., & Harriger, K. (2002). College students and deliberation: A benchmark study. *Communication Education, 51*(3), 237–253.

39. Harriger, K., McMillan, J., Buchanan, C., & Gusler, S. (2015). The long-term impact of learning to deliberate. *Diversity and Democracy, 18*(4). Retrieved from https://www.aacu.org/diversitydemocracy/2015/fall/harriger

40. Chapter 2, this volume, details this approach.

41. Nagda, B. A., Gurin, P., Sorensen, N., & Zúñiga, X. (2009). Evaluating Intergroup Dialogue: Engaging diversity for personal and social responsibility. *Diversity and Democracy, (12)*1. Retrieved from https://www.aacu.org/publications-research/periodicals/evaluating-intergroup-dialogue-engaging-diversity-personal-and

42. Ibid.

43. Twenge, J. (2017). *iGen: Why today's super-connected kids are growing up less rebellious, more tolerant, less happy—and completely unprepared for adulthood.* New York, NY: Atria.

44. Turkle, S. (2010). *Alone together: Why we expect more from technology and less from each other.* New York, NY: Basic Books.

45. Turkle, S. (2017). *Reclaiming conversation: The power of talk in the digital age.* New York, NY: Penguin Random House, p. 3.

History Matters: Against Romanticizing Student Affairs' Role in Inclusion

Dafina-Lazarus (D-L) Stewart

Penny Rue makes several assertions about the role of student affairs, the purpose of higher education, and the potential for interventions supported and facilitated by student affairs to foster inclusive environments for learning. Other than the role of social media over the last decade, many of Rue's arguments can be found in other founding philosophical documents in student affairs.[1] Unfortunately, these arguments are ill-equipped to help student affairs professionals truly understand the nature of the problems we face or what will be helpful in resolving them. In this response, I hope to offer what I feel to be a more authentic view of higher education, the role of student affairs, and how professionals in this field can evaluate the challenges besetting fostering inclusive environments for learning.

U.S. Democracy and Higher Education: A Deconstruction

From the founding of the earliest postsecondary institutions on the land that is now known as the United States, colleges and universities have participated in and profited from settler colonialism, racism, patriarchy, and capitalist exploitation of labor. Craig Steven Wilder[2] unpacks much of this history, which goes a long way toward challenging notions that the purpose of higher education has ever been aligned with democratic values. When Harvard was founded in 1636, it was made possible only through the forced removal and genocide of Indigenous peoples. This remains the case for every college founded prior to 1776, as well as for any college founded since. In my historical research on a set of private colleges in the Great Lakes region,[3] I noted a pattern of college founding dates closely following or concurrent with congressional legislation and treaties that removed Indigenous people from the states of Michigan, Ohio, Illinois, and Indiana.

Moreover, the history of higher education in graduate preparation programs is often portrayed in a positive light that defies the historical record. For instance, the role of the economics of enslavement in fortifying now elite colleges is typically overlooked or deemphasized.[4] The use of samples comprising predominantly White, middle class, and cisgender men to inform universalized theories of learning and development is also dismissed and ignored.[5] Additionally, these master narratives encourage continued dismissal of substantive long-standing issues of inequity and injustice in higher education. Both the historical record[6] and contemporary scholarship[7] have demonstrated the failure of colleges and universities—and the broad array of professionals within them—to substantively challenge underlying structures and systems that reproduce and support inequity in postsecondary education. As such, it is a gross overstatement to suggest, as Rue does, that higher education's purpose is intimately connected to or supportive of U.S. democracy.

Regarding the student affairs profession, we must remember that student affairs educators, functioning as deans of women and deans of men in the late nineteenth century, enforced rigid cishetero gender norms. The consequences of these norms included the oppression and expulsion of gay men from colleges and universities in the twentieth century.[8] Student affairs professionals supported and enforced racially segregated housing policies and prohibitions on interracial dating.[9] Student affairs professionals were also complicit in the attempt to silence and suppress student activism on both local and national levels during the civil rights movement and antiwar protests of the 1960s and 1970s.[10] Although student affairs professionals have espoused commitments to diversity, inclusion, and social justice advocacy over time,[11] minoritized student affairs professionals in marginalized campus roles largely have borne the burden of carrying out this work.[12] Professional associations have struggled to enact these espoused values within conference spaces.[13] Espousing values and enacting values are entirely different enterprises, and the failure to enact our values consistently has material effects for both minoritized professionals and students in student affairs.

As Rue notes, we have interpreted the rhetoric in our nation's founding documents to be aspirational; however, democracy has always been a flailing effort. To say that it is just now "undergoing significant stress and challenge"[14] or that the current "rise of White nationalism"[15] is thwarting our otherwise deliberate "progress toward equity"[16] reflects a view of this nation that does not withstand deep scrutiny. The whole of the twentieth century and these first decades of the twenty-first are flush with illustrations of stubborn resistance to any manifestation of the equitable and just democracy this nation's founders proclaimed. These examples include the rollback of Reconstruction Era advances for newly emancipated African

Americans; the concurrent rise of Jim Crow laws and racial terrorism affecting Indigenous peoples and Americans of African, Asian, and Latinx descent; the racially discriminatory awarding of GI Bill benefits to World War II veterans;[17] the rise of mass incarceration and the prison industrial complex;[18] the inhumane deportation of undocumented immigrants accelerated under President Obama;[19] the aggressive resegregation of public K–12 education led by affluent White parents;[20] the plodding advance of state-level legislative efforts to undermine access to legal abortion[21] and block the ability of transgender people to participate in public life;[22] and the decline in public support for postsecondary education as a public good as it has become more demographically diverse.[23]

The current public face of White nationalism has been operating largely uninhibited for most of the last half-century. Neither the 2016 presidential campaign rhetoric nor the White nationalists with their tiki torches in Charlottesville, Virginia, in August 2017 were the introduction of White nationalism in the United States. Though some may read this as overly cynical, such blunt critical and racial realism[24] is necessary if postsecondary educators ever hope to reckon fully with our persistent failure to foster environments supportive of diversity, inclusion, equity, or justice. Student affairs professionals need to reckon with the perverse and complicated history and present of the United States' societal structure to recognize its footprint within the practices and norms of our profession. Not doing so will render us continually ineffective in facilitating environments that foster equitable environments on our campuses and within our professional associations.

The False Rhetoric of Inclusion

The language of diversity and inclusion is not useful for realizing goals of equity and justice.[25] In fact, it often works at cross-purposes, as the interest convergence[26] that wins support for diversity and inclusion does not often find traction when it comes to the radical organizational transformation required to elicit equity and justice. For example, despite advertising affirmative hiring policies and nondiscrimination statements, hiring authorities and search committees often confront applicants from minoritized social groups with bias and hegemonic norms throughout the hiring process.[27] Having the appearance of diversity and inclusion through pursuing compositional diversity supposedly demonstrates institutional commitment to its espoused values, communicated through its nondiscrimination and equal opportunity statements. However, these same institutions are pursuing diversity and inclusion without dismantling hegemonic tacit assumptions that prevent that goal of increasingly more diverse compositional diversity from being realized.

Previously, I have also challenged the notion, seemingly supported by Rue,[28] that all ideas should find an audience within postsecondary institutions. Strident free speech proponents are usually only advocating for the rights of neoconservatives and bigoted speech to be propagated.[29] Whether to make ideas safe for students or students safe for ideas[30] is a false dichotomy. Rather, the issue is how institutional values should inform and evaluate policies about speech on campus in consideration of how that speech will make some populations vulnerable to harm.[31] Ethical principles in student affairs alone cannot determine how to resolve the ethical dilemma raised by the competing values of free speech and the profession's espoused value to do no harm.[32] In such cases, an ethical decision-making process needs to consider whether to subsume student safety and students' and professionals' perceptions of the campus climate to protect free speech.

Rue's essay also raises concerns for me about who she has in mind when she writes that young adults today are postracial, arriving with limited experiences with diversity, and intolerant of opposing ideas. Both academic scholarship and journalism have demonstrated that these characteristics are far more reflective of White, middle-class young adults than they are of young people generally.[33] This is important, as student affairs educators' assumptions about who they should be serving and who needs diversity interventions have led to inappropriate, harmful, and ineffective programming and policies. Missing from Rue's analysis is the reality that students minoritized by race, ethnicity, nationality, ability, gender, and sexuality have borne the brunt of the labor of diversity work on historically White, non-Native[34] colleges and universities to the detriment of their own learning and college experiences. Studies cited by Rue promoting the value of interracial friendships have been challenged by other scholarship that demonstrates that these positive effects are mostly seen for White students, not for racially minoritized students.[35] In light of this, student affairs educators must question who is really benefiting from the kinds of interventions that Rue extols.

Social Media

Rue supports her contention regarding the echo chambers that have hampered the public exchange of ideas by pointing to social media as a virtual environment that has facilitated and even created spaces absent of dissenting voices.[36] As a Gen Xer, I came up during the transition from rotary-dial to touchtone to dial-up Internet access, to the World Wide Web, to Google becoming both the name of a multibillion dollar global enterprise and a verb. I joined Facebook, Twitter, and Instagram (in that order) as an adult already in an academic career. Through that journey across the divide between late digital adopters and those born with a Facebook account, I have witnessed the echo chambers and the vitriol and abuse they produce that Rue decries. However, I have also seen minoritized young people find support, encouragement, and like-minded peers and adults who have supported their breath.[37]

Daloz Parks portrays a level of development in which young adults begin to seek a community that is open to others over one that is only filled with people like themselves.[38] This is a beautiful vision of what community can look like when there is mutual trust and empathy, but that is not the present reality. For people with minoritized identities, curating their online networks is a survival strategy. Rue's monolithic depiction of young adults does a great disservice to those with minoritized identities. Like their elders, young people with dominant identities have the privilege to form self-reinforcing cocoons and to extend them from virtual to physical spaces. Also, like their elders, young people with (multiple) minoritized identities daily face an onslaught of dehumanizing interactions, in person and online. It is naïve and dangerous to expect anyone to constantly withstand the barrage of trolling and abuse that is regularly visited upon users with minoritized identities. Student affairs educators should not deny the toll that kind of dehumanization exacts. The needs of our students who must learn to see beyond their privileged social identities should not be centered at the cost of minoritized students' needs for validation, belonging, and affirmation. Student affairs professionals therefore need to assess what student experiences with diverse perspectives have been and what specific things are needed to facilitate further critical thinking and critical consciousness-raising. This involves critical consideration of students' multiple minoritized and privileged identities as well as developing advanced awareness, knowledge, and skills in the professional competencies of social justice and inclusion and student learning and development.

The Role of Student Affairs

Rue supports her arguments with an array of sources by baby boomers and Gen Xers *about* Millennials and the generation following them ("Centennials"), but no sources reflect the voices of these young people about themselves. For the field of student affairs to become consistent, positive factors in the fostering of learning environments beyond inclusion, we must begin to listen to our students instead of listening to others talk about our students. I recommend reading Jesmyn Ward's edited collection[39] and Patrisse Khan-Cullors's memoir[40] and thoroughly reviewing website platforms such as Black Youth Project 100 (BYP 100)[41] to see what minoritized young people are saying about themselves. This independent education, coupled with listening to minoritized students at their own institutions, would broaden student affairs professionals' knowledge of the concerns, needs, and hopes of these young people for their higher education. I believe these insights would radically transform student affairs practice from one that centers the majority to one that centers and seeks to serve the most vulnerable members of our campus communities.

A Call to Action

It is not, as Rue asserts, that "existing structures built to support marginalized students" were instituted in a "less complex world."[42] For people with minoritized identities, the world has always been complex. Rather, those structures were not meant to facilitate transformational institutional change toward greater equity and justice. Today's students in U.S. higher education are no longer accepting modest evolutionary adjustments that ultimately preserve the status quo. Today's young people have seen the results of previous generation's efforts toward that end falter and are demanding revolutionary systemic change. The challenge for student affairs is whether it is willing to shake the very foundations of the field to bring about a new vision of higher education that is radically democratic in its pursuit of justice for all.

There are many ways in which student affairs professionals could contribute to this shaking and radical revisioning of higher education. I offer just a few of them here. First, independent reading is essential for broadening and challenging normative, functionalist versions of how higher education came to be. Empowered with such critical history, student affairs professionals can engage the kind of historical thinking that can see the footprints left on current professional theory and practice.

Second, as our scholarly foundation has expanded with contributions by researchers educated specifically in higher education, we have created professional and scholarly echo chambers that have isolated us from important and critically informed conversations happening elsewhere both within and beyond the academy. The result is that we must broaden our information networks to include critical perspectives that are not often represented in our professional and scholarly journals or are relatively inaccessible. For those engaged in social media, the hashtag #ScholarSunday on Twitter is a good place to learn of scholars doing critically engaged work throughout higher education.

Third, student affairs graduate preparation programs have a responsibility to review and revise their curricula intentionally to prepare new professionals for today's campus environments that, as Rue accurately points out, are fraught with division. Graduate preparation programs can begin to equip students to be change agents with the competence and capacity for enacting systemic change within their spheres of influence.

Fourth, identify your part and do that work. Recognizing and discussing systemic issues and the need for structural transformation can be overwhelming. However, each of us has daily opportunities to disrupt, challenge, and enact different futures. Work within the microclimates in which you have influence to shake tacit assumptions and practices that distance us from realizing our espoused values and aspirational goals. As you advance within your institution and the profession, continue that practice of disruption and of asking questions that redirect conversations toward equity. If all of us work within our spheres of influence, we will be involved in collectively shaking the foundations of our field. We will be able to do more than just imagine different futures; we will enact them.

Conclusion

In this essay I have gone to great lengths to uncover and expose the profession's failures to enact its espoused values throughout its history and its present. This critical view may strike some as cynical and hopeless. However, I agree with Rue that student affairs has aspired to value diversity, equity, and social justice—and held these positions often prior to their adoption by higher education institutions generally. In addition, some readers may see my essay as a condemnation of good people who are doing their best to reform oppressive systems. To this criticism, I acknowledge that people of good will can be—are needed to be—accomplices in this work of transformation.

Where Rue and I differ is that while Rue prioritizes how far the profession has come, I prioritize how far we have yet to go. While Rue points to external forces as major barriers to student affairs' ability to foster inclusive environments, I point to the internal forces that have persisted over time that challenge the profession from within. In doing so, I draw on James Baldwin defending his criticisms of the United States: "I love [this profession] more than any other and, for exactly this reason, I insist on the right to criticize [it] perpetually."[43]

These may seem to be mutually opposing perspectives to some readers—one hopeful, the other hopeless. On the contrary, they reflect different paradigms for approaching issues of diversity, equity, and justice.[44] Each of these perspectives has merit and validity—they are both authentic portrayals of our current situation. Rather than a binary approach, I urge student affairs professionals to embrace the critical dialectic of a both–and. Our aspirational goals are fundamentally important to inspiring collective calls to action, to not settle, to look within and not just without for the roots of our challenges.

We can do this, and, empowered by critical awareness, knowledge, and skills, we will.

Discussion Questions

1. What did you learn about the history and role of student affairs? How does what you have learned inform your assumptions about the possibility and reality of student affairs work related to inclusion and equity?
2. How can you diversify the perspectives you expose yourself to without requiring people with minoritized identities to do that labor for you?
3. What are some practices that you can begin, continue, or stop within your sphere of influence that would move your professional praxis beyond inclusion toward equity and justice?

Notes

1. Evans, N. J., & Reason, R. D. (2001). Guiding principles: A review and analysis of student affairs philosophical statements. *Journal of College Student Development, 42*(4), 359–377.

2. Wilder, C. S. (2013). *Ebony and ivy: Race, slavery, and the troubled history of American universities.* New York, NY: Bloomsbury.

3. Stewart, D.-L. (2017). *Black collegians' experiences in U.S. Northern Private Colleges: A narrative history, 1945–1965.* New York, NY: Palgrave McMillan.

4. Patton, L. D. (2016). Disrupting postsecondary prose: Toward a critical race theory of higher education. *Urban Education, 51*(3), 315–342; Wilder, *Ebony and ivy.*

5. Patton, Disrupting postsecondary prose.

6. Wilder, *Ebony and ivy.*

7. Patton, Disrupting postsecondary prose.

8. Dilley, P. (2002). *Queer man on campus: A history of non-heterosexual college men, 1945–2000.* New York, NY: RoutledgeFalmer.

9. Stewart, *Black collegians' experiences.*

10. Hutcheson, P., Gasman, M., & Sanders-McMurtry, K. (2011). Race and equality in the academy: Rethinking higher education actors and the struggle for equality in the post-World War II period. *Journal of Higher Education, 82*(2), 121–153; Stewart, *Black collegians' experiences.*

11. Reason, R. D., & Broido, E. M. (2017). Philosophies and values. In J. H. Schuh, S. R. Jones, & V. Torres (Eds.), *Student services: A handbook for the profession,* 6th ed. (pp. 39–55). San Francisco, CA: Wiley.

12. Stewart, D.-L. (2016). It matters who leads them: Connecting leadership in multicultural affairs to student learning and development. *About Campus, 21*(1), 21–28.

13. Stewart, D.-L. (2017, July 24). *Presence, absence, and the labor of being.* Retrieved from https://dafinalazarusstewart.wordpress.com/2017/07/24/presence-absence-and-the-labor-of-being/; Messmore, N. (2016, November 30). *An open letter to the open letter* [web log post]. Retrieved from https://danceswithdissonance.wordpress.com/2016/11/30/an-open-letter-to-the-open-letter/

14. Rue, P., this volume, p. 4.

15. Ibid., p. 4

16. Ibid., p. 4

17. Serow, R. C. (2004). Policy as symbol: Title II of the 1994 G. I. Bill. *The Review of Higher Education, 27*(4), 481–499; Turner, S., & Bound, J. (2003). Closing the gap or widening the divide: The effects of the G. I. Bill and World War II on the educational outcomes of Black Americans. *Journal of Economic History, 63*(1), 145–177.

18. Alexander, M. (2010). *The new Jim Crow: Mass incarceration in the age of colorblindness.* New York, NY: The New Press.

19. Chisthi, M., Pierce, S., & Bolter, J. (2017, January 26). *The Obama record on deportations: Deporter in chief or not?* Migration Policy Institute. Retrieved from https://www.migrationpolicy.org/article/obama-record-deportations-deporter-chief-or-not

20. Felton, E. (2017, September 6). The Department of Justice is overseeing the resegregation of American schools. *The Nation.* Retrieved from https://www.thenation.com/article/the-department-of-justice-is-overseeing-the-resegregation-of-american-schools/

21. Tracy, A. (2016, December 7). Ohio just passed the nation's most extreme anti-abortion bill. *Vanity Fair.* Retrieved from https://www.vanityfair.com/news/2016/12/john-kasich-ohio-anti-abortion-bill

22. Brabaw, K. (2017, March 31). Everything you need to know about "bathroom bills." *Refinery29.* Retrieved from http://www.refinery29.com/2017/03/148085/anti-transgender-bathroom-bills-what-you-need-to-know

23. Carlson, S. (2016, November 27). When higher education was a public good. *The Chronicle of Higher Education.* Retrieved from https://www.chronicle.com/article/When-College-Was-a-Public-Good/238501

24. Bell, D. (1992). Racial realism. *Connecticut Law Review, 24*(2), 363–379.

25. Stewart, D.-L. (2017, March). Language of appeasement. *Inside Higher Ed.* Retrieved from https://www.insidehighered.com/views/2017/03/30/colleges-need-language-shift-not-one-you-think-essay

26. Driver, J. (2011). Rethinking the interest-convergence thesis. *Northwestern University Law Review, 105*(1), 149–197.

27. Ahmed, S. (2012). *On being included: Racism and diversity in institutional life.* Durham, NC: Duke University Press; Spade, D. (2010). Be professional! *Harvard Journal of Law and Gender, 33*(1), 71–84.

28. "When students believe that it is a grave interpersonal risk to disagree with others, further retreat into their own digital cocoon is likely. [New paragraph.]

That echo chamber is being extended to the campus commons as well. Freedom of expression, long a cherished principle within American society and especially higher education, is under assault. Speakers considered to be offensive are disinvited, shouted down, or shut down. I am sympathetic to the concern, raised by some student activists, that to provide a platform to an offensive speaker is to create a psychologically unsafe environment on campus, yet these approaches make meaningful communication less likely, further deepening the challenge of creating true understanding," Rue, p. 10.

29. Serwer, A. (2017, September 26). A nation of snowflakes. *The Atlantic.* Retrieved from https://www.theatlantic.com/politics/archive/2017/09/it-takes-a-nation-of-snowflakes/541050/

30. Rue, p. 10.

31. Stewart, D.-L. (2017). Producing "docile bodies": Disciplining citizen-subjects. *International Journal of Qualitative Studies in Education, 30*(10), 1042-1046; Stewart, D.-L. (2018). Minding the gap between diversity and institutional transformation: Eight proposals for enacting institutional change. *Teachers College Record, 120*(14). Retrieved from http://www.tcrecord.org/library.

32. Kitchener, K. (1985). Ethical principles and ethical decisions in student affairs. H. J. Canon and R. D. Brown (Eds.), *Applied ethics in student services (New Directions for Student Services No. 30,* (pp. 17–30). San Francisco: Jossey-Bass.

33. Ewens, H. (2016, April 28). Why do we talk about Millennials like they're all middle class? *Vice.* Retrieved from https://www.vice.com/en_uk/article/qbxgxd/millennials-like-theyre-all-middle-class-lie-working-class-britain-class-war

34. Waterman, S. J., Lowe, S. C., & Shotton, H. J. (Eds.). (2018). *Beyond access: Indigenizing programs for Native American student success.* Sterling, VA: Stylus.

35. Byrd, W. C. (2017). *Poison in the ivy: Race relations and the reproduction of inequality on elite college campuses.* New Brunswick, NJ: Rutgers University Press; Nelson Laird, T. F., & Niskode-Dossett, A. S. (2010). How gender and race moderate the effect of interactions across difference on student perceptions of the campus environment. *Review of Higher Education, 33,* 333–356.

36. "More and more, we curate what we see and who we hear. We follow who we like on Instagram, and Twitter, and Facebook, and we receive targeted ads based upon what we already follow," Rue, p. 9.

37. waheed, n. (2014). *nejma.* Las Vegas, NV: CreateSpace.

38. Daloz Parks, S. (2000). *Big questions, worthy dreams: Mentoring emerging adults in their search for meaning, purpose, and faith.* San Francisco, CA: Jossey-Bass.

39. Ward, J. (2016). *The fire this time: A new generation speaks about race.* New York, NY: Scribner.

40. Khan-Cullors, P. (2018). *When they call you a terrorist: A Black Lives Matter memoir.* New York, NY: St. Martin's Press.

41. BYP 100 (2018). *Home page.* Retrieved from https://byp100.org/

42. Rue, p. 4

43. Goodreads (n. d.). Quotable quotes: James Baldwin. Retrieved from https://www.goodreads.com/quotes/1868-i-love-america-more-than-any-other-country-in-the

44. Strange, C. C., & Stewart, D. L. (2011). Preparing diversity change leaders. In D. L. Stewart (Ed.), *Multicultural student services: Building bridges, re-visioning community*. Sterling, VA: Stylus.

2

How Do Student Affairs Educators Help Students Learn to Engage Productively in Difficult Dialogue?

Learning Dialogic Skills for Effective Campus Conversations

Kelly E. Maxwell and Monita C. Thompson

There have been numerous contested issues throughout the history of American higher education. One of the first was "Who has access to higher education?" For over a century, especially in the last half-century, more and more women and people of color gained access to colleges and universities, raising another question about how these new populations would be integrated into predominantly white, initially male, institutions. As LGBT students came out, students with disabilities gained access, and undocumented students made their voices heard, this question remained paramount. As access opened for this newer wave of students, a further question surfaced about how higher education can truly become an inclusive place where all students can thrive. As these new voices emerged in larger numbers in the mid- to late twentieth century, we wondered how to communicate across these differences. People who brought different communication styles and norms, distinct life experiences and perhaps new and unique paths to universities, challenge many of the conventional ways of interacting, leading, teaching, learning, and communicating that were advanced in earlier days.

Moreover, questions we thought we had settled about who belongs and hurts that were on the mend have been exposed more recently as our national conversations have become more polarized. Painful though familiar wounds of exclusion and marginalization have been again revealed to those whose participation is in question and threatened. With the repeal of Deferred Action for Childhood Arrivals (DACA), our Dreamer students wonder whether they will be deported. African American students try to focus on their studies while walking across our campuses to find racist propaganda asserting long-debunked white supremacist myths. How can we communicate across that divide?

People of all political perspectives and people from both privileged and oppressed identities find themselves questioning, rightly or wrongly, whether "the other" recognizes and embraces their perspectives. These difficult topics about access, marginalization, and polarization might make it quite easy to walk away from people with whom we disagree. Dialogue is one avenue for bridging these divides. Dialogue is about being in relationship with others[1] where people are in a process together, learning and growing, although not necessarily agreeing. Dialogue also requires a safe environment for equity and civility. Notions of civility or how we view civility are culturally defined. A standard definition of *civility* often suggests respectful, polite discourse devoid of emotion. Conversely, incivility would be disrespectful, impolite, and fraught with emotion. Cortina posits that incivility can be a manifestation of bias, particularly with respect to gender and race.[2] Men, women, and people from different cultures may exhibit emotion differently; some may cry, others raise their voice, express anger, or become silent when tensions rise. Yet in true dialogue we must be willing to accept these cultural differences and embrace emotion (in all forms) to fully provide a safe and equitable learning environment.

Regrettably, the term *dialogue* has become overused. When communication occurs between at least two opposing groups, we often call it a dialogue. Yet there is a rich history of the dialogue movement in higher education that centers diversity and social justice. It is born out of the progressive educational movement of John Dewey and strengthened by the pedagogical innovations of social justice advocates like Paulo Freire and Myles Horton. It also arises from the serious social scientific inquiries catalyzed from the civil rights movement, feminist movement, gay rights movement, and disability rights movement.[3] Swayed by these progressive and academic innovations, corporations in the 1970s and 1980s began to understand the significance of a diverse workforce and sought to make their companies welcoming to all. Workplace diversity conversations also informed dialogue in higher education. Yet perhaps the most significant source stems from our students themselves. From the action and activism of the Black Action Movements and La Raza, to Peace Movements and Feminist Talk-Backs, our students led the way to call for dialogues with people from different groups and with differing and sometimes contentious perspectives.[4]

Given this history, connected directly to students and university life, student affairs educators have a responsibility to foster safe, civil, and inclusive learning environments for all students and provide models for students to talk with one another across their differences. One of the important first steps must happen at the leadership level. Vice presidents and deans should name the value of civil discourse and dialogue as core tenets of their work in student affairs. If we hope that students will have these tough conversations, are we having them? Do we model that agreement is the goal or that understanding multiple perspectives is valued? Do our planning processes involve opportunities for dialogue—for alternative voices to emerge and be valued and considered? Do we encourage professional development for our staffs to learn dialogic tools that they can use within their work and especially with students?

Intergroup Dialogue

Intergroup Dialogue is a form of dialogic communication that engages the different identities, ideas, and experiences of the students involved in it. This is the type of dialogue we do at the University of Michigan, which connects roughly equal numbers of students from two different social identity groups (e.g., race, ethnicity, gender, sexual orientation, and other groups) with a history of conflict and power differences to talk face-to-face about their experiences in the context of understanding identities, power, privilege, and oppression. The dialogues address Allport's contact conditions to maximize equality and minimize power differentials.[5] We do this by balancing numbers of participants from both identity groups so that no single student, particularly from marginalized identities, is tokenized in the space (e.g., in a race/ethnicity dialogue there are roughly equal numbers of students of color and white students). There are multiple people with multiple perspectives in any given identity , so it helps to build on commonalities and acknowledge differences within and across identity groups. Further, there are two trained undergraduate cofacilitators to help the students deeply engage in productive conversations with one another.[6] These dialogues take place over a semester as a credit-bearing course representing another of Allport's contact conditions: They are sanctioned by authorities, in this case, by the university itself.

The Intergroup Dialogue course follows a four-stage model of leading students through a process of creating a shared meaning of dialogue, understanding identities and social relationships through self-reflection and connection with others, examining social inequality through contemporary conflicts, and exploring ways to move forward individually and collectively.[7]

While intergroup dialogue may be applicable and even necessary in some instances, a semester-long course with balanced numbers of students from two identity groups may not be feasible or even desired in every setting. So how do we utilize some of the tenets of intergroup dialogue to create opportunities for face-to-face robust conversations among students, both proactively and amid conflict? How do we engage others in productive dialogue about contentious issues? We see these exchanges, sometimes called *difficult dialogues*, less as arduous chores and more as challenges that provide opportunities for growth and learning. The next section addresses a number of important considerations when creating opportunities for dialogues about any topic.

Setting the Stage for Dialogue

Setting expectations is a first step in the dialogue process. Just as our senior student affairs leaders must set expectations of their organizations, we, too, must set expectations for any dialogue encounter. Greater understanding (of one's own perspectives, of the issues at hand, of how others see the issues) can be an excellent goal but should be explicitly stated from the outset. If a solution is the stated expectation, be sure to provide time and space for problem-solving alongside the dialogue experience.

After defining the goals, the following components help us achieve the conditions necessary for dialogue. Most important, we believe that dialogue cannot be required. There must be openness to listening and contributing that cannot be achieved by compelling people to attend. Students often suggest that our Intergroup Dialogue course should be required of all students. We argue the opposite. Dialogue cannot be effective when it is mandatory. Another condition for dialogue is respecting others. Sometimes that is confused with respecting the perspectives that others hold—even when they are discriminatory or hurtful. The dialogue process is fundamentally about understanding, which comes from empathy. We must work to value the humanity of others in the room with whom we may vehemently disagree. Why might someone hold such opposing views? What life experiences have led them to that perspective? How can I connect their humanity to mine? This type of respect overrides agreement. Conflict and contentiousness can occur when we all value the humanity of "the other." If that human-to-human respect cannot occur (e.g., because the values one espouses demeans or devalues others) then true dialogue cannot occur.

Planning is another crucial component that supports the conditions of dialogue. While they can sometimes feel very spontaneous, the best dialogues have a loose structure and some key elements. First is deciding where to host it. Consider the issue. Is the dialogue based on a contentious campus issue? Who are the affected students? Do they come from identity groups that have different experiences with power? The location of the dialogue really matters. For example, suppose a predominantly white fraternity hosted a party where members were photographed in blackface and the Black Student Union is outraged. After the student conduct process has occurred and the reconciliation process has begun, perhaps several months later, both groups decide to meet and dialogue about the campus climate that led to the incident. The largely white fraternity feels it would be a nice gesture to host the dialogue in their expansive living room space. Help students consider how that location may in fact reify the marginalization that the Black students felt from the initial incident and how that might cloud the entire event. Instead, think carefully about a location that will support both groups. The second key element of planning for dialogue is the room set-up. Dialogues typically occur in a circle with 12 to 16 people. It is difficult to be in an intimate circle with 20 or more people. Participants have to speak louder than their typical speaking voice for people across the room to hear. Further, patterns of introversion and extraversion tend to play out, where some talk frequently while others hang back. Is it possible to create dialogic spaces with groups larger than 20? Yes, and thinking this through ahead of time is important. One option is to create smaller groups at round tables or consider the number of facilitators needed to break large groups into smaller units for dialogue.

The third key element is to consider facilitation. Who can and should facilitate the dialogue? We recommend cofacilitation when possible. Facilitators do not have to be topical experts but should have a strong foundation and perhaps hold differing perspectives on the topic or bring different identity experiences to the table. If cofacilitation is possible, what is the right combination? Are student or near-peer (perhaps graduate student) facilitators more appropriate? How might they get to the heart of an issue in ways that advisers, program directors, and mentors cannot? Would it be effective for a student affairs educator and a student to cofacilitate together? If others are facilitating, when is it appropriate for student affairs professionals to join the dialogue as participants? All facilitators should examine their own relationships to emotion and conflict. If one grew up in a culture where it was polite to get along and impolite to make waves, show emotions, or express dissent, what kinds of additional preparation are needed to lead these efforts? If easily mistrustful about dissenting viewpoints, how can a facilitator learn to invite those differing perspectives into the room? These are the types of questions to consider before hosting dialogues.

Thinking About the Dialogue Process

What happens during the dialogue process is crucial to the success of any dialogic engagement. Organizers should think ahead about the tone they set in the room, the emphasis on self-exploration and relationship-building, how and when to explore the issues at hand, and how to conclude the dialogue session. This next section explores each of these topics further.

Setting the Tone

Once the dialogue has begun, it is important to set the tone up front. Consider the length of the dialogue experience—several hours, several days (weekend retreat), over time? Attention to the length will help determine the depth of setting the tone. Regardless, we recommend attending to two things: creating a shared meaning of dialogue and group formation. Students have been in many discussions in and out of classrooms throughout their lives. Typical discussions may clarify issues but not deepen understanding. People participate in discussion to add their thoughts (like serial monologues) rather than to build on what others have contributed. Discussions happen with the assumption of an equal playing field for everyone (without overt attention to it). Dialogue is different, and the goals should be explained. Dialogue is collaborative, and the sharing of personal experiences is an important tool for greater self-awareness and overall understanding. Emotion is also a central part of dialogue. Specific attention is paid to the power dynamics in the room so that all people can participate on their own terms. (See the online supplement on the differences among dialogue, discussion, and debate for more on these distinctions.[8]) If the dialogue will run for a single session, facilitators can verbalize the differences in the types of communication and ask students to think about how these might look and feel different. Ask participants to be intentional throughout the gathering to notice whether they are staying in dialogue together. For a multisession dialogue, we might have students roleplay the distinctions among debate, discussion, and dialogue to help them recognize the differences.

Additionally, building group cohesion is important. Trust is vital to the process of dialogue. If conflict is a likely product of a dialogue, students must be prepared to trust the students sitting across from them in the circle. In a multisession dialogue, group formation is done through progressively more revealing icebreakers—from name games to deeper personal sharing like the five-minute poem.[9] All groups, regardless of length, should define some norms for how to talk together (see our Guidelines for Dialogue on p. 40). The most important aspect of using guidelines is to deepen trust and enhance the dialogue, not thwart it. Guidelines can be misused—especially by people who fear conflict or emotion, who are often the group with more privilege in the room—to tamp down conflict or avoid situations that bring disagreement. It is important to name these dynamics if they begin to occur and ask students to reflect on some of their most important learning moments. Chances are, they have come with dissonance or uncertainty. We want to promote spaces that allow students to be on their learning edges.

Creating guidelines for participation can be a great way to open conversations about safety. We always want students to be physically and psychologically safe in dialogue spaces. But that does not mean they will not experience dissonance, conflict, anger, or other strong emotions. *Contested issues* are by definition topics without agreement. It may take courage and fortitude to listen with empathy to perspectives one does not understand or that go against what one has learned throughout life or with which one wholeheartedly disagrees. Scholars refer to these as brave spaces that push us beyond our comfort zones to our learning edges—those spaces where dissonance combined with openness creates a framework for learning.[10] Only then can the dialogue truly be impactful. So, setting the stage for this openness is crucial to the process.

Self-Exploration and Relationship-Building

The next part of the dialogue experience asks three key questions: Who am I? Who are you? Why are we doing this together? This is the opportunity for self-exploration and relationship-building. Often people come to the dialogue with passion and openness but also with many un(in)formed perspectives and stereotypes about people with opposing viewpoints or differing identities.

This is a great time to help students build skills that are needed to make dialogue effective. In *Dialogue Across Difference*, Gurin, Nagda, and Zúñiga discuss several communication processes for intergroup dialogue.[11] Two of them are relevant here: engaging self and appreciating difference. When students are engaging themselves fully in the dialogue space, they are sharing their own stories and informed perspectives, they are following up on others' ideas to add their own, and they are suspending assumptions. Engaging oneself is an internal process of self-exploration and commitment.

Appreciating difference is more external. It involves participation with others by listening deeply, affirming one another, asking questions that seek to understand and taking the perspectives of others in the room. Depending on the length of the dialogue experience, facilitators might simply ask participants to be attuned to these self and other dynamics or they may engage in longer exercises that help build students' capacity for dialogue. As students engage in self-exploration and relationship building, they are learning crucial skills for the heart of the dialogue.

Exploring Contested Issues

After setting expectations, laying the groundwork, and learning important dialogue skills while exploring one's own perspectives and building relationships with others, students are prepared to examine the issue at hand. Exploring the contested issue is why many students want to engage in dialogue. They may be eager to skip the initial steps to get into the issue. Our advice is to "trust the process." Adequate skill-building and preparation benefits the dialogue process when discussing new or challenging issues with people who have differing views.

Facilitators need to consider a variety of questions when preparing for this part of the dialogue, such as the following:

- How do we get multiple perspectives on the table?
- How do we provide factual data to frame the conversation?
- How do we correct factual errors presented by participants?
- How do we handle emotion in the room?
- How do we balance airtime among participants?
- How do we avoid serial monologues and instead help students reach dialogue?

The heart of the dialogue should rely on inquiry—seeking to understand one another. Participants should be encouraged to ask questions and build on each other's responses to deepen the experience. The most effective facilitators also use inquiry methods to reach participants.[12]

Concluding the Dialogue Process

So, the dialogue has occurred—engaging, contentious, productive, touching, difficult, or even light-hearted. What now? The final step is to wrap up in a way that is consistent with the expectations described at the beginning. It is important to honor the dialogue process—even with all its complexities—by doing some kind of closing round of affirmations or takeaways to bring clo-sure to the experience. The wrap-up may also include answering the "so what" question. Why did we engage in this dialogue? What is different now? How are we changed? And, as a result of answering these questions is there something more that comes from this? All participants are changed by listening deeply to people with differing perspectives and having the opportunity to share their own experiences. That could be enough—knowing that we are thinking about the issues in new ways and interacting in the world with this newfound knowl-edge. However, the dialogue experience could lead to more self-exploration, more interpersonal interaction between individuals who found connection in the group, and even more collaboration and coalition-building across groups. Whether participants' expectations are fully met, helping students reflect on these opportunities is an appropriate conclusion to the dialogue experience.

Adapting Dialogue

This process, based loosely on the four-stage model of intergroup dialogue,[13] sets the conditions upon which a strong dialogue can occur. Yet at times, dialogue is not the right tactic. When contentiousness exists, emotions are too raw, or polarization is too great, we believe that dialogue will not be the best choice to proceed. And it is important for student affairs educators to understand the need to bring people together in ways that seek to address and resolve conflict, have student voices heard, and to discuss ways to work collectively with students.

Campus forums, town halls, workshops, focus groups, or restorative practices can be effective alternatives to dialogue. Forums and town halls allow students and the community at large to air feelings of frustration, fear, anger, and confusion, as well as provide clarifying information about the issue or situation. These types of venues can bring the campus community together to understand the various opinions and seek ways to provide the next steps—the "what now?"

While dialogue is distinct from these additional ways to address conten-tious issues on campus, dialogic techniques and methods can be used broadly with each of these alternatives. It is important for student affairs educators to recognize and use appropriate tactics that reflect the goals they seek to achieve. Forums or town halls can use practices such as small group discus-sions before large group sharing or exercises to surface concerns, questions, and thoughts and feelings in the room. Setting the tone and framing are still important, and the advice already given can also apply here. Utilizing dia-logic principles can still lead to effective communication, although it should not be mistaken for dialogue proper. Workshops are another way to help students explore issues and build skills. Workshops typically focus on skill building or a deeper understanding of particular concepts, such as giving and receiving feedback or understanding microaggressions. Workshop formats can use some of the same dialogic principles to foster good discussion and increased understanding. Focus groups can be productive ways for student affairs educators to gather information from selected groups about their experiences, feelings, thoughts, and ideas for moving forward after broad community concerns or campus climate issues. Restorative justice practices[14] can be used to address impact when community harm has been determined or when attempting to create a campus climate of inclusion after an unsettling incident. These practices may also use dialogic methods or techniques to create an environment of sharing, respect, support, and accountability.

Finally, as administrators, while we may want to host a dialogue with a particular group of students to learn more about their campus experiences, we recommend considering these steps when setting up and preparing for the event. Dialogue rarely occurs when there is a clear imbalance of power in the room. A small group of administrators are likely unwilling to make themselves vulnerable, share their own stories of pain or frustration, or truly be in dialogue with students from whom they are hoping to learn lessons. Relationship-building is more like rapport-building and is still a crucial part of the event. Yet it is not mutual or reciprocal like dialogue. Still, hearing students and listening to their concerns is important when contested issues are at play. The advice here can inform such conversations.

We are sometimes asked if power and privilege need to be addressed in a dialogue, workshop, or forum. We believe that being explicit about the relevance of power and privilege deepens the conversation and connection among students. The social group identities of individuals are always present in these interactions, whether acknowledged or not. There are significant obstacles to creating equity in the space when not attending to group identity, power, and privilege. First, marginalized students are keenly aware of their group identity and its impact on their lives and experiences. For some, not acknowledging how identity privilege and social power play out can leave them feeling that the interaction is inauthentic and real change will not happen. Attention to identity, power, and privilege in both the process of the experience (who is speaking, who is being listened to, whether there are cofacilitators of multiple identities, etc.) and the content of the interaction (directly talking about social identities and their impact on the discussion or perhaps even doing a social identity exercise) is important. Recognizing and attending to these dynamics is a good way to value students' time and experiences. It may also lead to deeper relationships among students who subsequently join in collective action to effect real institutional change.

Where Do We Go From Here?

As student affairs educators who seek to help students navigate the some-times unfamiliar landscape of dialogue, we must be prepared to engage our students and ourselves in these critical conversations. Sometimes contentious and conflictual, often rewarding and even fun, engaging in dialogue is central to educational practice both in and out of the classroom. Today's students must be prepared to think critically about difficult issues, build skills to listen and talk to people with whom they may have little in common or disagree, and build relationships to effectively work together even without whole-hearted agreement on issues facing society. But helping students learn these important skills begins with us. We, too, must be prepared to be in dialogue with our students. We must model and showcase the skills necessary to effec-tively speak with others across a variety of lines of difference including social identities, political ideology, disciplinary perspectives, and cultural differences.

As educators, we must do our own work, which begins with getting the skills to engage in dialogue along with understanding the impact of our social identities and the systems of privilege and oppression within which we operate. From listening to perspective taking, relationship-building to sharing our own experiences, we must attend conferences, seminars, workshops, and dialogues to build these skills. Often called *soft skills*, these are not frequently taught in graduate courses or through traditional academic endeavors. Professionals typically need to seek out opportunities to develop these proficiencies.

How can we effectively assess where we are and what we need in order to engage in productive dialogue? Self-reflection is key to doing our own work, and so is being in community. Are we surrounded by like-minded people whose perspectives reinforce our own or whose identities match ours? Do we have a trusted colleague from whom we can get honest feedback? We must activate our own learning edges as we seek to build the knowledge and skills to effectively dialogue with others. Doing our own work is about tak-ing a look at our multiple identities to learn more about them and how we are part of systems that advantage or disadvantage others or us. We need to closely examine our stories and experiences to look for patterns of inclusion or exclusion.[15]

Finally, we must simply try it out. Most of us in the United States do not grow up dialoguing with people who have different perspectives and identities. It may not feel any more natural or secure for us than for our stu-dents. We must find ways to practice dialogue personally and professionally. Building a culture of dialogue in staff meetings and professional develop-ment sessions is a beginning. Finding community engagement opportunities is another way to build skills. Even as we encourage our students to embrace their learning edges, student affairs educators, too, must learn the important tools to effectively dialogue across difference.

Guidelines for Dialogue

The following is a suggested list of guidelines to support effective dialogue.

1. We must ensure confidentiality. We want to create an atmosphere for open, honest exchange.
2. Our primary commitment is to learn from each other. We will listen to each other and not talk at each other. We acknowledge differences among us in backgrounds, skills, interests, and values. We realize that it is these very differences that will increase our awareness and understanding through this process.
3. We will not demean, devalue, or put down people for their experiences, lack of experiences, or difference in interpretation of those experiences.
4. We will trust that people are always doing the best they can. We will give each other the benefit of the doubt. We will assume we are all trying our hardest and that our intentions are good even when the impact is not.
5. Challenge the idea and not the person. If we wish to challenge something that has been said, we will challenge the idea or the practice referred to, not the individual sharing this idea or practice.
6. Speak your discomfort. If something is bothering you, please share this with the group. Often our emotional reactions to this process offer the most valuable learning opportunities.
7. Monitor your air time. Be mindful of taking up much more space than others. On the same note, empower yourself to speak up when others are dominating the conversation.
8. Don't freeze people in time. We are all a work in progress. We will not assume that one comment or one opinion made at one time captures the whole of a person's character.

These guidelines were developed by The Program on Intergroup Relations at the University of Michigan with acknowledgment to Melanie Morrison of Allies for Change and Shayla Griffin, 2012.

Discussion Questions

1. How do student affairs educators continue their own work—building content knowledge and process skills to engage in productive dialogue?

2. How important to the dialogue process is the examination of power in institutional and societal structures? Can effective dialogue only emphasize interpersonal relationships without examining power dynamics in social structures?

3. What are the considerations when two different groups want different outcomes from the dialogue experience?

Authors' Note

Throughout, we chose not to capitalize *white* in terms of race. This is an important deviation from many editorial styles that reimagines power where whiteness is not central (and therefore not capitalized) even while Black or other racial categories are capitalized.

Notes

1. Martin Buber calls it an "I–Thou" relationship. Buber, M. (1970). *I and Thou*. A new translation with a prologue "I and You" and notes by Walter Kaufmann. New York, NY: Scribner.

2. Cortina, L. (2008). Unseen injustice: Incivility as modern discrimination in organizations. *Academy of Management Review, 33*(1), 55–75.

3. Maxwell, K. E., & Thompson, M. C. (2017). *Breaking ground through intergroup education: The Program on Intergroup Relations (IGR), 1988–2016*. IGR Working Paper Series. Ann Arbor, MI: The Program on Intergroup Relations.

4. Ibid.

5. Allport, G. W. (1954). *The nature of prejudice*. Cambridge, MA: Addison-Wesley.

6. Zúñiga, X., Nagda, B. A., Chesler, M., & Cytron-Walker, A. (2007). *Intergroup dialogue in higher education: Meaningful learning about social justice* [Special issue]. *ASHE Higher Education Report, 32*(4).

7. Ibid.

8. Kachwaha, T. (2002). Exploring the differences between discussion, debate, and dialogue. The Program on Intergroup Relations. Retrieved from https://teaching.yale-nus.edu.sg/wp-content/uploads/sites/25/2016/04/Exploring-the-Differences-Between-Discussion-Debate-and-Dialogue.pdf

9. Tatum, B. D. (2007). *Can we talk about race? And other conversations in an era of school resegregation*. Boston, MA: Beacon Press.

10. Arao, B., & Clemens, K. (2013). From safe spaces to brave spaces. In L. M. Landreman (Ed.), *The art of effective facilitation: Reflections from social justice educators* (pp. 135–150). Sterling, VA: Stylus.

11. Gurin, P., Nagda, B. A., & Zúñiga, X. (2013). *Dialogue across difference: Practice, theory, and research on intergroup dialogue.* New York, NY: Russell-Sage.

12. Ibid.

13. Zúñiga et al., *Intergroup dialogue in higher education.*

14. Goldblum, A. (2009). Restorative justice from theory to practice. In J. Meyer Schrage & N. Geist Giacomini (Eds.), *Reframing campus conflict: Student conduct practice through a social justice lens* (pp. 140–154). Sterling, VA: Stylus.

15. Wong(Lau), K., Landrum-Brown, J., & Walker, T. E. (2011). (Re)Training ourselves: Professionals who facilitate Intergroup Dialogue. In K. E. Maxwell, B. A. Nagda, & M. C. Thompson (Eds.), *Facilitating intergroup dialogues: Bridging differences, catalyzing change* (pp. 85–97). Sterling, VA: Stylus.

Systemic Integration of Dialogic Skills: An Opportunity for Student Affairs/ Academic Affairs Partnerships

Jeannie Brown Leonard

As campuses and communities become more diverse, it makes sense to examine how higher education professionals prepare students for citizenship. Our democracy depends on inclusive participation, discussion, and evidence-based decision-making.[1] Our students come to us with a wide range of role models on ways to engage with others. In addition to diverse home and community contexts, students witness a host of intolerant exchanges through the news, reality TV, social media, and sporting events. Is it any wonder students struggle to be open to new perspectives and ideas? We cannot assume students know how to engage in civil discourse or dialogue. The word *dialogue* has a very specific meaning. Knowing a precise definition of *dialogue* is less meaningful than knowing how to leverage the skills used in dialogue to diffuse mistrust, promote listening, and improve understanding across difference. The challenge of helping students learn from others who are not like them provides opportunities for student affairs and academic affairs partnerships. In my response to Maxwell and Thompson I offer a path to integrating dialogic skills into two existing higher education structures, namely the formal curriculum and residential learning communities. Integrative learning approaches provide insight on how to help college students engage productively in difficult dialogues. That this engagement is important is far less contested than how we achieve it.

Dialogic Skills

Maxwell and Thompson draw from the literature and their experience with Intergroup Dialogue (IGD) as a foundation for how to help college students engage productively in difficult *dialogues*. These chapter authors succinctly and clearly provide the reader with context on the IGD program as it is practiced at the University of Michigan and elsewhere. IGD is a specific form

43

of engagement that promotes understanding across difference.[2] Their essay, however, is not a primer on IGD. The authors balance theory and practice in parsing out the critical elements of meaningful dialogue. I applaud Maxwell and Thompson for focusing on the dialogic skills at the foundation of IGD rather than insisting on IGD in its purest form. They recognize the challenge of emulating the IGD structure—a semester-long course dedicated to regular and sustained engagement with the right composition of students represented. They liberate the educator to borrow insights and techniques as needed. Creating the conditions for a successful dialogue is daunting, but the flexibility to adapt and adopt aspects of a well-established intervention is appealing and promising. Maxwell and Thompson address several contexts in which student affairs educators might be able to leverage dialogic skills, each with challenges and opportunities. I have clustered these applications into two types: reactive and proactive.

Reactive Situations

When responding to an incident on campus, senior administrators charge student affairs educators with resolving the conflict. This resolution might address perceptions of fundamental unfairness, involve restitution, or promote attitude and behavior change. Generally the goal is to achieve equilibrium and accord. Although there may be sustained engagement in these dialogues, there also is some coercion in bringing students together. The very act of bringing together students in conflict violates the voluntary criterion for successful dialogue. Similarly, if an incident is born out of distrust or hate, is it possible to engage in a process that requires a safe, nonthreatening environment?

Proactive Situations

When the goal is improved understanding of individual differences, dialogue promotes listening, learning, reflection, and action. This improved understanding creates an inclusive campus climate in which students from any background can thrive and learn from each other. There are logistical challenges to good dialogue. The need for small groups with balanced representation on the identity dimension under consideration makes intuitive sense, until one starts defining those dimensions. Our students, faculty, and staff inhabit multiple identities, and dialogue often does not accommodate these intersectionalities.[3] Additionally, the students who volunteer for these opportunities may be students who are already open and respectful of others. How can we bring to the discussion students who are intolerant of or inexperienced with perspectives different from their own?

Integrating Dialogue Into Educational Mission in the Formal Curriculum

To bring reluctant participants into the dialogue and to expand the scope of these interventions, I propose an integrated approach. There are two areas of the campus that, together, allow us to engage most or all of our undergraduates: the formal curriculum and living-learning communities (LLCs).

The Rise of Interdisciplinarity and Integrative Learning

The academy has embraced interdisciplinary approaches to teaching and learning, albeit without the definitional precision that some scholars prefer.[4] The term *interdisciplinary* often is used interchangeably with *multidisciplinary* and *integrative learning*. The problems facing our world are increasingly complex. These problems are beyond the scope of any one perspective; solutions often require leveraging insights and tools of two or more disciplines.[5] For example, using only economics to understand poverty ignores the vital insights from sociology, history, public policy, psychology, and finance. Interdisciplinary scholars focus on the contributions of different *disciplines* to understanding a problem. Integrative learning is more capacious: Disciplines as well as other perspectives inform solutions.[6] Interdisciplinary programs promote integrative learning and are growing at a fast pace on many campuses.[7] This growth provides a collaborative opportunity between academic affairs and student affairs in our shared goals of teaching students skills to engage with diverse others and promoting understanding of diverse perspectives.

There is remarkable overlap in the expectations for dialogue and how students become integrative learners. How can we expect our students to learn from diverse others without teaching them the tools for engagement? This teaching can occur in interdisciplinary classrooms with the help of dialogic skills. The steps of the interdisciplinary research process include understanding context, engaging with multiple perspectives, and identifying points of conflict and similarity to reach common ground.[8] By considering multiple perspectives on an issue, students can begin to see the merit in ideas with which they disagree. The goal is not to convert participants to one particular worldview. Rather, the goal is to recognize pluralism and invite respectful engagement across difference. "The more students encounter perspectives from other cultures, social classes, regions, nations, ethnicities, genders, sexual orientations, races, and religions as well as disciplines, the richer and more comprehensive their understanding of real-world issues."[9] This improved understanding allows for greater civility and safety on campus as well as evidence of improved learning.

Almost 20 years ago, Newell shared his views on how integrative learning can provide the pedagogical framework for holistic student development by embracing learning in all its contexts.[10] He invited student affairs educators to reinforce student growth and development by applying integrative learning approaches. Perhaps the tools developed by student affairs educators can inform and enrich faculty efforts at promoting integrative learning rather than the reverse. Faculty members engaged with interdisciplinary programs are likely allies in teaching the fundamentals of good dialogue.

By integrating dialogic skill instruction into the formal curriculum via interdisciplinary courses, the solution becomes systemic rather than ad hoc. The reactive approach described earlier aligns with the problem-solving goals of interdisciplinary courses: The problem exists; how do we address it? The proactive approach is a form of perspective taking and conflict resolution integral to integrative learning. Leveraging the dialogic skills of expectation setting, listening, empathy, and seeking common ground offers faculty more tools for teaching.

Residential Learning Communities

LLCs offer another area for integrating dialogue into the student experience. LLCs are residential housing structures where students with shared interests can engage in an intentional exploration of that interest, ideally blurring the boundaries of in-class and out-of-class learning.[11] Touted as a "high-impact practice,"[12] the National Study of Living Learning Programs (NSLLP) has produced empirical insights about the effectiveness of living-learning programs.[13] The most effective LLCs have a strong academic connection (usually accomplished via a shared course with clear student learning outcomes), shared oversight with academic affairs and student affairs, and extensive learning opportunities both inside and outside the classroom.[14] Using dialogic skills early in the year could build a foundation of understanding and trust among residents, contributing to community-building and improving learning outcomes. The NSLLP learned that students participating in LLCs "did not show differences in their appreciation for racial and ethnic diversity on their campus, nor did they say that they grew more than their non-LLP peers in terms of cognitive complexity, liberal learning, and personal philosophies."[15] LLCs are a potential venue for formal IGD experiences, which in turn may promote greater appreciation for difference and contribute to a culture that promotes equity, civility, and safety.

Next Steps

For decades higher education scholars have lamented the challenges of creating lasting and effective academic affairs and student affairs partnerships.

Taking a systemic approach to integrating dialogic practices into the formal curriculum and LLCs might lead to more productive collaborations. Resistance is likely. Faculty, traditionally, are not aware of the expertise of student affairs educators. Start by cultivating a few faculty champions; a good place to begin is with those teaching interdisciplinary courses. Teaching the skills of engagement should reduce the number and severity of incidents on campus that threaten diversity, civility, and safety.

Student affairs educators can partner with faculty in ways that are mutually beneficial. Share your expertise with the teaching and learning center on your campus. Offer workshops on using dialogue in the classroom. Invite faculty to shape the development of LLCs. There is great potential for students to learn dialogic skills in these residential contexts, which could help LLCs fulfill their potential.

Dialogic skills could promote understanding between academic affairs and student affairs professionals. By establishing common ground around shared goals of promoting student learning and success, collaborations across academic affairs and student affairs may improve. Maxwell and Thompson call this "doing our own work."[16] This collaboration is easier said than done, but it is worth the investment and effort.

Discussion Questions

1. In seeking collaborators for helping students learn to engage productively in difficult dialogue, whom might you approach? Which faculty members are engaged in integrative learning? Are there stand-alone programs in interdisciplinary studies or integrative studies where you might begin?

2. What learning outcomes are fostered by developing dialogic skills? How might an LLC teach these skills to residents? Who is best suited to teach these skills?

3. Reflect on your own personal and professional development. What might prevent you from finding common ground with someone from a different background?

Notes

1. Gutman, A. (1987). *Democratic education.* Princeton, NJ: Princeton University Press.

2. Zúñiga, X., Lopez, G. E., & Ford, K. A. (Eds.). (2012). *Intergroup dialogue: Critical conversations about difference, social identities, and social justice.* New York, NY: Routledge.

3. Abes, E. S., Jones, S. R., & McEwen, M. K. (2007). Reconceptualizing the model of multiple dimensions of identity: The role of meaning-making capacity in the construction of multiple identities. *Journal of College Student Development, 48*(1), 1–22.

4. Newell, W. H., & Green, W. J. (1998). Defining and teaching interdisciplinary studies. In W. H. Newell (Ed.), *Interdisciplinarity: Essays from the literature* (pp. 23–34). New York, NY: College Board; Association of American Colleges Universities. (2007). *College learning for the new global century: A report from the National Leadership Council for Liberal Education and America's Promise.* Washington DC: Association of American Colleges & Universities.

5. Committee on Facilitating Interdisciplinary Research, Committee on Science, Engineering, and Public Policy. (2005). *Facilitating interdisciplinary research.* Washington DC: National Academies Press. Retrieved from https://www.nap.edu/read/11153/chapter/1; Repko, A. F. (2008). *Interdisciplinary research: Process and theory.* Thousand Oaks, CA: Sage; Thompson Klein, J. (1999). *Mapping interdisciplinary studies.* Washington DC: Association of American Colleges Universities.

6. Taylor Huber, M., & Hutchings, P. (2004). *Integrative learning: Mapping the terrain.* Washington DC: Association of American Colleges & Universities & The Carnegie Foundation for the Advancement of Teaching.

7. Newell, W. H. (2008). The intertwined history of interdisciplinary undergraduate education and the Association for Integrative Studies: An insider's view. *Issues in Integrative Studies, 26,* 1–59.

8. Repko, *Interdisciplinary research.*

9. Newell, W. (1999, May/June). The promise of integrative learning. *About Campus, 4,* 17–23, p. 19.

10. Ibid.

11. Shapiro, N. S., & Levine, J. H. (1999). *Creating learning communities: A practical guide to winning support, organizing for change, and implementing programs.* San Francisco, CA: Jossey-Bass.

12. Kuh, G. D. (2008). *High-impact educational practices: What they are, who has access to them, and why they matter.* Washington DC: Association of American Colleges & Universities.

13. Inkelas, K. K. (2007). *National study of living-learning programs: 2007 report of findings.* Retrieved from http://hdl.handle.net/1903/8392

14. Brower, A. M., & Inkelas, K. K. (Spring 2010). Living-learning programs: One high-impact educational practice we now know a lot about. *Liberal Education, 96*(2), 36–43. Retrieved from https://www.aacu.org/publications-research/periodicals/living-learning-programs-one-high-impact-educational-practice-we

15. Ibid., para. 13.

16. Maxwell, K. E., & Thompson, M. C., this volume, p. 39.

Part Two

Cultivating Inclusive Learning Environments: Equity, Civility, and Safety

3

How Should Institutions Address Student Demands Related to Campus Racial Climate?

To Address Today's Student Demands for Racial Justice, Institutions Must Shift From Multiculturalism to Polyculturalism

Ajay Nair

Student demands related to campus racial climates are almost invariably calls for greater racial justice in higher education. To fully achieve that goal on our campuses requires a paradigm shift by colleges and universities from the traditional model of multiculturalism to one of polyculturalism manifested in communities of practice.[1] We must collaborate across institutional units and, equally important, we must reach out to and partner with today's students.

Most institutions traditionally employ a multicultural paradigm that, whether intended to or not, serves to resist change. Multiculturalism essentializes our complex individual identities; it oversimplifies them into categories based on a few narrow criteria like race, religion, and/or sexual identity. Thus, multiculturalism overlooks most of what makes each of us who we are.

Portions of this essay are adapted from a January 6, 2017, Huffington Post essay and other writings by the author.

51

For example, any one individual may self-identify as many things: straight, gay, or queer; Black, White, Asian, Latinx, a different racial/ethnic group, or a combination; differently abled; wealthy or middle or lower income; atheist, agnostic, or a member of one or more of any number of religious groups; native born or immigrant; from the eastern, western, northern, southern, or some other section of this or another country.

The point is that a vast array of identities intersects in each of us. No person is simply one or two or three identities. Ignoring our multiple intersecting identities, multiculturalism squanders opportunities for us to connect where we intersect, to learn from one another, to engage in constructive dialogue and debate that leads to lasting, systemic change.

By contrast, polyculturalism appreciates the myriad elements and intersections of our individual identities.[2] It reveals the intersections that connect us, and it invites us to engage in meaningful dialogue and debate. Importantly, a shift to a polycultural model calls us to community; indeed, it demands that we cultivate polycultural communities of practice on our campuses—communities grounded in shared principles such as cultural humility, equity, collaboration, debate and dialogue, transparency, and trust.

Throughout my 20 years as a higher education administrator and as a person of color, I've worked with students to negotiate hunger strikes, sit-ins, and many other forms of student dissent intended to advance racial justice on our campuses. Of course, students were mounting such protests long before I became an administrator—and, notably, their demands were much the same as those presented today by contemporary collegians.

Students of color and their allies from many backgrounds in the 1950s and 1960s fought for equal access—to integrate higher education institutions that were racially segregated. One of the demands of their heirs, including student activists at Emory and those in similar racial justice movements today, is equitable access to institutional resources and support services. Like their forebears and contemporaries, Emory students also demand that the university address, among other issues, achieving a sense of belonging for students of color, adequate academic and financial support for students from marginalized communities, equity in funding for student organizations, and recruitment and retention of faculty of color.

However, while students today may present racial justice demands similar to those of previous generations, their worldviews and strategies differ substantially. Today's students often operate largely outside higher education's dominant models. For example, they have been described as digital natives for whom social media and online engagement is a premium; meanwhile, many universities and colleges are still primarily focused on e-mail communication.

Similarly, today's students increasingly reject the still-dominant paradigm of multiculturalism. Experiencing firsthand far more diversity than any previous generation, polyculturalism is increasingly their norm. In response, we must be prepared to meet our students where they are and to be open to accepting the disjuncture between today's students and our hackneyed attempts to build diverse and inclusive communities.

Building on the important but incremental progress on racial and social justice issues over the years under multiculturalism, we have a unique opportunity today to reimagine the academy—not simply to move the margins closer to the center but to redefine the very center. To do so, we must move beyond institutional responses buried in yesterday's paradigms to finally achieving racial justice on our campuses.

Traditional Institutional Responses to Student Demands for Racial Justice

Historically, higher education has not been at the forefront on issues of racial justice. Too often, institutions have offered traditional response strategies to student demands for racially just campuses. One example is clinging to bureaucratic multiculturalism;[3] another traditional response, also among the most common, is the call for protesting students to provide quantitative evidence that supports their claims,[4] thus discounting the qualitative evidence of their lived experience. These typical responses are expressions of institutional resistance to change—the inherent, if sometimes unintentional, tendency to maintain the status quo.

Clinging to Bureaucratic Multiculturalism

With this traditional bureaucratic response, institutions implement multicultural programs and services to address student demands for social justice. This response typically reminds the community of what is already in place to support students of color. It also often describes bureaucratic, yet essential, processes (e.g., faculty governance, board approval, task forces) that will address students' remaining concerns.

In this scenario, significant resources are expended in attempts to create a more equitable community and obviate future disputes. This frequently involves institutions creating identity spaces, such as a Black Culture Center or Latinx Lounge. Such spaces are needed but too often are allocated insufficient resources. In this way, institutions unwittingly pit marginalized groups against one another in competition for limited resources. Moreover, and as noted previously, the outdated multicultural model does not fully consider the complexities of the individual polycultural identities that each student represents,[5] preferring to celebrate distinct groups. By failing to recognize our unique individual intersections with others across multiple identities, this response stifles dialogue across difference.

In these ways and others, bureaucratic multiculturalism resists the changes demanded by today's students, instead maintaining the status quo of the past half century. It rarely unpacks systemic issues and frequently results in a patchwork that only modestly improves the quality of life for students. Often, students settle for the patchwork because of their busy lives, short tenure at the institution, and frustration with the bureaucracy. Little or no systemic change results and, as suggested earlier, the demands of students today continue to echo those of their predecessors of generations past.

Calling for and Privileging Quantitative Evidence

Another typical institutional response to student racial justice demands is the worn-out trope of evidence-based decision-making, which calls for students to present quantitative "evidence" to support their claims. This is not to suggest that such evidence isn't important, that it does not exist, or that it cannot be produced.

Notably, however, those in power in the academy have historically privileged quantitative data over the qualitative evidence that can take into account the lived experiences of marginalized groups. Members of these groups may encounter subtle or not-so-subtle discrimination on a regular basis—experiences not shared by students from dominant groups or administrators in positions of power. Those who fit neatly into institutional structures are in a position to demand such evidence before acknowledging the need to reimagine the existing structures that privilege those in power.[6]

Individuals in privileged positions, unacquainted with the lived experiences of marginalized students, may also emphasize that higher education was nobly integrated a half century ago, implying, however naively, that the problem is solved. Some even suggest that people of color should express greater respect for these venerable institutions of higher education, as well as demonstrate more resilience in the face of adversity.[7] Such responses sidestep the realities of racial injustice and support the status quo.

The master higher education narrative reminds people of color that we are merely guests of these institutions—guests who are expected to assimilate into archaic systems. Respectability politics remind us that academic freedom for people of color comes with rules. Our opinions and ideas are valued as long as they do not challenge the master narrative, which renders people of color ersatz.[8] Calls for evidence become palisadelike barriers that marginalized groups must negotiate to become fully accepted into the academy.

Breaching Barriers: Embracing Polycultural Communities of Practice

Institutions seeking to create more racially and socially just communities must break with traditional responses to demands for racial justice and create communities of practice based on the new paradigm of polyculturalism. Such a community moves away from a predetermined political vision of a utopian multicultural community that is merely caring, celebratory, tolerant, and devoid of conflict.

Today's students are growing up in a wonderfully diverse, multicultural, global society that increasingly acknowledges and embraces our individual multidimensionality as complex beings, each with many identities. Yet, these students often find themselves living in an environment that limits their learning and development.

In contrast, a polycultural environment embraces the belief that cultures are dynamic and socially constructed through our interactions, influences, and exchanges with each other. At the same time, polyculturalism values the unique combination of the many individual identities that are equally salient to us—for example, sexual orientation, socioeconomic background, education, profession, ideology, and so much more.

Polyculturalism opens the doors to what today's students require: the opportunity to seamlessly traverse many cultural fields to discover new ways of knowing and understanding one another and the world around us. Polyculturalism resists the notion of postracialism; instead, it calls for support spaces to affirm our complex individual and group identities. It also allows our "safe spaces" to emerge to educate the broader community about histories and experiences that have been ignored or essentialized through multiculturalism's attempts to compartmentalize identities. It creates spaces of mobilization, nurtures a sense of belonging, and affirms individual and group identities.

A polycultural community of practice appreciates that each of us is the sum of many identities and requires us to struggle together to enunciate how we differ, where we connect, and how to live together. Such a community is regenerative. It leverages personal, local, national, and global resources to enact shared values, passions, and concerns in the interest of learning together and positively transforming individuals, our community, and the world.

Inevitably, there will be moments when a polycultural community of practice struggles with its own values and commitments due to the dynamic nature of communities and society. It will make mistakes, but we must be willing and able to show compassion and forgiveness and ultimately grow from these mistakes.

What would a framework for a polycultural community of practice look like? It might, for example,

- embrace polyculturalism, recognizing that cultures are dynamic and socially constructed through our interactions, influences, and exchanges with each other;
- forge inclusive community that includes students, faculty, staff, alumni, parents, families, and other stakeholders;
- encourage individuals from diverse backgrounds and perspectives to unite as one community to cocreate a shared sense of purpose, passion, concern, and commitment;
- ensure a sense of belonging for individuals and communities by engaging, embracing, and affirming the identities of all community members;
- encourage individuals to seamlessly traverse many cultural fields in authentic contexts as their authentic selves;
- enable freedom and growth through education that encourages lifelong exploration and the pursuit of truth;
- build trust and humility, essential components of community-building and learning; and
- Initiate community dialogue through physical proximity (e.g., town hall meetings and other initiatives that bring students together in the same physical space). Learning is more effective when it occurs in dialogue with others.

During my tenure at Emory University, which enjoys one of the most diverse student bodies among peer institutions, we began embracing this framework and reimagining ourselves as a polycultural community of practice. In 2015, our students afforded us a marvelous opportunity to put theory into practice—to undertake a grand experiment.

Emory's Grand Experiment: A Polycultural Community Responds to Student Demands for Racial Justice

During fall 2015, the Black Students of Emory movement, inspired by the nationwide Black Lives Matter movement, presented university administrators with 13 demands that ranged from curricular reform to increases in student organization funding. The goal of our students was and is to advance racial justice throughout the campus community. Their dissent and protest, like that of students on campuses nationwide, are responses to campus racial climates that are still failing students of color and, therefore, all campus members. Such racial climates have not adequately embraced social justice and its concomitant values, such as polyculturalism and cultural humility.[9] Our challenge as administrators was how to respond, as an institution aspiring to become a polycultural community of practice, to our students' demands for racial justice.

Within days of receiving the 13 demands, Emory officials, including myself in the role of senior vice president and dean of campus life, collaborated with student leaders to plan a retreat to address all issues set forth by our students. Our intent was to break with the kinds of traditional responses by higher education institutions cited earlier. Instead, Emory's goal was and is to implement a sustainable process to further racial justice at Emory. This is our grand experiment.

Most importantly, we did our best to meet our students where they were by acknowledging their demands as legitimate issues to be addressed. We listened to them, and they inspired us. Administrators accepted the evidence that the students offered, which was based largely on their lived experience on campus. We partnered with them and the larger university community to move Emory more intentionally and efficiently from the rhetoric of diversity and inclusion toward a new paradigm for racial justice.

Our students helped us to better understand that Emory's increasing diversity was outpacing university infrastructure and allocation of and access to resources and what that means academically and socially for our students and the larger university community.

Our experiment is a great success. We have hosted annual racial justice retreats and established a presidentially appointed Emory Commission on Racial and Social Justice, the centerpiece of our grand experiment. The commission, created by the university and composed of students, faculty, administrators, and staff, is doing something seen at very few institutions; it is challenging racial injustice and engaging all university stakeholders, from students to executives and faculty to frontline staff, to begin proactively dismantling oppressive systems. Working groups of students, faculty, and staff have addressed or are addressing each of the original demands, in some cases identifying additional areas requiring attention.

Through these efforts, we identified a range of needed initiatives, including new and enhanced programs and services as well as changes to policies, procedures, and practices. In addition, we have taken steps to institutionalize our movement toward a more just university community, challenging the status quo and pushing for systemic change. For example, we have reconfigured our bias-incident reporting system, increased staff diversity for counseling and psychological services, formed a working group to research macroaggressions and develop training materials for faculty, and formed a committee to address diversity issues in recruitment and retention of faculty.

The role of our students and student leadership, representing a cross-section of this diverse student body, has been invaluable in moving this great institution forward on the issue of racial justice. During the beginning of the campus movement, a student I knew well came to my office. She was visibly depressed. I asked her what was wrong. She responded, "Imagine what it's like to see Black bodies being murdered every day, bodies that look like you, and to go to your dorm room, away from family, and have to sit with those images. I need to do something. I need to take action in my community at Emory." And she did; she took an active role in forming and setting the agenda for the Commission on Racial and Social Justice.

At the height of the campus movement, another student asked whether we are serious about racial justice. My gut response was to emphatically say, "Yes." But then I considered what it would mean to truly prioritize racial justice. So, in the weeks that followed, I conversed with many of my colleagues. My first question—one that is being asked throughout higher education—was, "Is racial justice a priority for our institution?"

This question pointed to others. I encourage you to raise such questions at your institution. First, what are the values and principles of the community? Second, how does power operate in the university? How do we work within existing governance structures, refine structures, or create new structures? Third, what processes already work at the institution that can serve as a model? Fourth, how are we deploying resources? And fifth, if we know that past efforts have been unsuccessful, then shouldn't we consider new practices? Shouldn't we create best practices, experiment, and innovate?

From there, we embarked on a project that led us to the commission.[10] Every senior executive who deploys the resources of the university is now meeting routinely to discuss racial and social justice priorities. A range of programs and administrative practices are being examined, with many modified and enhanced, including bias incident reporting; counseling and psychological services; faculty evaluations; academic support for marginalized students; education of non-Black students; recruitment, compensation, and job security; and support for undocumented students.

In addition to implementing change that moves Emory toward a fuller realization of racial justice, the commission is helping to implement a paradigm shift to polyculturalism by embracing and practicing core values of polyculturalism in its ongoing work—values such as cultural humility, inclusivity and collaboration, and respectful dialogue and debate.

Redefining the Center

For some in higher education, today's racial justice movement, largely manifested in the Black Lives Matter movement, is a distraction, a moment in time that we must move beyond so we can get back to "business as usual." Ironically, the broad mission of U.S. colleges and universities—to develop, teach, and employ knowledge to serve the greater good—closely aligns with the new racial justice movement in higher education.

On a daily basis, faculty members drive innovation in a variety of disciplines. The same energy and passion are sorely needed around issues of racial justice. The cultural norms and traditions of our nation's institutions of higher education are impeding the necessary intellectual and financial resources required to apply our commitment to and knowledge of racial justice in the service of all humanity. Examples, as noted earlier, include the traditional preference for quantitative over qualitative evidence.

We must refocus the business of higher education on creating spaces where all members of our community are afforded opportunities to be liberated through knowledge and encouraged to pass on that knowledge to positively transform their communities and the world. Imagine an academy that prioritizes racial justice with the same *Shakti*[11] that we daily invest in other issues.

We can begin moving toward this goal with five basic steps:

1. *Establish a sustainable commitment to racial justice.* Promote a paradigm shift for institutions to embrace polyculturalism, which recognizes that each of us is a composite of many identities, and prioritize the racial justice that is fundamental to it.[12] Ensure ongoing and sustainable efforts to address issues of racial justice as an essential element of polyculturalism. Foster institutional memory among students, staff, and faculty; develop leadership skills; provide mentoring; and create advisory structures with actionable ideas, time lines, metrics, and accountability measures.

2. *Appropriately balance the agents of change.* Students often work toward change with minimal administrative support, although such support is essential if systemic change is to occur. Identify key administrators who

can provide assistance and guidance to students. Although there is an educational opportunity for students participating in activism, it often comes at a significant cost to their academic studies, a cost that we must mitigate.

3. *Partner with students and build trust with them.* Listen carefully and demonstrate compassion and care. Develop transparency by regularly and routinely communicating what is happening and where the initiative is headed. Help students develop the skills to successfully balance the needs of a culturally humble, socially just community with their own personal rights and desires.

4. *Cultivate coalition-building and engage all stakeholders in the change process.* Encourage engagement by the entire community, marginalized and nonmarginalized groups alike. This includes board and faculty members, alumni, students, and staff; all must have a voice for systemic change to occur. Encourage collaboration among marginalized groups so they can discover shared histories of oppression and develop shared agendas to promote racial justice. Promote a collaborative response between academic and student affairs to help deploy resources more effectively and foster a more holistic approach to addressing racial justice in our communities.

5. *Encourage debate and dialogue.* Open and honest engagement with evidence in its myriad forms—including qualitative and quantitative data—is critical to the productive exchange of ideas. However, the humanity of our community members should never be up for debate.

As educators, we can recognize that a commitment to these five steps brings substantial challenges and extraordinary opportunities. Most of us may also understand that an effective approach to addressing both is to cultivate a polycultural community of practice.

Conclusion

This is a watershed moment for higher education. We have a unique opportunity to reimagine our work on racial justice, learn from our history, and move beyond it by redefining our role as institutions of learning.

This moment affords us a chance to respond with sincere compassion and true justice, to finally transform into reality the vision of our campus communities as caring and diverse centers of learning where all students are afforded equitable access to opportunities to grow and learn and contribute to the greater good.

Discussion Questions

1. What three benefits would you cite in making a case to your supervisor or university administrator to enact a polycultural approach to campus racial justice?
2. What do you see as the three greatest obstacles to pursuing a campus-wide initiative such as Emory's grand experiment at the institution at which you are employed and/or studying?
3. Building on your responses to the first two questions, explain in broad terms how you would adapt the ideas presented in this essay to better suit them to your institution?

Notes

1. Wenger, E. (1998). *Communities of practice: Learning, meaning, and identity.* Cambridge, UK: Cambridge University Press.
2. Prashad, V. (2001). *Everybody was kung fu fighting: Afro-Asian connections and the myth of cultural purity.* Boston, MA: Beacon Press.
3. Prashad, *Everybody was kung fu fighting.*
4. Nair, A. (2016, January 6). Reimagining the university: A new paradigm for racial justice. *HuffPost.* Retrieved from www.huffingtonpost.com/ajay-nair/reimagining-the-universit_b_8921930.html.
5. Nair, A. (2015, December 9). Today's student activists illuminate path to progress. *NASPA.* Retrieved from www.naspa.org/about/blog/todays-student-activists-illuminate-path-to-progress.
6. Nair, Reimagining the university.
7. Ibid.
8. Stafford, Z. (2015 October 12). Respectability politics won't save the lives of Black Americans. *The Guardian.* Retrieved from www.theguardian.com/commentisfree/2015/oct/12/respectability-politics-wont-save-black-americans.
9. Tervalon, M., & Murray-García, J. (1998). Cultural humility versus cultural competence: A critical distinction in defining physician training outcomes in multicultural education. *Journal of Health Care for the Poor and Underserved, 9*(2), 117–125.
10. Nair, A. (Ed.). (2018, January 5). *Dialogue at Emory.* Retrieved from www.dialogue.emory.cdu/.
11. In Sanskrit, *Shakti* means sacred force, energy, or power.
12. Nair, Today's student activists illuminate path to progress.

Critical Considerations in Advancing Social Justice Agendas in Higher Education

Samuel D. Museus

Turbulent times evoke instability and uncertainty, but they also hold great promise. The current sociopolitical context can certainly be described as turbulent. While many of the core inequities permeating higher education have existed for centuries, shifts in the national climate in recent years have led to increased student movements, growing demands to address education's complex diversity problems, and expanding conversations about transforming education so that it serves all communities equitably. It is in such times that societies and systems determine whether they regress, rest on their laurels, or catapult into a new and more progressive era.

In chapter 3, Ajay Nair offers several suggestions regarding how higher education can advance justice within the aforementioned context, and I respond to these recommendations herein. In doing so, I utilize knowledge gained from over a decade of empirical research, teaching diverse undergraduate and graduate populations, and serving as director for the National Institute for Transformation and Equity (NITE), which has provided consulting, assessment, and support services to more than 100 college campuses seeking to advance their inclusion and equity efforts. I make the following main arguments. First, to advance social justice, postsecondary institutions must *prioritize equity over other values*. Second, to facilitate this prioritization, we should *cultivate a common vision* for an equitable education system that is aligned with core values of higher education's responsibility to communities and students. Third, we can choose to *use all tools* at our disposal to advance this common vision.

Prioritizing Transformation and Equity

There are several barriers that make it difficult to move toward a more socially just system, and they are too numerous and complex to cover thoroughly in one essay or even one book. However, Nair discusses some of the most critical challenges that can be the foundation for productive strategizing and the cultivation of a more robust vision for equity. One of these barriers is that the system of higher education has focused on values and priorities that distract us from—and are often in direct conflict with—social justice. These priorities include the quest for greater prestige, the need to ensure the financial exigency of institutions, and the increasing systems of surveillance and oversight that permeate colleges and universities.[1]

I have seen how these priorities can divert attention and energy away from any serious institutional investment in justice. For example, institutions continue to dedicate significantly more resources to science and technology scholarship than they devote to research that advances equity. Higher education organizations remain focused on what seems like a never-ending quest for advanced technology that results in educators spending exponentially increasing time navigating more complex technological systems at the expense of cultivating meaningful relationships with students from historically marginalized communities. Additionally, faculty are required to prioritize generating revenue over engaging in professional development that they hope will transform their teaching and advising to be more culturally relevant and responsive to diverse populations. Indeed, such priorities have been normalized, solidifying equity as a peripheral value on college campuses.

To make progress in advancing social justice, leaders must (re)center their focus on serving diverse communities and create campus support and reward systems that inspire, rather than discourage, efforts to advance an equity agenda. However, for institutions to make such a meaningful investment, leaders must shift their emphasis and resources away from revenue-generating activities that reinforce existing inequitable systems to those that are focused on advancing the well-being of historically marginalized communities. The question then becomes, why should those in power make this shift and how can we convince them to do so? We must ask—rather, demand—that higher education leaders and institutions face this conflict head-on and demonstrate how they are renewing their commitment to underserved communities and prioritizing this duty over goals that reinforce systemic inequities. In turn, leaders must be willing to take risks and spearhead this agenda, rather than passively support it.

Cultivating Common Vision

As institutions shift priorities, they must also cultivate a common vision for justice. Several years ago, a colleague and I argued that most campuses could be defined as multicultural organizations in which diverse subcultures increasingly emerge at the margins, while core institutional cultures remain Eurocentric.[2] Structures in which minoritized subcultures are fragmented and at the margins of the institution are likely a function of what Nair notes as a failure of multicultural organizations to unpack systemic issues, the tendency to rely on superficial patchwork strategies to create an image of "fixing" diversity problems at the expense of long-term, visionary, transformative change. This fragmentation and marginalization must be addressed or such organizations will fall short of creating more equitable systems.

One reason that institutions take a piecemeal approach to diversity is that they often lack a common vision for an equitable campus. Moreover, terms such as *diversity, inclusion, equity,* and *inclusive excellence* can be defined in many ways by many people, making efforts intended to advance them fragmented and sometimes divergent. Lacking a common vision, institutions often focus on de-escalating conflict and responding to climate tensions. Campuses do, however, have capacity to adopt an alternative approach that prioritizes long-term, deep, and pervasive transformation. Such an approach requires institutions to infuse equity into their mainstream cultures (e.g., values, assumptions, norms), structures, and practices. Nair offers an intersectional approach as one paradigm to advance such an agenda. Complementing this argument is an emerging movement to focus on building culturally relevant and responsive campuses.

Over the last decade, NITE has worked with campuses around the nation to cultivate a common vision for equity. Some of these institutions have adopted our Culturally Engaging Campus Environments (CECE; pronounced *see-see*) model, which was intentionally grounded in the voices of diverse populations and outlines nine critical elements of optimally inclusive and equitable environments. The framework is used to mobilize campuses to create environments where students have optimal access to spaces in which they can connect with people who understand them, learn about their own communities, give back to their own communities, engage meaningfully across cultures, and feel validated, as well as find critical collectivist, humanized, holistic, and proactive support.[3]

The movement to pressure higher education to provide a more culturally relevant and responsive education for marginalized communities is not a new one. Nair insightfully notes that students have been protesting since the 1950s, and the author underscores that many of their demands have not changed over time. It is also important to highlight that these student movements in the midtwentieth century were partly focused on demanding an education that was relevant to and served the communities of marginalized populations.[4] The failure of higher education to provide a curriculum that was in the best interest of the diverse communities catalyzed a movement to resist White supremacy and other forms of oppression. Many viewed a culturally relevant and responsive education as part of the solution—and many still hold this view today.

Engaging All Tools

To prioritize equity at the institution level and create a common vision for providing culturally relevant and responsive education on college campuses, it is important for us to consider the potential power of all tools that might help advance a social justice agenda. Nair astutely observes that, "those in power in the academy have historically privileged quantitative data over the qualitative evidence that can take into account the lived experiences of marginalized groups."[5] Moreover, major quantitative data systems often marginalize or completely ignore the voices of minoritized populations. For example, most U.S. Department of Education surveys collect data on diverse demographics (e.g., race, ethnicity, and gender), but include few, if any, questions related to concepts that are central to the experiences of minoritized populations (e.g., prejudice and discrimination, cultural assimilation and validation, culturally relevant education, etc.).[6] In sum, researchers rarely infuse perspectives of diverse communities into the core foundations of quantitative tools and data, making them inherently inequitable and ineffective at advancing equity agendas. Yet, this does not have to be the case.

Quantitative research is not inherently incapable of engaging the lived experiences of marginalized populations. In fact, scholars have recently created surveys and databases that can generate statistical evidence that centers the voices and priorities of marginalized populations.[7] If more researchers, assessment specialists, leaders, and educators utilize such tools in conversations about success and higher education's responsibility to the public, they can speak the language of quantitative researchers while making these conversations more equitable.

At NITE, we administer CECE surveys—which measure key elements of the CECE model discussed previously—to faculty, staff, and students on campuses across the country so that institutions can better understand their environments and utilize survey data to advance their equity efforts. These instruments are arguably among the first truly intersectional surveys because they prompt respondents to self-define and identify the multiple and often intersecting cultural communities and identities that are most salient to them. For example, respondents can indicate that both Asian American and low-income communities are most salient to them or clarify that Black, differently abled women are their primary community. Participants then answer survey items about the degree to which they have access to spaces that are relevant and responsive to these communities and identities.[8] However, the intersectional data collected are complicated and figuring out how to analyze and apply them to effect change is an even more daunting task. We need more voices to foster stronger national conversations about how to utilize this knowledge to effect positive systemic transformation.

Despite the unlocked potential of quantitative research in advancing equity, I deeply appreciate Nair's emphasis on the value of qualitative data. Indeed, students' stories are among the most powerful tools that can be used to transform educators' perspectives and effect positive change. Thus, it is important that we utilize stories from marginalized communities to illuminate the needs of minoritized populations and what allows them to thrive. These data and insights can be utilized in conjunction with more critical quantitative research to advance an equity agenda.

Conclusion

The instability of the current historical moment provides an opportunity for us to construct a collective vision for new and more equitable education systems. Nair catalyzes this transformative thinking through his essay. I aimed to build on and further complicate Nair's ideas, and I hope that readers will continue this discussion and feel empowered to invest more energy in advancing the equity agenda even further—for a vision of equity can only be achieved together.

Discussion Questions

1. What are the barriers to higher education shifting its emphasis to pursuing more complex and transformative justice or equity agendas?
2. What are some optimal ways in which campus leaders can utilize both qualitative and quantitative data to advance equity?

Notes

1. Lorenz, C. (2012). If you're so smart, why are you under surveillance? Universities, neoliberalism, and new public management. *Critical Inquiry, 38*(3), 599–629.

2. Jayakumar, U. M., & Museus, S. D. (2012). Mapping the intersection of campus cultures and equitable outcomes among racially diverse student popula-

tions. In S. D. Museus & U. M. Jayakumar (Eds.), *Creating campus cultures: Fostering success among racially diverse student populations* (pp. 1–27). New York, NY: Routledge.

3. Museus, S. D. (2014). The Culturally Engaging Campus Environments (CECE) model: A new theory of college success among racially diverse student populations. In M. B. Paulsen (Ed.), *Higher education: Handbook of theory and research* (Vol. 29, pp. 189–227). New York, NY: Springer.

4. Chung, A. Y., & Chang, E. T. (1998). From Third World liberation to multiple oppression politics: A contemporary approach to interethnic coalitions. *Social Justice, 25*(3), 80–100; Umemoto, K. (1989). "On strike!" San Francisco State College strike, 1968–69: The role of Asian American students. *Amerasia Journal, 15*(1), 3–41.

5. Nair, A., this volume, p. 54.

6. Berkner, L., & Choy, S. (2008). *Descriptive summary of 2003–04 beginning-postsecondary students: Three years later.* Washington DC: National Center for Education Statistics; Wei, C. C., Berkner, L., He, S., Lew, S., Cominole, M., & Siegel, P. (2009). *2007–08 National Postsecondary Student Aid Study (NPSAS: 08): Student financial aid estimates for 2007–08. First look.* Washington DC: National Center for Education Statistics.

7. Hurtado, S., Milem, J., Clayton-Pedersen, A., & Allen, W. (1999). *Enacting diverse learning environments: Improving the climate for racial/ethnic diversity in higher education.* [Special issue]. *ASHE-ERIC Higher Education Report, 26*(8); Museus, The Culturally Engaging Campus Environments (CECE) model; Museus, S. D., Zhang, D., & Kim, M. J. (2016). Developing and evaluating the Culturally Engaging Campus Environments (CECE) scale: An examination of content and construct validity. *Research in Higher Education, 57*(6), 768–793.

8. Museus, Zhang, & Kim, Developing and evaluating the Culturally Engaging Campus Environments (CECE) scale.

4

What Are the Responsibilities and Limits of Student Affairs' Roles in Preparing Students for Political Activism?

Student Affairs Educators' Brokering Role in Political Activism

Sandra Rodríguez

Higher education encourages the exploration of contested ideas, which makes student affairs fertile ground for political activism. At times, higher education acts as a socializing mechanism aimed at sustaining the status quo. Other times, it acts as a catalyst for change, critiquing existing power structures and facilitating innovation. Higher education provides students (a) a formal inculcation into the larger society (which is part of a larger reward system), (b) access to people and information (which provides access to power), (c) an awareness of larger societal structures (knowledge and social and cultural capital to ensure social mobility), and (d) expectations of approved behaviors (which sustains the status quo). In this mix of socialization and catalyst for change, students' responses to these opportunities vary. At times there is *dissonance* resulting from clashes between lived experiences and expectations. At times there is *reflection* as students reconcile clashes between ideology and reality. At times students *acquire voice*, which is an awakening of their conscious. And at times voice leads to *action*, which is a desire to be a catalyst for change. These are the four phases of transformation that underlie political activism.

Political activism usually involves the interaction of students (who are experiencing dissonance, reflecting, finding their voices, and acting to initiate change) and institutions (that fluctuate from sustaining the status quo to initiating change). While political activism is predictable on college campuses, the responsibilities and limits of student affairs' roles in preparing students and institutions for political activism are less certain.

Student affairs educators have a role in preparing both students and universities for activism. This brokering role is essential, and there are specific sources of knowledge, skill, and insight that educators need to possess to succeed: the knowledge to be a cultural interpreter to support both sides across borders that seem to divide during times of tension, the skills to facilitate communication across political and cultural divides and foster spaces for understanding and learning, and the insight to mediate unmet expectations between student demands and university structure.

It is through this role of brokering activism that student affairs can embrace its role as an educator for both the institution and the student. The core of our curriculum would utilize equity, civility, and safety to assist both sides in finding common ground. To find that common ground we must create spaces where we can listen, exchange ideas, construct solutions, and investigate possibilities.

In preparation for our brokering role, student affairs educators should embrace four key components. First, in any given tension-ridden situation we start by helping the diverse stakeholders recognize the gap between espoused and enacted values so that joint action can diminish that gap. We must acknowledge the gains, as many of these issues are complex and contended with on an ongoing basis. Second, we enter the brokering role with the intent of building student agency in contested spaces. The learning partnerships model offers one way to promote students' acquisition of voice through respecting their voices, helping them view experiences as opportunities for growth, collaborating with them to analyze their experiences, drawing them into the complexity of decisions, encouraging their personal authority, and working interdependently with them to solve problems.[1] If students have agency, good things result for all stakeholders. The quality of a dialogue with agentic stakeholders can develop tremendous results by balancing power between students and institutions.

Third, we create space to hear both the voices of proponents of the status quo and voices that offer minority or invisible views that demand change. It should be standard practice to build learning partnerships that respect multiple perspectives, encourage all students to develop their personal authority, and model sharing authority and expertise to solve complex issues.

Fourth, we create an understanding within the institution that activism on campus is necessary and there are specific actions that student affairs educators can take to broker positive change that benefits both the activist and the institution.

Student activism will always be present in higher education. It will exist as long as higher education refuses to appreciate students' lived narratives. It will remain as long as a disparity between espoused institutional values and institutional reality exists. It has been present in students for as long as a moment of dissonance has matured into a personal conviction. It is within that conviction that student affairs will find a student voice in need of advocacy and a platform for shared teaching and learning.

Evolution of Student Affairs' Engagement With Activism

Embracing our roles as educators to both the institution and the student activist stands in contrast to the early role of student affairs in higher education. Initially, our role was to get students to conform to codes of conduct and implement policy that upheld the concept of in loco parentis.[2]

Historically, student activism has been a powerful impetus on the evolution of the academy. Student political activism in American higher education has consisted of protestors; conscientious objectors; pacifists; feminists; radical theologists; social justice advocates; lesbian, gay, bisexual, trans, queer/questioning, intersex, and asexual or allied (LGBTQIA) activists; political ideologists; civil rights protestors; environmentalists; and nationalists of every stripe. It has a long history of causing institutional disruption and change that more accurately depicts the larger lived experiences of the society outside of the institution of higher learning including the civil rights movement of the 1960s. It has been rich in calling out the hypocrisy of institutional espoused values and teachings and the sociocultural, political, economic, and lived realities of society.

Initially, university administrators did not play a role of advocacy and development for the student body. American higher education established during the colonial period around religious principles yielded student activism against religious indoctrination and strict colonial codes of conduct. The role of administrators was one of the parent to ensure indoctrination in religious principles.[3] Creating agency in students through this formal inculcation in education was not part of the pedagogy. The first U.S. military draft act was passed in 1863, making colleges the main location for anticonscription campaigns. At the turn of the twentieth century, students were organizing on and off campus around socialism as a political agenda focused on issues of disarmament, free speech, and immigration—issues that today remain unsolved. Growth of activist student groups was slow because campus administrators could deny organization recognition based on their own conservative outlook.[4] Students viewed the concept of in loco parentis as overwhelmingly condescending. They challenged the issues facing society from within the institution by engaging in action that sought to change the larger narrative around individual rights, labor, politics, and social ills. The idealistic stand of a student activist has long called out the hypocrisy of espoused institutional values versus the lived reality of either the student or the society[5]—a pushback to "do as I say, not as I do."

The student political activism pendulum has swung from conservative, to apathetic, to radical over the last 200 years. Students have responded to campus, local, national, and international issues based on the larger issues of the time.[6] During times of war—the American Civil War, World War I, World War II, and the Korean War—student activism around conscription campaigns, conscientious objection, and disarmament existed but were overshadowed by nationalism. The apathy of the 1920s exemplified an activist focus of calling out the hypocrisy of institutional behavior while challenging social mores around sexuality. By the 1930s, radicalized student activists chose to organize, march against, and support larger national and international issues focused on political agendas (communism and socialism), civil rights, human rights, and equality.[7]

The 1960s solidified a departure for our profession from the role of in loco parentis, opening the door to our full participation in the learning process of university students. The student activism and conflict of that era both supported and demanded the transformation of our roles within the institution. In the push for students' legal rights, educators began to "see students in a different light—as maturing adults who wanted to have a say in the way the university and world worked—rather than as incapable of exercising good judgment and an entity over which the university had complete control."[8] Student affairs educators became increasingly involved in representing students, helping students represent themselves, and managing crises related to student activism.[9] Student activism focused on civil rights, free speech, the women's movement, ethnic studies, LGBT rights, and apartheid.[10]

Modern day activism, including the Black Lives Matter, #wearemizzou, and Deferred Action for Childhood Arrivals (DACA) movements, continues to shape our profession. In many ways, the shift in our roles is a response to the effects of student political activism. As Barr, Desler, and associates wrote, "Our field grew from the campus up, not from theory down."[11] It is this outlook that created our role as cultural interpreters brokering the contested space between the institution and the student activist. It is in our role as a student affairs educator that we can help the student activist work through the dissonance, reflection, acquisition of voice, and action.

Responsibilities and Limits of Student Affairs' Roles in Preparing Students for Political Activism

Times of institutional conflict magnify the inherent tension in creating a space for equity, safety, and civility. Democratic trauma—when the principles and tenets of the democracy intersect with the search for social justice, equity, and inclusion—can be a transformative experience for the institution. For example, higher education embraces democratic concepts like free speech. Democratic trauma occurs when that speech is diametrically opposed to the very existence of human beings who live the difference targeted by that speech. We are seeing that currently with the desire by the alt right to speak on college campuses composed of the very groups targeted by that speech. These circumstances often produce a clash for students between their lived experiences and expectations—*dissonance*.

Student affairs educators with a progressive pedagogy can help guide this dissonance by negotiating the inherent tension between the university and the valuable lessons that the student activist voice can teach us. Nowhere are our roles and responsibilities as a profession more critical than at this intersection. How we negotiate this intersection can define our professional roles with integrity. Our integrity lies in knowing and owning our own bias and prejudice as we teach and as we walk the path of our student's dissonance. Much like our individual intersections of race, class, socioeconomic status, and so on, the complexities of our professional intersections can be both a source of strength and exhaustion and can produce dissonance in the way we engage our role. Our negotiation of this complexity can also be an example of the civility necessary to name and negotiate the existence of status quo and its impact on difference within the academy. To bypass this intersection is an act of privilege our profession, our students, and our institutions cannot afford.

Understanding and Preparing the Individual Student Activist

Supporting students in learning through dissonance, reflection, acquisition of voice, and action requires understanding students' developmental pathways, knowing your student body, and knowing the student code of conduct.

Know Your College Student Development Theory

We have an obligation in student affairs to understand our students' development. This involves, in part, understanding college student development theory to understand the possible developmental pathways our students travel. It also involves understanding the geographical, social, political, class, race, and gender/nonbinary intersections that affect the day-to-day lives of our students. This requires the capacity to consume large amounts of information while discerning its validity. Understanding generational differences is key in the application of student development theory. Each generation brings with it individual nuances and lived experiences that influence how we apply the theory. Understanding development illuminates how students experience dissonance and engage in reflection, how much support and challenge is warranted to help them acquire their own voices, and how to partner with them to identify appropriate action.

Know and Own Your Student Body

The student body is a product of a connection to your institution. To believe otherwise is to dismiss 40 years of college student development theory. Activists do not just appear on our campus; they manifest, partially, in response to that connection (both positive and negative) with our institutions. Activism is a disruption of the self, of the issue, and of the institution—the status quo. Activists have a responsibility to name the problem and to offer solutions. Our pedagogy should encourage *reflection*—the clash between ideology and reality—on demands and the solutions student activists offer. We must challenge activists into spaces to dialogue about the problem to hear other points of view. It is in the reflection process that valuable reconciliation occurs between the lived experience and the changes sought.

Student conviction emanates from an awaking of the conscience—*acquisition of voice.* This produces the desire to name the problem and to disrupt the basis of the problem. Support the conviction by assisting the activist in grounding their voice in the available data, qualitative and quantitative. This prepares activists to teach through their voice. This prepares the institution to learn through activist narrative and supporting data. This intersection opens the door to solution-orientated discourse. As an educator, be present and in the moment when engaging concerns, demands, and proposed solutions. Acknowledge the activist dissonance and seek to understand the moment that materialized into conviction. This is the precise juncture from which student activists may draw the most strength. For example, our campus addressed recent incidences of racism by having student activists share their lived narrative while also creating space for a student researcher to share his qualitative data focused on student perceptions of our campus climate for students of color. Bringing an entire division of student affairs into a room to listen to student activist narratives and student-researched qualitative data was transformative. Always remain a student of students.

Know the Possible Consequences of the Activist Action and Communicate Them to the Student

Public administrative ethos dictates that we have an obligation to express concerns about and support for viable actions.[12] These actions can have both positive and negative consequences for the learning community and the activist. For example, student activists may know something we do not. Creating space to let their moral compass teach us brings the exchange full circle back to the teaching and learning mission of our institutions. However, the actions of student activists grounded outside of university policy can have negative consequences. For example, disrupting the ongoing teaching mission of the institution (e.g., classes, lectures) is not exercising free speech. It is a clear violation of the student code of conduct. Student affairs educators are responsible for engaging activists in exploration of consequences of their proposed actions and partnering with them to make appropriate choices. A desire to be a catalyst for change—*action*—can yield powerful results by grounding it in calculated action.

Understanding and Preparing the Institution

Moving the institution forward requires an understanding of institutional differences in culture and legal landscapes, political vistas and student body politic, institutional policies, and the professional ethos to guide student affairs professional's actions.

Know Your Institution

Private, public, and community colleges all have different cultures and legal landscapes. An important part of our academic preparation should be a history of case law. This is not to serve as legal counsel to the student activist or the institution, but rather to facilitate the dialogue around the intended institutional and student activist actions, demands, solutions, and institutional policy within precedent. We serve as cultural interpreters between the institution and the student activist in many ways. For example, I was facilitating a Black Lives Matter member and university police discussion about beginning a Black Lives Matter march on our campus and ending up in the downtown city plaza. The police asked several questions to which the student activist responded, "I'll speak to the members and get back to you." After three unanswered questions, I sensed the frustration on the part of university police. I took a moment to bridge this gap by explaining to university police that where police officers are used to working within models of hierarchical leadership, community-based groups tend to operate on a consensus model. The capacity to broker cultural gaps in dialogue is meaningful advocacy. Decoding institutional language and expectation empowers the student activist in the larger dialogue and develops their agency for full participation in discussions.

Know the Political Landscape and the Student Body Politic
Activism is about asking critical questions and then demanding answers. Activists engage the act of inquiry in different ways: silence, action, groups, solitude, absence, disruption of status quo, dismissing policy, and challenging administrative decision-making. Each of these forms is usually directed at our pedagogy, policy-making, campus climate, social issues, support for status quo, and an outright reaction to power. The onus is on our pedagogy as student affairs educators to situate the dissonance and the activism that results in reflective learning. For example, challenge student activists to ground their work in critical inquiry. They should thoroughly examine the resulting answers when received but also after the fact in reflection. Student affairs educators can engage students in a dialogue that raises awareness of the concepts they are attempting to analyze. Encourage them to apply the results in seeking solutions or making demands.

The body politic has an institutionalized student government mechanism. Universities assume the student government can represent all student points of view. While that ideal may exist, it is more likely that these formal structures represent the interests of the majority point of view. Therefore, student activists may actually view these representative bodies as a part of the institutional culture they are trying to reform. If student activists cannot see their goals or hear their voice within these structures, they become a point of estrangement, not support. Student activists should intentionally confront the disparity through communication that lists the deficits. Student affairs educators often serve as advisers to these formal student structures. It is within our purview to bring these parties to the table to communicate differences, deficits, and expectations. Further, these governing bodies often possess resources that should remain accessible to all student agendas, regardless of whether they align with the governing body's agenda.

Know the Policies and Your Interpretation, Communication, and Application Related to Public Space on Your Campus
We are not gatekeepers, nor should we ever interpret our job as such. To do so is a demarcation of a top-down approach to a pedagogy doomed to fail. We are caretakers of public space, and that integrity materializes by how we

interpret, apply, and communicate the policy on public space. The courts have decided that public universities can decide the time, place, and manner for use of space. Too often, administrators use this to silence points of view with which they disagree instead of educating student activists on how to maximize the use of public space to state their point of view effectively. Challenge both the institution and the student activist to embrace this intersection as a valuable teaching opportunity. Dominating a shared space (by either party) does not equate to effective teaching. Public space utilized to air community grievances brings our attention to problems that need solutions. It asks the community to redirect its priorities toward a collective effort.

Know That We Have an Obligation to Communicate Intended Activist Actions to Our Supervisor

This is not "playing both sides of the fence." It is a critical part of exemplifying the expectation to all parties involved of the value of open channels of communication. Nothing about our pedagogy should be covert. Likewise, we have an obligation to communicate an expectation of advocacy, where possible, by various university offices on behalf of the student activist. We must possess the agility to transcend cultural boundaries between the activist point of reference and the institutional structure and culture. This intersection can be difficult for us to negotiate as student affairs educators. Imagine the struggle for students.

Providing reasonable time limits to fill out forms, helping the student activist to navigate the complexity of the university bureaucracy, providing resources (e.g., sound amplification, tables, chairs), and interpreting complex university policies can guide your support for creating an effective teaching/learning environment. Strengthen channels of communication between the institution and the student activist by ensuring that valuable information is shared and processed equally by all parties. This alone can add to the civility at this crucial intersection. Always remain a student of institutions of higher learning.

Preparing Yourself for the Brokering Role

Our burden/joy and edification is to bear witness to student activist struggle—to witness the deadpan look in their eyes turn into a stare of solid conviction and agency. There is a fine line for us as administrators between advocacy and activism. In many ways, the line is defined by campus culture, upper administrative support (or lack thereof), and our own politics. Understanding your campus culture is key in the advising process and in knowing your boundaries as an administrator. We have an obligation to model the equity, safety, and civility in administrative oversight of student activism we seek to instill. Our pedagogy can ensure this standard. This means knowing our own biases and prejudices, because our role is to serve all students. Integrity also means educating yourself when blind spots in your knowledge present themselves. It means finding your own voice in learning to negotiate the students, their activism, university structure, and your pedagogy. I have many times found myself in my office with a student who believes an injustice is so great that he or she is willing to do whatever it takes to make a point. Making a point can last a moment even in this current age of social media. Teaching the point can have a lasting change within a learning community.

Brokering the engagement between student activism and the institution should move you into your own professional dissonance, reflection, acquisition of voice, and action necessary to make equity, civility, and safety a solid part of your pedagogy. Your commitment to lifelong learning will ensure this transformation happens over time, with experience and through learning partnerships. Always remain a student of your own professional development.

Implications

The profession we have chosen has been at the epicenter of some of the most profound student activist–led change in American history and partly shaped the responsibilities and limits of our roles in preparing students for political activism. Many student affairs professionals came before you to navigate the transformation of our profession from administrators to educators. Your goal is to broker positive change that evolves the institution and develops students within the context of a shared space. This is what distinguishes our interests as student affairs educators from the interests of the institution and the student activist.

Note that being a broker is always hard and contentious and can be perceived negatively. Conscientious objectors, pacifists, feminists, radical theologists, social justice advocates, LGBTQIA activists, civil rights protestors, environmentalists, and nationalists, while perceived during the conflict by those in power as antiestablishment, over time (postrevolution) are viewed as positive change agents.

Student affairs educators must know the responsibilities and limits of our roles in preparing students for political activism. To lend credence to activist voices can displace the history of the older voices, authority, and tradition from their place at the center of institutional culture, power, and socialization, causing a crisis that sends the institution into conflict. How we respond, in these circumstances, as student affairs educators can decide whether the institution remains entrenched in status quo or evolves.

Our leadership can be an antidote to the status quo and a socialization process that deflects the integration of the student activist narrative. Our teaching can bring espoused institutional values and actions into alignment by embracing and correcting our blind spots. Inherent in our advocacy will be the tension of embracing conflict as a catalyst for positive change.

Discussion Questions

1. What is the impact on student affairs educators who lend student activist voices legitimacy and support? How does that impact our standing in the profession, with our colleagues, and within the educational institution?
2. How are student affairs educators affected when we empower student activists to question status quo? Do we run the risk of having the legitimacy of our own voices damaged, disregarded, or even silenced?
3. What are the benefits to students' and institutions' learning in effective political activism?

Notes

1. Baxter Magolda, M. B. (2009). *Authoring your life: Developing an internal voice to navigate life's challenges.* Sterling, VA: Stylus, p. 251.

2. Miser, K. M. (1988). *Student affairs and campus dissent: Reflection of the past and challenge for the future* (1st ed.). Washington DC: National Association of Student Personnel Administrators.

3. Altbach, P. G., & Peterson, P. (1971). Before Berkeley: Historical perspectives on American student activism. *The ANNALS of the American Academy of Political and Social Science, 395*(1), 1–14.

4. Ibid.

5. Miser, *Student affairs and campus dissent.*

6. Altbach & Peterson, Before Berkeley.

7. Ibid.

8. Gaston-Gayles, J. L., Wolf-Wendel, L. E., Tuttle, K. N., Twombly, S. B., & Ward, K. (2005). From disciplinarian to change agent: How the Civil Rights Era changed the roles of student affairs professionals. *NASPA Journal, 42*(3), 263–268.

9. Ibid.

10. Miser, *Student affairs and campus dissent.*

11. Barr, M. J., Desler, M. K., & Associates. (2000). *The handbook of student affairs administration* (2nd ed.). San Francisco, CA: Jossey-Bass, p. 4.

12. Moore, M. H. (1995). *Creating public value: Strategic management in government.* Cambridge, MA: Harvard University Press.

Brokering Students' Political Activism: Expanding Student Affairs Professionals' Views

Cassie L. Barnhardt

The story of campus-based student activism is associated with students realizing their agency, voice, and capacity for perspective-taking and acquiring skills for direct engagement with collective social problems. The benefits that flow to students from their campus-based activism hold the potential to complement or extend the learning and developmental goals of postsecondary education. Campus activism contributes to students' civic commitments and holds links to students' civic and political participation and engagement beyond college.[1] Even so, to prepare student affairs educators for the inherent contention associated with students' campus-based activism and political mobilization, these phenomena must be considered in organizational and collective contexts.

Sandra Rodríguez rightly notes that student affairs educators can serve as brokers when students' political activism occurs on campus. As brokers, student affairs educators must operate as strategic political actors. They must be effective stewards of students' interests, and the campus/organization's interests (as specified in the professional competencies of the American College Personnel Association [ACPA] College Student Educators International and the National Association of Student Personnel Administrators [NASPA] Student Affairs Administrators in Higher Education) while also assessing the pressures and influences emanating from the broader sociopolitical environment, and their own self-interests.[2] My primary critique of Rodríguez's analysis of the student affairs professional's brokering role is that it underspecifies the sociological and organizational dynamics that are also critical to navigating episodes of campus-based political activism. Fittingly, and compatible with student affairs norms, Rodríguez privileges the psychological and developmental dimensions of administrative responsiveness, but this view can impose artificial limits on individuals' views of phenomena. Here, I propose criteria that complement and extend her ideas by revealing some of the driving organizational and sociological dimensions that can also shape student affairs educators' responses to displays of students' political activism.

Components and Structures of Campus-Based Political Activism

Student affairs educators can ready themselves to support students in exercising their agency and advise colleagues on responding to episodes of activism by understanding the features of social movements and activist phenomena writ large. Mobilization of any kind consists of four primary components: mobilizing groups, targets, tactics, and claims.[3] Together, these four elements coalesce to produce the relative level of intensity that flows from the mobilization/activism. Specifically, mobilizing groups are the parties who are seeking a change in a collective value or formal structure (policy, procedure); they hold some form of grievance and are taking action to address these concerns. (For the purposes of this essay, students are the mobilizing group.) Targets are the parties (e.g., persons, organizations) to whom the mobilizing group is directing its activist efforts; the target is often the university, but it can be the president, the governing board, elected officials, the bookstore, or a campus vendor, among others. Tactics are the specific types of behaviors and activities that a mobilizing group utilizes to communicate its positions and to express its grievances.[4] Tactics represent an array of possible actions, consisting of prototypical activities such as petition campaigns, demonstrations, rallies/marches, occupations of various kinds (e.g., sit-ins), protests, or hosting speakers/panels; to somewhat more novel tactics such as political theater or guerilla art installations, work stoppages or boycotts, or skywriting; to extreme approaches like using violence to communicate a political message. Claims (i.e., frames) are the substantive issues that inspire activists' grievances or the reasons that compel mobilizing groups to take action (e.g., campaigns to divest the endowment from fossil fuels, stop tuition hikes, enact fairness in assigning course registration times, improve campus climate, or have transparency in sexual assault reporting and accountability).

Together the elements of mobilization produce the relative degree of intensity that is experienced by targets, onlookers, or the campus as a site for the contention (even if it is not the target per se). Typically, intensity is determined by the size and duration of the event, along with the extent to which the tactics themselves convey feelings of intimidation or violence.[5] Being able to purposively create or anticipate the relative intensity of any instance of activism helps the organizers (students) and the target (university) to prepare and respond in their different roles. Student affairs educators can assist students in learning to be intentional with their organizing, using the lens of groups, targets, tactics, and claims as a framework to plan specific mobilization events or to pursue an overall campaign. Students are sometimes new to organizing and can learn skills and strategies that will assist them in effectively communicating their messages by being deliberate with these elements. Further, as campus educators formulate an administrative response to displays of activism, they can more precisely gauge or anticipate the level of intensity based on their analysis of how these four elements typically impact their campus community.

Tactics

Among the elements of mobilization, tactics have been given a prominent place in the discourse regarding campus-based student political activism.[6] Specifically, there are professional procedural guides noting the extent to which campuses possess legal authority to impose restrictions on activists' tactics.[7] Legal precedent allows campuses to regulate the time, place, and manner of campus-based expressions of free speech and assembly.[8] Campuses have also established internal procedural guidelines that consider movement tactics in determining the nature of police, campus safety, or other law enforcement entities' engagement at a particular mobilization event.

Public safety is important to campus officials because of the fear of tactical escalation. Prior displays of students' political activism have included violence and property damage, which stand out as scenarios campuses would like to avoid or prevent. Symbolically, the student deaths in the 1970 Kent State shootings represent the worst-case scenario, when National Guardsmen intervened during students' protest of the Vietnam War and President Nixon's order of the Cambodia invasion.[9] Similarly, the legacy of the Students for a Democratic Society's Weathermen advocacy of violence and adoption of bombing to communicate their antiwar position stands out as an iconic image of a possible public safety threat when students' political activism is at its most intense.[10] Nevertheless, these images represent the extremes, and not the norm. A 2010 survey of senior student affairs officers revealed that 92.2% perceive campus-based student activism on their campuses as being "orderly and peaceful," and just 5.2% indicate that it is typically "uncomfortable." The options of "violent or fearsome" were not utilized to describe students' activism that occurred between 1989 and 2010.[11] Comparatively, even at the height of the free speech, civil rights, and antiwar protests of the late 1960s, Long and Foster report that just 3% of campuses in their sample of 535 experienced violence, with more moderate tactics (sit-ins, picketing, marches, rallies, meetings, petitions, issuing demands) overwhelmingly serving as the norm.[12] More recently, while there has been an observable uptick in campus mobilization, remarkably few of the events are reported as including forms of physical or mortal violence (with notable exceptions of documented violence associated with protests occurring at the University of California, Berkeley in 2017; South Africa's University of Witwatersrand in 2016; and a rally that began on the University of Virginia campus and resulted in 1 dead and 19 injured in Charlottesville in 2017).

These cases and documented data communicate that violence attributable to campus political activism is a rare occurrence. Further, social movement scholarship reveals that violence is something that tends to progress incrementally, only after other, nonviolent forms of collective action fail to reach the intended target or prompt change.[13] If campus educators work to follow nascent and robust movement activities, they can, to a degree, anticipate the likelihood of escalation. Further still, while violence from campus protests is rare, McCarthy, Martin, and McPhail have observed dramatic increases in the odds (17.4 times) of police using restraining behavior during campus protests compared to police using this enforcement tactic during large, unplanned, convivial gatherings (bonfires, students celebrating in the streets after an athletic game).[14] These scholars also observed that the likelihood of police using force is greater when they are attempting to engage in crowd dispersal during campus protests (compared to the tendency to use force at convivial group gatherings). These patterns suggest there is a greater role for student affairs professionals to be brokers at the table for campus planning designed to anticipate tactical escalation to balance police presence with educational values. Moreover, movement history can serve as prologue, where the best way to avoid greater intensity (that includes the possibility of violence) is to heed Mueller's advice and to be responsive to early, more orderly forms of students' activism or civil disobedience.[15] Student affairs educators should carefully follow all forms of students' activism to ready the university for properly gauging the level and means of response.

Initiation

Following patterns of campus activism means that student affairs professionals need to become skillful in identifying patterns of movement initiation, to determine the opportune points of intervention to assert the campus's interests, assist students in voicing their viewpoints, or for determining where the campus, its subunits, or students might be strategic in cooperating with others to achieve maximum impact. There are many potential pathways by which students become linked to political activism. Activism can be motivated by students' ideological, personal, or political commitments, but the possibility exists for students to connect to movements or causes on account of their affiliations with organizations external to the campus environment as well. Certainly it is educationally important and responsible to encourage students' freedom to associate with entities within and beyond the campus environment. Campuses are heterogeneous places with varying people, ideas, and activities, and therefore they create opportunities for students to politically organize. Students' activism may be focused on issues internal to the university, but their political activism can also flow elsewhere with student activists targeting political entities (e.g., municipalities, the state/nation, elected leaders, government offices), as well as organizations outside of campus (e.g., businesses, community agencies, healthcare, or housing entities). In light of these complexities, it is important for student affairs educators to have a clear understanding about whether student activism is being initiated *by* students, compared to it being initiated *through* students; and whether student activism is initiated to make something happen *to* the university, or it is initiated *by* agents (students) of the university.

Beyond student-initiated campus-based political activism, external parties (including interest groups, partisan organizations, trade or labor groups, religious associations) have worked to actively recruit college students to advance their political agendas on and off campus.[16] The impetus of activism isn't always driven by the students first, but it can translate into student political activism. Alternately, external groups may not be entirely "external" to campuses, because some of them operate as parent groups to a campus-affiliated club or chapter.[17] The aim of these external parent groups can blur the lines of their student members' affiliations (e.g., localized versus federated affiliation) depending on the issue and what they are doing to advance the cause.[18] With respect to external parent groups engaged with students' political activism, some raise the prospect that students might be duped into advancing the agendas of external funders who seek to influence the public's view of a particular campus issue or want to shape the public's view of higher education in a particular way.[19] Student affairs professionals must be attentive to the possibility that external organizations may use the mask of student political engagement on campus as a means to indirectly access campus facilities, secure campus program funding to advance the external group's agenda (rather than the organically created students' political agenda), or are providing students with financial incentives or other resources that may allow them to exercise an outsized share of influence in the campus community compared to that wielded by typical student-led political organizations on campus. One of the stated aims of some ideological private philanthropic foundations has been to provide resources to campus-based student organizations who will advance their social or policy agendas, which includes funding, summer training for students, procedural guides, and field representatives to assist students.[20] The often cited adage to "follow the money" when seeking to identify sources of political influence can certainly be applied to the phenomena of students' political activism.

Lastly, beyond students' direct roles in political activism, college campuses are also targets of political activism. Associations and interest groups, the state, politicians, religious groups, and townspeople (among others) use activism to express their grievances with the university writ large, or with members of the university community (campus officials, faculty, students, staff, a particular campus program/initiative/office, or research center).[21] When activist efforts are aimed at the university or its stakeholders, these parties (which include students) could potentially engage in counter- or allied mobilization activities in response.[22] For example, if a religious group uses political activism to target a campus for their concerns with its procedural administrative practices of fairness, or employees' and students' access to reproductive healthcare, such actions may prompt students from a range of religious perspectives to engage in political action on their own or to link up with like-minded external parties.

Conclusion

It is not surprising that student affairs professionals might frame campus-based political activism as a matter suited for assisting the individual activist in acquiring agency and voice and extending their capacities for perspective-taking. However, students' political activism must also be framed through the more generalized sociological processes of movement phenomena. Here, I present the components of activism consisting of mobilizing groups, targets, tactics, and claims that reveal the ways in which organizing is a complex combination of factors that mediates its overall intensity. Finally, I focus on the use and impact of activists' tactics and the sources of initiation for students' political activism as critical pieces for making sense of how and where student affairs professionals can broker a campus response.

Discussion Questions

1. Reflecting on students' campus-based political activism in the past six months, what are the range of tactics utilized? Who are the mobilizing groups?
2. How does your campus assist students in exercising their own individual leadership and agency when working with external or parent organizations focused on political advocacy?

3. Independent of the sorts of claims or topics being advocated by various student political activists, what sorts of tactics prompt stakeholders to pay attention to activists' issues? Are senior administrators, faculty, students (peers), the public, or legislators evoked to respond by different approaches?

Notes

1. Barnhardt, C. L., Sheets, J. E., & Pasquesi, K. (2014). You expect what? Students' perceptions as resources in acquiring commitments and capacities for civic engagement. *Research in Higher Education, 56*(6), 622–644; Cole, E. R., & Stewart, A. J. (1996). Meanings of political participation among Black and White women: Political identity and social responsibility. *Journal of Personality and Social Psychology, 71*(1), 130–140; Stewart, A. J., Settles, I. H., & Winter, N. J. G. (1998). Women and the social movements of the 1960s: Activists, engaged observers, and nonparticipants. *Political Psychology, 19*(1), 63–94. For students' civic and political participation and engagement beyond college, see: Sax, L. J. (2004). Citizenship development and the American college student. In J.C. Dalton, T.R. Russell, & S. Kline (Eds.) *New Directions for Institutional Research, Assessing Character Outcomes in College* (Vol.122, pp. 65–80). San Francisco, CA: Wiley.

2. ACPA & NASPA. (2015). *Professional competency areas for student affairs practitioners.* Retrieved from http://www.naspa.org/programs/prodev/Professional_Competencies.pdf; ACPA. (2006). Statement of Ethical Principles and Standards. Retrieved from http://www2.myacpa.org/ethics/statement.php

3. Barnhardt, C. L. (2014). Campus-based organizing: Tactical repertoires of a contemporary student movement. In C. Broadhurst & G. L. Martin (Eds.), *Radical academia? Understanding the climates for campus activists* (Vol. 167, pp. 43–58). San Francisco, CA: Wiley.

4. Briscoe, F., Gupta, A., & Anner, M. S. (2015). Social activism and practice diffusion: How activist tactics affect nontargeted organizations. *Administrative Science Quarterly, 60*(2), 300–332.

5. Myers, D. J., & Caniglia, B. S. (2004). All the rioting that's fit to print: Selection effects in national newspaper coverage of civil disorders, 1968–1969. *American Sociological Review, 69*(4), 519–543; Snyder, D., & Kelly, W. R. (1977). Conflict intensity, media sensitivity, and validity of newspaper data. *American Sociological Review, 42*(1), 105–123.

6. Cowan, R., Newton, N., Smith, J., Brozen, A., Burger, N., & Homstad, M. (1995). *Campus organizing guide for social justice groups.* Retrieved from http://www.campusactivism.org/uploads/orgguide.pdf; Gora, J. M., Goldberger, D., Stern, G., & Halperin, M. (1991). *The right to protest: The basic ACLU guide to free expression.* Carbondale, IL: Southern Illinois Press; Smith, R. B. (1993). The rise of the conservative student press. *Change, 25*(1), 24–29.

7. Sun, J. C., Hutchens, N. H., & Sponsler, B. A. (2014). Responding to campus protests: A practitioner resource. Legal Links: *Connecting Student Affairs and*

Law, 1(2). Washington DC: NASPA Student Affairs Administrators in Higher Education.

8. Kaplan, W. A., & Lee, B. A. (2009). *A legal guide for student affairs professionals* (2nd ed.). San Francisco, CA: Jossey-Bass.

9. Brown, C., & Lewis, E. L. (1998). Protesting the invasion of Cambodia: A case study of crowd behavior and demonstration leadership. *Polity, 30*(4), 645–665.

10. Altbach, P. G., & Cohen, R. (1990). American student activism: The post-sixties transformation. *The Journal of Higher Education, 61*(1), 32–49.

11. Survey methods are described in Barnhardt, Campus-based organizing. Responses were drawn from a random sample of U.S. 4-year campuses. In total, 79 informed respondents (the most knowledgeable senior student affairs staff member) submitted responses to the survey, culminating in a 53% response rate. Responding campuses were representative of the sample on important structural dimensions including institutional type, size, selectivity, geographic location, history of prior activism, and types of statutory restrictions on dissent.

12. Long, D., & Foster, J. (1970). Levels of protest. In J. Foster & D. Long (Eds.), *Protest! Student activism in America* (pp. 81–88). New York, NY: William Morrow.

13. Benford, R. D., & Snow, D. A. (1992). Master frames and cycles of protest. In A. D. Morris & C. M. Mueller (Eds.), *Frontiers in social movement theory* (pp. 133–155). New Haven, CT: Yale University Press; McAdam, D. (1983). Tactical innovation and the pace of insurgency. *American Sociological Review, 48*, 735–754; Mueller, C. M. (1992). Building social movement theory. In A. D. Morris & C. M. Mueller (Eds.), *Frontiers in social movement theory* (pp. 3–26). New Haven, CT: Yale University Press.

14. McCarthy, J. D., Martin, A. W., & McPhail, C. (2007). Policing disorderly campus protests and convivial gatherings: The interaction of threat, social organization, and First Amendment guarantees. *Social Problems, 54*(3), 274–296.

15. Mueller, Building social movement theory.

16. Barnhardt, C. L. (2012). *Contemporary student activism: The educational contexts of socially-responsible student activism* (Unpublished doctoral dissertation). University of Michigan, Ann Arbor, MI; Bunnage, L. (2002). Freshman organizers: Can Union Summer become a year-round vocation? *New Labor Forum, Fall/Winter*, 92–97; Van Dyke, N., Dixon, M., & Carlon, H. (2007). Manufacturing dissent. Labor revitalization, Union Summer and student protest. *Social Forces, 86*(1), 193–214.

17. McCarthy, J. D. (2005). Persistence and change among nationally federated social movements. In G. F. Davis, D. McAdam, W. R. Scott, & M. N. Zald (Eds.), *Social movements and organization theory* (pp. 193–225). New York, NY: Cambridge University Press; McCarthy, J. D., & Zald, M. N. (1987). Resource mobilization and social movements. In M. N. Zald & J. D. McCarthy (Eds.), *Social movements in an organizational society* (pp. 15–47). New Brunswick, NJ: Transaction Books.

18. Binder, A., & Wood, K. (2012). *Becoming right: How campuses shape young conservatives*. Princeton, NJ: Princeton University Press; Crossley, A. D. (2017).

Finding feminism: Millennial activists and the unfinished gender revolution. New York, NY: New York University Press.

19. Dyke, Dixon, & Carlon, Manufacturing dissent.

20. Barnhardt, C. L. (2017). Philanthropic foundations' social agendas and the field of higher education. In M. B. Paulsen (Ed.), *Higher education: Handbook of theory and research* (Vol. 32). Cham, Switzerland: Springer; Binder, A., & Wood, K. (2012). *Becoming right: How campuses shape young conservatives.* Princeton, NJ: Princeton University Press; see also examples from the popular press: Kamenetz, A. (2018). Professors are targets in online culture wars; Some fight back. *nprED*. Retrieved from https://www.npr.org/sections/ed/2018/04/04/590928008/professor-harassment; Wilson, J. (2018, March 18). How to troll the left: Understanding the rightwing outrage machine—Recent events on US college campuses illustrate how the right has fine-tuned its formula for pushing progressives' buttons. *The Guardian Web Edition.* Retrieved from https://www.theguardian.com/us-news/2018/mar/18/how-the-right-trolls-the-left-college-campus-outrage

21. Clemens, E. S. (1997). *The people's lobby: Organizational innovation and the rise of interest group political in the United States, 1890–1925.* Chicago, IL: University of Chicago Press.

22. Zald, M. N., & Useem, B. (1987). Movement and countermovement interaction: Mobilization, tactics, and state involvement. In M. N. Zald & J. D. McCarthy (Eds.), *Social movements in an organizational society* (pp. 247–272). New Brunswick, NJ: Transaction Books.

5

What Does It Mean for Student Affairs Educators to Establish Safe and Just Responses to Campus Sexual Violence?

Moving Beyond Policy to Address Campus Sexual Violence

Chris Linder

Overrelying on policy and ignoring identity and power in efforts to address sexual violence has significant implications for campus educators and administrators. Although the need to comply with state and federal guidelines is real, compliance cannot be the only strategy to address campus sexual violence. To more effectively address campus sexual violence, I challenge administrators and educators to consider three specific strategies: view policy as necessary but insufficient, understand the history of sexual violence and its relationship to oppression, and employ an identity- and power-conscious framework in all sexual violence-related prevention and response strategies.

Although activists and advocates have been working for centuries to address sexual violence in the United States,[1] it has gained increased attention on college campuses in recent years. Increased attention to a complex, multifaceted issue is a double-edged sword. Having more people invested in addressing campus sexual violence may result in increased resources directed toward the problem; however, the urgency may also result in the development of less complex and nuanced strategies to address the problem. People in power frequently feel pressured to quickly develop one-size-fits-all policies. Unfortunately, there is no quick and easy fix to eradicate sexual violence—on campus or otherwise—and most policies address violence after it happens, rather than preventing it from happening in the first place.[2]

Policy Is Necessary, Yet Insufficient

The federal government established Title IX in 1972 to prohibit "sex discrimination in all educational programs and activities receiving federal financial assistance."[3] Through a complicated legal history and interpretation of a variety of case law and relationship to Title VII (sex discrimination in the workplace), Title IX became the policy through which campuses are held accountable for addressing sexual violence.[4] Unfortunately, in its current form and interpretation, Title IX incentivizes response to, rather than prevention of, sexual violence.

Like Title VII for employers, Title IX addresses institutional, rather than individual, misconduct. Title IX requires that campuses ensure safe and equitable learning environments for people of all genders. This means that if campus personnel (e.g., administrators, faculty, and staff) knew or should have known about practices or behaviors contributing to a hostile work or learning environment, they have a responsibility to address them. Because sexual violence disproportionately affects women[5] and transgender[6] people, campuses are not providing equitable access to education if over half of the population is at significant risk for sexual violence and campuses are not effectively addressing it.

Administrators, educators, and policy-makers genuinely want their campuses to be safe learning environments for all students, yet the pressure to comply with continually changing laws and guidelines impede them from considering what might work in their specific contexts. Guidelines for addressing sexual violence through Title IX change frequently. The Office of Civil Rights (OCR) has issued several sets of guidelines for interpreting and implementing policies related to sexual violence, including sexual harassment in line with Title IX, over the past few decades. The OCR issued a Dear Colleague Letter in 2011,[7] under the Obama administration, designed to change the ways campuses responded to sexual violence. Specifically, the letter provided additional guidance for adjudication processes on college campuses, including requiring campuses to use a preponderance of the evidence standard and clarity on the roles students and outside support people may take in adjudication processes. Recently, Betsy DeVos, the Secretary of Education in the Trump administration, issued a new set of guidelines[8] related to Title IX, rescinding the guidelines of the Obama administration. The new guidelines allow campuses to move from a preponderance of the evidence standard to a more strenuous clear and convincing standard of evidence in campus adjudication processes. A clear and convincing standard favors the respondent. Additionally, the new guidelines allow institutions to accept appeals from only the respondent, the respondent or the accusing party, or neither. Previous guidelines required institutions to include the respondent or accusing party in their appeals processes. Finally, the new guidelines allow institutions to use mediation to adjudicate sexual violence, an option unavailable in the previous guidelines.

Credit for the increase in attention to campus sexual violence goes to the student activists who organized a national movement to use Title IX to hold colleges and universities accountable for addressing sexual violence in the United States. In fall 2014, activists from across the country filed complaints with the OCR for violation of Title IX. At the time of this writing, students had filed over 450 complaints with the OCR,[9] illustrating the systemic nature of the problem. Although to date no school has been fined for Title IX violations,[10] the fear of a significant fine (upward of $200,000) and loss of federal funding resulted in campus administrators scrambling to interpret and comply with Title IX. Student activists (and survivors) who organized to file Title IX complaints with the OCR endured institutional betrayal upon reporting their experiences with sexual violence to the institution.[11] *Institutional betrayal* refers to the idea that a person suffers more trauma through "wrongdoings perpetrated by an institution against individuals who trust, or are dependent on that institution,"[12] than by the actual traumatic events. Student-survivors of sexual violence report that they endure more harm as a result of the way their institution handled (or did not handle) their report of sexual violence than they did as a result of the actual assault.[13] Further, student activists who filed OCR complaints conveyed a deep love and loyalty to their institutions—the activists wanted the institutions to better support students.[14]

From a place of harm, hurt, disappointment, anger, and hope, student activists advocated for campuses to respond more effectively to sexual violence. They used one of the few tools available to them—Title IX—to address the problem. Student activists demanded to be treated more equitably. Unfortunately, Title IX incentivizes response to, rather than prevention of, sexual violence. The primary liability risk for institutions under Title IX is for failing to appropriately investigate and adjudicate assaults after they happen, rather than for ineffective efforts to prevent assaults from happening in the first place.[15] Although many people argue that more effective response to sexual violence will reduce rates by removing current perpetrators and deterring future perpetrators, this has not yet proven true. Even with increased rates of incarceration for sexual violence,[16] rates of sexual violence have not decreased.[17] Another illustration that Title IX incentivizes response, rather than prevention, is that the 2011 OCR guidance dedicated 15 pages to response and a single page to prevention.[18]

Policy is a very important part of the puzzle of addressing campus sexual violence; however, complying with policy is a minimum expectation for effectively addressing campus sexual violence. Policymakers frequently develop routine responses to address a complex issue in a less-than-complex way. Although some policy is essential for ensuring that campus administrators and educators attempt to provide fair and equitable adjudication processes and provide alleged victims and perpetrators with appropriate resources, these policies must be considered the minimum, not the maximum requirements.

Unfortunately, policy leads many administrators and educators to get stuck on the "have to do" rather than the "should do" or "can do" in a compliance culture.[19] Campus administrators and educators frequently use compliance-related language to describe campus sexual violence efforts. For example, faculty and staff frequently discuss being a mandatory reporter, meaning that they "have to" report any instance of sexual violence that they are aware of, yet they do not really understand the principle behind mandatory reporting, which is to protect future victims of sexual violence from a known perpetrator. Failing to teach the why of a policy contributes to compliance culture, rather than a culture of preventing and effectively responding to sexual violence. Although "have to do" and "should do" need not be mutually exclusive, in today's litigious culture, the "have to do's" often come at the expense of the "should do's." It does not have to be this way. We can approach sexual violence from a both/and perspective. When we, as educators and administrators, find ourselves saying or feeling that we "have to" do something, we should stop and think for a minute. Even if we "have to do" something, what else "should" we be doing?

Despite the best intentions of policymakers, student activists, and educators, perpetrators of sexual violence still plague institutions of higher education with alarmingly high rates of sexual violence. Rates of sexual violence on college campuses have not improved during the past 60 years,[20] so existing strategies, including varied implementations of Title IX, do not work. Activists, educators, and administrators must work to change the culture on their campuses through avenues other than policy. Seeking new answers to old problems requires reflection, innovation, and creativity—three things administrators and educators do not have the luxury of—because of the forced focus on complying with ever-changing law and policy. In addition to overrelying on policy, compliance culture contributes to campus administrators and educators frequently failing to consider the roles of identity, power, and privilege in addressing campus sexual violence.

History and Roots of Sexual Violence

Sexual violence on college campuses has received unparalleled attention from media and policymakers over the past several years. Yet, sexual violence did not originate, nor does it solely exist, on college campuses. Sexual violence is a systemic tool of terrorization and violence,[21] and virtually no scholarship examines campus sexual violence through a historical lens. Further, most policy also fails to account for the roots of sexual violence. Failing to account for history results in activists, educators, and policymakers depicting sexual violence as a current problem, rather than a systemic issue with roots in colonization, exploitation, and economic control. Frequently referred to as a "national epidemic," researchers, journalists, and activists disassociate campus sexual violence from larger systems of power, privilege, and oppression. *Epidemic* implies a "short-term, isolated problem"[22] and does not consider how sexual violence has remained a constant form of power and control throughout history. In the United States alone, sexual violence has been used as a tool of colonization—White European settlers raped women in Native communities to exert power over them and to instill fear to get people to comply with White assimilation.[23] Additionally, White men have used rape as a tool of terrorization toward and economic control over communities in the United States for centuries. White slave owners frequently raped enslaved women as a way to increase their labor supply. Because the children of enslaved people became the property of the owner of the enslaved person, owners gained additional economic capital through raping enslaved women to attempt to impregnate them.[24] After legal slavery ended, White men continued to rape Black women, without repercussion, to illustrate their dominance and to instill fear, thereby maintaining power and control over Black communities.[25]

Just as sexual violence did not originate on college campuses, neither did efforts to eradicate it.[26] Women of color have been organizing to address sexual violence from an intersectional framework for centuries, yet their leadership and strategies are consistently ignored by mainstream White feminist organizations, who rely on the state to address interpersonal violence.[27] Campus policy has followed suit. Rather than seeking to learn from communities external to campus about ways to engage in accountability outside police and adjudication systems, campus administrators are required to comply with state and federal guidelines written from an identity-

and power-neutral perspective to address a problem that is anything but identity- and power-neutral. For example, some communities of color have used community accountability processes to address interpersonal violence for decades.[28] Community accountability is different from mediation—community accountability requires the participation of all members of a community to hold perpetrators responsible and help rehabilitate them as full members of a community. Mediation focuses on compromise, which is inappropriate for crimes like sexual violence, where the victim and perpetrator do not share an equal amount of power. Rather than shunning perpetrators, which frequently results in them going to another community to cause additional harm, some activists have worked to embrace perpetrators, name the harm they cause, and work to change their behaviors. Given the intimate nature of some campus communities, if done correctly and under the leadership of people thoroughly experienced with its practices, community accountability may also be appropriate for rehabilitating perpetrators, rather than sending them to other campuses to cause further harm.

A lack of attention to and awareness of history leads to ineffective and sometimes harmful strategies for addressing campus sexual violence. Ahistorical approaches to addressing sexual violence lead to superficial strategies to address the symptoms of a larger problem: oppression. Although it may seem like a lofty, academic exercise to engage in deep historical reflection and analysis about the ways in which sexual violence is a tool of terrorization and control with strong historical roots, it is not. Ahistoricism contributes to superficial strategies for addressing sexual violence, resulting in a failure to effectively change the culture related to sexual violence.[29] For example, rather than focusing on oppression and power, much of the scholarship about addressing campus sexual violence focuses on alcohol as a cause or a contributor to sexual violence.[30] Focusing on alcohol detracts from the roots of the problem: power and dominance. Given the long history of White men using sexual violence as a tool of power and control over marginalized communities, alcohol represents another distraction from addressing power. It is easier to say that college women should stop drinking so much than it is to challenge larger systems of power and dominance.

Challenging power and dominance means that people who have historically been entitled to assumptions of innocence (i.e., White people) will receive less of that benefit. Challenging power also means that White people (and other dominant groups) who enjoy a significant amount of comfort in relationship to power and equity may be uncomfortable facing their privileges and considering the ways in which they have unknowingly benefited from systems of dominance and power. However, this is our only choice. We cannot effectively address sexual violence at its roots without understanding the ways in which it has been used as a tool of power and dominance throughout U.S. and global history and working to interrupt a long history and legacy of power and dominance.

Power- and Identity-Conscious Approaches to Addressing Sexual Violence

Building on the need to understand the historical roots of sexual violence, we, as college and university educators and administrators, also need to better understand and interrupt identity- and power-neutral practices associated with addressing campus sexual violence. *Identity- and power-neutral* means that policies and practices do not consider the ways identities and the power associated with them influence people's experiences. For example, people with power have constructed Whiteness as the norm throughout U.S. history, resulting in White people having access to power and resources that people of color do not. Similarly, cisgender people—considered the norm in mainstream U.S. society—have access to safety and personal well-being in ways that transgender people do not.

Campus administrators and educators frequently fail to address oppression using a power-conscious framework. For example, we, as institutional agents, have attempted to address racism by working with and encouraging students of color to assimilate, rather than challenging White people to stop being racist. Similarly, sexual violence prevention efforts often focus on teaching potential victims (mostly cisgender women) to avoid being raped, rather than intervening with perpetrators and telling them to stop raping. Teaching people with less formal power to assimilate and protect themselves is far less threatening than challenging power and dominance. The root of sexual violence is power and dominance, and until we begin to address power and dominance at the core, we will not end sexual violence on campus or beyond.

Many people assume that policies and practices are power-neutral, meaning that they apply similarly to all people. However, when we construe issues as *neutral*, they automatically privilege dominant groups because of the ways we are socialized to accept dominant narratives if they are not explicitly interrupted. For example, a policy that has gender-neutral language (e.g., using *they* instead of *he* or *she*) may be attempting to interrupt gendered norms about sexual violence, including the idea that only women are victims and only men are perpetrators. However, if individuals do not know the purpose of gender-neutral language, they will likely default to their socialized assumptions of woman as victim, man as perpetrator. An identity- and power-conscious approach to writing a policy would include an explicit description of why the policy includes gender-neutral pronouns and examples and multiple pronouns to ensure that people of all genders are represented in the policy.

In addition to policies failing to consider identity and power, the implementations of those policies through response systems also frequently fail to consider identity and power. For example, one of the most common responses to addressing sexual violence after it occurs is to encourage victims to report the incident to police or a campus adjudication system; in fact, Title IX requires faculty or staff members who learn of sexual violence to immediately report to the Title IX officer. Although this policy is intended to protect students from perpetrators who may continue to assault people if not held accountable, the policy fails to achieve this goal, as perpetrators are rarely held accountable through campus adjudication systems[31] for a multitude of reasons, including a lack of understanding of the dynamics of sexual violence and the privilege most perpetrators enjoy. The lack of perpetrator accountability further harms victims and contributes to victims' feelings of institutional betrayal. Further, given that communities of color and queer communities have volatile relationships with police and similar systems,[32] the reporting mandate for responding to sexual violence harms many survivors. If survivors from minoritized communities report the violence to a campus adjudication or police system, they risk being further marginalized and harmed through racist and homophobic assumptions of identity- and power-neutral policies and practices. Examples of this include gay men being told their assault does not fall under the parameters of the campus sexual assault policy or women of color not being believed because people with power have constructed them as "rapeable" throughout history.[33]

Sexual violence disproportionately affects women of color,[34] transgender people,[35] and queer people,[36] yet research and strategies to address campus sexual violence almost exclusively focus on White, cisgender, heterosexual women.[37] In a study of 10 years of scholarship about campus sexual violence, less than 16% of 434 empirical articles included an analysis of data based on race, 5% based on sexual orientation, and 1% on disability. Similarly, only 6 articles included the option for participants to identify as a gender other than a binary gender (i.e., *male* or *female* or *man* or *woman*).[38]

Failing to account for the ways race, sexual orientation, and gender identity influence sexual violence results in limited attempts to address sexual violence. For example, bystander intervention has been hailed as an "effective" strategy to address sexual violence. The premise behind bystander intervention is that by training people to recognize potentially harmful situations and to intervene in those situations, overall rates of sexual violence will decline.[39] Although some research indicates that effective bystander training results in increased awareness of potentially harmful situations,[40] no research to date indicates a reduction in sexual violence where bystander intervention has been effectively employed.

Further, because most bystander trainings advocate a power-neutral perspective, meaning that they do not take into account the relationship between identity and power, bystander intervention may actually harm minoritized communities. One study concluded that White women were less likely to intervene in situations where the prospective victim was a Black woman.[41] Additionally, because the "stranger danger" myth (i.e., the idea that a person is most likely to be harmed by a stranger or "creepy" guy) is alive and well on most college campuses,[42] many students do not effectively identify acquaintance assault situations. Further, because the master narrative, rooted in a long history of racism, is that Black men are more likely to be perpetrators of sexual violence,[43] it is likely that many students fail to intervene in situations of sexual violence where the perpetrator is White or perceived as a "good guy" and perpetuate a hostile campus climate for men of color by assuming that they are likely to be perpetrators of sexual violence.

To more effectively incorporate power and identity in efforts to address sexual violence prevention and response, campus administrators and educators may benefit from employing a power- and identity-conscious framework, which requires them to consider the influence of identity and power in their work. Rather than writing policy with the most "typical" (i.e., what is represented in media and scholarship) cases of sexual violence in mind, write the policy with the most vulnerable victims in mind. For example, rather than focusing on a young, White, "innocent" and naïve woman as the typical victim, consider the ways that transgender students, students with a history of substance abuse, neuroatypical people, women of color, gay men, and students with disabilities might experience sexual violence. Does the policy cover all these experiences or is it written with only the (stereo)typical experience in mind?

Similarly, in educating about and responding to sexual violence, staff on campus must be trained to effectively understand the dynamics of sexual violence broadly, rather than only focusing on typical victims. Providing support and training that goes beyond Title IX compliance for staff and students affiliated with a wide variety of support services on campus is crucial. Engaging with staff and students affiliated with the identity-based organizations and offices on campus may also assist administrators and educators in having a deeper understanding of the dynamics of sexual violence and how it intersects with other forms of oppression. Title IX and victim advocate staff, as well as the staff and students facilitating prevention and education workshops, *must* be expected to and supported in engaging in professional development and training beyond that of compliance.

Reflection and Discussion

Given the current context of compliance, mandates, and litigation surrounding sexual violence on college campuses, administrators have been functioning from a place of crisis. Although policy provides administrators some guidance for addressing the problem, policy on its own is an incomplete and ineffective measure to eradicate sexual violence. Administrators and educators must move beyond compliance and effectively interrogate the power and identity implications of policy and practice as they relate to sexual violence on their campuses. Given that perpetrators continue to target victims—especially those with minoritized identities—at alarmingly high rates, the problem of campus sexual violence is urgent, yet not an epidemic. People with power have effectively interwoven sexual violence into the very nature of our world, making it difficult to eradicate through simple measures. Campus administrators and educators have a responsibility to engage fully and deeply with power to address sexual violence at its roots: power and dominance.

Discussion Questions

1. What is my relationship to power and dominance? In what ways have I knowingly or unknowingly benefitted from power and privilege?
2. What are my strategies for continuing to educate myself about power, privilege, and sexual violence? Who will hold me accountable for this education?
3. What is my role in addressing sexual violence on campus? What resources do I have access to and how can I leverage them to effectively interrogate and interrupt power dynamics on my campus?

Notes

1. Freedman, E. B. (2013). *Redefining rape: Sexual violence in the era of suffrage and segregation.* Cambridge, MA: Harvard University Press.

2. Silbaugh, K. (2015). Reactive to proactive: Title IX's unrealized capacity to prevent campus sexual assault. *Boston University Law Review, 95,* 1049–1076.

3. Tani, K. M. (2017). An administrative right to be free from sexual violence? Title IX enforcement in historical and institutional perspective. *Duke Law Journal, 66,* 1847–1903.

4. Silbaugh, Reactive to proactive.

5. Black, M. C., Basile, K. C., Breiding, M. J., Smith, S. G., Walters, M. L., Merrick, M. T., . . . & Stevens, M. R. (2011). *The national intimate partner and sexual violence survey.* National Center for Injury Prevention and Control,

Centers for Disease Control and Prevention. Retrieved from http://www.cdc.gov/violenceprevention/pdf/nisvs_executive_summary-a.pdf

6. Stotzer, R. L. (2009). Violence against transgender people: A review of United States data. *Aggression and Violent Behavior, 14*, 170–179.

7. Office of Civil Rights. (2011). *Dear colleague letter.* Retrieved from https://www2.ed.gov/about/offices/list/ocr/letters/colleague-201104.html

8. U.S. Department of Education. (2017). *Department of education issues new interim guidance on campus sexual misconduct.* Retrieved from https://www.ed.gov/news/press-releases/department-education-issues-new-interim-guidance-campus-sexual-misconduct

9. The Chronicle of Higher Education. (n.d.). *Title IX: Tracking sexual assault investigations.* Retrieved from https://projects.chronicle.com/titleix/

10. Hattersley-Grey, R. (2012, June 3). Not complying with Title IX could cost you. *Campus Safety Magazine.* Retrieved from https://www.campussafetymagazine.com/university/not-complying-with-title-ix-could-cost-you/.

11. Linder, C., & Myers, J. S. (in press). Institutional betrayal as a motivator for campus sexual assault activism. *NASPA Journal About Women in Higher Education.*

12. Smith, C. P., & Freyd, J. J. (2014). Institutional betrayal. *American Psychologist, 69*(6), 575–587.

13. Ibid.

14. Linder & Myers, Institutional betrayal as a motivator.

15. Silbaugh, Reactive to proactive.

16. Travis, J., Western, B., & Redburn, S. (2014). *The growth of incarceration in the United States: Exploring causes and consequences.* Washington DC: National Academies Press.

17. Black, Basile, Breiding, Smith, Walters, Merrick, . . . & Stevens, *National intimate partner and sexual violence survey.*

18. Silbaugh, Reactive to proactive.

19. Marine, S. B., & Nicolazzo, Z. (2017). *The rise of compliance culture: A dead end for ending campus sexual violence* [web log post]. Retrieved from https://jcshesa.wordpress.com/2017/06/27/the-rise-of-compliance-culture-a-dead-end-for-ending-campus-sexual-violence/

20. Adams-Curtis, L. E., & Forbes, G. B. (2004). College women's experiences of sexual coercion: A review of cultural, perpetrator, victim, and situational violence. *Trauma, Violence, & Abuse, 5*(2), 91–122.

21. Deer, S. (2015). *The beginning and end of rape: Confronting sexual violence in Native America.* Minneapolis, MN: University of Minnesota Press; Freedman, *Redefining rape.*

22. Deer, *The beginning and end of rape.*

23. Ibid.

24. Freedman, *Redefining rape.*

25. Ibid.; McGuire, D. L. (2010). *At the dark end of the street: Black women, rape, and resistance—A new history of the civil rights movement from Rosa Parks to the rise of Black power.* New York, NY: Alfred A. Knopf.

26. Ibid.

27. Bumiller, K. (2008). *In an abusive state: How neoliberalism appropriated the feminist movement against sexual violence.* Durham, NC: Duke University Press.

28. Bierra, A., Carrillo, O., Colbert, E., Ibarra, X., Kigvamasud'Vashti, T., & Maulana, S. (2006). Taking risks: Implementing grassroots community accountability strategies. In Incite! (Eds.). *Color of violence: The Incite! anthology* (pp. 250–266). Cambridge, MA: South End Press.

29. Harris, J. C., & Linder, C. (Eds.). (2017). *Intersections of identity and sexual violence on campus: Centering minoritized students' experiences.* Sterling, VA: Stylus.

30. Linder, C., Williams, B. M., Lacy, M., Parker, B., & Grimes, N. (2017, November). *A power-conscious content analysis of 10 years of scholarship on campus sexual violence.* Paper presented at the annual meeting of the Association for the Study of Higher Education. Houston, TX.

31. Lombardi, K. (2010, February 24). *A lack of consequences for sexual assault.* The Center for Public Integrity. Retrieved from https://www.publicintegrity .org/2010/02/24/4360/lack-consequences-sexual-assault

32. Richie, A. (2017). *Invisible no more: Police violence against Black women and women of color.* Boston, MA: Beacon Press.

33. Smith, A. (2005). *Conquest: Sexual violence and American Indian genocide.* Cambridge, MA: South End Press.

34. Porter, J., & McQuiller Williams, L. (2011). Intimate violence among underrepresented groups on a college campus. *Journal of Interpersonal Violence, 26*(16), 3210–3224.

35. Stotzer, R. L. (2009). Violence against transgender people: A review of United States data. *Aggression and Violent Behavior, 14,* 170–179.

36. Edwards, K. M., Sylaska, K. M., Barry, J. E., Moynihan, M. M., Banyard, V. L., Cohn, E. S., . . . & Ward, S. K. (2015). Physical dating violence, sexual violence, and unwanted pursuit victimization: A comparison of incidence rates among sexual-minority and heterosexual college students. *Journal of Interpersonal Violence, 30*(4), 580–600.

37. Linder, Williams, Lacy, Parker, & Grimes, *A power-conscious content analysis.*

38. Ibid.

39. Moynihan, M. M., & Banyard, V. L. (2011). Educating bystanders helps prevent sexual violence and reduce backlash. *Family & Intimate Partner Violence Quarterly, 3,* 293–304.

40. Katz, J., & Moore, J. (2013). Bystander education training for campus sexual assault prevention: An initial meta-analysis. *Violence and Victims, 28*(6), 1054–1067.

41. Katz, J., Merrilees, C., LaRose, J., & Edgington, C. (2017). White female bystanders' response to a Black woman at risk for sexual assault: Associations with attitudes about sexism and racial justice. *Journal of Aggression, Maltreatment, & Trauma.* Online first, http://www.tandfonline.com/doi/full/10.1080/10926771.20 17.1376238

42. Linder, C. & Lacy, M. (2017, March). *Stranger danger: College women's perceptions of campus safety.* Paper presented at the annual meeting of ACPA College Student Educators International. Columbus, OH.

43. McGuire, *At the dark end of the street.*

Abating Campus Sexual Violence Requires a Multifaceted Approach

Frank Shushok Jr.

From 2011 to 2017, I provided leadership for the Title IX Investigatory process at Virginia Tech. After 6 years as an insider to many gut-wrenching, life-altering cases involving sexual violence among college students, my heart is broken. It's one thing to hear the national statistics: that 1 in 5 women and 1 in 17 men are sexually assaulted in college; or that more than 90% of college students who experience sexual violence never report it.[1] It's another thing, however, to "see" the statistics—to know their names, understand their potential, meet their families, and observe their unrelenting trauma. The suffering of sexual violence is immeasurable, and the sheer reality that a full quarter of our student population experiences it should cause vicarious suffering for all of us. As I proclaimed in a 2017 *Washington Post* editorial, I had no idea—you might not either.[2]

Linder's thoughtful essay on sexual violence makes several important and compelling arguments with which I concur. I agree that the urgency of addressing sexual violence on college campuses often results in less complex strategies to address the problem.

In 2014, Governor Terry McAuliffe appointed me to Virginia's Task Force on Combating Campus Sexual Violence. During my year of service, I heard about far too many "silver bullets" for reducing the likelihood of sexual assault on college and university campuses. I often harkened back to a concept of requisite variety, an idea introduced to me during my graduate higher education organizational culture seminar. In summary, this concept argues that for organizations or people to deal effectively with the vast diversity of problems in society, the repertoire of nuanced potential responses must exceed the problems faced. Karl Weick puts it this way: "It's because of requisite variety that organizations have to be preoccupied with keeping sufficient diversity inside the organization to sense accurately the variety present in ecological changes outside it."[3]

What's clear to me about improving the plight of sexual violence in society in general, and college campuses in particular, is that simple solutions will not make meaningful progress. Instead, campus leaders must embrace a multifaceted approach that recognizes that policy development, political action, educational intervention, and cultural transformation must be pursued with equal vigor.

Policy as One of Many Prevention Strategies

As Linder points out, policy is insufficient, and yet, we must celebrate that serious policy development has been underway in the last decade. The Department of Education and its Office for Civil Rights 2011 Title IX Dear Colleague Letter,[4] for example, was a first and necessary step for bringing the topic of sexual violence the sense of urgency that has long been desperately needed. That 18-page document asserted the numerous ways colleges and universities must address and prevent sexual harassment to comply with Title IX, a law that prohibits discrimination on the basis of sex. While policies and procedures must undergo improvement and revision, these efforts represent critical steps forward. Yet even in the era after the 2011 Dear Colleague Letter, reporting of sexual violence remains inadequate. A 2015 analysis of Clery Act reporting, for example, revealed that a whopping 73% of primary campuses reported not a single instance of sexual violence in 2015.[5] National statistics on sexual violence bear out the improbability that this represents anywhere near reality.

Even at colleges where responding to reports of sexual violence had a robust infrastructure prior to 2011, the Dear Colleague Letter ushered in even greater commitment. Since 2011, Virginia Tech, known for its long-standing leadership around issues of sexual violence, experienced a 500% increase in sexual violence reporting after reformatting policies and procedures to comply with the 2011 guidance.[6] Baylor University, which has been the subject of national attention for failure to respond to a culture of sexual violence, had no Clery reports of sexual violence from 2008 to 2011. Unfortunately, Baylor, like many institutions, needed external pressure, including from the federal government, to address cultural realities that went unaddressed. In 2015, after the Department of Education and others intervened, Baylor received 23 reports of rape on campus.[7]

It is for this reason that I take exception with Linder's assertion that "changing laws and guidelines impede [campuses] from considering what might work in their specific contexts."[8] Without these external pressures, I worry progress would be far worse—in fact, nonexistent in many places. I posit that these laws often represent minimum standards upon which campus communities can build policies, procedures, and strategies. Colleges and universities too often bemoan federal oversight, yet it is precisely such pressure that prompts the action that our students deserve. Nothing highlights this unfortunate reality like the way civil rights legislation aided in removing racial barriers to opportunity in higher education from the 1960s to present. As Linder noted, Betsy DeVos has rolled back the Obama administration's 2011 guidance. In this environment, colleges and universities must demonstrate that they are committed to combating sexual violence, especially in the absence of federal pressure to do so.

Second, I agree that higher education's predominant strategy for addressing sexual violence leans toward responding, not preventing. Unfortunately, it's important to remember that responding is perhaps our greatest potential prevention strategy. As noted, there is evidence that many acts of sexual violence continue to go unreported. And if David Lisak, a clinical psychologist who has devoted his professional life to studying the causes and consequences of interpersonal violence, is correct that 90% of campus sexual assaults are undertaken by serial offenders who on average commit 6 rapes each, receiving reports of sexual violence, investigating them, and holding individuals accountable is clearly an effective prevention strategy.[9] Lisak isn't alone in his suggestion that predation is a problem. In a 2015 JAMA Pediatrics study of 1,642 men on 2 college campuses, nearly 25% admitted to being repeat offenders.[10]

Yet while response and adjudication are critical to addressing sexual violence, as Linder notes, too many survivors are revictimized by processes led by undertrained and undereducated administrators responsible for the Title IX investigation process. In a time when research shows unequivocal insight into the impact of trauma on victims, our response systems too often discredit victims of sexual assault for reasons that are scientifically explainable by neuroscience.[11] A failure of administrators to be educated about the tendency of trauma to fragment memory is a frequent cause for survivors to feel victimized.

I support Linder's assertion that the overreliance on policy, as well as the lack of attention to history and power, are serious issues that must be confronted as part of a nuanced response to sexual violence. To "interrupt identity- and power-neutral practices associated with addressing campus sexual violence,"[12] as Linder compellingly argues we need to find approaches to working with one another undergirded by a spirit of generosity, listening, and learning.

It's also of fundamental importance that men be invited to contribute meaningfully to the conversation—which will require recognizing that learning is in progress and their participation will involve inadvertent missteps in language, philosophy, and perceived inadequacy in knowledge. As a man, sexual violence was mostly a cognitive reality framed by statistics for far too much of my life. I'm truly sorry about this unfortunate reality. If you're one of the fortunate ones who has been personally unscathed by sexual violence, don't assume that means you are off the hook. Decide not to ignore the sexual violence unfolding all around you. Start by educating yourself. As you begin to express interest in and care about the issue, you may be surprised by those who feel safe disclosing how sexual violence has impacted their lives. And you may begin to see how our larger culture plays out on our campuses. One starting book I recommend is Jon Krakauer's *Missoula: Rape and Justice in a College Town.*[13]

Facing the Realities of Our Culture

As I have considered my tenure working with hundreds of Title IX cases, I worry that our important policy work and even vigorous accountability measures are doing too little to influence cultural change. I am convinced that the sort of meaningful change we desire will demand far more of our time and resources than online training programs, robust policies, and educational programs for faculty, staff, and students. Instead, we will need to embrace the reality that the foundation of our problems rests squarely in cultural assumptions and ways of knowing that must be deconstructed, held up, looked at, evaluated, and put back together in a new way. This will require a campus infrastructure that is well resourced and equipped to engage students in ongoing, relational conversation about culture, power, oppression, gender, gender roles, sexuality, and even biology. In addition, since men are by far the most likely perpetrators of sexual violence, we must be relentless in creating opportunities for students to deconstruct acculturated patterns of belief influencing their behavior.

Albert Bandura's social learning theory[14] may prove useful to educator's efforts to reduce sexual violence on college and university campuses. Bandura's theory suggests learning occurs within a social context from observation, modeling, and imitation. Bandura argues that modeling reinforces the behavior of others and, similarly, the environment reinforces modeling. While direct experience promotes learning, most of it first occurs vicariously by observing others' actions.[15] The modeling of behavior, of course, also extends to what is observed in mass media. Media, therefore, is having a profound shaping effect on the perceived reality of students. From locker rooms, to movies, to the Internet, American youth receive repeated and relentless messaging about gender, sexuality, and perceived expected behavior (scripts). Upon arriving on campus, enacting these engrained scripts often becomes the real-life storyline of a sexual assault. And nothing has demented our views of gender, sexuality (and related behavior) like the ubiquitous nature of online pornography. In *Pornland: How Porn Has Highjacked Our Sexuality*, Gail Dines argues that porn creates a rape culture by "normalizing, legitimizing, and condoning violence against women."[16]

Social or sexual scripting theories assert that people acquire and internalize, both consciously and unconsciously, systems of belief about what should or should not happen in a social context. Sexual scripts are "culturally available messages that define what counts as sex, how to recognize sexual situations, and what to do in a sexual encounter."[17] As Linder argues, understanding the history of sexual violence, and especially its relationship to power and oppression, is an essential component of any potentially effective prevention strategy. Unfortunately, my experience is that most students are unaware of the scripts activating their daily behavior, which, at worst, turns into abusive power plays, oppression, and violence. Even more disappointingly, few colleges and universities have developed thoughtful interventions to engage students in the work required to deconstruct the scripts influencing them.

As I am writing this essay, there has been an onslaught of reports of powerful leaders in business, government, and entertainment who have been involved in some of the most revealing, repetitive, and repulsive sexual harassment behavior to come to light in recent years. These disturbing events have unfolded despite decades of policies and training around sexual harassment in these industries. Like Linder, I believe our policy development strategies have done little to unearth the oppression and power structures that fuel our acculturation and, ultimately, large swaths of sexual violence in our environments. Prevention strategies that have the greatest potential for meaningful progress, therefore, will require an altogether new approach whereby colleges and universities invest in an infrastructure to walk alongside students as they are guided in deconstructing the cultural beliefs (and scripts) that have bombarded them for 18 years or more before they arrive on a college campus. How can students change behavior if they are unconscious of the deep-seated assumptions often guiding it?

Too many of our students are arriving on campus with well-developed but warped scripts playing in their heads about gender roles, sexuality, and college life. And nothing has the potential to unleash these dangerous role-plays like the effects of alcohol. Unfortunately, these narratives have been given to our current generation of students by all of us who have gone before them. We've collectively created a culture reinforced with pornography; gendered and sexualized humor and media; locker room talk; stereotypes; victim blaming; and, worst of all, complacent acceptance of the status quo.

Discussion Questions

1. What cultural messages about power and identity have you unconsciously internalized that promote sexual violence? How can you identify, deconstruct and reconstruct these messages?
2. What strategies can you use to help students identify, deconstruct, and reconstruct the cultural messages they have internalized that promote sexual violence?

Notes

1. Smith, S. G., Chen, J., Basile, K. C., Gilbert, L. K., Merrick, M. T., Patel, N., . . . Jain, A. (2017). *The national intimate partner and sexual violence survey (NISVS): 2010–2012 state report.* Atlanta, GA: National Center for Injury Prevention and Control, Centers for Disease Control and Prevention.

2. Shushok, F. (2017, April 6). I had no idea: Sexual assault awareness begins on campus. *The Washington Post.* Retrieved from https://www.washingtonpost .com/news/grade-point/wp/2017/04/06/i-had-no-idea-sexual-assault-awareness-begins-on-campuses/.

3. Weick, K. E. (1979). *The social psychology of organizing.* New York, NY: McGraw-Hill, p. 188.

4. U.S. Department of Education. (2011). *Dear colleague letter.* Retrieved from https://www2.ed.gov/about/offices/list/ocr/letters/colleague-201104.html

5. American Association of University Women. (2017). 89% of colleges report zero incidents of rape in 2015. Retrieved from https://www.aauw.org/article/ clery-act-data-analysis-2017/

6. Virginia Tech. (2015). *Title IX annual report for student-on-student sexual harassment and sexual violence.* Blacksburg, VA: Virginia Tech.

7. Baylor University records significant increase in sexual assault reports. (2016, October 16). *Campus Safety Magazine.* Retrieved from https://www .campussafetymagazine.com/news/significant_increase_in_sexual_assault_reports_ recorded_by_baylor_universit/

8. Linder, C., this volume, p. 90.

9. Lisak, D., & Miller, P. M. (2002). Repeat rape and multiple offending among undetected rapists. *Violence and Victims, 17*(1), 73–84.

10. Swartout, K. M., Koss, M. P., White, J. W., Thompson, M. P., Abbey, A., & Bellis, A. L. (2015). Trajectory analysis of the campus serial rapist assumption. *JAMA Pediatrics, 169*(12), 1148–1154.

11. Ullman, S. E. (2010). *Talking about sexual assault: Society's response to survivors.* Washington DC: American Psychological Association.

12. Linder, C., this volume, p. 95.

13. Krakauer, J. (2015). *Missoula: Rape and the justice system in a college town.* New York, NY: Doubleday.

    14. Bandura, A. (1977). *Social learning theory.* Englewood Cliffs, NJ: Prentice-Hall.

    15. Bandura, A. (1986). *Social foundations of thought and action: A social cognitive theory.* Englewood Cliffs, NJ: Prentice Hall.

    16. Dines, G. (2010). *Pornland: How porn has hijacked our sexuality.* Boston, MA: Beacon Press, p. 96.

    17. Frith, H., & Kitzinger, C. (2001). Reformulating sexual script theory: Developing a discursive psychology of sexual negotiation. *Theory & Psychology, 11*(2), 209–232, p. 210.

6

How Do Student Affairs Educators Navigate the Tension Between the First Amendment Right to Free Speech and the Expression of Ideas That Create a Hostile Campus Climate?

Free Expression, Civic Education, and Inclusive Campuses

Rafael E. Alvarado

If there be time to expose through discussion the falsehood and fallacies, to avert the evil by the processes of education, the remedy to be applied is more speech, not enforced silence.

—Whitney v. California, *1927*

I n May 2017, Tennessee became the country's leader in enacting modern free-speech legislation, and no fewer than 10 other states are currently fielding their own versions.[1] In the coming months and years, administrators will need to create or revisit policies on the topic to ensure compliance with federal and state laws. By faithfully implementing existing constitutional law, spurring dialogue on topics of academic freedom and civic education, and providing students with challenge and support for difficult conversations, student affairs professionals can meet their legal duties while enhancing an inclusive campus environment.

The Modern Free-Speech Crisis in Higher Education

Affirming the First Amendment in an era of pluralism and multiculturalism, especially during a demographic shift toward a heterogeneous American society, is a challenge that colleges and universities must face. Student activism on campus has been a regular headline in the mainstream media for the last several years.[2] Beginning with two important student movements, one at the University of Missouri and one at Yale University, student activism drew critical attention from both the political left and right; often, media and politicians characterized the demonstrations as the actions of coddled and entitled students who would rather disinvite controversy or violently shut down opposing viewpoints than engage in civil debate over disputed issues. Importantly, both sides of the political spectrum categorized the movement as an attack on free speech and expression,[3] a cornerstone of our liberal democracy captured in the First Amendment of the Constitution.

In the decade leading up to these student movements, students and student organizations across the country filed lawsuits decrying so-called free-speech zones—areas set aside in public places for the purpose of political protesting—on public university campuses as unconstitutional.[4] In these federal cases, judges held that free speech zones were subject to the same laws governing traditional public forums, such as town halls and sidewalks. The court decisions marked important victories for both conservative-leaning groups, who argue that universities and colleges have become liberal havens, and free-speech purists, who advocate for minimal restrictions on expression.[5]

These related movements substantially influence the ongoing free-speech legislation in various states, which addresses free speech and expression as well as academic freedom. By delineating state policy, legislatures hope to protect free expression so that students may learn various, opposing, and perhaps controversial ideas before making up their own minds and deciding their belief systems free of indoctrination or groupthink. Administrators, in turn, should familiarize themselves with the relevant legal rules and standards, seeing them as restrictions on public action as well as educational tools for students and colleagues alike.

Legal Issues

Freedom of belief, speech, expression, and assembly are cornerstones of liberal democracies such as our own; indeed, these freedoms are so important that the country's founding political generation enshrined them in the first official amendment to the United States Constitution. The First Amendment reads

> Congress shall make no law respecting an establishment of religion, or prohibiting the free exercise thereof; or abridging the freedom of speech, or of the press; or the right of the people peaceably to assemble, and to petition the Government for a redress of grievances.[6]

Despite the seemingly clear language of the First Amendment, laws forbidding or regulating speech are commonplace.[7] This body of constitutional law has made important distinctions between the content and the manner of expression and has paid close attention to the location where speech occurs. Supreme Court decisions dating back to the late 1950s deal specifically with college and university students and faculty and are important examples of the knowledge required to understand the restrictions and requirements on public institutions. The Supreme Court has spilled a significant amount of ink on issues related to student speech and expression, and its opinions undergird our contemporary understanding of academic freedom. It is important to note that, although the First Amendment only reaches public institutions and courts afford wider latitude in controlling the speech of students and faculty at private institutions, the importance of expression within the framework of academic freedom is such that all colleges and universities, regardless of governance, should consider the implications and effects of barring speech based on content.

Student Speech, Expression, and Association

College students' right to free speech finds its basis in a conflict between elementary school students and a school faculty. In *Tinker v. Des Moines Independent Community School District*,[8] the Supreme Court addressed the issue of students wearing black armbands to school as a sign of political protest. The Supreme Court held that students do not "shed their constitutional rights to freedom of speech or expression at the schoolhouse gate" and that these displays did not substantially interfere with the educational operations of the school and were therefore protected speech. This important precedent applies across educational contexts and is foundational in college students' right to free speech.

Later, the Supreme Court heard a case involving a college's refusal to recognize a student organization due to the controversial message members valued and espoused. In *Healy v. James*,[9] the decision was reached that colleges and universities could not bar recognition of a student group absent evidence that the organization would constitute a substantive disruptive force on campus. This approach marks the beginning of school laws that demand content- and value-neutrality when recognizing and endorsing student organizations and their endeavors; it also requires that colleges and universities have strong evidence that the recognition of a group be an imminent threat to the educational process before disallowing the organization.

In the vein of *Healy*, *Widmar v. Vincent*[10] expanded student access to available university facilities despite a student organizations' religious affiliation. The Supreme Court held that the university had "opened its facilities for use by student groups," and that it could only establish "reasonable time, place, and manner regulations" moving forward. For example, administrators can regulate the times people can speak to accommodate public conveniences such as traffic and residential housing; they can regulate the places people can speak, provided the school designates the area for other legitimate educational uses; and they can regulate the manner in which people communicate when the mode of expression would obstruct the space's legitimate use or cause public inconvenience or property damage. These three cases, taken together, form the foundation for student voice and organization on campuses; administrators, offices, and departments must apply content-neutral principles when determining which individuals they do and do not allow to speak on campus.

Academic Freedom

Academic freedom is a special concern of the First Amendment—but it has not received much elaboration since the Supreme Court laid out its basic contours in *Sweezy v. New Hampshire*.[11] In a divided opinion, the Supreme Court found that a state legislature's attempt to intervene in the lectures and research of a faculty member was an unconstitutional exercise of power. The Supreme Court's opinion cited the importance of academic freedom for individuals: "Teachers and students must always remain free to inquire, to study and to evaluate, to gain new maturity and understanding; otherwise our civilization will stagnate and die." A concurring opinion agreed that the legislature overstepped its constitutional boundaries but provided an alternative reasoning: Rather than focusing on individual academic freedoms, this opinion affirmed the "exclusion of governmental intervention in the intellectual life of a university." These two perspectives on academic freedom—individual and institutional—overlap significantly and in fact empower administrators to enact programs in support of designated values and goals, which will become important when fashioning responses to offensive speech.

In more recent history, the Supreme Court has restated the importance of academic freedom when deferring to academic decisions; often, it states this in the context of institutional controversies and reinforces the idea that universities and colleges have the right to pursue significant interests as an exercise of that freedom. Most prominently and importantly, the Supreme Court has deferred to institutional decision-making regarding affirmative action, but the language of the opinions highlights general acquiescence to academic decisions by universities.[12] Although not dispositive, these decisions lend heavy weight to an ongoing recognition of institutional academic autonomy, where a judge would defer to an institutional decision that has made its way before a court.

Policy Recommendations

Recognizing the significant and important body of existing constitutional law is critical to frame institutional responses to new and forthcoming legislation. In light of relevant laws and campus politics, I recommend that administrators implement those changes that fall within their purview while incentivizing faculty members to meet and act so that they may install academic regulations. Additionally, these interventions should be iterative and reflexive,[13] identifying inputs and outputs and using this information to make ongoing adjustments in light of a changing legal and social climate. Although the emphasis of this book is on student affairs, universities need to address this topic on an institutional level. Therefore, my recommendations address academic affairs as well as student affairs. Individuals in both realms of university life should communicate and collaborate on this effort to ensure uniform compliance throughout the educational environment.

Academic Affairs

Academic leaders should create policies addressing speech and expression in classrooms; the faculty should create neutral definitions of what constitutes a disruption to the educational environment before, not after, an incident arises that requires attention. Top-down implementation on campus often results in faculty contempt for and distrust of an administration,[14] so administrators should be careful to exercise their limited power in the realm of academic affairs and instead allow the faculty time to deliberate. In addition to on-campus and in-classroom findings, faculty should create policies discussing the implications of off-campus and online speech, such as distinguishing action in an official capacity from action in a private capacity.[15]

Furthermore, this faculty dialogue on the meaning of academic freedom should not limit itself to faculty members and instructors but consider the freedoms—and corresponding responsibilities—for students. Faculty members should empower students to make their own decisions about what, when, and how they study, even in courses that fulfill mandatory requirements; to do this, they may provide flexible curricular requirements or expand options for general requirements, and in classrooms they may give students discretion to choose topics for papers or presentations.[16] This perspective promotes a proactive approach to student learning, one that adopts the intention of creating independent, critical thinkers rather than indoctrinated automatons. It also encourages amendment to or reconstruction of the institution's curriculum, which will prepare students to engage in dialogue without disturbing the First Amendment.

In conjunction with clarifying their stance on students' academic freedom, chief academic officers should consider integrating civic education into the general curriculum. As it stands, many university missions address building basic skills and developing broadened perspectives; many schools enact these imperatives through mandatory courses in rhetoric and reasoning, as well as general course requirements in scientific, social, historical, and artistic realms. These general requirements, and the reasons undergirding them, echo the popular notion of upholding critical and independent thinking as the hallmark of a proper education. By introducing civic education into the general requirements, colleges and universities can prepare students to not only deal with laissez-faire free-speech policies on campus but also meet such goals as creating politically active citizens and leaders and building the capacity to engage in respectful dialogue across differences.

Civic education encompasses the preparation of citizens and focuses on installing dispositions rather than substantive beliefs: a disposition to obey the law, a disposition to engage in political participation to achieve justice, and a disposition to engage in public reasoning with respect.[17] Administrators can incorporate these goals into the curriculum through required coursework, the identification of general options, or widespread integration throughout the institutional curriculum;[18] outside of the classroom, administrators can develop programs and initiatives that expose students to the foundations of liberal democracy, bring in speakers to discuss the myriad ways that freedom of expression on campus has been beneficial for social progress, and host workshops teaching students the skills necessary to respond to offensive speech. These requirements would help students recognize the importance of free speech in the broader mosaic of civic participation, empower them to exercise their rights appropriately, and reinforce the institution's commitment to free speech and expression, all without imparting a specific idea, value, or belief.

Although it is becoming increasingly unwise to establish formal codes of civility on campus, administrators can still educate students on the importance of civil discourse and encourage these constructive behaviors as an important element of the campus—and broader public—culture.[19] As Uecker argues, restricting speech "fails to address the ideas and meanings that lie beneath controversy,"[20] encouraging students to hide their beliefs—and failing both at building common ground for conversation and at following the mandates of our Constitution. By focusing on methods of civil discourse rather than the content of speech, colleges and universities can promote dialogue without running afoul of the law or mandating a specific mode of interaction. This blueprint for civil discourse can also include the college or university's time, place, and manner regulations, aligning various institutional policies to increase constructive dialogue on campus.

Student Affairs

As for students' rights and restrictions, the existing body of constitutional law addressing freedom of speech, expression, and association strongly apply. Senior student affairs officers should learn about the construction of content- and value-free regulations on the time, place, and manner of speech or assembly; they should then train all employees whose work relates to these recognitions and permissions, building the institution's capacity to sustainably follow the law.[21] As previously stated, public colleges should recognize and identify any venues on campus that serve as public or designated forums because their regulation must be neutral. Especially in public outdoor spaces, colleges and universities need to allow students to freely gather and express their ideas, provided that the demonstration or speech does not substantively interfere with the educational operations of the university or create imminent physical harm. Institutions should consider removing all preexisting regulations of speech or expression; in their place, they should adopt a uniform policy on student and faculty speech that simply states that the school will adhere to applicable laws when regulating campus speech, expression, and assembly.

Institutions must also devise crisis management plans to deal with any possible expressions, speakers, or symbols that cause disruptive controversy on the campus. These plans should serve a purpose—addressing significant and potentially disruptive controversy resulting from protected expression—and have clear lines of authority and action steps.[22] By establishing communication methods and campus protocol in advance, administrators can fairly apply plans to any campus crisis; it will also serve as a legal defense if the college or university must interfere with otherwise protected speech, demonstrating that its response was not reactionary or motivated by the content of the speech. Part of developing these plans should be the consideration of the school's capacity to provide security at all events; if unable to cover all events, campus security should establish a value- and content-neutral formula for providing security at assemblies. This formula can consider things such as expected student turnout, presence of guests and community members, and methods of demonstration, and shall make no inquiry into the precise content of the speech or expression.

Also, administrators from the top to the bottom should identify and excise any definitions of *harassment* that do not mirror existing federal, state, or local laws; instead, they can establish a single disciplinary procedure to investigate and adjudicate issues that arise. Colleges and universities, if they have not already, should also fill their disciplinary staff, which is responsible for adjudicating these procedures, with individuals knowledgeable about and capable of legal analysis, as the trend toward formalistic and legalistic methods of dispute resolution in higher education continues.[23] Next, the school should delineate value- and content-free reasons that may justify disinviting a speaker, as previously noted, and apply these rules uniformly if future issues require such action.

Finally, and perhaps most importantly in these politically divided times, colleges and universities should enhance and promote the services available to their diverse campus student body, especially to students of color, queer students, students with disabilities, international students, and religious minority students.[24] Although the present-day controversies that have dominated media and politics resulted largely from conservative movements that rally against efforts by these historically marginalized populations,[25] they do not deprive the institution from pursuing diversity, and the educational benefits that flow therefrom, in all aspects of campus.

While the approaches taken to recognize and grant students access to various resources are value- or content-neutral there is nothing preventing a university from itself promoting values, and in fact many do so through their mission statement. Familiarity with the values espoused can inspire and motivate administrators to provide resources to students on campus, as well as to incentivize students to engage in counter-speech whenever there is an incident of permissible speech that may been harmful or offensive.

It is also important for administrators to note that, although the recent cases that have erupted across campuses demonstrate a growing conservative voice in higher education, the multicultural divide on campus is both less deep and less wide, with greater homogeneity between different groups and greater diversity within individual groups; indeed, many students on college campuses recognize and value the benefits of a demographically diverse student body.[26] While this policy of increasing support for certain populations may cause controversy among students, administrators, and faculty who deny any benefits of demographic diversity,[27] it does not run afoul of a university's constitutional rights; indeed, it can further many colleges' espoused values of advancing diversity and inclusion. By explicitly valuing democratic engagement in addition to other espoused values, schools and administrators can ground their policies in content-neutrality and support free and equal citizenship.

For these marginalized voices on campus, many of whom may become increasingly subject to ideas and statements questioning their inherent value or worth, the spike in controversial speech and expression on campus may seem counterproductive and perhaps even destructive to the civil rights gains made in previous decades. However, college students maintain a right to adopt bigoted beliefs based on stereotypes,[28] and the First Amendment guarantees that no public institution may require that they change or retreat from these ideas. Indeed, the history of our legal system shows that these neutral values have been helpful in creating spaces for the historically marginalized.[29] While offensive speech runs counter to many universities' explicit approval of diversity and inclusion, it also provides an opportunity for administrators, faculty, and students to engage in critical dialogue by exposing sources of prejudice, questioning stereotypes, and identifying systemic relationships between language and action.[30] Again, a college need not abandon its own interest in receiving the educational benefits that flow from a demographically diverse student body, and it may act affirmatively to formally address protected but controversial demonstrations and assemblies by issuing statements, enacting programming, or revisiting the curriculum.

Discussion Questions

1. What speech or expression policies exist at your current institution? Are they commonly known or are they hidden from students, staff, and faculty? Are they applicable throughout the university or limited to certain offices or departments? Are they effective? Are they within the bounds set by the Constitution?
2. What are the costs of allowing controversial speech on campus? What are the benefits? Who benefits from laissez-faire public-speech policies?
3. What constitutes a "substantive" interference with the educational environment? Who makes this determination? Are there ever times where a substantive interference is appropriate? Why or why not?

Notes

1. Quintana, C., & Thomason, A. (2017, May 15). The states where campus free-speech bills are being born: A rundown. *The Chronicle of Higher*

Education. Retrieved from http://www.chronicle.com/article/The-States-Where-Campus/240073

2. For example, Chadwell, C. C. (2017, May 2). Michigan senator launches new bill concerning university free speech codes. *Michigan Daily,* p. 1; Flaherty, C. (2017, May 15). Critics of proposed legislation on First Amendment rights at Wisconsin public universities says it goes too far. *Inside Higher Ed.* Retrieved from https://www.insidehighered.com/news/2017/05/15/critics-proposed-legislation-first-amendment-rights-wisconsin-public-universities; Kristoff, N. (2015, November 11). Mizzou, Yale, and free speech. *The New York Times.* Retrieved from https://www.nytimes.com/2015/11/12/opinion/mizzou-yale-and-free-speech.html; Simon, C. C. (2016, August 1). Fighting for free speech on America's campuses. *The New York Times.* Retrieved from https://www.nytimes.com/2016/08/07/education/edlife/fire-first-amendment-on-campus-free-speech.html?_r=0.

3. Papandrea, M.-R. (2017). The free speech rights of university students. *Minnesota Law Review, 101,* 1801–1861.

4. Roberts v. Haragan, 346 F. Supp. 2d 853 (N.D. Tex. 2004); Univ. of Cincinnati Chapter of Young Americans for Liberty v. Williams, 2012 U.S. Dist. LEXIS 80967 (S.D. Ohio 2012).

5. Kitrosser, H. (2017). Free speech, higher education, and the PC narrative. *Minnesota Law Review, 101,* 1987–2058.

6. U.S. Const. amend. I.

7. Shiffrin, S. H., Choper, J. H., & Schauer, F. (2015). *The First Amendment: Cases—comments—questions* (6th ed.). St. Paul, MN: West Academic.

8. 393 U.S. 503 (1969).

9. 408 U.S. 169 (1972).

10. 454 U.S. 263 (1981).

11. 354 U.S. 234 (1957).

12. Regents of the University of California v. Bakke, 438 U.S. 265 (1978); Grutter v. Bollinger, 539 U.S. 306 (2003); Fisher v. University of Texas, 579 U.S. (2016).

13. Lattuca, L. R., & Stark, J. S. (2009). *Shaping the college curriculum: Academic plans in context* (2nd ed.). San Francisco, CA: Jossey-Bass.

14. Hendrickson, R. M., Lane, J. E., Harris, J. T., & Dorman, R. H. (2013). *Academic leadership and governance of higher education: A guide for trustees, leaders, and aspiring leaders of two- and four-year institutions.* Sterling, VA: Stylus.

15. Amar, V. D., & Brownstein, A. E. (2017). A close-up, modern look at First Amendment academic freedom rights of public college students and faculty. *Minnesota Law Review, 101,* 1943–1984; Levy, R. E. (2014). The tweet hereafter: Social media and the free speech rights of Kansas public university employees. *Kansas Journal of Law and Public Policy, 24,* 78–135; Sun, J. C., Hutchens, N. H., & Breslin, J. D. (2013). A (virtual) land of confusion with college students' online speech: Introducing the curricular nexus test. *University of Pennsylvania Journal of Constitutional Law, 16,* 49–96.

16. Macfarlane, B. (2012). Re-framing student academic freedom: A capability perspective. *Higher Education, 63*(6), 719–732.

17. Brighouse, H. (2006). *On education*. New York, NY: Routledge.

18. Lattuca, L. R., & Stark, J. S. (2009). *Shaping the college curriculum: Academic plans in context* (2nd ed.). San Francisco, CA: Jossey-Bass.

19. Uecker, T. W., & Sardelli, K. (2011). How do campus administrators go beyond the First Amendment in achieving balance between free speech and civil discourse? In P. M. Magolda & M. B. Baxter Magolda (Eds.), *Contested issues in student affairs: Diverse perspectives and respectful dialogue* (pp. 354–364). Sterling, VA: Stylus.

20. Uecker, T. W. (2011). Putting the hammer down. In P. M. Magolda & M. B. Baxter Magolda (Eds.), *Contested issues in student affairs: Diverse perspectives and respectful dialogue* (pp. 354–364). Sterling, VA: Stylus

21. McDonnell, L. M., & Elmore, R. F. (1991). Getting the job done: Alternative policy instruments. In A. R. Odden (Ed.), *Education policy implementation* (pp. 157–183). Albany, NY: State University of New York Press.

22. Rollo, J. M., & Zdziarski, E. L., II. (2007). Developing a crisis management plan. In E. L. Zdziarski II, N. W. Dunkel, & J. M. Rollo (Eds.), *Campus crisis management: A comprehensive guide to planning, prevention, response, and recovery* (pp. 73–95). San Francisco, CA: Jossey-Bass.

23. Areen, J., & Lake, P. F. (2014). *Higher education and the law* (2nd ed.). St. Paul, MN: Foundation Press.

24. Harper, S. R., & Quaye, S. J. (2015). Making engagement equitable for students in U.S. higher education. In S. J. Quaye & S. R. Harper (Eds.), *Student engagement in higher education: Theoretical perspectives and practical approaches for diverse populations* (pp. 1–14). New York, NY: Routledge.

25. For example, Hartocollis, A. (2016, March 24). Professors' group says efforts to halt sexual harassment have stifled speech. *The New York Times*. Retrieved from https://www.nytimes.com/2016/03/24/us/professors-group-says-efforts-to-halt-sexual-harassment-have-stifled-speech.html; Mele, C. (2016, November 28). Professor watchlist is seen as a threat to academic freedom. *The New York Times*. Retrieved from https://www.nytimes.com/2016/11/28/us/professor-watchlist-is-seen-as-threat-to-academic-freedom.html.

26. Levine, A., & Dean, D. R. (2012). *Generation on a tightrope: A portrait of today's college student*. San Francisco, CA: Jossey-Bass.

27. For example, Subotnik, D. (2016). How diversity training hurts. *Academic Questions, 29*, 198–204; Wood, P. (2016). The architecture of intellectual freedom: A statement of the National Association of Scholars. *Academic Questions, 29*, 119–148.

28. Moore, W. L., & Bell, J. M. (2017). The right to be racist in college: Racist speech, White institutional space, and the First Amendment. *Law & Policy, 39*(2), 99–120.

29. For example, Gay Students Organization of the University of New Hampshire v. Bonner, 509 F.2d 652 (1st Cir. 1974).

30. Goodman, D. J. (2011). *Promoting diversity and social justice: Educating people from privileged groups* (2nd ed.). New York, NY: Routledge; Schulzke, M. (2016). The social benefits of protecting hate speech and exposing sources of prejudice. *Res Publica, 22*, 225–242.

Balancing Free Speech and Inclusive Campus Environments: A Worthy Yet Complicated Commitment

Naomi Daradar Sigg

Alvarado provides an apt prescription of what institutions of higher education should do to create a more harmonious balance between the preservation of the First Amendment and the duty to foster an inclusive community with his statement: "By faithfully implementing existing constitutional law, spurring dialogue on topics of academic freedom and civic education, and providing students with challenge and support for difficult conversations, student affairs professionals can meet their legal duties while enhancing an inclusive campus environment."[1] However, the implementation of his recommendations can be complex and daunting. How can we ensure administrators are knowledgeable of their institution's legal obligation to protect free speech and expression and equipped with tools to advance civil discourse in classrooms and beyond? What skills do administrators need to practice and teach so communities can engage in civil, authentic, and transformational dialogue? Most importantly, how do we treat everyone with human dignity and respect so each community member has equal opportunity and space to both contribute and learn in a mutually beneficial and inclusive community? In this essay, I offer ideas to equip administrators with the legal grounding on the First Amendment, along with knowledge of university policies supporting this constitutional duty. I provide dialogue skills as a practical strategy to provide the brave space needed to engage in topics that are divisive and polarizing. I discuss the importance of providing support for all students including those from underrepresented and marginalized communities.

Strategies for Faculty and Staff Development

Administrators all need development in a variety of capacities. In order to create a better balance between free speech and campus inclusion, we must understand our identities, become knowledgeable on the legalities in student affairs concerning free speech, and learn how to engage in civil discourse with colleagues and students. As an Asian American immigrant woman, I was socialized to listen, accommodate, and make space for others in a way that minimized my voice. As a student, and early in my profession, I was hesitant to share my ideas and push for what I believed to be in the best interest of others and myself. Today, I recognize the internalized oppression that prevented me from recognizing that my voice and ideas, though different, were valuable and necessary in creating innovative solutions and initiatives. As administrators, we must reflect on our identities, values, and biases and gain the awareness, skills, and knowledge to be effective educators fostering an inclusive and equitable culture. This particular work is an inward journey. As lifelong learners, we need to catapult ourselves into the same introspection that we ask and sometimes expect of students. This work is a journey where no one ever fully arrives. Thus, we need to be ever humble, nimble, and vigilant as we model self-discovery and provide space to hear the experiences and perspectives of others.

In addition to understanding our personal identities, administrators must keep a pulse of the current issues and topics that affect their roles, including the legal implications of our work. Alvarado provides a legal and historical overview setting the stage with fundamental court cases with which all student affairs professionals should be familiar. Too often, administrators and faculty find out about these while developing policies during the aftermath of a negative campus incident. Campuses disseminate information during challenging times instead of through proactive university-wide communication, professional development, or training. The list of administrators knowledgeable on these legal topics should not be limited to conduct officers, advisers, diversity offices, and legal counsel, but should extend to all student affairs professionals and faculty. Administrators should learn this information during departmental or divisional orientations, professional development, and compliance mechanisms. Additionally, university leaders need to communicate both the value and duty of upholding the First Amendment in their diverse learning communities. Universities can host campus speakers and panels on free speech and send more information on the topic through campus newsletters or e-mails.

Although I believe that positive change in the form of policies can arise out of these moments, the more important systemic change needs to come in the form of well-established community expectations and skills for effective dialogue. In recent conversations with colleagues, I asked if they felt knowledgeable and skilled enough to navigate and facilitate controversial dialogues. Without hesitation, and with the same defeated expression, many disclosed that they felt ill equipped and frozen in these moments. In addition to feeling deskilled, many professionals believe that they do not have the permission to engage in dialogue on topics that are divisive or provocative. A few years ago, I sat in a room with colleagues listening to a webinar on the racial tensions in our nation and on our campuses following the protests in Ferguson, Missouri, after the shooting of Michael Brown. The room was full, but few people shared their thoughts during the first 20 minutes of our dialogue following the webinar. I firmly believe in naming dysfunctional group dynamics and quickly noted that folks appeared hesitant to share their perspectives and asked if others felt this particular vibe in the room. One colleague spoke up and said that they did not know if they were allowed to talk about these things at work since we had not received communication from upper-level administrators. My colleagues were fearful to engage both students and other professionals because they did not know how to navigate these dialogues and because they feared negative pushback from peers and supervisors. The fear in the room was real and shared by many. My colleagues needed institutional permission along with training on dialogue skills to engage in spaces just like this one.

Utilizing Dialogue to Promote Free Speech and Campus Inclusion

Developing and utilizing strong communication skills are important for students and administrators alike. As Alvarado points out, students need "challenge and support for difficult conversations."[2] Almost every student will encounter someone with a different perspective or lived experience. Some exchanges will be unpleasant and just plain disheartening. To uphold free speech on campus, students need skills to engage effectively across difference, express and defend their viewpoints, and be open to learning even in moments of discomfort. In my first professional role, one of my favorite responsibilities was running a campus retreat focused on identity and community building. We began the retreat with ground rules. One rule was to take others' words as gifts. The notion that words of another person could be a gift perplexed many students. I claimed that everything you hear from another person can do one of two things. It can help you change your mind, learn something new, or challenge you to change your thinking or behavior. Conversely, you may disagree with what they say, but this is also a gift because even in this circumstance, their words can help you reaffirm your own beliefs and values.

Just as we did at the retreat, campuses need to develop community expectations and strategies that cultivate productive dialogue. Sardelli states, "We must set aside taking a restrictive or reactionary approach to speech and expression on campus in favor of a proactive community-based approach to an educational exchange of ideas."[3] As a member of a campus community that both institutionally defines and practices *dialogue* in myriad ways through our membership in the Sustained Dialogue Campus Network, I see how dialogue can transform the way we engage with each other. Dialogue provides opportunities to address contentious topics while serving as a restorative practice during incidents involving harm caused by the speech or expression of others.

Sustained Dialogue Institute founder Hal Saunders defines *dialogue* as

> a process of genuine interaction through which human beings listen to each other deeply enough to be changed by what they learn. Each makes a serious effort to take others' concerns into her or his own picture, even when disagreement persists. No participant gives up her or his identity, but each recognizes enough of the other's valid human claims that he or she will act differently toward the other.[4]

Students and administrators alike appreciate this definition. It calls for authenticity, vulnerability, and a willingness to change. Moreover, this definition focuses on content, identity, and relationship. Our community teaches this model of dialogue during student orientation and professional development sessions. This definition urges community members to engage with people regardless of similarity or difference with the goal of upholding everyone's right to express ideas in a framework that encourages civil discourse.

Supporting Students While Creating the Balance

It is critical for campuses to have community expectations on how to engage with each other that reflect the values of the institution while still upholding free speech for every community member. Moreover, institutions should have clear guidelines and support systems in place when the speech or expression of some individuals undermines the dignity and worth of others. I recall sitting nervously next to a law professor and general counsel waiting to be ushered into the room to join our chief diversity officer in presenting information to our board of trustees on free speech and campus climate. The topic was timely, contentious, and multifaceted. Just months earlier, news journalists described university campuses as war zones[5] after violent and destructive protests erupted following several speaking engagements by controversial commentators at the request of student groups. During the panel discussion, I realized how complicated this topic was and that there were high-stakes implications for policies, campus climate, academic affairs, and student retention and success. As trustees asked questions regarding space reservations, speaker invites, and other university policies, I fixated on one question directed toward me. A board member asked me how the university was supporting students who felt vulnerable, targeted, or victims of microaggressions. I answered the question by sharing the many university support services, programs, student groups, and dialogue initiatives, but I also ended with the fact that we needed to do more to equip students with skills to respond and engage in precisely these types of moments.

As universities move toward creating brave spaces[6] in the classroom and elsewhere on campus, it is imperative that they also provide proper support to underrepresented and marginalized identities. Though all students can benefit from listening to diverse perspectives, the discomfort experienced by students forced to listen to statements that challenge the core of their identity or human dignity can have a cumulative impact. Students may experience *microaggressions,* defined by Derald Wing Sue as "brief and commonplace daily verbal, behavioral, and environmental indignities, whether intentional or unintentional, that communicate hostile, derogatory, or negative racial, gender, sexual-orientation, and religious slights and insults to the target person or group."[7]

Though all community members have the right to share their thoughts, including thoughts that are bigoted, they also need to remember the responsibility they have as a member within a community that espouses certain values like inclusion, equity, and social justice. Furthermore, all community members must remember that their speech has impact and may prompt additional questions and further engagement that necessitate their listening to other points of view as well. After a bias incident on campus, we held a community dialogue allowing participants with varying viewpoints on the incident to listen to each other. These interactions foster understanding and promote a culture where all voices are heard even when grappling with difficult content.

Conclusion

Student affairs professionals may find themselves perplexed as they try to reconcile free speech and expression while safeguarding the inclusive and equitable student experience many of us try to foster. Many find this balance to be tenuous at best. However, if universities approach this task as a community, with everyone bearing equal responsibility toward the goal of free speech and the creation of an inclusive community, the needle can shift toward balance. The work is difficult and it is important. Therefore, we must continue in dialogue as we grapple with how to create this balance with all members of our institutions, engaging faculty, staff, and students as we all learn in this journey together.

Discussion Questions

1. What common dialogue or communication strategies are taught to students, faculty, and staff? How can you utilize dialogue skills to mitigate contentious and polarizing interactions?
2. What support structures, policies, or practices are in place to address campus incidents where free speech and expression cause harm to others? How do you communicate support to those exercising their rights while addressing potential microaggressions or bias incidents?

Notes

1. Alvarado, R. E., this volume, pp. 109–110.
2. Alvarado, R. E., this volume, p. 109–110.
3. Sardelli, K. (2010). Drafting a community-wide blueprint for civil discourse. In P. M. Magolda & M. B. Baxter Magolda (Eds.), *Contested issues in student affairs: Diverse perspectives and respectful dialogue* (pp. 365–370). Sterling, VA: Stylus, p. 367.
4. Saunders, H. (2001). *A public peace process: Sustained dialogue to transform racial and ethnic conflicts.* New York, NY: Palgrave, p. 82.
5. Steinmetz, K. (2017, June). Fighting words: A battle in Berkeley over free speech. *TIME.* Retrieved from http://time.com/4800813/battle-berkeley-free-speech/
6. Arao, B., & Clemens, K. (2013). From safe spaces to brave spaces: A new way to frame dialogue around diversity and social justice. In Landreman, L. (Ed.), *The art of effective facilitation: Reflections from social justice educators* (pp. 135–150). Sterling, VA: Stylus.
7. Sue, D. (2010). *Microaggressions in everyday life: Race, gender, and sexual orientation.* Hoboken, NJ: Wiley, p. 5.

7

How Should Institutions Redefine and Measure Student Success?

Student Success as Liberal Education Escapes Definition and Measurement

Laura Elizabeth Smithers

The question structuring this chapter begins with the presumption that we should define and measure *student success*. The perspective missing from this question is: *What possibilities exist for versions of student success in excess of its definition and measurement?* Measurements ask us to standardize definitions of *success*—say, four-year graduation—and work to produce all students in this image. As a former academic adviser, I can read a university catalog and tell you the quickest pathways to graduation a university has to offer. This makes me an asset to institutions that place a value on student success as measured by graduation rates, but does shuttling students to majors with comparatively lax degree requirements produce an expansive version of student success? I am the last person to argue that metrics of student success such as college graduation lack all meaning. However, when measurements of achievements like college graduation become the focus of student affairs practice, they warp our institutions and our students in their image.[1] I use *graduation* here as it is the most frequently cited definition of student success today, but this logic follows no matter what definition you substitute in its place. In what follows, I argue that definitions and measurements of *student success* construct student realities in ways that are counterproductive to liberal education, and liberal education is the ineffable outcome of higher education that produces students capable of changing the structures of our profoundly problematic world.

The Association of American Colleges & Universities (AAC&U) defines *liberal education* in part as "an approach to learning that empowers individuals and prepares them to deal with complexity, diversity, and change."[2] When framed as an *approach to learning*, a liberal education perspective on student success emphasizes process and practice, not measurable outcomes. Accordingly, liberal education notions of student success cannot be defined in advance and cannot be measured through increasingly complex scientific and predictive metrics. As John Dewey noted over 100 years ago, the ultimate outcome of education is "just the process of living itself."[3] Contrary to calls for student affairs educators to come into cultures of measurement,[4] student affairs professionals must create spaces for students to escape such measurements. Paradoxically, it is only in the refusal of measurement that we create the conditions for students to access a liberal education. In what follows, I renarrate the history of student success in higher education through this lens, and I offer the following provocations for an everyday student affairs practice that holds student futures radically open: (a) refusal, (b) embracing alternative ways of knowing, and (c) the imperative to go rogue.

Student Success in Higher Education

Student affairs was born in the union of early advising services and the scientific study of student success.[5] Both halves of this union have been present within the field, with varying degrees of influence, ever since. Today, the scientific study of student success eclipses holistic understandings of students, instrumentalizes higher education to the attainment of scientific measurements, and in both perpetuates inequality and exclusion.

The Science of Graduation

The field of student affairs came into its own 80 years ago with several publications, including *The Student Personnel Point of View*,[6] that called for the scientific study of the new problem of student dropouts. Integral to this new scientific approach was the development and use of standardized student record forms. This standardization facilitated the comparison of student-level information between universities; in fact, the first scientific studies of students were single-year, multi-institutional studies.[7] Even with this scientization, early student affairs researchers did not think that the results of these studies could be used on their own to guide services. Scientific management provided one of many forms of knowledge necessary for practice. For the next several decades, individualized student support and the scientific study of student progress were considered two separate domains of knowledge that were both necessary.[8]

By the dawn of the 1970s, this two-pronged approach to student affairs began to change. The first major synthesis of the student affairs literature, Kenneth Feldman and Theodore Newcomb's *The Impact of College on Students*, called for an increased use of longitudinal studies utilizing more sophisticated statistical analyses.[9] Shortly thereafter, directly citing Feldman and Newcomb's call, Alexander Astin published *The Methodology of College Impact*, a two-part essay that introduced the Input-Environment-Output (I-E-O) model to higher education research.[10] In this model, students can be understood as a collection of measurable characteristics upon arriving to the university (I), and the university environment itself (E) can also be understood as a collection of measurable characteristics. Under these assumptions, the output (O) of the university environment—student attainment of a specified desirable outcome, such as graduation—can be studied through scientific measurement, and university programming (E) can be adjusted accordingly to optimize the attainment of a desirable outcome. This methodology gave shape to the scientific study of college students through impact, or the measurable effect of the university environment (E) on student outcomes (O). This logic of scientific measurement now dominates legitimized knowledge production within higher education and student affairs. Twenty-first-century references to definitions and measurements of *student success* are extensions of this now commonsense science of college impact.

Student Success in the Twenty-First Century

Higher education's current focus on student success is due in part to the influence of *Learning Reconsidered*, whose object of inquiry is learning, and George Kuh's work on student engagement. *Learning Reconsidered*, the widely influential 2004 NASPA and American College Personnel Association (ACPA) joint publication, explicitly reconnects the work of higher education and student affairs to the education of the whole student. It does this through defining and measuring desired student outcomes to produce what is variously termed *student learning, transformative liberal education*, and *student success*.[11] Kuh and associates state that what matters in student success can be classified into three categories: precollege experiences, the college experience, and postcollege outcomes.[12] In *Learning Reconsidered*, as in Kuh's research, student success is known through Astin's I-E-O model.

Data-driven[13] research has become the commonsense method of knowledge production in student affairs, operationalized variously through the study of learning, engagement, student success, and other outcomes. This common sense governs the field to a greater extent than does any single definition or measurement of *student success*. When we know students through data, we know parts of students (e.g., GPA, academic standing, declared major) as extracted from the messy, complicated, and overflowing persons we know through our practice. Modern student success research *knows* and *creates* success through the optimization of student data points under the implicit assumption that practitioners, administrators, and researchers can manufacture success if only we can produce students with the right combinations of data.

Student success has also notably become the clarion call of many foundations and centers, including Complete College America, EAB (formerly the Educational Advisory Board), the Lumina Foundation, and Postsecondary Success at the Gates Foundation. These groups advocate for specific interventions to increase student success as retention and graduation through funding and publishing internal and external research. Some produce solutions that many institutions purchase for millions of dollars, at the opportunity cost of hiring dozens of staff, providing millions of dollars in student aid, adding orientation sessions in multiple languages, and so on. These foundations and centers host conferences and meetings of senior administrators on student success, and they deliver a steady stream of data-driven student success e-mails to inboxes across higher education. Student affairs professional organizations are also involved in student success research and practice, which reflects both the salience of the concept to practitioners as well as organizational ties to external foundations.[14] Not to be left out, the U.S. Department of Education has also called for higher education to shift toward defining and measuring student outcomes in the name of student success.[15] Foundation and government-sponsored literature on student success is abundant, and it tips heavily in the direction of data-driven research to improve retention and graduation rates.

Dividing Scientific Measurements and Holistic Justifications

Universities, research centers, and foundations across the country firmly believe that student affairs practice is or should be student-centered.[16] At the same time, educators and researchers justify centering data, or evidence, in the name of being student-centered. This is not student-centered practice; this is data-centered practice.[17] Student affairs educators are the final frontier of university employees who still know students as persons—rather than simply as data. Increasingly, in order to be recognized as competent, student affairs practitioners are also asked to know our students through data and as data.

Placing the focus of researcher and practitioner efforts on the pursuit of predefined outcomes, no matter how broadly stated, limits success to what can be imagined in the present and achieved during the confines of the work. Alongside positive college outcomes like graduation are those that no one can foresee at matriculation and that the longest of longitudinal studies cannot capture. These outcomes live outside the boundaries of predefined outcomes and their measurements.[18] To engage these possible futures, a different approach to student success is required.

Provocations Toward Success as Liberal Education

Scientific definitions and measurements of *student success* produce useful knowledge but cannot by themselves lead student affairs educators to assist in the production of values that escape advance definition and measurement. Our worlds contain items we can code, measure, name, and predict, as well as items that are ephemeral, escape coding and measurement, resist naming, and exist in a possible future unknown to us in the present. There are (at least) two sides to student success: the definition and measurement of desired outcomes, and the wide open possibilities of success that we and our students can never (re)present as a present day measurement. The first side is marked by the manipulation of data to maximize the impact of the institution on the achievement of student outcomes. The second is marked by liberal education, the practices of success that resist capture by definition and measurement. A conception of student success outcomes marked by liberal education includes outcomes (e.g., autonomy, happiness) often in conflict with dominant definitions (e.g., credits earned, graduation). Consider a student who is successful by all current measurements but would rather be in cosmetology school than at your two- or four-year institution. I struggle with measurements that would mark this student's on-time graduation as the outcome that earns the label of *success*, while dropping out would likely mark the student's living and learning program, residence adviser, and academic advisers as deficient. Yet even considering such defiant examples of student success outcomes—outcomes errantly marked as successful that defy a student's experience or the reverse—does not fulfill the promise of success as liberal education. Liberal education shifts the gaze of student success from the definition of outcomes to practices of educational experimentation.[19] A focus on the practices of student success pulls practitioners away from data and toward their university communities. This is a success that is made in and through communities of practice, influenced by but irreducible to any retention rate, predictive analytic, practitioner, or budget line. Student success as liberal education paradoxically holds open possibilities for the attainment of *student success* outcomes that include and are in excess of *retention and graduation.*

Student success pursued overwhelmingly through prescriptive outcomes or metrics denies our students a liberal education and accordingly the open futures they deserve and our world so desperately needs. I have no set of prescriptions for practitioners to get outside of this; prescriptions are the problem. In what follows, I offer a few provocations and experimentations for new and established student affairs educators interested in creating their students, departments and universities differently.

Refusal

I am willing to bet that new student affairs professionals know that their students are more than their measurements in short order of the start of their first graduate assistantship. I am also willing to bet that those with years of experience in student-facing student affairs positions recognize that the measurements that shape their work do not fully capture the students with whom they work. From my own experience, I realized as both a graduate assistant and a supervisor that student-level measurements were insufficient sources of knowledge about the students with whom I worked. However, without another language of valid practice, I centered student-level measurements of success—or risk—in my time as a practitioner. One possible way to center success as liberal education is to refuse such measurements and honor our knowledge that something is not quite complete with the depiction of our students that measurements provide, or the worlds that measurements reshape in our institutions. Eve Tuck and K. Wayne Yang name the importance of refusal in ending the reproduction of settler colonial futures in education, contending that "refusal is a generative stance, not just a 'no,' but a starting place for other qualitative analyses and interpretations of data."[20] Refusal in student affairs practice can open up the space required to practice student success differently. Programs that refuse to use predictive analytics or standard student information system data to gather their participants take a step toward seeing their offices' constituents and communities differently. For example, career services educators who refuse to use tagged student interest data to target outreach open space for students to see themselves differently within potential career fields. One strategy to begin to create student success differently is to refuse its scientific operation.

Embracing Alternative Ways of Knowing

To grant validity only to knowledge produced within scientific or quasiscientific studies is to subordinate the knowledges contained within communities of practice as well as Latinx, queer, Black, indigenous, and borderlands ways of knowing.[21] This subordination of knowledges is dismissive at best, and profoundly racist, sexist, and cisheteronormative at its core. Scientific knowledge created queer folks as deviant and produced scientific racism through the eugenics movement. In fact, founding student affairs documents explicitly connect our field with scientific racism, stating that the responsibility of those in student affairs to the individual student and the scientific study of the student was in fact a "dual responsibility: to the welfare of the individual as well as to the culture and learning of the race."[22] Scientific data collection and production shaped our modern understanding of nationality as well as nationalism and xenophobia.[23] We recognize these shortcomings of scientific measurement, yet we continue to let science dictate which students are most in need of advising support, which students are most likely to graduate with a microgrant from the university, and what cocurricular changes will best support student success as four-year graduation. A focus on student success as liberal education might draw upon queer theory's treatment of identity as fluid, in contrast to the fixed and measurable frameworks of identity prevalent in I-E-O impact studies, to design programs that support the student transition to university.[24] A practice of student success as liberal education might include knowledges from ethnic studies in organizational decision-making before implementing suggestions from EAB policy audits.[25] Practices of student success as liberal education would experiment with ways of knowing student achievement outside of grades and credit accumulation. None of these suggestions are codeable within university databases; none create knowledges that are easy to extract from their environments and distribute to offices around campus. This is precisely the point. Data-driven systems will chug along, feeding neoliberal imperatives for data-informed decision-making. In their interstices, student affairs educators who engage students with knowledges and practices that resist extraction as data points engage in the practice of liberal education.

The Imperative to Go Rogue

To begin a student affairs practice outside of measurement, practice outside of measurement. Utilizing alternate ways of knowing and being will render you invisible to data extraction in the most productive of ways. To produce students capable of creating our world differently, go rogue; enact an "ongoing experiment with the informal."[26] In your work as an adviser, find ways to know which students are most in need of your time outside of at-risk metrics. Center your community-building with students, practitioners, and faculty across campus, and come into your advising loads through these relationships. If you work in cultural centers, work with your communities in ways that are occasionally invisible to administrators who treat your work as data points to include in marketing materials. If you currently work alongside cultural centers, ask around. Chances are your colleagues' offices already engage in such rogue conduct as a means of survival and resistance.[27] If you work in student conduct, try restorative justice practices outside of your university's academic honesty procedures and deny the data points of failure in student records. This flies in the face of what administrators likely want or require of you; as such, rogue practices place you in a precarious position. Those who occupy bodies, identities, and positions of power hold the largest responsibility to go rogue. For those who occupy bodies and identities that already render them precarious, lean on coalitions of practitioners to cocreate rogue spaces. Going rogue does not require that you confess your rogue transgressions. Going rogue means capitalizing on the invisibility of practices outside of data to create university environments, and the students who come into relation with them, differently.

Our systems of measuring student success create the conditions necessary for institutions of higher education to become credentialing factories. We believe in graduation as an outcome because of its association with all sorts of positive outcomes. However, in the rush to produce graduates and other definable and measurable values of higher education, we sideline those values that carry the potential to create students capable of making our world different. If you think that what makes a student successful exceeds what we can possibly measure, then go rogue.

Futures of Measurement and Excess

Measurement of student success is a way to know, within the boundaries of measurement science, if desired outcomes are achieved. Student success as liberal education shifts the focus of the field from knowledge to practice, and in doing so, produces encounters with success that escape definition and measurement.[28] These encounters are not in need of replacement with science. They are the production of student success as liberal education, the practices of success that a focus on our relationships with students outside of definition and measurement incites. Institutional student success initiatives that crowd out the exploration of this excess of measurement fail to live up to the holistic aims of the field.[29]

Student affairs must work in the interstices of cultures of data, evidence, and accountability that lend legitimacy only to outcomes that can be defined in advance and measured. In doing so, we practice a student success that queers data-driven practice beyond easy recognition. The next generation of student success work must emphasize local student affairs practices that live in an unyielding experimentation. We presently spend far too much time perfecting our definitions and measurements of student success on the bodies of students to the exclusion of experimentations with practices that carry expansive possibilities of successes that escape all attempts to advance definition and measurement. Our current challenge is not to replace student success measurements with pure experimentation, but to tip current data-driven practices away from bounded productions of success and toward visions of success rooted in the unbounded possibilities of liberal education.

Discussion Questions

1. What values do you place on the college experience?
2. What do current definitions and measurements of student success produce?
3. Where current definitions and measurements cannot produce your values, how might you alter your practice?

Notes

1. cf. Barad, K. (2003). Posthumanist performativity: Toward an understanding of how matter comes to matter. *Signs: Journal of Women in Culture and Society, 28*(3), 801–831.

2. AAC&U. (2017). What is a 21st century liberal education? *Liberal Education and America's Promise.* Retrieved from https://www.aacu.org/leap/what-is-a-liberal-education, para. 1.

3. Dewey, J. (1916). *Democracy and education: An introduction to the philosophy of education.* New York, NY: Macmillian, p. 281.

4. cf. Culp, M. M., & Dungy, G. J. (2012). *Building a culture of evidence in student affairs: A guide for leaders and practitioners.* Washington DC: NASPA—Student Affairs Administrators in Higher Education.

5. cf. the Foreword in ACE. (1937). *The student personnel point of view* (American Council on Education [ACE] Studies, Series 1, Vol. 1, No. 3). Washington DC: ACE. Retrieved from https://www.naspa.org/images/uploads/main/Student_Personnel_Point_of_View_1937.pdf

6. American Council on Education. (1949). *The student personnel point of view* (American Council on Education Studies, Series 6, No. 13). Washington

DC: ACE. Retrieved from https://www.naspa.org/images/uploads/main/Student_Personnel_Point_of_View_1949.pdf

7. Hopkins, L. B. (1926). Personnel procedure in education: Observations and conclusions resulting from visits to fourteen institutions of higher learning. *The Educational Record Supplement no. 3.* Washington DC: American Council on Education [ACE]; McNeely, J. H. (1938). *College student mortality* (Office of Education Bulletin 1937, No. 11). Washington DC: Government Printing Office.

8. American Council on Education, *The student personnel point of view.*

9. Feldman, K. A. & Newcomb, T. M. (1969). *The impact of college on students: Vol. 1, An analysis of four decades of research.* San Francisco, CA: Jossey-Bass.

10. Astin, A. W. (1970). The methodology of college impact, part one. *Sociology of Education, 43*(3), 223–254; Astin, A. W. (1970). The methodology of college impact, part two. *Sociology of Education, 43*(4), 437–450.

11. National Association of Student Personnel Administrators [NASPA] and American College Personnel Administrators [ACPA]. (2004). *Learning reconsidered: A campus-wide focus on the student experience.* Washington DC: NASPA. Retrieved from https://www.naspa.org/images/uploads/main/Learning_Reconsidered_Report.pdf

12. Kuh, G. D., Kinzie, J., Buckley, J. A., Bridges, B. K., & Hayek, J. C. (2006). *What matters to student success: A review of the literature.* Washington DC: National Postsecondary Education Cooperative. Retrieved from https://www.ue.ucsc.edu/sites/default/files/WhatMattersStudentSuccess(Kuh,July2006).pdf

13. Or data-informed, these terms do the same work as it relates to my analysis. cf. McCormick, A. C., & McClenney, K. (2012). Will these trees *ever* bear fruit? A response to the special issue on student engagement. *The Review of Higher Education, 35*(2), 307–333.

14. Burke, M., Parnell, A., Wesaw, A., & Kruger, K. (2017). *Predictive analysis of student data: A focus on engagement and behavior.* Washington DC: NASPA—Student Affairs Administrators in Higher Education. Retrieved from https://www.naspa.org/images/uploads/main/PREDICTIVE_FULL_4-7-17_DOWNLOAD.pdf

15. U.S. Department of Education. (2015). *Fact sheet: Focusing higher education on student success* [Press release]. Retrieved from https://www.ed.gov/news/press-releases/fact-sheet-focusing-higher-education-student-success

16. *Student-centered* appears in the mission statements and statements of core values of the student affairs units at many American universities. For an example of a research center and a foundation teaming up to promote student-centered practice, see ACE (2017, July 10). ACE, Lumina Foundation to establish Alliance for Global Innovation in Tertiary Education. *American Council on Education.* Retrieved from http://www.acenet.edu/news-room/Pages/ACE-Lumina-Foundation-to-Establish-Alliance-for-Global-Innovation-in-Tertiary-Education.aspx

17. cf. Deleuze, G. (1992). Postscript on the societies of control. *October, 59,* 3–7.

18. cf. Deleuze, G. (1990). *The logic of sense*. New York, NY: Columbia University Press; Springgay, S., & Truman, S. E. (2017). On the need for methods beyond proceduralism: Speculative middles, (in)tensions, and response-ability in research. *Qualitative Inquiry, 24*(3), 203–214.

19. Manning, E. (2016). *The minor gesture*. Durham, NC: Duke University Press; Mazzei, L. A. (2017). Following the contour of concepts toward a *minor inquiry*. *Qualitative Inquiry, 23*(9): 675–685; Springgay & Truman, On the need for methods beyond proceduralism.

20. Tuck, E., & Yang, K. W. (2014). Unbecoming claims: Pedagogies of refusal in qualitative research. *Qualitative Inquiry, 20*(6), 811–818, p. 812.

21. Anzaldúa, G. (1987). *Borderlands/la frontera: The new mestiza*. San Francisco, CA: Aunt Lute Books.

22. Lloyd-Jones, E. M., & Smith, M. R. (1938). *A student personnel program for higher education*. New York, NY: McGraw-Hill, pp. 38–39.

23. Ngai, N. M. (2004). *Impossible subjects: Illegal aliens and the making of modern America*. Princeton, NJ: Princeton University Press.

24. cf. Butler, J. (1990). *Gender trouble: Feminism and the subversion of identity*. New York, NY: Routledge.

25. Ethnic studies is my colloquial approximation of Roderick Ferguson's *interdisciplines*; cf. Ferguson, R. A. (2012). *The reorder of things: The university and its pedagogies of minority difference*. Minneapolis, MN: University of Minnesota Press; EAB. (2016, April 19). *Academic policy audit: Tools for identifying and prioritizing institutional barriers to success*. Retrieved from https://www.eab.com/research-and-insights/academic-affairs-forum/toolkits/academic-policy-diagnostic

26. Harney, S., & Moten, F. (2013). *The undercommons: Fugitive planning and black study*. Wivenhoe, UK: Minor Compositions, p. 74.

27. Also known as *survivance*; cf. Brayboy, B. M. J. (2006). Toward a tribal critical race theory in education. *The Urban Review, 37*(5), 425–446.

28. The arguments here lean heavily on assemblage theory; cf. Deleuze, G., & Guattari, F. (1987). *A thousand plateaus: Capitalism and schizophrenia*. Minneapolis, MN: University of Minnesota Press.

29. Baxter Magolda, M. B. (2009). The activity of meaning making: A holistic perspective on college student development. *Journal of College Student Development, 50*(6), 621–639; as read through Deleuze, *The logic of sense*.

Redefining Student Success to Foster More Inclusive Learning Environments

Molly Reas Hall

In the preceding essay, Smithers contends that defining and measuring *student success* is not compatible with liberal education and offers student affairs educators alternative courses of action such as "going rogue" when tasked with measuring student success. In my response, I argue the benefits of measuring student success and advocate that, by broadening the definition and measurement of *student success*, measuring student success can foster both liberal education and more inclusive learning environments. More specifically, I present a different interpretation of liberal education, share challenges and opportunities from the body of literature on "academic quality," advocate for the use of more qualitative and locally defined measures of student success, and offer a concrete example of how defining and measuring student success may be able to foster more just and inclusive learning environments. As a full-time professional working in academic assessment, I know firsthand that measuring student success in meaningful ways can be difficult but is worth doing.

Defining and Measuring *Liberal Education*

While Smithers references part of the American Association of Colleges & Universities' (AAC&U's) definition of *liberal education* in her essay, a more comprehensive definition provided by AAC&U is as follows:

> Liberal Education is an approach to learning that empowers individuals and prepares them to deal with complexity, diversity, and change. It provides students with broad knowledge of the wider world (e.g., science, culture, and society) as well as in-depth study in a specific area of interest. A liberal education helps students develop a sense of social responsibility, as well as strong and transferable intellectual and practical skills such as communication, analytical and problem-solving skills, and a demonstrated ability to apply knowledge and skills in real-world settings.[1]

In contrast to Smithers's view that liberal education is elusive—escaping definition and measurement—I contend that multiple aspects of a liberal education are measurable. Based on the full AAC&U definition, measures associated with a liberal education can address breadth of knowledge (e.g., students' experiences in their general education curriculum); depth of knowledge (e.g., students' experiences in their academic major); student learning outcomes (e.g., critical thinking and written communication skills); vocational outcomes (e.g., employment rates and types of jobs secured); and social responsibility outcomes (e.g., community engagement).

AAC&U has been at the forefront of operationalizing tenets of liberal education into measurable outcomes, leading the creation of 16 different Valid Assessment of Learning in Undergraduate Education (VALUE) rubrics for student learning outcomes such as problem-solving, intercultural knowledge and competence, ethical reasoning and action, and global learning. While these VALUE rubrics have their detractors[2] as well as their proponents,[3] thousands of higher education institutions from all over the world have utilized the AAC&U VALUE rubrics to measure a wide variety of outcomes commonly associated with a liberal education.[4]

I agree with Smithers that we cannot predefine all outcomes associated with a liberal education; however, the aspects of a liberal education that AAC&U describes can be—and have been—measured. I assert that, if done well, measuring what *can* be defined and measured provides higher education institutions with valuable information to inform decision-making and improvement so that we may better educate and serve students. For example, if a major institutional goal is to increase student engagement in experiential learning, collecting data on students' experiences related to activities such as undergraduate research, study abroad, internships, and service-learning can help inform the institution's next steps. Measuring student success does not need to be perfect to be valuable.

Challenges Associated With Measuring Student Success

Challenges associated with measuring student success (or *academic quality*, as it is often referred to in academic affairs) are well documented in the research literature. One of the biggest concerns in the academic quality literature regarding measurement is that what gets measured tends to be what gets done.[5] For example, if a student affairs division decides to measure student attendance at certain types of programs, then units may focus their efforts on increasing attendance at these events rather than focusing on the quality of the programs offered. Another common issue is that measurements frequently consist of what is *easy* to measure rather than what is *most important* to measure.[6] An example here would be when a wellness unit measures student knowledge at the end of an educational program even though the unit is more interested in measuring the extent to which students, in the future, apply the knowledge they gained. Since it is considerably easier to measure student knowledge when a program is implemented than to follow up with students months or years afterward, it is much more common for units to measure the former than the latter. A final issue I'd like to highlight here is using *quantities* to measure *qualities*. As Barnett argued, "to believe that we can say something of real insight about the quality of an educational process by describing it in numerical terms is an illusion. Qualities and quantities are different kinds of entities."[7] While quantitative metrics such as student GPAs and time to degree provide valuable information to institutions, I advocate that data related to student success should encompass more than numbers.

Informing Improvement and Meeting Standards

In the academic quality literature, tensions between the primary purposes of assessment—(a) to inform continuous improvement and (b) to meet external standards—are well documented.[8] Although I strongly believe that the primary reason to measure student success should be to inform improvement (e.g., improvements to student learning and/or the student experience), I would be remiss not to mention that the vast majority of higher education institutions in the United States are required to measure student success in order to gain and keep accreditation that enables them to receive federal financial aid and certain types of external funding. Although meeting external standards is a secondary motivation, it is another compelling reason to measure student success and to do it well. If educators are going to spend valuable time and energy collecting and reporting data on student success to accrediting bodies, then let's collect and report data that are meaningful to our campuses and can inform continuous improvement. Leading regional accrediting bodies such as the Southern Association of Colleges and Schools Commission on Colleges (SACSCOC) allow colleges and universities to define what *student success* means for their particular institution and student body,[9] so let's take advantage of it.

Developing Local Definitions of *Student Success*

I agree with Smithers that defining *student success* solely in terms of graduation and retention rates is both narrow and problematic. While I can certainly understand why educators may opt to "go rogue" when faced with measuring student success, another potential course of action is for student affairs educators to work with their campus communities to create local definitions of *student success* that extend and/or counter the current definitions related to graduation and retention rates preferred by government bodies such as state legislatures. For measurements of student success to be meaningful, colleges and universities would be well served to expand their definitions of student success and adopt more qualitative measures such as observations of student behavior, focus groups, interviews, blog posts, and ePortfolios. This course of action aligns with Smithers's suggestion to embrace "alternative ways of knowing."[10] In my view, shifting the definition away from retention and graduation rates toward student learning (which can be defined broadly, encompassing learning in both the curriculum and the co-curriculum) would be a good start. If what gets measured is really what gets done, then it is vital that we measure aspects of student success that we believe are critical to the growth and development of students and our work as educators.[11]

Smithers argues "that definitions and measurements of *student success* construct student realities in ways that are counterproductive to liberal education."[12] I respectfully disagree; student success measurements do not have to narrowly define the student experience. To illustrate my point, I offer an example of a student affairs division that is defining and measuring student success in ways that not only go beyond retention and graduation rates but also have the potential to foster more inclusive learning environments. In 2010, the Division of Student Affairs at Virginia Tech broadened its notion of student success by adopting the following five aspirations for student learning:[13]

1. Committing to unwavering *curiosity*—Virginia Tech students will be inspired to lead lives of curiosity, embracing a life-long commitment to intellectual development.
2. Pursuing *self-understanding* and *integrity*—Virginia Tech students will form a set of affirmative values and develop the self-understanding to integrate these values into their decision-making.
3. Practicing *civility*—Virginia Tech students will understand and commit to civility as a way of life in their interactions with others.
4. Preparing for a life of *courageous leadership*—Virginia Tech students will be courageous leaders who serve as change agents and make the world more humane and just.
5. Embracing *ut prosim* (That I May Serve)[14] as a way of life—Virginia Tech students will enrich their lives through service to others.

Thus, the division's definition of *student success* now includes curiosity, self-understanding and integrity, civility, courageous leadership, and *ut prosim*.

Developing and implementing the five aspirations for student learning at Virginia Tech was an extensive administrative process. Over the course of several years, the meaning of each aspiration was discussed in detail, followed by lengthy discussions on how each aspiration could be operationalized for programming and measurement purposes. These latter discussions resulted in division-wide learning outcome frameworks that provide effective roadmaps for designing campus programs and measuring student growth related to the aspirations. Each student affairs unit currently submits an annual assessment report that includes data on at least one measure specifically related to the aspirations for student learning.[15]

Measuring the aspirations for student learning requires student affairs units to work collaboratively across the division, to reframe their work in new ways, and to implement more direct measures of student learning.[16] This effort also requires student affairs educators to view their work as part of a larger student life curriculum. For example, Recreational Sports has reframed sportsmanship as civility, and the Leadership Education Collaborative has reframed servant leadership as *ut prosim*. In Housing and Residence Life, hall directors asked student staff to design bulletin boards that invited residents to share their thoughts on the aspirations for student learning. Students were given aspirations sticky notes on which they provided their own definitions of the aspirations (e.g., "How do you define *curiosity*?") and then posted the notes on the bulletin boards. Hall directors took pictures of the completed bulletin boards and used the responses as assessment data for the unit.

In summary, I agree with Smithers that "a different approach to student success is required"[17] and offer Virginia Tech's Division of Student Affairs as an example of a unit that has "embraced alternative ways of knowing"[18] by defining and measuring *student success* in ways that better support liberal education. Was the process Virginia Tech engaged in to develop and operationalize its aspirations for student learning easy? No. Was it quick? No. Do I think it serves as an example of how defining and measuring student success may foster more inclusive learning environments? Yes, I do. While I feel this approach has great potential to foster student learning and development on college campuses, it takes time to create local definitions of *student success* and then measure student success in meaningful ways. In order for this type of work to be implemented at other colleges and universities, it is important for institutions to both value and reward this work.

Discussion Questions

1. How does your campus currently define *student success*? How may this definition be broadened to foster more inclusive learning environments?
2. What challenges have you experienced with measuring student success?
3. What competencies are needed for student affairs educators to adopt more qualitative and/or locally defined measures of student success?

Notes

1. Association of American Colleges & Universities. (n.d.). *What is liberal education?* Retrieved from https://www.aacu.org/leap/what-is-a-liberal-education

2. Anson, C. M., Dannels, D. P., Flash, P., & Housley Gaffney, A. L. (2012). Big rubrics and weird genres: The futility of using generic assessment tools across diverse instructional contexts. *The Journal of Writing Assessment, 5*(1). Retrieved from http://journalofwritingassessment.org/article.php?article=57

3. For example, Suskie, L. (2018). *Assessing student learning: A common sense guide* (3rd ed.). San Francisco, CA: Jossey-Bass.

4. Association of American Colleges and Universities. (n.d.). VALUE. Retrieved from https://www.aacu.org/value

5. Dew, J. R., & Nearing, M. M. (2004). *Continuous quality improvement in higher education*. Westport, CT: Praeger.

6. Jones, J., & de Saram, D. D. (2005). Academic staff views of quality systems for teaching and learning: A Hong Kong case study. *Quality in Higher Education, 11*(1), 47–58; Kleijnen, J., Dolmans, D., Willems, J., & van Hout, H. (2011). Does internal quality management contribute to more control or to improvement of higher education? A survey on faculty's perceptions. *Quality Assurance in Education, 19*(2), 141–155.

7. Barnett, R. (1994). The idea of quality: Voicing the educational. In G. D. Doherty (Ed.), *Developing quality systems in education* (pp. 68–82). London, England: Routledge, p. 75.

8. For example, Sachs, J. (1994). Strange yet compatible bedfellows: Quality assurance and quality improvement. *Australian Universities Review, 37*(1), 22–25.

9. Southern Association of Colleges and Schools Commission on Colleges. (2018). *The principles of accreditation: Foundations for quality enhancement*. Retrieved from http://www.sacscoc.org/pdf/2018PrinciplesOfAcreditation.pdf

10. Smithers, L. E., this volume, p. 128.

11. Dew & Nearing, *Continuous quality improvement in higher education*.

12. Smithers, L. E., this volume, pp. 127–128.

13. Virginia Tech Division of Student Affairs. (n.d.). *Aspirations for student learning*. Retrieved from http://www.dsa.vt.edu/aspirations/aspirations.php

14. Adopted in 1896, *ut prosim* is Virginia Tech's motto, which translates from Latin to "That I May Serve."

15. Each unit develops its own outcomes and measures in consultation with the division's assessment and professional development unit.

16. Direct measures of student learning enable someone to directly observe if a student has achieved the knowledge, skill, ability, or competency identified in a learning outcome.

17. Smithers, L. E., this volume, p. 131.

18. Smithers, L. E., this volume, p. 128.

8

What Are the Risks of Assuming the Sharing of Proper Pronouns Is a Best Practice for Trans* Inclusion?

More Than Pronouns: Problematizing Best Practices of Trans* Inclusion

Kathryn S. Jaekel and D. Chase J. Catalano

Over the past decade, university educators have increased their attention on trans* college students.[1] As this attention has increased, so too has research outlining how to best support and serve trans* students. For example, Spade outlines basic principles to create an inclusive and welcoming environment for students[2]: offering key suggestions such as avoiding roll call, asking students' proper pronouns, and allowing students to self-identify their gender and names. At many institutions, and specifically within the field of student affairs, these suggestions have taken hold; in fact, it's become the trend that pronouns (e.g., she, her, hers; he, him, his; ze, hir, hirs; they, them, theirs) now appear on institution and conference name badges, e-mail signatures, and business cards. Moreover, the inclusion of pronouns during introductions comes from the best intentions: to allow individuals the agency to name their gender.

The pervasiveness of giving pronouns within the field of student affairs is likely because our field values personalization and relationship development. Introductions are a necessary part of forming a group dynamic, whether as part of a student organization meeting, an introductory staff meeting, or the first class of the semester. Introductions in these spaces usually include people's names and personal information (e.g., hometown, major, previous institution). These spaces are increasingly using the "best practice" that encourages everyone to share their pronouns as an act of self-clarification and self-determination.[3]

While many student affairs professionals utilize the practice of asking for pronouns to signal trans* inclusion, increasingly, this best practice concerns us. Our concern is twofold. First, pronouns are merely presumptive of one's gender and, as such, may give false understandings of one's gender identity and experiences. Second, asking for pronouns at the start of meetings and class sessions is a mere performance of inclusivity and not an actual strategy for inclusion. Put another way, the act of pronoun introduction *could* be an act of inclusion *if* facilitation includes context (self-disclosure as agency and revelation of normative gender assumptions) and the practice surfaces in other classroom strategies to name trans* oppression.[4] In short, we must address the conundrum that the simple asking of pronouns is necessary, insufficient, and potentially harmful in efforts toward trans* inclusion and liberation. As such, we explore the potential unseen risks of asking for pronouns as a means of engaging in trans* inclusion. We expand upon our concerns alongside information about how we identify to help readers better contextualize how we interpret these concerns and perspectives. We conclude with discussion questions to trouble the discussion about "best practices" and offer other ways of participating in trans* liberation and inclusion.

A Note on Terminology

Before moving forward, we first discuss some terminology regarding gender and gender identity. We recognize that there are a variety of ways these terms are understood and used. As such, we offer here how we understand and operationalize these terms. *Biological sex*, often assigned at birth (i.e., male, female, intersex), is different from *gender identity* (i.e., gender queer, woman, man, trans*) and *gender expression* (i.e., masculine, feminine, androgynous, gender nonconforming). For instance, a person assigned male at birth who grows up to identify as a man and expresses his gender in ways that align with masculinities is *cisgender*.

Trans* oppression functions under the assumption that all people are cisgender (the invisibility of trans*ness). Trans* oppression manifests as individual, institutional, and cultural forms of oppression for those whose gender identity or gender expression does not conform with the gender binary (woman/man).[5] Trans* oppression reminds us that while often people assume that one's biological sex defines one's gender, such is not the case. Transgender identities (e.g., trans*, trans woman, trans man, gender non-conforming, agender) are vast and complex. Moreover, the constellation of gender identities and gender expressions remind us that gender liberation is about finding the language and expression to define our own genders. Importantly, we use the term *trans**, denoted with the asterisk, in this essay both to be inclusive of a spectrum of gender identities as well as to provide a visual disruption. Because in so many ways our gender identities provide disruption, we use the asterisk to provide a similar disruption.

Trans* in Higher Education

As the body of literature that centers trans* topics expands in higher education, individuals have identified recommendations and best practices to engage in inclusive efforts of trans* college students. Scholars have called for better housing options for trans* students,[6] better access to gender-inclusive restrooms,[7] inclusion of gender identity in nondiscrimination policies,[8] and inclusion of trans* topics into curricula.[9] The origins of these suggestions are campus climate studies that illuminate transgender, trans*, and gender nonconforming students face more discrimination than their lesbian, gay, bisexual, and queer (LGBQ) peers.[10] Research centering on trans* collegians has shown these students often face discrimination both inside and outside of the classroom.[11] These studies offer stories about students being misgendered, being called by names with which they do not identify, and engaging in often hostile interactions with faculty, staff, and peers around issues of gender. To address these forms of discrimination, researchers have suggested that colleges and universities engage in inclusive initiatives that center on gender inclusive language. This includes the act of asking individuals for their "preferred" pronouns at the start of meetings and/or classes.[12]

In light of this scholarship, colleges, universities, and particularly student affairs divisions have produced a flurry of handouts, PowerPoint presentations, and statements on best practices aimed at greater gender inclusion. A quick Internet search results in hundreds of what we characterize here as *quick fix* documents, all purporting inclusive strategies for implementation in contexts ranging from student affairs meeting spaces to classrooms. Nearly all of these documents begin with the "best practice" of asking for everyone to name their pronouns at the start of meetings, classes, and even in e-mail signatures and on name tags.

The alleviation of trans* oppression cannot be achieved through quick fixes—in this case, simply asking individuals to identify their pronouns. Instead, we posit that the quick-fix approach of asking for pronouns is an unexamined process that serves mostly cisgender people, allowing them to alleviate their anxiety about misgendering others. Asking about pronouns, especially as an introductory activity, provides others with a quick and easy-to-remember linguistic marker of gender (which is well intentioned) *and still* does not provide adequate gender understanding. After participants have collected personal pronouns, the significance of gender-inclusive conversations is rarely revisited. This is likely because the "inclusion" (i.e., asking of pronouns) has "been dealt with."

Masking the Complexities of Gender

Both authors of this chapter struggle when asked for our pronouns and with the notion that our pronouns reveal any meaningful insights about our gendered experiences. Like so many others, simply revealing our current pronouns does not provide accurate information about our genders or gender identities. In many respects, when asked about pronouns, it often feels like forced vulnerability that cisgender individuals seldom experience in those spaces. Our genders come with a context and complexity and refuse the tidiness of pronouns.

In some ways, the act of pronoun sharing seems to center the edification of cisgender people and their reflection. Those who are cisgender tend to expect others to be cisgender. They might feel surprised by the act of naming their pronouns because they think it is obvious. Naming their pronouns could cause new learning about trans*ness, reflection on trans* oppression, and disrupt cisgender expectations of gender normativity. Simultaneously, the lack of attention to presumptions of what trans*ness "looks like" (e.g., the expectation that all trans* people do not meet normative gender expressions) means some trans* people who are perceived as gender conforming are ignored or not seen as "trans* enough." Yet, those with more noticeable transgressions of gender norms are often overly scrutinized during an innocuous introduction.

For example, I (Katy), identify as a gender-nonconforming queer woman. Even when writing about my gendered experiences, I struggle with how to identify my gender as well as what terms I should use and/or with which I identify. While I'm a woman, I am not a typical woman in that I wear what are socially understood as "men's" clothes, brandish a "man's" haircut, and have masculine body movements. As such, I am a different type of woman—one who is often mistaken for a man and is expected to engage in a manner consistent with masculinity. I'm frequently misgendered, both in the workplace and in social contexts. Giving my pronouns, regardless of what they might be, gives little indication of my past experiences.

I am also someone whose gender often shifts based on spaces I am in, as I inhabit different spaces at my university. My gender, how I'm seen, and how colleagues address me in a meeting is vastly different than how my students perceive me. Offering different sets of pronouns in different spaces is a chore, for both me as well as those who do not realize that pronouns can shift based on environments. As such, there are no pronouns I find suitable to convey who I am and how I should be addressed. Instead, the act of asking for my pronouns is a form of performance (i.e., it's been deemed the "right" thing to do), as well as a means to "accurately" verify and ascribe my gender to ensure others do not feel confused and/or uncomfortable in an event where they must speak about me.

Oddly, I (Chase) feel pressure to share my pronouns and ask students their pronouns at the start of each semester. This is due to my own belief that this is a helpful activity to eliminate trans* oppression.[13] At the time when I coauthored a chapter on trans* oppression, others viewed my gender as incoherent.[14] To ask for "he/him/his" pronouns was an act of agency and self-determination (I did not consistently pass as a man). Pronoun recognition was the strongest demand I was willing to make in the early stages of my social and biomedical transition; they were my declaration that I was no longer a woman. For similar reasons, once I could grow what I consider nice-looking facial hair, I was reluctant to clean shave my face. My facial hair was also a declaration of my gender and my achievement to reach a recognizable masculine aesthetic. *And* it was my fear that without facial hair, my feminine (whatever that means) facial features would be too apparent. Thus, I would not be recognized as I saw myself. Now, in classroom settings, unless I state otherwise, people read me as a cisgender White man. In some ways, this is an achievement, right? I pass, and I pass *so well* that I get the well-intentioned feedback, "If you didn't tell me, I would never know you are trans*." The problem is that I am and always will be trans*. My gender, regardless of the perception of others, does not align with ciscentrism.[15] A simple declaration of my pronouns completely erases my years of struggle, self-advocacy, discomfort, and biomedical interventions. My pronouns, without other gender contextualizing efforts, give others the power to determine my gender story and ascribe privileges that do not align with my life. My socialization for more than 25 years was as a girl/woman, *and* I (still) find masculinity is an ill-fitting garment.

We understand the origins and intentions that spawned the culture of pronouns as a part of introductions (or name tags or e-mail signatures), which is to surface assumptions of equating perceived embodiment with gender identity and expression. Additionally, pronoun assertion disrupts the idea that our gender identities and expressions are clear from a glance at our bodies. Assumptions about how bodies must align with gender identities and gender expressions is a form of trans* oppression, and we should draw attention to these assumptions in our resistance to reifying how bodies and genders must align to be "normal."

Concurrently, declaring pronouns, as part of introductions by a facilitator, relieves trans* people of the responsibility of initiating this practice into each group they inhabit. The complexity is that pronouns matter and they also do not matter. We posit that more in-depth discussions about the negative impact of pronouns must be a part of an introduction process. For instance, consider the following:

- Do we address the fact that many people give their attention to the person(s) they perceive as gender incoherent and pay little attention to the pronouns of those they perceive as cisgender?
- Do we acknowledge that trans* oppression means each group begins with the expectation we are all cisgender?
- How do we acknowledge that trans*ness requires exposing ourselves to vulnerabilities?
- Do we remind cisgender people who forget to name their pronouns (cisgender privilege)?
- Do we interrogate what it means when cisgender people claim no pronoun preference because they have never been misgendered in a way that causes violence or exploitation or fear?

As the preceding questions elicit, trans*ness is still a curiosity[16] that enlivens people to examine their gender in ways previously unconsidered. Thus, our goal is for those who facilitate introductions to consider these questions when choosing to include pronouns in an introduction activity.

Minimizing the Work of Inclusion

In addition to our concern regarding the false assumption that pronouns appropriately and adequately represent gender identity, we remain concerned with the ways that the rhetoric of inclusion obscures actual acts of inclusion. Asking for pronouns risks minimizing the ongoing, often hard work of trans* inclusion. Specifically, Ahmed argues that college and university approaches to diversity (i.e., policies, statements, and other initiatives) often obscure the actual act of inclusion.[17] That is, by communicating the desire to be inclusive, by naming policies and acts, it instead communicates to individuals that these topics and issues have been "dealt with" and, as such, need no further discussion.

I (Katy) served on a commission at my university that was supposed to advocate and center the experiences of lesbian, gay, bisexual, transgender, and queer (LGBTQ) students, staff, and faculty. Our mission was to promote and develop equitable inclusive practices for queer and trans* university communities. The commission met once a month and consisted primarily of cisgender, straight individuals who self-selected to be on the commission. Meetings began with sharing names and pronouns. Despite this act of inclusion and the mission of the commission, members consistently misgendered each other. Moreover, the meetings routinely occurred in a building that did not have gender-inclusive restrooms (though those facilities were available on campus). Despite the goals of the commission and the adherence to pronoun sharing at the start of each meeting, it's troubling that larger issues were ignored, such as correcting each other when an individual was misgendered and providing access to inclusive restrooms. Overwhelmingly, in this meeting space, the act of "inclusion" only took place through inquiring about pronouns. After the act of sharing pronouns ended, trans* issues were ignored and pronouns were seldom honored. As such, while the commission's goals and mission reflected the rhetoric of inclusion, the performance of that mission was not achieved.

We have seen the effects of the minimization of inclusion manifested through trans* students' low expectations of their colleges and universities.[18] While I (Chase) was a director of an LGBT Resource Center, I sought to create campus traditions about trans* liberation; create programs for, and not just about, trans* identities; advocate about the importance of gender inclusive restrooms; and facilitate trainings on social justice and inclusion. However, I found students often focused on what I consider minimal forms of inclusion about personal dignity: pronoun recognition, name recognition, and restroom access. To be sure, these are essential components for students to function in their day-to-day life, to relieve stress of potential violence, and as an acknowledgment of their personhood. For students, the bar of inclusion was set so low that liberation seemed to end at pronouns. As such, offering pronouns at introductions became their end goal in the cultural shift of the institution, rather than questioning the structures and practices that might create a more holistic and inclusive campus. The notion that inclusion means merely asking for pronouns rather than actions concerns us. We believe colleges and universities can and should do more.

Considerations for Professional Praxis

We see trans* inclusion as far more than asking pronouns. Rather, it's a call for structural inclusion embedded throughout the institution. Structural inclusion consists of changes to curriculum, policies, and physical structures that lead to greater gender inclusivity and trans* liberation. For many, the practice of asking of pronouns is the extent of their attempts toward trans* inclusion, whereas for us, it's just the beginning.

Pronouns function as a part of trans* epistemology and how we come to name ourselves. Hailed as brave and inspirational by the risks we take to name ourselves, pronoun sharing doesn't acknowledge that trans* oppression is seemingly insurmountable.[19] Nicolazzo argued that pronoun sharing during introductions, like other "best practices," is a reinforcement of trans* oppression by the simplistic assumption that dismantling trans* oppression is achievable by the "correct" practices.[20] We know that pronouns are not a panacea toward trans* inclusion. We recognize gender as rooted in characteristics, affects, and signs vaster than the gender binary, and thus we need complex strategies, not quick fixes, to change the climates on our campuses. We start with pronouns and we must not end with pronouns. We must explain why we ask, what the pronouns mean, and how knowing them is a form of accountability for liberation.[21]

Thus, to foster trans* inclusion and lead to trans* liberation, we believe there must be a commitment to go beyond pronouns. Instead, we believe that there should be a shift from "practices" to critical professional praxis.[22] Here, critical professional praxis serves as an approach that recognizes the power-laden nature of actions and practices and challenges individuals to engage in critical reflection to address inequities. As such, student affairs practitioners must be aware of what they can do on the individual and institutional levels. On the individual level, student affairs practitioners can be integral to their trans* college students' success by researching trans* histories, examining and reflecting upon bias (both their own and that of others), advocating for trans* students' needs, and enacting a commitment to think beyond and complicate their understanding of the gender binary.

On the institutional level, student affairs practitioners can be advocates for inclusive policies, practices, and spaces. They can serve as advocates for students and help students navigate institutional culture and help connect students to resources. They can remember that trans* inclusion is the responsibility of everyone in all areas of the institution, even if it's not an explicit part of their functional area.

Conclusions

The efforts of student affairs educators to create conditions of trust and authenticity, which allow gender identity and expression to holistically exist across various campus contexts, need to be the core objective of why pronouns are part of an introduction activity. If we are to engage in trans* inclusive practice, then we must move beyond symbolic recognition, catering to cisgender expectations of gender conformity, and hold gender as a complicated lived practice.[23] The tension, as we see it, is that pronoun sharing at the start of group formation is both about self-determination and produces anxiety. Creating campus communities that are open to the constellation of potential genders means we must think about why we use pronouns in introductions and how that knowledge informs group development. The focus must be beyond personal pronouns, instead attending to what it means to invite gender into our spaces. Pronouns serve a basic function and somewhere they became the extent of trans* inclusion rather than a starting place.

Our focus is to offer trans* liberation in praxis for those who facilitate welcome activities and introductions in various spaces across campuses. We aim to help others consider how they construct and understand pronoun uses and to consider their role in trans* inclusion. We offer these discussion questions to begin further trans* inclusion conversations that examine how student affairs practitioners can reflect and act beyond pronouns.

Discussion Questions

1. Do you have knowledge of trans* students/colleagues in your sessions/classes/meetings? If so, have you done any work to consider their comfort level with pronoun sharing in a decontextualized space?

2. How might you utilize pronouns as an introductory tool to go deeper than the articulation of pronouns themselves? How can you frame introductions as the first step toward understanding others and inviting gender exploration, examination, and analysis into your work?

3. What strategies can you use to engage in trans* inclusion within your sphere(s) of influence beyond pronouns?

Notes

1. Nicolazzo, Z. (2017). *Trans* in college: Transgender students' strategies for navigating campus life and the institutional politics of inclusion*. Sterling, VA: Stylus. We further detail how we understand and use this term in the section, "A Note on Terminology."

2. Spade, D. (2011). Some very basic tips for making higher education more accessible to trans students and rethinking how we talk about gendered bodies. *The Radical Teacher, 92*(1), 57–62.

3. Beemyn, B., Curtis, B., Davis, M., & Tubbs, N. J. (2005). Transgender issues on college campuses. In R. Sanlo (Ed.), *Gender identity and sexual orientation: Research, policy, and personal perspectives* (New Directions for Student Services, no. 111, pp. 49–60). San Francisco, CA: Jossey-Bass; Nicolazzo, *Trans* in college*; Spade, Some very basic tips.

4. Catalano, D. C. J., & Griffin, P. (2016). Sexism, heterosexism, and trans* oppression: An integrated perspective. In M. Adams, L. A. Bell, D. J. Goodman, & K. Y. Joshi (Eds.), *Teaching for diversity and social justice* (3rd ed., pp. 183–211). New York, NY: Routledge.

5. Ibid.

6. Kortegast, C. A. (2017). "But it's not the space that I would need": Narrative of LGBTQ students' experiences in campus housing. *Journal of College and University Student Housing, 43*(2), 58–71.

7. Seelman, K. L. (2014). Recommendations of transgender students, staff, and faculty in the USA for improving college campuses. *Gender and education, 26*(6), 618–635.

8. Marine, S., & Catalano, C. (2014). Engaging transgender students on college and university campuses. In S. J. Harper and S. R. Quaye (Eds.), *Student engagement in higher education: Theoretical perspectives and practical approaches for diverse populations* (2nd ed., pp. 135–148). New York, NY: Routledge.

9. Jaekel, K. S., & Nicolazzo, Z. (2017). Teaching trans*: Strategies and tensions of teaching gender in student affairs preparation programs. *Journal for the Study of Postsecondary and Tertiary Education, 2*, 165–179.

10. Garvey, J. C., & Rankin, S. R. (2015). The influence of campus experiences on the level of outness among trans-spectrum and queer-spectrum students. *Journal of Homosexuality, 62*(3), 374–393.

11. Ibid; Pryor, J. T. (2015). Out in the classroom: Transgender student experiences at a large public university. *Journal of College Student Development, 5*(56), 440–455; Jaekel & Nicolazzo, Teaching trans*.

12. Beemyn et al., Transgender issues on college campuses.

13. Catalano, D. C. J., McCarthy, L., & Shlasko, D. (2007). Transgender oppression curriculum design. In M. Adams, L. A. Bell, & P. Griffin (Eds.), *Teaching for diversity and social justice* (2nd ed., pp. 219–246). New York, NY: Routledge.

14. Ibid.

15. Anon. (2017, August 2). Invalid measures invalidate us: Ciscentrism and ableism in the trans autism literature [web log post]. Retrieved from https://www.writewhereithurts.net/

16. Pusch, R. S. (2005). Objects of curiosity: Transgender college students' perceptions of the reactions of others. *Journal of Gay and Lesbian Issues in Education, 3*(1), 45–61.

17. Ahmed, S. (2012). *On being included: Racism and diversity in institutional life*. Durham, NC: Duke University Press.

18. Catalano, D. C. J. (2015). Beyond virtual equality: Liberatory consciousness as a path to achieve trans* inclusion in higher education. *Equity &*

Excellence in Education, 48(3), 418–435; Nicolazzo, Z. (2017, March 8). Imagining a trans* epistemology: What liberation thinks like in postsecondary education. *Urban Education,* 1–26. Retrieved from http://journals.sagepub.com/doi/10.1177/0042085917697203

19. Nicolazzo, Imagining a trans* epistemology.

20. Ibid.

21. Love, B. (2010). Developing a liberatory consciousness. In M. Adams, W. J. Blumenfeld, R. Castañeda, H. W. Hackman, M. L. Peters, & X. Zúñiga (Eds.), *Readings for diversity and social justice* (2nd ed., pp. 599–603). New York, NY: Routledge.

22. Croom, N. N., & Kortegast, C. A. (2018, May 23). When ignoring difference fails: Using critical professional praxis. *About Campus.* Retrieved from http://journals.sagepub.com/doi/abs/10.1177/1086482218765765

23. West, C., & Zimmerman, D. H. (1987). Doing gender. *Gender and Society, 1*(2), 125–151.

What Happens to a Dream Deferred? Sharing Proper Pronouns as an Act of Gender Self-Determination

Z Nicolazzo

"What happens to a dream deferred?"[1] I have taken a public stance in my research and writing regarding the notion of best practices.[2] Simply put, my stance has been—and continues to be—that "best practices" are oversimplified, created without attention to cultural contexts or histories, and suppose easy solutions to what are often complex problems. In a field where "creating best practices seems like a best practice,"[3] my beliefs make me a bit of an outsider. However, my research continues to indicate that the implementation of these "best practices" is wholly insufficient in counteracting the trans* oppression present in higher education.

And still, despite their insufficiency as a "best practice," I assert that the inclusion of sharing one's proper pronouns during introductory activities for meetings and classes is necessary to forward trans* inclusion. Specifically, sharing proper pronouns allows trans* people to (pro)claim our agency and humanity in whatever form(s) we want it to take. We can also do this (pro) claiming differently depending on time and context, taking into account issues of safety, vulnerability, and personal comfort, all without suggesting that we are lying or confused about who we are as trans* people.

In responding to Jaekel and Catalano's essay, I start with a personal story about my evolving understanding and usage of pronouns. I then introduce LeeAnn Bell's notion that "social justice is both a process and a goal"[4] as well as Angela Y. Davis' notion that "freedom is a constant struggle."[5] In so doing, I argue that if we as student affairs educators intend to hold fast to our values regarding social justice and inclusion,[6] we should—where and when possible—continue to view the sharing of proper pronouns as necessary to forward trans* inclusion. In essence, I argue that inviting people to assert their proper pronouns in whatever way is safe and comfortable for them during introductory activities for classes and meetings is an important act of gender self-determination; one that forwards the heretofore deferred dream of trans* liberation in higher education and student affairs.

My Personal Pronoun Story

Ever since coming into my own trans* sense of self, I have used the pronouns *ze* (pronounced like the letter Z, and used in place of *he, she,* and *they*) and *hir* (pronounced like the word *here,* and used in place of *him, his, her, hers,* and *theirs*). However, in the spring of 2017, I began wondering if perhaps I wanted to start using different pronouns. At the suggestion of a friend, I sent an e-mail to a small group of people asking them to use *she, her,* and *hers* when referring to me. I asked that they do this only with others who were on the e-mail, which made sense given that all the people on the e-mail knew and were in regular contact with one another. Sending this e-mail provided me a safe platform from which I could "test drive" these new-to-me pronouns, allowing me to gauge my own feelings when others used them in referring to me.

Over time, I began to feel more comfortable using my new pronouns in public venues. For example, when referring to myself on Twitter, I would sometimes use *her* rather than *hir.* I also began experimenting with using my new pronouns when I would go to other campuses to give talks about my research. Although I did not share them in all spaces, or with everyone with whom I met and interacted—choices I made based on how I perceived my levels of risk, safety, and the potential to have to do the emotionally taxing work of explaining and defending my pronouns—sharing my pronouns as a way of introducing myself to others became a deeply liberating experience. The process of exploring and (pro)claiming my new-to-me pronouns has felt so liberating, in fact, that I am now ready to write about them in this book, which may have a wide readership.

As with everything, my choice-making regarding my pronouns is always framed by structural privileges and oppressions. My Whiteness, for example, protects me in ways that trans* women and feminine-of-center[7] people of color cannot assume in a U.S. society steeped by White supremacy and anti-Blackness. For example, it should come as no surprise that of the known murders of trans* people in the United States, most are trans* women of color. I also am highly cognizant that my economic and educational privilege, coupled with my secure employment as a tenure-track faculty member, provides me a level of protection as a transfeminine person that many of my trans* sisters do not have.[8] And still, in a highly conservative field such as education,[9] and in a profession like student affairs that has an extreme lack of trans* professionals,[10] (pro)claiming my pronouns, and determining when, where, and with whom I use them, makes this (pro)claiming all the more affirming and important.

Simply put, I agree with Jaekel and Catalano when they proclaim, "We see trans* inclusion as far more than asking pronouns."[11] However, I argue trans* inclusion must begin with providing spaces in which, and opportunities for, trans* people to self-determine our own genders in our own ways. If we do not have spaces or platforms to be who we are on our own terms, then we continue to lack agency in how we might (pro)claim our genders, and our dream of being seen as who we are is, yet again, deferred. Thus, I argue that while it certainly is not a panacea in and of itself—a point Jaekel and Catalano make—providing space for sharing one's pronouns can be a deeply liberating and vitally important platform in a U.S. cultural context replete with trans* oppression.

Social Justice, the Struggle Toward Freedom, and Our Commitment to Inclusive Practice

In 2015, members of the American College Personnel Association (ACPA) and NASPA collaborated to update the professional competency areas for the field of student affairs. One of the competency areas included in this revision was titled Social Justice and Inclusion, and parrots Bell's writing by explicitly defining *social justice* "as both a process and a goal that includes the knowledge, skills, and dispositions needed to create learning environments that foster equitable participation of all groups and seeks to address issues of oppression, privilege, and power."[12] In framing social justice as both process and product, student affairs educators recognize the ongoing importance of seeking equity, even if that seeking does not lead to perfect solutions.

Further implicit in the field's framing of social justice is the notion that equity, justice, and freedom for marginalized populations, including trans* people, will continue to be a constant struggle.[13] Jaekel and Catalano rightly point to the ongoing struggle of assuming the sharing of proper pronouns can be a stand-in for trans* inclusion. However, if one is to recognize the constant struggle of trans* liberation, and if one is to embrace movements toward social justice and inclusion as "both a process and a goal," then do we not owe it to those most on the margins to have spaces and opportunities to (pro) claim ourselves as fully human? And, moreover, does this not start with our abilities to assert our proper pronouns in whatever way we want, knowing we can change, augment, or shift these in various contexts and at various times? I greatly appreciate Jaekel and Catalano interrogating how people have used the sharing of proper pronouns as the one and only practice toward trans* inclusion. *And* I wonder, if we do not start with this practice, then how can we get where we all must go? It is not the *only* practice we must do, but it is *an important* practice as we struggle toward the dream of trans* inclusion.

What Happens to a Dream Deferred?

I began my response to Jaekel and Catalano's essay with a line from a Langston Hughes poem that asks the question: What happens to a dream deferred? In thinking about my life and work, I have a variety of dreams. I dream of trans* liberation in higher education, complete with environments, programs, offices, and curricula that center our needs and desires as a highly marginalized community.[14] I dream of worlds in which I and other trans* girls, women, and feminine people do not have to encounter the systemic sexism, racism, colonialism, classism, and trans* oppression that requires us to defend who we are as women and feminine people. I dream for my gender to not engulf or consume all of who I am. I dream of seeing more women, girls, and feminine people like myself live their days free from myriad forms of violence that too readily frame our existence. And I dream for my fellow student affairs educators to do what the small group of queer, trans*, and accomplice friends who I e-mailed in the spring of 2017 did: Provide me the space, time, and ability to explore who I am as a trans* person.

I also have many worries about what happens when the dreams I and other trans* people have are deferred in higher education. Going back to Hughes' words, I worry the deferral of our dreams will cause them to "dry up … fester like sores … sag like a heavy load … or explode."[15] I worry that the effects of our dreams of trans* liberation will mean the continuation of negative consequences for our health and well-being,[16] to say nothing of our continued disengagement from educational environments[17] or continued risk and alienation throughout the public sphere.[18] I also worry that—as Jaekel and Catalano argued—talking about those things that are heralded as "best practices" in student affairs (e.g., gender-inclusive bathrooms, proper pronoun and name policies, and including gender identity/expression in nondiscrimination policies) may be increasing in frequency but is doing little to impact the livability of trans* students' lives.

And with all my dreams, and despite all my worries, I argue that if we are to recognize social justice as a process and a goal, and if we are to continually engage in the constant struggle toward freedom, we may do well to view the sharing of proper pronouns during introductory activities as a necessity. This does not mean we as trans* people must always share of ourselves, nor does it mean we must do so in ways that are unsafe, or with people we know will not recognize us as worthy of dignity and respect. However, it means that we view the sharing of proper pronouns as an act of self-care, which, as Audre Lorde wrote, "is not self-indulgence, it is self-preservation, and that is a [necessary] act of political warfare."[19]

Discussion Questions

1. If you share/ask others to share their proper pronouns, why do you do so? If you do not, why not?
2. How can you create strategies and practices where sharing your proper pronouns is a part of an educational process rooted in unlearning binary notions of gender?
3. How can these essays about the "best practice" of using proper pronouns during introductory activities be transferred to interrogate other "best practices" and/or binaries in student affairs and higher education?

Notes

1. Hughes, L. (1969). *Selected poems of Langston Hughes* (5th ed.). New York, NY: Alfred A. Knopf, p. 268.

2. Nicolazzo, Z. (2017). *Trans* in college: Transgender students' strategies for navigating campus life and the institutional politics of inclusion.* Sterling, VA: Stylus; Nicolazzo, Z. (2016). "Just go in looking good": The resilience, resistance, and kinship-building of trans* college students. *Journal of College Student Development, 57*(5), 538–556.

3. Nicolazzo, *Trans* in College*, p. 140

4. Bell, L. A. (2007). Theoretical foundations for social justice education. In M. Adams, L. A. Bell, & P. Griffin (Eds.), *Teaching for diversity and social justice* (2nd ed., pp. 1–14). New York, NY: Routledge.

5. Davis, A. Y. (2016). *Freedom is a constant struggle: Ferguson, Palestine, and the foundations of a movement.* Chicago, IL: Haymarket Books.

6. ACPA & NASPA. (2015). *Professional competency areas for student affairs educators.* Washington DC: Authors. Retrieved from https://www.naspa.org/images/uploads/main/ACPA_NASPA_Professional_Competencies_FINAL.pdf

7. For a definition of *feminine-of-center*, as well as other (trans*)gender-related terminology, please see Nicolazzo, *Trans* in College*, pp. 165–170.

8. Grant, J. M., Mottet, L. A., Tanis, J., Harrison, J., Herman, J. L. & Keisling, M. (2011). *Injustice at every turn: A report of the national transgender discrimina-*

tion survey. Washington DC: National Center for Transgender Equality and National Gay and Lesbian Task Force.

9. Pinar, W. F. (1998). Introduction. In W. F. Pinar (Ed.), *Queer theory in education* (pp. 1–47). Mahwah, NJ: Lawrence Erlbaum Associates.

10. Jourian, T. J., Simmons, S. L., & Devaney, K. (2015). "We are not expected": Trans* educators (re)claiming space and voice in higher education and student affairs. *TSQ: Transgender Studies Quarterly, 2*(3), 431–446.

11. Jaekel, K., & Catalano D. C. J., this volume, p. 151.

12. ACPA & NASPA. *Professional competency areas for student affairs educators*, p. 30.

13. Davis, *Freedom is a constant struggle.*

14. Spade, D. (2015). *Normal life: Critical trans politics, administrative violence, and the limits of law* (2nd ed.). Durham, NC: Duke University Press.

15. Hughes, *Selected Poems of Langston Hughes*, p. 268.

16. Grant et al., *Injustice at every turn.*

17. Nicolazzo, Z, Marine, S. B, & Galarte, F. J. (2015). Introduction. *TSQ: Transgender Studies Quarterly, 2*(3), 367–375.

18. Landsbaum, C. (2017, February 24). Laverne Cox explains why anti-trans bathroom legislation isn't really actually about bathrooms. *The Cut.* Retrieved from https://www.thecut.com/2017/02/laverne-cox-explains-what-bathroom-laws-are-really-about.html

19. Lorde, A. (1988). *A burst of light, essays.* Ann Arbor, MI: Firebrand Books, p. 131.

9

How Should Institutions Support Students With Marginalized Identities? What Practices Are Essential for the Establishment of Safe and Inclusive Learning Environments?

What Is Equitable? Engaging the Four Is of Oppression to Support Students of Color

Jonathan A. McElderry and Stephanie Hernandez Rivera

Colleges and universities across the country continue to struggle supporting students with marginalized identities, including (but not limited to) gender, race, ethnicity, sexual identity, ability level, socioeconomic status, religious identity, and citizenship status. The creation of safe and inclusive learning environments necessitates the adoption of equitable policies and practices. In this essay, we assert that equity-oriented organizational transformation requires understanding oppression as functioning on multiple levels: ideological (perpetuation of dominant narratives), institutional (policies and practices that enact and reinforce dominant ideologies), interpersonal (the way groups and individuals interact), and internalized (how ideologies are internalized).[1] Recognizing multiple levels of oppression allows student affairs educators to gain a more holistic understanding of student success impediments, which in turn promotes engagement in interventions that dismantle oppression, support students, and create inclusive environments. In this essay, we provide examples of the four Is of oppression and identify equity-oriented policies and practices that can be implemented at each level. Considering the immense scope of this topic, this essay centers people of color, while simultaneously incorporating the ways different interlocking identities affect how students are treated and oppressed on campus. It is necessary for student affairs educators to develop an understanding of students' experiences of oppression in a way that is holistic and considers multiple forms of oppression.

The Four Is of Oppression

Current conversations on supporting students of marginalized identities have focused on how to create more inclusive spaces/environments. When reflecting on what inclusion represents, we must consider who it is for. The practice of inclusion, perceived as serving marginalized communities, has also been used to make dominant groups more comfortable with including the "other." Our professional experiences in higher education range from working at small, private liberal arts institutions to large, flagship, predominantly White institutions within the functional areas of cultural centers; diversity, equity, and inclusion; Greek life; student conduct; and student organization advising. Through these experiences we have witnessed that identity-focused centers intended to serve the needs of a specific community (or communities) also feel they must communicate to the public that "everyone is welcome in this space." This rhetoric allows dominant-identity students to feel more comfortable with marginalized student populations having their own space, hence making inclusion something that is contingent on the approval of dominant groups. Examining the four Is of oppression encourages an interrogation of how institutions and those who work within them foster inequitable and hostile environments for students, centering efforts to attend to the needs of the marginalized over the comfortability of the privileged. Although the scope of transformational change needed to foster equitable higher education institutions may exceed the influence of student affairs educators, it is important to note that we do have power. We suggest ways student affairs educators may harness their power to address the four Is of oppression, which are often overlapping and intersectional within higher education, rarely operating in isolation.

Ideological Oppression

Colleges and universities must acknowledge and be held accountable for the history of oppression experienced by different communities within institutions of higher education. Examples of institutional practices that perpetuate dominant ideologies of exclusion include founding date celebrations that don't acknowledge different dates of institutional access for diverse groups of students and mascots that honor colonial and racist imagery. Policies and practices for naming campus buildings and erecting monuments also serve as a form of ideological oppression. Building names and campus memorials recognize individuals who have been identified (mainly by those with privileged identities) as making contributions to society or the institution; however, in some cases, these individuals have also committed atrocities against specific groups, espoused oppressive beliefs, or engaged in discriminatory practices. Preserving building names and monuments that honor individuals who advocated racism and discrimination is a form of ideological oppression that upholds dominant historical narratives.

It is also necessary for institutions to consider the ways they have continued to benefit from colonization and existence on land stolen from Indigenous populations. Recognizing Christopher Columbus Day and Thanksgiving are examples of ways institutions continue to participate in national efforts to reinforce dominant ideological narratives and make invisible the experiences of Indigenous students. When colleges and universities institutionalize Indigenous images and people as mascots and symbols within their campus, they neglect to recognize the historical trauma experienced by Indigenous groups.[2]

In recent years, many students and faculty have challenged higher education institutions to acknowledge their racist histories and take tangible actions to create safe and inclusive learning environments. For example, in 2017, Duke University received media attention for removing a statue of Confederate general Robert E. Lee from the Duke Chapel. Before acting, Duke University's president, Vincent E. Price, sought counsel from the board of trustees, students, faculty, and staff. President Price stated, "I took this course of action to protect Duke Chapel, to ensure the vital safety of students and community members who worship there, and above all to express the deep and abiding values of our university."[3] The University of Texas at Austin also removed several Confederate statues in the middle of the night, 10 days before fall 2017 classes were to begin. The university president justified the actions by stating that the statues "run counter to the university's core values."[4] He later elaborated that institutions cannot choose their history but do have a hand in how it is celebrated on each of their campuses.

Changing building names and removing statues disrupts ideological oppression by showing that the ideals and sentiments of those previously honored are in direct conflict with the current culture, mission, and vision of the institution. Student affairs educators must also acknowledge and disrupt the perpetuation and reinforcement of dominant ideologies in their work (e.g., review and alter policies for honoring individuals, program selection criteria, etc.). Additionally, professionals can call attention to and interrupt ideological oppression by actively participating in committees charged with planning campus celebrations, developing institutional recognition policies and establishing university protocols.

Institutional Oppression

Institutional oppression occurs when campuses adopt policies and practice that enact and reinforce dominant ideologies. Student affairs professionals can address institutional oppression by identifying and challenging oppressive department/division policies, media content, events, and programs. For example, Sara Ahmed describes *document diversity* as using documents such as mission statements, admissions materials, and/or websites to give the appearance of inclusive environments without actually engaging in the action or effort needed to truly foster inclusion and equity on campus.[5] An institution can claim a value of "respect" and describe itself as "an open, inclusive, supportive, and sustainable community" in a mission statement yet refrain from implementing practices and policies that intentionally support those who experience racialized or other forms of oppression. Policies and practices should reflect the values an institution espouses, and websites and printed materials should not attempt to showcase diversity without the adoption of policies and practices that support students of color. These actions can create an atmosphere of distrust among current and prospective students who observe campus departments or the broader institution using them as a marketing tool.

In addition to interrogating document diversity practices, student affairs professionals can also intervene in institutional oppression and support students of color by critically analyzing the policies and practices that guide their work. An example of reflective practice centered on institutional oppression is a student conduct professional's critical analysis of how marginalized students are supported through disciplinary policy and practice, particularly in the adjudication of hate speech and acts. *Hate speech* has been defined in various ways. Pulling from a diverse set of definitions, we describe it as speech and acts that cause harm to target marginalized identity groups through "intimating discrimination and violence."[6] The effects of hate speech and acts can cause emotional and mental harm and distress. Additionally, hate speech is not just dislike for a specific historically marginalized group, but represents an antigroup discourse of exclusion and inferiority.

Hate speech is a contentious topic; claims of censorship arise in response to calls for bans on hate speech.[7] The First Amendment "protects" freedom of speech and assembly and prevents the government from limiting the expression of citizens and their personal views, regardless of how unpopular the opinion may be.[8] However, the government can regulate or hold speech accountable when it constitutes "fighting words" and has the potential to incite violence;[9] the government can also regulate speech or assembly by limiting the time, place, or manner in which the speech is made. Accommodationists have urged a middle ground approach;[10] however, that is difficult to accomplish when hate speech holds both material and psychological implications.

At times, institutional policies protect students of privilege who participate in hate speech and acts by encouraging "teachable moments" in the form of an educational sanction as a form of punishment. However, a teachable moment can also come in the form of a material consequence. Institutions should develop policies that hold students accountable when their actions and language do not reflect the values of the institution, particularly when these acts and behaviors mentally, emotionally, or physically target historically marginalized groups and hold the potential to incite violence. Requiring students to attend a cultural event or write a reflective response on their hate language and acts is not a severe enough consequence, especially when that language can impact their peers' success and overall well-being. In this example, an analysis of student conduct sanctioning policies and protocols may reveal the role the student code of conduct plays in perpetuating institutional oppression.

Another example of institutional oppression emerges upon examination of the University of Missouri's response to the fall 2015 campus protests organized primarily by Black students. In the aftermath of the protests, the institution updated its policies relating to freedom of speech. One of the policies states that individuals should not "interfere with, or prevent (a) the orderly conduct of a University function or activity,"[11] which includes meetings and classes. Should individuals participate in this behavior, they will be susceptible to arrest.[12] This policy update falls in accordance with the law as freedom of speech can be regulated to specific places and times. In the case of the University of Missouri, however, one must ask if these policies criminalize Black students with the threat of arrest for exercising their freedom of speech, particularly since the revision of these policies occurred post-fall 2015.[13] The updated policies were distributed to the entire campus community and one policy specifically referenced "Camping on Campus," which was a tactic used by student protesters in the fall of 2015. Although two instances of Black students being called the n-word on campus were one of several contributing factors that sparked the fall 2015 campus protests, the university didn't seem to respond to the use of this discriminatory language with the formation of a committee to define *hate speech* and the various consequences that could be supported by law. Additionally, these incidents of overt racism did not prompt the university to send a mass e-mail that communicated to the community what hate speech was or how students could be held accountable for it, similar to the freedom of speech policy updates distributed in response to the campus protest.

Freedom of speech and expression is important; however, it should not be used to protect students with privileged identities at the expense of students with minoritized identities. It would be irresponsible for institutions to confuse freedom of speech with hate speech. Dominant ideologies are present throughout institutions and policies and practices send messages to the campus community regarding what is acceptable. When the behavior of individual students and organizations creates a hostile and even potentially violent campus climate for others, campus policies and protocols should be leveraged to inform immediate action. A lack of clear campus policies on issues related to hate speech, for example, perpetuates institutional oppression, allowing students to assume that they can engage in these acts and behaviors without consequence, even if that is not necessarily the case. Student affairs educators should actively seek to participate in campus conversations to define, differentiate, and create policies that establish clear measures of accountability and demonstrate what is acceptable within an institution and what is not. Disrupting institutional oppression necessitates developing protocols and practices that protect student dignity and promote student learning, even if it means expelling students. Additionally, campus administrators should be cautious of developing policies that criminalize particular groups, while protecting others.

Interpersonal Oppression

Interpersonal dynamics, defined as patterns of interaction and communication between campus community members, represent another level of oppression that must be addressed in the interest of supporting students with marginalized identities. Interpersonal oppression is manifested in many forms, including harassment, microaggressions, and stereotypes perpetuated by faculty, staff, and peers. Dominant ideologies that exist about students of color make them susceptible to microaggressions that can cause them to feel inferior or *othered*. Responding to questions such as "What are you?"

to determine one's racial identity, fending off requests to touch one's hair because it is "different," or absorbing descriptions of a women's behavior as "aggressive" are just a few of many examples of microaggressions that marginalized students continually face. For students of color, microaggressions are exhausting and mentally and emotionally burdensome. Student affairs educators should work to educate themselves on the various ways students of color can be microaggressed and find strategies of intervening when applicable. They can also work to educate students and colleagues they work with on understanding microaggressions, their impact, and possible interruptions and responses. Microaggressions occur in interactions every day and they detract from the well-being of students of color and their ability to feel like they belong in the campus community.

Students of color can also face more overt forms of interpersonal oppression through harassment. Increased usage of social media among college students has unearthed and shined a national spotlight on racist events occurring on college campuses. In November 2017, a White female student at the University of Hartford was expelled and faced criminal charges after her social media post documenting harassment of her Black roommate went viral. The expelled student stated in the video, "After one and half months of spitting in her coconut oil, putting moldy clam dip in her lotions, rubbing used tampons on her backpack, putting her toothbrush places where the sun doesn't shine, I can finally say goodbye to Jamaican Barbie."[14] The expelled student's roommate had reported feeling unwelcome in the room and sought medical attention because she was ill. In a second example of a viral video garnering national headlines, members of the Sigma Alpha Epsilon chapter at the University of Oklahoma were captured on camera in February 2015 using racialized language, vowing to never let a Black person into the fraternity and making references to lynching, sparking conversations on race and its intersection with Greek organizations on college campuses.[15] Soon after the release of the video, the university expelled two members of the fraternity and removed the Sigma Alpha Epsilon chapter from the campus.

These examples of hostile campus climates point to the need for a larger conversation about the impact of interpersonal oppression on sense of belonging for students of color. The unchecked perpetuation of microaggressions may lead to more overt acts of racism such as those witnessed at the Universities of Oklahoma and Hartford. When students aren't held accountable for their language and behaviors, it creates an environment of hostility for students of color and will likely influence the ways White students and students of color formulate relationships with each other. As previously mentioned, campus administrators must send a message that these behaviors are unacceptable through appropriate accountability measures; in the cases of the University of Hartford and the University of Oklahoma, accountability was achieved through expulsion.

There are many programs, initiatives, and retreats that can be developed to foster critical consciousness among students. Student affairs educators can provide a space for students to address interpersonal interactions such as micro-aggressions through group training or one-on-one interactions. Professionals can also demonstrate their support for students of color by working to establish rapport and building genuine relationships, attending events hosted by cultural student organizations, and collaborating on programs. Investing in the well-being of students of color is likely to increase their comfort in seeking support when negative interpersonal interactions do occur.

Additionally, there are numerous national and local conferences in higher education that allow student affairs professionals opportunities to expand their critical consciousness and strengthen their capacity to disrupt interpersonal oppression. Each year thousands of higher education professionals attend national and regional events sponsored by American College Personnel Association (ACPA)–College Student Educators International, NASPA–Student Affairs Administrators in Higher Education, Critical Race Studies in Education Association (CRSEA), National Conference on Race and Ethnicity (NCORE), and Creating Change to present best practices in the field, as well as learn from practitioners and scholars doing the work. When conferences are not financially accessible to student affairs educators, self-education through books, articles, and online resources is always an option. The onus is on individuals to seek out professional development and learn from their colleagues within the field; this essay references a vast number of resources that student affairs educators can examine in the interest of developing their critical consciousness and ability to support students. Professionals can impact interpersonal interactions within their spheres of influence when they consider the ways they facilitate critical thinking in their work.

Internalized Oppression

The internalization of oppressive ideologies occurs in both dominant and marginalized communities. Student affairs professionals must examine the ways they have internalized dominant ideologies, stigmas, and representations of various groups and how these internalized beliefs manifest themselves in their interpersonal interactions, as well as the development of institutional policies and practices that perpetuate oppression. Student affairs professionals who are White can internalize dominant ideologies in ways that reaffirm their own privilege and prevent them from working to understand

and dismantle the structures in place that privilege their communities while marginalizing others.

For example, internalized, color-blind ideologies allow individuals to deny racism as a factor that can impede the success of communities of color, contributing to the development of advising relationships and practices (e.g., admissions criteria that prohibit the race-conscious review of applications) that fail to acknowledge the lived experiences of oppression of students of color.[16] Additionally, internalized deficit notions of thinking regarding specific communities of color, such as Black, Latinx, and Indigenous students, can affect the ways professionals think about and provide services to these students.[17] Interpersonal interactions between staff who have internalized deficit views and students of color may lead students to internalize deficit notions of thinking about themselves and their own communities. Hence, it is imperative for student affairs professionals to provide advising, counseling, and services that consider the ways students have internalized oppression, but also how the professionals themselves have internalized ways of thinking about particular communities.

The community cultural wealth model addresses the ways that perceived deficits placed upon communities of color are actually assets and sources of wealth.[18] The model minority myth, often associated with different communities in the Asian diaspora, can also have detrimental effects on students.[19] These myths have placed Asian communities in closer approximation to Whiteness and in doing so have masked the varying forms of racism experienced by those within this diaspora. This can lead student affairs educators to fail to consider the racism and pressures experienced by Asian students and prevent them from providing services and initiatives that focus on this community. Additionally, it can affect the ways professionals counsel and advise Asian students based on expectations they have of their community.

Professionals of color must also work to grapple with their own internalization of dominant ideologies that has manifested itself in different ways. Professionals of color may need to work to disrupt their own deficit ways of thinking about themselves and their communities and in this recognize not only how they are oppressed by a system but also how they may be oppressing students who have shared racial and/or ethnic identities and students of color outside of their identities. As professionals, we both have had to grapple with our own internalization of dominant ideologies as well as how we have perpetuated these ideologies onto our students. It is necessary to continue to find pathways of education and critical reflection in order to disrupt dominant ideologies, but also prevent continued harm to students of color.

Women of color, queer students of color, transgender students of color, low-income students of color, and others who identify with multiple marginalized, intersecting identities face unique challenges as they navigate institutional structures that oppress multiple dimensions of their identities. Dominant ideologies and narratives are socialized and ingrained within all people, and it takes a commitment and purposefully created space to think about ourselves and how we ingest and perpetuate oppression. Microaggressions and overt acts of racism/sexism can psychologically affect a student's experience through forms of racial battle fatigue, exhaustion, taxation, and imposter syndrome.

Implementing spaces where students can discuss the internalization of these oppressions and how they navigate them is beneficial for students with marginalized identities. Counterspaces and self-preservation spaces have been utilized by communities of color to communicate their experiences in a way that will be validated by those with similar or shared experiences. Gloria Anzaldúa also discusses the complexity of interlocking identities as a queer Chicana and visibly Brown woman and the development of consciousness and cultural *choques* (or clashes) happening in a borderland.[20] These borderlands allow for the development of critical consciousness and creating transformation. In our professional roles within identity centers, we have facilitated and developed these types of spaces, including women of color initiatives and Black men initiatives, utilizing theory and literature to support our work and consider the complexity of identity.[21] These spaces can be utilized intentionally for marginalized students to discuss the ways they internalize and experience oppression.

Rather than relying on students to create their own space, student affairs educators should proactively develop these spaces in collaboration with students. Additionally, professionals should be conscious of their identity and how it can positively and negatively influence interactions with students of color. For example, a White woman can support women of color in creating a space focused on their identity, but the content and what the students need that space to look like should be determined by the students. Understanding the experiences of marginalized students can be achieved by researching literature on their experiences, utilizing theory, hearing their voices, and developing genuine relationships.

Conclusion

If institutions seek to support students of marginalized identities, it becomes their responsibility to ask "What is equitable?" Equity ensures that we aren't simply making or creating space to include others, while maintaining the status quo, but that institutions undergo a process of transformation. This requires commitment, time, patience, and willingness to engage in the critical examination of ideological, institutional, interpersonal, and internalized forms of oppression. Student affairs professionals can begin this work by advocating within their sphere of influence, educating themselves and engaging in a self-reflexive practice, collaborating with campus colleagues to examine the four Is of oppression, and speaking up and out when necessary. The work needed to truly support students of marginalized identities means a commitment from the entire campus community; it requires a divestment from structures that subordinate and a commitment to critical thought and an ideology of equity. This collective commitment, however, does not remove the individual accountability of student affairs educators to examine their own investment in oppression. It is appropriate for student affairs professionals to reflect on all the ways they perpetuate dominant ideologies, cultivate oppressive institutional cultures, foster oppressive interpersonal dynamics, and enact internalized oppression as a way of life. The four Is framework serves as a productive starting point for identifying policies, practices, initiatives, and documents that need to be dismantled, created, and/or changed in the interest of constructing more equitable and inclusive environments for students of color.

Discussion Questions

1. In what ways do you see the four Is of oppression manifested in your campus community? In the specific area where you work?
2. When reflecting on the four Is of oppression, what is within your sphere of power and/or control with respect to fostering change? What are some of the ways you can make short and long-term change related to disrupting the four Is of oppression?
3. What books, articles, documents, and blogs could you review over the next year to enhance your awareness and consciousness related to supporting students from marginalized communities?

Notes

1. Chinook Fund by COFIE. (2010). The four "Is" of oppression. *Colorado Funders for Inclusiveness and Equity.* Retrieved from http://www.coloradoinclusivefunders.org/uploads/1/1/5/0/11506731/the_four_is_of_oppression.pdf

2. Evans-Campbell, T. (2008). Historical trauma in American Indian/Native Alaska communities: A multilevel framework for exploring impacts on individuals, families, and communities. *Journal of Interpersonal Violence, 23*(3), 316–338.

3. Price, V. (2017, August 19). Duke removes Robert E. Lee statue from chapel entrance. Retrieved from https://today.duke.edu/2017/08/duke-removes-robert-e-lee-statue-chapel-entrance

4. Watkins, M. (2017, August 21). UT-Austin removes confederate statues in the middle of the night. *Texas Tribune.* Retrieved from https://www.texastribune.org/2017/08/20/ut-austin-removing-confederate-statues-middle-night/

5. Ahmed, S. (2007). "You end up doing the document rather than doing the doing": Diversity, race equality, and the politics of documentation. *Ethnic Racial Studies, 30*(4), 590–609.

6. Walrdron, J. (2012). *The harm in hate speech.* Cambridge, MA: Harvard University Press.

7. Massaro, T. M. (1990). Equality and freedom of expression: The hate speech dilemma. *William and Mary Law Review, 32,* 211.

8. https://www.aclu.org/united-states-bill-rights-first-10-amendments-constitution#firstamendment

9. Massaro, Equality and freedom of expression.

10. Ibid.

11. Basi, C. (2017, April 27). New policies designed to help campus community, visitors understand rights related to protests and use of public spaces. Retrieved from: http://munews.missouri.edu/news-releases/2017/0427-new-policies-designed-to-help-campus-community-visitors-understand-rights-related-to-protests-and-use-of-public-spaces/

12. Ibid.

13. In the fall of 2015, the University of Missouri became national news when a graduate student went on a hunger strike to combat the rampant racism on campus. Through his work and many other students on campus, the president of the University of Missouri system resigned, as well as the chancellor of the local campus.

14. Bailey, C. (2017, November 2). Hartford student expelled, faces hate crime charge for harassing black roommate. *NBC News.* Retrieved from: https://www.nbcnews.com/news/nbcblk/hartford-student-expelled-faces-hate-crime-harassing-black-roommate-n816556

15. DeSantis, N. (2016, February 16). Fraternity releases findings on racist chant by Oklahoma chapter. *The Chronicle of Higher Education.* Retrieved from https://www.chronicle.com/blogs/ticker/fraternity-releases-findings-on-racist-chant-by-oklahoma-chapter/108548

16. Bonilla-Silva, E. (2010). *Racism without racists: Color-blind racism and the persistence of racial inequality in the United States.* Lanham, MD: Rowan & Littlefield.

17. Solorzano, D., Ceja, M., & Yosso, T. J. (2000). Critical race theory, racial microaggressions, and campus racial climate: The experiences of African American college students. *Journal of Negro Education, 69*(1/2), 60–73.

18. Yosso, T. J. (2005). Whose culture has capital? A critical race theory discussion of community cultural wealth. *Race Ethnicity and Education, 8*(1), 69–91.

19. Wing, J. Y. (2007). Beyond black and white: The model minority myth and the invisibility of Asian American students. *The Urban Review, 39*(4), 455–487.

20. Anzaldúa, G. (2012). *Borderlands/La frontera: The new mestiza.* San Francisco, CA: Aunt Lute.

21. Moraga, C., & Anzaldúa, G. (1983). *This bridge called my back: Writing by radical women of color.* New York, NY: Kitchen Table, Women of Color Press.

Intersectionality, Culture, and Mentoring: Critical Needs for Student Affairs Educators

Julie A. Manley White

McElderry and Rivera's use of the four Is of oppression is a useful framework to address the questions of how colleges can best support students with marginalized identities and identify essential practices for establishing safe and inclusive learning environments. I read their essay in the context of my own experience, with over 25 years as a student affairs educator, including in roles such as health educator, women's center leader, club adviser to a variety of student organizations (e.g., feminist groups, lesbian, gay, bisexual, transgender, and queer [LGBTQ] groups, sororities), and diversity trainer.

I find several points of agreement with McElderry and Rivera, including the distinction between equity and inclusion. I, too, have experienced and witnessed pressure on identity-focused centers to make members of dominant identity groups feel comfortable, even when they express hostile viewpoints about the identity group being served. While *diversity, equity,* and *inclusion* are often used interchangeably, it is useful to work from common definitions, and student affairs educators would be wise to seek out campus definitions or to engage in conversations to develop such definitions. Some helpful examples have been developed by California State University East Bay and the University of Michigan.[1]

I would extend McElderry and Rivera's discussion of supporting students and building an equitable campus on three fronts. First, intersectional approaches must also recognize the often overlooked perspectives and identities of students living in poverty and coping with economic inequities and, related, the experiences of many of these students as parent, family caregiver, and/or full-time worker. Second, in their efforts toward equity and inclusion, student affairs educators must attend to the organizational culture of their campus and navigate unspoken social and political norms. Third, new student affairs educators must receive mentoring in order to develop the capacity to effectively engage in this work.

Inclusion of Economic Inequities in Intersectional Approaches

I am in full agreement with McElderry and Rivera that colleges must acknowledge how they benefit from their histories of colonialism and slavery and continued positions of privilege. McElderry and Rivera also emphasize intersectionality and the multiple marginalized identities that students may hold. This is especially important for colleges with strong access missions that serve disproportionate numbers of students from marginalized groups.

Generally, McElderry and Rivera's examples are from predominantly White institutions. A discussion of how best to serve students from marginalized communities would benefit from examining colleges and universities who serve larger numbers of those students, such as community colleges, regional public colleges, tribal colleges, and historically Black colleges and universities. In my experience as a community college educator, a student's most salient identity may not be one of those we typically discuss, such as race or ethnicity; it may be an identity as a person living in poverty or a single parent or a working student. As Gail Mellow, president of LaGuardia Community College, noted when asked about whether her students were likely to protest the types of issues discussed in the preceding essay, "Our students don't have time for that."[2] Mellow explains that many of her students are working two or three part-time jobs just to be able to afford college and support their families. In fact, the profile of today's college students demonstrates that they do not reflect the "traditional" profile typically found at more selective colleges and universities. They tend to fall in the following categories:

- More than one-third are over the age of 25.
- Nearly half are independent from their parents.
- Nearly half are enrolled part-time.
- More than one-third are Black, Hispanic, Asian/Pacific Islander, or American Indian/Alaska Native.
- Forty percent are from families with a total family income of less than 200% of the Federal Poverty Line.
- Three-quarters are working either full-time (32%) or part-time (43%).
- Nearly 1 in 4 are parents, and 1 in 8 are single parents.[3]

Economic injustice and its material effects on students' lives are rarely discussed in the media coverage of college students, who are instead depicted as entitled and swaddled.[4] Likewise, McElderry and Rivera do not discuss how institutions can achieve inclusive and equitable environments for students struggling with financial needs. Economic inequity must be addressed, in light of findings that 61% of college students surveyed met the federal definition of *food insecurity*, and 1 in 4 community college students said they had not eaten for a full day because they didn't have enough money. Further, 28% of community college students in this study were unable to pay their mortgage or rent on time during the past year, and 10% had lost utility services at some point during the past year.[5] These students are far from the well-worn stereotype of poor people as lazy and entitled; one-third of community college students experiencing food and/or housing insecurity were both working and receiving financial aid.[6] Recently, Governor Cuomo introduced legislation requiring food pantries at all New York state public colleges.[7] While this is an important recognition of food insecurity among college students, it must be paired with more comprehensive programs and services to support students with financial need,[8] and these programs must consider how to serve the whole student, who may have multiple marginalized identities. An intersectional approach must be inclusive of the varying and interacting ways in which classism, racism, sexism, heterosexism, ableism, and other forms of marginalization affect students' access to resources. For example, just as student affairs educators must be sure that programs and services are fully accessible to those with differing means of mobility (whether walking or using a wheelchair or another assistive device), we can offer financial supports to students, such as transportation passes, access to healthy food, or child care services. On the policy level, institutions and/or systems can follow the lead of New York, which has allocated funding for comprehensive wraparound services for students, including child and elder care, transportation, health care services, family and employment counseling, and legal aid.[9]

Navigating Organizational Culture

McElderry and Rivera focus their discussion on early-career professionals' roles. While they do not make their rationale explicit, research supports their claims. Early-career student affairs educators sometimes have difficulty navigating campus issues related to oppression, generally coming to a campus job after experiencing mainly theoretical discussions in the graduate classroom, with little exposure to often highly politicized organizational cultures.[10]

As a case study of an incident that could challenge even the most senior student affairs educator, consider the following example. Monroe Community College (MCC) found itself with a labor dispute after a student sent a racist tweet regarding vandalism of the Confederate flag on his truck.[11] The MCC Faculty Association took issue with the president's initial response, which was to state that there could be no disciplinary action because the tweet came from a personal account off-campus.[12] The faculty criticized the lack of force of the statement and two-day gap between the tweet and the president's response. Additionally, the faculty stated that they were not adequately involved in the development of the college's subsequent action plan for inclusion.

This case provides many opportunities for student affairs educators to be involved, including revisions of the code of conduct; providing programs about racism and the history and symbolism of the Confederate flag; and supporting students of color in the aftermath of the tweet. However, given the tensions between faculty and administration, student affairs educators in this kind of scenario would benefit from developing broad coalitions and seeking advice from senior leaders as they strive to support marginalized students.

The Importance of Mentoring

When it comes to institutional politics, early-career student affairs educators often enter a vastly different culture, whether they are coming from a role outside higher education or directly from a preparatory graduate program. As Renn and Jessup-Anger found, "the political nature of student affairs surprised and dismayed many new professionals; one wrote, 'I was disheartened to discover the highly volatile political nature of the campus in which I work.'"[13] While Renn and Hodges recommend that student affairs graduate programs include "more discussion of the potential impact of organizational culture on their transition into a new position and their ability to be a change agent in their new environment,"[14] new professionals will still need mentoring and support from more seasoned professionals on campus.

Early-career student affairs professionals often expect their supervisor to be their mentor; however, a supervisor is often focused on day-to-day operational needs and may not always be able to step back and offer a broader perspective.[15] Seasoned student affairs leaders should develop models that help new professionals connect with mentors who can help them acculturate to the institution and translate theory into practice. For example, new student affairs educators can be matched with a more senior staffer at the institution and/or mid-level and senior leaders can mentor staffers from areas outside their own, so that new staff can benefit from an additional perspective beyond their supervisor. New student affairs educators should also proactively seek mentors who can provide diverse experiences and points of view as they acculturate to a new campus.

In closing, student affairs educators working for fully equitable and inclusive campuses must use an intersectional approach that recognizes often overlooked identities and experiences, including economic inequities; learn to navigate organizational cultures; and participate in mentoring in order to be effective in their efforts.

Discussion Questions

1. Imagine yourself as a student affairs educator in one of the real-life examples described in this essay. How would you respond to support students with marginalized identities? How would you identify and deal with any organizational obstacles that may affect your response?
2. How can student affairs leaders best mentor new student affairs educators? What types of mentoring programs would be most helpful?

Notes

1. Operational definitions for diversity, equity and inclusion and cultural competence. (n.d.). Retrieved from http://www.csueastbay.edu/about/diversity/files/docs/pdfs/operational-def-diversity-equity-inclusion.pdf; University of Michigan, Institute for Social Research. (n.d.). Diversity, equity, and inclusion defined. Retrieved from http://home.isr.umich.edu/diversity/dei-defined/

2. Willen, L. (2015). Amid national diversity protests, community college students dare to dream of debt-free life. *The Hechinger Report*. Retrieved from http://hechingerreport.org/amid-national-diversity-protests-community-college-students-dare-to-dream-of-debt-free-life/

3. U.S. Department of Education. (2015). *Demographic and enrollment characteristics of nontraditional undergraduates: 2011–12*. Washington DC: National Center for Education Statistics, Institute of Education Sciences. Retrieved from https://nces.ed.gov/pubs2015/2015025.pdf

4. Willen, Amid national diversity protests.

5. Wisconsin Hope Lab. (2016). *What we're learning: Food and housing insecurity among college students*. Madison, WI: Wisconsin Hope Lab. Retrieved from http://www.wihopelab.com/publications/Wisconsin_HOPE_Lab_Data%20Brief%2016-01_Undergraduate_Housing%20and_Food_Insecurity.pdf

6. Goldrick-Rab, S., Richardson, J., & Hernandez, A. (2017). *Hungry and homeless in college: Results from a national study of basic needs insecurity in higher education*. Washington DC: Association of Community College Trustees. Retrieved from http://ww.wihopelab.com/publications/Hungry-and-Homeless-in-College-Report.pdf

7. Lederman, D. (2018, January 2). Cuomo wants food pantries at all public colleges. *Inside Higher Ed*. Retrieved from https://www.insidehighered.com/quicktakes/2018/01/02/cuomo-wants-food-pantries-all-public-colleges

8. Goldrick-Rab, S. (2018, January 14). It's hard to study if you're hungry. *The New York Times*. Retrieved from https://www.nytimes.com/2018/01/14/opinion/hunger-college-food-insecurity.html

9. State University of New York. (2016, January 5). *Governor Cuomo expands community schools programs to Adirondack and Onondaga Community Colleges.* Retrieved from https://www.suny.edu/suny-news/press-releases/october-2016/10-5-16-community-schools-program/10-5-16-community-schools-program.html

10. Renn, K. A., & Hodges, J. P. (2007). The first year on the job: Experiences of new professionals in student affairs. *NASPA Journal, 44*(2), 367–391; Renn, K. A., & Jessup-Anger, E. R. (2008). Preparing new professionals: Lessons for graduate preparation programs from the national study of new professionals in student affairs. *Journal of College Student Development, 49*(4), 319–335.

11. Roll, N. (2017, November 7). The racist tweet that won't go away. *Inside Higher Ed.* Retrieved from https://www.insidehighered.com/news/2017/11/07/how-student%E2%80%99s-tweet-led-faculty-labor-dispute

12. Ibid.

13. Renn & Jessup-Anger, Preparing new professionals, p. 326.

14. Renn & Hodges, The first year on the job, p. 38.

15. Ibid.

10

What Role Should Student Affairs Educators Play in Supporting Undocumented Students in the Current Political Climate?

Confronting Anti-Immigration Rhetoric on Campus: A Student Affairs Imperative

Susana M. Muñoz

September 5, 2017, is forever etched in my heart. Before the Trump Administration rescinded the Deferred Action for Childhood Arrivals (DACA) Executive Order, my colleagues and I texted back and forth with each other with analyses of potential glimmers of hope and doom provided by myriad media outlets. I watched Attorney General Jeff Sessions's announcement as it streamed live. Tears of sadness and anger rolled down my face as I heard him describe immigrants as "illegal aliens," misinform the American public, and fuel the anti-immigration rhetoric, stating that the DACA program "denied jobs to hundreds of thousands of Americans by allowing those same illegal aliens to take those jobs."[1] That day I authored two op-ed pieces. The first argued that, "The announcement had nothing to do with national security but more with upholding the values of White supremacy."[2] I illuminated and complicated how elements of the United

States' xenophobic past (e.g., the Chinese Exclusionary Act of 1882 and the Mexican Repatriation Act of 1930) are upheld by contemporary framing of immigrants. The second op-ed essay urged college presidents to act courageously to support DACA students on their college campuses. I explained, "I have witnessed students go through great lengths to fight for their humanity and for their families. College presidents, I urge you to do your part. Higher education can no longer be a spectator in the fight for immigration rights."[3]

While college presidents may set the tone for supporting undocumented students, it is student affairs professionals who execute the work. In my decade of work with undocumented college students, I have witnessed variation in degree of support and awareness of undocumented students on college campuses. While some student affairs professionals will offer compassion and support, on a number of occasions I have received comments such as, "I thought I was supposed to report them [undocumented students]," which clearly illustrates how the anti-immigration rhetoric in U.S. society has influenced student affairs practice. The aim of this essay is to provide the reader with an understanding of issues and challenges facing undocumented students and illuminate how anti-immigration sentiments seep into student affairs practice. Given our sociopolitical climate, the field of student affairs must work diligently to fight anti-immigration rhetoric, which is rooted in White supremacy.

Policy and State Contexts

Readers of this contested issue may have limited awareness about undocumented students. Let me begin by providing an overview of undocumented students in the United States to contextualize this essay. Currently, there are approximately 11.4 million undocumented immigrants living in the United States; children account for about 1.8 million. Each year, high schools in the United States graduate between 50,000 and 65,000 undocumented students.[4] Many undocumented high school students navigate college access in isolation with little to no support or with high school counselors who do not have knowledge about or awareness of college access issues.[5] Context plays an important role in how undocumented students navigate college access. For example, only 19 states (California, Colorado, Connecticut, Florida, Hawaii, Illinois, Kansas, Maryland, Minnesota, Nebraska, New Jersey, New Mexico, New York, Oklahoma, Oregon, Rhode Island, Texas, Utah, and Washington) have passed in-state resident tuition policies that make certain undocumented students eligible for in-state tuition. California, Colorado, New Mexico, Texas, and Washington have also enacted policies that allow undocumented and DACA students to receive state financial aid, making college access more feasible given that applying for federal financial aid is not an option.

Conversely, nine states (Alabama, Arizona, Georgia, Indiana, Missouri, Montana, North Carolina, Ohio, and South Carolina) have passed legislation to prohibit undocumented students from paying in-state tuition rates. In fact, Alabama, Georgia, and South Carolina have enacted policies that specifically bar undocumented students from enrolling in some or all of its public higher education institutions. It is important to highlight these varying state contexts because student affairs administrators' support of undocumented college students can depend on local context and anti-immigration sentiments. Variability can be found even within a particular state. Contreras addressed the experiences of undocumented students in the state of Washington by specifically questioning variability of experiences by institutional type.[6] Her study revealed community colleges and four-year institutions varied in levels of financial need and support, awareness of support services and resources, and quality of validation from campus professionals. This variability inadvertently categorizes institutions as undocufriendly or hostile campuses for undocumented students. Faculty and staff play an important role in shaping these campus environments.[7] In some instances, student affairs administrators develop fears of job retaliation for serving undocumented students. Student affairs professionals must question, "Are these my own personal fears or are these fears reproduced within my work or institutional culture?" Acknowledging that fears may be rooted in anti-immigration sentiments allows for one to consider the ways in which White supremacy is reproduced. What administrators, faculty, and staff need to keep in mind is that if a campus has opened its door to undocumented students, then it has an ethical obligation to ensure undocumented students receive adequate services and support. Not doing so constitutes institutional negligence.

Issues Facing Undocumented Students

Support for undocumented students must consider multifaceted campus contexts and the intersectional nature of students' social identities. While most undocumented students are Latinx, first generation, and have lived in the United States the majority of their lives, the lived experiences of undocumented immigrants are heterogeneous. To frame our understanding of support, I address three areas of need: access to higher education, how students make meaning of their legality, and campus climate. I also share short narratives from the undocumented students who have participated in my previous studies to contextualize these topics. As a caveat, I acknowledge that I collected these data before the 2016 presidential election and before DACA was rescinded.

Access to Higher Education

Even when higher education institutions implement state policies regarding undocumented student access, there is no real accountability as to how higher education institutions are employing, training, and tracking their effectiveness related to these policies. For example, Jaen from New Mexico—one of the first states to pass an in-state tuition policy—experienced challenges gaining information and access to college.[8] He recalled, "They [high school counselors] never informed me, they never told me, they never said, 'You know what, if you're undocumented you can attend any college as long as you graduate from a high school in New Mexico'."[9] I remember the frustration in his voice as he talked about the myriad barriers he faced in just obtaining accurate knowledge about the college-going process for undocumented students.

Many undocumented students either navigate the college access process through peer support and networks or investigate options on their own. On occasion, students mention a teacher or mentor who helped them to navigate the college access process, but that support was seldom highlighted or openly advertised. Currently, I am noticing a positive change; high schools are paying greater attention to college access for undocumented students. In 2015, during a keynote address for the "Keeping the Dream Alive" conference (where the audience was mainly high school guidance counselors), I fielded numerous questions from audience members, such as the following:

- How do we gain trust from undocumented students?
- How can the state of Colorado centralize financial resources for undocumented students?
- Where can we locate support resources for undocumented students while they are in college?

These questions provided me a sense of hope because so many counselors seemed eager to assist their students in meaningful ways. Student affairs administrators who work in college access sectors should forge relationships with high school personnel around supporting undocumented students by connecting with teachers and counselors who work closely with undocumented students.[10] Admissions officers may also consider forging relationships with community organizations that advocate for immigrant human rights by facilitating college admissions or financial aid workshops. Yet, the question remains, are colleges and universities ready to welcome undocumented students to their campuses?

Making Meaning of Legality

During a Coming Out of the Shadows rally in Chicago, Illinois, I saw undocumented activists stand in front of a podium in the middle of Daley Plaza to retell their narratives with conviction and passion as they self-proclaimed themselves as "undocumented, unafraid, and unapologetic." I stood in awe and wondered how they arrived at that juncture of being "unafraid" and how they made meaning of their legality. These questions became the focus of my book, *Identity, Social Activism, and the Pursuit of Higher Education*, which documented the lives of 13 participants who self-identify as "undocumented and unafraid."[11] From this research, I learned that many of their first messages about their legal status came from their parents and families. As a well-intended gesture, these students were told to hide their status because it may implicate their households to deportation. But more often than not, students talked about the fact that they always knew they didn't have "papers" but never understood the magnitude of its meaning. The meaning-making process of their legal status for some came when they wanted to apply for a driver's license or apply to financial aid to attend college. Not having a social security number meant potential missed opportunities to certain scholarships, ineligibility for federal loans and grants, and inability to study abroad. For many, making sense of their legal status occurred in isolation or with limited knowledge, as Juan from Florida explained:

> I would never say anything at work. I would never say anything to my peers. When I went to [four-year college] I often kept quiet about the stuff. I would rather just deal with it on my own, with my computer, because I just felt that first I had to hide it because again I didn't want the university to find out.[12]

Before many of these social activists discovered other undocumented peers, community organizations, or advocates, active concealment of their legal status was not necessarily by choice. Many students chose to conceal their status because of internalization of stigma, the realities of deportation, and the lack of visible support mechanisms. This poses an important question for student affairs professionals: In what ways do you make your support for undocumented students visible in your work?

The process of disclosing legal status is complex. I encourage student affairs educators to view disclosure of legality as a continuum. Depending on the context, students who self-identify as "unafraid" may also not feel comfortable disclosing their legal status in all spaces and places. As a student activist who participated in civil disobedience in Senator John McCain's office, Yahaira also had to be privy to her context as she navigated her legal status, as she stated:

> For example, just last night I was asked [by someone at work], "You're going to vote, right? I mean you're moving but you're going to vote." And even though I'm very open [about status] I'm thinking about my business and I do some interpreting at courts, so in this context people don't know that I'm undocumented. And I mean I'm not fond of it, but I have to pay the bills somehow, and so kind of finding myself in this situation of, I don't know how to answer this question.[13]

This example depicts the contextual situations in which undocumented students are placed in a "revolving door" mode of disclosure depending on their own risk assessment. For students in my book, civic engagement also facilitated their ability to make meaning of their legality through experiential knowledge of their peer group or by viewing disclosure as a political act of resistance.[14] Some students used their legal status as an educational opportunity, and these students wanted to make an impact in their community. Some wanted to be role models for the younger generation, as David stated:

> I know there are other folks behind me who are thinking about going to school and being able to act as a role model really motivates me and letting them know that they are capable of reaching their goals and going to college. . . . I don't think it's [legal status] hindered me in any way. It's been the opposite. It's fueled me even more. . . . It's a self-empowering feeling of knowing that you are taking initiative to start a conversation, to do workshops—in particular, knowing that you are educating others about a topic they are passionate about.[15]

While undocumented students are often used for educational purposes by having them (re)tell their lived experiences, student affairs professionals need to recognize the emotional labor that is placed on undocumented students by positioning them as the "educators" for their campus community. The ability to (re)tell their lived experiences can be an empowering act; however, students should decide if disclosure is indeed empowering within their particular context.

Another element of legality is its intersection with other salient identities like race, gender, and sexual orientation. I vividly remember Alex questioning, "How do I deal with [W]hite people and how do I make queer people understand immigration?"[16] It is important to note that immigration is a feminist issue, a multirace issue, a multiethnicity issue, and a queer issue, to name a few. While popular media may portray one image of undocumented immigrants, student affairs professionals must recognize intersectionality as part of understanding legal status as a salient identity. For undocumented students to disclose their legal status to student affairs professionals, practitioners need to be seen as visible allies, which means active engagement within the community (inside and outside the walls of higher education). The current political climate has also produced shifts among undocumented students. For some, students who were once comfortable with their legal status are now more cautious about their surroundings and spaces given the anti-immigration rhetoric and heightened presence of deportation. For others, the political climate has motivated them to be more vocal and open about their legal status. College is the most opportune time for students to delve deeply into their salient identities. Student affairs professionals should offer a venue, an opportunity, and a space for undocumented students to grapple with their legality. By creating peer groups around their legality, undocumented students can strengthen their sense of belonging, their ability to unpack their lived experiences and develop agency as they learn to navigate their college environments.

Campus Climate and Institutional Change

Today, colleges and universities differ considerably in how they support undocumented students. For example, in the state of California, University of California System President Janet Napolitano mandated that all institutions in the system create physical offices to support undocumented students. These Dream Resource Centers provide a structural presence for undocumented students and provide support services, such as legal service and financial support. The University of California's structural support is the exception, not the rule, however, as campus support for undocumented students varies widely and depends on leadership, commitment, and resources. For the past three years, I and my research team (Darsella Vigil and Elizabeth Jach) have examined how undocumented/DACA students experience their campus climate at public, private, and community colleges in the state of Colorado, and we have concluded that campus ideology significantly influences how and why student affairs professionals act or don't act in support of undocumented students. In our preliminary findings, senior administrators expressed fear and a belief that their institutions would not protect them if they were to create programs specifically for undocumented students. Some were concerned about backlash from donors and constituents. Lately, I have seen more college presidents support the DACA program and reiterate their institutional commitment to equity and inclusion. The importance of understanding the college president's position on issues related to undocumented students is crucial in creating dialogue and direct action to provide more institutional support and infrastructure to improve college persistence and retention of undocumented students. Possible actions for student affairs professionals include creating a campaign of support by placing "I support undocumented students and families" stickers or posters outside of campus offices, working closely with undocumented student organizations to gauge their needs, providing free legal services for their immigration cases, and establishing an emergency financial fund.

In our climate and culture study, we learned that many campuses displayed forms of racist nativist microaggressions such as institutional ignorance, which helps to uphold White supremacy. Institutional ignorance describes the ambivalent stance colleges and universities take in supporting undocumented students. If student affairs administrators lack knowledge about undocumented students, they may be ill-informed or ill-equipped to serve this population. In one case, undocumented students were classified as international students by their campus. Silvia explained, "They always label me as an international student, I hate that. . . because their experience is completely different than mine." The majority of undocumented students have obtained most of their education in the United States, and placing them in an office that serves students who reside in other countries erases their lived experiences in the United States. Many undocumented students detailed incidents where they had to explain to student affairs administrators the nuances of DACA, which places additional emotional labor on the student. The lack of knowledge and feelings of invisibility leaves students feeling hesitant to disclose their legal status. One way to remedy this issue is to bring together a university team to conduct DREAMzone ally training. This training could specifically discuss the national landscape of immigration as well as college- and university- specific resources, support, and initiatives. Colleges and universities should consider incorporating trainings about undocumented college students as part of new faculty and staff orientation.

What Does Support Look Like for Undocumented Students?

With the end of DACA, undocumented students are struggling to make sense of their future while simultaneously trying to complete their college degrees. This section illustrates actions student affairs educators can take in order to support undocumented students. Again, support for undocumented students varies across institutions and state contexts. While these tips are not exhaustive, I encourage faculty, provosts, vice presidents of student affairs, and college presidents to meet with undocumented students to gauge their specific needs and challenges. Targeting these specific areas primes the campus environment for campus-wide efforts and multiple access points, rather than solely relying on singular efforts from a couple of student affairs units.

Since undocumented students do not qualify for federal financial aid, they enter college on an unequal playing field. Without DACA, many students will lose the employment that has afforded them the ability to pay for their schooling. Colleges and universities should create a student aid fund that could offset diminished earning potential. I also encourage administrators to work with students to review their scholarship awards and institutional aid packages and assist them in securing funding for the remainder of their enrollment in college. The inability to work may create food insecurity and housing affordability concerns. It is imperative that resources and information are available to students. Undocumented immigrants do not qualify for any federally funded social programs to support individuals experiencing poverty. Many community-based programs may be able to assist individuals without legal status.

Undocumented immigrants have always lived under the dark cloud of possible deportation. The difference I see in the policies enacted by the Trump administration is that there is little discretion in how deportation is prioritized. This is evident when hospitals and courthouses are used as targets to apprehend undocumented immigrants.[17] These events may impact how undocumented students perceive law enforcement, and they may be hesitant to report crimes on and off campus. Student affairs professionals can help to facilitate dialogues between campus and community police around how to protect immigrant communities. On my campus, administration has communicated clearly that local and university police will not ask about immigration status and will not collaborate with Immigration and Customs Enforcement (ICE) unless a verified court warrant is presented to the institution. However, college administrators need to understand that the presence of ICE on campus property is disruptive and unhealthy for all students. Researchers have linked immigration raids to increased anxiety and stress.[18] Thus, leaders of institutions of higher education need to think strategically and methodically about how to handle the presence of ICE on campus grounds as it could have long-standing implications for the entire university community.

Mental health needs for undocumented students will increase over the next few years. At this time, it is important for administrators to evaluate the knowledge and awareness of current mental health clinicians on campus. In my interactions with undocumented college students, many hesitate to utilize counseling services because the students assume that "they [counseling] will not know how to help me." Or, when students do use counseling services, they become frustrated that counselors are unaware of the issues and concerns associated with living without legal status in the United States. Counselors should be well trained in the areas of family separation and the trauma associated with deportation, and they should have a keen understanding of immigration rights. I also caution student affairs professionals to avoid overutilizing students to educate the greater university community without any compensation of their time. Some students gain agency when they can use their narrative to create change, but this is emotional work that is often left uncompensated.

Undocumented students will need assistance with their employment planning. They will benefit from guidance from the career center on whether they could possibly establish a limited liability company (LLC) to gain legal employment. Legal services on college campuses are vital to assisting students understand their rights as college students. On my own campus, we have partnered with a local immigration lawyer to work with students on their individual cases or with their families. Knowing the limited capacity of our own campus legal services, my campus has also hired two immigration lawyers to visit with students on a bimonthly basis. We have also opened this service to any current employee. Legislative bills are rapidly being introduced in Congress, so colleges and universities should be keeping a close eye on this progress as well as connecting with their legislative advocates.

Similar to ending sexual assaults on campus, assisting undocumented students should be a campus priority. This means organizing a group of university individuals who have direct contact with the president's leadership to set an agenda and priorities for cultivating an inclusive environment for undocumented students. Undocumented students should no longer struggle in silence on our college campuses. They need authentic support systems, and even more importantly, they need to feel less invisible. Campus leaders need to think deeply about institutionalizing change that includes addressing the campus climate for undocumented students and creating solidarity spaces for students to grapple with their legal identity. Student affairs professionals should be holding their senior leadership accountable by sharing anecdotal data about the experiences of the students they serve. At minimum, all student affairs professionals should have a healthy awareness and understanding of undocumented students on their campuses. Moving toward change and action requires student affairs professionals to question if their unit and programmatic efforts are indeed inclusive of and accessible to undocumented students.

Conclusions

I remember feeling quite defeated in 2010 when the U.S. Senate filibustered the DREAM Act. However, the lessons since that time have been foundational to today's immigration rights movement. We need to give thanks to undocumented and unafraid activists who have inspired a nation to listen and act. These leaders have encouraged undocumented individuals to be unashamed of their legal status and to use their cultural knowledge to resist the anti-immigration rhetoric. Seven years ago, the issue of undocumented youth was barely on anyone's radar. Now, the whole world is paying attention. Higher education has an opportunity to create societal change not only for undocumented college students but also potentially for the 11 million undocumented immigrants living in the United States. We no longer fear engaging in these important conversations within our university community. Can higher education stop the xenophobia and racism that continues to permeate the fabric of our country? Perhaps not, but that does not mean we should stop trying. If higher education is a microcosm of society, then perhaps colleges and universities need to model what we believe society can become: a more just and democratic space. This requires a critical examination of our own historical legacies of White supremacy and how they continue to be upheld on our college campuses. This is no small endeavor, but certainly a necessary change to address the inequities plaguing the United States.

Discussion Questions

1. What is the status of undocumented students' access to higher education and financial aid in your state?
2. What formal supports, if any, are available to students on your campus? What opportunities are there for student affairs professionals to connect undocumented students with these supports?
3. Develop a plan for how to support undocumented students on your campus. Consider one action you can take today, next week, next month, and next semester. How can these steps work toward a vision of supporting undocumented students?

Notes

1. Teague, R. B. (2017, September 5). We cannot admit everyone. Transcript of Jeff Sessions' remarks on ending the DACA program. *Time Magazine.* Retrieved from http://time.com/4927426/daca-dreamers-jeff-sessions-transcript/

2. Muñoz, S. (2017, September 5). White supremacy shows its reach with end of DACA. *The Global Post.* Retrieved from http://www.theglobepost.com/2017/09/05/white-supremacy-us-daca-immigration/

3. Muñoz, S. (2017, September 5). An open letter to college presidents about DACA. *Diverse Issues in Higher Education.* Retrieved from http://diverseeducation.com/article/101138/

4. Pew Research Center. (2015). *5 facts about illegal immigration in the U.S.* Retrieved from http://www.pewresearch.org/fact-tank/2015/11/19/5-facts-about-illegal-immigration-in-the-u-s/

5. Muñoz, S. M. (2015). *Identity, social activism, and the pursuit of higher education: The journey stories of undocumented and unafraid community activists.* New York, NY: Peter Lang.

6. Contreras, F. (2009). Sin papeles y rompiendo barreras: Latino students and the challenges of persisting in college. *Harvard Educational Review, 79*(4), 610–631.

7. Suárez-Orozco, C., Katsiaficas, D, Birchall, O., Alcantar, C. M., Hernandez, E., Garcia, Y., . . . Teranishi, R. T. (2015). Undocumented undergraduates on college campuses: Understanding their challenges and assets and what it takes to make an undocufriendly campus. *Harvard Educational Review, 85*(3), 427–463.

8. Muñoz, *Identity, social activism, and the pursuit of higher education.*

9. Ibid., p. 45

10. Storlie, C. A., & Jach, E. A. (2012). Social justice collaboration in schools: A model for working with undocumented Latino students. *Journal for Social Action in Counseling and Psychology, 4,* 99–116.

11. Muñoz, *Identity, social activism, and the pursuit of higher education.*

12. Muñoz, *Identity, social activism, and the pursuit of higher education,* p. 60.

13. Ibid., p. 64.

14. Ibid., p. 65.

15. Ibid., pp. 77–78.

16. Ibid., p. 110.

17. Yee, V. (2017, October 27). The U.S. nursed an undocumented 10-year-old. Now it may deport her. *The New York Times.* Retrieved from https://www.nytimes.com/2017/10/27/us/immigrant-girl-surgery-detained.html; Yu His Lee, E. (2017, November 15). Immigration arrests at New York courthouses up 900 percent, advocates say. *ThinkProgress.* Retrieved from https://thinkprogress.org/courthouse-arrests-immigrants-00-percent-b15d5155d5bf/

18. Lopez, W. D., Kruger, D. J., Delva, J., Llanes, M., Ledón, C., Waller, A., . . . & Israel B. (2017). Health implications of an immigration raid: Findings from a Latino community in the midwestern United States. *Journal of Immigrant Minority Health, 19*(3), 702–708.

Emphasizing Institution-Wide Strategies to Support Undocumented Students in Higher Education

Maria Sanchez Luna and Mei-Yen Ireland

What should I do? Are they going to change their minds again? Should I send in my renewal application now? How do I know when I should send in my application? If my DACA expired one month ago, what should I do? Will I still qualify for in-state tuition when my DACA expires? What financial resources are available to support my education? Will my scholarships be revoked if DACA is rescinded? When should I tell my employer that my DACA status ended? If DACA ends, will I lose my job? Should my mom and siblings move since the government has my address? What should my family do to stay under the radar?

These are questions undocumented and Deferred Action for Childhood Arrivals (DACA) students confront daily, made even more prominent in the sociopolitical context since the election of President Trump. Susana Muñoz's essay provides an important foundational understanding that we hope all student affairs professionals draw upon in their support of undocumented and DACA students, particularly in this uncertain and vitriolic sociopolitical context. In this response essay we expand upon several of Muñoz's points and perspectives, specifically the new reality of the Trump era, the complexity and diversity within the undocumented community, and the need for institution-wide approaches to supporting undocumented and DACA students.

A New Reality for DACA Students

The discourse of then-candidate Trump's campaign fueled anti-immigrant rhetoric by making xenophobia and fear pillars of his political message. Confronting the uncertain possibility of Trump winning the presidential election, many DACA students were left pondering a series of "what if" scenarios regarding their immigration status. Much of the anti-immigration rhetoric that Trump spewed during the campaign is now a reality. On September 5, 2017, then Attorney General Jeff Sessions announced the end of DACA, leaving many DACA beneficiaries' lives in limbo.

Webs of stressors emerge when wide-ranging immigration policy reform such as the repeal of DACA is announced. Those who applied and were approved for DACA face the possibility of losing their status or deportation and the undoing of the economic, educational, and work-related progress they have made. They must also navigate confusion about immigration deadlines, application costs, and lawyers' fees. There is also fear tied to DACA students' family members, who may now be in danger because their addresses were given to United States Citizenship and Immigration Services during the application process. The new reality of the Trump-era immigration policy is a constant state of confusion and uncertainty about whether to renew or wait for reapplication, what new policies may be enacted or rescinded, and the implications for education tuition and employment.[1] Since DACA began in 2012, DACA students have advanced their education, attained better job prospects, and made important financial decisions. Without DACA status, all gains (e.g., job, education, financial security) will be simultaneously forfeited.

A study investigating undocumented and DACA community college students' emotional reactions to Trump's presidential victory revealed that students experienced intense emotions including shock, fear, sadness, and terror.[2] Students' visceral reactions stem from fear about what's going to happen next, the uncertainty about Trump's policies or the impact of his overt racism, and fear for family members. The current sociopolitical context magnifies and heightens the stressors and anxiety experienced by undocumented and DACA students. The current reality is that undocumented and DACA students "find themselves on continuously shifting ground, calibrating each decision they make in accordance with or as a strategic reaction to the existing sociopolitical context."[3] The Trump era is marked by fear, uncertainty, and perpetual limbo as the topic of immigration reform is batted between the executive office, Congress, and judicial rulings, no closer to a clear direction. The potential for inflections of crisis points for students as immigration reform continues to swing between progress and setbacks is even greater in this new reality. Heightened chronic stress has the potential to impact students' learning and engagement on campus and demands ongoing attention by higher education administrators and educators. Institutional and educator efforts to support undocumented and DACA students must acknowledge diversity within the student immigrant community.

Complexity and Diversity Within the Community

Estimates from the National Center for Educational Statistics show that nearly 24% of all undergraduate students are immigrants or second-generation U.S. citizens.[4] As many as 225,000 higher education students are undocumented.[5] These students must navigate legal, racial, ethnic, linguistic, and religious barriers to their success. While there is much in their experiences that is similar, it is important to emphasize that undocumented and DACA students' experiences vary widely throughout the country. Undocumented and DACA students are diverse in their racial/ethnic and cultural backgrounds as well as across myriad other factors. Their educational trajectories into higher education range from earning their GED, coming straight from high school, or stopping-out after high school. Their family compositions and familial responsibilities range from being the only person in their family in the country to caretaking for undocumented parents or younger siblings. The socioeconomic levels of undocumented immigrants in the United States range from 14% of the undocumented population living below 50% of the poverty level to 36% of the undocumented population living above 200% of the poverty level.[6]

While the majority of undocumented individuals came from Mexico and Central and South American countries, immigrants from Asian countries have steadily increased.[7] Of the 10.9 million undocumented immigrants in the United States, 14% (1.5 million) are from Asia, with the highest representations from China, India, the Philippines, and Korea.[8] Undocumented Asian Americans have underutilized DACA, constituting about 6% of the DACA-eligible population but representing only 2.8% of DACA applicants.[9] Even within the Latinx experience in the United States we often ignore and exclude Afro-Latinx; lesbian, gay, bisexual, transgender, and queer (LGBTQ); and Indigenous identities.

Given the chronic portrayal in the sociopolitical context of undocumented immigrants as Mexicans crossing the border, misinformation is the norm. Undocumented and DACA communities are not homogenous. DACA recipients come from many different nationalities, races, and cultural backgrounds, and their experiences will reflect those diverse backgrounds. Within each of these identities there are even more unique stressors in addition to their immigrant identity. We emphasize the diversity and complexity of the undocumented and DACA community to remind educators about the danger and possibility of diminishing and erasing the complexities of their lives.

We also want to note for student affairs educators that not all undocumented students are or desire to be activists. While the activism among undocumented and DACA students is inspiring and a significant factor in the lives of many students, we encourage educators to be sensitive to and support students who are not activists and those who prefer to stay under the radar. This does not mean students do not want to be involved in what is going on in the immigrant community, but they might have reason to be wary or may be more introverted and prefer not to share their status. Whether activists or not, undocumented students experience challenging physical and mental health issues from the ongoing stress and anxiety.

The Need for Whole-College Efforts

All students, particularly undocumented and DACA students, come to college engaged with and influenced by factors outside the control of higher education. From "bathroom bills" targeting transgendered individuals to ongoing police violence that gave rise to the Black Lives Matter movement, the larger U.S. sociopolitical context impacts students despite seeming to take place outside the "bubble" of campus. More attention is needed on the ways in which the sociopolitical context surrounding undocumented immigrants produce cultural forces that affect higher education policy and the campus environment. Awareness of the fact that higher education is a cog in the sociopolitical context should inspire greater attention to the ways that colleges can create opportunities, foster access, and institutionalize a stronger structure of support.

When considering the myriad strategies for supporting undocumented students, we encourage educators to consider the intersections of structural, social, and spatial factors and the need to address how they support undocumented students across and throughout the whole institution. Structural factors play out through the policies and processes that limit access to higher education including in-state tuition policies, access to financial aid or scholarships, and other admission requirements. Structural factors reinforce the external sociopolitical context and establish an environment in which subsequent social and spatial factors thrive.

Social factors are particularly pronounced through vitriolic discourse on immigration seen in the media and repeated through interactions on campus. For many undocumented students, colleges are places where they want to exist and flourish but may fear others discovering their immigration status or using it against them. DACA recipients and undocumented students can face hostility from fellow students, professors, and staff members inside and outside the classroom. Seemingly innocuous debates about immigration in class, under the guise of practicing the skills of debate or persuasive writing, can weigh heavily on undocumented and DACA students.

Spatial factors represent the interconnectedness of political and economic powerlessness with a person's perception of fear.[10] Campuses can be places that exacerbate a sense of fear for undocumented and DACA students given that they routinely confront social, ideological, and structural power differentials as they navigate administrative processes, engage in class discussions, interact with peers and faculty who have preconceptions about immigrants, weigh their participation in "normal" college experiences like study abroad or internships, and balance the demands of college and family responsibilities. Structural, social, and spatial factors can create and sustain campus as a place of fear and exclusion, which requires intentional and institution-wide attention.

Strategies for Student Affairs Educators

We must institutionalize efforts to support undocumented and DACA students to address structural, social, and spatial factors so that all students experience the support they need to be successful. Without a comprehensive, college-wide approach, departments or staff knowledgeable about the experiences of and resources for undocumented students may exist, but students may struggle to locate these sources of information and advocacy. Here we identify a series of strategies for student affairs educators to consider as they champion the work of supporting undocumented and DACA students through institution-wide efforts.

Establish and Then Move Beyond an Office and/or Position With the Authority to Advocate for Undocumented and DACA Students

While there has been an important surge in designating an office or position on campus that focuses on supporting undocumented students, we caution student affairs professionals away from viewing this as sufficient support. Care must be taken to ensure that the office and/or position has sufficient resources, authority, and connection to institutional leadership to be an effective advocate for undocumented students. Additionally, charging one person or office with supporting undocumented and DACA students has the potential to become a structured way to put a bandage on an issue and avoid committing the resources and visible, cross-campus support needed to truly address the needs of undocumented and DACA students.

Foster a Culture and Provide the Resources and Trainings Necessary to Ensure That "It Isn't Optional to Learn About Undocumented Students' Experiences and the Policies That Impact Them"[11]

We encourage all student affairs educators to consider what is needed to collectively become knowledgeable mentors and sources of support for students. We commend the emergence of "safe zone" programs to help students identify the faculty and staff to whom they can entrust their stories; however, there is a danger that such a program will only attract those with a passion (and compassion) for supporting undocumented students, giving a pass to those who may choose not to participate and therefore not producing a change in the overall campus climate. Emphasis must be given to creating a campus environment that reduces the fear that undocumented students may feel from any staff and peers.

Conduct a Policy Audit From the Perspective of Undocumented and DACA Students to Identify the Structural and Process Components of the Student Experience That Are Barriers to Undocumented and DACA Students
No matter what department you work in on campus, we encourage student affairs educators to scrutinize policies and procedures in their department that reinforce structural, social, or spatial dimensions of undocumented and DACA students' experience. From study abroad applications and messaging to financial aid forms and procedures or policies about access to student organization funding, conducting a policy analysis from an undocumented or DACA student perspective is critical to surface hidden factors that impact students' belonging, access, and success.

Ensure Campus Leadership Provides a Visible and Ongoing Commitment to Offering Support for Undocumented Students That is Meaningful, Comprehensive, and Diffused Through the Institution
Leaders must "build an infrastructure that prepares educators for a diverse student body."[12] This includes commitment around funding options for students; setting a tone and sustained focus on undocumented students that adapts to their needs in this uncertain time; and establishing clear expectations for faculty, staff, and students that includes required cultural competency goals that are embedded into performance or annual reviews or are a part of required credit-bearing courses.

Conclusion

Supporting undocumented students is an issue of equity and access and requires colleges and universities to institutionalize safe places of support, easy-to-access information, fiscal resources, and institution-wide professional development. When discussing supports for specific student populations, we tend to focus on developing individual capacity—advancing professional knowledge and cultivating the professional's compassion and approachability. While this approach has merit, it is insufficient. If undocumented students are to truly experience the campus as a safe space to pursue their dreams, student affairs professionals must lead the charge for developing cohesive, campus-wide efforts focused on attending to the structural, social, and spatial dynamics of campus life.

Discussion Questions

1. What are the demographics of undocumented and DACA students in your state and at your institution? How might the intersections of their identities impact their experience?
2. What steps are needed for your institution to take a whole-college approach to supporting undocumented and DACA students?

Notes

1. Frequently asked questions on DACA Termination. (2017). National Immigrant Law Center and United We Dream. Retrieved from http://weareheretostay .org/resources/frequently-asked-questions-on-daca-termination/

2. Andrade, L. M. (2017). "The war still continues:" The importance of positive validation for undocumented community college students after Trump's presidential victory. *Journal of Hispanic Higher Education*. Retrieved from http://www.smc.edu/StudentServices/Documents/The%20War%20Still%20 Continues.pdf

3. Chang, A. (2017). *The struggles of identity, education, and agency in the lives of undocumented students: The burden of hyperdocumentation.* Cham, Switzerland: Palgrave Macmillan, p. 47.

4. Arbeit, C. A., Staklis, S., & Horn, L. (2016). *New American undergraduates: Enrollment trends and age at arrival of immigrant and second-generation students.* Washington DC: The National Center for Educational Statistics. Retrieved from https://nces.ed.gov/pubs2017/2017414.pdf

5. Suarez-Orozco, M. M., Teranishi, R., & Suarez-Orozco, C. E. (2015). *In the shadows of the ivory tower: Undocumented undergraduates and the liminal state of immigration reform.* Los Angeles, CA. Retrieved from https://escholarship.org/uc/ item/2hq679z

6. Migration Policy Institute. (2014). *Profile of the unauthorized immigrant population: United States.* Washington DC: Author. Retrieved from https://www .migrationpolicy.org/data/unauthorized-immigrant-population/state/US

7. Passel, J. S., & Cohn, D. (2014). *Unauthorized immigrant totals rise in 7 states, fall in 14: Decline in those from Mexico fuels most state decreases.* Washington DC: Pew Hispanic Center. Retrieved from http://www.pewhispanic.org/ files/2014/11/2014-11-18_unauthorized-immigration.pdf

8. Migration Policy Institute, *Profile of the unauthorized immigrant population.*

9. Buenavista, T. L. (2018). Model (undocumented) minorities and "illegal" immigrants: Centering Asian American and US carcerality in undocumented student discourse. *Race Ethnicity and Education, 21*(1), 78–91.

10. Whitzman, C. (2007). Stuck at the front door: Gender, fear of crime and the challenge of creating safer space. *Environment and Planning, 29,* 2715–2732.

11. Chang, *The struggles of identity, education, and agency,* p. 99.

12. Ibid., p. 101.

11

How Does Social Class Influence Student Learning and the Work of Student Affairs Educators?

Social Class Complexities in Curricular and Cocurricular Learning: Options Do Not Mean Access

Sonja Ardoin

Education in the United States has always been a class-based process[1] and the academy still contributes to social class stratification and reproduction today. Higher education began as an effort to bring White, Christian men from affluent families together for education and training because, as Frederick Rudolph notes, "the state would need competent rulers, the church would require a learned clergy, and society itself would need the adornment of cultured men."[2] The first institutions—Harvard, Yale, and so on—were considered to be finishing schools of sorts for this particular population, centered around the mission of developing these men as both scholars and well-mannered gentlemen.[3] Because of their purpose and population, the early U.S. colleges and universities were "shaped by aristocratic traditions and . . . served the aristocratic elements of colonial society."[4] As such, higher education neither allowed nor appealed to poor or working-class populations because of financial and labor costs, locations, and the absence of practical application. In short, the system was, and is, set up to sustain the broader social constructs of class stratification—championing the rich to get richer, in not only finances but also culture and connections.

Although several higher education and governmental leaders in the 1830s expressed the desire for higher education to serve as a conduit for social and economic mobility,[5] the elite nature of higher education continued well into the nineteenth century. It was not until the Morrill Acts of 1862 and 1890 that the U.S. federal government, led by Justin Morrill from Vermont, made an attempt to broaden the purpose of higher education and increase access for additional populations of people. John Thelin notes that these new institutions initially shifted their focus to "affordable, practical higher education."[6] Even with the establishment of state and, later, city colleges, there was a persistent issue of higher education focusing on the rich and, as Rudolph states, "the American university [was] . . . an agency for democratizing aristocratic values."[7] This means that even when poor and working-class individuals engaged in higher education, they were expected to learn and assimilate to beliefs, values, and ways of being that were likely different from their own.

To combat this reputation and reality, in the early 1900s there was focused growth on teachers' colleges and junior colleges to reduce costs and increase convenience for poor and working-class populations, with the added hope of showcasing how higher education could contribute to broader social mobility.[8] Yet, the Higher Education Act of 1965—passed 329 years after the founding of the first U.S. college—was still trying to prevent access to higher education being dependent on social class and, correspondingly, created federal student financial aid programs (e.g., the Pell grant) to increase access for poor and working-class individuals.[9] While there were gains for poor and working-class students in what Amy Stich calls the "massification of [U.S.] higher education" after World War II, primarily through the Servicemen's Readjustment Act of 1944 and Civil Rights Act of 1965, most of the advances occurred at open-access or less selective two-year and four-year institutions.[10] This reinforced social class stratification in higher education by creating a system in which particular institutional types serve specific social classes, funneling poor and working-class students into less selective institutions and protecting the prestige of selective institutions for affluent students.

It is for these reasons that some, including me, still argue that higher education continues to focus on serving the privileged.[11] Many colleges and universities in the United States center their values and purpose on bourgeois philosophies and behaviors which favor those from middle- and upper-class backgrounds; for example, institutions often assume students have access to basic needs, pretend everyone has similar knowledge with which to navigate the academy, teach particular verbal and written communication methods while ostracizing others, and reinforce distinct definitions of *success*. Stich and Carrie Freie note, "the working classes arguably remain devalued and pathologized within our contemporary [higher education] context."[12] Research from Allison Hurst[13] and Krista Soria,[14] among others, highlights how many policies, practices, and cultures in higher education reproduce the status quo, contribute to class stratification, and exhibit classism.

As educators, while we know that many options for learning exist, we also need to recognize that not everyone has equitable access to those options. Jerome Karabel summarizes it well, saying there is a distinction between equality of opportunity and equality of condition.[15] I argue that, even when individuals from different social class identities access higher education, the complexity of social class identity influences students' curricular and cocurricular learning and, subsequently, their collegiate experience.

The Broadness and Complexity of Social Class Identity

When someone mentions or is asked to define *social class* the first thing that often comes to folks' minds is some characterization of money. We have been socialized to conceive social class by the amount of money we have in the bank or the material goods we own. This is not wrong; it is an easy approach to conceptualizing social class. However, it is only a partial portrayal of social class identity.[16] Alfred Lubrano describes the broadness of social class as "nearly everything about [a person]," serving as a "script, map, and guide . . . tell[ing] us how to dress, how to hold ourselves, how to eat, and how to socialize."[17] This broadens our understanding of social class by encouraging us to think of all the ways this dimension of our identity shapes how we move through the world.

Will Barratt further highlights social class complexity by sharing the following components of this identity—(a) class of origin; (b) current, felt class; and (c) attributed class—and describing the social class that people grew up in, the way people feel about their social class in the moment at hand, and what others assume or perceive about people's social class.[18] When these three components do not align, we can experience dissonance about our social class identity, thus making it even more challenging to understand or discuss. These illustrations of social class demonstrate how this dimension of identity is broad; complex; and, to the dismay of many, without an agreed-upon definition in the literature.[19]

Coded and Limited Language

In higher education, we do not often talk about social class identity, considering it a taboo topic because of how most of us were, and continue to be, socialized. Scott Thomas and Angela Bell note that "class. . . is not carefully tracked in higher education."[20] Rather, in attempting to collect data on this dimension of identity, institutions yield to definitions and language that are both coded and limiting—such as *Pell-eligible, low-income,* or *need-based aid.* All of these terms operationalize social class as only one aspect of the identity—financial resources or wealth. This is a problem in higher education because it assumes that if a student's financial need is met, then equity of opportunity has been achieved. If only it were that simple. William Ming Liu and colleagues encourage the view of social class as a cultural construct, rather than merely a demographic variable.[21] Institutions can utilize several conceptual models to broaden their understanding of this construct and, hopefully, increase advocacy and action around social class identity. I highlight two of these models in the next section.

Social Class Identity Conceptual Models

In addition to financial resources, social class includes one's attitudes, experiences, knowledge, resources, and opportunities. Liu and colleagues' social class worldview model (SCWM)[22] and Tara Yosso's community cultural wealth model[23] are two conceptual models that can assist students and student affairs educators in developing a more complex and profound understanding of social class identity in its entirety and how it influences student learning.

Liu and colleagues' SCWM[24] provides a framework incorporating individuals' perceptions and experiences of social class through the capital accumulation paradigm, which includes three types of capital—social, human, and cultural—and five interrelated domains—consciousness, attitudes, and salience; referent groups; property relationships; lifestyle; and behaviors. These domains capture self and others' awareness, emotions, and significance about social class identity and systems; the people who influence one's social class worldview, including group of origin, peer group, and group of aspiration; one's material possessions and presentation of social class; how one spends one's time and resources (e.g., cultural capital); and how one acts, or an "observable manifestation of a social class worldview."[25] Liu and colleagues offer this combination of capitals within these domains as a "lens through which people perceive their world."[26]

The SCWM demonstrates the complex layers that one has to explore and recognize to gain a deeper understanding of social class identity. It also provides student affairs educators with an outline from which to assess office- and campus-level policies, practices, and culture and to build support structures for students from poor and working-class identities. For example, if a student's referent group of origin belittles higher education, the student may be wary of returning to campus for the second year. Or, if a student hears of all the glamorous locales where others spend spring break or summer while the student works at a local restaurant, their sense of belonging on campus may wane because of the lifestyle differences between the individual and the referent peer group.

To pair with the SCWM, Yosso's community cultural wealth model[27] focuses on "the array of cultural knowledge, skills, abilities and contacts possessed by socially marginalized groups that often go unrecognized and unacknowledged" and features the following forms of capital: (a) aspirational, (b) familial, (c) linguistic, (d) navigational, (e) resistant, and (f) social. Aspirational capital is one's ability to set future goals and remain focused despite challenges. Familial capital is a combination of kinship and culture through connections to one's family and community. Linguistic capital is the skill of being bi- or multilingual or bi- or multidialectical. Navigational capital is perseverance and movement through institutions and systems. Resistant capital is recognizing inequity and acting to challenge it. Social capital is an individual's network of connections and resources.

Each form of capital can, and should, be viewed as a valuable set of skills and experiences that students bring to campus that can be built upon during the college experience. For example, student affairs educators can help students frame their capitals on applications, résumés, and cover letters to showcase unique knowledge, skills, or experiences. Yosso's model repositions all forms of capital—those derived from any social class identity—as helpful to one's development, rather than as a deficit to overcome, and useable for disrupting social stratification. Rather than student affairs educators perceiving poor and working-class students as empty buckets to fill, their perspective can shift to recognize all students as having valuable capitals to share.

Although these conceptual frameworks allow for deeper and broader understanding of social class, it is important to note that social class identity is not experienced in isolation. Rather, individuals combine social class with their other dimensions of identity (e.g., race/ethnicity, gender, ability). Thus, how I experience my working-class identity as a White, straight, temporarily able, Catholic, cisgender woman is likely different than someone who identifies as a working-class woman of color or a working-class gay man. Our lens of social class is contextual. This means that both students and student affairs educators need to be cautious of assuming that all students from a similar social class have uniformly experienced that dimension of their identity.

Social Class and Student Learning

As a first-generation college student who comes from a working-class background; a student affairs educator; and, now, a faculty member, I experience the influence of social class on student learning through both personal and professional lenses. Sure, colleges and universities are now offering a multitude of academic areas of study, research opportunities, student organizations and campus events, and support services, but that does not mean students from all social classes have equitable opportunities to utilize these options. Social class shows up in how folks engage in the campus community, in both curricular and cocurricular spaces, and, as such, influences their learning opportunities.

Curricular

Formal, or academic, learning is not social class neutral. Stich argues, "knowledge is neither of equal social value, merit, nor form; nor is it dispensed within institutions in equal measure. Knowledge is rather, much like the social system itself, differentiated and classed."[28] For example, whether or not we have books in our home as children, and what kind of books those are, can be rooted in social class identity.[29] It also shapes what types of PK–12 schools we attend, including curricular and extracurricular offerings and access to guidance counselors that frame the college access and choice processes.[30] In short, social class identity influences our curricular learning in all sorts of ways. In the higher education environment, social class tends to influence students' choices about where and what to study and how they engage in the curricular life of the institution. It can also determine whether, or how much, faculty choose to include this identity in course content and, thus, whether students see their experience represented in the curriculum or learn about social class identity at all.

The college access and choice process is where social class first influences student learning in higher education. There are a multitude of institutional types in the United States and, in the myth of meritocracy, those are all theoretically accessible; however, in reality, many students from poor and working-class backgrounds are concentrated in community colleges and less-selective four-year institutions, while affluent students are overrepresented at four-year and elite institutions.[31] This happens not only because of college costs but also because of factors such as college knowledge, location, peer influence, and family and community expectations. Social class can also direct students' choice of academic study; many poor and working-class students lean toward the professional majors that directly relate to employment upon graduation (e.g., education, engineering), while students from other social classes are open to pursuing the liberal arts. Even once the decisions of where and what to study are made, Krista Soria points out that students from the poor or working class face barriers in obtaining the items they need for curricular learning—including but not limited to books, other course materials, and technology and software—and may have less time to devote to studies because of the need to work at part- or full-time jobs[32] or serve as caretakers for their families.

Research also shows that faculty and peers often have lower expectations for poor and working-class students;[33] this can influence students' aspirational capital, their desire to build relationships with or seek help from some faculty members, and students' peer interactions on collaborative projects or study groups. Correspondingly, social class can also sway whether or not students pursue opportunities for undergraduate research, internships, study abroad, and graduate school. Students from poor and working-class backgrounds may not believe opportunities like this are for "people like them"[34] (aligning with the SCWM's attitudes, referent groups, and behaviors domains) or may face hurdles to participation because of familial, navigational, or social capital (see Yosso's community cultural wealth model).

Communication styles, as a component of social class (see Yosso's linguistic capital and Liu and colleagues' behaviors), can also influence students' learning. Higher education, like many fields, not only has its own language of terms and acronyms[35] but also expects students, administrators, and faculty to speak in certain ways—what I deem *academic speak* and Soria terms the *hidden curriculum*.[36] This academic speak benefits certain populations while providing the hidden message that specific accents, word choices, tones, and nonverbals are not welcome in the academy, usually those of poor and working-class folks and people of color. This can discourage participation from poor and working-class students during courses and, as such, impact their learning, leading to feeling "lost" or "left behind."[37] Favoring certain ways of speaking and behaving reproduces the status quo and contributes to class stratification in higher education. In addition, Kenneth Oldfield explains that the presence, and sometimes expectation, of discussion and debate—including with faculty—as a form of inquiry and learning may be new for poor and working-class students.[38] It is critical to inform students that this type of communication and dialogue is beneficial and help students become comfortable with verbally testing their own and others' ideas and opinions.

Finally, curricular learning can be influenced based on what is not represented in the curriculum or only represented from a deficit perspective. Since social class is often seen as taboo, it is rarely a topic that students explicitly explore or discuss in their courses. This can reinforce that social class is off-limits, send a message that it is not important enough to study, and deter poor and working-class students from voicing their experiences or those of their family and friends. Additionally, if individuals from poor or working classes are only shown in the curriculum from a deficit perspective, it can negatively shape opinions about students from those social class identities—both for those students themselves and from their peers. Faculty can foster more learning for students from all social classes if they support examination of this identity from a place of value and encourage students to draw from their personal experiences in course discussion and assignments. This can validate students' knowledge and capitals, nurture their confidence, and advance their ability to both share and further develop.

Cocurricular

Social class influences student learning in cocurricular spaces as well. In addition to financial resources that can determine one's ability to engage, some students come to college with more information and different attitudes about student groups and campus services than others.[39] This impacts everything from where one lives and eats—on- or off-campus—to how one spends one's "free" time. Student engagement levels vary along social class identity lines, with affluent students more apt to live on-campus (specifically in the "nice" residence halls) and join student government, fraternities and sororities, and other high-powered organizations on campus that align with and further their social and cultural capital and lifestyle. Georgianna Martin's research highlights how students from poor and working-class backgrounds recognize that they might compromise résumé-building (e.g., expanding their capitals) when their jobs, families, or academic studies leave little time for cocurricular engagement.[40] Additionally, campus services, such as learning/tutoring centers, health centers, and counseling centers, may be utilized inequitably based on social class. Students may not know these center's services are generally included in student fees, thus being "prepaid," or they may have an aversion to seeking help, which can be seen by some as a form of weakness.

Student affairs educators need to consider how they might be impeding some students' ability to learn in cocurricular environments with fees and dues, assumptions that students know how to access information about campus engagement or services, or scheduling events for hours which may only fit with particular students' schedules. We should also consider how to cultivate more social class equity on campus through facilitating intergroup dialogue sessions around social class, instituting language diversity appreciation programs, sharing more information about opportunities and refraining from using jargon and "campus speak" in marketing and promotion, expanding living-learning communities around social class identity, and/or establishing class identity centers on campus (similar to other identity-based centers).[41] Advisers to student groups should also encourage those groups to examine their policies, practices, and culture to determine if their membership and events appeal to students from all social classes.

Preceding equity challenges in curricular and cocurricular spaces, students from the poor or working classes may face barriers with learning because of struggles with basic needs. Sara Goldrick-Rabb[42] and Clare Cady[43] are raising awareness and calling for action around issues of homelessness and food insecurity in higher education.[44] It is Maslow's hierarchy of needs: If a student does not have shelter or food, how can we expect them to fully engage in the learning process? Educators are being called to "increase awareness of resources, create workshops to support basic needs, provide dedicated spaces for students to store and prepare food, and develop and train crisis response teams."[45]

Addressing Classism in Higher Education

Throughout this chapter I have showcased some of the ways that classism occurs in higher education, including assuming that, because opportunities and options exist, students have equitable access to them. To address classism, institutions and those who work within them need to critically reflect upon and analyze campus policies, practices, and culture and determine how to shift or change these to create equitable experiences for students from all social classes. Part of this will include student affairs educators examining their own identities, biases, and privileges and letting go of stereotypes and assumptions about social class identity. For example, we should not assume that all students have laptops or smart phones to engage in classrooms or take assessments—that is classist. We should also consider what it means to charge students to attend on-campus conferences or pay fees or dues for student groups—this can be classist. We cannot set up a system to advantage certain populations (e.g., affluent, privileged students) and still applaud ourselves for all the options we have on campus. Until those options are equitably accessible, they are not real options; rather, they are methods of affirming the status quo and furthering class stratification. There is much more work to be done in exploring the influence of social class identity throughout the academy, including the work of student affairs educators, and I plan to contribute to that body of scholarship. I hope others choose to as well. At the very least, we can all increase the conversation about social class identity.

Discussion Questions

Student affairs educators, along with students, other higher education administrators, and faculty members, can continue the conversation around social class influences on student learning through three potential first steps:

1. *Consider social class identity*—How do you identify your social class? And, how do students and colleagues with whom you work identify? If you don't know, why? If you do know, why might you avoid sharing your social class identity with others?
2. *Converse about social class identity*—How can we talk more about social class identity on campus? What curricular and cocurricular spaces can incorporate dialogue on social class identity? How can we train student affairs educators to facilitate these discussions?
3. *Comprehend classism*—How might your program, office, department, division, or institution be creating structural barriers (e.g., financial, social, cultural) for poor and working-class students or favoring affluent students through policy, practice, or culture? How might obstructions or preferentialism be reduced or eliminated?

Notes

1. Hurst, A. L. (2012). *College and the working class: What it takes to make it.* Boston, MA: Sense.
2. Rudolph, F. (1990). *The American college and university: A history.* Athens, GA: The University of Georgia Press, p. 6.
3. Ibid., p. 7.
4. Ibid., p. 7.
5. Ibid., pp. 215–217.
6. Thelin, J. R. (2011). *A history of American higher education* (2nd ed.). Baltimore, MD: The John Hopkins University Press, p. 75.
7. Rudolph, *The American college and university*, p. 465.
8. Ibid.
9. Higher Education Act of 1965, retrieved from http://legcounsel.house .gov/Comps/HEA65_CMD.pdf
10. Stich, A. E. (2012). *Access to inequality: Reconsidering class, knowledge, and capital in higher education.* Lanham, MD: Lexington Books, pp. 5–7; Thomas, S. L. & Bell, A. (2008). Social class and higher education: A reorganization of opportunities. In L. Weis (Ed.), *The way class works: Readings on school, family, and the economy* (pp. 273–287). New York, NY: Routledge, pp. 273–287.
11. Hurst, *College and the working class.*

12. Stich, A. E., & Freie, C. (2016). The working classes and higher education: An introduction to a complicated relationship. In A. E. Stich & C. Freire (Eds.), *The working classes and higher education* (pp. 1–9). New York, NY: Routledge, p. 3.

13. Hurst, A. L. (2010). *The burden of academic success: Loyalists, renegades, and double agents.* Lanham, MD: Lexington Books.

14. Soria, K. (2015). *Welcoming blue-collar scholars into the ivory tower: Developing class-conscious strategies for student success.* Columbia, SC: National Resource Center for The First-Year Experience and Students in Transition.

15. Karabel, J. (2006). *The chosen: The hidden history of admissions and exclusion at Harvard, Yale, and Princeton.* New York, NY: Houghton Mifflin.

16. Stitch & Freie, The working classes and higher education.

17. Lubrano, A. (2004). *Limbo: Blue-collar roots, white-collar dreams.* Hoboken, NJ: Wiley, p. 5.

18. Barratt, W. (2011). *Social class on campus: Theories and manifestations.* Sterling, VA: Stylus.

19. Martin, G. L. (2015) "Tightly wound rubber bands": Exploring the college experiences of low-income, first-generation White students. *Journal of Student Affairs Research and Practice, 52*(3), 275–286.

20. Thomas & Bell, A social class and higher education, p. 278.

21. Liu, W. M., Soleck, G., Hopps, J., Dunston, K., & Pickett Jr., T. (2004). A new framework to understand social class in counseling: The social class worldview model and modern classism theory. *Journal of Multicultural Counseling and Development, 32*(2), 95–122.

22. Ibid.

23. Yosso, T. (2005). Whose culture has capital? A critical race theory discussion of community cultural wealth. *Race Ethnicity and Education, 8*(1), 69–91.

24. Liu et al., A new framework to understand social class in counseling.

25. Ibid., p. 106.

26. Ibid., p. 107.

27. Yosso, Whose culture has capital?

28. Stich, *Access to inequality*, p. 49.

29. Ardoin, S. (2017, August 11). What you need to know about the reality of social class on campus [web log post]. Retrieved from http://www.presence.io/blog/what-you-need-to-know-about-the-reality-of-social-class-on-campus/

30. Ardoin, S. (2018). *College aspirations and access in working-class, rural communities: The mixed signals, challenges, and new language first-generation students encounter.* Lanham, MD: Lexington Books; Aronson, P. (2008). Breaking barriers or locked out? Class-based perceptions and experiences of postsecondary education. In J. T. Mortimer (Ed.), *Social class and transitions to adulthood* (New Directions for Child and Adolescent Development) no. 119, 41–54. Hoboken, NJ: Wiley; Thomas & Bell, Social class and higher education.

31. Poutré, A., Rorison, J., & Voight, M. (2017). *Limited means, limited options: College remains unaffordable for many Americans.* Washington DC: Institute for Higher Education Policy; Martin, "Tightly wound rubber bands."

32. Aronson, Breaking barriers or locked out?; Soria, *Welcoming blue collar scholars into the ivory tower*; Thomas & Bell, Social class and higher education.

33. Soria, *Welcoming blue collar scholars into the ivory tower.*

34. Archer, L., & Leathwood, C. (2003). Identities, inequalities, and higher education. In L. Archer, M. Hutchings, & A. Ross (Eds.), *Higher education and social class: Issues of exclusion and inclusion* (pp. 175–191). New York, NY: Routledge Falmer.

35. Ardoin, *College aspirations and access in working-class, rural communities.*

36. Soria, *Welcoming blue collar scholars into the ivory tower.*

37. Archer, L., & Leathwood, C., Identities, inequalities, and higher education, p. 190; Aronson, Breaking barriers or locked out?

38. Oldfield, K. (2007, January/February). Humble & hopeful: Welcoming first-generation, poor and working-class students to college. *About Campus*, pp. 2–12.

39. Barratt, *Social class on campus.*

40. Martin, "Tightly wound rubber bands."

41. Ardoin, S. (2018). Straddling social classes: Helping working class students create a sense of belonging in both their hometowns and higher education. In G. Martin (Ed.), *Social class identity in student affairs* (New Directions for Student Services, pp. 75–86). San Francisco, CA: Jossey-Bass.

42. Goldrick-Rab, S. (2017, August 7). Basic needs security and the syllabus. Retrieved from https://medium.com/@saragoldrickrab/basic-needs-security-and-the-syllabus-d24cc7afe8c9

43. Cady, C. (2017, August 14). Your student leaders are back. *Medium.* Retrieved from https://medium.com/@saragoldrickrab/your-student-leaders-are-back-c01ba552b619

44. Yavorski, K. (2017, September 10). The number of starving college students is shockingly high. *The Week Magazine*. Retrieved from http://theweek.com/articles/723090/number-starving-college-students-shockingly-high

45. Ibid., para. 30.

Disrupting Educational Privilege: Partnering With Students and Communities to Create True Inclusion

Angela Cook

During an event called Three Acts in Over-the-Rhine,[1] community leaders[2] of Cincinnati, Ohio's Over-the-Rhine shared stories of this vibrant and embattled neighborhood. One speaker, Dorothy Darden, asked a compelling question: How do you build an inclusive community when people cannot afford to live there? In the context of social class in higher education, Darden's words translate: How can educators truly include students and communities of all social classes when many still experience barriers to access? As student affairs educators, we have a mission and a responsibility to support students from diverse socioeconomic backgrounds. Educators should strive to understand their students deeply and holistically through awareness of their individual stories, strengths, and goals. In addition, student affairs educators must do more to disrupt the isolation and elitism that often characterizes higher education. Educators must cultivate communities not only on campus but also within off-campus neighborhoods. Higher education has tremendous power to create positive change, and we must embrace our role as community partners. Only then will we dismantle higher education's legacy of serving and promoting "White, Christian men from affluent families,"[3] and create empowering learning communities for all people.

Impacts of Social Class on Learning

Ardoin provides a well-researched conceptual framework for social class in higher education, and several of her observations capture what I have witnessed as a student affairs educator. Social class involves more dimensions than money; social capital, for example, contributes heavily to opportunities for advancement. Working as an assistant director in a business school, I regularly observe familial and personal connections that lead to internships, lucrative jobs, and business contracts. Students of lower social class are less likely to have existing connections, causing them to face more obstacles than their privileged peers. Simply increasing scholarship funding cannot rectify educational inequities. Despite dedicated scholarships for underprivileged students, the business college struggles to recruit and retain them. Educators can create a space where students of lower socioeconomic backgrounds see themselves represented and supported. Colleges can connect students to engaged alumni who serve as mentors, provide financial support to attend conferences and networking events, and help students comprehend what social capital they may not realize they possess.[4]

Ardoin also noted that colleges and universities continue to uphold systems that "focus on serving the privileged."[5] In each education institution where I have worked, trainings and department initiatives have consistently omitted the impact of social class on student learning. Miami University has a history of attracting students of higher socioeconomic status. Rarely did we explicitly discuss supporting students of lower social class. During the University of Cincinnati's recent Equity and Inclusion conference, few presentations examined social class. Including socioeconomic status alongside other identities such as race, gender, and sexual orientation can be a challenge, and we must identify more effective ways to approach inclusion.

Cultivating Inclusion on Campus

I advocate a combination of strategies to create fully inclusive institutions: (a) review available research from a variety of identities, methodologies,[6] and perspectives; (b) benchmark other institutions to see what initiatives they have tried;[7] (c) survey and assess students to hear their unique voices; and (d) critically examine who is still missing from our schools and what actions will bring them into our educational community. Ardoin tackles the first strategy and provides numerous resources for exploration of the second. I will spend the remainder of my response exploring the last two strategies.

As busy practitioners mired in the day-to-day of higher education, our limited time and resources often expire before we can fully engage in research and benchmarking. In such circumstances, these approaches should take lower priority than assessing one's own students. For the knowledge from research and benchmarking to have any merit, they must be representative of and fully reflect the truths of our institution's students.[8] To create inclusive institutions, the highest investment we can make is to hear our students' unique stories, voices, and contexts. Educators cannot spend all their limited time studying theories of the impact of social class on learning. They must attempt to understand how it manifests for the students who attend their institution and then transform that knowledge into inclusive activism.

In pursuit of understanding students' stories, educators should identify a representation of students from various social identities, including class; conduct individual interviews, focus groups, and surveys; and create a committee of student representatives tasked with identifying solutions to marginalized students' needs. Such actions maximize students' strengths and contributions for the benefit of the entire community while also providing them with hands-on learning and leadership opportunities. Students who have voice and ownership over their own education and support system will practice personal responsibility, self-regulation,[9] and agency. Older adult students, who are accustomed to leading independent and self-driven lives, would value the flexibility and trust to determine for themselves what is most beneficial to their learning.[10]

New Strategies for True Inclusion: Community Partnerships

Despite all our efforts to provide students with equitable support and services, we still do not truly disrupt higher education's predilection for privileging White, affluent, Christian men. We must constantly ask: "Who is not here? Who is *still* not represented in our institution?" The next step after Ardoin's research is to examine who never arrives on college campuses. What happens that they do not or cannot come to our institutions? What systems of privilege and oppression are damaging our communities? We must disrupt our current systems and cultivate institutions that strive to answer and act upon these questions. We must challenge the traditional roles we have always assumed for education and how it functions within our communities. Just like any individual resident, business, or organization, our colleges and universities are members of a community. We must acknowledge our membership and take ownership of our role in the larger community, and then actively collaborate to promote our mutual welfare and success.

Over the last few years, we have had to confront the consequences of neglecting our community partnerships. The 2016 presidential election has exposed the deep divide between higher education and Americans who do not have access to our colleges and universities.[11] Across all political affiliations, America's low-income communities have suffered because of unequal access to education at every level. I have witnessed this in elementary education in low-income African American communities in the Deep South, in my predominantly White hometown that has been hit hard with the opioid epidemic, and in three varied college towns where the university was one of the largest employers.[12] Educational inequity is all around us, and it especially manifests around lines of race and class.[13]

Educators can help empower surrounding communities by using similar strategies as listening to and partnering with their students. Establish town halls between the institution and community members.[14] Gather the voices and perspectives from every neighborhood, representing the area's full diversity. Engage in dialogue to comprehend and respect one another's circumstances, needs, and goals. Collaborate with community leaders to determine what partnerships would best serve all participants.[15] Find opportunities to bring the institution's neighbors to campus and cultivate occasions for students to meaningfully engage in diverse off-campus communities.[16] From my experience in education ranging from primary school to undergraduate and graduate students to adult learners, I urge higher education institutions to get involved with their community K–12 schools. By the time students reach college age, some are so far off track that higher education would never happen for them. If we want true equity, we need to significantly reform every level of education in our communities, including communities of color and low-income neighborhoods.

Rather than upholding higher education's legacy of isolation in an ivory tower,[17] true change can come when we turn colleges and universities inside out, bringing surrounding communities into the opportunities that higher education can offer. Even for those institutions that possess robust town-gown relationships, educators should consider what more they can do. There is always something more we can do to build common understanding, service, and respect. Education is crucial to the future of our world. If we do not do more to educate and advance ourselves and everyone around us, our troubles and conflicts will only deepen the divide.

Conclusion

Toward the end of her story, Dorothy Darden woke the room with her words: "I'm not fearful of change. I'm fearful of extinction."[18] She expressed the urgency facing our marginalized communities, not just in Cincinnati but across the nation and globe. As educators, we must disrupt the privilege that allows us to ignore the plight of our most impoverished communities. Working in and attending higher education is an advantage that so many neighbors never can access. Those of us who occupy educational spaces must leverage our positions and advocate for the survival and empowerment not only of our low-income students but also of our surrounding low-income communities and communities of color. This will help us bring true inclusion into education.

Discussion Questions

1. How will you collect your students' backgrounds and perspectives to better understand their experiences?
2. What partnerships can you create with students to address their needs, interests, and goals?
3. How can you replicate this work in your institution's surrounding communities, with the goal of creating new collaborations for inclusion in our neighborhoods and in higher education?

Notes

1. This event was planned by Tiffany Cooper, board member of the Over-the-Rhine Museum, and was hosted at Chatfield College in Over-the-Rhine. As a colleague and friend, I owe many thanks to Tiffany for teaching me about race, social class, and community in my new Cincinnati home.

2. For more details on the event and its three speakers, please see the event page: https://www.facebook.com/events/910743072440207/

3. Ardoin, S., this volume, p. 203.

4. Black, W. (2018, April). *Lean on me: Coaching students through society and the workplace.* Conference presentation at the University of Cincinnati Equity and Inclusion Conference, Cincinnati, Ohio.

5. Ardoin, this volume, p. 204.

6. For example, Indigenous methodologies assert research should be a partnership and serve the advancement of those studied. Smith, L. T. (2012). *Decolonizing methodologies: Research and Indigenous peoples* (2nd ed.). London, UK: Zed Books.

7. Explore relevant professional organizations, journals, e-publications, and conferences that highlight theories and best practices for your functional area.

8. See, for example, Bauer-Wolf, J. (2018). How to "not be rich." *Inside Higher Ed.* Retrieved from https://www.insidehighered.com/news/2018/04/16/new-crowdsourced-student-affordability-guide-goes-viral-university-michigan?utm_source=Inside+Higher+Ed&utm_campaign=afb9e1329f-DNU20180111&utm_medium=email&utm_term=0_1fcbc04421-afb9e1329f-199681981&mc_cid=afb9e1329f&mc_eid=26aae8678a.

9. Nilson, L. B. (2013). *Creating self-regulated learners: Strategies to strengthen students' self-awareness and learning skills.* Sterling, VA: Stylus.

10. Knowles, M. S., Holton III, E. F., & Swanson, R. A. (2005). *The adult learner: The definitive classic in adult education and human resource development* (6th ed.). London, UK: Elsevier.

11. For statistics on voter breakdown by education see: Castillo, W., & Schramm, M. (2016). How we voted—by age, education, race and sexual orientation. *USA Today College.* Retrieved from http://college.usatoday.com/2016/11/09/how-we

-voted-by-age-education-race-and-sexual-orientation/; Silver, N. (2016). Education, not income, predicted who would vote for Trump. *FiveThirtyEight*. Retrieved from http://fivethirtyeight.com/features/education-not-income-predicted-who-would-vote-for-trump/

12. Ashland University, Miami University, and University of Cincinnati.

13. Kozol, J. (1991). *Savage inequalities: Children in America's schools*. New York, NY: Broadway Books.

14. Schedule them on campus, out in the surrounding areas, and virtually. Engage in a variety of ways that work well for the needs of your diverse communities.

15. Smith, *Decolonizing methodologies*.

16. However, be constantly aware of the potential pitfalls associated with bringing students to impoverished neighborhoods. Partner with community members to create authentic experiences that avoid poverty tourism, superficial service opportunities, and perpetuating privilege. For an example of creating empowering partnerships, see Mtawa, N., & Wilson-Strydom, M. (2018). Community service learning: Pedagogy at the interface of poverty, inequality and privilege. *Journal of Human Development and Capabilities, 19*(2), 249–265.

17. The documentary of the same name explores affordability and the value of college within the context of rising tuition costs, which is another crucial topic for inclusion in higher education. Rossi, A. (Producer & Director), & Braun, B. (Producer). (2014). *Ivory tower* [Motion picture]. United States: Participant Media, Paramount Pictures, Samuel Goldwyn Films.

18. Three Acts in Over-the-Rhine.

12

What Is the Role of Student Affairs Educators in Helping Students Whose Learning Is Complicated by Experiencing Trauma?

Navigating the Complex Space of Supporting Student Survivors of Trauma

Tricia R. Shalka

In the spring of 2003 I was living an idyllic existence. I was a sophomore studying abroad in Lyon, France, and I kept pinching myself about the seemingly fairytale moments that filled my days. The sun would filter through my window in the mornings, and I would stick my head out to marvel at the ancient city beneath me. To the right I could see La Sâone River and Vieux Lyon rising up the hill, where Roman ruins still speckled the old city. Directly in front of me was the building in which Antoine de Saint-Exupéry, the author of *Le Petit Prince*, was born. My walk to school meandered down a cobblestone street named after Victor Hugo, and my afternoons were often spent in rituals of eating and exploring with friends. I savored every warm crêpe filled with melted Nutella.

However, that fairytale soon came to a sudden halt when I arrived in the proverbial wrong place at the wrong time. While traveling through southern

France, I abruptly awoke in the middle of the night to the smell of smoke and the realization that I was trapped inside a burning hotel. My body instantly snapped into survival mode and a state of incredible clarity. I understood completely that I might not make it out alive that night, but I was intent on fighting with everything I could to circumvent that outcome. By the time help arrived, I had already sustained damage to my lungs and second- and third-degree burns over one-third of my body. I remained in an induced coma for two weeks and began the difficult physical part of my recovery surrounded by my dad and an amazing medical team at Hôpital Lapeyronie in Montpellier, France.

The physical recovery from my traumatic experience was grueling, but the psychological impacts were equally if not more challenging at various stages. Early on, I faced the daunting decision of whether or not to return to college for my junior fall, slightly less than five months after the fire. I was still in recovery, but I knew I would have the professional care I needed at Dartmouth. The greater challenge was determining whether or not I was ready to confront the scariest battle of all—resuming a "normal" life.

I took the leap and returned to school. However, as I sat on the bus with my mom at Boston's South Station bound for Hanover and Dartmouth, I suddenly felt overcome with anxiety and unsure if I could continue. For the first time, it occurred to me that I might not fit at Dartmouth any more. The fire had changed me—would I relate to my friends and surroundings with the same exuberance I once had? Would people stare when they realized I was back? Would they be unsure what to say to me? Would I see people whispering and pointing as I went by? Would the fact that I was almost entirely covered by clothing to disguise my scars on a hot September day draw even more attention? All I wanted to do was blend in, and yet I knew even under normal circumstances that was improbable at a small college.

Shortly after arriving in Hanover I realized returning was the right decision, largely because of the tremendous support system that surrounded me. I was struck by how wonderful it felt to be back with friends and interacting so naturally. It felt amazing to laugh again. The phenomenal generosity and compassion from so many administrators and faculty on the campus overwhelmed both my mom and me. Faculty and staff made promises of support to me that week. As that week turned into the remaining two years of my time as a student, those promises proved far from empty. Indeed, one of the primary reasons I thrived rather than simply survived was because of remarkable administrators and faculty members who encouraged me, supported me, and believed in me.

Trauma in Higher Education

In recent years, trauma has emerged as a hot topic in higher education. Certainly, trauma has been in the fabric of students' lives as long as higher education has existed, but contemporary developments in federal policy have brought its prevalence to the forefront of assumed knowledge for higher education professionals. Specifically, a report by the White House Task Force to Protect Students From Sexual Assault under the administration of President Obama drew explicit attention to trauma in parallel to the crisis of continued sexual violence on college campuses and called for institutions to approach their work through a trauma-informed lens.[1] However, for many student affairs practitioners, trauma and trauma-informed approaches can be difficult topics for a variety of reasons, both personal and professional. Yet, as my own experience suggests, educators hold tremendous power to make a difference in the lives of student survivors of trauma. In what follows, I offer an overview of different ways to conceptualize trauma as well as how it might show up in our work with students. Finally, I address the role of student affairs educators in supporting students impacted by trauma and various dilemmas that can complicate this work.

What Is Trauma?

Trauma is an inherently subjective experience that impacts individuals in diverse ways. Even when two people survive a similar trauma and are traumatized by the experience, the ways that traumatic response manifests may vary.[2] As inclusive as our attempts may be, we probably will not capture trauma in all its forms. We could brainstorm an exhaustive list of potentially traumatizing experiences (e.g., natural disasters, terrorism, racism, life-threatening illnesses, community violence, abuse), and yet we will likely miss some. We could generate an equally exhaustive list of symptoms we might witness in someone who is traumatized by an experience (e.g., flashbacks, hypervigilance, sleep disturbances, avoidance, difficulties concentrating, numbing), and yet we will likely miss some.

Historically, *trauma* has been defined primarily as a serious physical or psychological injury that results from an experience that overwhelms the body's physical and/or psychological capacities for survival.[3] This definition is incomplete. Rather, trauma impacts a person or community at a variety of levels including individual, relational, and cultural.[4] Although many envision trauma as resulting from a singular experience (e.g., a sexual assault, a car accident), this paradigm must be expanded to include non-event-based traumas. These traumas may be more insidious or pervasive in presentation and include states such as historical trauma, microaggressions, or persistent neglect or abuse.[5]

What is sometimes missing from conversations about traumatic experience is the interplay of systemic oppression.[6] The inequities of our society can be sources of trauma, as is the case for experiences of racial trauma, extreme poverty, intergenerational trauma, and other conditions of bias that overwhelm the human condition. Additionally, those who endure the daily effects of marginalization are often at a higher baseline stress level as a result.[7]

As educators, our responsibility to student survivors is that of developing a heightened understanding of the intersecting role of power and privilege in traumatic experience. Restrictive and political definitions of *trauma* complicate the healing process for many survivors. For example, sometimes there is a conflation of the term *post-traumatic stress disorder* (PTSD) with trauma. Rather, PTSD is a specific psychiatric diagnosis and just one possibility out of many reactions to *trauma*. The challenge of PTSD's prominence in our social language is that its criteria for diagnosis contain a very particular and restrictive definition of trauma that leaves out many people who are indeed suffering from traumatic experiences.[8] I have witnessed this in my research when students struggle because their personal knowing tells them what they have experienced is traumatic and yet they do not fit into the "traditional definitions of trauma" box. Part of our work in student affairs, then, must explore what boundaries our personal understandings or our institutional policies and practices have created around what "counts" as trauma and how this influences those who may be struggling outside of these socially constructed lines.

How Might Trauma Show Up in Our Work With Students?

Trauma arises in our work with students in varied ways, sometimes overtly and sometimes less so. We may notice something in a class we teach, a student group we advise, a program we host, or a student we mentor. Or we may not. Sometimes a student may directly disclose trauma. At other times, disclosure may be more tentative and concealed, if it happens at all. A participant in a previous research study told me the way she worked through much of her trauma was to write about it in class assignments, though sometimes abstractly. In other words, her disclosure was there, but perhaps not always obviously so to the person reading and evaluating her assignments.

Sometimes trauma is truly invisible. It may profoundly impact the spaces in which we engage with students, and yet we may not have any conscious awareness of its presence. However, learning to recognize some common signs of how trauma may manifest can help us to be more attentive to how we structure various environments and interactions with students when trauma is present.

In moments of trauma in which physical or psychological survival may be challenged, an individual may go into a physiological response pattern that is often referred to as fight, flight, or freeze.[9] There are also many forms of trauma that do not fall into the pattern of a singular event and rather build collectively over time. Regardless, what may develop following traumatic experiences are traumatic stress responses. Although conversations about traumatic reactions naturally gravitate to many of the negative impacts, it is also important to recognize that resilience and growth can and do happen in parallel to the many difficulties that trauma survivors may endure. Indeed, researchers have documented the possibility of posttraumatic growth in which survivors may experience positive changes in terms of sense of self, sense of relationships, and philosophy of life.[10]

Broadly speaking, many scholars and clinicians talk about traumatic stress reactions in terms of two dominant presentations—hyper and hypo responses.[11] Hyperarousal responses to trauma are those with which we may be more familiar. In this context, an individual is "experiencing too much activation."[12] When we witness someone in a state of hyperarousal they may appear agitated, overwhelmed, hypervigilant, and/or unable to relax as a result of intrusive thoughts and emotions.

Conversely, trauma can also induce a contradictory response. In this manifestation, individuals may experience hypoarousal in which they are in a state of "too little activation."[13] A lack of sensation and emotion characterize hypoarousal responses. When someone is hypoaroused they may be numb, passive, or appear distanced. This presentation can be more challenging to discern if we associate trauma with dramatic responses. Instead, a person in a state of hypoarousal may float under the radar in many of our campus environments.

These extreme arousal states offer a connection to how trauma can negatively influence students' learning experiences. These responses complicate the capacity for students to metabolize information and take part in community,[14] two outcomes we are particularly interested in within higher education environments. For example, imagine a student in resident assistant training consumed by intrusive memories of a previous trauma. In moments of hyperarousal, that student is likely unable to focus on the content being delivered, let alone feel connected to his/her/their surroundings. Or imagine a student attending a leadership development workshop in a state of hypoarousal, withdrawn and checked out of what is happening in the room. That student might be unable to meaningfully participate in the goals of the workshop, and someone observing the student may falsely assume the student is disinterested, if the student is noticed at all.

What Is Our Role as Student Affairs Educators in Effectively Supporting Students Through Trauma?

Many student affairs educators were drawn to the field for the capacity to make a difference in students' lives. As well intentioned as those aspirations may be, defining what it means to support students is contested terrain and evokes dilemmas and complications centering on how best to do our work while remaining well ourselves. It seems that obvious responses of how to best support student survivors of trauma would include items like "be a good listener" and "help connect students to needed resources." Those are great starting points, but the act of being good support for the journey through trauma is complicated. In what follows, I highlight a few dilemmas that student affairs educators may encounter and conclude with some thoughts on what we can do to be helpful to student survivors.

Dilemma 1: Should I Incorporate Trigger Warnings in My Work With Students?

Much debate has emerged in higher education environments about the use of *trigger warnings*, which are defined as, "[statements] cautioning that content (as in a text, video, or class) may be disturbing or upsetting."[15] Often, university educators conceptualize trigger warnings in relation to course syllabi; however, we can expand these boundaries to imagine other situations where trigger warnings might be worth considering. For example, should we consider them before trainings that include potentially sensitive topics? What about before screening a movie that contains possibly traumatic content?

The debate regarding trigger warnings is expansive.[16] Some emphasize the psychophysiological effects of trauma and either argue in favor of warnings, given harmful triggering effects that can occur for survivors, or against warnings, maintaining that exposure to stressors is part of the healing process. In another camp, some argue that trigger warnings amount to coddling that threatens the aims of higher education. Another perspective offers that trigger warnings acknowledge the very real differences that exist in student experiences, often due to inequitable power structures. Meanwhile, still others contend that a certain amount of anxiety has always been part of the learning process. Ultimately, trauma researchers have suggested that appropriate and manageable amounts of anxiety may be very different for those who have been traumatized.[17]

No matter where individuals situate themselves in this debate, the reality is that we can never anticipate all that could be a trigger for someone who survived trauma (assuming we even know the particular trauma experience), because sometimes the trigger is literal while other times it can be more symbolic.[18] Additionally, survivors are navigating a world replete with triggers as part of their ongoing process of recovery. Weighing the options of what to do as student affairs professionals must include some reasonable considerations. If there are obvious triggers that we have reason to believe would be harmful to a student, it seems reasonable to consider articulating those in advance. Meanwhile, those very desires to spare anxiety may themselves be anxiety-provoking, particularly when they put students into a situation of forced disclosure if they are opting out of a certain activity. Thus, while our assessments may be grounded in considerations of avoiding significant harm to students, there are many contextual judgments we will make along the way about what is in the best interest of a student in a particular situation.

Dilemma 2: How Do I Navigate Mandatory Reporting?

The complexities of mandatory reporting, particularly around sexual violence, have greatly complicated the work of student affairs professionals with student survivors. Student affairs educators frequently find themselves in the position of being supports and confidants to students. Yet, many student affairs staff members face the possibility of legal obligations to report instances of sexual violence of which they are made aware. This puts many professionals in a complicated situation.

First, it is important to get informed about the specific requirements that apply to your situation, as reporting requirements may vary and can change as government and institutional policies evolve. For example, federal laws such as Title IX obligate certain "responsible employees" to report instances of sexual violence,[19] while the Cleary Act requires that any "campus security authority" report applicable crimes, such as sexual assault.[20] Meanwhile, some states and institutions have interpreted mandatory reporting obligations broadly and their policies reflect wider reach in terms of which employees need to report instances of sexual violence.[21]

Second, it is critical to consider the importance of control for survivors of trauma. When student affairs professionals are mandatory reporters for their campus, they need to make this known to students who may want to disclose situations of sexual violence—their own or those of others. This is also why clarity about specific reporting requirements is useful so students can be provided accurate information about what you may need to disclose. Key in this process is maintenance of a climate of trust in which students can make their own decisions about what they want to do with the information they have to share.

Dilemma 3: How Do I Support Students When I'm Personally Affected by Their Trauma?

The ways in which others' trauma can affect us is well documented in helping professions literature. Often this is framed through the lens of secondary traumatic stress or vicarious trauma.[22] Secondary traumatic stress results when a helper's engagement with another's trauma causes behaviors that mimic symptoms associated with PTSD such as hypervigilance, intrusive thoughts, avoidance behaviors, nightmares of the other person's trauma, and difficulty with concentration. Vicarious trauma negatively impacts the helper's cognitive landscape, including shifts in self-concept, self-efficacy, worldviews about safety and trust, and/or spiritual beliefs. Helpers can also be impacted by someone else's trauma in more beneficial ways. This type of secondary trauma effect is known as vicarious resilience and accounts for the ways in which a helper may experience positive outcomes by engagement with another person's resilience and coping mechanisms to overcome adversity.[23]

Proactive self-care is a foundational component of supporting others through trauma, and occurs on multiple dimensions. First, engaging in critical self-assessment allows for identifying the actual limits of what you are and are not able to handle. Once you identify these limits, it is helpful to develop strategies that simultaneously help you recognize when you are reaching these boundaries and how to honor them. Second, identify your own support resources. Indeed, counseling literature points to how important it is for those engaged in work with survivors of trauma to have outlets to process their own reactions and feelings to what they are witnessing.[24] Third, it cannot be underscored enough that those in helping roles need to engage in strong self-care behaviors to support their own well-being, whether that is through, for example, exercise, healthy eating, time with friends or family, therapy, or spiritual support.

What Can We Do?

Student affairs educators are uniquely positioned to provide effective support to student survivors of trauma. While this assistance can take many forms, I outline some key examples of how student affairs professionals can structure their work to effectively support student survivors of trauma.

Holding Supportive Space

One of the most significant things we can do to support survivors is the simple and complicated work of being a good listener. Critically, we must take cues from survivors for their readiness to discuss their trauma or not.[25] However, if a student survivor wants to open up about their experience and we are capable of listening, holding supportive space for that student is one of the most powerful things we can do.

Many aspects of traumatic experiences carry with them negatively charged emotions for survivors that can distance them from others. Feelings of shame, guilt, or fear may be strongly present for those who have endured tremendous adversity and distance survivors from the supportive others they ultimately need to heal.[26] Thus, when a survivor is ready and wants to share his/her/their experience, the act of sharing that story with a supportive other can be a critical component of the healing process.

Conscious and Informed Referrals

Effective support is a balancing act. At one extreme is the possibility of disengaging completely. You may witness this in colleagues who, at the sheer mention of a potentially sensitive subject, refer students to someone else, often a counselor, and end the conversation. Overreferring can burden college counseling centers that may already be challenged in meeting the volume of student needs. At the other extreme is overinvolvement. An example of this scenario is a colleague who is taking phone calls from a distraught student day and night. This constant contact can ultimately be harmful to both the professional and student.

Certainly, there are times when these examples are intermittently appropriate. Colleagues may be aware of their limits and know when a student discloses a particular trauma that it is a personal trigger and something they cannot handle. Alternatively, colleagues may be overinvolved for a contained period of time during which they are connecting the student with other resources to ensure their safety.

We need to consider not only the process of referring but also how to engage in conscious and informed referring. This includes self-awareness work on our parts. Why do we want to refer a student (i.e., is it a matter of our own unexplored discomfort or a legitimate need to involve a mental health professional?)? Why do we *not* want to refer a student (i.e., are we playing the martyr or is the situation under control and we are easing the burden on other colleagues?)?

What Else Might Be Going On?

Part of our work in supporting students through trauma is developing better capacities to "see" trauma in the lives of those around us. We've already discussed the ways in which traumatic experience is subjective and how traumatic stress responses can manifest in both hyper and hypo responses. In other words, it might not be obvious to the untrained eye that what is happening in front of us is a response to trauma as opposed to just a difficult student who seems to get frustrated with minor changes or a star student who seems to do everything perfectly.

If there is one thing to advocate for in helping to support students through trauma, it is professionals who get in the habit of asking themselves, "What else might be going on here?" Taking a pause to ask this question in practice and policy is paramount to effectively supporting students who are battling the challenges of trauma. What might this look like in practice? Fundamentally, it is about slowing down. It is about noticing the student who seems very upset by a particular classroom environment and asking, "What else might be going on?" It is about interrogating the policy that mandates students write an essay to explain their falling grades to remain in an honors program and asking, "What would it be like for the student to self-disclose if the reason is trauma?" It is about observing the student who seems perfectly composed and controlled and asking "What could I be missing?" The answers in these scenarios may have nothing to do with trauma, but it might. Leaving open the possibility of trauma is what allows space for students to heal.

Conclusion

Trauma is a persistent component of many students' experiences on our campuses. Although it is unlikely we can change that reality, there is tremendous potential the work we can do in effectively supporting student survivors as they seek to engage in the positive learning and development experiences of our campus environments. The path of walking alongside survivors of trauma is not always easy or comfortable, but it is through our work to be good partners in the journey that comfort and recovery are possible.

Discussion Questions

1. How do you define *trauma*? What might your definition mean in terms of trauma that you readily "see" and forms that you do not? What are the implications in your work?
2. Identify some existing policies or practices in your work and interrogate them through a trauma-informed lens. What effectively supports student survivors? What might be challenging or harmful to student survivors?

Notes

1. White House Task Force to Protect Students From Sexual Assault. (2014). *Not alone: The first report of the White House task force to protect students from*

sexual assault. Retrieved from https://obamawhitehouse.archives.gov/sites/default/files/docs/report_0.pdf

2. Briere, J. N., Scott, C., & Jones, J. (2015). The effects of trauma. In J. N. Briere & C. Scott, *Principles of trauma therapy: A guide to symptoms, evaluation, and treatment* (2nd ed., DSM-5 update, pp. 25–61). Thousand Oaks, CA: Sage.

3. Erikson, K. (1995). Notes on trauma and community. In C. Caruth (Ed.), *Trauma: Explorations in memory* (pp. 183–199). Baltimore, MD: Johns Hopkins University Press.

4. Levers, L. L. (2012). An introduction to counseling survivors of trauma: Beginning to understand the context of trauma. In L. L. Levers (Ed.), *Trauma counseling: Theories and interventions* (pp. 1–22). New York, NY: Springer.

5. Hyatt-Burkhart, D., & Levers, L. L. (2012). Historical contexts of trauma. In L. L. Levers (Ed.), *Trauma counseling: Theories and interventions* (pp. 23–46). New York, NY: Springer; Brown, L. S. (2008). *Cultural competence in trauma therapy: Beyond the flashback*. Washington DC: American Psychological Association.

6. Brown, *Cultural competence in trauma therapy*; Stevens, M. E. (2016). Trauma is as trauma does: The politics of affect in catastrophic times. In M. J. Casper & E. Wertheimer (Eds.), *Critical trauma studies: Understanding violence, conflict and memory in everyday life* (pp. 19–36). New York, NY: New York University Press.

7. Supin, J. (2016, November). The long shadow: Bruce Perry on the lingering effects of childhood trauma. *The Sun, 491*, pp. 4–13.

8. Brown, *Cultural competence in trauma therapy*.

9. van der Kolk, B. A. (2014). *The body keeps the score: Brain, mind, and body in the healing of trauma*. New York, NY: Viking.

10. Calhoun, L. G., & Tedeschi, R. G. (2013). *Posttraumatic growth in clinical practice*. New York, NY: Routledge.

11. Levers, An introduction to counseling survivors of trauma; Supin, The long shadow.

12. Ogden, P., Minton, K., & Pain, C. (2006). *Trauma and the body: A sensorimotor approach to psychotherapy*. New York, NY: W. W. Norton, p. 26.

13. Ibid.

14. van der Kolk, *The body keeps the score*.

15. Trigger warning. (2017). *Merriam-Webster's online dictionary*. Retrieved from https://www.merriam-webster.com/dictionary/trigger%20warning

16. Knox, E. J. M. (2017). Introduction: On trigger warnings. In E. J. M. Knox (Ed.), *Trigger warnings: History, theory, context* (pp. xiii–xxi). Lanham, MD: Rowman & Littlefield.

17. Supin, The long shadow.

18. Taylor, H. (2017). Accessibility on campus: Posttraumatic stress disorder, duty to accommodate, and trigger warnings. In E. J. M. Knox (Ed.), *Trigger warnings: History, theory, context* (pp. 22–36). Lanham, MD: Rowman & Littlefield.

19. United States Department of Education, Office for Civil Rights. (2014). *Questions and answers on Title IX and sexual violence*. Retrieved from https://www2

.ed.gov/about/offices/list/ocr/docs/qa-201404-title-ix.pdf; United States Department of Education, Office for Civil Rights. (2001). *Revised sexual harassment guidance: Harassment of students by school employees, other students, or third parties.* Retrieved from https://www2.ed.gov/about/offices/list/ocr/docs/shguide.pdf

20. Napolitano, J. (2014). Only yes means yes: An essay on university policies regarding sexual violence and sexual assault. *Yale Law & Policy Review, 33*(2), 387–402.

21. Sokolow, B. W. (2013, September 23). Mandatory reporting for Title IX: Keep it simple. *The Chronicle of Higher Education.* Retrieved from http://www.chronicle.com/article/Mandatory-Reporting-for-Title/141785

22. Newell, J. M., & MacNeil, G. A. (2010). Professional burnout, vicarious trauma, secondary traumatic stress, and compassion fatigue: A review of theoretical terms, risk factors, and preventive methods for clinicians and researchers. *Best Practices in Mental Health, 6*(2), 57–68.

23. Hernández-Wolfe, P., Killian, K., Engstrom, D., & Gangsei, D. (2015). Vicarious resilience, vicarious trauma, and awareness of equity in trauma work. *Journal of Humanistic Psychology, 55*(2), 153–172.

24. Knight, C. (2013). Indirect trauma: Implications for self-care, supervision, the organization, and the academic institution. *The Clinical Supervisor, 32*(2), 224–243.

25. Supin, The long shadow.

26. van der Kolk, *The body keeps the score.*

A Focus on Relational and Narrative Aspects of Trauma: Challenges and Opportunities for Higher Education

Kelli D. Zaytoun

There is no grief like the grief that does not speak.[1]

We must bear witness to what our bodies remember. . . . These narratives serve not just as self-nurturing "therapy," but actually change reality.[2]

Given the multitude of complex issues associated with supporting student survivors of trauma, Shalka's introduction to the topic aptly homes in on the essentials with which all student affairs educators should be familiar: definitions and manifestations of trauma; current discussions related to our work; and how to best support students by listening well, making referrals, and carefully examining the efficiency of policies and procedures. Part of the effectiveness of Shalka's essay lies in her sharing of her personal story, which not only informs the reader of her firsthand knowledge of trauma but also is a reminder of how trauma comes in an endless variety of specific forms. Importantly, testimonies like Shalka's are a critical part of trauma recovery, a process that involves the survivor, family members, friends, and society at large. As Judith Herman states, "Remembering and telling the truth about terrible events are prerequisites both for the restoration of the social order and for the healing of individual victims."[3] Shalka's appropriately broad-sweep introduction makes room for this more focused response, one that concentrates on the relational and narrative or "account-giving" aspects of trauma and trauma recovery. More specifically, this essay underscores the vastness of the interpersonal and societal conditions within which trauma and its implications and recovery occur and the role that truth-telling plays in healing from trauma on individual and collective levels. Lastly and accordingly, given these considerations, I reflect on how student affairs educators are poised to take responsibility for and aid in trauma recovery processes.

The Relational Context of Trauma: Interpersonal Effects and Systemic Conditions

Trauma is too often understood as an individual, unspeakable, secret experience and burden that no one can possibly understand, but trauma and its repercussions occur in profoundly collective and ever-present contexts. As a friend who works with refugee populations recently said to me, "Trauma lives alongside us."[4] Although trauma's effects are deeply individual and personal, leaving lasting psychological and bodily traces, the families and communities within which victims are enmeshed are connected to the trauma in complicated ways; here we find support for survivors but also sometimes the sources of the trauma. We—and those we love, mentor, teach, and work with—might carry trauma, in wide ranges of degrees and severity, and with it, a variety of means for responding to it, and those responses have effects that ripple through communities and generations. The effects of trauma extend beyond our direct experience with it when we witness, try to help, and are touched in other ways by someone's traumatic pain. Additionally, new research even indicates that those who experience trauma can pass epigenetic effects on to their children.[5] No realm of experience—psychological, physiological, social, or spiritual—is beyond trauma's reach. Healing from trauma, therefore, is not an individual task or responsibility given this complex, relational, broad context.

In addition to considering how family and community affect and are affected by a person's traumatic experience, understanding the relational context of trauma involves a serious look at systemic oppression on institutional and societal levels. Although most of us think of trauma as being caused by one unimaginable circumstance, trauma can also occur slowly over time, not only to individuals but also to collectives. Trauma inflicted by extreme circumstances garners more attention than trauma endured by everyday ones, like microaggressions and emotional neglect.[6] Instances of cultural displacement, isolation, and erasure, for example, might not be as easy to identify as trauma-inducing as other immediately life-altering events, like those caused by a natural disaster, violent injury, or the sudden death of a loved one. Some populations are more vulnerable to traumatic circumstances, including women; children; people with disabilities; and racial, ethnic, and sexual minorities.[7] Such circumstances and vulnerabilities affect many of our students. Shalka makes a critical point, one I seek to expand, in mentioning that systemic oppression is overlooked in discussions of trauma. Attention to how groups of people are traumatized by systems of power and politics is crucial to addressing and eliminating trauma. Institutions of higher education can play a major role in studying, and educating the public about, such phenomena. Certainly, student affairs educators can take the lead in helping to ensure that institutional oppression is identified and addressed and that support systems are in place for those who experience marginalization and discrimination. For example, student affairs educators are often those who are charged with or who initiate the establishment of a university-wide social justice task force that identifies problems in and strategies and policies for addressing issues of diversity and inclusion.

A supportive network in the form of family and friends is necessary for individual trauma survivors; for groups of people who experience particular types of trauma, such networks come in the form of political movements.[8] Indeed, "in the absence of strong political movements for human rights, the active process of bearing witness inevitably gives way to the active process of forgetting. Repression, dissociation, and denial are phenomenon of social as well as individual consciousness."[9] Herman identifies three times in the twentieth century that particular types of traumas—hysteria, combat neuroses, and effects of domestic and sexual abuse—received public attention due to political movements that advanced the study of those traumas *and* moved society in the direction of eliminating those trauma's sources (war and sexism). This work is immense and still ongoing; I write this essay in the midst of 2018's #MeToo movement, which has given way to millions of women speaking out about having suffered from sexual harassment and assault. Addressing trauma, therefore, often involves and requires not just caring for individual victims; it involves wide-ranging community efforts and activist activity. Student affairs educators support institutional efforts, including those that are student led, that raise awareness about and demand change around issues like sexual, gender-based, and racial harassment and violence. In this regard, colleges and universities are at the vanguard of social redress.

Narrational Aspects of Trauma

Discussion of the complicated contextual and collective aspects of trauma, however, must take place alongside attention to trauma's deeply personal effects. I focus here on just one of the major, necessary tasks of trauma recovery and how student affairs educators can play a positive role in the healing process: the individual act of telling stories of trauma. According to Susan Brison, "*saying* something about a memory *does* something to it"[10] allowing the survivor to begin to take control over the experience in its aftermath. Brison suggests that, although trauma dismantles one's concept of self, deeply disturbing the process of memory, sense of time, and even sense of one's own body, recovery of the self is possible in the presence of those who compassionately bear witness to the survivor's story. Judith Herman agrees:

"Recovery can only take place in the context of relationships; it cannot occur in isolation."[11] To be clear: No one should be forced to share their stories, and I do not wish to diminish the horrors that trauma inflicts by highlighting the possibilities for overcoming it; my emphasis on the role of narrating traumatic experience in healing is meant to focus on the opportunities that can be present in the context of a safe, supportive, higher education environment. Indeed, as Shalka mentions, resilience can ensue. Survivors can discover ways to cope and flourish, and supporters feel the benefits of having helped and having learned from the survivor. The broad point here is that processes of healing, learning, and growing are *relational*; they are communicative endeavors. As educators we will likely be in the position of witnessing our students, and perhaps even ourselves, work through trauma, whether we welcome it or not. One way to begin to approach the presence of trauma in our work is, quite simply, to recognize it, "to 'see' trauma in the lives of those around us,"[12] as Shalka puts it, to help give it a voice, and to take responsibility for becoming a part of the healing process when it is appropriate and when we can. Of course, some of us are in better positions, professionally and emotionally, to do this than others, but paying attention to how trauma manifests itself in individuals, *and* to how healing from trauma is a relational, community process is an important step for higher educational professionals.

Higher education, in a variety of ways, in and outside of the classroom, lends itself to important, specific forms of learning and expression that, even unwittingly, facilitate the two-way process of giving and witnessing testimony: reading, writing, listening, and speaking. One way to approach how an educator might play a role in the individual truth-telling step of trauma recovery is to explore how that educator is in a position to facilitate one of these four forms of expression. Advisers and counselors, resident hall directors, and directors and coordinators of programs might have more opportunities than the faculty for individual conversations with students, but faculty have the chance to interact with students by reading and responding to their writing, including students' responses to what they read. Some student affairs educators, particularly, are in positions that warrant their being trained in trauma assessment and invention. All institutions should have point persons trained for immediate response to trauma victims. Professors of certain fields, like literature, composition, psychology, and women, gender and sexuality studies, might see stories of trauma surface in students' work or their reactions to certain texts. Students will also turn to a professor as someone they can talk to and trust. As Shalka suggests, being a good listener and making referrals are at the foundation of what we can do for student survivors, and this task is not to be taken lightly, as needs and what it takes for someone to feel safe enough to share their story, vary. Victims might be dealing with repression, disassociation, and/or sensory flashbacks, just to name a few of the serious consequences that can be associated with traumatic experience. Student affairs educators should be familiar with these implications and the professionals on and off-campus that can treat students presenting psychological and physical symptoms.

In addition to emphasizing our duty to listen well and make referrals, given the systemic conditions of trauma discussed earlier, I seek to extend our sense of responsibility to include being a part of the systemic change needed for institutional and cultural shifts in attention to trauma, change that insists that society, on large-scale levels, "hold traumatic reality in consciousness."[13] Educators in the position to make standards, policies, and procedures can identify risks and barriers, *and* create effective resources and responses for those at risk for trauma and for trauma survivors. Historically, university women's and lesbian, gay, bisexual, transgender, queer/questioning, allied/asexual (LGBTQA) centers and Black cultural centers, for example, offer cutting-edge resources and programming in this regard for campus and community members, with events like V-Day: A Global Movement to End Violence Against Women and Girls, and the Clothesline Project, and the national demands of the Black Liberation Collective, just to name a few. The violation, violence, and destruction of trauma in its many forms can't be kept secret; indeed, attempts to deny or bury it are always futile and damaging, to individuals, to vulnerable populations, communities, and society as a whole, and the effects last for generations.

The relational and contextual nature of trauma and self, and the narrative aspects of healing emphasized in this essay indicate vast challenges, but also opportunities, for educators. It behooves us to take on trauma, give it a voice, as unspeakable as those traumas might seem, in order to bring them to the surface, give victims acknowledgment and control, and finally, stop cycles, secrecy, and the diminishment, pain, and erasure of persons and peoples. Shalka closes with a hopeful statement, saying that "comfort and recovery are possible" for survivors when we are "good partners in the journey."[14] We can do that in many ways, as listeners, advocates, educators, and activists, bringing relief and help to individual students and being a part of the larger changes that are necessary for reducing and preventing instances and sources of traumatic experience.

Discussion Questions

1. How can you contribute to making institutional improvements that minimize the traumatic effects of systemic marginalization and oppression, like microaggressions and cultural isolation?

2. What strengths do you have as a student affairs educator that can help facilitate the process of giving and witnessing testimonies of trauma, in oral and written forms?

3. What opportunities exist on your campus to raise awareness about and prevent traumatic incidents, like those for which college students are at risk, including sexual and intimate partner violence? What policies and resources are in place to assist survivors? How might they be improved?

Notes

1. Wadsworth Longfellow, H. (1839). *Hyperion*. New York, NY: Samuel Coleman, p. 108.

2. Anzaldúa, G. (2015). *Light in the Dark/Luz en lo Oscuro: Rewriting Identity, Spirituality, Reality*. Durham, NC: Duke University Press, p. 21.

3. Herman, J. (1992). *Trauma and recovery: The aftermath of violence—From domestic abuse to political terror*. New York, NY: Basic Books, p. 1.

4. E-mail conversation on December 10, 2017, with Sally Lamping, Lecturer in Literacy, School of Teacher Education, Charles Sturt University, Bathurst, NSW, Australia.

5. Hurley, D. (2013). Grandma's experiences leave a mark on your genes. *Discover Magazine*. Retrieved from http://discovermagazine.com/2013/may/13-grandmas-experiences-leave-epigenetic-mark-on-your-genes

6. Pantas, S., Miller, S. A., & Kulkami, S. (2017) P.S.: I survived: An activism project to increase student and community trauma awareness. *Journal of Teaching in Social Work, 37*(2), 185–198.

7. Ibid., p. 187.

8. Herman, J. (1992). *Trauma and recovery*.

9. Ibid., p. 9.

10. Brison, S. (2002). *Aftermath: Violence and the remaking of the self*. Princeton: Princeton University Press, p. xi.

11. Herman, J., *Trauma and recovery*, p. 133.

12. Shalka, T. R., this volume, p. 229.

13. Herman, J., *Trauma and recovery*, p. 9.

14. Shalka, T. R., this volume, p. 230.

13

Why Is Religion a Difficult Issue in American Higher Education and How Should Student Affairs Respond?

Balancing Competing Interests Through Principled Practice

P. Jesse Rine and Brian D. Reed

"**R**eligion and academia have never had an easy relationship."[1] So begins an essay by Louis Betty for *Inside Higher Ed* in response to the news that Vandy Catholic, a 500-member faith-based student organization at Vanderbilt University, would abandon its official university status and move off campus for the upcoming academic year. The impetus for Vandy Catholic's decision was the strict application of a university nondiscrimination policy that required registered student groups to comply with two mandates. First, membership had to be extended to "all comers," a condition already met by the group. Second, all student members had to be eligible to run for leadership positions, regardless of their personal beliefs. In an official statement, the university highlighted the institutional value of inclusivity it sought to uphold by enforcing the nondiscrimination policy:

> As a higher education institution, Vanderbilt encourages and supports diversity of thought and opinion among our students, faculty, and staff—this is one of the cornerstones of an academic environment. We also recognize

that student organizations help enrich the out-of-classroom experience for our campus community and want to be certain that all of our students have an opportunity to participate in the student organizations that interest them. We are committed to making our campus a welcoming environment for all of our students.[2]

After much deliberation, the student board of Vandy Catholic determined that compliance with the second requirement in the nondiscrimination policy would fundamentally alter the group's identity as a faith-based organization. In a letter to supporters, the group's chaplain shared the board's rationale for leaving campus and relinquishing the benefits of being a registered student organization: "A Catholic student organization led by someone who neither professes the Catholic faith nor strives to live it out would not be able to serve its members as an authentically Catholic organization."[3] Those sympathetic to Vandy Catholic's position argued that by expanding student participation rights beyond membership to include eligibility for leadership positions, the university had actually limited the freedoms of the student organizations themselves. In his essay, Betty posited, "Not allowing a religious organization to stipulate who can be a leader would seem tantamount to denying it the freedom to define itself how it chooses."[4]

The Vandy Catholic case is instructive because it raises larger questions about diversity, inclusivity, and religion on campus. How can college administrators cultivate an array of campus organizations that reflect both the diversity of student interests and the commitments of the institutions they serve? Is the best way to demonstrate institutional inclusivity by honoring difference across official student groups or by mandating difference within said groups? Who adjudicates when institutional values come into conflict with the long-standing beliefs and practices of existing campus religious organizations, and on what basis should decisions be made? Finally, amid such tensions, how should student affairs educators navigate this complex terrain while attending to individual and collective student development?

As these questions illustrate, religion can be one of the most challenging subjects with which college administrators must grapple. The college years are intended to be a time when big ideas—the nature of truth, the meaning of life, the relation of self to community, and the good society—are explored. Yet students come to campus already shaped by their own life experiences and personal beliefs. For many, faith has played a deeply formative role in their identity development, providing a sense of purpose and a framework for understanding the world. When individuals from different religious backgrounds present divergent expectations for their college experience, student affairs educators must often make difficult choices. In many situations, hard and fast answers prove elusive.

   This essay provides the resources necessary for student affairs educators to approach the issue of religion on campus in an informed and equitable manner, one that acknowledges the historical, cultural, and practical dimensions of this deeply personal subject. We begin by chronicling the role of religion in higher education, from the founding of the first universities whose religious nature informed the foundational concepts and structures that would eventually be adopted by the early American colleges, to the philosophical and societal shifts that have shaped college life today. We then turn attention to three key aspects of our contemporary context, namely, the differing institutional purposes that animate the American postsecondary landscape, the state of religious belief among today's collegians, and the role of student affairs educators in fostering holistic student development. We conclude by outlining four principles for practice that can empower student affairs educators to act with integrity and professionalism, make meaningful contributions to their particular institutional contexts, and prepare the students they serve to live authentically and respectfully within a pluralistic society.

Historical Precursors

To fully appreciate the multifaceted nature of religion in American higher education, one must first become acquainted with the historical precursors to the contemporary academy. Although a complete treatment of religion's role in the development of American higher education falls beyond the scope of this essay, a brief overview of four consequential eras reveals the complex dynamics inherited by today's colleges and universities.

The Medieval Era

The earliest epoch of note is the medieval era, a thousand-year period following the fall of the Roman empire and preceding the European Renaissance. It was during this time that the first European universities were founded. The medieval era was defined largely by the Roman Catholic Church and its Christian worldview, which held that truth was unified and singular, God was its ultimate source, and faith was a necessary precondition to knowledge. The dominant philosophy of the day was scholasticism, a form of Christian rationalism that employed deductive and dialectical reasoning to craft a systematic approach to theology. The scholastic method animated the cathedral schools, which were established by the Roman Catholic Church to educate its clergy.

   Initially, instruction in cathedral schools consisted of basic literacy training through the study of scriptural collections, church documents, and devotional materials.[5] Over time, however, the Roman Catholic Church's perspective on the study of pagan writings started to shift. Originally understood as a threat to Christian belief, secular sources came to be viewed as potential contributors to the unified field of knowledge that ultimately pointed to the Creator. Reflecting this conviction, ecclesiastical authorities began to require that cathedral schools teach the seven liberal arts—grammar, rhetoric, logic, arithmetic, geometry, music, and astronomy—in addition to, and in service of, theology.[6] This curricular shift coincided with the rise of the first universities in the late eleventh and early twelfth centuries, most of which grew out of the cathedral schools.

Going forward, three key institutions—the civil government, the church, and the university—would shape the character of medieval society and direct its course. However, as the recognized guardians and purveyors of official knowledge, universities exerted a unique degree of influence in that they educated the persons who would lead the other two institutions.[7] Centuries later, the earliest American colleges would be founded for the same purpose—to train clerics for the church and administrators for the state— and would adopt an explicitly religious identity as well.

The Colonial Era and the Antebellum Era

American institutions of higher education took root during the colonial era and the antebellum era, a period beginning with the arrival of the first European settlers and continuing until the eve of the American Civil War. Various motivations spurred relocation to the New World, not the least of which was the lure of religious freedom. The Protestant Reformation had challenged the religious order of medieval Europe and brought forth scores of new Christian denominations, many of which faced religious persecution. The New World, however, offered the prospect of freely practicing one's personal faith.

Immigrants from a wide range of religious sects inhabited the New World, including Dutch Calvinists, English Puritans, French Huguenots, German Lutherans, and Scottish Presbyterians, and many of these groups would eventually found colleges. In 1636, English Puritans established Harvard College and modeled it after Emmanuel College at Cambridge, one of the great medieval universities. Harvard's character was religious, and its purpose was dual—to train clergy and to educate civic leaders—a formulation echoing medieval forerunners and replicated by every other college founded in America prior to the Revolution.[8]

After securing its independence from England, the infant nation grew, and its population expanded westward. New colleges sprouted up all across the American frontier, as Christian denominations sought to evangelize newly formed communities. By 1810, colleges founded by Congregationalists, Presbyterians, and Episcopalians accounted for more than 85% of all postsecondary enrollment in America.[9] Two additional Protestant denominations, the Baptists and Methodists, benefited from membership surges following the Second Great Awakening and rapidly raised new colleges across the country.[10] On the eve of the American Civil War, Protestant denominations had founded more than 80% of the nation's colleges.[11]

The Era of Transformation

Following the American Civil War, American higher education entered an era of transformation, during which the purposes and composition of the existing system shifted significantly. As the nation industrialized throughout the first half of the nineteenth century, demand for formal education in the practical arts intensified. In response, the Morrill Act of 1862 provided federal land to states for the purpose of establishing colleges that would offer courses in agricultural, technical, and mechanical studies. The resulting proliferation of state colleges normalized the expansion of the college curriculum beyond the traditional liberal arts disciplines.

For decades after their founding, the land grant colleges continued to reflect the country's broader Protestant cultural consensus in their institutional structures and practices. For example, most state colleges required students to attend chapel services as late as the 1890s.[12] However, the religious character of American higher education would eventually wane in the wake of new approaches to teaching and learning, new purposes for the educational enterprise, and new perspectives within the academic disciplines.

One significant catalyst for change was the importation of the German model of higher education and its modernist outlook. In contrast to the medieval formulation of faith seeking understanding, the German model emphasized the objective pursuit of truth through empirical investigation. In 1876, the Johns Hopkins University became the first American institution of higher education intentionally modeled after the German research university. As the land grant and colonial colleges grew into universities, many followed Johns Hopkins's example.[13]

As institutional forms evolved, so too did institutional functions. American universities increasingly viewed their social purpose in economic, rather than religious, terms. Consequently, clerical training moved to the periphery of collegiate life, while preparation for the industrial workforce took center stage. In addition, moral philosophy gradually displaced Christian theology as the primary framework for defining the educational enterprise.[14]

Religious influence further diminished with the rise of new schools of thought that undermined the established Christian worldview. Higher criticism sought to interpret scripture within its sociocultural context, a method implying that the Bible was of human, rather than divine, origin. Logical positivism rejected supernatural explanations in favor of empirical analysis, while relativism argued that truth could be grasped only in local, but not universal, forms. Darwinian evolution called into question accepted understandings of human origins.[15]

New institutional forms, new educational purposes, and new academic perspectives all contributed to a general secularizing trend in American higher education during the era of transformation. One important effect of this trend was the eventual disengagement of religious colleges from their founding denominations.[16] This phenomenon would continue into, and help define, the fourth and final consequential era.

The Era of Multiplicity

At the close of World War II, the American system of higher education entered an era of multiplicity, during which colleges and universities diversified across a number of dimensions. The long-standing trend toward secularization fostered further variation among the ranks of religiously affiliated institutions, with most of these colleges falling somewhere between faithful adherence to and complete abandonment of their founding missions. In addition, many elite private and land grant universities that had adopted the German research model eventually morphed into "multiversities," or loose confederations of varying interests that "served multiple purposes, centers of power, and clienteles."[17] These diverse interests cohered not by a unified vision of education, but by the common task of knowledge production, a project whose modernist foundations would eventually be called into question.

The second half of the twentieth century gave rise to postmodernism, a movement that rejected the modernist belief in language as a stable and unbiased transmitter of truth. In contrast, postmodernists argued that meaning shifts across sociocultural contexts, and those contexts are ultimately shaped by power relations.[18] As postmodern thought gained currency in the American university, attention turned to ensuring that historically marginalized perspectives received representation within the college curriculum. As a result, new academic disciplines emerged—such as Black studies, women's studies, and postcolonial studies—and many institutions added multicultural course requirements to their general education programs.[19]

American higher education was becoming increasingly multifaceted, as was the society it served. Though certainly not monolithic, most of the early

Americans shared a Western European cultural and religious heritage. Near the start of the era of transformation, new waves of immigrants arrived from southern and eastern Europe and brought with them new languages, cultures, and religions.[20] Many of these people groups subscribed to Roman Catholicism, Eastern Orthodoxy, and Judaism, traditions differing significantly from American Protestantism but sharing multiple points of intersection as monotheistic, Abrahamic religions.

The range of cultural diversity supplied by new immigrants expanded even further during the era of multiplicity, when Congress passed the Immigration and Nationality Act of 1965. This law eliminated previously established quotas based on national origin that privileged Western Europeans and provided new opportunity to immigrants from Africa, Asia, and Latin America. Shortly thereafter, immigration from Asia and Latin America soared, and by 1990 the majority of new immigrants to the United States came from countries outside Europe.[21] Consequently, the United States became more religiously diverse during this period, adding followers of world religions such as Buddhism, Hinduism, and Islam.

The Present Landscape

Today, the American system of higher education is distinguished by its remarkable diversity, a widely recognized strength that nevertheless contributes to institutional, individual, and professional complexity, and this complexity often renders religion a difficult issue to navigate. At the institutional level, colleges and universities in the United States take multiple forms and serve varying purposes. Three basic types of four-year institutions illustrate this reality: public, nonsectarian, and religiously affiliated. Although many once reflected the religious character of their initial social context, public institutions presently embody a secular ethos that allows but does not formally establish any particular religious expression. When compared to their private counterparts, public colleges and universities enroll a proportionately greater number of students and therefore tend to be larger (see Table 13.1). The other two basic institutional types—nonsectarian and religiously affiliated—are private and therefore not legally bound to maintain a stance of religious neutrality.[22] Nonsectarian institutions choose not to privilege a specific religious tradition, even though many were founded by Christian denominations and often retain vestiges of their original religious identity, such as campus chapels. In contrast, religiously affiliated institutions are explicitly connected to a particular church or religious denomination, though practice at these institutions can vary significantly across dimensions such as public rhetoric, membership requirements, and governance.[23]

TABLE 13.1
Total Four-Year Institutions and Undergraduate Enrollment by Type

Type of Institution	Fall 2015		
	Total Four-Year Institutions	Total Undergraduate Enrollment	Average Undergraduate Enrollment
Public	555	6,053,708	10,908
Nonsectarian	362	1,160,239	3,205
Religiously Affiliated	576	1,336,005	2,319

Source: United States Department of Education, Institute of Education Sciences, National Center for Education Statistics, Integrated Postsecondary Education Data System (IPEDS). Retrieved from https:// nces.ed.gov/ipeds. Counts are for public and private not-for-profit baccalaureate, master's, and doctoral institutions in the United States.

Religiously affiliated institutions number more than their public and non-sectarian peers, yet they tend to be the smallest of the three types.

At the individual level, today's college students bring a wide range of religious preferences to campus, even as the majority increasingly expresses a desire for spiritual development. For example, a national study found that 83% of college students identified with a particular religious tradition, including Seventh-Day Adventism, Buddhism, Eastern Orthodoxy, Hinduism, Islam, Judaism, Mormonism, Roman Catholicism, Unitarianism, and 8 different Protestant Christian denominations.[24] The same study found that 81% of college students attended religious services at least occasionally, 80% expressed an interest in spirituality, and nearly 50% thought it was essential or very important to seek out opportunities for spiritual growth.

It is perhaps little surprise that this institutional and individual diversity introduces complexity at the professional level. From its origin in the late nineteenth century, the student affairs profession has consistently seen its role as facilitating holistic student development, including spiritual growth. And yet, much like American higher education as a whole, religious influence in the student affairs profession has gradually declined. For decades, it was not unusual for student affairs educators to have some type of religious or theological training. However, as the profession codified its preparation standards during the midtwentieth century, concerns over the separation of church and state led many to question the professional value of religious training. Consequently, most student affairs training programs failed to adequately address spiritual development, and fewer persons with religious expertise were hired as student affairs educators.[25] Although the field has witnessed increased interest in spirituality of late, the profession's reticence to engage issues of religion persists, even as many of today's college students wish to explore spiritual matters from a multitude of faith traditions.

Principles for Practice

In the midst of this multilayered complexity, student affairs educators may wonder how exactly to respond. Matters of personal belief often present a challenging terrain to traverse, but the following four principles for practice provide a way forward. First and foremost: *Student affairs educators should understand and honor their institutional contexts.* As noted earlier, the ways in which religious traditions are acknowledged and engaged by a particular college or university will depend largely upon its institutional type (i.e., public, nonsectarian, religiously affiliated). In addition, student affairs educators should attend to two other consequential dimensions of institutional context: mission and culture. An institution's mission defines its identity within the postsecondary landscape, declares its purpose for existence, and provides direction for future action, while an institution's culture emerges from the widely accepted symbols, ideals, assumptions, and beliefs its members collectively use as an interpretive lens for behavior.[26] Institutional type, mission, and culture all contribute to norms and expectations for the treatment of religion on campus, and the most effective student affairs educators are those who clearly understand and align with these structures, norms, and expectations. This assessment begins with the job search process, during which candidates should acknowledge that institutional cultures are often slow to change and should honestly ask themselves whether they can fully support the existing mission and values of the institution. Although the candidate need not perfectly align with the institution, it is important to consider the personal and professional strain that can result from being at odds with one's employer before accepting any job offer. Moreover, because administrative staff do not enjoy the privileges of academic freedom in the same manner as their faculty colleagues, they must exercise great wisdom and care regarding how to appropriately voice their discontent with existing structures, norms, and expectations. Challenges to institutional culture are more likely to be successful if they are viewed as advancing rather than undermining institutional mission.

Shifting focus from institutional to individual concerns reveals a second principle for practice: *Student affairs educators should personally cultivate the self-awareness, integrity, and authenticity they hope to instill in the students they serve.* Indeed, before they can appropriately engage students in the process of spiritual development, student affairs educators must first come to grips with their own inner lives. Self-awareness serves as a prerequisite to truly knowing and serving others, and it is cultivated by critically examining one's own personal identity, or "the moving intersection of the inner and outer forces that make me who I am."[27] Personal disciplines such as reflective journaling can create space for regular self-assessment, while intentional dialogue with trusted colleagues can sharpen one's own perceptions through honest yet supportive critique. Once self-awareness has been achieved, the next step is to commit to personal integrity. Individuals with integrity command the respect of others because they "are consistent with a personally owned value structure, over time and across varied contexts."[28] Turning lastly to the outward presentation of the self, student affairs educators should endeavor to lead authentic lives. Authenticity builds trust in relationships, because it presents one's personal orientations, motives, and biases in a forthright manner.[29] When student affairs educators know themselves well, apply their personal values consistently, and conduct their lives with candor, they are most able to guide students along their chosen paths of spiritual discovery.

Moving from care of self to care for others leads to a third principle for practice: *Student affairs educators should take an individualized approach to fostering student spiritual growth.* Individualized approaches are preferable because they recognize student uniqueness, provide a sense of agency, and encourage self-authorship. Moreover, individualized approaches have the added virtue of adaptability across institutional contexts and religious traditions. For instance, one commendable individualized technique is motivational interviewing, a method which offers an effective framework for walking alongside students in their moments of contemplation. The hallmark of motivational interviewing is the honor it affords to individual autonomy and the trust it places in a person's natural wisdom and desire to grow in a positive direction.[30] In this approach, the student affairs educator serves as a partner seeking both to evoke what is present rather than supply what is missing and to elicit from within rather than impose from without. By asking open-ended questions and practicing reflective listening, the motivational interviewer empowers interviewees to choose, plan, and act of their own volition. Regardless of the chosen technique, when student affairs educators adopt individualized approaches to fostering spiritual growth, they serve as advocates who place student interests above their own.

Turning attention from the individual to the collective highlights the fourth and final principle for practice: *Student affairs educators should aim to achieve religious pluralism rather than theological agreement on their campuses.* The college years present a unique opportunity for emerging adults to come into close contact with persons whose ideas, beliefs, and convictions differ significantly from their own, and to learn how to live in harmony with others without compromising fundamental aspects of their own personal identities. Student affairs educators can work toward this goal by endeavoring to foster understanding and social cooperation, rather than complete theological agreement, among different religious groups on campus. This balance is best achieved by recognizing the right to hold exclusivist truth claims ("my belief is true and your belief is false") while also requiring respect for the rights of others ("their beliefs are as precious to them as mine are to me").[31] Exercises such as perspective taking, facilitated negotiation, structured interfaith dialogue, and interfaith service projects bring students into contact with religiously diverse others, promote greater understanding of difference, and require some degree of social cooperation, but they do not demand theological uniformity. This approach fosters both civility and equity, because it enables the student affairs educator to prepare students for the pluralistic world they will inherit even as they progress along their preferred religious—or nonreligious—pathways.

Conclusion

Historical precursors, societal shifts, and sector diversity all contribute to the complex nature of religion in American higher education. Although this complexity often translates to challenge for the student affairs educator, it also presents a tremendous opportunity for those who recognize the richness that religious faith offers to its adherents. By seeing the college years as an exceptional period of life for self-determination and spiritual development—rather than an occasion for religious disabuse or deprogramming—student affairs educators can champion all students as they undertake their unique explorations of being and becoming.

Discussion Questions

1. Are the colleges where you have studied public, nonsectarian, or religiously affiliated, and how did these institutional identities shape their approach to religion? Did you find yourself in alignment or conflict with these approaches? What effect did that have on your student experience?
2. Imagine that a situation similar to the one described at the beginning of this essay occurred on your campus. Which individuals, groups, and/or institutional policies would you consult in the decision-making process? What resources for resolution currently exist on your campus, and which would you like to implement that are not currently in place?

3. Which of the four recommended principles for practice strikes you as most helpful? What steps might you take to implement this approach more fully in your role as a student affairs educator? Which would you find most challenging to adopt, and why?

Notes

1. Betty, L. (2012, May 4). Sending Catholics running for cover. *Inside Higher Ed.* Retrieved from https://www.insidehighered.com/views/2012/05/04/essay-impact-vanderbilt-policies-catholic-students

2. Statement from Vanderbilt University (2011, September 15). Retrieved from https://news.vanderbilt.edu/2011/09/15/statement-from-vanderbilt-university/

3. University Catholic. (2012). *About.* [Letter to alumni, parents, and friends of Vanderbilt Catholic] Retrieved from https://universitycatholic.org/vanderbilt-catholic-will-not-re-register

4. Betty, Sending Catholics running for cover.

5. Lucas, C. J. (2006). *American higher education: A history.* (2nd ed.). New York, NY: Palgrave Macmillan.

6. Ibid.

7. Axtell, J. (2016). *Wisdom's workshop: The rise of the modern university.* Princeton, NJ: Princeton University Press.

8. Lucas, *American higher education.*

9. Cohen, A. M., & Kisker, C. B. (2010). *The shaping of American higher education: Emergence and growth of the contemporary system.* (2nd ed.). San Francisco, CA: Jossey-Bass.

10. Ringenberg, W. C. (2006). *The Christian college: A history of Protestant higher education in America.* (2nd ed.). Grand Rapids, MI: Baker Academic.

11. Axtell, *Wisdom's workshop.*

12. Marsden, G. M. (1994). *The soul of the American university: From Protestant establishment to established nonbelief.* New York, NY: Oxford University Press.

13. Rudolph, F. (1990). *The American college and university: A history.* Athens, GA: The University of Georgia Press.

14. Marsden, *The soul of the American university.*

15. Ringenberg, *The Christian college.*

16. Burtchaell, J. T. (1998). *The dying of the light: The disengagement of colleges and universities from their Christian churches.* Grand Rapids, MI: Eerdmans.

17. Axtell, *Wisdom's workshop,* p. 340.

18. Bloland, H. G. (1995). Postmodernism and higher education. *The Journal of Higher Education, 66*(5), 521–559.

19. Rine, P. J. (2013). Christian college persistence in the postmodern turn. In A. B. Rockenbach & M. J. Mayhew (Eds.), *Spirituality in college students' lives: Translating research into practice* (pp. 69–87). New York, NY: Routledge.

20. Tindall, G. B., & Shi, D. E. (1997). *America: A narrative history.* (4th ed.). New York, NY: Norton.

21. Ibid.

22. Kaplan, W. A., & Lee, B. A. (2014). *The law of higher education: Student version.* (5th ed.). San Francisco, CA: Jossey-Bass.

23. Benne, R. (2001). *Quality with soul: How six premier colleges and universities keep faith with their religious traditions.* Grand Rapids, MI: Eerdmans.

24. Astin, A. W., Astin, H. S., Lindholm, J. A., Bryant, A. N., Szelényi, K., & Calderone, S. (2005). *The spiritual life of college students: A national study of college students' search for meaning and purpose.* Los Angeles, CA: Higher Education Research Institute, UCLA.

25. Dalton, J. C. (2005). The place of spirituality in the mission and work of college student affairs. In A. W. Chickering, J. C. Dalton, & L. Stamm (Eds.), *Encouraging authenticity and spirituality in higher education* (pp. 145–164). San Francisco, CA: Jossey-Bass.

26. Renn, K. A., & Patton, L. D. (2017). Institutional identity and campus culture. In J. H. Schuh, S. R. Jones, & V. Torres (Eds.), *Student services: A handbook for the profession* (pp. 58–72). San Francisco, CA: Jossey-Bass.

27. Palmer, P. (2007). *The courage to teach: Exploring the inner landscape of a teacher's life.* San Francisco, CA: Jossey-Bass, p. 14.

28. Chickering, A. W. (2005). Our orientation. In A. W. Chickering, J. C. Dalton, & L. Stamm (Eds.), *Encouraging authenticity and spirituality in higher education* (pp. 5–36). San Francisco, CA: Jossey-Bass, p. 9.

29. Ibid.

30. Miller, W. R., & Rollnick, S. (2013). *Motivational interviewing: Preparing people for change.* (3rd ed.). New York, NY: Guilford Press.

31. Patel, E., & Meyer, C. (2010). Defining religious pluralism: A response to professor Robert McKim. *Journal of College & Character, 11*(2), 1–4.

Supporting Interfaith Climates and Outcomes: Considerations and Practices for Student Affairs Educators

Benjamin S. Selznick

In his seminal work *A Common Faith,* John Dewey wrote: "I make no claim to knowing how far intelligence may and will develop in respect to social relations. But one thing I think I do know. The needed understanding will not develop unless we strive for it."[1] It is in this spirit of moving toward a shared, needed interfaith understanding that I consider important questions associated with creating campus environments that foster equity, civility, and safety for students holding increasingly diverse worldviews.

To begin, I provide a brief response to the historical account offered in the previous essay, highlighting the potential challenges that stem from working at and/or attending institutions with religious traditions encoded into their DNA. I then introduce perspectives on how student affairs educators might consider religion in connection with students' precollege experiences, institutional climates, and postsecondary outcomes.[2] I close with additional thoughts and applications connected to these topics. Throughout, I am guided by a sincere desire to meaningfully inform action, aiming to provide student affairs educators opportunities and language that can directly inform substantive conversations and guide intentional practices on their campuses.

A Christian History

A primary reason that religion is a difficult issue on American college campuses is that many institutions of higher education were not founded to be places for interfaith exchange and expression. Instead, as presented in the preceding essay, institutional founders often designed colleges to explicitly support Christian worldviews, transfer knowledge rooted in Christian epistemologies and ethics, and reinforce Christian social codes. This "broader Protestant cultural consensus"[3] Rine and Reed refer to is notable and merits a closer examination. Consider again that at the founding of many institutions under the Morrill Act of 1862, chapel attendance was not merely desirable or preferred, but rather *required*—a mandatory component of one's public postsecondary education, in a building that likely still holds a prominent location on campus, in a nation whose constitution explicitly prohibits laws establishing religion.[4]

As institutions enter what Rine and Reed refer to as the era of worldview multiplicity, many do so holding distinctively Christian histories. Institutionally, artifacts of this legacy often continue to dictate students' lives in pronounced ways. Consider the common academic calendar at many public and private nonsectarian institutions. Jewish students living by this calendar, for example, must explicitly request course time off for Rosh Hashanah and Yom Kippur. However, ample time is provided for travel and celebration of Christmas, with its symbols and expressions (e.g., trees, lights, music) often being unquestionably demonstrated throughout campus in anticipation of this holiday.[5]

This essay reminds readers how this living Christian history complicates equity with respect to religion from an institutional perspective. When approaching issues of religion—especially on public and non-religiously affiliated private campuses—it is important to recognize not only the extent to which historical and cultural expressions may marginalize students but also how an institutions' religious trajectory might not be considered in its discourse or questioned in its decision-making.

Students, Climates, and Outcomes

I provide additional perspectives that nuance the recommendations Rine and Reed introduced by asking the following questions: (a) Who are our students? (b) What campus climates are we creating? and (c) What outcomes are associated with religion? I encourage student affairs professionals to reflect on their own worldview identity development, their collegiate experiences, and their roles as student-facing and community-building educators while reading this section.

Our Students

Just as institutions enter the era of multiplicity from their own trajectories, students come to college reflecting a broad diversity of perspectives with respect to religion and their own worldview identity development. While there are many facets to this conversation, including intersectional approaches to identity,[6] I focus on one aspect that is essential to cultivating civility: contact with religious others.[7] A sustained line of scholarly inquiry has considered the importance of interfaith contact—supported exchanges between individuals of differing worldviews—in promoting civility with respect to religion.[8] Given demographic realities, geographic factors, and individual preferences, we have in the United States and abroad areas of very low and very high contact between individuals of different religious traditions and worldview perspectives.[9] While it is possible for students to have met, attended classes, and socialized with members of other religious backgrounds, it is also possible for students to have never interacted with an individual from a different worldview, be this someone expressing another religious tradition or proclaiming no religious affiliation at all.

In striving to create campus spaces of civility and safety, it is necessary that student affairs educators recognize and purposefully engage such initial differences.[10] Student affairs practices (e.g., fostering diverse worldview expressions in cocurricular spaces, training interfaith peer-educators)[11] are especially important and timely given the recent rise in hateful rhetoric directed toward members of non-majority religious groups (e.g., Muslims, Jews) that has the harmful potential to replace a desire for authentic interactions with fear, prejudice, and divisiveness that ultimately compromise safety for all.

Our Climates

According to a recent research study, one in four college students experienced religious intolerance during the 2015–2016 academic year.[12] Acknowledging and addressing this reality, an emerging body of literature has begun to investigate the extent to which the campus climate—especially its psychological and behavioral dimensions—can promote productive exchanges across diverse religious viewpoints.[13] Emphasizing the importance of student–student interactions, having educationally and environmentally supported provocative exchanges with others of differing worldviews (e.g., learning about another student's worldview, having interfaith discussions that positively support one's own worldview identity development) consistently appears to benefit students across the worldview spectrum. Unsupportive and negative exchanges often have the opposite effect, engendering campus climates perceived as being insensitive and divisive.[14]

How are positive campus climates for worldview expression created? Several research-to-practice findings and approaches have been offered, converging on a general consensus: Both formal and informal aspects of the collegiate experience can and should be engaged. An increasingly widespread practice—one in which student affairs practitioners are often relied upon to be participants, facilitators, and organizers—has been programmatic efforts aimed at opening up interfaith and interworldview dialogue. Initiating such dialogue outside of the classroom (e.g., through interfaith dinners or facilitated interfaith dialogues) "can alter [students'] feelings or perceptions of being marginalized, particularly if the recommendations derived from those conversations influence institutional policies and practices."[15]

Certainly, one role of student affairs educators can be to initiate and lead programming connected to such conversations, establishing spaces in which students feel comfortable expressing their own worldview assumptions in the spirit of dialogue and shared learning. Student affairs educators can also be instrumental in promoting the idea that when interfaith work is left purely to chance and/or unsupported by educators, such exchanges could have a negative effect on students or simply not happen at all.[16] Additionally, it is important for students to have dedicated space on campus (e.g., club meeting space, prayer room) for expressing their own worldview, connecting with others to have distinctive shared experiences and opportunities for personal and group reflection. Taken together, creating and sustaining a healthy balance between cultivating interfaith exchange and providing dedicated space for collective expression may indeed be the optimal engagement approach that can be supported by cocurricular educators.[17]

Our Outcomes

Rine and Reed placed significant emphasis on the processes by which professionals and students alike develop with respect to religion. Offering another presentation, I introduce an outcome-focused narrative that can further inform practice. Drawing on multiple developmental theories, and emphasizing outcomes presented in recent research efforts (e.g., the Interfaith Diversity Experiences & Attitudes Longitudinal Survey),[18] we might consider three distinct, albeit interdependently related, outcomes:

1. *Self-authored worldview commitment.* As Mayhew and Rockenbach describe, "a self-authored individual would have an informed, critical understanding of his or her worldview, would describe him or herself in ways consistent with such an understanding, and would relate to others in a manner also consistent with that understanding."[19] It is important to recognize that, similar to holistic perspectives on development toward self-authorship—"the internal capacity to define one's beliefs, identity, and social relations"[20]—college can spur students toward achieving this understanding and equitably interacting with others from a position of having thoughtfully grappled with intrapersonal tensions and developed competencies and strategies for continuing this purposeful worldview development over the lifespan.

2. *Appreciative attitudes.* Coming to hold appreciative attitudes toward specific religious groups is an outcome that can promote civility, moving from mere *tolerance* toward expressed and informed *appreciation* of other worldview identities and their adherents. As Eck profoundly observes: "Tolerance is too thin a foundation for a world of religious difference and proximity. It does nothing to remove our ignorance of one another, and leaves in place the stereotype[s]. . . that underlie old patterns of division and violence."[21] Several recently published papers looked at such attitudes toward specific groups (e.g., Muslims, atheists), finding that aspects of campus climate can indeed influence the appearance of such outcomes.[22]

3. *Pluralism orientation.* Whereas appreciative attitudes might pertain to one or another religious group or worldview, pluralism orientation reflects a comprehensive understanding that commitment to one's personal development and peaceful exchange across worldviews can productively coexist. People with a highly pluralistic orientation is able to find truth in worldviews other than their own, believing that individuals can productively and authentically collaborate toward achieving shared goals even when their worldviews are different. Given its encompassing nature, pluralism orientation might be considered a foundational component in ensuring safety, both psychological and physical, within and beyond campus communities.[23]

Considered collectively, examining student characteristics, environments, and these three outcomes in an interdependent and interconnected way might also address a potential challenge presented by the individualized approach suggested in the Rine and Reed essay. Namely, while individualized approaches to student development are desired, they are not always feasible in practice given resource constraints of time, space, and dedicated personnel. Adopting a more integrative approach that establishes clear relationships between campus environments and outcomes, with attention to students' entering characteristics, may help alleviate this concern by equipping the student affairs educator with scalable practices targeted toward achieving specific goals.

Conclusion

As Rine and Reed accurately summarize, the college years can be "an exceptional period of life for self-determination and spiritual development."[24] Operating under this shared assumption, I have further examined the contexts and factors influencing the extent to which these years do, in fact, prove exceptional with respect to religion.

Returning to the guiding question for this chapter, I close by offering that perhaps religion is a difficult and contested issue because both students and institutions encounter this dimension of the human experience animated by interconnected and profoundly influential historical contexts. These include personal histories of development; histories of geography, demography, and policy; histories of relationships between students and postsecondary institutions; physical histories of what gets built where; and social histories that shape the wider relationship between the university and society. Moreover, these histories are dynamic, responsive to changes in individuals, postsecondary institutions, and the sociopolitical cultures in which each operates.

One overarching approach that student affairs educators can adopt in responding to these layers of historical complexity is to understand, embrace, and activate their potential to serve as educational partners in creating campus climates that positively promote student outcomes. Although engaged in the project of achieving what the prior essay refers to as "religious pluralism rather than theological agreement on their campuses"[25] this approach goes even further by suggesting that it is incumbent upon student affairs educators to play leadership roles in moving religion *away* from being a difficult issue *toward* being an issue that can unite individuals across lines of difference with the shared goals of creating equitable, safe, and civil campuses for all religious and worldview expressions.

One strategy student affairs professionals may adopt in practice comes from the religious studies pedagogy literature: *neutral enthusiasm*. As Simmons describes this instructional practice: "neutral enthusiasm means that I can be openly enthusiastic about religious phenomenon yet remain neutral and nonjudgmental."[26] Applied broadly to cocurricular contexts, this approach suggests that student affairs professionals can be enthusiastic about promoting interfaith and interworldview understandings without privileging any one tradition or perspective.

Given their student development mandate and unique institutional positionality, student affairs educators are perhaps in an optimal place to exercise and champion neutral enthusiasm with respect to religion and worldview. Practices might include facilitating and continuously improving intergroup dialogue connected to religious and worldview difference;[27] developing and implementing effective peer-educator training curricula; vigorously working to help students ensure religious accommodations and institutional membership recognition; becoming familiar with religious resources, both on campus and in the community, and helping students navigate toward these places and spaces; and celebrating religious diversity and expressions in residence halls. Whatever forms this work takes, I close by paraphrasing Dewey and emphasize that a shared understanding, one grounded in the principle that all benefit from campus climates that proactively and intentionally support religious expressions and worldview development, will not emerge unless *you*—individually and collectively—strive for it.

Discussion Questions

1. How do the historical trajectories introduced in this chapter shape the context and practices of your current institution? Institutions you have previously attended? Institutions at which you aspire to work?
2. What are additional considerations for religion and worldview with respect to (a) students' background characteristics; (b) campus climate expressions; (c) student outcomes; (d) and the dynamic relationships among students' entering characteristics, climates, and outcomes?
3. To what extent do you agree that student affairs educators can productively engage the practice of neutral enthusiasm? What benefits might this mind-set provide to you and your students? What challenges could be associated with enacting this approach?

Notes

1. Dewey, J. (1934). *A common faith*. New Haven, CT: Yale University Press, p. 76.
2. Astin, A. W. (1993). *What matters in college: Four critical years revisited*. San Francisco, CA: Jossey-Bass; Mayhew, M. J., Rockenbach, A. N., Bowman, N. A., Seifert, T. A., & Wolniak, G. C. (2016). *How college affects students: 21st century evidence that higher education works* (3rd ed.). San Francisco, CA: Jossey-Bass.
3. Rine P. J. & Reed B. D., this volume, p. 243.
4. The First Amendment to the United States Constitution includes the following text, known commonly as the free exercise clause: *Congress shall make no law respecting the establishment of religion, or prohibiting the free exercise thereof.*
5. Seifert, T. (2007). Understanding Christian privilege: Managing the tensions of spiritual plurality. *About Campus, 12*(2), 10–18.
6. Museus, S. D., & Griffin, K. A. (2011). Mapping the margins in higher education: On the promise of intersectionality frameworks in research and discourse. In K. A. Griffin & S. D. Museus (Eds.), *Using mixed-methods approaches to study intersectionality in higher education: New Directions for Institutional Research* (pp. 5-13). San Francisco: Jossey-Bass.
7. Allport, G. W. (1954). *The nature of prejudice*. Reading, MA: Addison-Wesley.

8. For example, Rockenbach, A. N., Mayhew, M. J., Morin, S., Crandall, R. E., & Selznick, B. (2015). Fostering the pluralism orientation of college students through interfaith cocurricular engagement. *The Review of Higher Education, 39*(1), 25–58.

9. See *U.S. religion census 1952–2010*. Retrieved from http://www.usreligion census.org/

10. Mahaffey, C. J., & Smith, S. A. (2008). Creating welcoming campus environments for students from minority religious groups. In S. R. Harper & S. J. Quaye (Eds.), *Student engagement in higher education: Theoretical perspectives and practical approaches for diverse populations* (pp. 81–98). New York, NY: Routledge.

11. Renn, K. A., & Reason, R. D. (2013). *College students in the United States: Characteristics, experiences, and outcomes.* San Francisco, CA: Jossey-Bass.

12. Fosnacht, K., & Broderick, C. F. (2017, November). *Religious intolerance on campus: A multi-institutional study.* Paper presented at the annual meeting of the Association for the Study of Higher Education (ASHE), Houston, TX. Retrieved from http://nsse.indiana.edu/pdf/presentations/2017/ASHE_2017_Bro derick_Fosnacht.pdf

13. Rockenbach, A. B., & Mayhew, M. J. (2013). How the collegiate religious and spiritual climate shapes students' ecumenical orientation. *Research in Higher Education, 54,* 461–479.

14. Rockenbach et al., Fostering the pluralism orientation of college students through interfaith cocurricular engagement.

15. Ahmadi, S., & Cole, D. (2015). Engaging religious minority students. In S. R. Harper & S. J. Quaye (Eds.), *Student engagement in higher education: Theoretical perspectives and practical approaches for diverse populations* (2nd ed., pp. 171–185). New York, NY: Routledge.

16. See Rockenbach, A. N., Mayhew, M. J., Correia-Harker, B. P., Dahl, L., Morin, S., & Associates. (2017). *Navigating pluralism: How students approach religious difference and interfaith engagement in their first year of college.* Chicago, IL: Interfaith Youth Core.

17. Mayhew, M. J., Bowman, N. A., Rockenbach, A. N., Selznick, B., & Riggers-Piehl, T. (2018). Appreciative attitudes toward Jews among non-Jewish U.S. college students. *Journal of College Student Development, 59*(1), 71–89.

18. Rockenbach et al., *Navigating pluralism*; see also Patel, E. (2016). *Interfaith leadership: A primer.* Boston, MA: Beacon Press.

19. Mayhew, M. J., & Bryant Rockenbach, A. N. (2013). Achievement or arrest? The influence of the collegiate religious and spiritual climate on students' worldview commitment. *Research in Higher Education, 54,* 63–84; see also Mayhew, M. J., Rockenbach, A. N., & Bowman, N. A. (2016). The connection between interfaith engagement and self-authored worldview commitment. *Journal of College Student Development, 57*(4), 362–379.

20. Baxter Magolda, M. B. (2008). Three elements of self-authorship. *Journal of College Student Development, 49*(4), 269–284; see also Renn & Reason, *College students in the United States.*

21. Eck, D. L. (2006). *What is pluralism?* Retrieved from http://www.pluralism.org/pluralism/what_is_pluralism

22. Bowman, N. A., Rockenbach, A. N., Mayhew, M. J., Riggers-Piehl, T. A., & Hudson, T. D. (2017). College students' appreciative attitudes toward atheists. *Research in Higher Education, 58*(1), 98–118; Rockenbach, A. N., Mayhew, M. J., Bowman, N. A., Morin, S. M., & Riggers-Piehl, T. (2016). An examination of non-Muslim college students' attitudes toward Muslims. *The Journal of Higher Education, 88*(4), 479–504.

23. Rockenbach et al., Fostering the pluralism orientation of college students through interfaith cocurricular engagement; Rockenbach & Mayhew, How the collegiate religious and spiritual climate shapes students' ecumenical orientation.

24. Rine P. J. & Reed B. D., this volume, p. 249.

25. Rine P. J. & Reed B. D., this volume, p. 248.

26. Simmons, J. K. (2006). Vanishing boundaries: When teaching about religion becomes spiritual guidance in the classroom. *Teaching Theology and Religion, 9*(1), 37–43; see also Gravett, E. (2018). Lost in the great divide: Motivation in the religious studies classroom. *Teaching Theology and Religion, 22,* 1–32.

27. Edwards, S. (2017). Intergroup dialogue and religious identity: Attempting to raise awareness of Christian privilege and religious oppression. *Multicultural Education, 24*(2), 18–24.

14

What Is the Student Affairs Educator's Role in Navigating Tensions Between Legislative Action and Institutional Policy?

From Guns to Transgender Students' Rights: When Policy and Personal Positions Do Not Align

Amelia Parnell and Jill Dunlap

he current political and cultural landscape in the United States of America has revealed difficult issues that affect individuals and groups in myriad ways. The country has witnessed how quickly topics can inflame national conversations that impact everyone, regardless of income, citizenship status, or level of formal education. The increased use of social media and online news outlets has provided fertile ground for dialogue and debate, and anyone with access to the Internet can participate in conversations. Public policy is now more relevant than ever, as local, state, and federal systems will be the levers that spur change, especially regarding America's higher education system. Specifically, student affairs educators now find themselves grappling with serious policy issues at the state and federal level that negatively impact the students our profession is committed to supporting. From the repeal of the Deferred Action for Childhood Arrivals (DACA) program to proposed travel bans that have inspired renewed anti-Muslim rhetoric on college campuses, student affairs educators are now faced with the difficult challenge of navigating these complex issues, somehow simultaneously following the law and institutional policy and supporting minoritized and targeted students. Similarly, the absence of federal guidance related to guns has left states responsible for developing laws and policies that govern how institutions should address students' right to bear arms. As a result of such policy developments, student affairs educators are called upon to foster equitable, inclusive, and safe campus environments within the frameworks of state law, as well as enact their espoused personal and professional values.

Student affairs educators are very interested in public policy, as the two primary associations for the profession, NASPA—Student Affairs Administrators in Higher Education and the American College Personnel Association (ACPA)—College Student Educators International, have made visible efforts to elevate the voice of student affairs in federal and state policy discussions. For example, both organizations regularly draft and support statements and other correspondence to Congress that address the impact of proposed legislation and regulatory developments on the higher education community.[1] Student affairs educators are actively engaged in advocacy at all levels on topics that range from college access and affordability to data privacy and governance. While such engagement and close connection to issues is in many ways positive, some professionals are experiencing associated challenges, especially as they navigate the tension between legislative action and institutional policy.

When institutional policies do not align with student affairs educators' personal views, those educators must balance multiple responsibilities: adhering to protocol; advocating for the students they serve, and living their personal values. Tensions arise for many student affairs educators when they are obligated to adhere to discriminatory policies or laws that negatively impact many of their most vulnerable students. Of focus in this essay are two contested policy issues confronting college campuses today: transgender rights and guns. Both discussions describe how regulatory and legislative activities shape how student affairs educators work on college campuses, particularly in regard to reconciling, in some instances, differences in their professional roles and personal values.

While many higher education administrators will argue that federal or state intervention into institutional policies is a bad thing, in recent years, such regulations have also provided long-needed protections for vulnerable students ranging from sexual assault survivors to transgender students. And as the industry has witnessed in recent months, deregulation can also leave institutions' most vulnerable students feeling unsettled and even more minoritized. Guns on campus and transgender rights are two critical issues that have resulted in high volume state-level discussions and policies. For example, North Carolina and Indiana enacted legislation that regulated how transgender individuals access public restrooms. The direct impact on college campuses is evident. Similarly, Kansas and Georgia enacted legislation that permitted guns on campus. Many institutions modified their campus policies in ways that both adhered to the laws and ensured a safe learning environment. The role of student affairs educators in these public policy discussions will be increasingly critical, especially in terms of reconciling personal positions on these issues while ensuring student support and safety. Legislative action, particularly regarding contested issues such as guns and transgender rights, creates an obligation for campus professionals to do hard work that includes expanding one's knowledge of public policy; creating safe and brave spaces for dialogue; diffusing hostile environments; elevating student voices in policy conversations; and engaging in proactive policy advocacy at the institutional, state, and federal level. This essay describes the current political environment on these issues and offers suggestions for how student affairs educators can navigate ever-changing regulatory and legislative activity.

Transgender Rights on Campus

A prominent contemporary tension between legislative action and institutional policy centers on issues of equity and inclusion for transgender students, particularly their rights. Recent research suggests that 25% of transgender students in particular experience discrimination in the college environment, as reported by their lesbian, gay, and bisexual (LGB) peers.[2] Amid increasing activism on the part of transgender rights advocates, it is not surprising that the issue was taken up by the Office of Civil Rights in recent years.

Federal (De)Regulation

In May 2016, Catherine Lhamon, then assistant secretary for civil rights in the U.S. Department of Education, issued a Dear Colleague Letter outlining protections for transgender students in any "educational programs and activities operated by recipients of Federal financial assistance."[3] Although guidance from the department does not "carry the force of law," it is an instrument the department uses to determine whether an institution is in compliance with its legal obligations.[4] The department used this guidance document to include transgender students under the umbrella of Title IX to include protection for a student's gender identity and transgender status, in addition to the traditional view of Title IX as prohibiting gender discrimination. Importantly, this guidance specifically addressed institutions' obligations to provide a safe and nondiscriminatory environment for transgender students; identify transgender students by the use of their indicated pronoun rather than simply those on their educational documents; allow students to use the restroom, housing, and athletic facilities aligning with their identified gender; and ensure the privacy of transgender students' educational records.

Some college and university administrators expressed concerns[5] about how to implement the new guidance.[6] For schools that had not proactively addressed transgender students' rights issues, the Dear Colleague Letter seemed like an incredibly difficult regulatory burden to meet. Other institutions, including the University of California system, had already begun addressing transgender student concerns by way of a transgender task force. Similar task forces at institutions across the country are beginning to address the myriad challenges facing transgender students on campus, from nondiscriminatory housing policies to access to gender neutral bathrooms to policies allowing students to change their names on official educational documents. Student affairs educators, particularly those working in lesbian, gay, bisexual, and transgender (LGBT) resource centers, were well positioned to begin the work of compliance with the 2016 Dear Colleague Letter. However, as is often the case when new guidance requires compliance, some compliance officers and high-level administrators struggled to get the appropriate staff with expertise involved in the conversation.

Within months of being elected to office, President Donald Trump's administration, under the direction of education secretary Betsy DeVos, repealed the May 2016 Dear Colleague Letter in a joint statement with the Department of Justice. According to the repeal notice, the Obama-era guidance documents did not "contain extensive legal analysis or explain how the position is consistent with the express language of Title IX, nor did they undergo any formal public process."[7] The letter further expresses that both departments will defer to the states in the establishment of educational policy, and that LGBT students continue to be protected from discrimination under the Department of Education's Office of Civil Rights. The decision to repeal the 2016 transgender rights guidance was a major blow to social justice educators and transgender students, faculty, and staff on campuses across the country. This gap in protections for transgender students at the federal level meant that many student affairs educators in states attempting to pass discriminatory "bathroom bill" legislation found themselves struggling with how to reassure transgender students that they are welcome and supported on campus.

Transgender Rights on Campus: Current Status of Legislation

The repeal of the federal transgender guidance did not occur in a vacuum. State legislation promoting discriminatory policies aimed at transgender students abounded in the first half of 2017. According to state tracking work by the National Conference of State Legislatures, state-level analysis indicates that during the 2017 legislative session, 14 states considered legislation that would limit transgender students' rights at school; another 16 states considered legislation aimed at restricting access to multiuser restrooms or other sex-segregated facilities considering gender or sex only as that which was assigned at birth.[8] North Carolina was the only state to pass discriminatory legislation, House Bill 2, which the legislature later repealed after significant backlash by business and sports associations. Texas was the only other state to come close to passing similar legislation targeting transgender students' rights. Texas House Bills 2899, 46, and 50 all failed to move forward during the 2017 legislative session.

Student affairs educators across the country, especially in states with proposed discriminatory "bathroom bills," continued to find ways to support transgender students who were suddenly feeling targeted by both state and federal policymakers. If there is good news to be found about this topic, it is that legislators seemed singularly focused on bathroom issues, which leaves campus administrators with a host of other strategies to support transgender colleagues, faculty, staff, and students at their institutions.

NASPA conducted a preliminary survey of student affairs educators on the issue of support for transgender faculty, staff, and students. Initially designed as a way to measure compliance with the 2016 Obama administration guidance, after the repeal, NASPA continued this survey research as a way to assess how student affairs educators have implemented transgender supportive policies and practices in spite of the repeal. The initial survey drew responses from student affairs administrators in 25 states, with the largest portion of responses from California, Massachusetts, and Texas. More than 66% of respondents indicated that their institutions have bias incident response protocols that include the option to report transgender bias incidents, although most respondents were not aware of how many such incidents had been reported during the previous reporting period. Another 21% of respondents indicated that their institutions have transgender inclusiveness working groups to examine ways to support transgender students that included representatives from a range of offices, including health centers, counseling centers, community LGBT advocacy groups, women's centers, and multicultural offices, among others. Perhaps surprising to some, of those campuses that indicated they had a transgender inclusiveness working group, 66% indicated that their working group existed prior to the 2016 Dear Colleague Letter. Forty-one percent of respondents indicated their institutions have policies in place by which students can change the gender listed on their educational documents or identification cards, while another 23% indicated that their policy only allows for those changes in specific circumstances. Another 34% of respondents indicated that there is a policy in place protecting students' abilities to use the housing, locker room, and restroom facilities in alignment with their gender identity, rather than their sex assigned at birth. Finally, respondents also indicated other measures in place to support transgender students, faculty, and staff at their institutions, including insurance coverage for transgender students' medical needs, campus climate surveys addressing transgender bias, and adding gender identity to the institution's nondiscrimination policy.

These survey results provide hope that despite challenging political climates at both the state and federal level, campus administrators, led by student affairs professionals, are committed to recruiting, retaining, and supporting marginalized students. Student affairs educators have focused on outreach to transgender students and the LGBT community to develop ways to support transgender students, while complying with troubling and discriminatory federal and state legislation. For example, if institutions were worried about running afoul of pending state legislation about bathrooms, they can forge ahead with revising housing's or records' name-change policies that are supportive of transgender students' experiences. In addition to the work of supporting students, student affairs educators must also understand how this work supports colleagues from these marginalized groups as well. Student affairs educators recognize that students are not the only ones whose lives are touched by discriminatory legislation restricting bathroom usage or who stand to benefit from name change policies at institutions of higher education. One transgender respondent's comments highlight this need particularly well.

> I think it's worth noting how precarious it is for trans employees to advocate for trans-inclusion in higher education. I'm the one most trans students come to when they run into barriers on campus, and I'm responsible for leading most of the transgender advocacy work, which is exhausting. It's difficult to be fighting transphobic systems while also being directly impacted by them and employed by them.[9]

While the fight for transgender protections has centered on students, it is also clearly affecting the faculty and staff who provide expertise to institutions on these issues and who bear the heavy load of supporting transgender individuals who feel targeted by these federal and state efforts.

Respondents also indicated a number of challenges in balancing the work of supporting students in the face of constantly changing and often harmful federal and state guidance and legislation. Student affairs educators, as the ones most closely working on student support services, often see the effect of policymakers' decision on a personal, individual level. Student affairs staff find themselves at the front edge of the battle lines being drawn on equity, inclusion, and social justice issues that affect the students at institutions of higher education. Whether the issue is one of free speech with the potential to harm minoritized students, protecting Deferred Action for Childhood Arrival (DACA) students (i.e., DACA-mented students), or supporting transgender students, faculty, and staff in the face of discriminatory legislation, student affairs staff will continue to champion the rights and safety of students from marginalized populations. If there is any group up to the task of finding work-arounds or innovative ways to support students despite a troubling civil rights climate, it is the dedicated field of student affairs. These issues are not the first civil rights questions to be presented to campus administrators, and they certainly will not be the last. Complying with problematic federal and state policies that serve to discriminate against students can be difficult for student affairs educators. Rather than simply complying with these troubling policies, student affairs educators are finding creative ways to reach out to transgender populations and raise awareness of the other myriad, supportive policies on campus for this vulnerable population.

Legislative Action and Institutional Policy: Tensions Related to Guns on Campus

The Second Amendment to the United States Constitution states that "a well-regulated Militia, being necessary to the security of a free State, the right of the people to keep and bear Arms, shall not be infringed."[10] Melear and St. Louis[11] suggest that the language of the Second Amendment has resulted in much debate regarding its applicability collectively or individually to citizens. One underlying question is whether the possession of firearms on a campus, by persons who are not responsible for law enforcement, contributes to or detracts from a safe learning environment. Debates about the issue typically involve questions regarding whether the allowance of guns on campus could lessen the likelihood of campus shootings or increase the number of incidents of accidental injury or suicides. Many violence prevention professionals are also concerned about the effect of weapons in situations of domestic violence and sexual assault.

Also at the center of the discussion is whether the presence of guns quells the free expression of ideas in both classroom and cocurricular environments. For example, there is the possibility of a "chilling effect" in that students or other members of the campus community may feel hesitant to express their views in the presence of someone who has a weapon. It appears that campus leaders may not perceive guns on campus favorably; a 2013 survey of college presidents revealed that of the 400 respondents, nearly all (95%) were against concealed weapons on college campuses.[12] However, increased state legislative activity regarding concealed carry suggests that institutions not yet affected by concealed carry legislation should prepare for the possibility that guns may be allowed on their campuses in the future. Now is the time for student affairs educators to become more knowledgeable of public policy, more critical of campus policy, and more proactive in advocacy.

Guns on Campus: Status of Legislation

The National Conference of State Legislatures (NCSL), which tracks state legislation on campus carry laws, has reported that all 50 states' legislatures allow citizens to carry concealed weapons if they meet certain requirements; however, in regard to higher education institutions, 16 states currently ban carrying a concealed weapon on a college campus (i.e., California, Florida, Illinois, Louisiana, Massachusetts, Michigan, Missouri, Nebraska, Nevada, New Jersey, New Mexico, New York, North Carolina, North Dakota, South Carolina, and Wyoming).[13] Ten states allow carrying concealed weapons on college campuses (i.e., Arkansas, Colorado, Georgia, Idaho, Kansas, Mississippi, Oregon, Texas, Utah, and Wisconsin). However, states vary regarding whether concealed weapons are allowed in all areas of the campus or only certain spaces. For example, Georgia law authorizes individuals with a concealed carry license to carry weapons on the property of any public institution of postsecondary education, except for buildings or property used for athletic events or student housing.[14] In Arkansas, individuals who complete a concealed carry training may possess a concealed handgun in the buildings and on the grounds of public institutions. Twenty-three states allow each institution to individually decide whether to ban or allow concealed carry weapons on the campus (i.e., Alabama, Alaska, Arizona, Connecticut, Delaware, Hawaii, Indiana, Iowa, Kentucky, Maine, Maryland, Minnesota, Montana, New Hampshire, Ohio, Oklahoma, Pennsylvania, Rhode Island, South Dakota, Vermont, Virginia, Washington, and West Virginia).[15] As institutions in these states determine whether guns should be allowed on their campus, there is an opportunity for student affairs educators to proactively use research to inform their advocacy. For example, proponents of concealed carry may argue that the allowance of guns could make students feel safer. However, some research suggests that the opposite may occur, as a 2014 study found that in states where firearm restrictions were loosened, the number of aggravated assaults increased.[16] Student affairs educators can also gather their campus climate data to determine the rates at which violent acts are occurring.

The issue of guns on campus has likely led to tension at higher education institutions across the country, regardless of whether state legislation was introduced, enacted, or vetoed. One tension that could occur on campuses, particularly those that allow guns, is the challenge of acknowledging one's personal views and complying with the responsibilities of the role. A second tension is difficulty in leveraging relationships between multiple campus units that are responsible for addressing gun violence.

As mentioned earlier, members of the campus community have expressed concern that permitting individuals to have concealed carry at the institution would make the environment less safe. For example, Deborah Ballad-Reisch, a professor at Wichita State University in Kansas, wrote in a blog post that she could not "work in a climate in which students are fearful to claim their voices because the person next to them in my classroom may have both different views and a gun."[17] Ballard-Reisch added that she found the Kansas law that permits concealed carry on college campuses to be the "antithesis of everything a civil society stands for."[18] For student affairs educators, these sentiments reflect tensions caused by the requirement to be present in spaces that may be more dangerous and the acceptance of responsibilities that are unfamiliar, such as dissecting the intersections of state law and campus policy.

Brunson, Stang, and Dreessen[19] state that in times of campus crisis, student affairs professionals will need to sometimes assume leadership roles and responsibilities that go beyond their job descriptions. Considering the potential for violence that guns on campus can create, student affairs educators will need to take the lead in proactively addressing the issue in multiple ways. For example, professionals at residential institutions should create mandatory training for residence hall staff to understand campus gun policies and the process by which they can share concerns. Professionals at all institutions should regularly discuss the institution's gun policy with students, display the policy in frequently used facilities, and provide ways for students to report activities that violate the policy. In instances where these trainings and feedback sessions reveal significant areas for which the institution should modify its policies, student affairs educators should advocate for such changes. Though these responsibilities may often require student affairs educators to reconcile their personal views on guns, the absence of these activities jeopardizes the safety and well-being of the campus community.

Although the presence of a weapon on campus does not automatically result in violence, the very nature of the topic is one that can quickly lead campus professionals into a discussion of procedures should an unexpected gun-related event occur. One relationship that is critical in gun-related scenarios is that of law enforcement and student affairs. This relationship requires the negotiation of responsibilities and levels of authority, as law enforcement officers, both on- and off-campus, may not interact with students as regularly as student affairs professionals do. Similarly, student affairs educators may not have the levels of training that law enforcement officers have to stabilize an emergency situation. As a result, legislative action that allows guns on campus could make it very difficult for campus professionals to collaboratively select strategies for adhering to the law, ensuring a safe environment, and promoting high engagement and dialogue for everyone. States may continue to introduce new gun legislation each year. Accordingly it appears that student affairs educators will need to expect these tensions to continue.

Conclusion

Considering the significance of contested and divisive issues such as concealed carry and transgender rights on our campuses, it is reasonable to assume that no student affairs educator may agree with every state or federal policy that impacts the lives of students. However, tough policy issues provide opportunities for student affairs educators to honor their personal positions by making campuses safe and supportive for all students. Although the task of managing the tension between legislative action and institutional policy may always be complex, tiresome, and ambiguous, one thing that the student affairs community can do is increase its direct engagement in advocacy. Legislators and Department of Education personnel, at both the state and federal level, would benefit from information about the lived experiences that occur on America's college campuses. Student affairs educators are in a good position to provide such context for elected and appointed officials, and this is a good time to engage in purposeful dissemination of information to these parties.

We already have examples of successful advocacy in the student affairs community. During the 2017 NASPA annual business meeting, the association's board of directors presented a resolution to formally express support for the rights and protections of transgender individuals and denounce efforts to suppress their freedom to use restroom facilities of their choice.[20] During the previous year's annual meeting, scores of student affairs educators marched to the Indiana state capital in a peaceful demonstration to address pending legislation that would negatively affect transgender individuals. As student affairs educators continue to keep up with the fast pace of today's public policy environment, it is likely that the tensions between legislative action and institutional policy will remain. However, contested issues such as transgender rights and guns on campus present an opportunity for student affairs educators to influence the development of thoughtful and respectful campus policies and procedures. Though higher education may continue to wrestle with these and other difficult topics, student affairs educators, to the extent that they can accept the many intersections of their personal and professional priorities and values, can be exemplary in helping the field respond and thrive.

Discussion Questions

1. What role should federal guidance or state legislation have in advancing civil rights and adequately addressing concealed carry on college campuses?
2. What role do student affairs educators have in advancing civil rights for marginalized students on campus when federal guidance or state laws do not yet exist? What is your role in complying with or challenging federal or state laws that target vulnerable student populations?
3. How can student affairs educators use open dialogues or town halls with students regarding the presence of guns, transgender rights, or other critical issues on campus?
4. How often does the institution require cross-functional training for addressing difficult issues? Which functional units and professionals are involved in the development and delivery of the training?

Notes

1. American Council on Education. (2017, September 12). Comments to the U.S. House of Representatives and Senate leadership regarding Deferred Action for Childhood Arrivals. Retrieved from http://www.acenet.edu/news-room/Documents/Letter-to-Congress-on-DACA-Sept-2017.pdf

2. Harvard T. H. Chan School of Public Health, Robert Wood Johnson Foundation, & National Public Radio. (2017). *Discrimination in America: Experiences and views of LGBTQ Americans*. Retrieved from: https://cdn1.sph.harvard

.edu/wp-content/uploads/sites/94/2017/11/NPR-RWJF-HSPH-Discrimination-LGBTQ-Final-Report.pdf

3. Lhamon, C., & Gupta, V. (2015, May 13). *Dear colleague letter on transgender students.* Department of Education, Office for Civil Rights. Retrieved from https://www2.ed.gov/about/offices/list/ocr/letters/colleague-201605-title-ix-transgender.pdf

4. Ibid.

5. Malone, S. (2016, June 10). College dorms a new front in U.S. battle over transgender rights. Reuters. Retrieved from https://www.reuters.com/article/us-usa-lgbt-education/college-dorms-a-new-front-in-u-s-battle-over-transgender-rights-idUSKCN0YW15P

6. Horsley, S. (2016, May 13). White House sends schools guidance on transgender access to bathrooms. NPR. Retrieved from https://www.npr.org/sections/thetwo-way/2016/05/13/477896804/obama-administration-to-offer-schools-guidance-on-transgender-bathrooms

7. Battle, S., & Wheeler, T. E. (2017, February 22). *Dear colleague letter.* U.S. Department of Education, Office for Civil Rights. Retrieved from https://www2.ed.gov/about/offices/list/ocr/letters/colleague-201702-title-ix.pdf

8. Kralik, J. (2017, July 28). Bathroom bill legislative tracking. Retrieved from http://www.ncsl.org/research/education/-bathroom-bill-legislative-tracking635951130.aspx

9. NASPA—Student Affairs Administrators in Higher Education. (2017). Unpublished survey data.

10. U.S. Constitution, Second Amendment. (1791).

11. Melear, K. B., & St. Louis, M. (2015). Concealed carry legislation and changing campus policies. In B. Hephner LaBanc & B. O. Hemphill (Eds.), *College in the crosshairs: An administrative perspective on prevention of gun violence* (pp. 59–60). Sterling, VA: Stylus.

12. Price, J. H., Thompson, A., Khubchandani, J., Dake, J., Payton, E., & Teeple, K. (2014). University presidents' perceptions and practice regarding the carrying of concealed handguns on college campuses. *Journal of American College Health, 62*(7), 461–469.

13. National Council on State Legislatures. (2017, May 5). Guns on campus: Overview. Retrieved from http://www.ncsl.org/research/education/guns-on-campus-overview.aspx

14. Education Commission of the States. (2017). Policy snapshot: Postsecondary campus safety. Retrieved from https://www.ecs.org/ec-content/uploads/Policy_Snapshot_Postsecondary_Campus_Safety.pdf

15. National Council on State Legislatures, Guns on campus.

16. Aneja, A., Donohue, J. J., & Zhang, A. (2014, September 4). *The impact of right to carry laws and the NRC Report: The latest lessons for the empirical evaluation of law and policy* (Stanford Law and Economics Olin Working Paper No. 461. Retrieved from https://papers.ssrn.com/sol3/papers.c...act_id=2443681

17. Flaherty, C. (2017, July 5). Another professor leaves over campus carry. *Inside Higher Ed.* Retrieved from https://www.insidehighered.com/quicktakes/2017/07/05/another-professor-leaves-over-campus-carry

18. Ibid.

19. Brunson, J., Stang, M., & Dreessen, A. (2010). Essential student affairs services in a campus crisis. In B. O. Hemphill & B. Hephner LaBanc (Eds.), *Enough is enough: A student affairs perspective on preparedness and response to a campus shooting* (pp. 108–109). Sterling, VA: Stylus.

20. NASPA—Student Affairs Administrators in Higher Education. (2017). Recap of resolutions passed by board of directors. Retrieved from https://www.naspa.org/about/blog/naspa17-marked-the-passing-of-three-resolutions-reflecting-critical-moments

Passion and Policy: How Student Affairs Educators Navigate Their Roles in the Face of Legislative Restrictions

R. Bradley Johnson

The ability to work with and advocate for students is one of the primary reasons many student affairs educators choose to enter the profession. But as Parnell and Dunlap acknowledge, student affairs educators sometimes face challenges in their work when they must uphold state and federal laws and regulations while simultaneously serving as advocates for targeted and marginalized students on their campuses. Values such as altruism, equality, aesthetics, freedom, human dignity, justice, truth,[1] and community[2] have been identified by student affairs educators as foundational to their work. These values are sometimes challenged when legislative policies and actions impose restrictions on how students are supported on campus, threatening the sense of equity, safety, and civility upon which collegial communities are built.

I agree with Parnell and Dunlap's argument that the student affairs profession needs to increase its direct engagement in advocacy. Public policy advocacy can take many forms (e.g., social media posts, protest marches, calls to Congressional leaders). Depending on the type of institution where one works (public versus private), advocacy efforts may be subjected to regulation. For example, many public institutions have political activity guidelines in place that restrict the nature of political work carried out by an employee (e.g., no political activity during work time, no use of institutional resources to carry out political activity, no institutional apparel or use of institutional name by the employee that could be construed as endorsement of views by the institution). Even if a student affairs professional does wish to engage in public policy advocacy, exhausting work demands may limit their ability to become politically engaged beyond their institution. In these situations, it is important for student affairs educators to utilize institutional relationships and resources to navigate tensions between legislative action and professional practice. In this essay, I draw upon the example of North Carolina's HB2 "Bathroom Bill" to illustrate both political tensions encountered by student affairs professionals and productive negotiation strategies.

Legislative Actions and Policies

Recent legislative actions have created politically charged campus environments that student affairs educators must navigate in their efforts to support and advocate for students. Examples of federal and state policy efforts demanding student affairs attention include President Trump's call to end the Deferred Action for Childhood Arrivals (DACA) program;[3] federal travel bans targeting individuals from specific Muslim nations;[4] state legislation authorizing guns on campus;[5] and state policy attacks on the equity and safety of lesbian, gay, bisexual, transgender, queer plus (LGBTQ+) individuals.[6]

My home state, North Carolina, has encountered controversy and challenges associated with many of these legislative actions and policies. For example, North Carolina entered the national spotlight in March 2016 when state legislation was passed that severely threatened the rights of LGBTQ+ individuals within the state. The Public Facilities Privacy & Security Act, more officially titled "An Act to Provide for Single-Sex Multiple Occupancy Bathroom and Changing Facilities in Schools and Public Agencies and to Create Statewide Consistency in Regulation of Employment and Public Accommodations" (more commonly known as House Bill 2, HB2, or its nickname, "The Bathroom Bill"),[7] was a piece of legislative action called "the most anti-LGBT law in the U.S."[8] because of its power to override local ordinances concerning wages, employment, and public accommodations. HB2 consisted of five parts;[9] however, the most controversial component and the one that garnered the greatest media attention addressed the use of public facilities (hence the nickname "The Bathroom Bill"). HB2 regulated the use of public facilities (i.e., bathrooms), mandating individuals use the bathroom corresponding to the sex on their birth certificate. The legislation imposed discriminatory regulations on transgender individuals, requiring them to use bathrooms that corresponded with their assigned biological sex, not the gender with which they currently identified. For its proponents, HB2 was intended to "prevent an imminent crisis of straight men putting on dresses to view women in women's restrooms."[10] However, if implemented, this legislation would have required a transgender man (assigned female at birth) who was taking testosterone, had a full beard, and was dressed in men's clothes to use a female-designated bathroom. This situation would likely have been more shocking or surprising than if this same transgender man entered a male-designated bathroom.

An important part of HB2 was that there was no mechanism for enforcement articulated in the legislation nor were there penalties or consequences for anyone who violated the act. The president of the University of North Carolina (UNC) System, Margaret Spellings, noted the enforcement oversight in her response to the legislation on behalf of the UNC System, saying that HB2 was "hastily drawn, perhaps without fully considering all the implications" and that "if it were up to me, I would not recommend" the passing of the bill.[11] Although Spellings stated that the UNC system would follow HB2 (more specifically the public facilities use portion), in a memo to UNC system institutions, she indicated that "constituent institutions must continue to operate in accordance with their nondiscrimination policies and must take prompt and appropriate action to prevent and address any instances of harassment and discrimination in violation of university policies."[12] At institutions which had adopted nondiscrimination policies, especially those that protected sexual orientation and gender identity and expression, transgender community members could be protected from the discriminatory state legislation by referencing institutional policy and interpreting the legislation from different perspectives. For example, an institution's police or campus safety department could purposefully choose to not patrol bathroom facilities looking for violations of HB2. As illustrated in this example, when interpreting legislative actions and policies through the principles of social justice, equity, and nondiscrimination, student affairs educators can work with campus partners to navigate legal responsibilities while maintaining a safe and supportive community for all.

Navigating Tensions Between Professional Values and Legislative Actions

As a student affairs educator in North Carolina as well as a member and advocate for the LGBTQ+ community, the HB2 legislation deeply affected me on a personal and professional level. The discriminatory legislation presented my student affairs colleagues and me with the challenge of upholding our commitment to advocating for "diverse groups of students and their unique needs in every venue of the institution"[13] while simultaneously fulfilling our professional responsibilities as institutional agents charged with implementing state law and campus policy. The passage of HB2 required North Carolina student affairs educators to interpret and integrate personal values, professional competencies (e.g., the *Professional Competency Areas for Student Affairs Educators* published by the American College Personnel Association [ACPA] and the National Association of Student Personnel Administrators [NASPA]), ethical standards, and public policy. The capacity to ethically and productively navigate tensions that arise from the adoption of federal, state, and/or institutional policy counter to one's personal values and political ideologies is an essential student affairs professional competency,[14] one that both new and seasoned student affairs educators are called upon to demonstrate with increasing frequency. Rather than waiting for public policy challenges such as HB2 to arise before developing an advocacy plan, I encourage student affairs educators to adopt a proactive stance, building productive campus partnerships and engaging in ongoing collection of relevant student data so they can effectively attend to students' needs in politically charged campus environments.

Build Campus Partnerships

A valuable legislative action and public policy resource on my campus is the director of strategic initiatives. This position serves as the primary liaison with federal and state elected and appointed officials and keeps the institution well-informed on developments in governmental affairs via the *Government Relations* website and an active and engaged Twitter account. The director of strategic initiatives also provides the institution guidance when proposed legislation and policies hold potential harmful consequences for members of our community. When HB2 passed, the director of strategic initiatives consulted with university counsel and informed our chancellor of the scope of the legislation's influence on campus. Our chancellor then issued a community-wide e-mail to update the campus on the status of the legislation as well as affirm the institution's commitment to equal opportunity and nondiscriminatory policies. In the case of campuses without a dedicated governmental affairs position, student affairs educators should identify the individual (or individuals) within the president or chancellor's council who engages in government relations work and seek their guidance on the possibility of setting up a website with up-to-date information on policies and legislation affecting higher education. Student affairs professionals might also advocate for the government relations liaison to attend a department or division meeting to update staff on the political climate in the state and how pending legislation could affect the student experience and professional responsibilities. Proactively building relationships with institutional government affairs staff and facilitating department/division public policy conversations will increase staff capacity to effectively respond when confronted with legislative mandates like HB2.

Collect Relevant Data

Student demographic data serves as another valuable resource for student affairs educators to leverage when seeking to navigate tensions between legislative actions and campus policy. Demographic information about students is critical to making sure their needs are met and issues are addressed. However, for some institutions, the collection of student demographic data may not be as complete as one would like or hope. Having incomplete student demographic information creates an environment where resources may not be properly allocated to serve student needs. As Shane Windmeyer stated:

> Colleges and universities are responsible for the education and safety of all students, including their LGBT students. A school cannot provide necessary services or maintain proper safety and campus climate without first knowing who are the out-LGBT students attending their school. Demographic questions asking students about their sexual orientation and gender identity give university administrators the data they need to properly implement LGBT-inclusive policies and practices.[15]

Returning to the HB2 example, when confronted with the challenge of implementing the discriminatory legislation, a more concerted effort to communicate with students identifying as transgender could have been made by student affairs professionals if they had proactively developed a practice of collecting specific demographic information on the student body. The ability to quickly identify trans-identified students on campus would have allowed student affairs educators to adopt a more personal approach with respect to helping students feel safe and supported on campus. Without these data, student affairs educators on my campus relied primarily on smaller, personal networks and connections with transgender students as well as broader messages sent to the campus community by the chancellor to convey institutional support for students facing discrimination under HB2.

Student demographic information is typically collected via the admissions application, whether it is an institution-specific document or a multicampus application such as the Common Application or the Universal College Application. A concern for student affairs educators is that their institution may not accurately capture all aspects of a student's identity in the college application process, including information about sexual orientation or gender identity and expression. Fortunately, the Common Application and the Universal College Application now allow questions about gender identity and expression to be included within the core set of questions;[16] however, for institutions who do not use these admission forms or do not ask about these student demographics, there exists a critical information gap. Without access to this data, it is difficult for student affairs educators to identify students who might be affected by harmful legislation or institutional policies. This was certainly the case for many institutions in North Carolina when HB2 passed, as information about student sexual orientation and gender identity or expression was not readily available in a report from the institution's mainframe database. Specific data on students who identified as transgender would have allowed student affairs educators the opportunity to provide a more personalized form of outreach with respect to supporting students as they navigated the campus environment post-HB2. If employed at a campus that does not collect student demographic information related to diverse dimensions of identity, I urge student affairs professionals to advocate for the collection of this missing information. Data speak volumes—especially in an age of metrics, assessments, and evaluations.

Conclusion

Parnell and Dunlap state that "it is reasonable to assume that no student affairs educator may ever agree with every state or federal policy that impacts the lives of students" but when contested issues arise, an opportunity presents itself for "student affairs educators to influence the development of thoughtful and respectful campus policies and procedures."[17] I wholeheartedly agree with this assertation. It is our purpose and obligation to ensure that we have the resources we need to work with and meet the needs of students in our care. And while there may be instances where legislative and/ or institutional policies arise that challenge us in our work, it is our underlying commitment to the welfare and development of our students that will sustain us in our roles as student affairs educators.

Discussion Questions

1. How can your institution best gather data on marginalized student populations to better understand and advocate for the needs of these students?
2. What resources are available at your institution to help you keep abreast of state and governmental policies and laws affecting higher education? By what other means could you supplement these resources to be better aware of policies and laws that potentially could affect your students?

Notes

1. Young, R. B., & Elfrink, V. L. (1991). Essential values of student affairs work. *Journal of College Student Development, 32*(1), 45–55.
2. Roberts, D. C. (1993). Community: The value of social synergy. In R. B. Young (Ed.), *Identifying and implementing the essential values of the profession*

(New Directions for Student Services, no. 61, pp. 35–45). San Francisco, CA: Jossey-Bass; Young, R. B. (1993). Essential values of the profession. In R. B. Young (Ed.), *Identifying and implementing the essential values of the profession* (New Directions for Student Services, no. 61, pp. 5–14). San Francisco, CA: Jossey-Bass.

    3. American Immigration Council. (2017, September 6). The Dream Act, DACA, and other policies designed to protect dreamers. Retrieved from https://www.americanimmigrationcouncil.org/research/dream-act-daca-and-other-policies-designed-protect-dreamers; U.S. Citizenship and Immigration Services. (2017, October 6). Consideration of Deferred Action for Childhood Arrivals (DACA). Retrieved from https://www.uscis.gov/archive/consideration-deferred-action-childhood-arrivals-daca; Valverde, M. (2018, January 22). Timeline: DACA, the Trump administration and a government shutdown. *Politifact.* Retrieved from http://www.politifact.com/truth-o-meter/article/2018/jan/22/timeline-daca-trump-administration-and-government-/

    4. Exec. Order No. 13769, 3 C.F.R. 8977-8982 (2017).

    5. Ewing, M. (2017, April 5). Campus carry: The movement to allow guns on college grounds, explained. *The Trace.* Retrieved from https://www.thetrace.org/2017/04/campus-carry-movement-to-allow-guns-on-college-grounds-explained/

    6. Human Rights Campaign, www.hrc.org

    7. General Assembly of North Carolina, Second Extra Session 2016, Session Law 2016-3, House Bill 2. (2016, March 23). Retrieved from http://www.ncleg.net/Sessions/2015E2/Bills/House/PDF/H2v4.pdf

    8. Tan, A. (2016, March 24). North Carolina's controversial anti-LGBT bill explained. *ABC News.* Retrieved from http://abcnews.go.com/US/north-carolinas-controversial-anti-lgbt-bill-explained/story?id=37898153; Yang, J. (2016, March 24). How North Carolina signed a bill dubbed the most anti-LGBT law in the U.S. *PBS News Hour.* Retrieved from https://www.pbs.org/newshour/show/how-north-carolina-signed-a-bill-dubbed-most-anti-lgbt-law-in-the-u-s

    9. General Assembly of North Carolina, Second Extra Session 2016, Session Law 2016-3, House Bill 2. (2016, March 23). Retrieved from http://www.ncleg.net/Sessions/2015E2/Bills/House/PDF/H2v4.pdf; Lloyd, H. (2016, May 13). McCrory's House Bill 2: A brief outline of its five "parts." *Huffington Post.* Retrieved from https://www.huffingtonpost.com/harold-lloyd/mccrorys-house-bill-2-a-b_b_9966020.html

    10. Lloyd, McCrory's House Bill 2.

    11. Newsom, J. (2016, April 8). UNC system president: HB2 "hastily drawn." *Greensboro News & Record.* Retrieved from http://www.greensboro.com/news/schools/unc-system-president-hb-hastily-drawn/article_2154e351-6a96-50d5-843f-fbf8e0e03a80.html

    12. Newsom, J. (2016, April 8). The syllabus: The UNC system and HB2 (updated). *Greensboro News & Record.* Retrieved from http://www.greensboro.com/blogs/the_syllabus/the-syllabus-the-unc-system-and-hb-updated/article_903d2069-a3d5-5504-b66b-2c6b131a69b3.html

13. Komives, S. R. (2015). Shaping the future: Lessons from the past. *About Campus, 20*(1), 4–12, p. 9.

14. ACPA & NASPA. (2015). *Professional competency areas for student affairs educators*. Washington DC: Author.

15. Windmeyer, S. L. (2012, March 19). To ask or not to ask: LGBT identity on college admission forms. *The Huffington Post*. Retrieved from https://www.huffingtonpost.com/shane-l-windmeyer/college-admission-forms-sexual-orientation_b_1346593.html

16. Schubert, A. (2016, May 9). Common Application, Universal College Application add gender identity question. *USA Today College*. Retrieved from http://college.usatoday.com/2016/05/09/common-app-universal-college-app-add-gender-identity/

17. Parnell, A., & Dunlap, J., this volume, pp. 270, 271.

PART THREE

Cultivating Professional Capacities to Foster Inclusive Learning Environments

15

Given the Complexity Associated With Fostering Equitable, Civil, and Safe Learning Environments, How Should Graduate Preparation Programs Prepare Students to Work in Higher Education?

Advancing Power- and Identity-Conscious Student Affairs Graduate Programs

Rosemary J. Perez

People often ask me what led me to become a faculty member in a higher education and student affairs (HESA) graduate preparation program. It is easy to talk about my passion for working with new practitioners and for improving graduate education so that it is more equitable and inclusive. But if I am honest, I wanted to become a HESA faculty member because I struggled at times in my master's program at a historically and predominantly White institution. My White faculty members did not always understand my experiences, but I knew they cared deeply about me. And when tensions ran high in my Cultural Pluralism class, my White instructor did not ignore them. Rather, she adapted in ways that I could not have imagined. She created space for racially minoritized students to deepen our relationships and our understandings of ourselves as we worked with a community organizer who challenged us on our internalized dominance. Concurrently, she worked closely with the White students in caucus to talk about White privilege and to address White fragility.

Many years later, I can now say that my experience in that Cultural Pluralism class at age 23 transformed me. During that class, my anger, sadness, and frustration were validated and I felt more seen and empowered than I had before. I also was increasingly appreciative of my colleagues who were willing to do the hard work of examining how privilege and oppression were operating in our cohort, at our institution, and in society. When our class "blew up" and met in racial caucuses for a period of time, it had the potential to be ugly and damaging. But instead, my instructor's humility and passion for social justice coupled with my cohort's commitment to doing the hard work it takes to be in community created an experience that was ultimately healing. While I do not remember the course objectives, I do remember the course's outcomes, which have shaped my understanding of what HESA programs can do for and with students when they acknowledge students' multiple intersecting social identities and acknowledge how privilege and oppression operate in classrooms. My experience demonstrated the complexity of fostering equitable, civil, and safe learning environments in HESA preparation programs and highlighted the need for graduate education to be more consistently power and identity conscious. To create HESA programs that work in service of social justice and inclusion, there is a need to continuously examine the underlying assumptions of our field and consistently use critical pedagogy and create opportunities to advance students' capacities to understand and engage across differences in socially constructed identities, values, beliefs, and ideologies.

Graduate Education in Student Affairs

If we are to create more power- and identity-conscious graduate preparation programs, it is vital that we first explore the role of these programs in student affairs. With this in mind, an overview of graduate education in student affairs and an examination of the notion of competency in the field are provided.

Purposes of Student Affairs Graduate Training

In concept, HESA training programs equip graduate students with the knowledge, habits of mind, and skills needed to work in the field.[1] They serve as powerful agents of socialization that inform individuals' values and beliefs about the nature of "good practice" and how the field's stated commitment to concepts such as social justice and inclusion[2] should be enacted on our campuses and in our professional communities. Thus, HESA programs, like all educational spaces, have the potential to be spaces that foster social change while also acting as tools of social reproduction. Faculty design programs to impart the knowledge, values, and skills that ground the field, while concurrently creating space for individuals to explore their personal identities, identify their interests, and clarify their approaches to practice.

Ideally, the multiple aims of HESA programs are aligned, but they can be in competition with each other, particularly when graduate students' socially constructed identities, values, and ways of knowing are not reflective of the dominant culture (e.g., White, middle class, heterosexual, Christian). My experience in my Cultural Pluralism course highlighted the tensions among these multiple aims of graduate education. In working to enhance students' cultural competency, those with racially minoritized identities found ourselves struggling to learn and to feel valued. Had our instructor not adapted her approach to the course, it is likely that my White peers would have seemingly increased their cultural competency and their understandings of Whiteness and privilege at the cost of their peers of color.

Complicating Competency

While the student affairs field relies on HESA programs to prepare the next generation of professionals, there has not always been consensus on the essential knowledge and skills required of student affairs educators. The lack of agreement about how to train student affairs professionals reflects the realities that (a) our field emerged as faculty roles and responsibilities evolved and (b) a graduate degree in higher education and student affairs is not required to work in the field.[3] Furthermore, the work of student affairs educators, and in turn the field itself, continues to evolve as the needs of students and campuses change across the intersection of historical, social, and political contexts.

While the American College Personnel Association (ACPA) and NASPA *Professional Competency Areas for Student Affairs Educators* and Council for the Advancement of Standards (CAS) in Higher Education Standards[4] have signaled increasing agreement about what knowledge and skills are essential for contemporary student affairs practice, how to gauge what it means to be "competent enough" to work in the field is not always clear. Specifically, it can be challenging to assess and to make fine distinctions when gauging degree of competency. We are able to recognize the extremes in performance but may find it more challenging to tease out the nuanced difference in how student affairs educators demonstrate their knowledge and skills. Ultimately, the complexities of meeting the multiple aims of graduate education in student affairs coupled with evolving understandings of core knowledge, values, and skills required to work in dynamic educational contexts only add to the challenge of providing educators with a foundation for creating equitable, safe, and civil learning environments.

Social Justice and Inclusion in Graduate Preparation Programs

While the field espouses a commitment to social justice and inclusion, graduate preparation programs have not consistently enacted our stated commitments. Prior to the emergence of the ACPA and NASPA competencies, HESA programs did not always include focused coursework related to equity, diversity, inclusion, and/or social justice.[5] Thus, there are practitioners deemed by HESA faculty as adequately prepared to work in student affairs who have very little or limited understanding of power, privilege, and oppression. Yet, these individuals are in positions to teach, supervise, and mentor newer professionals.

Programs now tend to include at least one diversity-oriented course, yet a stand-alone course, while necessary, is insufficient for preparing student affairs educators to advance social justice and inclusion. Commitments to equity, inclusion, and social justice need to be woven throughout HESA curricula and reflected in faculty members' teaching and advising practices. Even if social justice is infused into HESA curricula, this doesn't mean that all students are served well by our HESA programs. Faculty and students with marginalized and minoritized identities often do the heavy lifting within courses and conversations related to equity, diversity, inclusion, and social justice, which is mentally and emotionally taxing. Furthermore, racially minoritized students in HESA preparation programs have reported experiencing microaggressions in their classes and in their workplaces.[6] Although graduate preparation programs are spaces for learning and development, those with dominant identities often learn at the expense of their minoritized peers.

It is vital that HESA faculty do a better job of using what we know about promoting increasingly complex understandings of social justice and inclusion across domains of development in our own graduate training programs. Specifically, we need to leverage the rich body of research on diverse learning environments to inform graduate education. In theory, HESA programs have strong potential to advance learning about and across differences in power and socially constructed identities since students engage with diversity in the curriculum and they may have informal opportunities to build relationships with peers and colleagues who hold different identities and beliefs from them.[7] Yet, some of our programs lack the compositional diversity across socially constructed identities that will enrich formal and informal interactions across differences. Additionally, there is a need for HESA faculty members to assess and actively work to create inclusive climates within their programs. Enacting our stated commitments to social justice and inclusion ultimately requires moving beyond inclusive programs to ones that are power and identity conscious, because this shift centralizes social justice.

Moving Toward Power- and Identity-Conscious Graduate Programs

Given the complexities of fostering equitable, safe, and civil learning environments, I assert that HESA preparation programs need to be consistently power and identity conscious. To this end, I explore key steps toward developing such programs.

Reexamining Programmatic Aims and Outcomes

For HESA programs to better prepare educators to foster equitable, safe, and civil learning environments, we need to be honest about our aims. What kinds of practitioners do we really want to train in our individual programs? Are HESA programs designed to cultivate socially just practitioners? Critically conscious practitioners?[8] Practitioners who are inclusive? Practitioners who celebrate diversity? The field broadly desires to foster social justice and inclusion, but does scrutiny of our individual courses, our pedagogical choices, and the structures of programs show that we are really doing that work?

HESA curriculum and pedagogy in programs that desire to train critically conscious practitioners should be different from programs that are designed solely to hone practitioners' awareness of diversity. While diversity, inclusion, equity, and social justice are related to each other, they are distinctive in the ways they acknowledge the existence of power, privilege, and oppression within social systems and how they in turn affect individuals' lived experiences. Being transparent about program aims requires that HESA faculty actively work to enact their values and that they are held responsible for the extent to which they reinforce and contest systems of oppression within their learning communities.

If we foreground power, privilege, and oppression in HESA curricula, then we are moving toward cultivating critically consciousness educators. These individuals not only understand power structures and their roles within them but also actively work to disrupt oppression and work toward creating educational environments and systems that are more equitable. Organizing our curricula to foster critical consciousness moves us beyond talking about social justice and inclusion as a competency toward doing work that is in service of liberation and adjusting our curricular content and structure accordingly.

Creating HESA programs that work in service of social justice challenges us to rethink the notion of competency and to ask: Who is taught and what is taught? Who decides how *competency* is defined and how it is manifested? How do we center the voices and experiences of the marginalized and minoritized in our scholarship and practice? To what extent does my work perpetuate narratives of professionalism that constrain and devalue minoritized students and educators? How am I contributing to and how am I contesting systems of oppression? Reflective questions such as these are vital for both HESA students and faculty to consider since they provide opportunities for us to acknowledge power dynamics within our programs and to honor the knowledge and expertise we all contribute to our learning communities. They also push us to consider how we collectively develop learning opportunities that foreground developing critical consciousness and taking action as educators to advance social justice. If we create HESA curricula that actively engage students in the coconstruction of knowledge and that acknowledge their multiple intersecting identities and how we are collectively affected by power, privilege, and oppression, we will model how to create learning environments that are power and identity conscious and that promote equity, civility, and to a lesser extent safety. By this, I mean we work to build trust and respect, but all members of the learning community will be challenged, which can lead students to feel "unsafe," particularly if they experience dissonance.

Furthermore, fostering critical consciousness among student affairs educators requires us to attend not only to learning but also to the process of unlearning. For HESA faculty and curricula to contest dominant ways of knowing, we need to surface our assumptions, biases, and beliefs and interrogate how these viewpoints reinforce deficit perspectives of minoritized communities and, in turn, systems of oppression. This kind of self-work is ongoing and should not end when students complete their HESA program. As such, HESA faculty need to initiate the process and emphasize that the process of learning and unlearning is continuous. In this regard, we are continuing to socialize HESA graduate students to habits of mind that will affect how they approach the process of creating learning environments where equity, civility, and safety may work in harmony or where they may be in tension with each other.

Teaching in Service of Social Justice and Inclusion

Creating HESA programs that are consistently power and identity conscious requires that we also reevaluate how instructors teach in service of social justice and inclusion. Specifically, we need to shift to centering critical perspectives in curriculum and pedagogy, cultivating inclusive learning communities, and fostering complex thinking.

Shift to Centering Critical Perspectives in Curriculum and Pedagogy

To more effectively prepare student affairs educators to navigate the complexities of fostering equitable, safe, and civil learning environments, we need to infuse varying perspectives on equity, diversity, and inclusion into our curriculum and applied experiences (i.e., assistantships, practica). For example, we need to use critical perspectives[9] and critical pedagogies[10] throughout HESA programs rather than reserving them for diversity courses. Critical pedagogies are designed to create connections among ideology, power, culture, curriculum, and pedagogy; in doing so, they contest dominant ways of knowing and they centralize the voices of those who are marginalized and minoritized. Examining how power, privilege, and oppression manifest themselves and how they affect students' experiences is applicable to all HESA course content and applied field experiences.

Ideally, if we integrate critical perspectives throughout the curriculum and partner more closely with those who supervise assistantships and practica, we can engage students more regularly in conversations about praxis[11] or linking their reflections with actions to transform inequitable social structures. Often, we ask students to evaluate what others are doing to promote social justice and inclusion or to hypothesize what they will do in the future. Instead, HESA faculty and practicum and assistantship supervisors could collaborate to support students' efforts to engage in praxis throughout their graduate training experiences. Creating these linkages may better enable graduate students to navigate the tension between translating thoughts into action and to examine the organizational and systematic barriers that may limit or penalize us for taking action to promote equity and inclusion.

Yet, shifting toward critical approaches to pedagogy and praxis is not without its challenges since resistance is likely to manifest itself in many forms. For example, some may argue that centering critical perspectives is an effort to indoctrinate emerging professionals into prioritizing social justice in student affairs practice over other knowledge and skills needed in the field (e.g., assessment, supervision). Others may resist the use of critical perspectives and pedagogies because they erroneously believe HESA faculty are teaching students that there is only one way to approach social justice in student affairs. Furthermore, HESA faculty who use critical pedagogies may receive lower course evaluations if they challenge students' privileges, and this may affect their abilities to earn tenure or be renewed as a course instructor. Although HESA faculty who use critical perspectives and pedagogies in their praxis are likely to encounter resistance, I assert that centering the voices and experiences of those who are marginalized and challenging systems of oppression are necessary if we are to train student affairs educators who are truly committed to serving all students and advancing social justice.

Cultivating Inclusive Learning Communities

For HESA programs to leverage the strengths of critical pedagogies, we need to be intentional about how we create and cultivate inclusive learning communities. Although many programs use a cohort model, membership in a cohort does not mean that students feel as though they are part of a community. With this in mind, we need to create shared expectations about how we will engage with each other as we learn, regardless of class format (i.e., face-to-face, online, hybrid). While we tend to prioritize creating community in face-to-face courses, similar approaches to cultivating relationships can be used in online and hybrid courses if instructors are intentional about creating space and opportunities for students to engage with each other, ideally in a synchronous format. The practice of setting expectations in classrooms or in diversity trainings is common, and it can feel meaningless unless it is grounded in service of creating community rather than assuming one is already present.

Rather than asking students what they expect of each other, I have begun asking students the following questions: What do you need to learn within this community? What are you willing to give to others within this community? This subtle shift in questions requires students to articulate their needs and to demonstrate reciprocity for their peers. In the process of setting community learning expectations in my courses, I urge students to move beyond generalities and to explore what we want community to look and feel like. We also talk about creating brave spaces[12] where we can take risks and lean into discomfort. In these brave spaces, individuals can strongly disagree with each other and maintain respect for each other. They can feel angry and frustrated but still allow space for forgiveness and compassion. I have found that as I have shifted how we talk about learning community expectations, students have been increasingly willing to take risks, accept challenges, make mistakes, and accept responsibility for when they have hurt or harmed others. Also, I have been mindful of the extent to which I uphold the learning community expectations and how I model being vulnerable and taking responsibility for my impact on others rather than my intentions.

Creating inclusive learning communities requires paying equal attention to content and process. What we learn is as important as how we learn together. Attending to how we engage within our HESA programs should happen beyond the day we discuss course expectations. Fostering equitable, safe, and civil spaces for learning includes addressing and naming when we observe microaggressions, fragility, and centralizing the needs and interests of those with dominant identities. When instructors name how inequality and oppression operate in our classroom spaces, an opportunity to learn emerges and there is potential for us to advance our understanding of our identities, our privileges, and our subordination. In these moments, we model various ways to navigate the tensions of creating learning spaces that are equitable, safe, and inclusive. Though we might be imperfect, choosing to intervene or returning to the conversation at a later point is necessary since it is difficult for a group to collectively move forward and to support each other's learning if we ignore how we have negatively affected members of the community.

Fostering Complex Thinking

The work of creating learning communities that are equitable, safe, and civil requires abilities to see multiple perspectives, to hold tension and contradiction as a way of being, and to understand there may not be a right or best answer. As previously noted, HESA programs can advance the complexity of students' thinking by consistently asking them to reflect on their experiences in a structured manner. In particular, we can challenge students to make connections between course content and their lived experiences by using scholarly personal narratives and praxis journals as assignments. We can also enhance critical thinking by creating opportunities for students to examine their underlying assumptions and how they affect their practice.

As we promote increased complexity across the cognitive, intrapersonal, and interpersonal domains of development, students may need additional challenge and support to work though the discomfort of not always having a right or best answer as they engage in practice. In particular, students should be challenged to reflect on questions such as the following: Why do I need one answer? Who do I look to as sources of authority and why? How am I affected when I don't know the "right answer" or "best way" to navigate complex situations? How do my identities and relationships affect what I think I should do? While students may find ambiguity uncomfortable, coming to understand that it is an inherent part of student affairs work is valuable. Rather than looking for answers, coming to see oneself as creating change is an important part of promoting social justice and inclusion in dynamic environments. However, one may not see oneself as capable of enacting change unless learning opportunities are scaffolded to build a developmental bridge[13] meaning adequate challenge and support is needed to shift from prior to new, more complex ways of knowing.

Conclusion

Ultimately, if HESA faculty are to enhance student affairs educators' abilities to foster equitable, civil, and safe learning environments, we must create graduate training programs that are power and identity conscious. To do this, we need to scrutinize our work, our assumptions, and our beliefs so that we can leverage the strengths of critical pedagogy. We also need to work diligently to create inclusive communities and to foster increased complexity across cognitive, intrapersonal, and interpersonal domains of development. By centralizing social justice and inclusion in our work, HESA programs have the potential to be empowering and liberating spaces that may in turn affect how educators advocate for and advance equity and inclusion on our campus and in our communities.

Discussion Questions

1. How would your graduate preparation program experience change if it were more power and identity conscious?
2. What has your graduate preparation program helped you learn related to social justice and inclusion? What has your program helped you begin to unlearn?
3. What training is needed in doctoral programs to prepare faculty members who teach within power and identity conscious student affairs graduate preparation programs?

Notes

1. Perez, R. J. (2016). A conceptual model of professional socialization within student affairs graduate preparation programs. *Journal for the Study of Postsecondary and Tertiary Education, 1*, 35–52.

2. American College Personnel Association and National Association of Student Personnel Administrators, Professional Competencies Task Force. (2015). *Professional competency areas for student affairs educators*. Retrieved from http://www.myacpa.org/professional-competency-areas-student-affairs-practitioners.

3. Hevel, M. S. (2016). Toward a history of student affairs: A synthesis of research, 1996–2015. *Journal of College Student Development, 57*(7), 844–862; Thelin, J. R. (2011). *A history of American higher education* (2nd ed.). Baltimore, MD: Johns Hopkins University Press.

4. American College Personnel Association and National Association of Student Personnel Administrators, Professional Competencies Task Force. *Professional competency areas for student affairs educators*; Council for the Advancement of

Standards in Higher Education. (2015). *CAS professional standards for higher education* (9th ed.). Washington DC: Author.

5. Flowers, L. A. (2003). National study of diversity requirements in student affairs graduate programs. *NASPA Journal, 40*(4), 72–81.

6. Flowers, L. A., & Howard-Hamilton, M. F. (2002). A qualitative study of graduate students' perceptions of diversity issues in student affairs preparation programs. *Journal of College Student Development, 43*(1), 119–123; Linder, C., Harris, J. C., Allen, E. L., & Hubain, B. (2015). Building inclusive pedagogy: Recommendations from a national study of students of color in higher education and student affairs graduate programs. *Equity & Excellence in Education, 48*(2), 178–194.

7. Gurin, P., Dey, E. L., Hurtado, S., & Gurin, G. (2002). Diversity and higher education: Theory and impact on educational outcomes. *Harvard Educational Review, 72*(3), 330–366.

8. Freire, P. (1970). *Pedagogy of the oppressed.* New York, NY: Continuum.

9. Abes, E. S. (2016). Situating paradigms in student development theory. In E. S. Abes (Ed.), *Critical perspectives on student development theory* (New Directions for Student Services, no. 154, pp. 9–16). San Francisco, CA: Jossey-Bass.

10. Nesbit, T. (2004). Class and teaching. In J. A. Sandlin & R. St. Clair (Eds.), *New Directions for Adult and Continuing Education,* Vol. 2004, No. 120: Promoting critical practice in adult education (pp. 15-24). San Francisco, CA: Jossey-Bass.

11. Freire, P. *Pedagogy of the oppressed.*

12. Arao, B., & Clemens, K. (2013). From safe spaces to brave spaces: A new way to frame dialogue around diversity and social justice. In L. M. Landman (Ed.). *The art of effective facilitation: Reflections from social justice educators* (pp. 135–150). Sterling, VA: Stylus.

13. Baxter Magolda, M. B. (2001). *Making their own way: Narratives for transforming higher education to promote self-development.* Sterling, VA: Stylus.

A Systemic Approach to Enacting Equitable, Civil, and Safe Learning Environments

Jessica C. Harris

erez demonstrated the complexity of fostering equitable, civil, and safe learning environments in higher education and student affairs (HESA) preparation programs. To address this complexity, she suggested that HESA programs foster social justice and inclusion by continuously examining underlying assumptions of the field, consistently using critical pedagogy, and creating opportunities to advance students' capacities to understand and engage across difference. While I agree with many of Perez's arguments, she often suggested individual, microlevel approaches to addressing in/equitable, un/safe, and un/civil learning environments in HESA programs. This microlevel approach does little to address the multiple and intersecting systems of domination that influence, and often stifle, one's everyday experiences with and enactment of learning environments. In this essay, I interrogate how sociohistorical systems of domination and institutional and programmatic structures often influence HESA learning environments and, subsequently, may shift many of Perez's microlevel recommendations. To address and identify the complexities of fostering inclusive learning environments, structures and systems must be addressed prior to and/or in tandem with the individual suggestions Perez detailed.

Sociohistorical Systems of Domination

Perez's essay makes clear that social justice, inclusion, and identity and power consciousness are focal points in creating learning environments. Yet, I was struck by Perez's lack of naming systems of domination, such as racism, sexism, ableism, heterosexism, and their connection to enacting safe, civil, and equitable learning environments. The discounting of systems of domination through scholarship not only falls short in acknowledging the pervasiveness of dominant ideologies, such as White supremacy, in society and the HESA classroom but also renormalizes these ideologies and upholds the status quo.[1] To be sure, Perez is one of many scholars to stop short in naming systems of oppression and the ways in which they manifest in postsecondary contexts.[2] Yet, in order to enact inclusive learning environments in HESA programs, educators must name and address the systems of domination that inherently inform in/equitable, un/safe, and un/civil learning environments.

For example, I have taught student affairs courses in which the majority, if not all, of the students in the course identified as people of color. While these courses included structural racial diversity, Whiteness continued to work within these classroom environments. I perceived White ideologies to manifest through students' internalization of racism and through different forms of racism, such as monoracism, or "a social system of psychological inequality where individuals who do not fit monoracial categories may be oppressed on systemic and interpersonal levels because of underlying assumptions and beliefs in singular, discrete racial categories."[3] For example, a Black student expressed that a Black and White multiracial student in their cohort might not "fully" understand the Black experience because they were not "full" Black. This example connects to monoracism, a product of White supremacist ideology. Additionally, I have observed students' internalization of racist stereotypes, even if joking, e.g., "I was admitted to this program because of affirmative action."

To address an inequitable, unsafe, and uncivil learning environment educators must ask, "How are students' microlevel interactions connected to macrolevel and dominant ideologies of identity that HESA students have learned throughout their educational journeys?" As educators, we must acknowledge that all individual interactions within the classroom are identity specific and are manifestations of centuries of violence, control, and dominant ideologies.[4] Due to this history and the embeddedness of oppression, educators must re/read research, often outside of higher education, that explores these systems and histories so that we might better understand and address the manifestation of systems of domination in the HESA classroom.

Educators should also dialogue with students about ways in which systems of domination influence classroom dynamics. After observing tense cohort interactions during one specific class session, I posed the question, "How are we perceiving White supremacy to work in this space?" It is imperative that faculty name these systems (e.g., racism, White supremacy) to disrupt their normalization. Furthermore, for students to have this conversation, they must be knowledgeable of systems of domination, which requires faculty to include course readings that name, define, and disrupt these systems. Because scholars of higher education may not often name systems of domination,[5] faculty must assign readings from higher education and other academic disciplines (e.g., history, ethnic studies, women's studies) to engage students in learning about and thinking through how systems of domination manifest in postsecondary contexts, including graduate classrooms. Attempts to enact these learning environments may continue to fall short if educators and students remain normalized to the systems of domination that influence individuals' everyday experiences both inside and outside of the learning environment.

Institutional Structures

Perez acknowledged, "Although HESA faculty who use critical perspectives and pedagogies in their praxis are likely to encounter resistance, I assert that centering the voices and experiences of those who are marginalized and challenging systems of oppression are necessary."[6] While I somewhat agree with Perez's statement, I also acknowledge that centering minoritized voices and challenging systems of domination takes a toll on and comes at a great cost for faculty members with minoritized identities.[7] For example, scholars[8] have explored how women of color faculty members often face gendered racism in the classroom, which may manifest in disrespectful and threatening behavior from White male students. Furthermore, many faculty members with minoritized identities are more likely to receive poor student teaching evaluations because they diverge from students' hegemonic perceptions of what a faculty member should embody.[9] In short, for some HESA faculty members, particularly those with minoritized identities, the learning environment is always already inequitable, unsafe, and/or uncivil. These learning environments are a manifestation of ideologies and social systems (as previously discussed) that inform institutional structures, such as mission statements, policies and procedures for tenure and advancement, and institutional reward structures.[10]

Institutional leaders must foster equitable, safe, and civil working environments for HESA faculty members so that they might feel free to enact similar environments for students. Institutional mission statements must explicitly state their valuing of diverse perspectives and ramifications for disrespect of this diversity, particularly as it relates to faculty members. Policies and procedures for tenure and advancement, specifically the evaluation of teaching, must be interrogated. Institutions can rework evaluation processes to account for the ways in which students may discriminate against and scrutinize minoritized faculty through these evaluations.[11] Some scholars have suggested that a rubric, in which faculty members list the teaching practices they use and how these practices correlate to student success, may be a more appropriate assessment of teaching and learning in higher education.[12] Scholars have also suggested that women faculty be given a "boost" on their teaching evaluations; the "boost" or bonus would be "determined by average gender bias in teaching evaluations at [faculty members'] institution or national averages. Professional reviews should then be based on these adjusted data, not those laden with unconscious (and possibly conscious) bias."[13] Finally, if universities expect faculty members to foster safe, civil, and equitable learning environments, institutional structures must reward them for doing so. For example, the University of California 10-campus system recently instituted a tenure and advancement policy that states, "Teaching, research, professional and public service contributions that promote diversity and equal opportunity are to be encouraged and given recognition in the evaluation of the candidate's qualifications."[14]

Programmatic Structures

Perez suggested the reexamination of programmatic aims and outcomes so that power, privilege, and oppression are foregrounded in HESA curricula to cultivate inclusive learning communities that promote equity, civility and, to some extent, safety. When I read Perez's suggestion, I was reminded of the intriguing findings from my recent research with HESA faculty members and their approaches to teaching student development theory courses. The majority of the 18 HESA faculty members involved in the research explored how programmatic structures constrained their abilities to teach student development theory in manners that fostered critical thinking and cultivated social justice, inclusion, and praxis. For example, several junior faculty members relayed how comprehensive exams and the necessity to teach to these exams constrained their ability to urge students to "think outside of the box" when it came to theory. Although faculty members craft comprehensive exam questions and institute exams as a requirement of HESA programs, several junior faculty explained that it was difficult to convince other, often senior, faculty members to shift the nature of exams, let alone do away with the comprehensive exam. In short, the re/socialization that many participants encountered throughout their time in HESA stifled their ability to shift the curriculum and cultivate critical consciousness in the learning environment.

While foregrounding power, privilege, and oppression in HESA curricula is an excellent commitment, it is nearly impossible to do so when programmatic structures—which are influenced by institutional and societal structures—prohibit faculty members from doing so. Thus, when reexamining programmatic aims and outcomes, as Perez suggested, it is necessary to ask questions that interrogate the structures of programs and connect to microlevel issues. For example, how might comprehensive exams stifle the actualization of equitable, safe, and civil learning environments? What are the structures of socialization, including anticipatory (graduate students) and organizational (faculty members), that are embedded throughout HESA programs and work to stifle social justice and inclusion? How might educators disrupt and/or shift these structures so that HESA learning environments are supported in fostering equity, safety, and civility?

Conclusion

Educators must account for, and connect, macrolevel structures to microlevel, everyday experiences within HESA programs. HESA graduate students must also learn the importance of accounting for and connecting the macro to the micro because they will soon be teaching courses, planning programs, and/or conducting research that must acknowledge how the individual exists within, and is influenced by, systems of domination. Educators must make the connection between systems, structures, and individual experiences to foster equitable, safe, and civil learning environments in HESA programs.

Discussion Questions

1. What programmatic structures might constrain your ability to teach and/ or learn in manners that foster critical consciousness and social justice and inclusion?
2. How do sociohistorical systems of domination manifest in the HESA learning environment? How do you maintain these systems?
3. In what ways do institutional structures influence your teaching/learning within the HESA classroom?

Notes

1. Harper, S. R. (2012). Race without racism: How higher education researchers minimize racist institutionalized norms. *The Review of Higher Education 36*(1), 9–29.

2. Ibid.

3. Johnston, M. P., & Nadal, K. L. (2010). Multiracial microaggressions: Exposing monoracism in everyday life and clinical practice. In D. W. Sue (Ed.), *Microaggressions and marginality: Manifestation, dynamics, and impact* (pp. 123–144). New York, NY: Wiley, p. 125.

4. Pérez Huber, L., & Solórzano, D. G. (2015). Racial microaggressions as a tool for critical race research. *Race, Ethnicity and Education 18*, 297–320.

5. Harper, Race without racism.

6. Perez, R. J., this volume, p. 291–292.

7. McGowan, J. M. (2000). African-American faculty classroom teaching experiences in predominantly White colleges and universities. *Multicultural Education, 8*(2), 19–22; Patton, L. D., & Catching, C. (2009). "Teaching while Black": Narratives of African American student affairs faculty. *International Journal of Qualitative Studies, 22*(6), 713–728; Pittman, C. T. (2010). Race and gender oppression in the classroom: The experience of women faculty of color with White male students. *Teaching Sociology, 38*(3), 183–196.

8. Ibid.

9. Ford, K. A. (2011). Race, gender, and bodily (mis)recognition: Women of color faculty experiences with White students in the college classroom. *The Journal of Higher Education, 82*(4), 444–478.

10. Pérez Huber & Solórzano, Racial microaggressions as a tool for critical race research.

11. Ford, Race, gender, and bodily (mis)recognition.

12. Wieman, C. (2015). A better way to evaluate undergraduate teaching. *Change, 47*(1), 6–15.

13. Pritchard, S. B. (2015). Should female faculty get bonus points to correct gender bias in student evaluations? *Higher Ed Jobs*. Retrieved from https://www.higheredjobs.com/articles/articleDisplay.cfm?ID=692

14. University of California, Los Angeles. (2018). UCLA Academic Personnel Office–Diversity. Retrieved from https://apo.ucla.edu/cap-guidance/diversity

16

What Professional Development Opportunities Are Necessary to Ensure That Professionals Have the Capacities and Competencies to Make Good Decisions When Faced With the Unknown?

Trust Your Instincts, Pack a Compass, and Never Hike Alone

Cynthia H. Love

To face the unknown and effectively meet the needs of college students, student affairs educators must have good intentions, inspiration, and energy in the form of a professional development plan. While often thought of as an annual job requirement dictated by supervisors, this plan instead should be a self-given gift frequently consulted and revised throughout your career. A detailed professional development plan informed by honest self-assessment of your goals and competencies serves as a compass and catalyst for deliberate, active, and necessary change. This evolving document helps identify current knowledge, skills, and dispositions as well as essential areas for growth within a profession characterized by shifting demographic, technological, political, and economic forces. Enacting a professional development plan is analogous to hiking in the wilderness. Your path will likely be unmarked, unpredictable, challenging, and rewarding. At minimum, you will need to trust your instincts, make sure you pack a compass, and seek the wisdom of an experienced guide along the way.

Higher education educators struggle with difficult trails that have become increasingly challenging during the twenty-first century, like the seemingly intractable persistence of racism and sexism in the academy. Janina Montero, former vice chancellor of student affairs at the University of California, Los Angeles (UCLA) captures this context:

> Students are bringing new historical and cultural experiences: new meanings of borders, migration, refugees, social justice, humanitarian assistance; the #BlackLivesMatter movement; the Occupy movement; the impact of international terrorism on civil rights. We are living these trying times together, trying to make sense of the many seismic shifts in demographics and the evolving sociocultural connections and interactions.[1]

Montero names many of the unmarked trails student affairs educators must transverse. To ensure equity, civility, and safety in the academy, educators must commit to their own professional evolution, grounded in principles, standards, and competencies informed by best practices and healthy work environments.

Guides to Optimizing Professional Development

In this essay, the compass is a metaphor for the following sources of direction when crafting a professional development plan: (a) Evan and Reason's guiding principles for student affairs;[2] (b) the Council for the Advancement of Standards (CAS) in Higher Education;[3] (c) the American College Personnel Association (ACPA) and NASPA *Professional Competency Areas for Student Affairs Educators*;[4] and (d) yourself. The advice to never hike alone encourages educators to trust their judgments, and seek guidance from colleagues, supervisors, and mentors. I offer four specific examples that reveal ways for educators to make good decisions in these complex times.

Evans and Reason's Guiding Principles

Evans and Reason identify the following principles that are useful guides to optimize professional development: (a) focus on students—the primary purpose of our work; (b) recognize the role of the environment in a student's collegiate experiences; (c) acknowledge the importance of intentional, empirically grounded practice; and (d) be responsible to the broader society.[5] These principles are drawn from Evans and Reason's thematic analysis of 13 foundational student affairs documents such as *Student Personnel Point of View*, published in 1937, and *Powerful Partnerships*, published in 1998. These principles have stood the test of time despite dramatic changes in the nature and scope of student affairs work. As such, the principles provide a solid foundation upon which to build a professional development plan.

Evans and Reason's first principle focuses on collegians. Supporting and advocating for students is challenging, because students are ever changing. Knowledge generated and disseminated even a decade ago is woefully outdated today. Theories that student affairs educators learned, for example, during their graduate studies must be continually updated and augmented. Remaining professionally competent means continually redefining what it means to be an educator, which takes conviction, courage, and a passion for lifelong learning. Professional development plans guided by the principle of focusing on students chart a course for student affairs educators to engage in continuous, self-directed learning centered on understanding and appreciating emergent student development theory and practice as well as environmental, organizational, and political knowledge that shapes the student experience. Book clubs, podcasts, conferences, newsletters, and webinars are just a few resources you can draw upon to guide your student-focused professional development journey.

Evans and Reason's second principle recognizes that larger social systems influence campus environments and these campus environments influence student affairs educators as well as the students they serve. For example, in 2017, national and state policies on the rights and protections of undocumented students have had a profound and rippling effect on campus policies, student affair educators' advocacy roles, and undocumented students' pursuit of a college degree. Many senior university administrators felt let down by legislators and government agencies. Likewise, immigration mandates from campus administrators—rooted in their inability to balance the external stakeholders' demands and policies with internal stakeholders' desires— disappointed many student affairs educators and undocumented students. Educators need to understand not only how external influences shape campus politics and policies but also how to advocate for students within these contexts.

I offer an example to further illuminate what a professional development plan guided by a commitment to student advocacy looks like. In 2017, a new professional working in Texas wanted to attend a workshop hosted by Southerners on New Ground (SONG), a queer liberation organization comprising people of color; immigrants; undocumented people and those with disabilities; and working-class, rural, and small-town residents in southern communities. The governor prohibited the spending of state funds on certain types of diversity training, so the university refused to fund the request. I encouraged the individual to take release time and self-fund the workshop. The person sold gear on craigslist.com and identified friends attending the training to share transportation and youth hostel expenses. This example reveals one way to adhere to institutional policy, navigate competing demands, and advocate for the less powerful (as well as support a new professional's development plan even if it cannot be institutionally financed).

Evans and Reason's third principle recognizes the importance of empirically grounded practice. Trying to understand students, external campus influences, and campus politics and policy necessitates educators' familiarity with and willingness to contribute to higher education research. This means blurring an age-old and dysfunctional binary of *scholar-practitioner*. It is essential for educators to be both learners and teachers by staying up-to-date on empirical research as well as generating and disseminating knowledge. A purposeful professional development plan can help achieve this aim.

Attending and presenting at regional and national conferences is an obvious way to teach and learn. Attending both student affairs (e.g., ACPA, NASPA) and non-student affairs sponsored conferences (e.g., Creating Change[6] hosted by the National Task Force, the Social Justice Training Institute,[7] Lead365,[8] and the Centre for Global Inclusion[9]) constitute professional development opportunities that expand educators' intellectual horizons. Choices regarding which conferences to attend and which sessions to engage in should be guided by frequent self-assessments of your knowledge gaps and the strategic selection of opportunities to fill them—reflective tasks embedded in the process of creating and updating your professional development plan.

Educators must not only consume knowledge to enhance practice but also generate and disseminate their local knowledge worldwide. Navigating crisis is an example of a topic about which many student affairs educators have valuable insight to share. Student affairs educators are called upon to support students during tragic events, both local and national. We've learned a lot from these losses and recoveries. Campus responses to events such as Hurricane Katrina, the Virginia Tech massacre, unrest in Ferguson, and the Orlando Pulse shootings provide vitally important insights that must be disseminated. Digital platforms like ACPA Video on Demand[10] have made it possible to share knowledge beyond traditional scholarly publications. Following the death of Michael Brown in Ferguson, Missouri,[11] ACPA staff members travelled to St. Louis and filmed interactions around the city, which resulted in a video series entitled *Deconstructing Racism in the Academy*.[12] Ventures such as this one reveal the benefits of purposefully interacting with colleagues, supervisors, and mentors resulting in a supercharged professional development opportunity (rooted in networking, dialogues across difference, and best practices) that can be shared with others beyond the borders of your campus. However, in order to engage in empirically grounded practice, you must carve out time for this work. Professional development plans can help you prioritize and identify strategies for achieving your research and knowledge dissemination goals (e.g., attend a writer's retreat, submit an institutional research grant proposal).

Evans and Reason's fourth principle centers on a belief that student affairs educators have a responsibility to society and must take an active role in cultivating the civic capacities of college graduates. Student affairs' civic development work has taken on new meaning and complexity in the current political moment. Robert Arnove in *Philanthropy and Cultural Imperialism* charges:

> A central thesis is that foundations like Carnegie, Rockefeller, and Ford have a corrosive influence on democratic society, represent unregulated and unaccountable concentrations of power and wealth, buy talent, promote causes, and, in effect, establish an agenda of what merits society's attention. They serve as "cooling-out" agencies, delaying and preventing more radical, structural change. They help maintain an economic and political order, international in scope, which benefits the ruling-class interests of philanthropists.[13]

Dynamics such as these have a profound influence on higher education. Faculty members, such as Arnove, often act as public intellectuals. Their scholarship not only benefits students and colleagues but also transcends the academy to educate and challenge society. Student affairs educators devote a disproportionate amount of time to the development of students and the profession, often shunning larger societal responsibilities.

It is necessary but insufficient for educators to simply recognize these corrosive power dynamics Arnove points out. Student affairs educators can engage students in discussing these power dynamics as well as conduct and disseminate research that counters these perspectives. They (and the students with whom they work) must act on this knowledge to improve society.

It is important to note that, although social justice is not explicitly mentioned in Evans and Reason's framework of foundational student affairs principles, Reason and Broido[14] do identify social justice advocacy as a guiding professional principal, highlighting empirical research on student affairs professional values; the articulation of equity, diversity, and inclusion outcomes in the *ACPA/NASPA Professional Competency Areas for Student Affairs Educators*; and the increasing influence of critical social theory (e.g., critical race theory) within student affairs professional preparation and practice.

Evans and Reason's four principles (rooted in social justice) serve as a compass to guide engagement in activities that can help you answer the question posed at the outset of this chapter, "What professional development opportunities are necessary to ensure that professionals have the capacities and competencies to make good decisions when faced with the unknown?"

CAS Professional Standards

The CAS in Higher Education (founded in 1979) is an invaluable resource for mapping a professional development plan. Guided by a philosophy of self-regulation and a commitment to collaboration,[15] CAS publishes self- and institutional assessment guides for providing quality programs and services that foster student learning and development. The adoption of the CAS philosophy and self-assessment process benefits the individual, the division, and the whole institution by contributing to a culture of accountability and continuous improvement.[16]

The guiding principles for CAS, which mirror those that inform the work of educators, highlight five areas of emphasis: (a) students and their environment, (b) diversity and multiculturalism, (c) organization, leadership, and human resources; (d) health-engendering environments, and (e) ethical considerations. Led by these principles, CAS has developed a diverse array of tools and resources designed to help individuals and organizations assess alignment with national best practices. Engaging in frequent reflection on your ability to demonstrate the CAS Characteristics of Individual Excellence,[17] design programs aligned with relevant functional area CAS Standards, and/or enact the CAS Statement of Shared Ethical Principles[18] will guide you in the articulation of professional development goals and strategies that reflect with the collective wisdom of the 41 higher education professional organizations which comprise CAS. For example, if upon reflection you find yourself struggling to provide multiple examples of ways in which you consistently enact the CAS characteristic of individual excellence ("Values differences among groups of students and between individuals; helps students understand the interdependence among people both locally and globally"[19]), you can seek the guidance of a trusted mentor to help you identify specific professional development goals and strategies focused on strengthening your capacity to facilitate learning opportunities that empha-size local and global interdependence.

ACPA and NASPA Professional Competencies

In 2010 (and again in 2015), an ACPA and NASPA Joint Task Force on Professional Competencies and Standards reached a consensus on professional competencies. Competencies define broad professional knowledge, skills, and attitudes expected of student affairs educators, regardless of their area of specialization or positional role. The 2015 *ACPA/NASPA Professional Competency Areas for Student Affairs Educators* include personal and ethical foundations; values, philosophy, and history; assessment, evaluation, and research; law, policy, and governance; organizational and human resources; leadership; social justice and inclusion; student learning and development; technology; and advising and supporting.[20]

Student affairs educators should possess a foundational understanding of these competencies, which prepares them to navigate issues of safety, civility, and equity. Common strategies for engaging with these competencies include: attending national conferences, forming divisional/departmental reading groups, and participating in virtual professional development programs (e.g., blogs, webinars) aligned with specific competencies. Programs such as ACPA's Compliance U™ certificate program[21] or NASPA's Certificate Program in Student Affairs Law and Policy[22] align with the professional competency in law, policy, and governance and offer significant support to the growing demands for compliance in many campus areas.

To guide the development of a competency-oriented professional growth plan, ACPA and NASPA translated the competency document into a set of rubrics[23] that student affairs educators can use to self-assess professional competence and chart professional growth at the foundational, intermediate, and advanced levels. In addition to providing the rubric templates, ACPA and NASPA also offer guidance for using the rubrics in a variety of contexts, including professional development, supervision, and professional associa-tion engagement. When attending a conference, student affairs educators might use their professional competency rubrics to decide which sessions to attend. Additionally, professionals can use the competency rubrics to frame conversations with mentors and/or supervisors regarding areas for growth and relevant professional development opportunities.

The significance of the ACPA/NASPA professional competencies is underscored in Magolda and Carnaghi's reconceptualization of professional development in student affairs:

Professional development must be knowledge-driven and based on competencies, so that participants can be theoretically informed as they assume roles as administrators, advocates, activists, counselors, assessors/evaluators, advisers, technologists, disciplinarians, free speech experts, public safety officers, referral agents, crisis managers, leadership developers, arbitrators, ethicists, and role models.[24]

Self-Reflection

If we are to take seriously our own professional development, we must augment externally defined guides such as the aforementioned principles, standards, and competencies (that focus on knowledge and skills) with internally defined self-reflection. Kolb and Yaganeh argue

the learning way is about approaching life experiences with a learning attitude. It involves a deep trust in one's own experience and a healthy skepticism about received knowledge. It requires the perspective of quiet reflection and a passionate commitment to action in the face of uncertainty.[25]

A commitment to lifelong teaching and learning requires a revolution of the heart and mind[26] that educators must undertake as part of their professional development. This change involves increasing the breadth and depth of one's knowledge and skills as well as developing an internal voice to guide one's professional development and actions.[27] Educators must take responsibility for their own professional development and not wait for others to provide content or structure. It is also important for student affairs educators to reflect on the context of their professional development, exploring alignment with their personal values and institutional values.

For example, when I reflect on my own experience as a White woman growing up in the south, I recognize the intentional processes I went through to eliminate unconscious bias against and fear of people of color. It was not until I was 20 that I recognized, understood, articulated, and rejected the false assumptions of White supremacy and its enduring effects on American culture. While in college, I encountered for the first time feminist and Black studies scholarship. These readings introduced me to concepts such as social location, stigma, and unconscious bias and improved my skills as an activist and advocate.

It took me 40 years to continually reflect upon and begin to understand my Whiteness. This self-awareness started to shift in my early twenties when I accepted my first professional job as an educational diagnostician in public K–12 education. The assessment tools available at the time to test children were all normed on White students, which resulted in low scores for non-White students (particularly those who did not speak English as their primary language). I discovered the System of Multicultural Pluralistic Assessment (SOMPA). Non-White students tested with the SOMPA had significantly higher scores.

The west Texas school district for which I worked refused to fund my SOMPA training. I borrowed funds to enroll in the training and used vacation days for the required travel to California. After achieving certification and incorporating SOMPA into my testing protocols, the number of non-White students on my caseload—who were being forced into special education classes—decreased by 50%.

Colleagues criticized my decision to pursue this professional development opportunity because it made them look bad. I had to deal with this reaction professionally and personally, but it did not change what I believed I had to do in behalf of the students and their families. Without this internal voice I would have been hard pressed to stand up to this pressure.

The gap between my values and the values of the school district were wide. Self-reflection—a critical professional development navigational tool—brings to the forefront of one's consciousness the value gap between self and institution. There is never total congruence, but too wide a gap can result in consternation. My capacity to reflect and act on these reflections contributed to this powerful professional development opportunity. Purposeful participant-observation of self and work environment can reveal these value gaps and the determination to develop professional capacities necessary for advancing an activist agenda.

In *The Career Architect Development Planner*, Lombardo and Eichinger suggest that 70% of our professional growth happens at work.

> Development generally begins with a realization of current or future need and the motivation to do something about it. This might come from feedback, a mistake, watching other people's reactions, failing or not being up to a task—in other words, from experience. The odds are that development will be about 70% from on-the-job experiences—working on tasks and problems; about 20% from feedback and working around good and bad examples of the need; and 10% from courses and reading.[28]

Rather than wait for such a realization to occur, student affairs educators can intentionally monitor their practice to identify and maintain a productive professional development plan. In addition to using the principles and self-assessment of competencies described earlier, educators can purposefully reflect on their developmental goals simultaneously. Taylor and Baxter Magolda outline a seven-step plan that addresses knowledge, skill, and developmental capacity to practice effectively in ambiguity.[29] Their plan guides educators through identifying challenging contexts, establishing appropriate learning goals, recognizing the developmental capacities that the learning goals require, establishing developmental goals accordingly, and finding ways to individually support one's own growth as well as seek out partners and colleagues to do so. Understanding one's self and continually monitoring the fit between self and work is foundational to ensuring that educators have the capacities and competencies to make good decisions when faced with the unknown. You do not need to leave campus to experience meaningful growth and professional development.

Never Hike Alone

Higher education is replete with wilderness treks on unmarked trails. No road maps exist. However, as Aesop's fable, "The Bundle of Sticks," reminds us, "there is strength in union."[30] This passage is a useful reminder of the importance of colleagues, supervisors, and mentors in the context of professional development. As we hike these unmarked wilderness trails, the need for support, feedback, and guidance is obvious. Being part of a professional community that has good colleagues and mentors and encourages continuous learning is essential. However, professional communities do not automatically translate to good colleagues and mentors. Even when others (e.g., supervisors, colleagues) have good intentions to support professional growth, they are often unaware of how to do so effectively. When educators engage in reflection and craft a personally relevant professional development plan, they are better able to seek out appropriate partners and mentors and help those partners understand what kind of support they need. A supervisor is in a much better position to help a supervisee achieve their professional goals if the supervisee clearly articulates desired areas for growth and opportunities for development. Taylor and Baxter Magolda's model advocates seeking out *learning partners*, defined as partners who collaborate to support an educator's development by taking the back seat of the tandem bicycle while giving the educator the captain's seat to direct the journey.

Ralph Waldo Emerson argues, "What we fear most is usually what we most need to do."[31] Finding and cultivating good colleagues, supervisors, and mentors, can both ease fears and confront and address issues we usually avoid.

Conclusion

Student affairs educators must situate professional development at the epicenter of their work on a daily basis. Magolda and Carnaghi identify principles to guide professional development; the following are particularly relevant: (a) good intentions are never enough, (b) lifelong learning is essential, and (c) embracing change is scary and necessary.[32]

First, as noted earlier, knowledge must augment good intentions. Having a sincere interest in and concern for collegians without possessing requisite knowledge (e.g., cultural competencies) is risky business. Second, staff development or career-long learning is essential for educators to continue to build upon their existing wisdom and cultivate their intellectual curiosities. Third, change is difficult. We must change ourselves before we can expect others to change. A comprehensive professional development plan framed by guiding professional principles, competencies, standards, and self-reflection, can assist in this process.

To carry out the hope and possibility of our work, we need to care for ourselves as well as others. The Midwest Academy for Organizing for Social Change gives great advice for the journey:

> Care for yourself, learn to appreciate your abilities and develop a vision that provides center, grounding, and meaning for your work. We've chosen this work, not just as a job, but as a commitment to a better world. We can change history. Justice can govern if we take the future into our own hands.[33]

Discussion Questions

1. Take stock of your current knowledge using the principles, standards, competencies, and self-reflection described in this essay. What goals emerge from your assessment?
2. What opportunities can you identify and what resources can you attract to help you meet these goals?
3. How can you describe your goals to supervisors, mentors, and colleagues to enlist their support and assistance in reaching them?

Notes

1. Patel, E., Montero, J., Love, C. H., & Glass, M. E. (2016). Navigating conflicts related to religious and non-religious identity. *Journal of College and Character, 17*(3), 190–196, p. 192.

20. American College Personnel Association & National Association of Student Personnel Administrators, *ACPA/NASPA professional competency areas.*

21. Welcome to Compliance U™. (2018). Retrieved from https://complianceu .org/home

22. Student Affairs Law and Policy. (2008–2018). Retrieved from https:// www.naspa.org/focus-areas/law-and-policy

23. ACPA: College Student Educators International & NASPA: Student Affairs Administrations in Higher Education. (2016). *ACPA/NASPA professional competencies rubrics.* Washington DC: Authors.

24. Magolda, P., & Carnaghi, J. E. (2017). Evolving roles and competencies: Professional development reconsidered. In J. Schuh, S. R. Jones, & V. Torres (Eds.), *Student services: A handbook for the profession* (6th ed., pp. 532–549). San Francisco, CA: Jossey-Bass.

25. Kolb, D., & Yaganeh, B. (2011, Sept. 13). *Deliberate experiential learning: Mastering the art of learning from experience* (WP-11–02). Cleveland, OH: Case Western Reserve University, Weatherhead School of Management. Retrieved from http://weatherhead.case.edu/departments/organizational-behavior/workingPapers/ WP-11–02.pdf

26. Parks, S. D. (2005). *Leadership can be taught: A bold approach for a complex world.* Boston, MA: Harvard Business School Press.

27. Baxter Magolda, M. B. (2009). *Authoring your life: Developing an internal voice to navigate life's challenges.* Sterling, VA: Stylus.

28. Lombardo, M. M., & Eichinger, R. W. (1996). *The career architect development planner.* Minneapolis, MN: Lominger, p. 4.

29. Taylor, K. B., & Baxter Magolda, M. B. (2015). Building educators' capacities to meet twenty-first century demands. *About Campus: Enriching the Student Learning Experience, 20*(4), 16-25.

30. Aesop. (n.d.). The father, his sons, and the bundle of sticks. *Fables of Aesop.* Retrieved from https://fablesofaesop.com/the-father-his-sons-and-the-bundle-of-sticks.html

31. Emerson, R. W. (n.d.). Quotes. Retrieved from https://www.goodreads .com/quotes/7966602

32. Magolda & Carnaghi, Evolving roles and competencies.

33. Bellah, R., Madsen, R., Sullivan, W., Swidler, A., & Tipton, S. (1991, July 12). The good society: Shaping the institutions that shape us. *Commonwealth Magazine*, p. 425.

Professional Development as a Healing Community Practice

Michelle M. Espino

When did professional development become such a burden? When did it begin to feel extraordinary, something outside of the purview of daily practice? Why does professional development seem insurmountable? When did our profession develop rhetoric of professional development as dusty books on a shelf, as selfish time amid the "real" work, of the last priority amid critical moments that cannot afford a break for reflection?

I raise these questions out of deep concern that generations of student affairs colleagues are denying themselves, and those they supervise, opportunities for deeper reflection, for the creation of safe(r) and brave spaces in which to tackle issues that cannot be neatly listed on flip charts or read about in books about competencies, values, and the foundation of our profession. Tension resides in what we have declared as professional development and whether it is enacted, supported, or integrated into daily practice. Tensions are present in what I teach and hope for as I educate the next generation of student affairs educators and impart the importance of professional development. In this chapter, I argue that the guiding principles described in Love's essay set the foundation for *formal* professional development. However, they do not address the more personal, contextual, or culturally responsive aspects that define the profession of student affairs for everyone, especially people from marginalized and minoritized backgrounds. The professional development that I describe is dynamic and engaging. It is a living text that grows through communion with others, and yet is not always fully embraced by our profession.

Moving Beyond Tradition

I marvel at the excitement and curiosity with which graduate students wrestle with ideas of who we are supposed to be on college campuses, of our obligations and responsibilities to support and challenge students in

316

their development and to question policies and practices that hinder that development. I appreciate learning from these emerging professionals who are developing and honing the critical consciousness that is essential to craft new interpretations of our foundational documents (including the countless chapters about what professional development is supposed to be about) to draw strength to serve an ever-changing student body within shifting educational and political landscapes.

In her essay, Love explains that there are at least four guides that can lead us in the best direction with our practice; three of these are essential documents in our profession and the fourth is the self. What seem to be missing are relationships and community. A compass is often needed when you are wandering and have lost your path. It is difficult to follow a particular direction while navigating the higher education landscape when colleagues no longer remain committed to honing their skills and knowledge base, are reticent to move beyond what they have known and practiced for years, or forgo institutionalizing professional development through funding and paid leave. Eventually, the so-called realities of entry-level positions temper a sense of wonder about the student affairs profession. Early-career professionals may not fully understand the hierarchies and systems of power at play that limit what they can do and are willing to forsake for the benefit of students. Various work environments may not reflect a professional community that engages in critical dialogue; employs evidence-based practices; actively seeks to refine growth edges in their learning; or delves deeply into unlearning racism, sexism, heteronormativity, and additional forms of oppression inherent in our traditions, programming, and assessment/evaluation methods. Reflection and learning are viewed as luxuries rather than daily habits that enhance body/mind/spirit.[1]

The compass becomes problematic if our true North is not the same as that of those in our offices. What if our true North centers on dismantling oppression in our policies, in our practices, in how we mentor our colleagues and students? Where can we find safe(r) spaces, our *comunidad*?[2] Rather than viewing professional development as yet another competency to be achieved, what if we viewed it as a space for healing?

Professional Development as a Healing Practice

Professional development has been a source of healing for me as a first-generation college student and Chicana feminist who moved from a student affairs position to life on the tenure track as a faculty member. During my master's program, I became familiar with formal professional development through the national conferences for our professional associations. As I pored over the conference booklets and organized my schedule, what was most vital was finding community. As 1 of only 2 Latinas in a cohort of 40, I hungered for *cultura*, for a sense of place and belonging that was beyond developing assessment skills or learning best practices.

I was relieved to find networks and knowledge communities centered on Latina/o/x professionals. I sought resources that could make sense of the numerous students of color who began visiting my office because I was the only one. I needed sources of support external to my institution because few well-intentioned colleagues could enhance my development as a professional without first understanding the tensions I felt—especially if I could not yet put into words the cultural taxation I experienced, the long hours, the neglect of my own well-being. At a moment when I was uncertain whether the profession was the right path for me, I talked with seasoned practitioners who validated the struggles and challenges and offered hope.

Professional development was about the community that I began to build and, a decade later, would lead. The informal version of professional development was prioritized. I was part of a national network where we found respite in one another. We did not have to attend national conferences to be in communion with each other. I only had to call or e-mail to find professionals who reflected my lived experience and buoyed me when I grew weary of being the first or the only one in my office. Those national networks were also localized by region, state, and city. We became each other's touchstones. Eventually, we would take the leadership positions within the associations and share ideas through presentations and individual mentoring sessions. We crafted curricula for preconferences, drive-ins, lunch-and-learn programs, knowing that each could be the first opportunity someone had to learn from someone who looked like them, who could validate their lived experience with a smile and a gentle nudge to keep moving forward.

Even when I shifted to my role from a student affairs practitioner to a faculty member, I could not leave my community behind. I remain rooted to this network because of our *comunidad*, because I am intellectually challenged and kept grounded in what is pressing on my colleagues in their practice. They nourish my spirit. In Love's essay, the self is one of the most valued guides, but for me and for many minoritized practitioners, the self is in relationship with others who understand and value the assets that our cultures and lived experience bring to the profession.

Professional Development as a Community of Practice

Professional development is not just about keeping current on the latest research, although the scholarly discourse is an important venue for honing our practice. In my journey in this profession, the type of professional development that has been the most meaningful and has retained my minoritized colleagues is found within the *comunidad* that we have created. Our community was and is a space for "emancipatory reflective practice, [a space for] reclaiming of one's story and personal power, and individual and collective agency."[3] Professional development should move beyond an individualized process to a more collective space in which we can create communities of practice.[4] If we can create these healing spaces for our own learning and engagement, we will be able to strengthen our approaches to supporting students.

Communities of practice are sites for learning and engagement among a group of people who are passionate about a topic and are seeking avenues to deepen knowledge and understanding.[5] In the context of higher education, communities of practice can develop through cross-departmental interactions, division-wide projects based on shared interests (e.g., assessment, diversity, first-year experience, to name a few), or through informal gatherings with colleagues across the campus community. As a form of "situated learning,"[6] communities of practice have the potential to "drive strategy, generate new lines of [inquiry], solve problems, promote the spread of best practices, develop people's professional skills, and help recruit and retain talent."[7] The following dimensions are necessary in cultivating a community of practice: (a) social interaction among members that will drive the norms and expectations of the community; (b) mutual understanding of and movement toward a common goal; and (c) cultivation of (in)tangible "communal resources" such as "language, routines, artifacts and stories."[8] Learning, cooperation, and knowledge transfer only occur when there is trust and open communication.[9]

Communities of practice are evident in our local, regional, and national networks where we gather together based on interests, experience, identity(ies), and functional areas. Professional development is enacted through community; it should not be viewed as tedious or irrelevant. Disrupting traditional notions of professional development is necessary to embrace our role as generators of knowledge who apply theory (informal and formal) in our daily practice, who will challenge ourselves and our colleagues to create emancipatory spaces for expression and engagement. Professional development through community helps us to adapt to the changes occurring on our campuses and our interactions with the social world. It is dynamic and fluid, with an agenda that is set by the community. In other words, professional development is ethical, evidence-based practice rooted in authentic community.

Professional development is meant to help us recalibrate, to add knowledge and skills to our repertoire, to help us make sense of change that is inevitable on our campuses, to see beyond the horizon to the value of our work in the years to come. We must be in communion with one another to continue in our developmental journeys. Professional development is a living text that challenges traditional standards of development, reframes our guiding principles, promotes an ethic of care, and requires a mutual understanding and knowledge of social inequities and injustice. It is not a burden; it is an honor and a shared responsibility.

Discussion Questions

1. Reflect on your professional relationships and networks. In what ways can you develop a community of practice with existing relationships that occurred organically and invite your growth?
2. What steps would you take to find healing, mutual understanding, and validation for yourself and others through a community of practice?
3. What forms of professional development nourish your spirit?

Notes

1. Lara, I. (2002). Healing sueños for academia. In G. Anzaldúa & A. Keating (Eds.), *This bridge we call home: Radical visions for transformation* (pp. 433–438). New York, NY: Routledge.

2. Most research on professional development for minoritized student affairs professionals is in dissertation research. I offer the following published articles for reference: Bertrand Jones, T., Scott Dawkins, L., McClinton, M. M., & Hayden Glover, M. (Eds.). (2012). *Pathways to higher education administration for African American women.* Sterling, VA: Stylus; Roberts, D. M. (2007). Preferred methods of professional development in student affairs. *NASPA Journal, 44*(3), 561–577; West, N. M. (2017). A decade of a student affairs preconference program: Perceptions and characteristics of African American women's summit participants. *College Student Affairs Journal, 35*(1), 69–85.

3. López Figueroa, J., & Rodriguez, G. (2015). Critical mentoring practices to support diverse students in higher education: Chicana/Latina faculty perspectives. In C. Turner (Ed.), *Mentoring as transformative practice: Supporting student and faculty diversity* (pp. 23-32). New Directions for Higher Education, 2015(171), p. 25.

4. Wenger, E., McDermott, R., & Snyder, W. (2002). *Cultivating communities of practice: A guide to managing knowledge.* Boston, MA: Harvard Business School Press.

5. Cumming-Potvin, W. M., & MacCallum, J. (2010). Intergenerational practice: Mentoring and social capital for twenty-first century communities of practice. *McGill Journal of Education, 45*(2), 305–323; Taylor, K. B., Baxter Magolda,

M. B., & Haynes, C. (2010). Miami University's collective journey toward discovery-based learning. *Learning Communities Journal, 2*(2), 1–26.

6. Roberts, J. (2006). Limits to communities of practice. *Journal of Management Studies, 43*(3), 623–639.

7. Wenger, E. C., & Snyder, W. M. (2000). Communities of practice: The organizational frontier. *Harvard Business Review, 78*(1), 139–145, p. 140.

8. Roberts, Limits to communities of practice, p. 624.

9. Roberts, Limits to communities of practice.

17

What Responsibility Does Student Affairs Have to Help Graduate Assistants Navigate the Ambiguity Between Their Student and Professional Roles?

Navigating Two Worlds: Supporting Graduate Students in Their Dual Roles as Students and Professionals

Jessica Gunzburger

Student affairs graduate education has immense potential to create opportunities for transformational learning and prepare student affairs professionals to promote equity, civility, and safety in higher education contexts. I look back on my own master's experience with great fondness and nostalgia, having made lifelong friends and learned an immense amount about the profession and myself. However, graduate school is also *difficult*. Even in ideal circumstances, graduate students are called on to be students and professionals, all while learning about themselves and the profession. This essay explores the responsibility that the student affairs profession, in particular graduate assistantship supervisors and faculty, has to graduate students in the field as they navigate the ambiguity of their roles. I argue that student affairs professionals have a responsibility to help graduate students navigate the challenges of their dual roles as students and emerging professionals. However, this responsibility is not easily fulfilled, and as a profession we often fall short. I outline four key ways that faculty and supervisors can support graduate students in their dual roles and possibilities for how they may approach this work.

Core to my argument is the recognition that graduate students exist in two worlds. They are students in a graduate program, actively engaging in the classroom to learn about themselves, their students, and higher education. Concurrently, graduate students are engaged in day-to-day student affairs work through their assistantships, internships, and/or practica experiences. It is the intersection of these two worlds where the greatest potential for their learning exists. When practical work and coursework complement each other and there is adequate and developmental support, graduate student learning can be immense and effective. However, when there is little support or congruency between the experiences, the ambiguity and stress may be beyond what many graduate students are equipped to manage. The goal for the student affairs profession should be to provide graduate students with the best of both worlds rather than the worst of them.

Helping graduate students navigate these two roles as emerging student affairs professionals is an adaptive challenge.[1] Heifetz describes adaptive challenges as problems that are in and of themselves difficult to define, and there is no clear, step-by-step solution. Supporting graduate students is such an adaptive challenge. There is no manual of steps we can follow to effectively help every graduate student navigate the ambiguity of their experiences, and I make no attempt to offer such a list. Rather, I outline how student affairs professionals can help graduate students navigate their dual roles as professionals and students through (a) appropriately scaffolded responsibilities, (b) identity-conscious support, (c) communication between assistantships and faculty, and (d) quality supervision.

Situating Graduate Study in the Student Affairs Field

Before I discuss the responsibility student affairs faculty and assistantship supervisors have to help graduate students navigate their roles as both students and professionals, I provide some context on student affairs graduate programs. Graduate school is a critical time in the socialization and preparation of upcoming student affairs professionals.[2] Graduate students are learning about different functional areas and theories, as well as who they are as people. This process can be exhilarating and exciting, but also challenging and difficult.[3] Ideally, the content that students learn in their academic program aligns well with their assistantship and internship experiences.[4] Learning occurs in both places for students, and both have an important impact on their experience.

So who are these graduate students? New professionals make up 15% to 20% of the professionals in the field, and these professionals primarily graduate from over 125 student affairs master's programs.[5] In this essay, I address primarily full-time graduate students in a master's program who hold part-time assistantships (approximately 15–30 hours per week). Most of these individuals graduated from their undergraduate institutions within the past 5 years and are likely to be in their 20s. This group of students is unique because of the swift transition many of them experience from their undergraduate careers to serving in professional capacities within their assistantships.

Although the students I address here share these general characteristics, graduate students even within these parameters are not a monolithic group. Students vary in their identities across race, gender, sexuality, ability, class, spirituality, ethnicity, familial education history, family structure, and immigration status. Students also vary in terms of their undergraduate institution, work history, involvement experience, and undergraduate major. Different aspects of an individual influence how each approaches and makes meaning of the graduate experience.

Beyond the individuals themselves, graduate experiences differ across programs and assistantships. Academic programs can vary in their foci, curriculum, and rigor. There are different requirements regarding original research, comprehensive exams, and number of credits required. Even within the same program, graduate student experiences may vary significantly depending on the assistantship they hold, in terms of both the hours expected of them and the demands of their work. Some graduate students are in assistantships that correlate to their interests and passions, while others accept positions that do not directly relate to their professional goals as a means of funding their education.[6]

Assistantships can be particularly important to the graduate student's experience[7] in terms of content and time commitment. Responsibilities vary from mostly administrative tasks with very little student contact to significant autonomy in coordinating student programming or a residence hall. Many of the graduate students who are tasked with these responsibilities were undergraduate students themselves mere months before beginning their graduate experiences. These students are asked to do a great deal, and the support they are given is critical. However, as a profession we often fall short of providing the support that graduate students need to navigate their dual roles as students and professionals.

Effectively Supporting Graduate Students in Their Dual Roles

Graduate students have responsibilities as both students and professionals, each difficult and complex adaptive tasks. Given the challenge of each of these roles, current graduate student supervisors and faculty have a responsibility to help graduate students navigate these dual roles. I now outline four key ways that faculty and supervisors can support graduate students. For each point I discuss the importance of the area, challenges to providing that support, and suggestions for improving practice for graduate students' experiences.

Appropriately Scaffolded Responsibilities

Graduate students are often eager to take on significant work and responsibility as a part of their assistantships, practica, and internships, and many institutions rely on graduate students' contributions to keep their programs functioning. When these responsibilities are appropriately scaffolded, this relationship can be mutually beneficial to both the department and the graduate student. However, when responsibilities are not intentionally constructed it can be exploitative and harmful both to the graduate students and the individuals they serve.

Appropriately scaffolded responsibilities are a fit for a graduate student's *growth edge*.[8] This is a mental space where an individual is at the limit of their current developmental capacity or understanding and can grow in that capacity with support from a supervisor. An individual's developmental capacity represents the meaning-making structure used to make sense of their world.[9] In the case of graduate student responsibilities, developmental capacity will affect how a student approaches work and fulfills responsibilities. Faculty and supervisors must actively assess and consider a student's developmental capacity both to provide sufficient support and assign appropriate tasks to a student. As faculty and supervisors make these decisions, there may be strong pulls from both the graduate student and institutional needs to give the graduate student more responsibility or work than is appropriate. However, it is critical that faculty and supervisors take into account the graduate student's developmental capacity and knowledge base when determining what an appropriate task or responsibility is for that graduate student.

To better illustrate the importance of assessing developmental capacity when assigning tasks, consider a graduate student who has responsibilities to assist with training for orientation leaders on campus. The work this graduate student takes on should align with their current capacities. A graduate student who operates from a socialized perspective will rely heavily on their supervisor for direction and seek the "right" way to approach a situation.[10] Putting such a student in charge of facilitating complex discussions with orientation leaders with much ambiguity and the requirement of sorting through multiple viewpoints where no one is "right" would be beyond that student's growth edge and not set them up for success. However, this task would be ideal to promote developmental growth for students who are constructing their internal voice and beginning to operate from a self-authored perspective. This opportunity would allow students to hold multiple perspectives and further reflect on their own.[11] Ultimately, faculty and supervisors should ask themselves if the graduate student has the developmental capacity necessary to meet the challenges of a given task and, if not, if there is reasonable support from faculty member or supervisor that can fill in those gaps. For more on how to assess developmental capacity and appropriately coach individuals of different meaning making structures, see Baxter Magolda and King's *Assessing Meaning Making and Self-Authorship: Theory, Research, and Application*[12] and Berger's *Changing on the Job.*[13]

A graduate student's knowledge base also affects what responsibilities and tasks are appropriate. For example, a graduate student who is advising a student government association needs a specific knowledge base to be effective in the role. Does this student have the knowledge of university policies and procedures necessary to responsibly advise this group as they plan initiatives? Does the graduate student have an understanding of how oppression functions so that when a microaggression occurs during an executive board meeting they are able to effectively recognize it and intervene? Does the graduate student have the experience in event planning to make sure that the students organizing an event have adequately prepared for possible issues with the event implementation? Without adequate support and guidance from supervisors, graduate student decisions may contribute to physical and emotional harm of the individuals with whom they work. The graduate student's supervisor must ask themselves if the graduate student has the necessary knowledge and experience to fulfill their responsibilities and, if not, if they are able to prepare the student with that knowledge.

Identity-Conscious Support

Graduate students' identities and the institutional context in which they work fundamentally influence the support and guidance that individuals may need to successfully navigate their dual roles as students and professionals. To ignore the role of identity and systems of oppression is to deny graduate students an equitable experience, particularly when graduate students with minoritized identities are navigating both the graduate experience *and* systemic oppression. Providing identity-conscious support is challenging given that supervisors and faculty are not always trained to do so, particularly when it is a supervisor or faculty member with a dominant identity working across a power structure to supervise an individual with a minoritized identity. Additionally, identity-conscious support is not often the norm in the field of student affairs, so supervisors and faculty may be going against the grain as they try to embrace such equitable practice. Despite these challenges, identity-conscious support is necessary both for individuals navigating their minoritized identities in student affairs and their dominant ones.

Supervisors and faculty have a responsibility to support students with minoritized identities within their departments and programs. Fundamental to this support is the recognition that these students consistently face oppression in their work and lives. All interactions and support of students with minoritized identities must take this into account. For instance, supervisors should recognize that an individual with an oppressed identity might spend more time supporting students with the same identity on campus. A hall director who is transgender may spend more time talking with transgender residents of their building because those students seek them out, something their cisgender counterparts do not spend time doing. Supervisors must recognize this additional work that graduate students with minoritized identities often assume on their campuses.

Supervisors and faculty also have a responsibility to provide coaching and mentoring that help graduate students with minoritized identities navigate systems of oppression that permeate student affairs. For instance, one participant in my dissertation study on racism in supervision shared how a White supervisor supported her as a Black woman. This supervisor told her to "never get the copies" so she was not seen in a service role, but instead as an equal member of the leadership team.[14] This supervisor recognized that the participant's journey to being a professional and negotiating relationships in the office would be different for her than for her White male peers and provided helpful coaching to help navigate her role.

Faculty and supervisors also have a responsibility to provide identity-conscious support and coaching to students with dominant identities, particularly those supervisors and faculty who share the dominant identity of the graduate student. These authority figures can help graduate students with dominant identities learn how they are complicit in systems of oppression. For example, a White male faculty member may help a White male student realize how he is participating at length in class discussions and taking up a significant portion of the discussion time in class. This conversation can help this White male student see how he is exerting dominance, perhaps without realizing it, and reinforcing systems of power. In another example, supervisors and faculty can help students with dominant identities recognize the privilege they hold within their graduate programs and student affairs. For instance, graduate students are often told that a master's program is a time of growth where mistakes are an acceptable and a necessary way to learn. However, individuals with marginalized identities often have less space to make mistakes than their peers with privileged or dominant identities. A Black woman who makes a mistake, for instance, often cannot do so without it reflecting on others with her identity. A White male making the same mistake, however, does not reflect on his White male peers. Supervisors can help students with dominant identities recognize the privilege they hold and recognize how this may affect their interactions with peers and students with minoritized identities.

Communication Between Assistantship Supervisors and Faculty

At their best, graduate experiences have near-seamless integration between assistantship and classroom experiences. Research indicates that when this integration occurs, graduate students are best prepared to advance into full-time professional work.[15] The cycle of learning between the classroom and assistantship creates many opportunities for learning but can only be maximized when assistantship supervisors and faculty communicate and coordinate to intentionally shape a graduate experience. If this intentional communication is not present, these two facets of the experience can be at odds rather than synergistic.

There are multiple reasons that make strong communication between assistantship supervisors and faculty difficult. Time is a limiting factor for all involved. Few student affairs professionals have extra time in their schedules to reach out to faculty members. For faculty, it can be time intensive to coordinate with multiple assistantship departments and supervisors. Additionally, the work of coordinating with assistantship supervisors is not typically rewarded in tenure processes. In short, there are competing priorities for both faculty and assistantship supervisors that make communication challenging.

Despite these challenges, faculty and assistantship supervisors can make strides in improving communication in a number of ways. First, these two groups can make sure they have clear expectations for graduate students that do not conflict between assistantships and academic programs. For instance, a graduate student may want to participate in a Black Lives Matter protest on their campus. They may receive contradictory messages from assistantship and academic departments on whether it is appropriate or allowed to participate in a protest given the student's dual staff and student status. Faculty and student affairs professionals can alleviate the stress and challenge that graduate students may face in trying to navigate these contradictory expectations by communicating proactively with each other.

Another reason for consistent and clear communication between assistantship providers and faculty surrounds the many and sometimes competing expectations and tasks for graduate students. Managing multiple priorities is difficult for many seasoned student affairs professionals, let alone graduate students new to the field. Handling workloads from assistantships, internships, practica, and coursework challenges many graduate students.[16] Student affairs professionals can support graduate students by making sure each aspect of their graduate school experience has reasonable expectations that complement each other. This coordination does not mean that each assistantship experience needs to be the same—there will be natural variety among assistantship experiences.

There are many ways communication between assistantship supervisors and faculty may take shape, and the exact approach will depend on many factors (e.g., number of assistantship sites, number of students in the program, number of faculty). However, a few approaches may be helpful. Faculty and assistantship supervisors can hold meetings two to three times a year to talk about big-picture issues that face graduate students in their programs and departments, such as the expectations and time commitment clarifications already outlined. A part of these conversations can be establishing points of contact in anticipation of concerns arising throughout the year. It may also be helpful for each student to have an assistantship contract outlining their responsibilities and the hours they spend working on a weekly basis. This approach may help students from going down the slippery slope of working far more hours within their assistantship than intended.

Quality Supervision

Thus far I have repeatedly brought up the role that supervisors within assistantships, internships, and practica play in graduate students' lives. Although supervision has been frequently mentioned, it bears explicit and individual discussion here as well. Many individuals have substantial influence on a graduate students' experience, but supervisors have the unique opportunity to be in frequent and individual communication with graduate students through one-to-one meetings and assistantship work on a daily basis. Multiple studies point to how much influence a supervisor has on a supervisee's experience,[17] and this may be particularly true for graduate students and new professionals.[18]

Supervision is itself an adaptive challenge, one that demands a great deal of graduate students' supervisors. Moreover, many supervisors of graduate students were recently graduate students themselves and still grapple with some of the same growth challenges as the individuals they supervise. On top of all of this, student affairs professionals are rarely prepared to be good supervisors. Despite the ubiquitous nature of supervision in our field, little attention is paid to good supervision in the literature, graduate preparation programs, or training.[19] This lapse in supervisor preparation means that graduate students' supervisors are often ill-prepared to support them in their roles and the immense growth they are experiencing.

Providing quality supervision is a nuanced and complex task and beyond the scope of this essay. What I focus on instead is how, as a field, we need to increase the time and energy we spend on preparing supervisors so they can most effectively support graduate students. Key to this effort is investing in the development of student affairs professionals as supervisors. This can begin in graduate preparation programs as individuals learn about themselves and others (e.g., developmental capacity, social identities). Once in the field, professionals need to engage in ongoing training and development. This can take the form of reading groups, workshops, webinars, conference sessions, and individual development in one-to-one meetings.

The Best of Two Worlds

Many graduate students face significant challenges navigating their roles as students in an academic program and professionals in their assistantships, pracitca, and internships. Although difficult, existence in these two worlds provides myriad opportunities for learning and growth. Although graduate school can certainly be a time of intense growth, growth does not need to be traumatic or consistently overwhelming. As a student affairs profession, we have a responsibility to help graduate students navigate these multiple roles so they get the best of both of these worlds rather than the worst of them. This can happen in many ways, including appropriately scaffolded responsibilities, identity-conscious support, communication between assistantship supervisors and faculty, and provision of quality supervision. Given that graduate students continue on to become the leaders of our profession and have profound influence over how undergraduate students learn within our higher education institutions, the field of student affairs has a responsibility to help them navigate the ambiguity of their roles in order to maximize their learning and continue to be at their best throughout their years in the profession.

Discussion Questions

1. For graduates of student affairs master's programs, how did your own graduate experience shape how you perceive the graduate experience for current master's students?
2. How do/did your social identities shape your master's program experience?
3. For supervisors of graduate students, in what ways do you need to grow in order to provide the graduate student support outlined in this essay?

Notes

1. Heifetz, R. A. (1994). *Leadership without easy answers.* Cambridge, MA: Belknap Press.
2. Gansemer-Topf, A. M., Ewing Ross, L., & Johnson, R. M. (2006). Graduate and professional student development and student affairs. In M. J. Guentzel & B. E. Nesheim (Eds.), *Supporting graduate students and new professionals: The role of student affairs* (New Directions for Student Services, Issue 115, pp. 19–30). San Francisco, CA: Jossey-Bass.
3. Nesheim, B. E., Guentzel, M. J., Ganswemer-Topf, A. M., Ewing Ross, L., & Turrentine, C. G. (2006). If you want to know, ask: Assessing the needs and experiences of graduate students. In M. J. Guentzel & B. E. Nesheim (Eds.), *Supporting graduate students and new professionals: The role of student affairs* (New Directions for Student Services, Issue 115, pp. 5–18). San Francisco, CA: Jossey-Bass.
4. Renn, K. A., & Jessup-Anger, E. R. (2008). Preparing new professionals: Lessons for graduate preparation programs from the national student of new professionals in student affairs. *Journal of College Student Development, 49,* 319–335.
5. Ibid.
6. White, J., & Nonnamaker, J. (2011). Supervising graduate assistants. In L. D. Roper (Ed.), *Supporting and supervising mid-level professionals* (New Directions for Student Services, Issue 136, pp. 43–54). San Francisco, CA: Jossey-Bass.
7. Ibid.
8. Berger, J. G. (2012). *Changing on the job: Developing leaders for a complex world.* Stanford, CA: Stanford Business Books.
9. Ibid.
10. Ibid.
11. Ibid.
12. Baxter Magolda, M. B., & King, P. M. (2012). *Assessing meaning making and self-authorship: Theory, research, and application* (ASHE Higher Education Report, vol. 38, no. 3). San Francisco: CA: Jossey-Bass.
13. Berger, *Changing on the job.*
14. Gunzburger, J. G. (2017). *"Get it together, damn it!": Racism in student affairs supervision* (Unpublished doctoral dissertation). Miami University, Oxford, OH.

15. White & Nonnamaker, Supervising graduate assistants.

16. Grube, S. A., Cedarholm, K., Jones, C., & Dunn, M. (2005). Master's student life: The balance between student and professional. *The College Student Affairs Journal, 24,* 152–161.

17. Barham, J. D., & Winston, R. B., Jr. (2006). Supervision of new professionals in student affairs: Assessing and addressing needs. *The College Student Affairs Journal, 26*(1), 64–68; Tull, A. (2006). Synergistic supervision, job satisfaction, and intention to turnover of new professionals in student affairs. *Journal of College Student Development, 47*(4), 465–480; Winston, R. B., Jr., & Creamer, D. G. (1997). *Improving staffing practices in student affairs.* San Francisco, CA: Jossey-Bass.

18. Cooper, D. L., Saunders, S. A., Winston Jr., R. B., Hirt, J. B., Creamer, D. G., & Janosik, S. M. (Eds.) (2002). *Learning through supervised practice in student affairs.* New York, NY: Routledge.

19. Perillo, P. A. (2011). Scholar practitioners model inclusive, learning-oriented supervision. In P. M. Magolda & M. B. Baxter Magolda (Eds.), *Contested issues in student affairs: Diverse perspectives and respectful dialogue* (pp. 427–432). Sterling, VA: Stylus; Winston & Creamer, *Improving staffing practices in student affairs.*

Caught in the Middle: A Stable Anchor for Graduate Students Amid a Discursive Struggle

Hoa Bui

Taking a developmental focus, Gunzburger argues that due to ambiguous dual student-professional roles, student affairs needs to pay attention to graduate students' holistic professional and identity-based personal development through proactive and constant communication between the academic program and the assistantship sites. I agree with Gunzburger that graduate student struggles are the rule rather than the exception. Many aspects of the work expose graduate assistants to external stakeholders (e.g., academic affairs campus partners, parents, students), who might expect a competency level that does not match the developmental and professional stage of graduate students. No buffer zone exists between learning and doing. Because student affairs is a small field, graduate students and new professionals have one chance to make a good impression and build or burn bridges. The stakes seem high; mistakes, costly. Gunzburger's suggestions are important for the daily sanity of graduate students.

I am concerned, however, that Gunzburger's proposed resolutions to the issue of graduate students' dual roles imply a technical conceptualization of the problem, which calls for the selection and use of "a large collection of available rules . . . that will help them achieve a particular given end."[1] Within student affairs, the structures already exist to implement Gunzburger's suggestion. The logical inference is that university departments simply need to do a better job of executing of these goals. Having more techniques to do better in the areas Gunzburger points out is necessary because ideological changes take time, require organizational buy-in, and can be overwhelming. Additionally, concrete techniques are encouraging because well-intentioned student affairs faculty and practitioners can inch toward lessening the graduate students' struggle.

The duality of being a student affairs graduate assistant comes about because narratives of the student role and narratives of the professional role supposedly exist independently yet actually bleed into one another: A knowledge gap in the classroom can become an unfixable detriment to the assistantship, a mistake made at the assistantship is attributed to the short-comings of the academic program or the student. Managing this duality requires much developmental maturity, role management skills, and ideological clarity. Gunzburger's technical suggestions would address developmental and skill building dimensions of graduate students' dual roles but do little to advance graduate students' ideological stance.

In responding to the guiding question framing this set of essays, I draw upon a political lens and the notion of ideological discourses that enable people and organizations to reproduce and harness power, control, and status to protect the interests and position of those in power. Ideological discourse is a system of specific narratives reproduced and enforced by power.[2] These narratives are widely promoted, and hence accepted, not by merit but rather by usefulness to those in power. For example, a dominant ideological discourse of success in the United States draws upon the tightly integrated concepts of meritocracy, the American dream, individualism, and free will. This ideological system informs debates regarding health care, immigration, tax cuts, and higher education policy. A technical approach to the graduate student dual-role dilemma is insufficient and destructive when ideological discourse is left untouched. "Ideology . . . thrives *beneath* consciousness"[3] and "saturates everyday discourse in the form of common sense."[4] To know what discourse dominates is to know the source of pressures that our field (mostly) unconsciously and unintentionally places on our graduate students to fit in. Critical and continual reflection on discourses is imperative for ensuring that well-intentioned techniques do not come from the convenient common sense and end up reinforcing the political struggles of graduate students.

In this essay, I identify four discourses shaping the lived experiences of student affairs graduate assistants. To illustrate this discursive struggle, I analyze the example of how a student affairs division responded to graduate students' desire to join a grassroots campus protest. I argue that among those discourses, student affairs as a field must bolster and commit to two specific discourses: Graduate students are critical stakeholders and graduate assistants are an essential investment for the future of the field.

Governing Discourses of the Student Role and the Professional Role

Multiple discourses exist to inform the answer to the question, "What does it mean to be a student affairs graduate assistant?" Here are a few discourses on the student role:

- Graduate students as unprepared, fragile snowflakes: *Snowflake* refers disparagingly to "millennials who were allegedly too convinced of their own status as special and unique people to be able (or bothered) to handle the normal trials and travails of regular adult life."[5] As "fragile snowflakes," graduate students are inexperienced yet idealistic in their activism and romantic about their resistance (against systemic oppression). This makes them either unfit for or unproductive in involvement in institutional-level decision-making.
- Graduate students as stakeholders: Graduate students are important members of the higher education system. To engage graduate students in important decision-making processes is the best way to teach them how to live out the values and purposes of the field.

Following are discourses governing the professional role:

- Graduate employees as liabilities: Graduate assistants' inexperience and political presence may bring trouble to the university through lawsuits or bad (i.e., radical or "controversial") publicity. A mistake made by graduate employees is not an opportunity to learn but rather a risk to manage.
- Graduate employees as investments for the field that advocates for empowering employees by supporting their development and contributing to their employees' priorities:[6] The time in graduate school is the time our future crop of professionals learns the vocabulary and culture of our field. The same way that the orientation experience shapes first-year students' college experience, graduate school experience greatly influences how young professionals see themselves in the field.

The following case example demonstrates how these four discourses manifested for graduate assistants in my residence life office in a midsize public university. When graduate students advocate for their rights and challenge a decision from the institution's leadership, people of different roles employ these discourses to justify their opinions, and graduate students are caught in the middle of a discourse war for prominence.

Protesting and Organizing Against "the System"

As the start of the school year approached, a Facebook event for a march organized by a student group (unrecognized by the university) to fight against White supremacy appeared on many student affairs professionals' newsfeed.

Hundreds of students (including resident assistants and graduate students in different departments) and faculty members expressed interest or virtually committed to attend the march. On the event page, the organizers referenced the recent counterprotesters in Charlottesville, Virginia, after the "Unite the Right" White supremacist protest. The day before the march on my campus, the full-time and graduate staff in the residence life office received a directive from our supervisor that (a) resident assistants could participate during the march because they are students first and (b) full-time and graduate assistants could not join the protest. Our supervisor provided multilayered reasons. First, the university did not sanction the protest. Second, after Charlottesville, as a state university, the university did not want to open itself up for any kind of criticism if its employees might potentially be seen not being neutral in a politically charged event. My supervisor acknowledged that the protest's purpose aligned with the institution's values, such as diversity and inclusion, yet any participation was "strongly discouraged" (no elaboration existed on the specific consequence if an employee defied the discouragement). This expectation for the full-time staff was reasonable, as full-time staff *are* the institution and in a different political-professional position to address White supremacy. However, just as is the case with resident assistants, graduate students are students first, given that their assistantship roles are a direct result of their admission to a graduate program.

When protests erupt, universities look to student affairs professionals to release an official statement, serve as observers in case of escalation, and provide information and support for students directly or indirectly. Senior campus administrators expect student affairs professionals (including graduate students) to act as experts and become the face of the institution. An additional ideological expectation is to remain "objective." Any indication that graduate students are aligned with a particular side is allegedly an indicator that these staff members cannot support (i.e., provide care services to) all students (i.e., the customer), which opens the organization up to criticism, negative public image, and lawsuits. Graduate students who publicly express their political views become a liability. Meanwhile, undergraduate students can protest (if they desire) because they are institutional stakeholders and protesting is a legitimate exercise of their rights and a positive sign of active engagement.

Given that the supervisor's directive came at the last minute, the graduate students were disheartened but also not surprised, knowing the conservative political climate of the university and the university's risk-averse proclivity. Nonetheless, the graduate students requested clarification from the university leaders—the director of the office, vice president of student affairs, and the general counsel—regarding their student role. Many graduate students also processed this issue with their professors, and the director of the student affairs program advocated for the students' right to protest. A week later the leaders of the department and vice president of student affairs responded; they decided to increase emphasis on the "student role" of graduate assistants in the organizational structure in the interest of managing the risk of graduate students' right to protest. Specifically, residence life graduate assistants had to give up previously granted professional autonomy, with their direct supervisor assuming a more hands-on role in their student staff meetings, resident assistant supervision, and resident assistant employment decisions. Additionally, the leaders clarified that graduate students can only protest issues "directly related to their position as graduate students." For example, they can protest for better health insurance policy *for* graduate students but cannot protest against White supremacy "in general." The decision became a hot topic of discussion in multiple circles. More than once I heard the "wisdom," "They/you [graduate students] just don't know the field enough yet." Full-time staff infantilized graduate students by taking the stance that to involve graduate students in the decision-making process is unproductive because either "they just wouldn't get it (i.e., the decision)" or "they are not ready for this (i.e., the process)." Therefore, following the fragile snowflake discourse, graduate students' "naiveté" in organizational understanding, reality, and politics became the "obvious" explanation for the trigger of their original resistance, the justification for the leaders to decide to emphasize their students' role while deemphasizing their professional role, and the reason for their ineffective self-advocacy. Graduate assistants know and live their ambiguous student-professional role, yet the student affairs division here shielded them from the discussion and learning of their own reality. Essentially, graduate students challenged the institution and leaned on the stakeholder discourse, yet the institution counterreacted by framing their action as that of fragile snowflakes.

The Reframing Responsibility of Student Affairs

As Gunzburger described, most student affairs graduate students are recent college graduates. During the graduate school socialization process, young professionals learn what is appropriate and right—the common sense of student affairs—not by hearing what is explicitly said but by observing and reacting to what unintentionally, unconsciously, and subconsciously happens. In the campus protest example, the predominant discourses on graduate assistants are of liability and fragile snowflakes, and "balancing" the student role with the professional role means that one is neither student (with protesting right) nor professional (with supervisory autonomy). The problem here is not with graduate students themselves but with the way we frame them as the problem. Those discourses disempower graduate assistants during the critical formative period of their professional journey. The field has to name this political reality: Having language to describe an experience is empowering, as the language legitimizes the experience. Once the language is shared, the field should proactively advocate for graduate students as rightful stakeholders as students and as a worthy investment as employees. To reinforce these discourses, when graduate students raise an issue, rather than having their concerns diluted through a long chain of supervision, assistantship sites should meet with them directly and involve them in the decision-making process. Rather than assuming that graduate students are not ready for the reality and politics of the field, student affairs faculty and supervisors have to arm graduate students with strategies and knowledge, give them the chance to make informed choices, and let them make mistakes on their own. This process might be uncomfortable for supervisors and the faculty, but avoiding such discomfort robs graduate students of the opportunity for learning and feeling empowered to improve the field. Graduate students of student affairs are the future; to treat them as stakeholders is to accept and to hold space for them *because of* their inexperience and distinct priority. Committed investment might come at a price. However, just as responsible parents do not resent the investment they provide their children, if the field is serious about producing innovative and resilient incoming professionals to serve changing student demographics and adapt to challenging sociopolitical landscapes, graduate students need to believe that they matter. So, too, does the profession need to believe they matter!

Discussion Questions

1. What discourses on the roles of student affairs graduate students and professionals have you encountered?
2. Involving every stakeholder on campus (including graduate students) in important decisions is not always possible. What are some ways student affairs could involve graduate students more?
3. What are some reasons for graduate students to not be involved in important decision-making process even if they are invited?

Notes

1. Quantz, R. A., O' Connor, T., & Magolda, P. M. (Eds.). 2011. *Rituals and student identity in education: Ritual critique for a new pedagogy.* New York, NY: Palgrave Macmillan, p. 139.

2. Jackson, A. Y., & Mazzei, L. A. (2012). *Thinking with theory in qualitative research: Viewing data across multiple perspectives.* New York, NY: Routledge.

3. Hebdige, D. (1979). *Subculture: The meaning of style.* London: Routledge, p. 11.

4. Ibid., p. 12.

5. Merriam-Webster. (n.d.). No, "snowflake" as a slang term did not begin with *Fight Club*: The lost history of "snowflake." *Merriam-Webster.* Retrieved from https://www.merriam-webster.com/words-at-play/the-less-lovely-side-of-snowflake

6. Bolman, L. G., & Deal, T. E. (2013). *Reframing organization: Artistry, choice, and leadership* (5th ed.). San Francisco, CA: Jossey-Bass.

18

How Should Student Affairs Professional Preparation Programs Address Discrimination and Bias in the Graduate Classroom?

No Struggle, No Progress: The Complexities of Pretenure Minoritized Faculty Addressing Bias, Discrimination, and Oppression in Student Affairs Graduate Preparation Programs

David Pérez II

Nearly three years passed before I developed the confidence to address bias and discrimination in graduate classrooms within the student affairs in higher education (SAHE) program at Miami University (MU). Hearing these words may be surprising and perhaps disconcerting for individuals I have instructed, supervised, or mentored in student affairs. Before drawing erroneous conclusions, continue reading this essay, which reveals complexities inherent in addressing bias and discrimination in graduate classrooms. I have witnessed how efforts to promote inclusion in student affairs are undermined by faculty, staff, and graduate students. Yet, I maintain that faculty must be willing to acknowledge bias and discrimination, share responsibility for dismantling systems of oppression, and support educators who foster social justice and inclusion within higher education.

To my knowledge, I am the first (and only) cisgender Latino man to serve as a tenure-track assistant professor in MU's Department of Educational Leadership. While I have grown accustomed to representing the 3.5% of Latinx faculty on campus, the underrepresentation of faculty of color at MU has heightened my experience of *onlyness*, which is defined as "the psychoemotional burden of having to strategically navigate a racially politicized space occupied by few peers, role models, and guardians from one's same racial or ethnic group."[1] Although Harper's study focused on Black male undergraduates, the perspectives they shared on onlyness helped me to better understand how I have endured bias and discrimination as an educator in the classroom. Similar to participants in Harper's study, I have devoted considerable time and energy to prove that I was qualified. Based on MU's promotion and tenure guidelines,[2] I completed midsemester course evaluations, invited tenured faculty from other departments to observe my instruction, and used this feedback to adjust my pedagogy and the curriculum to establish "multiple indicators of teaching effectiveness." Yet, these indicators concealed how bias and discrimination manifested in my courses.

Despite efforts to promote social justice and inclusion in student affairs, faculty and students with minoritized identities continue to endure bias and discrimination in higher education, in general, and in the classroom, in particular. An essential question that warrants an answer is, "How should student affairs preparation programs address bias and discrimination in the graduate classroom?" Adhering to the American College Personnel Association (ACPA) and the National Association of Student Personnel Administrators' (NASPA's)[3] professional competencies, most student affairs preparation programs focus on preparing graduate students to advance social justice and inclusion (SJI). The SJI competency is "both a process and a goal which includes the knowledge, skills, and dispositions needed to create learning environments that foster equitable participation of all groups while seeking to address and acknowledge issues of oppression, privilege, and power."[4] Student affairs educators demonstrate competence by meeting the needs of underserved students, raising the social consciousness of colleagues, and redressing historical and contemporary inequities that maintain systems of oppression. Yet, aspiring student affairs educators who claim to be SJI advocates often fail to recognize their biases and discriminatory actions in student affairs graduate preparation program classrooms.

During my first two years as a faculty member, I was reluctant to address bias and discrimination in classrooms for myriad reasons. While I do not liken my experiences to cisgender women faculty of color, Pittman[5] helped me to identify the subtle ways White students undermined my role as an educator—comparing my instruction to other SAHE faculty, questioning my intellectual competence when they earned a B on an assignment, and threatening to give me unfavorable teaching evaluations. Instead of challenging students, I remained silent because I wanted them to feel comfortable discussing other controversial issues in my seminars. Nevertheless, I intuited that some students were hesitant about and resistant to engaging in dialogue about bias and discrimination. Similar to participants in Turner-Kelly and Gaston Gayles' study,[6] graduate students complained that faculty placed too much emphasis on race but seldom expressed outrage related to racism. I feared that any attempt to address these issues directly with students would confirm negative stereotypes about Latino men as aggressive and domineering.[7] I assumed the burden of tending to *White fragility*, which DiAngelo defined as "a state in which even a minimum amount of racial stress becomes intolerable, triggering a range of defensive moves."[8] For example, White students complained to my colleagues in private when they were held accountable or struggled to disengage from conversations related to racism in class. Instead of redirecting students to me or sharing insights from these conversations, faculty made offhand remarks such as, "I heard about what happened in your class," or "That reminds me of how students treated Dr. [woman faculty of color]," when I shared concerns about my courses. This led me to question my colleagues' commitment to SJI. Despite my apprehensions, I began to voice my concerns about bias and discrimination with SAHE graduate students and faculty in the department.

When I accepted the invitation to contribute an essay to this book, I did so with the intent of supporting other pretenure assistant professors with minoritized identities in student affairs and higher education programs. My hope is that this essay provides insights to support faculty of color who experience bias and discrimination based on other intersecting minoritized identities (e.g., gender, sexual orientation, ability). Additionally, I hope that after reading this essay, graduate students are enlightened and empowered to take greater ownership for advancing social justice and inclusion. Our failure to address these matters in graduate preparation programs reinforces a culture that perpetuates hostile classroom climates. If we are unable to talk about oppression in the classroom, how can we expect aspiring student affairs educators to demonstrate the foundational, intermediate, and advanced competencies that foster social justice and inclusion?[9]

To illuminate the magnitude and complexity of these issues, I present excerpts from a letter I e-mailed students in EDL 676: Foundations of Student Affairs in Higher Education. I wrote this letter in response to two students of color challenging an evangelical Christian White woman who appeared disengaged when they repeatedly expressed concerns about oppression in class. I, too, noticed these dynamics. On one occasion, this White woman opened her laptop and surfed the Internet as a peer disclosed that they were "afraid of being gunned down by police simply for being big, Black, and gay." Even now, my chest tightens as I contemplate the risks this queer Black man took to educate his peers about oppression. After meeting independently with the three students directly involved in this incident, I contemplated how to engage seminar participants. I wrote a letter, which in part read:

> In all honesty, I have been struggling to find the "right words" to share with you all. What do I say when so much has already been said. When delivering the West India Emancipation speech, Frederick Douglass stated: "The whole history of the progress of human liberty shows that all concessions yet made to her august claims have been born of earnest struggle. The conflict has been exciting, agitating, all-absorbing, and for the time being, putting all other tumults to silence. It must do this or it does nothing. If there is no struggle there is no progress. Those who profess to favor freedom and yet deprecate agitation are men who want crops without plowing up the ground; they want rain without thunder and lightning. They want the ocean without the awful roar of its many waters."
>
> You may be asking yourself, "Where is David going with this?" Lean in with me. . . . There are a few things I want to draw attention to in Douglass' remarks that are relevant to what occurred in class today.[10]

I never anticipated sharing these words with students, faculty, or staff outside of the SAHE program, but this letter alludes to three strategies that student affairs preparation programs should take in addressing bias and discrimination in graduate classrooms.

Acknowledge Bias, Discrimination, . . . and Oppression

Faculty should acknowledge how bias and discrimination perpetuate oppression in student affairs. This can be challenging for faculty members who desire to create *safe spaces* or learning environments that allow students to engage in honest and respectful dialogue about controversial issues.[11] Creating safe spaces for students to engage in dialogue is essential, but I have come to recognize the classroom as a contested space that requires faculty to "help students better understand—and rise to—the challenges of genuine dialogue on diversity and social justice issues."[12] *Brave spaces* are designed to promote civil discourse about controversial issues that advances an anti-oppressive agenda in student affairs and higher education.[13] While brave spaces are desirable, faculty must be willing to take risks in order to create and sustain these learning environments. In another section of the letter I sent to my students, I took a risk by challenging them to reflect on how their silence was perpetuating oppression:

> Silence has the potential to communicate lots of things. This semester, students have taken risks by sharing very personal details about their lives (i.e., racism, sexual assault, homophobia). At times, these moments were met with silence. Please note that I am not pointing any fingers. . . . My sense is that people were silent, because they may have been unsure how to respond. We don't want to say anything that is harmful, so we remain silent while listening to the experiences of students who are marginalized on a daily basis. Unfortunately, our silence can communicate different messages—"I agree that [-ism] is not a problem" or "I don't care about [-ism]."
>
> We may not know what to say, but even acknowledging that can be helpful. "I am lost for words. I can't even imagine what that is like for you. . . . I am committed to disrupting [-ism], but I am not sure how to do this." And as Wilson Okello, a SAHE doctoral student, suggested to Bethany,[14] "Please excuse my language, while I find my voice." Your voices are all important. Disrupting racism requires White people to speak up. Addressing sexism requires men to voice their concerns. This isn't easy, but it is necessary.

Students' responses to my letter encouraged and surprised me. Whereas some students apologized for their silence, others asked for advice on how to better support their peers. Although more than half of the students in this course recognized their biases, they never acknowledged how discrimination was perpetuated in our classroom. Only one White cisgender woman, Becky, accused me of reverse racism. I was surprised by her response considering the rapport we established. Becky was not my advisee, but I met with her periodically to process personal, academic, and professional challenges she experienced as a first-year SAHE student. I assumed *invisible labor* or what Williams described as "the pressure faculty members of color feel to serve as role models, mentors, even surrogate parents to minority [and White] students, and to meet every institutional need for ethnic representation."[15] While Becky referred to me as a "mentor" during our individual meetings, she questioned my competence as an educator in class. When I met with students to process my letter, Becky maintained that she "did not learn anything in this course." Students appeared shocked by her comment, but they remained silent—I did, too. Instead of debating this issue with her, I redirected my attention to engaging students in dialogue about how to create and sustain brave spaces in the classroom. Once final grades were submitted, I met with Becky to address concerns about her classroom remarks and to encourage her to read several articles I shared with students in response to this incident.[16]

Share Responsibility for Dismantling Systems of Oppression

Faculty with minoritized identities should not bear sole responsibility for dismantling systems of oppression. In "Fostering Cultures of Inclusion in the Classroom," Quaye and Chang[17] integrated three theories—the learning partnerships model, critical race theory, and mattering and marginality[18]—to reveal ways faculty can shift "the culture of the classroom from one in which students may feel out-of-place to one in which students matter and construct knowledge [that] fosters new possibilities for academic and social success among diverse populations."[19] Coconstructing learning environments with graduate students has been not only personally and intellectually gratifying but also emotionally demanding as we critically examine our privilege and/ or marginalization. In my letter, I encouraged students to reflect on how they struggled and progressed as a cohort:

> We all struggle with [-isms] based on our privileged and marginalized positions. I was reminded of this when Ronnie shared his struggles with engaging others in dialogue about spirituality. I, too, struggle with conversations that are related to my privileged identities. As an educator, I do not want to say or do anything that perpetuates -isms experienced by marginalized students. . . . Yet, I have come to recognize that these conversations are complex, messy, and unsettling but worth the struggle. I'm not suggesting that we approach these conversations haphazardly. We should be mindful about what we say and how we say it, but this should not hinder us from joining the struggle. This is essential to making progress.
>
> I imagine that some of you may be feeling like the progress we've made this semester has been lost. That depends . . . on how we proceed forward as a learning community. I know the verbal exchange that took place toward the end of class was challenging for everyone—particularly those directly involved—but I've heard that some progress has already been made. My understanding is these individuals have [already] reached out to each other. . . . This is encouraging, but I feel compelled to ask, "Are we going to continue to lean on each other or will we become silent again?" I refuse to be complicit in this process.

To foster a culture of inclusion in this foundations of student affairs seminar, I invited graduate students to revise assignments, readings, and other parts of the curriculum to address oppression for the remainder of this course. For example, some students submitted weekly journal entries after assessing their SJI competence using different inventories (e.g., Project Implicit, ACPA/NASPA Professional Competencies Rubric).[20] In full disclosure, I am not sure this enhanced the climate in our classroom, but this process provided graduate students with the foundational knowledge to interrogate and begin dismantling systems of oppression.

Support Educators Who Advance SJI

Tenured faculty should support educators who advance SJI in student affairs preparation programs. In response to the challenges I experienced, several colleagues suggested that I invite a tenured professor to observe my interactions with graduate students. I was told that this professor would provide departmental faculty with "additional context" for understanding the dynamics in my classroom. In addition to providing constructive feedback on my pedagogy, the professor agreed to document how bias, discrimination, and oppression manifested in these seminars. After e-mailing students, I shared the full letter as well as students' responses with this tenured professor and other faculty in my department. Colleagues praised me for my "authenticity" and "beautiful words" via e-mail, but the department's promotion and tenure committee members' evaluations of my teaching revealed how faculty of color are subjected to racist teaching evaluations. In my annual evaluation they wrote, "Given the concern that you were perhaps 'cohorted'[21] in previous years as a result of racism that impacted your student evaluation scores, [the college] offered to assign a master teacher to serve as a mentor . . . for your course in Fall 2015." This was a total misrepresentation of what occurred. I did not request a White woman to serve as a "master teacher" or "mentor" in dealing with racism. My personal, educational, and professional experiences at predominantly White institutions left me well prepared to cope with oppression.

Although my colleagues acknowledged the positive contributions I made as an assistant professor both inside and outside of the classroom, they did not acknowledge how bias and discrimination undermined my experience as a Latino educator.[22] Based on students' responses to my letter, I anticipated the department's promotion and tenure committee would document my efforts to address oppression and to foster inclusion in this course. Additionally, I would have appreciated the committee documenting how other pretenure, women, and/or faculty of color endured similar treatment in the SAHE program. However, their response conveyed that some faculty members were complicit in perpetuating oppression. While I felt unsupported by my colleagues, I found comfort in rereading the concluding thoughts I shared with graduate students in my letter to them:

I want to reiterate [that] you are making progress. . . . The struggles and progress you've made have not been in vain. This has not been absent of challenges, but Frederick Douglass never said "plowing up the ground" would be easy. This process requires us to remove deeply embedded weeds (i.e., racism, sexism, classism), to plant seeds with care, and to sustain environments that bear fruit in the future. This process requires a great deal of patience and care. It will require patience when our privileged colleagues say, "Please excuse my language, while I find my voice." Moreover, it will require patience when our marginalized colleagues say, "Please excuse my language, while I share (and heal from) my pain." Remember. . . . If there is no struggle there is no progress.

I never anticipated sharing these words with graduate students or faculty in student affairs graduate preparation programs, but my hope is that this essay inspires others to acknowledge bias and discrimination and to share responsibility for dismantling systems of oppression, regardless of whether your efforts are supported.

Conclusion

Despite efforts to promote social justice and inclusion, faculty continue to wrestle with how to effectively address bias, discrimination, and oppression in graduate classrooms. Like many student affairs graduate preparation programs, my department and academic program has focused on increasing the representation of faculty and students from underrepresented populations. Conversations related to SJI resulted in new course offerings such as intergroup dialogue, student success, and critical Whiteness studies. Yet, these efforts have not transformed how my students and I continue to experience the classroom. These experiences are not unique and in fact are quite pervasive.[23] Yet, I wonder how faculty and students might address similar concerns in other student affairs graduate preparation programs.

In retrospect, my biggest regret is that I did not acknowledge bias and discrimination sooner. While I am not responsible for redressing racism, I could have coconstructed learning experiences that prepared students to work toward dismantling oppression. Before answering this call to action, I implore both graduate students and pretenure faculty of color to read Dafina-Lazarus Stewart's proverbial love letter to first-year faculty with minoritized identities.[24] Ze emphasized, "Your life may inform your teaching, [but] you do not have to teach your life. . . . Your heart is not a 16-week curriculum for others' [sic] to attain their learning outcomes through the toil of your devastations." Stewart suggested that we set boundaries, which I endeavored to do when sharing my letter with SAHE students and faculty. Although I expected backlash from some students, I never anticipated that my colleagues would remain silent or perpetuate racism. Ze reminded me that "the best anecdote to . . . biased systems is excellence . . . not a call to assimilation, but rather to doing the work, consistently, thoroughly, and at such a high level of quality that your haters [are] silenced." I took risk in challenging SAHE students and faculty, which also demanded that I exceed their expectations in the areas of teaching, research, and service. At the time of writing this essay, the content had the potential to undermine my promotion to associate professor with tenure in the Department of Educational Leadership at MU, but I refused to be complicit in perpetuating bias, discrimination, and oppression in student affairs graduate preparation programs.[25]

Discussion Questions

1. To what extent are you complicit in perpetuating bias and discrimination in the classroom?
2. How can faculty members and students coconstruct learning environments that help to dismantle systems of oppression?
3. In what ways can tenured faculty support pretenure assistant professors with minoritized identities in advancing social justice and inclusion?

Notes

1. Harper, S. R. (2013). Am I my brother's teacher? Black undergraduates, racial socialization, and peer pedagogies in predominantly White postsecondary contexts. *Review of Research in Education, 37*(1), 183–211, p. 189.

2. Miami University. (n.d.). *Promotion and tenure guidelines for dossier preparation: 2014-2015*. Retrieved from http://www.miamioh.edu/_files/documents/secretary/Promotion_Tenure_Guidelines.pdf

3. ACPA & NASPA. (2015). *Professional competency areas for student affairs educators*. Washington DC: Authors.

4. Ibid., p. 14.

5. Pittman, C. T. (2010). Race and gender oppression in the classroom: The experiences of women faculty of color with White male students. *Teaching Sociology, 38*(3), 183–196.

6. Turner Kelly, B., & Gaston Gayles, J. (2010). Resistance to racial/ethnic dialog in graduate preparation programs: Implications for developing multicultural competence. *College Student Affairs Journal, 29*(1), 75–85.

7. Hurtado, A., & Sinha, M. (2016). *Beyond machismo: Intersectional Latino masculinities*. Austin, TX: University of Texas Press; Pérez II, D. (2017). In pursuit

of success: Latino male college students exercising academic determination and community cultural wealth. *Journal of College Student Development,* 58(2), 123–140; Sáenz, V. B., & Bukoski, B. E. (2014). Masculinity: Through a Latino male lens. In R. A. Williams (Ed.), *Men of color in higher education: New foundations for developing models of success* (pp. 85–115). Sterling, VA: Stylus.

8. DiAngelo, R. (2011). White fragility. *International Journal of Critical Pedagogy,* 3(3), 54–70, p. 54.

9. ACPA & NASPA, *Professional competency areas for student affairs educators,* pp. 30–31.

10. Library of Congress. (n.d.). *Two speeches by Frederick Douglass: West India Emancipation address and Dred Scott decision.* Retrieved from https://www.loc.gov/resource/mfd.21039/?sp=1&st=gallery

11. Arao, B., & Clemens, K. (2013). From safe spaces to brave spaces: A new way to frame dialogue around diversity and social justice. In L. M. Landreman (Ed.), *The art of effective facilitation: Reflections from social justice educators* (pp. 135–150). Sterling, VA: Stylus.

12. Ibid., p. 136.

13. Ali, D. (2017). *Safe spaces and brave spaces: Historical context and recommendations for student affairs professionals.* NASPA Research and Policy Institute: Washington DC.

14. With the exception of Becky, all students granted me permission to use their names in this essay. Becky is a pseudonym.

15. Williams J. A. (n.d.). *The invisible labor of minority professors.* Retrieved from http://www.chronicle.com/article/The-Invisible-Labor-of/234098

16. Yosso, T. J., Smith, W. A., & Solórzano, D. G. (2011). Challenging racial battle fatigue on historically White campuses: A critical race examination of race-related stress. In R. D. Coates (Ed.), *Covert racism: Theories, institutions, and experiences* (pp. 211–238). New Milford, CT: Brill; Williams, *The invisible labor of minority professors.*

17. Quaye, S. J., & Chang, S. H. (2012). Fostering cultures of inclusion in the classroom. In S. D. Museus & U. M. Jayakumar (Eds.), *Creating campus culture: Fostering success among racially diverse student populations* (pp. 88–105). New York, NY: Routledge.

18. Baxter Magolda, M. B. (2004). Learning partnerships model: A framework for promoting self-authorship. In M. B. Baxter Magolda & P. M. King (Eds.), *Learning partnerships model: A framework for promoting self-learning partnerships: Theory and models of practice to educate for self-authorship* (pp. 37–62). Sterling, VA: Stylus; Delgado, R., & Stefancic, J. (2001). *Critical race theory: An introduction.* New York, NY: New York University Press; Schlossberg, N. K. (1989). Marginality and mattering: Key issues in building community. In D. C. Roberts (Ed.), *Designing campus activities to foster a sense of community* (pp. 5–15). (New Directions for Student Services, 28) San Francisco, CA: Jossey-Bass.

19. Quaye & Chang, Fostering cultures of inclusion in the classroom, p. 95.

20. ACPA & NASPA. (2016). *ACPA/NASPA professional competencies rubrics.* Washington DC: Authors; Harvard University. (n.d.). *Project implicit.* Retrieved from http://www.chronicle.com/article/The-Invisible-Labor-of/234098

21. In this instance, the term *cohorted* was used to describe how SAHE graduate students historically, collectively, and intentionally give faculty of color unfavorable teaching evaluations.

22. Solórzano, D. G. (1998). Critical race theory, race and gender microaggressions, and the experience of Chicana and Chicano scholars. *International Journal of Qualitative Studies in Education, 11*(1), 121–136; Turner, C. S. V., González, J. C., & Wood, J. L. (2008). Faculty of color in academe: What 20 years of literature tells us. *Journal of Diversity in Higher Education, 1*(3), 139–168; Urrieta, L., Méndez, L., & Rodríguez, E. (2015). "A moving target": A critical race analysis of Latina/o faculty experiences, perspectives, and reflections on the tenure and promotion process. *International Journal of Qualitative Studies in Education, 28*(10), 1149–1168; Zambrana, R. E., Harvey Wingfield, A., Lapeyrouse, L. M., Dávila, B. A., Hoagland, T. L., & Valdez, R. B. (2017). Blatant, subtle, and insidious: URM faculty perceptions of discriminatory practices in predominantly White institutions. *Sociological Inquiry, 87*(2), 207–232.

23. Gildersleeve, R. E., Croom, N. N., & Vasquez, P. L. (2011). "Am I going crazy?!": A critical race analysis of doctoral education. *Equity & Excellence in Education, 44*(1), 93–114; Truong, K. A., Museus, S. D., & McGuire, K. M. (2016). Vicarious racism: A qualitative analysis of experiences with secondhand racism in graduate education. *International Journal of Qualitative Studies in Education, 29*(2), 224–247; Turner Kelly & Gaston Gayles, Resistance to racial/ethnic dialog in graduate preparation programs.

24. Stewart, D.-L. (2016, September 8). *Just because you're magic: A love letter to minoritized faculty in your first year.* Retrieved from https://dafinalazarusstewart.wordpress.com/2016/09/08/just-because-youre-magic-a-love-letter-to-minoritized-faculty-in-your-first-year/

25. After submitting the original draft of this essay but before publication of this book, MU granted me tenure and promoted me to associate professor.

You Are Not Alone: Graduate Preparation Programs' Responsibility and Commitment to Addressing Discrimination and Bias in Classrooms and Beyond

Bridget Turner Kelly

In this essay, I provide feedforward for Pérez's essay, introduce ideas the essay sparked based on my own experiences in graduate preparation programs, and close with questions to spur further dialogue. The central idea the essay sparked was that program-level change and support are needed to create the structures, practices, and culture essential for supporting marginalized faculty and systematically addressing bias and discrimination in the classroom and beyond. Where Pérez's essay focused on classroom-based strategies he took as a faculty member, my response calls on the graduate preparation program community of faculty, students, and student affairs educators to transform the program to be more equitable for all.

Feedforward for Pérez's Essay

I respond to Pérez's thoughtful essay in the spirit of feedforward. I largely agree with and hope to extend Pérez's points by pointing out areas of strength and what I believe his work calls us to consider.

Pérez and I share similar stories of "onlyness," as I have entered every graduate preparation program as the only and the first faculty member of color. Being untenured as one of 3.5% Black women faculty nationally in higher education[1] felt like being a unicorn, especially as I have done so at historically White universities. The unicorn experience helped me agree with Pérez that "faculty must be willing to acknowledge bias and discrimination, share responsibility for dismantling systems of oppression, and support educators who foster social justice and inclusion within higher education."[2] His essay eloquently demonstrates that there are inequitable consequences for untenured faculty who hold marginalized identities and who openly acknowledge bias and discrimination. Along with jeopardizing tenure, marginalized faculty are often accused of derailing important content by focusing on bias and discrimination. They are rarely supported by leadership in their program when they address bias and discrimination. Pérez eventually brought his concerns to students and faculty colleagues, and I agree he should have done this at the outset. One of the best pieces of advice I got from a mentor was "be yourself as you go through the tenure process, because you are deciding whether you want to be there just as they are deciding whether they want you there." Students and academic programs are harmed when faculty are not empowered to act for justice and equity.[3]

Pérez's excerpted letter demonstrated vulnerability, courage, and the sound pedagogical practice of using classroom dissent as a learning opportunity for students. I applaud the letter imploring silent students to use their voices to affirm and demonstrate active listening with those who shared stories of oppression. I did not see in the excerpts of the letter whether he encouraged silent students to contribute to the learning environment by sharing their own stories of privilege and roles as the oppressors—acknowledging their active or complacent roles in perpetuating bias and discrimination. Once this acknowledgement happens, students can decide if their complicity with oppression aligns with their ideals, values, and beliefs, and if not, focus on ways to stop oppressive attitudes and behaviors. Recognizing the oppressor within also may allow a student to really hear, affirm, and actively listen to stories of others being oppressed. For those students who share stories of oppression, being truly heard can promote healing and open space for the whole class to discuss causes, effects, and solutions. When some students do not feel heard, other students remain silent, and some students get into contentious discussions, the tendency of faculty is to calm people down and/or move onto something else. When I have been in those circumstances as a faculty member, my skin gets hot, my legs shake, and my heart races. Years of practicing and sitting with my discomfort have taught me to dive in deeper. It is scary, but I have asked students to stay longer in class so we could air as many feelings and thoughts as possible. Active listening, waiting in silence until people are compelled to speak, sharing my stories of privilege and marginalization, and being prepared to not have all the answers is some of how I have dealt with instances of bias and discrimination in the graduate classroom. Like Pérez, I engaged, but I wondered how it would affect my tenure.

Pérez expertly discussed what faculty and students could do to address bias and discrimination in the graduate preparation classroom. His focus was rightly on students' growth and learning—but at what cost to the faculty—particularly, faculty with marginalized identities? Who in the program is supporting untenured faculty members and faculty members with marginalized identities in their work inside the classroom? When I dived deeper into contentious discussions of bias and discrimination I did so at great risk to my career, especially when I was untenured. I did it anyway because I held the privileged status of having a partner and family that could financially support me if I lost my job. I did it because at the time, I thought the risk of getting fired was worth it if it helped students learn how to think and feel through bias and discrimination. I ultimately did not lose my job and found support from program directors, department chairs, and deans when students complained to them about me being too critical and asking too many questions about identity, equity, and oppression in class. What would have happened if I did not hold the class privilege I do or if administrators did not support my teaching content, pedagogy, or style? My central argument is that it should not be left solely to the faculty member to create environments to openly and bravely discuss issues connected to bias and discrimination.

Community Approach to Addressing Bias and Discrimination

What struck me most about Pérez's essay was his isolation. Yes, he should address these issues in the classroom, but not in an isolated context. Instead of support, he felt the need to prove himself to his faculty colleagues because of their reactions to the incidents in his classroom. As the first and only cisgender Latino assistant professor in his program, Pérez was without support and without models for addressing bias and discrimination in the classroom. Without seeing examples of how to do it well, especially in that particular program, without being able to discuss it with other marginalized faculty in his program, and without having ample empirical research on the topic to read—how could he learn to do it well?

In my case, as someone who has visible marginalized identities of being a Black woman, I relied on senior faculty of color in other departments to get models of how to address issues of bias and discrimination in the classroom. I sought peer mentors from Black women I met at professional conferences and called on them when difficulty arose in my classroom. I read works by Black women (e.g., Beverly Daniel Tatum, bell hooks) to get assistance on how to do faculty life as an untenured Black woman. I also connected with student affairs educators on campus who were knowledgeable about privilege and oppression and who supervised students in the program through assistantships and internships. Without this external help I feared I would not earn tenure and, even worse for me, that students would not learn what they needed to from the courses I taught. Out of worry that they would not fully support me in the tenure process, I never went to my program director, department chair, or dean to ask for support in the classroom.

Leverage Privilege for Power

As a tenured, associate professor and program chair of higher education, I held different perspectives on the topics of bias and discrimination in the classroom. I held privilege not only in my position but also in my intersecting identities (e.g., cisgender, heterosexual, Christian, middle class, to name a few) and knowledge of the graduate preparation community. Privileges should be leveraged for power to make the program a more equitable environment for all. I agree with everything Pérez wrote in his essay that addresses what he could do inside the classroom, but from my perspective there is more that must be done by those who hold privilege and power in the program. The director of the program, tenured faculty, and student affairs educators in Pérez's program could proactively provide the support needed by leveraging their privilege and power for a more equitable and transformative program. For instance, there is power in providing models for untenured marginalized faculty to see how others deal with bias and discrimination. Program directors may invite faculty and student affairs educators with marginalized identities who excel in creating equitable classroom environments to share their experiences in teach-ins. Other ways those with power in the program may leverage it for change are:

- Carefully assess how marginalized faculty and students are treated by examining your own biases and discriminatory behavior (could range from reflective practice with supervisors to program-wide empirical surveys);
- Ensure those hired in the program have a demonstrated commitment to addressing bias and discrimination (seek evidence in résumés and ask interview questions about actions/works, not just philosophies/beliefs);
- Discuss empirical research on addressing bias and discrimination in the classroom and program at meetings and in division of student affairs' in-services (secure experts to facilitate, if needed);
- Educate faculty, search committees, and other leadership bodies on bias and discrimination manifesting differently for marginalized, untenured faculty (provide evidence from literature to decision-making bodies);

- Ask prospective students to address their understanding of bias and discrimination in their personal statement/admission packet (align recruitment efforts with stated aim of social justice/equity focus of program);
- Educate students through curriculum infusion, program-wide speakers, workshops on bias and discrimination (cultivate resources for promoting social justice/equity).

These ideas are not new. Scholars in student affairs have documented bias and discrimination in and out of the university classroom.[4] What keeps this list from being enacted fully is that it requires a fundamental shift in the program curriculum and practices that are embedded often unconsciously by those in power. Rather than focusing on how Pérez could alter himself to fit the environment, the list asks the program to examine how the environment can transform to proactively address bias and discrimination, particularly for people with marginalized identities. To amplify the list, I will share a few examples of creating and being a part of transformative environments in graduate preparation programs.

Ensure Staff Commitment to Reducing Bias and Discrimination

Prior to taking my current position, I was the first and only person of color in every program I had joined in higher education and student affairs. Through collaborative work with program directors, deans, and student affairs educators who demonstrated a commitment to equity and excellence, I was not the last. At every university, faculty of color were hired after me in those programs, and the faculty increased their colleagues and students' knowledge of issues of bias and discrimination.

Ensure Admissions Process Reduces Bias and Discrimination

I began my career at the University of Vermont (UVM) graduate program in higher education and student affairs. At the time there were 2 cohorts of students: roughly 13 first-year master's students and 15 second-year master's students. There was a single student of color across both cohorts. With constant discussions, sharing of research, collaborating with the division of student development, and years of work on race, in particular, the cohorts when I left the university 4 years later were 50% students of color.

Ensure That Curriculum and Pedagogy Reduces Bias and Discrimination

Addressing bias and discrimination was still difficult to address, but there was a supportive environment for me to do the work as an untenured, cisgender,

Black, woman assistant professor at UVM. There was a required class on cultural pluralism that explicitly addressed topics such as bias and discrimination. There also were more faculty of color and student affairs educators of color in the university to talk with, and that gave me energy and support to do the equity work I felt called to do with students.

While I worked at Loyola University Chicago, I directed a program of all faculty of color and over 50% students of color, among other marginalized identities, in the master's and doctoral programs. This is no accident.[5] The faculty redesigned the curriculum to include both a required course in privilege, oppression, and social justice, *and* we infused the remaining required classes with attention to equity, inclusion, and social justice. Students address social justice in their applications to the program. Changing the demographics of who was teaching and learning in the classroom and ensuring the curriculum followed inclusive pedagogy enabled us to more effectively address issues of bias and discrimination in the classroom as marginalized faculty.

Conclusion

Pérez stated that his actions, or even the actions I described previously, do not alone transform how bias and discrimination in the classroom is discussed. Addressing some of the items on the list enabled me to be in supportive communities while still operating in larger systems of oppression. Transformation takes commitment from the entire community, especially those with power. It is not the responsibility of faculty alone to address bias and discrimination in the classroom. The graduate preparation program community needs to prepare the way through equitable and engaged admissions, curriculum, professional development, and critical assessment of policies and practices. It is the responsibility of all to dismantle systems of oppression and rebuild graduate preparation programs with equity and social justice.

Discussion Questions

1. How can students, faculty, and student affairs educators engage in discussions that transform the way bias and discrimination is addressed in and out of the classroom?
2. What program efforts could transform how those with marginalized identities are supported in addressing bias and discrimination in the classroom and beyond?

Notes

1. National Center for Education Statistics (NCES), U.S. Department of Education. (2016). Table 315.20 Full-time faculty in degree-granting postsecondary institutions, by race/ethnicity, sex, and academic rank: Fall 2011, fall 2013, and fall 2015. In U.S. Department of Education, National Center for Education Statistics (Ed.), *Digest of Education Statistics* (2015 ed.). Retrieved from https://nces.ed.gov/programs/digest/d16/tables/dt16_315.20.asp?current=yes

2. Pérez, this volume, pp. 341–342.

3. NCES, U.S Department of Education, Table 315.20 Full-time faculty in degree-granting postsecondary institutions, by race/ethnicity, sex, and academic rank: Fall 2011, fall 2013, and fall 2015.

4. Ferguson, A., & Howard-Hamilton, M. F. (2000). Addressing issues of multiple identities for women of color on college campuses. In N. J. Evans & V. A. Wall (Eds.), *Toward acceptance: Sexual orientation issues on campus* (pp. 283–297). Washington DC: ACPA; Gasman, M. (2016). The five things no one will tell you about why colleges don't hire more faculty of color. *The Hechinger Report.* Retrieved from http://hechingerreport.org/five-things-no-one-will-tell-colleges-dont-hire-faculty-color/; Gaston Gayles, J., & Kelly, B. T. (2007). Experiences with diversity in the curriculum: Implications for graduate programs and student affairs practice. *National Association of Student Personnel Administrators Journal, 44*(1), Article 11; King, P. M., & Howard-Hamilton, M. F. (2000). Becoming a multiculturally competent student affairs professional. *Diversity on Campus: Reports from the field* (pp. 26–28). Washington DC: National Association of Student Personnel Administrators.

5. Squire, D., Jourian, T. J., Kelly, B. T., Byrd, A., Manzano, L., & Bumbry, M. (2018). A critical race feminist analysis of men of color matriculating in a higher education doctoral program. *Journal of Diversity in Higher Education, 11*(1), 16–33.

19

What Is the Value of Student Affairs Research as It Relates to Issues of Equity, Civility, and Safety?

The Value and Disconnect of Student Affairs Research Related to Equity, Civility, and Safety

JoNes R. VanHecke

> *In Theory everything is possible. Unfortunately, I live in Practice and the road to Theory has been washed out.*
>
> —Anonymous

While working on my PhD, I often told people that I aspired to become a scholar practitioner, the mythical student affairs educator who simultaneously challenges and supports students developmentally while contributing to the field's literature with robust, methodologically sound, and thoughtful publications. During my coursework, I enjoyed reading assigned books and research articles. Those days were a heady, productive thinking time. I looked for interconnectivity. I spent time thinking about the implications of research in practice. Thanks to a strong master's degree program and more than a decade working in student affairs, the topics of diversity, equity, and inclusion were never far from my thoughts. Concepts of civility and safety as we experience them on today's college campuses, however, had only begun to percolate as the issues we now experience in contemporary American higher education.

It is because I have such a positive regard for research and theory that I am sincerely confounded by what I see as a lack of utilization of research by student affairs educators as we struggle to address issues of civility, equity, and safety on our college campuses. Why don't we turn to the latest journal articles to make decisions about helping our students find a balance between free speech and accountability when someone yells bias-laden insults from a moving car at a student perceived as belonging to a historically under-represented group? Why don't we reach for the latest research when the Republican and Democrat student organizations are both feeling attacked by the other group's sidewalk chalkings? Why are senior administrators more likely to turn to an external media consultant when faced with student pro-test rather than grounding their response in student development theory? While long gone, my graduate student days are not forgotten. I still believe in the importance of research-informed practice, particularly regarding the issues that vex us as student affairs educators. Research must play a valuable role in addressing issues of equity, civility, and safety, but student affairs educators must also consider context when utilizing research and theory to inform decision-making. In addition to context, student affairs educators and researchers alike must be diligent and creative in utilizing all resources available that can assist us in accomplishing this important work.

In this essay, I discuss the complexities that student affairs educators face as we lean into issues of equity, civility, and safety on our college campuses and examine some of the obstacles associated with using research and theory to address these challenges. First, however, I consider existing models that explore the overarching questions about the tension between research/theory and practice. We must understand the theory-practice disconnect before we can use research to inform our decision-making.

Consideration of Existing Student Affairs Models

Theory is abstracted practice, and practice is applied theory. Both are necessary and interrelated. Individuals in practice often claim that those who concentrate on theory and research are detached from the real world. Individuals in research and theory development assert that those in practice lack a fundamental grounding for why they do what they do, resulting in incongruous practices. Even student affairs researchers can't agree on the right balance between research and practice, as is evidenced in the existence of three distinct models.

In his model, Love currently[1] suggests that student affairs is ruled by the supposition that only formal theory should be applied to practice. Love reflects upon the idea that this assumption causes practitioners to feel that they must choose between their lived experiences and formal theory. He argues that there is an inherent incongruity between *formal theories of learning and development,* defined as "public, conscious, explicit, and organized conceptions of defined and related phenomena,"[2] and informal theories utilized by practitioners. Love proposes that practitioners should incorporate their own values and assumptions instead of using formal theory. An example of this is a scenario where formal theory has not yet caught up to what is occurring on college campuses. To date, college student theorists have not posited ways to frame the unique experiences of students with autism spectrum disorder in college. *Autism spectrum disorder* is defined as "any of a group of developmental disorders such as autism and Asperger's syndrome marked by impairments in the ability to communicate and interact socially and by the presence of repetitive behaviors or restricted interests."[3] Because of social and communication challenges, students on the autism spectrum sometimes present in ways that leave their peers concerned for personal safety. As a result, campus behavioral assessment teams are asked to apply rubrics designed to assess social interactions and related behaviors to those with developmental disabilities. How do administrators tasked with assessing safety respond when models fail to exist? Love would argue that student affairs educators must be freed from thinking associated with formal theory and instead rely on their own values and assumptions.

In response to Love, Evans and Guido[4] wrote that the use of informal theories alone may result in unintended problems caused by practitioners relying on faulty assumptions about student growth and development. Evans and Guido have

> no issue with the use of informal theory as a mediator between formal theory and practice. We do have an issue with using informal theory by itself to guide practice, given that it is impossible to determine the accuracy of an individual's assumptions or sense making.[5]

Instead they insist that the use of formal theory is necessary to ensure that a practitioner's decision-making is effective and proactive. To return to the example of the behavioral assessment team evaluating the student on the autism spectrum, Evans and Guido urge educators to consider existing theory in addition to our own values and assumptions. While not aware of developmental theory specific to students on the autism spectrum, some aspects of existing developmental theories may apply. For example, Sanford and Adelson's theory of challenge and support[6] is certainly relevant to working with students with developmental disabilities and could be taken under advisement during the behavioral assessment team's process.

Reason and Kimball[7] propose a compromise between the two models by suggesting that

> both Love (2012) and Evans and Guido (2012) are correct in crucial aspects while expanding on each of their arguments: Student affairs professionals have need for both formal and informal theories. The way student affairs professionals think about the connections between formal theory, informal theory, and practice will determine their success as student affairs professionals.[8]

Reason and Kimball propose a four-step model: formal theory, institutional context, informal theory, and practice with feedback loops to acknowledge the critical nature of assessment in student affairs work. "These feedback loops afford student affairs practitioners the opportunity to engage in reflective practice and ensure that the conversion from rigorous formal theory to the adaptive needs of practice (driven by informal theory) does not result in undesirable outcomes."[9]

Where Reason and Kimball's model drives to the core of the theory-and-practice tension is found in their understanding that a "successful theory-to-practice translation requires the rigorous application of formal theory as modified by local context."[10] Accounting for context grounds this model in significant ways. Reason and Kimball define *institutional context* broadly as "the way in which environment informs institutionally supported student development goals and provide guidance to student affairs professionals about how these goals are best achieved."[11] Too often as a senior student affairs officer, I've heard complaints from staff about the lack of relevancy of a research article to the specific work we are doing at our institution. Models that account for institutional context help address those concerns. As student affairs educators, it is our responsibility to reflect on our own unique campuses when we utilize research to inform our practice. If our first question is "What research and theory could assist us in making sense of this situation?" then the second question needs to be, "What do I know about my campus and students that further informs my decision-making?"

When I asked my colleagues across the country to think with me about the value of student affairs research as it relates to issues of equity, civility, and safety and why there is a disconnect between research and practice, most began their responses to me with a contextualization from their own institutions. For example, Sarah Westfall, vice president for student development and dean of students at Kalamazoo College, wrote, "I work on a campus that has become very diverse very quickly, and it has been a bumpy ride in terms of equity, civility, and safety."[12]

Lisa Landreman, assistant vice president/dean of student life at Roger Williams University, began by writing, "I have many hard-working student affairs folks who have been at the institution a long time."[13] Consistent with Reason and Kimball's model, these practitioners lead with institutional context. It is critical that if we intend to use all resources available to us to inform our decision-making, we will need to account for the importance of institutional context to practitioners.

Theory and research or practice standing alone are not adequate for addressing the complex developmental realities unearthed when working with today's college students around issues of civility, equity, and safety. Henry Toutain, recently retired dean of students from Kenyon College, underscores the importance of institutional context when he writes,

> Success, I believe, depends upon many factors, including the sensitivity, sensibility, skill, and persistence of practitioners, as well as contextual circumstances, from institutional culture to student demographics and prevailing social trends.[14]

Each college or university campus has a unique history, background, and set of triggers specific to their own institution. If we are to successfully meet the challenges of civility, equity, and safety presented on our college campuses, this context must be at the forefront of administrative decision-making.

Equity, Civility, and Safety

The work of student affairs educators is complex, and, in my opinion, the current issues of equity, civility, and safety are particularly challenging. Why is this? Sarah Westfall writes eloquently about the difficulties of grappling with these issues:

> One of the challenging parts about the moment we're in is that some deeply personal issues related to identity are informing and driving some very public, community behavior. Useful research and writing on the nexus of these issues has had a hard time keeping up with the reality of how students and institutions are responding.[15]

Often on our campuses, equity and safety are concerns expected to be met by institutional action. Revising policy, providing resources, and engaging people all happen at the institutional level. But as Henry Toutain points out, "civility demands much more than institutional action. Civility focuses on individual conduct and values (respect, intellectual freedom, open inquiry) more than institutional action."[16] Sarah Westfall takes it one step further when she observes that

> unlike other causes (fossil fuel divestment, food justice, as examples) the issues of equity, safety, and civility seem especially charged because, I think, equity, civility, and safety have been defined in very personal ways. It is hard for communities to fully meet the very personal, competing demands of individuals.[17]

Often equity and safety are framed in individual terms and pit people or groups against each other. How some benefit and others don't or how some feel safe while others are afraid too often means that, for student affairs educators addressing a conflict, the response appears to favor one side over the other.

Landreman concurs when she writes that

> the safety issue is becoming harder. It has evolved beyond setting guidelines to help facilitate productive, respectful conversations on difficult issues. It's gone from minoritized folks feeling frustrated with White fragility and people from privilege conflating "safety" with feeling uncomfortable to our current climate where minoritized students literally feeling that their physical safety may be at risk.[18]

Westfall's and Landreman's observations—that individuals with highly personalized and sensitive concerns expect an institutional response—suggest that the stakes are high for student affairs educators to respond in skillful and informed ways. This critical moment lays a clear path to the importance of utilizing all resources available and underscores the significance of looking to Reason and Kimball's model that calls on us to use formal theory, institutional context, informal theory, and practice along with feedback loops to get it right. By proposing a model that features theory, context, and practice, Reason and Kimball suggest a way forward for student affairs educators seeking a balanced approach. Unfortunately, in my experience, utilizing this model doesn't necessarily help us overcome the obstacles associated with utilizing research.

We're Too Busy and Other Reasons

What is it that gets in our way and keeps us from using formal and informal theory, institutional context and feedback loops when responding to conflicts arising from issues of civility, equity, and safety? In this section of the essay, I examine five reasons student affairs educators refrain from connecting research/theory and practice: failure to prioritize the work, failure to see the work as our own, timing to publication, writing to the wrong audience, and failure to stand for our own convictions.

Toutain identifies many factors that perpetuate a disconnect between theory and practice; however, he also touches on what, in my experience, is the most frequently cited reason—namely that practitioners say they are just too busy to stay abreast of new research and theory developments. Toutain suggests it is that "because we're frequently so consumed with executing practice—and our colleagues are almost universally focused on practical impacts on campus—that we miss opportunities to share sound research/theory."[19] Landreman echoes that concern when she writes about her efforts to educate staff. "Some are interested but say that they don't have time to stop doing the work to read, research, or seek out professional development."[20] Practitioners often feel pushed to the limit. Today's higher education reality means more governance guidance, increased accrediting body expectations, and more pressure from internal and external constituencies. It does feel like there is precious little time available to stay abreast of research and thoughtfully apply it to daily work.

Of course, as tough as it is to admit, saying "I'm too busy" is also just a way of saying that "I'm prioritizing other things." Every day I prioritize my work. I decide that I'll call back the president before I respond to an e-mail from a vendor. I decide that engaging in a conversation with a distressed first-generation student is more important than attending a faculty committee meeting. Cognizant of making a choice or not, I'm always making a choice. Our successful future depends on prioritizing the importance of using the research and theory available to us.

Perhaps an equally prevalent but more disappointing reason that many struggle to engage practice with research is that not all student affairs educators see civility, equity, and safety as "their work." Landreman shared that she has talked with practitioners who voice that engaging with the research in this area isn't critical to them because they have so few students of color, international students, or other historically underrepresented groups on their campus. "It feels like an area of specialization that people can opt out of (e.g., I'm into social justice issues and another staff member is into learning communities) rather than some baseline competencies that we all need."[21] When we adopt the limiting mind-set that the Diversity Center or Residence Life Office staff are the people responsible for dealing with civility, equity, and safety on our campus, we allow our professional specialization to override the essence of what is at the core of student affairs work, namely that, regardless of where you work on campus, be it the Career Center, the Well-Being Office, or Student Activities, educating students about civility, equity, and safety belongs to all of us. In our enthusiasm for specializing our work, let us not forget that the teachable moment presents itself in many ways and in many varied conversations. As dedicated student affairs educators, we must be ready to seize those moments by anticipating them and that includes understanding what the research says and how theory can be applied.

While much of this essay is practitioner focused, it is important to address the fact that there are also things that researchers and theorist can do: specifically, time to publication and intentional connection with practitioners. Research is often a year or older by the time it is published. Yet practitioners experience issues of safety, equity, and civility as rapidly evolving and changing quickly and regularly on our campuses. Last year's best research may not aid us in understanding today's campus protest. These things are happening now, and thanks to social media and technologies that facilitate instant connections, the protest of the day on campus A quickly becomes next week's protest on campus B. This chain reaction is happening before student affairs educators have a chance to compare notes or researchers begin to devise studies. Research that won't be published until a year from now may not inform practice in the ways that we need it to. Of course, if practitioners are not committed to reading that research, time to and timing of publication quickly become moot points.

Who researchers are writing for is the fourth concern. Although writing about the field of public health, but also relevant to student affairs, Green and colleagues[22] posit that the underlying problem is that

> the production of evidence is organized. . . with highly centralized mechanisms, whereas the application is highly decentralized. This social distance prevails because scientists are more oriented to the . . . audiences of other scientists for which they publish than to the needs of practitioners.

In my experience, too many scholars skip the most important step of their research: implications for practice. During the five years I served as the associate editor for the *Journal of Student Affairs Research and Practice's* Innovations in Practice feature, the single most frequent criticism offered to the authors was that they needed to provide a stronger exploration of how their research can inform practitioner thinking and action.

Finally, we must also reflect on the responsibility practitioners bear for the disconnect between student affairs theory and practice when we fail to have the courage of our own convictions. One practitioner, who wishes to remain anonymous, told me that as the senior student affairs officer, this can manifest itself when a senior colleague or the president suggests a course of action that runs counter to our research/theories/principles of civility, equity, or safety. For example, we may choose not to advocate on behalf of students who want to bring to campus diversity programming such as *The Vagina Monologues*[23] or a drag show because it might be considered controversial. Refusal to share campus statistics on bias and hate incidents for fear of creating a perception of the campus as an unwelcoming place is another example. As the anonymous administrator pointed out, to the degree that we sacrifice principle for the sake of senior staff comity, we are complicit in undermining the potential positive impact of sound theory/research.

What We're Doing and Can Do in Response

Many student affairs professionals are committed to engaging around these difficult issues. I asked my colleagues across the country to share with me some of the ways that they are addressing equity, civility, and safety on their campuses. The good news is that we are trying many approaches—some new innovations and some variations on the tried and true—to find the ones that work the best on our campuses. "Food For Thought" professional development luncheons, divisional common reading and discussion sessions, the review of American College Personnel Association (ACPA)/NASPA competencies and CAS Standards, monthly meetings with campus social justice educators, passive education poster campaigns, movie and discussion series, renewed commitment to mediation, and partnering with faculty on teaching civil discourse skills are just a few of the ideas being tried on college campuses.

Increasingly, we see concerns about civility, equity, and safety manifest themselves on our campuses as turbulent conflicts. When these conflicts make the news, all too often the goal for senior administrators is to diffuse the crisis. While I understand the impetus behind such responses, our work as student affairs educators and the theory and research that forms our professional foundations tells us that instead we need to be focused on intentionally bringing our community together. Our priority must be first and foremost for the educational benefit of our students.

If, as researchers, we are committed to our research contributions living beyond the journal and the next round of citations and instead shape the work of the profession, then we need to invest time in the thoughtful development of a strong implications for practice section in all of our research manuscripts. Researchers should consider partnering with practitioners in developing those implications.

Publishing a study should only be the *initial* step to making research known to the community. Other proactive measures need be taken to encourage the uptake of theory and research. Consider distributing results to college and university administrators with whom relationships have been forged. Making a commitment to presenting research findings at practitioner attended conferences is another good step. The Association for the Study of Higher Education is an important organization for higher education researchers but its ability to reach practitioners pales in comparison to organizations such as NASPA or ACPA. Regional and other functional area-specific conferences are also excellent venues to consider.

Professional associations must do more to make cutting edge research a focal point for conferences and find new models to allow researchers to present without the burden of costly conference attendance. The afternoon poster session is not succeeding as the answer to this dilemma. It's time to think out of the box for ways to help important research and theory development reach practitioners.

Finally, student affairs educators must prioritize the consumption of current research and theory. Actively seek ways to support each other in this important effort. Host a book discussion or a colleague coffee break focused on a new article. Schedule time on your calendar every other week to peruse journals and other publications. Ask your counterparts at neighboring institutions what recommendations they might have for insightful research. Search out new colleagues, especially those who are coming from masters and PhD programs, for conversations about what they have been reading. Create opportunities to talk with others about what you've been reading and how you're making sense of it.

Conclusion

There is important work for everyone, researchers and practitioners alike, as we shepherd this latest generation of students through their college years, never more so than when it comes to equity, civility, and safety. If practitioners are serious about doing our best possible work, then we must prioritize staying abreast of the latest research and literature. We must make time to read and comprehend theory. We must actively apply theory and we must use the research in our practices. Researchers need to purposefully engage with practitioners and seek ways to connect our work to practitioners. Nowhere in American higher education is this more important than research and practice related to equity, civility, and safety.

Discussion Questions

1. Does one of the three models (Love, Evans and Guido, Reason and Kimball) resonate more than the others with you? If so, which one and why?
2. What obstacles stand in your way when it comes to regularly reading the latest research in student affairs?
3. What strategies do you and your colleagues have for prioritizing your commitment to engaging with the latest research?

Notes

1. Love, P. (2012). Informal theory: The ignored link in theory-to-practice. *Journal of College Student Development, 53*(2), 177–191.
2. Ibid., p. 179.
3. https://www.merriam-webster.com/dictionary/autism%20spectrum%20disorder
4. Evans, N. J., & Guido, F. M. (2012). Response to Patrick Love's "informal theory": A rejoinder. *Journal of College Student Development, 53*(2), 192–200.
5. Ibid., p. 199.
6. Sanford, N., & Adelson, J. (1962). *The American college: A psychological and social interpretation of higher learning.* New York, NY: Wiley.
7. Reason, R. D., & Kimball, E. W. (2012). A new theory-to-practice model for student affairs: Integrating scholarship, context, and reflection. *Journal of Student Affairs Research and Practice, 49*(4), 359–376.
8. Ibid., p. 360.
9. Ibid., p. 373.
10. Ibid., p. 372.
11. Ibid., p. 368.
12. S. Westfall, personal communication, September 15, 2017.
13. L. Landreman, personal communication, September 10, 2017.
14. H. Toutain, personal communication, September 14, 2017.
15. S. Westfall, personal communication, September 15, 2017.
16. H. Toutain, personal communication, September 14, 2017.
17. S. Westfall, personal communication, September 15, 2017.
18. L. Landreman, personal communication, September 10, 2017.
19. H. Toutain, personal communication, September 14, 2017.
20. L. Landreman, personal communication, September 10, 2017.
21. L. Landreman, personal communication, September 10, 2017.
22. Green, L., Ottosson, J., Garcia, C., Hiatt, R., & Roditis, M. (2009). Diffusion theory and knowledge dissemination, utilization, and integration in public health. *Annual Review of Public Health (30)*, 151–174, p. 171.
23. Ensler, E. (1996). *The vagina monologues.* New York, NY: Dramatists Play Service.

Considering the Practical Usefulness of Higher Education Research and Theory in Promoting Equity, Civility, and Safety

Nicholas A. Bowman

At the risk of sounding uncritical and biased (as I have known JoNes VanHecke for more than 15 years), I agree with most of the arguments advanced in her essay. In particular, I concur with the major factors she identified as contributing to student affairs educators' under-utilization of research: failure to prioritize the work, failure to see the work as one's own, researchers writing to the wrong audience, and failure to stand for one's own convictions (timing of publication is perhaps less important than those other reasons). I also appreciated her insightful points about some people "opting out" of engaging meaningfully with issues of equity, civility, and safety as well as the importance of institutional contexts in shaping the consideration of research and theory within practice. She presented several authors' perspectives on the role of informal theory and appeared to lean toward the views of Reason and Kimball;[1] I would do the same.

However, I have two major issues that I want to add to this conversation. First, as a faculty member who spends a great deal of time conducting research and reading other scholars' work, researchers deserve far more of the blame than VanHecke has assigned them. Second, although this chapter is technically about research, VanHecke talked quite a bit about theory and its use. I think this subtle scope shift is important, and I agree with the implicit assumption that theory is often more useful than specific research findings in terms of informing day-to-day practice.

Casting Blame on Researchers

Toward the beginning of her essay, VanHecke poses several questions about the use of theory. The first one jumped out to me: "Why don't we turn to the latest journal articles to make decisions about helping our students find a balance between free speech and accountability when someone yells bias-laden insults from a moving car at a student perceived as belonging to a historically underrepresented group?"[2] Frankly, I think this is because the latest journal articles are nearly useless for addressing the important question of how to respond to this incident. An ideal research study related to this issue could examine (a) the impact of the adoption of an institutional free speech or hate speech policy on the frequency of such incidents, or (b) the impact of a specific intervention designed either to help the victim or to deal with the offender on subsequent outcomes for those students. Unfortunately, scholars conduct this type of research far less often than they should.

Instead, most research focuses on a broader level of abstraction about whether a particular type of intervention is helpful, and my own research is no exception. For example, I can tell you with some confidence that college diversity workshops enhance civic outcomes six years after graduation,[3] but those findings provide no insight into what exactly that workshop should entail, how long it should be, or who should facilitate it. Knowing that diversity workshops have long-term effects is certainly important for practitioners who want to engage in evidence-based practice, but student affairs educators need guidance above and beyond knowing that a type of intervention is effective, especially when it can be implemented in many different ways.

VanHecke talked about the lengthy publication process for peer-reviewed research, which is certainly a concern. Some major higher education journals have (or have recently had) a two-year delay between the acceptance of a manuscript and publication in the journal. I recently had a paper under review at a journal for nine months before we received an initial decision; the decision was that we needed to make some revisions, resubmit the updated paper to the journal, and then wait for the next decision. This challenge certainly needs to be addressed, and some journals are doing so by shortening the review time and by publishing recently accepted articles online before they appear in a printed issue. However, the research questions examined in these journal articles are generally not so time-sensitive that this problem negatively affects practitioners, since the articles often do not focus on practical concerns of the day. Some researchers may argue that this is a chicken-and-egg problem: Why would researchers focus on studying time-sensitive questions when their work may not be quickly available to the practitioners who would benefit from reading it? There are certainly faster ways to share findings than publication in selective peer-reviewed journals (e.g., blogs, conference presentations), and researchers should share their work through these outlets more frequently. That said, existing reward structures strongly favor the types of research dissemination that are generally the slowest.

VanHecke also discussed the important problem of research papers not providing enough implications for practice. Two additional problems related to implications are noteworthy. First, researchers frequently provide implications that their study simply does not support (these implications are often supported instead by previous studies). Second, in a potentially related problem, the implications provided in the paper are simply not new. Papers on equity and safety almost invariably call for greater attention to relevant issues and increased efforts to assist students, especially those who need it most. These points can and should be repeated, but what concrete implications can be offered that were not already well established from previous research? When I write a paper that shares new research results, I have a personal goal to provide at least one implication that is truly novel. This feels like a shockingly low bar, but many research papers never reach that threshold.

As is often true, pointing out problems is much easier than creating solutions. To start, journal editors and reviewers need to require that research papers provide better practical implications for a paper to be published. Studies that explore important problems of practice in a rigorous manner should also be more greatly valued by academic journals and by university promotion and tenure committees. In addition, doctoral programs that train future faculty can play a key role in this process, because they can help students determine not only meaningful research topics but also how to make sense of the usefulness of these findings.

Practical Usefulness of Theory Versus Research Findings

The influential social psychologist Kurt Lewin famously stated, "There is nothing so practical as a good theory."[4] Despite the widespread discussion about the theory–practice divide, I tend to agree with this statement. Research findings may be useful for discovering which practices are effective, but theory is essential for knowing why these practices are successful and how best to design them. Whether consciously or not, student affairs educators are drawing upon some theory or belief structure that informs how they engage with students during advising appointments, disciplinary meetings, informational workshops, and other interactions. In some ways, the findings of individual research studies are—and should be—less important in guiding one's actions in those moment-to-moment encounters than are theories about moral development, self-authorship, and/or learning and cognition.

In the domains of equity, civility, and safety, various theories may inform understanding of student experiences and productive actions; some of these examine campus climate for diversity, learning from diversity engagement, social stratification, psychological needs, and college student attrition. Returning to the diversity workshop example, multiple theories can provide important insights into the ideal design of a workshop. Informed by these perspectives, productive approaches would likely include the use of real-world personal examples, facilitation of meaningful intergroup interactions, incorporation of different types of activities, and attention to both cognitive and emotional pathways of learning.

As an additional problem with incorporating research findings, some studies reach different conclusions about whether a certain practice actually promotes a desired outcome. First-year seminars provide a great example of this issue. According to a recent systematic review of the literature, over 180 studies have examined the link between taking a first-year seminar and retention to the second year of college.[5] With that much research, you might assume (or hope) that we would know exactly whether and when first-year seminars promote student retention. Sadly, we do not. That extensive review found a small, positive relationship overall, which is consistent with the findings from two other reviews.[6] However, these reviews found different results across studies, such that individual researchers do not agree on how effective this practice might be or whether it is effective at all.

A final cautionary note about the use of research findings relates to whether writers are using the literature and their own work to provide an in-depth understanding of relevant research versus using them to prove a predetermined viewpoint. As we consider campus civility and safety, considerable theory and research supports the importance of experiencing a campus climate that is safe emotionally and physically, and considerable evidence also exists for the importance of having one's viewpoints challenged for fostering learning and growth.[7] Therefore, an argument that is in favor of upholding all free speech, or conversely of avoiding all controversial viewpoints, is likely missing important nuances that should inform practice.

So how can student affairs educators identify trustworthy research? No approach is foolproof, but some tips may be helpful. First, studies that have been published after going through a peer-review process, which occurs at many journals, are more likely to have trustworthy results. Some of the most selective journals also publish some of the strongest studies. Second, be cautious when reading research from an organization or authors that have something to gain from the findings ("collegestudyguides.com found that buying their products leads to higher grades!"). Third, systematic reviews of the literature can combine the results of individual studies and examine how these are similar or different across a variety of students, institutions, and research designs. As a result, a strong literature review may provide the best source of available knowledge.

Conclusion

This response sought to expand upon VanHecke's excellent discussion of using student affairs research and theory in practice. In summary, higher education researchers—in terms of individual scholars and broader systems in which that scholarship occurs—deserve a fair bit of blame for the underuse of research and theory. Moreover, the application of theory is crucial for guiding effective practice; this use is generally more important and productive than drawing upon the findings of individual research studies, especially at the microlevel of how to implement policies and practices as well as how to work with students.

Discussion Questions

1. How do you use research and theory in your own work?
2. What research topics and issues do you want to learn more about, especially those related to equity, civility, and safety?
3. How can you and your colleagues work together to facilitate this learning and application?

Notes

1. Reason, R. D., & Kimball, E. W. (2012). A new theory-to-practice model for student affairs: Integrating scholarship, context, and reflection. *Journal of Student Affairs Research and Practice, 49*(4), 359–376.

2. VanHecke, J. R., this volume, p. 360.

3. Bowman, N. A., Denson, N., & Park, J. J. (2016). Racial/cultural awareness workshops and post-college civic engagement: A propensity score matching approach. *American Educational Research Journal, 53*(8), 1556–1587.

4. Lewin, K. (1943). Psychology and the process of group living. *Journal of Social Psychology, 17*, 113–131, p. 118.

5. Permzadian, V., & Credé, M. (2016). Do first-year seminars improve college grades and retention: A quantitative review of their overall effectiveness and an examination of moderators of effectiveness. *Review of Educational Research, 86*(1), 277–316.

6. Mayhew, M. J., Rockenbach, A. N., Bowman, N. A., Seifert, T. A., Wolniak, G. C., with Pascarella, E. T., & Terenzini, P. T. (2016). *How college affects students: Vol. 3, 21st century evidence that higher education works.* San Francisco, CA: Jossey-Bass.; Robbins, S. B., Oh, I. S., Le, H., & Button, C. (2009). Intervention effects on college performance and retention as mediated by motivational, emo-

tional, and social control factors: Integrated meta-analytic path analyses. *Journal of Applied Psychology, 94*(5), 1163–1184.

7. Hurtado, S., Alvarez, C. L., Guillermo-Wann, C., Cuellar, M., & Arellano, L. (2012). A model for diverse learning environments. In M. B. Paulsen (Ed.), *Higher education: Handbook of theory and research* (Vol. 27, pp. 41–122). New York, NY: Springer.

20

How Can/Should Student Affairs Educators Use Assessment to Improve Educational Practices Related to Equity, Civility, and Safety?

Using Deconstructed Assessment to Address Issues of Equity, Civility, and Safety on College Campuses

Gavin W. Henning

Issues of equity, civility, and safety continue to be paramount issues on college campuses. Access and success in higher education will continue to be important as long as entrance rates and graduation rates are lower for minoritized students. Despite a decrease in crime on college campuses,[1] safety remains an ever-present concern for students and parents. Sexual assault and other forms of violence, such as microaggressions, persist.[2] Following the 2016 presidential election in the United States, civility has become a growing concern in higher education.

Assessment is commonplace on college campuses. With increased calls for return on investment, assessment is required to ensure accountability in student learning and success as well as program effectiveness. While vital to these purposes, assessment can be expanded to help understand how power and oppression impact student experience in higher education.

Assessment has been growing in acceptance, with many in higher education using it to investigate the effectiveness of programs and services. Current and traditional approaches to assessment examine issues of equity, civility, and safety. However, these methods center on prevalence and effectiveness of programs and services related to these issues. What they fail to do is uncover the basis for these issues in a way that provides opportunities to address them. A new approach to assessment that moves beyond its positivist beginnings and reframes the purpose of assessment is needed. Assessment can be a powerful tool in understanding and addressing equity, civility, and safety. But, to do so, it must undergo a radical transformation moving beyond its traditional use and deconstruct social structures that perpetuate oppression, which undergirds these issues.

History and Evolution of Assessment in Higher Education

Purposes for assessment are changing. The historical evolution of assessment began with program evaluation, as outlined in the 1937 and 1949 publications of the *Student Personnel Point of Views*, by the American Council on Education.[3] Research regarding student learning and development was added as a purpose of assessment during the 1960s and the 1970s.[4] Between 1970 and 1990, stakeholders outside education (e.g., legislatures) furthered the assessment movement by calling for accountability, but the focus remained rooted in evaluation of student learning and programs. In other words, assessment addressed the extent to which programs and services achieved their goals and added to the value of higher education.

Student affairs assessment evolved in the 1980s and 1990s and proliferated into the early 2000s. In addition to program evaluation, assessment was also utilized for program development as higher education professionals and student affairs educators realized the benefit of outcomes to inform the program creation process. Assessment was taking on a more primary role as it became integrated with program development, not simply an activity performed after a program had been implemented. As the use of assessment grew, so did literature to support this emerging subfield. Between 1996 and 2006, 3 books on the subject of assessment were published by scholars. In contrast, between 2006 and 2016, 11 books were published on this topic. These resources primarily focused on assessment methods and processes, rather than underlying values and philosophy.

Assessment arose and matured because of the need to evaluate programs for accountability and improvement. The landscape of higher education is changing and new approaches to assessment are necessary. Assessment should continue to focus on student learning and program evaluation, but it must also begin to examine the underpinnings and structures that impact higher education and student experience.

Assessment Functions, Philosophy, and Methodology

Two main functions of assessment are accountability and improvement.[5] These purposes have been rooted in a positivistic paradigm that focuses on objectivity and has kept a "safe" distance between the assessor and the assessment domains, with the intent of providing more truthful or rigorous assessment results. In positivism, the knower is separate from the known.[6] Objectivity has been viewed as a critical characteristic of rigorous assessment. Current traditions of assessment embedded in a positivistic paradigm are limited in impact because objectivity is a barrier to fully understanding a phenomenon.

Emerging approaches to assessment provide opportunities to expand the scope and enhance the impact of the practice. Some scholars advocate for assessment to be considered inquiry.[7] Inquiry is both a function of assessment and a methodological approach. Different than past approaches to assessment, inquiry emphasizes reflection, as assessment often ends up comprising data collection, analysis, and reporting with little opportunity for reflection. Bourke furthers the concept of inquiry by describing it as answering questions through seeking information, positioning assessment as a learning process grounded in curiosity rather than documentation driven by accountability.[8] An inquiry approach to assessment builds upon constructivist and interpretivist philosophical paradigms rather than a positivistic one. Unlike positivism, which centers on objectivity, the constructivist and interpretivist perspectives embrace subjectivity as the belief that individuals cannot be distanced from a phenomenon. Individuals construct and interpret reality based on their values, beliefs, and experiences. Effective inquiry also needs to consider values, beliefs, and experiences. Assessment that embraces subjectivity as well as objectivity would be able to provide a more complete picture of oppressive structures in higher education.

Positivist approaches to assessment are useful when evaluating programs and services related to equity, civility, and safety. They also enable understanding the prevalence of issues on college campuses related to these topics. Positivistic approaches would focus on perspectives such as how many sexual assaults occur on campus and how those have changed over time, what the climate is like on campus for minoritized groups, the effectiveness of an orientation program regarding consent in reducing sexual assaults, or the effectiveness of individual outreach in helping minoritized individuals access academic support services. However, effectiveness and pervasiveness only tell part of the story. These methodological approaches cannot help explain the underlying factors influencing phenomenon.

An inquiry methodological approach to these three issues would question why sexual assault is happening on campus, why minoritized groups access support services less frequently than majority students, and why there is an increase in discussions around free speech and what students are allowed to say. Assessment, in the traditional sense, can help understand these questions, but it may not dig deep enough into an issue to uncover underlying factors.

To understand how power and oppression impact equity, civility, and safety a new philosophical approach to assessment and thus a new methodological approach, building on the concept of assessment as inquiry, must be taken.

Inquiry as an assessment methodology is based upon a constructivist/interpretivist philosophical perspective. DeLuca Fernandez[9] takes this approach a step further. She frames assessment through a critical theory lens, suggesting that assessment should interrogate and address equity questions in higher education, asserting that power, privilege, and structures must be exposed by assessment.[10] This approach moves past inquiry, evaluation, and prevalence approaches to examining phenomena. Since power and privilege are rooted in history, cultural norms, and societal contexts, assumptions regarding how society works must be made explicit. In other words, society's social structures impact phenomena and how they are experienced and understood by individuals. Without this deconstruction, underlying oppressive structures cannot be known and thus remedied. Advancing a critical theory approach to assessment necessitates a subjective methodology that seeks a broader understanding of a phenomenon considering how individuals and their interpretation and understanding of the phenomenon are understanding of the phenomenon is influenced by social structures such as power and oppression. Equity, civility, and safety are subjects that benefit from this critical theory-based approach to assessment.

Critical Theory and Poststructuralism

Critical theory and poststructuralism philosophical paradigms are frames for understanding the impact of power and oppression on assessment.

Critical Theory

Critical theory, based on Marxism, arose between World War I and World War II as a critique of society and a rejection of positivism and phenomenology.[11] It is one point on a continuum of philosophy of knowledge. The continuum starts with positivism, followed by postpositivism, interpretivism, constructivism, and then critical theory. A central tenet of critical theory is that individuals' reality cannot be separated from forms of oppression. Critical theory seeks to expose the hidden assumptions of how society works. In addition to understanding how oppression influences reality, its goal is the liberation of individuals from the constraints of social structures such as power and oppression. Critical theory introduces reflection as a tool to make oppression and other societal structures (e.g., power and privilege) explicit.

Investigating the influence of societal and campus oppression on colleges' reality is critical to assessing equity, civility, and safety. Reflection and thus critique are methodological tools of critical theory. Building on inquiry, reflection is a useful tool for exploring issues of equity, civility, and safety.

Poststructuralism

Poststructuralism follows critical theory on the continuum of philosophies of knowledge and extends critical theory's analysis of the link between knowledge and power.[12] While constructivism challenges positivism for not considering the individual in knowledge creation, poststructuralism confronts the assumption of positivism that the world can be perceived without investigation of the assumptions underlying the phenomenon.[13] Poststructuralism centers on wholeness and connection rather than disconnection between experience or knowledge and psychological and sociological structures and influences.[14] These structures include social norms, institutionalized power, privilege, and oppression.

Poststructuralists posit that both the phenomenon and the systems of knowledge that produced it must be examined when studying a phenomenon. Poststructuralists maintain that unconscious and hidden structures and forces govern behavior, even if people are unaware of them,[15] which is why it is essential to expose those structures and forces. Unconscious biases are one such force. Through unconscious biases, people act in ways that are microaggressions against minoritized populations. These microaggressions then influence how minoritized students experience college.

As discussed earlier, using a positivist lens to assess equity, civility, and safety would center on prevalence and effectiveness of programs to address these three issues. A positivist approach to assessment does not necessarily consider how individuals interpret their experience. An example of assessment through an interpretivist perspective would be assessing not only the prevalence of issues related to civility but also how individuals make sense of the experience and how it impacts their life as a college student. If a student were the victim of racist graffiti on their door, this new approach to assessment would examine how this graffiti affected the student in the moment as well as in everyday life. Poststructuralism delves deeper than individual interpretation to uncover social structures that impact phenomenon. A poststructuralist approach to assessment of equity, civility, and safety would attempt not only to explain how power and oppression impact how people experience these issues, which is a critical theory approach, but also reason how social structures influence how oppression manifests. In the same racist graffiti example, assessment would investigate structural components such as campus culture, policies regarding bias incidents, and past administrative responses to such behaviors. In regard to equity, a poststructuralist assessment approach may try to understand campus culture and how norms and values influence how oppression is expressed.

Like critical theorists, poststructuralists argue that reflection is vital to understanding how social structure influences oppression, which then impacts individuals' experiences. However, reflection must intentionally deconstruct a phenomenon to uncover social structure influences. Thus, poststructuralism, through the use of deconstruction, is both a facilitator of and an opportunity for reflection.[16]

Application of Poststructuralism to Assessment

Supplementing the positivist paradigm of assessment with a poststructural paradigm has profound implications for assessment practice. A poststructural approach to assessment centers on deconstruction, but in two different forms: product and process. Assessment as product is the analysis of the phenomena being assessed. A deconstructed process of assessment is an intentional method to achieve the specific goal of uncovering and addressing oppressive social structures that influence the phenomenon. With this approach, assessment furthers equity and social justice and is not just a data process. The product of deconstructed assessment is an analysis of a phenomenon that exposes the social structures that shape power and oppression. An example would be an assessment of an orientation program. The assessment focuses on how the structure and operation of the orientation program perpetuates oppression. The process may involve examining how orientation leaders are selected, with the product an analysis regarding how the selection process for orientation leaders is implicitly biased to privilege majority students.

McArthur suggests that a question assessment must answer is "for whom and by whom?"[17] Questions such as this seek to expose underlying assumptions of the assessment process and deconstruct the positionality of those involved. This student-centered approach uses reflection to suggest that there may be hidden assumptions in the assessment process. Assessment performed "on" students by practitioners or instructors establishes an additional power structure within the larger social system, as students are subjects being studied. The assessment process changes when students are collaborators. Involving students as assessors empowers them to contribute to and interpret their experience.

Deconstructed assessment is more than a technical procedure[18] or a procedural process.[19] While methodological steps are implemented, a concurrent goal of deconstructed assessment is social justice through interrogating how social structures such as power, oppression, and privilege influence programs and services, and finally how those programs and services affect students.

Deconstructed assessment seeks to make explicit the biases of individuals conducting assessments. Assessors bring their experience, identity, and privilege to the assessment process. A positivist approach promotes objectivity through the enactment of a methodology that separates the assessor from the phenomenon. When guided by a poststructural paradigm, a goal of the assessment process is unmasking the impact assessors' experiences and assumptions have on the assessment process.

With a deconstructed approach to assessing an orientation program, the "for whom" is the students, not the program directors. By exploring how they experience the orientation program, it becomes possible to question how an orientation program may be inequitable.

Characteristics of Deconstructed Assessment

Deconstructed assessment has five characteristics distinguishing it from other approaches to assessment.

Assessment as inquiry is the first characteristic of deconstructed assessment. Reflection is a key element of critical theories, including poststructuralism.[20] Individuals performing assessment need to consider and make explicit their own subjectivities as well as their relationships with the data and the people represented in the data.[21] Failure to recognize what assessors bring to the assessment limits its impact; more critically, unexamined subjectivity can also reinforce privilege and oppressive power structures. An inquiry approach to deconstructed assessment naturally lends itself to qualitative rather than quantitative methods, particularly narrative as a tool to represent findings. When assessing orientation, reflection would be built into the process. Assessors would first examine their own biases about programs such as these. They would engage in reflection through journaling or memo writing. In the data collection process, they would encourage reflection on experience from participants and organizers.

A second characteristic of deconstructed assessment is an activist/social change approach to assessment not only to uncover power and relation issues inherent in social structures that impact various phenomena but also to effect change to dismantle oppression through assessment. Deconstructed assessment brings to light the social structural components influencing issues of equity, civility, and safety so that these are not just topical issues but symptoms of more complex power relations. A deconstructed approach to assessing an orientation program would investigate effectiveness by exploring student experience and how social, campus, and program structures maintain oppression. This examination would result in changing structures to minimize or eradicate oppression in the program.

A third characteristic is increased emphasis on the use of qualitative assessment methods. Quantitative methods such as surveys would still be used, as there would still be a need for larger scale data collection.[22] However, to be able to deconstruct phenomena to understand the underlying assumptions as well as uncover how societal structures influence a phenomenon, qualitative tools such as interviews, case studies, and narratives must be used to deconstruct phenomena to understand the underlying assumptions as well as uncover how societal structures influence a phenomenon. Deconstructed assessment will also more frequently employ multiple methods. Triangulation of data through multiple methods provides a more complex and nuanced picture of a phenomenon than a single method of data collection. Any assessment of orientation would emphasize data collection techniques such as interviews, focus groups, or journaling to gather deep, rich, narrative data regarding individual experience.

A fourth characteristic of deconstructed assessment is student involvement in the assessment process. Students are equal partners in the assessment process, from design to analysis to change promotion. Deconstructed assessment would mirror participatory action research, where assessors partner with community members to identify an issue for exploration, collaborative investigation, and interpretation of findings. Involving students in assessment can increase support for any changes that result from the findings, because students have been a part of the process to deconstruct their experience and recommend changes.

A fifth characteristic of deconstructed assessment is what Montenegro and Jankowski call *cultural responsiveness*, a pedagogy where instructors use an asset-based approach to teaching that includes students' cultures.[23] Culturally responsive assessment assures that the assessment process, from outcome development to findings interpretation, is considerate of students' cultures and differences. In addition, culturally responsive assessment uses varying assessment methods appropriate for the different ways students may demonstrate their learning.[24] Assessment that does not consider culture or equity can privilege some types of learning over others.[25] Deconstructed assessment of orientation would include data collection that explored how the program was developed and implemented to honor students' cultures and experiences. A variety of assessment techniques would be used and cultural context would be a lens during data analysis.

Using Deconstructed Assessment to Improve Practices Related to Equity, Civility, and Safety

Given that a poststructural approach to assessment uncovers and examines how power, privilege, and oppression are products and processes, it is well suited to address issues of equity, civility, and safety on college campuses.

Deconstructed Assessment as Product

As a product, deconstructed assessment assesses the effectiveness of programs and services to address equity, civility, and safety. When assessing effectiveness, deconstructed assessment will investigate how social structures such as power, privilege, and oppression influence programs and services.

Another way deconstructed assessment can be a product is through assessing student learning and development. To truly understand college student learning and success, students' experiences must examine invisible influences from social structures and underlying assumptions about college, structures, and experiences. Through this approach, the effects of equity, civility, and safety on students' learning and development can be known.

Through deconstructed assessment, assessors can seek to understand the intersectionality of student social identities, as this understanding will assist practitioners and instructors in meeting students' needs. Social identities are largely influenced by society's power structures. To provide the most useful programs and services, student affairs educators need to understand students' multiple identities within current power and social structures.

Deconstructed Assessment as Process

Deconstructed assessment focuses on reflection, which can be integrated throughout the process, beginning with positionality of assessors to How social structures influence the way data are collected, analyzed, and interpreted. Rather than simply describing equity, civility, and safety, assessors can use deconstructed assessment to analyze the component parts of each issue and understand the assumptions regarding the issues and the impact of social structures on those issues.

Deconstructed assessment employs multiple methods, with strong reliance on qualitative methods. Qualitative data gathered through multiple methods can provide a fuller perspective of a phenomenon that affords an opportunity for deconstruction. In addition, storytelling can be employed by using narrative to capture student assumptions and interpretation of experiences.

Finally, deconstructed assessment should approach the assessment process through a social justice lens. It will be important to understand the impact of language, particularly gender-inclusive language. Also critical is the inclusion of all voices, or at least of representative voices, when assessing a phenomenon. As noted earlier, all data should be disaggregated to understand the experience of specific groups of students.

Political Implications

Assessment is inherently a political practice as it involves resource allocation.[26] As such, there will be political implications using a deconstructed assessment approach. Politics are also infused throughout deconstructed assessment, as it is an inclusive process that seeks to uncover the assumptions and influence of social structures. With a point of uncovering assumptions and impact of structures, there will likely be impact on institutional priorities. Assessment findings may suggest the need to provide additional resources to specific groups of students, dismantle power structures that impede student success, or establish more inclusive learning environments.

Competencies Needed

Proficiency in all American College Personnel Association (ACPA)/NASPA professional competency areas is critical in addressing issues of equity, civility, and safety. The intersection of two of these areas is particularly salient when assessing around these issues. The knowledge and skills addressed in the social justice competency are key prerequisites for engaging in deconstructed assessment. These competencies address knowledge of how systems of oppression operate, how oppression can be systemic and integrated within a structure, and how to effect change. Without this skill and knowledge, it is difficult to use assessment to understand how social structures impact oppression, which affects individual experience at college. The assessment competency area covers the skills and knowledge to perform assessment as a method. As currently framed, the assessment skills and knowledge articulated do not enable someone to effectively engage in deconstructed assessment, where individuals must have a set of skills that intersect these two competency areas. Individuals having skills in both areas would understand systems of oppression and structures that contribute to it as well as strategies to address oppression. They would also have skills to effectively execute assessment methods.

Conclusion

Deconstructed assessment is a new approach to assessment that serves as both product and process. In addition to understanding the effectiveness of programs and services, using a poststructuralist lens for assessment transforms it from a transactional procedure of collecting and analyzing data into a transformational process for decision-making and social justice to expose systems of power, privilege, and oppression to address issues of equity, civility, and safety on college campuses.

Discussion Questions

1. Deconstructed assessment is a powerful approach to assessment that is both product and process. How can you implement deconstructed assessment in your work?
2. Involvement of students is a key characteristic in deconstructed assessment. In what ways can you involve students in the assessment process in your work?
3. Deconstructed assessment seeks to expose and address power, privilege, and oppression in student affairs. How can you envision using deconstructed assessment to address equity, civility, and safety by exposing and addressing the influences of power, privilege, and oppression on these issues?

Notes

1. National Center for Education Statistics. (n.d.) *College crime.* Retrieved from https://nces.ed.gov/fastfacts/display.asp?id=804

2. Godderis, R., & Root, J. (2017). Addressing sexual violence on post-secondary campuses is a collective responsibility. *Teaching and Learning Journal, 9*(3), 1–9.

3. American Council on Education. (1937). *Student personnel point of view.* Washington, DC: Author.

4. Ewell, P. (2002). History and current status of assessment. In T. Banta & Associates (Eds.), *Building a scholarship of assessment* (pp. 3–25). San Francisco, CA: Jossey-Bass.

5. Ibid.

6. Agger, B. (2004). Critical theory, poststructuralism, postmodernism: Their sociological relevance. *Annual Review of Sociology, 17,* 105–131.

7. Newhart, D. (2015). Positioning the *Journal of Student Affairs Inquiry. Journal of Student Affairs Inquiry, 1*(1), 1–4; Bourke, B. (2015, November 15). Inquiry and the assessment cycle [Web log post]. Retrieved from https://www .linkedin.com/pulse/inquiry-assessment-cycle-brian-bourke

8. Bourke, Inquiry and the assessment cycle.

9. DeLuca Fernandez, S. (2015, December 5). *Critical assessment.* Webinar presented at Student Affairs Assessment Leaders Structured Conversations.

10. Bronner, S. (2011). *Critical theory: A very short introduction.* New York, NY: Oxford University Press.

11. Ibid.

12. Peters, M., & Burbules, N. (2004). *Poststructuralism and educational research.* Lanham, MD: Rowman and Littlefield.

13. Agger, Critical theory, poststructuralism, postmodernism.

14. Peters & Burbules, *Poststructuralism and educational research.*

15. Ibid.

16. Besley, C. (2002). *Poststructuralism: A very short introduction.* New York, NY: Oxford University Press.

17. McArthur, J. (2016). Assessment for social justice: The role of assessment in achieving social justice. *Assessment and Evaluation in Higher Education, 41*(7), 967–981, p. 978.

18. Agger, Critical theory, poststructuralism, postmodernism.

19. McArthur, Assessment for social justice: The role of assessment in achieving social justice.

20. Peters & Burbules, *Poststructuralism and educational research.*

21. Bourke, B. (2017). Advancing toward social justice via student affairs inquiry. *Journal of Student Affairs Inquiry, 2*(1), 1–18.

22. Montenegro, E., & Jankowski, N. A. (2017, January). *Equity and assessment: Moving towards culturally responsive assessment* (Occasional Paper No. 29). Urbana, IL: University of Illinois and Indiana University, National Institute for Learning Outcomes Assessment (NILOA).

23. Ibid.

24. Ibid.

25. Ibid.

26. Henning & Roberts, *Student affairs assessment.*

Assessment as Power: Using Our Privilege to Center the Student Voice

Abby C. Trout

avin W. Henning advances a compelling argument in support of an inquiry- and critical theory-based approach to assessment in higher education. Embracing this ideology allows student affairs educators to evolve assessment practice beyond conventional program evaluation and toward culturally responsive social change that privileges students' voices. Given the power of assessment, data, and research described by Henning, using deconstructed assessment lifts student voices otherwise excluded from assessment's powerful position in the decision-making landscape of higher education. In this essay, I affirm particular tenets of deconstructed assessment and advocate for the need for students, especially from marginalized identities, to be collaborators in assessment. Then, I discuss questions for student affairs educators to consider to use deconstructed assessment with persistence, care, and accountability in practice.

Assessment as Power

The power of assessment resonated for me years ago when I conducted an assessment on what students learn as a result of completing internships. In particular, I learned the importance data has not only in improving student services but also in communicating and advocating for the needs of students to powerful administrators. Ideas, rooted in assessment data, carry weight in higher education. A phenomenon presented as a result of assessment carries a certain amount of assumed objectivity that gives that phenomenon legitimacy in the eyes of many decision-makers.

Throughout my assessment, I used data from student journals written by approximately 100 student interns throughout their summer internships as well as from internship supervisors' performance reviews of the students, and data from several focus groups and individual interviews I conducted with student interns. A colleague in institutional research, a team of student researchers, and I analyzed the data and created themes centering on student learning outcomes. One theme that emerged was professionalism as a concept and the need for interns to better understand and navigate office and professional culture. Administrators embraced this issue and we brainstormed ways to incorporate teaching students about professionalism into our programs and services.

However, the dominant conceptualizations of professionalism are laden with unwritten rules that reinforce norms based on heterosexual, able-bodied, White, cis men. If we had used a deconstructed assessment approach, we still would have used the students' essays, focus groups, and interviews, but perhaps our next step would have examined the concept of professionalism from and guided by the perspectives of minoritized student populations and how it reinforces existing power structures. The results of this assessment would have lifted the student voice to a level that senior administrators may be more likely to hear and subsequently focused on exposing prejudice and discrimination in a commonly taught subject in career services. The more administrators understand the political capital created in assessment findings, the more we can use assessment to subvert and eradicate oppressive structures.

Henning rightfully asserts that traditional assessment methods—focused on objectivity, aggregated data, and effectiveness based on the trends of the majority—are limited in scope and when used alone sustain the status quo. I concur with the way Henning connects privilege and historical and societal context to the product and process of assessment calling for a broader and more critical approach to assessment—one that explicitly deconstructs the role of power and oppression within phenomena. The inclusion of the student perspective and voice throughout the assessment process and as a key outcome of assessment disrupts power-laden and oppressive structures and evolves assessment beyond just a data process.

The Imperative Need for Centering the Student Voice

Including student voice in assessment best tells the story of student learning and development because narratives come from the source. If our intention with deconstructed assessment is to make the student experience more just and inclusive, then we need to challenge the power dynamics we occupy as administrators and collaborate with students. Partnering with students in the assessment process acknowledges their rightful status as experts about the student experience and honors their agency to guide and influence data collection and analysis.[1]

Reflecting on my assessment of internship student learning outcomes, to future career services professionals I now recommend coconstructing the assessment infrastructure (e.g., goals, methodology, feedback loops) with student partners from marginalized backgrounds to dissect the structures in professionalism within internships. The students' experiences and perspectives around the definition of *professionalism*, the ways in which that perception of professionalism maintains the status quo on and off campus, and the needs of students from marginalized identities would make up the assessment efforts versus a traditional focus on the perspectives and experiences from internship employers or career services staff. Additionally, Henning highlights the importance of disaggregating data. Disaggregating data centers marginalized populations and creates space to highlight their voices outside the confines of statistical significance.[2] As we seek to lift the voices of those marginalized groups that are smaller in number, in terms of a data sample size, this is imperative. Thus, I would look to the student partners to provide input on which populations are excluded in internships and examine how we could advance social justice in redefining professionalism through that lens. With the added focus of maintaining confidentiality, using assessment as advocacy in these ways allows those stories in the numerical minority to illuminate what the majority never could.

Obstacles and Strategies

Despite endorsing Henning's critical and deconstructed approach to assessment, I explicitly discuss two limitations for all student affairs educators to consider when implementing these methods. First: How do we manage the volume of data with a deconstructed assessment approach? Second: How do we invite in students from marginalized identities as collaborators in assessment without adding to their emotional labor? I explore these questions and offer modest recommendations to address these issues.

Managing Volume

Deconstructed assessment uses several qualitative tools such as narrative and triangulating data gathered through multiple methods to achieve many different outcomes. While I support the use of these methods, they produce vast quantities of data, which can easily overwhelm student affairs educators. Becoming overwhelmed with data may result in abandoning the assessment process and never using the data. Outcomes such as these stunt the progress of deconstructed assessment. I see this in my own practice as well as across higher education. However, managing the volume of data by constructing a sustainable data management system and process can help to ensure assessment data will be used. While I recognize that addressing the problem of proper data management may seem trivial in comparison to the other issues identified in this essay, as a practitioner this is a primary reason I see staff struggle to engage in assessment. If we do not complete our assessment or analyze our data we risk forfeiting one of our main goals in student affairs, to expose and eradicate oppression for silenced collegians.

Using technology and collaborating with colleagues across campus to create a user-friendly data management system have greatly increased my ability to engage in assessment. For example, in my assessment on intern learning outcomes I partnered with institutional research and university information technology services to code large amounts of qualitative data and create a database from which I or my colleagues could more easily query the data. These partner departments had the resources, knowledge, and infrastructure to help not only me but also my colleagues use and apply the data we collected. Every campus has different resources, so I encourage you to find colleagues with shared values but complementary skill sets to enhance your efforts.

The Emotional Drain on Students

Students from minoritized groups daily shoulder emotional and cognitive labor from society at large in addition to the expectations of college. Adrienne Green[3] notes this in her reflection on the emotional toll she and other students of color experience in the tension of processing racism in their own life on top of the demands of being a student. These labor demands will be increased if student affairs educators invite students to collaborate in assessment arenas. Some students may find the invitation to tell their story in deconstructed assessment to be another expectation for students from marginalized identities to educate the majority,[4] especially in light of the ever-present reality that campus politics may stunt any meaningful change. Throughout American history there has been an undeniable pattern that, when progress advances the rights of the oppressed, there is a backlash by those in power, thus compounding the costs on the oppressed.

To clarify—students are the narrators of their own stories and need to be respected as such. I do not point out this potential limitation to suggest otherwise. As I hold a number of privileged identities, the story of the emotional drain on people of marginalized identities by those in power is not mine to tell. However, it would be unethical and naive to not honestly acknowledge the potential for prejudicial backlash and emotional drain on students as well as other campus members (e.g., staff and faculty) of marginalized communities in using deconstructed assessment.

As educators, we can begin to address this limitation in many ways, although I will focus on three. First, we must acknowledge our responsibility for the backlash on students that often accompanies social justice progress. In using assessment as advocacy, "we have to be prepared to learn some ugly truths about ourselves."[5] We cannot merely react to the politics that may try to continue silencing the student stories amplified through deconstructed assessment. Instead we need to use what power and privilege we hold as administrators to proactively clear a space among the organizational structure of higher education for students to be heard. Second, we must provide students varying levels of participation. Outline what serving as a collaborative partner in assessment could look like at different levels of emotional and time investment. This could allow students to decide the degree to which they partner with the project without having to forfeit the opportunity to be heard. Third, we must proactively provide support to students throughout the process. Again, consider how you can utilize your privilege as an administrator to compensate and replenish in some way the energy you will ask student partners to expend.

Conclusion

An inquiry- and critical theory-based approach to assessment in higher education provides students from marginalized identities platforms to control the story of their experience and interpret how that impacts programs and services on campus. By evolving the power of assessment to the pursuit of social justice as the product and process, inviting students to be collaborators in assessment and centering their voice, and disaggregating data to better focus on the needs of specific groups, assessment addresses more than program evaluation and effectiveness. With the added focus of practitioners proceeding with effective data management, strategic leadership in the face of campus politics, and accountability to minimizing the emotional drain on marginalized communities, deconstructed assessment can shine light on and seek to interrogate silencing structures to take action toward change.

Discussion Questions

1. How can you better manage your data and campus resources to utilize your assessment to its highest social justice potential?
2. How can assessment practitioners use their power and privilege to support student partners in assessment?

3. What other limitations exist from your perspective in using decon-structed assessment, and how might you address them?

Notes

1. Heiser, C., Prince, K., & Levy, J. (2017). Examining critical theory as a framework to advance equity through student affairs assessment. *The Journal of Student Affairs Inquiry, 2*(1), 7–10.

2. Ibid.

3. Green, A. (2016, January 21). The cost of balancing academia and racism. *The Atlantic.* Retrieved from https://www.theatlantic.com/education/archive/2016/01/balancing-academia-racism/424887/?utm_source=atlfb

4. Lorde, A. (1984). *Sister outsider: Essays and speeches.* Trumansburg, NY: Crossing Press.

5. Bourke, B. (2017). Advancing toward social justice via student affairs inquiry. *The Journal of Student Affairs Inquiry, 2*(1), p. 7.

21

What Would It Take for Student Affairs Educators to Facilitate a Personal Learning Design Approach That Enhances Equity, Civility, and Safety?

Pursuing Equity, Civility, and Safety Through Personal Learning Design

Taran Cardone

Student affairs educators face the wicked problem[1] of equipping students for a diverse world both during and after college. A *wicked problem* is a complicated issue with unclear solutions and far-reaching implications. The current higher education landscape has many students from privileged backgrounds who have had minimal exposure to difference and the unknown.[2] Additionally, students from marginalized backgrounds, having only recently gained access to higher education, need significant support.[3] These complex issues necessitate student affairs educators to fashion more comprehensive approaches that serve *all* students.[4] Such an approach must address these issues in a manner as complex as the problem itself. I propose that personal learning design[5] is an approach that matches the level of complexity needed to address this wicked problem. Personal learning design is a structural approach in that it is incorporated into as many aspects of a student's life as possible. This model invites students to continually consider how they might use their personal goals to drive which experiences they choose and how they engage therein. Through ongoing reflection and design thinking, students connect their personal learning to campus community goals such as inclusion and equity. An approach that originated in the business sector, design thinking involves intentionally creating an experience through inspiration, ideation and implementation.[6]

To transform our current approach and, thereby, address our wicked problem, adaptive learning[7] is critical for students and educators alike.[8] Adaptive learning allows us to grow our abilities to handle increasingly complex situations; instead of just acquiring more skills and knowledge, we learn more innovative ways of engaging with the world than we had previously, including how to see situations differently (i.e., cognitive capacity), how to see ourselves and our role in situations differently (i.e., intrapersonal capacity), and how to relate to others in situations differently (i.e., interpersonal capacity). To shift and grow in these ways requires *trans*formational learning,[9] which allows us to expand our developmental capacities, changing the actual structure[10] or framework for how we know, who we are, and how we navigate relationships. *In*formational learning, in contrast, allows us to increase our knowledge and skill competencies, informing the actual content of what we know and can apply.

As our capacities grow, we become more fluid in how, where, and with whom we can apply competencies. For example, with civility, there are pertinent skills (e.g., listening, observing, and facilitating conversation) and, in order to use those skills effectively within a range of contexts with diverse people, we need underlying developmental capacities. King and Baxter Magolda used the term *intercultural maturity* to describe the mature developmental capacities needed for civility.[11] Embodying intercultural maturity requires transformation of one's developmental capacities over time as is consistent with the development of self-authorship.[12] *Self-authorship* is the ability to face outer complexity (e.g., how to address constantly changing issues of equity, safety and civility) with inner complexity (e.g., having an inner compass for handling challenging situations where there are no clear formulas and we need to draw on our own authority). According to Baxter Magolda and King, learning partnerships are critical to helping learners develop self-authorship.[13] Learning partnerships empower learners to use complexity as a vehicle, growing their ability to use what they know to shape their experience.

Given the interconnection between self-authorship and intercultural maturity,[14] it is critical to promote these complex capacities instead of just instilling competencies. We often think of inclusion as it relates to *content* within disparate programs. We aim to promote intercultural maturity but do not always realize that, by pursuing these goals in a disconnected fashion, we may actually be worsening our wicked problem! We believe that, if we provide students with enough informational learning, it will yield the transformational learning necessary for intercultural maturity. However, focusing on content and acquisition of competencies is necessary but insufficient. I remember learning this lesson as a resident assistant when I organized a program for my residents to discuss stereotypes. I hoped they would apply what they learned to being compassionate community members. Instead, I found myself confronting culturally driven roommate conflicts, where students struggled with cultural differences in their living environments, and identity-related bulletin board violations, where students directed demeaning messages toward cultural groups. These incidents revealed the limitations of stand-alone programming. Despite a significant investment in similar intercultural competency programming, incivility is unrelenting[15] and students are in over their heads or facing challenges for which they have yet to develop the required complexity.[16] These realities convey the need to integrate content (i.e., promoting competencies) with structure (i.e., expanding developmental capacities), tailoring our practice to developmental readiness. Enacting this shift through an integrated structure such as a personal learning design approach will allow us to advance interconnected goals of promoting self-authorship and intercultural maturity. As a result, students will be not only poised to engage with any number of complex situations but also further equipped to navigate equity, safety, and civility.

What Is Personal Learning Design?

Personal learning design is an approach in which learners intentionally coordinate and shape their experiences, creating their college experience over time and, thereby, building the capacity to navigate life. Since a personal learning design approach extends across the entire college journey, it allows students to learn content deeply while growing in their capacity to meaningfully apply this content both in and out of the classroom. In order for personal learning design to facilitate this kind of experience, student affairs areas must collaborate to integrate their goals, practices, and resources, reinforcing for students the interconnectedness within their own college experience. Having overseen the development and implementation of personal learning design initiatives at two very different universities, I can attest to its potential in promoting interconnectedness within student affairs so that we may, in turn, inspire interconnectedness. Toward this end, personal learning design consists of several key components that allow educators and learners to accomplish these overall goals, including a name, shared learning outcomes grounded in a shared developmental process, and anchor learning experiences with reflection and design tools.[17] To illustrate this concept, I share the story of Dakota, an alumna who engaged in bLUeprint, a personal learning design initiative at my former institution, Lehigh University. I then speak to how each of these components and personal learning design overall can contribute to equity, safety, and civility.

From the moment Dakota stepped on campus, she was introduced to bLUeprint as a framework and tool for engaging in her college experience as an interconnected journey. During orientation, she received her Draft Book, a journal for reflection on her personal goals and bLUeprint's learning outcomes, the five foundations for student success: creative curiosity, identity development, collaborative connections, inclusive leadership, and professional growth and success. Dakota then shared her reflections with her orientation group, first-year seminar course, and residential community, where she created a personal bLUeprint during her first hall community meeting, utilizing her Draft Book. In Dakota's own words, a personal bLUeprint is "an open-ended plan or map for how you want to envision or craft your unique college experience."[18] A bLUeprint is an example of how a personal learning design approach involves learners in creating their own unique personal learning designs. These designs represent what an individual learner hopes to learn through their experience. Sharing her bLUeprint with peers in a facilitated dialogue allowed Dakota to share what was important to her and learn what mattered to others. After creating her personal bLUeprint, she discussed it further with her resident assistant (RA) and attended Community Development Experiences, hall events where she engaged in dialogue around the foundations.

As Dakota engaged with the rest of campus, she interacted with bLUeprint in a variety of settings and with various educators. After a conduct incident, Dakota received bLUeprint reflection questions from her conduct hearing officer. As a student leader, she used the Draft Book 2.0 journal to reflect on the foundations in her role as a head RA, sorority member, and president of Student Senate. Dakota also collaborated with peers to create organizational bLUeprints, establishing team goals for the year corresponding with the foundations. They then connected these organizational bLUeprints back to their personal bLUeprints in an effort to align shared goals and talents.

Components of Personal Learning Design and Their Connection to Equity, Civility, and Safety

Facilitating personal learning design requires several components that have the potential to advance inclusion through a structural approach.

Naming Personal Learning Design Efforts: What Is Our Shared Work as a Community?

A personal learning design initiative's name elucidates what educators and learners ought to consider as they begin engaging in their experience. For example, the name and theme of bLUeprint helped Dakota realize that she ought to create and revise her college experience. Also, the Draft Book reflection questions and personal bLUeprint conversations helped Dakota frame her college experience within her goals and the foundations. A personal learning design initiative's name grounds the college experience within a common theme, illuminating aspects of the journey that might go unnoticed.

From an inclusion perspective, it is important to find a name and a theme broad enough for all individuals and groups to see themselves within. Since the personal learning design initiative will guide how educators and students design and assess learning experiences, its theme should reinforce that individuals should not strive to become one type of person or do their experience in one narrow way. The theme reinforces that, when engaged in any kind of experience, we all navigate our way differently; in and of itself that reality need not be feared nor does it need to diminish how any one person engages that experience in comparison to others. There are few opportunities to engage in that conversation with college students. In a climate of loneliness,[19] students rarely explore their shared challenges, let alone strategize in the face of them. A lack of common experiences, connecting meaningfully within and across learning experiences, contributes to the growing sense of disconnection we have from ourselves, to each other, and between our different groups. The less integrated and connected that we feel, the greater the risk of seeing each other as less human, which does not bode well for equity. A personal learning design initiative's name can invoke connectedness and remind learners of the value of their supportive community.

Shared Learning Outcomes Within a Shared Developmental Process

A personal learning design initiative's learning outcomes reflect both content and structure. In terms of content, they include a variety of skill sets and knowledge to be learned and applied in a variety of contexts. In terms of structure, they mirror the advanced capacities that guide how individuals use their competencies and in what kinds of contexts. The personal learning design initiative's learning outcomes are transparent in naming the campus community's most important aspirations for their graduates. They should elaborate on values that the college holds, helping learners situate their skills within broader community conversations and human capacities. Although community members will have different interpretations of each learning outcome, the community engages in recursive[20] dialogue, utilizing these learning outcomes as a source of inspiration and accountability. In Dakota's story, she continually engaged with the foundations throughout her college experience. As a result, she became clearer on what the university expected of her and what she expected from herself. These insights informed how she revised her personal bLUeprint and engaged as a learner, community member, and leader.

A personal learning design initiative's learning outcomes should also invite community members to grow their cognitive, intrapersonal, and interpersonal capacities, developing the capacity for self-authorship and intercultural maturity.[21] Since foundational developmental capacities are at the heart of inclusion,[22] it is critical to include a learning outcome for each dimension of self-authorship. Growth in each outcome could, then, support capacities that contribute to intercultural maturity. bLUeprint's learning outcomes mirror capacities for self-authorship in that creative curiosity aligns with the cognitive dimension, identity development aligns with the intrapersonal dimension, and collaborative connection aligns with the interpersonal dimension.

Since content and structure (as described earlier) are intertwined in developmentally tailored practice, a common language or shared developmental process is helpful for offering how learners might grow in each outcome. We often expect and share our advanced outcomes but do not always articulate a process for learners to actualize them. A shared developmental process guides the following: (a) learners' self-assessment of their own learning, and (b) how educators might engage learners depending on where they are in their learning. With bLUeprint, the developmental process is called the learning cycle and involves an introductory to advanced process in which learners discover, explore, connect, and apply their learning within any experience. It is not meant to be a linear process; however, the cycle does embody a natural unfolding toward complexity. In discover, a learner gains exposure, whereas, in explore, they go deeper within an experience and identify pathways. In connect, a learner makes connections between experiences, whereas in apply, a learner translates learning to new experiences. With Dakota, we were able to see how she discovered a variety of learning experiences, explored pathways within each of those experiences, connected her various experiences, and applied her learning to new experiences over time. Learners, therefore, continually use the developmental process to identify where they are in their learning and articulate where they might grow based on their self-assessment.

If we combine these components to advance inclusion, student affairs educators would help students grow in shared learning outcomes, utilizing a shared developmental process. For example, bLUeprint invited Dakota to develop her cognitive, intrapersonal, and interpersonal capacities through the respective learning outcomes of creative curiosity, identity development, and collaborative connections. Based on the previously mentioned self-authorship and intercultural maturity literature, at the initial level (i.e., discover as it relates to bLUeprint), individuals would struggle with recognizing the legitimacy of different worldviews, making it hard to learn about others' experiences. At an intermediate level (i.e., explore as it relates to bLUeprint), would begin to see legitimacy in different worldviews, but would find it difficult to evaluate them beyond what external authorities have told them. At a mature level of development (i.e., connect and apply as it relates to bLUeprint), they would be able to negotiate how they engage with different worldviews based on what they learn from diverse individuals with whom they interact.

If educators challenged learners with increasingly deeper interactions, learners could not only grow developmental capacities for self-authorship but also strengthen their capacity for intercultural maturity. Ideally, through their entire college experience, learners could better understand why they operate the way they do; how it is perfectly reasonable for others to do the same; and how, through dialogue, it is possible to arrive at mutually beneficial goals. Also, transparency regarding how these learning outcomes might unfold allows learners to remember that there is a learning process and they are unique learners with personal strengths from which to draw. In Dakota's example, she described how sharing open-ended personal bLUeprints helped her gain deeper insight into herself, her peers, and the foundations, leading to deeper understanding and a willingness to leverage resources toward shared goals.

Anchor Learning Experiences With Embedded Reflection and Design Tools: How Will We Ensure That Our Personal Learning Design Initiative and Its Learning Outcomes Are Integrated Throughout the Student Experience?

To ensure that learners are continually engaging the shared learning outcomes across their various experiences, it is critical to embed reflection and design tools throughout the college experience. The nature of these particular tools will vary depending on access to interactions with students, student and institutional culture, and the name of the personal learning design initiative. With bLUeprint, it is critical for students to design their personal bLUeprints throughout their college experience. Dakota's story highlights anchor learning experiences across the student affairs division where she utilized these different tools (e.g., bLUeprints, Draft Books 1.0 and 2.0).

These reflection and design tools can provide support for a variety of student populations. For students who are more involved, the tools offer ongoing coaching from peer and professional educators. Utilizing consistent tools and processes across experiences helps learners reinforce the interconnectedness of their experiences and synthesize feedback across contexts to inform their overall development. For less involved students, the tools are a way to form a learning partnership with them, providing access to resources that could enhance their college experience. Moreover, the tools provide a way for discerning, communicating, and advocating for what one needs from a learning experience, especially because many learning environments are not designed with marginalized groups in mind.[23]

What Does This Mean for Educators?

Personal learning design creates a developmental bridge[24] wherein learners' experiences build upon each other across learning environments, allowing students to develop a broad range of capacities and competencies. Building such a bridge requires zooming out beyond traditional departmental boundaries to design the larger student experience in a way that best supports *all* students. Instead of individual departments vying for students to involve themselves in their activities exclusively, this approach prioritizes the larger story of the student experience. Practically, this means realigning our division's work through the lens of learners and what *they* need rather than through the lens our respective departments and what *we* need. Success, in this metaphor, requires that educators engage in boundary spanning leadership[25] for the sake of student learning.

This shift to focusing on learners coordinating and shaping learning experiences, instead of offices and educators managing the educational process, is important to recentering learners' voices, goals, and meaning-making in their college experience. In this way, it is different than a traditional division-wide learning outcomes framework or residential curriculum[26] that is often hidden from learners and based on one-sided educational outcomes. Although well intended, these models of practice tend to perpetuate the traditional power dynamics found in the academic classroom, where experts drive the experience. Although we pride ourselves on our commitment to equity, we do not often consider how our notions as student affairs educators can foster power imbalances with learners. If our practice is consistently centering our own voices and expertise as educators instead of negotiating power

and meaning with learners, then our commitment to equity is tenuo
help learners build confidence in their abilities to withstand differenc
must help learners recognize and connect to their authentic power in b,
able to navigate their lives and develop capacities to face the unknown.
must engage them in learning-centered environments where they develo
their own plans and draw their own conclusions as opposed to teaching-
centered environments where external authorities tell them what to do and
what to think.[27]

Transforming in these ways has political implications for us as student
affairs educators. It requires looking at ourselves and the rationale for our
current systems, practices, and ideologies. By upending how we think about
our work with students, we create questions around how we negotiate power
and meaning with them. Moreover, families and students may be wondering
why they are paying us a lot of money for their students to only be self-directed!
If our leadership or colleagues don't see the value in this approach, it may
complicate whether or not we are "successful" or affect established campus
partnerships. We may even find ourselves in over our heads with a need for
bigger developmental capacities![28] I know firsthand because I have encountered
these complications in this work. Even so, the potential for this approach as a
complex solution for wicked problems far outweighs the risks. If we want to
tackle these issues at the root, we must get underneath and rethink the whole
system. We have a real opportunity to maximize our resources, role model
vulnerability for our colleagues and students, and grow our own and others'
developmental capacities to face the complexity of the world. It begins with us.

Discussion Questions

1. How can you develop the advanced capacities required for self-authorship
   and intercultural maturity?
2. How can you create learning environments that support learners' development of advanced capacities?
3. In what ways can you support the development and facilitation of a personal learning design initiatve to address equity, safety, and civility at
   your institution?

Notes

1. Heifetz, R. A., Grashow, A., & Linsky, M. (2009). *The practice of adaptive leadership: Tools and tactics for changing your organization and the world.* Boston, MA: Harvard Business Press.

10. Helping students explore their privileged identi-
ty. Washington DC: American Association of Colleges &
from www.diversityweb.org/DiversityDemocracy/vol13no2/

. 2016. Marginalized majority: Nontraditional students and the
ve. Diversity & Democracy. Washington DC: American Association of
Universities. Retrieved from https://www.aacu.org/diversitydemocracy
.nter/scobey

4. Tanaka, G. (2005). *The intercultural campus: Transcending culture and
er in American higher education.* New York, NY: Peter Lang.

5. Cardone, T. (2018). *Embracing customization in higher education: Leveraging personal learning design to promote design thinking and self-authorship.* Manuscript submitted for publication.

6. Brown, T., & Wyatt, J. (2010). Design thinking for social innovation. *Stanford Social Innovation Review, 8*(1), 30–35.

7. Ibid.

8. Baxter Magolda, M. B. (2014). Enriching educators' learning experience. *About Campus, 19*(2), 2–10; Taylor, K. B., & Baxter Magolda, M. B. (2015). Building educators' capacities to meet twenty-first century demands. *About Campus, 20*(4), 16–25.

9. Mezirow, J. (Ed.). (2000). *Learning as transformation: Critical perspectives on a theory in progress.* San Francisco, CA: Jossey-Bass.

10. Baxter Magolda, M. B. (2001). *Making their own way: Narratives for transforming higher education to promote self-development.* Sterling, VA: Stylus; Baxter Magolda, M. B. (2009). *Authoring your life: Developing an internal voice to navigate life's challenges.* Sterling, VA: Stylus; Baxter Magolda, M. B. (2009). The activity of meaning making: A holistic perspective on college student development. *Journal of College Student Development, 50*(6), 621–639; Berger, J. G. (2012). *Changing on the job: Developing leaders for a complex world.* Stanford, CA: Stanford Business Books; Kegan, R. (1994). *In over our heads: The mental demands of modern life.* Cambridge, MA: Harvard University Press; Kegan, R., & Lahey, L. L. (2009). *Immunity to change: How to overcome it and unlock potential in yourself and your organization.* Boston, MA: Harvard Business Press; Kegan, R., & Lahey, L. L. (2016). *An everyone culture: Becoming a deliberately developmental organization.* Cambridge, MA: Harvard Business Review Press.

11. King, P. M., & Baxter Magolda, M. B. (2005). A developmental model of intercultural maturity. *Journal of College Student Development, 46*(6), 571–592.

12. Ibid.

13. Baxter Magolda, M. B., & King, P. M. (Eds). (2004). *Learning partnerships: Theory and models of practice to educate for self-authorship.* Sterling, VA: Stylus Publishing.

14. Ibid.

15. Wong, A., & Green, A. (2016, April 4). Campus politics: A cheat sheet. *The Atlantic.* Retrieved from https://www.theatlantic.com/education/archive/2016/04/campus-protest-roundup/417570/

16. King, P. M., Baxter Magolda, M. B., & Massé, J. C. (2011). Max learning from engaging across difference: The role of anxiety and meaning m. *Equity & Excellence in Education, 44*(4), 468–487.

17. Cardone, *Embracing customization in higher education.*

18. D. DiMattio, personal communication, December 6, 2017.

19. Bruni, F. (2017, September 2). The real campus scourge. *New York Time* Retrieved from https://www.nytimes.com/2017/09/02/opinion/sunday/college-freshman-mental-health.html

20. Harris, M., Hill, R. R., & Cullen, R. *The learner-centered curriculum: Design and implementation.* San Francisco, CA: Jossey-Bass.

21. King & Baxter Magolda, A developmental model of intercultural maturity.

22. Ibid.

23. Ladson-Billings, G. (1995). Toward a theory of culturally relevant pedagogy. *American Educational Research Journal, 32*(3), 465–491; Maher, F. A., & Thompson, M. K. (2001). *The feminist classroom: Dynamics of gender, race and, privilege.* Lanham, MA: Rowman & Littlefield.

24. Kegan, *In over our heads.*

25. Ernst, C., & Chrobot-Mason, D. (2010). *Boundary spanning leadership: Six practices for solving problems, driving innovation, and transforming organizations.* New York, NY: McGraw-Hill Education.

26. Kerr, K. G., Tweedy, J., Edwards, K. E., & Kimmel, D. (2017). Shifting to curricular approaches to learning beyond the classroom. *About Campus, 22*(1), 22–31.

27. Tagg, J. (2003). *The learning paradigm college.* Boston, MA: Anker.

28. Taylor & Baxter Magolda, Building educators' capacities to meet twenty-first century demands.

...earning Design Approach:
...nt Affairs Educators Ready?

Matthew R. Johnson

I appreciate Cardone's essay for the following reasons: (a) attention to developmental capacities required for student learning, (b) the intentional effort to displace dominant student affairs practice, and (c) boundary-spanning thinking. Cardone's three elements are important not only to the field as a whole but also to me as an individual because they inform both my practice and my research Student development is the dominant lens through which I view my work as a graduate faculty member. As a professor researching the effects of various experiences on students' capacities to engage in a diverse democracy, I have become increasingly critical regarding current practices in higher education and student affairs specifically. I worry that many collegiate experiences offer little value for student learning. In this essay, I offer five unresolved issues I noted after reading Cardone's essay that educators engaged in a personal learning design approach should consider. I want to be clear that such an approach advances equity, civility, and safety, but I have reservations about the feasibility of its implementation.

Unresolved Issues in a Personal Learning Design Approach

I address the following five unresolved issues to consider when adopting a personal learning design approach: questioning the impact of various learning experiences, limited capacities for conversations about differences, underdeveloped capacities for perspective taking, issues with shared resources, and difficulty in developing shared language.

Questioning the Impact of Various Learning Experiences

The first unresolved issue that I had after reading Cardone's essay was how a personal learning design approach accounts for experiences that seemingly hold power for student learning but offer little impact or deleterious effects. My scholarship examines the effectiveness of *high-impact practices* (HIPs), which Kuh defines as teaching practices (e.g., service-learning, study abroad) that are strongly associated with student learning, especially for marginalized students.[1] HIPs have become common vernacular in higher education, with student affairs educators becoming somewhat evangelical in their quest to increase students' involvement in them. However, unlike Kuh's contention, I (and others) have found HIPs do not yield universal outcomes, especially when we account for students' precollege capacities.[2] The effectiveness of educational experiences like HIPs are directly related to the ways in which they are implemented and how individual student differences are engaged. I often liken the ways in which educators discuss HIPs to chicken noodle soup in that whenever someone is sick, the invariable advice to get well is to consume chicken noodle soup. Such advice neither withstands empirical scrutiny nor is inclusive of individual differences. In fact, people are often enthusiastically forceful in such advice, which I also often see in higher education surrounding HIPs. These practices are nearly universally lauded as powerful sites for learning and recommended enthusiastically for all students. However, just like chicken noodle soup, we give little attention to the evidence for the effectiveness of HIPs; the nature of these experiences; and, germane to Cardone's thesis, how these HIPs are part of a larger landscape of students' experiences. What remains unclear to me, especially in a personal learning design approach, is how HIPs—especially those that do not benefit student learning—fit into personal learning designs. How do architects of a personal learning design approach decide which experiences to include, especially within a fervent environment that universally positions HIPs as the chicken noodle soup that cures all that ails students? And further, what do they do with experiences like service-learning[3] that have been shown to be problematic for student learning? If educators myopically focus on involving students in various educational experiences like HIPs at the expense of focusing on how these are implemented, the success of a personal learning design approach is likely limited.

Limited Capacities for Conversations About Differences

A personal learning design approach centers the role of student affairs educators as facilitators of "meaning-making,"[4] as Cardone aptly notes. While this is important, I worry about student affairs educators' capacities to engage in critical conversations that help students make meaning about their experiences. As students move through a personal learning design that provides intentional support to help them grow in their journey toward self-authorship, the skills required of student affairs educators to support their development similarly increases. Educators struggle with facilitating conversations about and across differences for several reasons, including difficulty navigating their roles, lack of institutional support, and feelings of unpreparedness.[5] Further, student affairs educators must be careful to ensure that when engaging students in meaning-making about their experiences, the learning of those with privileged identities does not benefit at the expense of minoritized populations, which has been shown to occur in diversity-related experiences.[6] If student affairs educators are serious about implementing a personal learning design approach, they will need to engage in the necessary work of building the capacities of faculty and student affairs educators to engage in dialogue about and across differences to ensure that all students learn and benefit similarly.

Underdeveloped Capacities for Perspective Taking

The success of a personal learning design approach is directly tied to social perspective taking, which is one's ability to accurately infer the thoughts and feelings of others, as well as incorporate them into one's own worldview.[7] The capacity for perspective taking is critical given that it functions as an important mediating outcome for higher order learning outcomes.[8] Perspective taking in a personal learning design approach is important for not only students but also student affairs educators, as they help students connect various experiences across campus. A comprehensive examination of the climate for perspective taking found that only about one-third of faculty and student affairs educators believe their institutions make perspective taking for students a major focus.[9] Roughly only one in four college seniors believed their campuses made perspective taking a major focus. Particularly troubling was that, as students progressed through college, they were more likely to report that their campuses did not make perspective taking a major focus. This same study found that just over half (52%) of students reported an increased ability to learn from diverse others while in college.

As Cardone argues, a personal learning design approach is a paradigmatic shift that requires student affairs educators moving "beyond traditional departmental boundaries to design the larger student experience in a way that best supports *all* students."[10] The Association of American Colleges & Universities' (AAC&U's) report referenced previously found that only about one-third (36%) of students said that student affairs educators frequently promote perspective taking. Additionally, only 43% of student affairs educators believe senior campus administrators publicly advocate for perspective taking on their campuses. If the success of a personal learning design approach is predicated on fostering perspective taking in both college students and student affairs educators, these results should prompt pause.

Several years after this report, I conducted a study with colleagues examining which collegiate experiences were positively associated with perspective taking among college students.[11] Using a multi-institutional sample of 21,548 college seniors, we found no cocurricular experiences (e.g., service-learning, study abroad) were positive predictors of perspective taking once we accounted for the perspective taking capacities students brought to college. These results were troubling and led us to conclude that experiences that promote perspective taking are on the margins of student affairs practice, and student affairs educators need to drastically rethink their practice if perspective taking is ever to be at the center of our work. The extent to which a personal learning design approach helps address this issue by centering perspective taking remains to be seen. At the very least, the success of a personal learning design approach would be in how it centers perspective taking as a pedagogical strategy woven throughout the design. To center perspective taking, educators might first explicitly name perspective taking as a learning outcome or value of their learning communities (e.g., graduate preparation program, division of student affairs). Next, they should find ways to bolster self-awareness through journaling, self-reflections, discussion, and similar methods. Leveraging the learning that comes with self-awareness and incorporating the viewpoints of others into a personal learning design approach should follow.

Issues With Shared Resources

Implementing a personal learning design approach also comes with political ramifications. End of the year assessment reports often mirror the isolated structures Cardone details in her essay. Student affairs educators regularly face pressure to prove that their programs and services positively impact student learning. Administrators often tie such assessment efforts to resource allocation, such that programs that demonstrate significant impact, either in learning, satisfaction, or participation, receive positive funding support, and others do not. Senior administrators who control resources naturally want to fund efforts that demonstrate positive effects, especially in times of financial constraint. Within a personal learning design approach, this modus operandi would have to evolve. Doing so would require student affairs educators to set aside the self-interests of their programs and pet projects for a larger good (i.e., personal learning design approach) that may or may not benefit them directly.

Difficulty in Developing Shared Language

Cardone provides important cautions about the difficulty in ensuring a common understanding for the various outcomes that might comprise a personal learning design approach. At my current institution, I have been involved in ongoing efforts to bolster student leadership development. Having watched myriad conversations where students, faculty, and student affairs educators talk past one another concerning leadership, I shuddered at the thought of being charged with building coherent and shared understandings of additional complex outcomes across campus. Those implementing a personal learning design approach face a tall order in galvanizing coherent, distinct, and meaningful understandings of capacities they seek to foster in students, especially those related to diversity, equity, and civility. The feasibility of such a task, especially in a field plagued by high turnover, is worth questioning. Compounding this concern is that many student affairs educators do not come from student affairs preparation programs, which limits their understanding of student development theory. Building their capacities for engaging in a personal learning design approach no doubt requires a tremendous investment of time and financial resources through meetings, workgroups, and professional development.

Shared understandings of outcomes we hope to foster in students is also rife with power differentials. For instance, in thinking about outcomes related to students' understandings of difference, most educators are likely more comfortable talking about diversity (e.g., how students are different) and multiculturalism (e.g., how students work with people different than themselves) than equity (e.g., disrupting unequal power structures that oppress minoritized populations). On the campuses where I have worked and consulted, colleagues who advocate for diversity and multiculturalism are plentiful, while those willing to prioritize and pursue equity are sparse. In seeking to coalesce around shared understandings, equity-based perspectives may get lost in majority voices seeking safer options in diversity and multicultural frameworks. As arduous as it may be, considerable collective time should be spent with faculty, student affairs educators, and students to flesh out the meanings of various constructs. Such conversations might be aided by selected readings that theorize and delineate their meanings. Another possible strategy would be to frequently revisit the question "What would this look like?" when forging shared understandings to help shape and crystalize what students should learn. Additionally, facilitators should be careful to implement pedagogical strategies that ensure everyone's voices are heard (e.g., individual writing, small group discussions). While such conversations may not always result in consensus, there is still tremendous value in finding points of agreement and surfacing tensions and differing perspectives in the ongoing work of a personal learning design approach, as Cardone eloquently notes.

Conclusion

My hope is that I have highlighted some important tensions in developing a personal learning design approach, especially as they relate fostering a climate of equity, civility, and safety. As I stated from the outset, I believe deeply in the power of student development as a lens to promote student learning. If student affairs educators believe in the power of a personal learning design approach, they should seek to mitigate the inherent tensions in doing so.

Discussion Questions

1. How can on-campus programs and experiences that offer little impact on student learning be altered to better align with a personal learning design approach?
2. If perspective taking is required for a personal learning design approach to be successful, how might it be centered in student affairs practice given research that suggests it currently is not?
3. How can we bolster student affairs educators' capacities to have conversations about and across differences in the pursuit of helping students make meaning of their experiences?

Notes

1. Kuh, G. D. (2008). *High-impact educational practices: What they are, who has access to them, and why they matter.* Washington DC: Association of American Colleges & Universities.

2. Soria, K. M., & Johnson, M. R. (2017). The role of high-impact educational practices in the development of college students' pluralistic outcomes, *College Student Affairs Journal, 35*(2), 100–116; Kilgo, C. A., Ezell Sheets, J. K., & Pascarella, E. T. (2015). The link between high-impact practices and student learning: Some longitudinal evidence. *Higher Education, 69*, 509–525.

3. Butin, D. W. (2006). The limits of service-learning in higher education. *The Review of Higher Education, 29*, 473–498.

4. Cardone, T., this volume, p. 402.

5. Quaye, S. J., & Johnson, M. R. (2016). How intergroup dialogue facilitators understand their role in promoting student development and learning. *Journal on Excellence in College Teaching, 27*(2), 29–55.

6. Chang, M. J., Astin, A. W., & Kim, D. (2004). Cross-racial interaction among undergraduates: Some consequences, causes, and patterns. *Research in Higher Education, 45*, 529–553.

7. Gehlbach, H. (2004). A new perspective on perspective taking: A multidimensional approach to conceptualizing an aptitude. *Educational Psychology Review, 16*, 207–234.

8. Baxter Magolda, M. B., & King, P. M. (Eds.). (2004). *Learning partnerships: Theory and models of practice to educate for self-authorship*. Sterling, VA: Stylus.

9. Dey, E. L., Ott, M. C., Antonaros, M., Barnhardt, C., & Holsapple, M. A. (2010). Engaging diverse viewpoints: What is the campus climate for perspective-taking? Washington DC: Association of American Colleges and Universities.

10. Cardone, T., this volume, p. 402

11. Johnson, M. R., Dugan, J. R., & Soria, K. M. (2017). Try to see it my way: What influences social perspective taking among college students? *Journal of College Student Development, 58*, 1035–1054.

22

How Do Student Affairs Educators Integrate Personal and Professional Identities in Digital Spaces/Social Media?

Orchestrated in Harmony or Forced With a Disconnect

Josie Ahlquist

Orchestras are like people. They're the sonic embodiment of their community.[1]

On the surface, social media appears simple enough: free platforms, most with easy-to-navigate interfaces. You could set up a Facebook or Twitter account within minutes. However, soon after you've chosen your profile picture and added a few choice words to your bio, the complexity of these digital spaces becomes clear. Tools like Facebook, Twitter, and Instagram immediately recommend people for you to follow from public life—news sources and celebrities—to your personal life—friends, family, maybe even your students or supervisor. You immediately face decisions that present a wealth of opportunities to connect with others through your life's personal and professional adventures, but possibly at the cost of disconnecting parts of your identity.

Can student affairs educators keep their personal and professional identities in harmony on social media? While it welcomes you into a constantly networked and even fun community, social media presents unknowns: public perception, colleagues' high expectations, and identity inequalities. Is an integrated identity in student affairs even possible, with or without social media? This essay answers these questions. Minimal research has been performed on integrating personal and professional social media identities, and few best practices for navigating the twisting, turbulent, fast-moving nature of digital communication have received widespread adoption in any industry, let alone student affairs. However, I believe that by com-posing a blended digital identity based on Bronfenbrenner's developmental model, which bridges the individual and the environment, student affairs educators can find a way to not just survive, but thrive on social media. A blended digital identity approach tasks professionals to recognize and navi-gate environments and systems, but also points to the power individuals have in shaping and even amplifying their digital impact through the lenses of individuality, congruency, and leadership.

Social Media Status Update

It's becoming more difficult to precisely define *social media*. A variety of definitions exist, but for the sake of clarity, I use the following broad one: "An Internet-based platform that allows the creation and exchange of user-generated content, usually using either mobile or web-based technologies."[2] While dozens of platforms meet this definition, I highlight three of the most prominent ones based on the Pew Research Center's 2016 social media usage statistics: Facebook (79%), Instagram (32%), and Twitter (24%).[3]

Facebook has the widest adoption to date, with more than 1.59 billion active monthly users around the world at the end of 2016.[4] Pew researchers Greenwood, Perrin, and Duggan called Facebook a "starting platform," as 88% of Internet users at least have an account, 76% report that they log on daily, and 55% scroll their activity feeds throughout the day. The young adult age group (18–29-year-olds) has the highest percentage of Facebook users (88%).[5]

If Facebook is a starting platform, then Instagram and Twitter are sec-ondary ones. In 2017, Instagram reported having 600 million accounts, and in its 2016 survey, the Pew Research Center discovered that 32% of adult Internet users are on Instagram.[6] Considering only young adults' Instagram usage, this number surges to 59%.[7] In 2016, Twitter reported having 313 million monthly users,[8] and the 2016 Pew survey found that 24% of adult Internet users are on Twitter.[9] Like Instagram, Twitter is more popular with a younger demographic, as 36% of 18–29-year-olds are on the platform.[10]

Research on how general social media usage statistics compare with student affairs-specific usage statistics is still emerging. For example, in a study on digital experiences of higher education professionals, we found that among our 420 survey respondents Facebook was the platform with the highest adoption rate, followed by Twitter, then Instagram.[11] However, for younger and entry-level student affairs professionals, Snapchat ranked among the top three platforms.

These sets of data are evidence of the accelerated rate of change within social media, with usage statistics and even available platforms changing yearly. What remains constant among them is the fact that social media provides an open channel for communicating directly with students, an opportunity that now has been recognized by leaders in the student affairs field.

Going Digital in Student Affairs

Within our society, with students, and within the field of student affairs, social media has been met with both progress and pushback. Publications from 2000 to 2016 still describe an overall tension between technology and higher education, with Barrett describing the relationship as "oil and water."[12] However, a reconciliatory shift arrived in 2015 when Student Affairs Administrations in Higher Education (National Association of Student Personnel Administrators [NASPA]) and College Student Educators International (American College Personnel Association [ACPA]) updated their Professional Competency Areas for student affairs educators to create a stand-alone competency for technology (Tech) because their planning group recognized that "student learning and success spans environments that are both physical and virtual."[13]

The Tech competency features the following terms that are important to define:

- *Digital identity* is basically what you are posting in digital spaces and what others have posted about you; the aggregate of all this digital content is your digital identity.
- *Digital reputation* is others' perceptions of your digital identity, in addition to your intentional curation of what you want this to be.
- *Digital communities* are networks in local, national, and global virtual environments, many times facilitated by social media platforms.

These terms are woven throughout the foundational, intermediate, and advanced levels of the Tech competency. To meet its expectations at the foundational level, student affairs educators should "demonstrate awareness of one's digital identity and engage students in learning activities related to responsible digital communications and virtual community engagement as related to their digital reputation and identity."[14] Self-awareness is the focus at this level, as well as educating students on responsible usage of social media. At the intermediate level, the expectation elevates to "proactively cultivate a digital identity, presence, and reputation for one's self and by students that models appropriate online behavior and positive engagement with others in virtual communities."[15] At this level, awareness is now paired with action. At the advanced level, digital leadership is proposed beyond self-awareness or role modeling to collective community action. Furthermore, these competencies expect leaders to infuse community and institutional values into social media practices.[16] The primary themes threaded through all of these skill levels are knowledge of digital presence, role modeling for students, and educating the campus community on online engagement.

While adding the Tech competency was a significant step forward for the student affairs profession, it has major weaknesses: it's vaguely worded, lacks examples, and doesn't recognize individual or institutional differences. For example, who decides what modeling "appropriate online behavior" is? Every institution differs on social media guidelines, policies, and even contracts for administrators and faculty; what would be commonplace to post on social media at one institution might be a fireable offense at another. The next section discusses this issue further: Who is actually empowered to meet the Tech competency expectations, and what examples from actual student affairs educators can we learn from?

The Digital Disconnect in Student Affairs

Networked technology creates rough terrain for education professionals to navigate. Remember that digital identity includes not only what you produce but also how others interpret your contributions (i.e., your digital reputation). We can't always control or even know these perceptions, which are influenced by position/title, gender, age, race, and ethnicity. Sonja Ardoin, program director and clinical assistant professor of higher education administration at Boston College, explained how these perceptions can lead to inequity:

> First, as a straight, cisgender, White woman who is able-bodied and identifies as Catholic, I have privilege in many spaces and, as such, my identities, personality, and beliefs often align with others' social constructs and expec-

tations. Conversely, as someone from a poor and working-class, rural background, I sometimes feel obligated to "code switch" in the higher education environment, masking my Southern, rural accent and refraining from talking about class identity, which is known to be taboo is some spaces. So, while I try to be as real as possible (online and in person) and believe I am mostly successful in that, I also recognize that my level of real varies based on privilege, marginalization, and context.[17]

Tensions and even risks are amplified for an educator who is outspoken online and is from a marginalized identity, which has created a new digital divide. On one side of it, educators from privileged identities have the freedom to cultivate digital identities and form online networks, while educators from marginalized identities, especially people of color, may be silenced. Global statistics show that physical characteristics, like gender, and personal characteristics, like political views, are also likely to draw online harassment.[18] Working in higher education, you maneuver even more complicated layers of privileged professionalism, serving in public positions where your employment could be at risk based on not only factors outside of your control, like budgets, but also your personal actions, like something you tweet.

For example, student affairs educator Jonathan Higgins posted tweets about racial injustice, calling out Whiteness, White supremacy, and police brutality. Higgins was offered and had accepted a position as the director of the Resource Center for Queer Students at Pomona College; however, students discovered his tweets, and reprinted them in the student newsletter, *College Fix*.[19] They also directly approached Pomona's administration with their concerns, and Higgins's employment offer was rescinded without Pomona making direct connections to his Twitter activity.[20] In response, the Facebook group Student Affairs Professionals rallied to Higgins's aid, posting an open letter to the Pomona administration that called the firing a "gross injustice."[21] This story exposed a rift between what society and the field of higher education purport to be free speech, what issues can be discussed and challenge and by whom.

Because of this digital disconnect, it's important to consider your values and apply reflection skills so that you can fully stand behind everything you post in digital spaces, even when you are publicly called out for it. Fredrick Smith, director of the Cross Cultural Centers at California State University–Los Angeles, tries "to be responsible in my posts, reposts, and likes, making sure that I vet sources, see who/what the sources are linked to, what their agendas are. I try to pose questions rather than post just opinions."[22] This level of intentionality is key to effectively cultivate a blended digital identity. However, it's a difficult balancing act, as Juhi Bhatt, assistant dean of students for community standards and student involvement at SUNY Fashion Institute of Technology, has recognized:

> Each and every person holds the power of access in their hands. It truly is up to us what others know about us. The difficulty in keeping everything to ourselves is that we may miss out on building some amazing connections and relationships.[23]

In the next section, I explain how to navigate through the disconnect and orchestrate this balance within multiple systems, including on social media, so that you don't miss out on building these connections and relationships.

Composing Your Blended Approach to Social Media

Spaces for engaged digital community members in higher education aren't all filled with the gifs, memes, and cat videos that typically flood social media. In the Internet's public spaces, you'll interact with companies and users who are both known and unknown to you. In some cases, your posts might be seen by audiences who aren't even on the platforms. How, then, do you confidently compose your blended identity while being aware of the actual audiences around you and knowing the context in which you're connecting with them? Peter Konwerski, previously the vice provost and dean of student affairs at The George Washington University (GW), stated, "I try to show students (as well as faculty, staff, parents, family, alumni, and friends of GW) that I'm a real person with real, genuine interests, a family, two dogs, hobbies etc." However, he is aware that his online activity is under scrutiny:

> I'm also always representing GW by using the handle I use and speaking [as] GW's dean of students—so people watch that and will monitor what I say and react if they think my position is at odds with the university or is problematic.[24]

Konwerski is a fluid composer: constantly aware of his audience, campus responsibilities, and the value of sharing about his real life. While taking the blended approach to social media means that your messaging shouldn't be completely unrehearsed, it also shouldn't be overly produced. To strike this balance, I remix developmental theory into digital practice.

Connecting Self, Social Media, and Systems

The social media approach I discovered and propose in this essay is "a blended digital identity and leadership approach that is strategic, yet values based, to interact with the entire campus community."[25] To visualize this application and recognize its influence on both the individual and the environment, I applied Bronfenbrenner's developmental ecology model; this remix is illustrated in Figure 22.1. Although Bronfenbrenner's model has already been applied to digital communities[26] and digital college student development,[27] it is new to student affairs practice on social media.

While Bronfenbrenner's model was originally produced to explain student identity development, it's also relevant to a blended approach to social media, which bridges the individual and the environment. Bronfenbrenner's model recognizes that individual behavior is connected to how people interact with their environment and vice versa, so as you place communities in the context of the ecology model, you see the microsystem, mesosystem, exosystem, and macrosystem. Evans and colleagues stated, "These systems are where the work of development occurs as an individual's developmentally instigative characteristics inhibit or provoke reactions—forces and resources—from the environment in the course of proximal processes."[28] Social media tools

Figure 22.1. Bronfenbrenner's ecological theory of development.

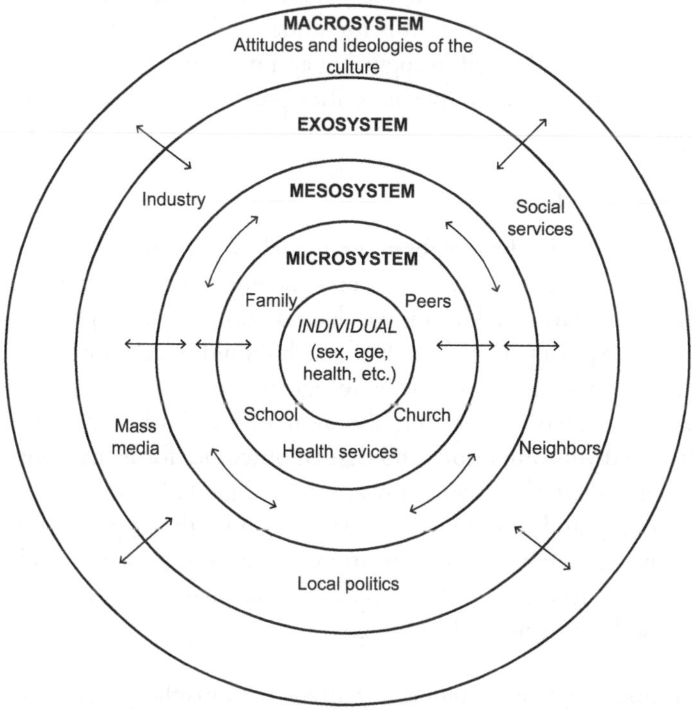

Note. Reprinted from *Wikimedia Commons*, by Hchokr. Retrieved from https://commons.wikimedia.org/w/index.php?curid=50859630 (CC BY-SA 3.0).

and digital communities are woven into each of these systems for student affairs educators, interacting with their personal and professional lives.

For example, at the center of the model is self, interacting with a micro-system of close contacts and colleagues, spanning face-to-face and online mediums. These are your everyday and close-knit relationships. Within the mesosystem are links that connect you to different settings, for example, the processes between being a resident director during workdays and a graduate student on weekends. On social media platforms, your mesosystems are mashed together with every status update; systems and contexts collapse on each other as family, friends, supervisors, students, and even celebrities roll through your feed. An exosystem, like the government (through Internet regulations) or phone provider (through major hardware or software changes), affects a platform like Facebook in ways outside our control and interacts with the model's other systems. At the same time, macrosystems made of societies' beliefs and views swirl around all of these systems.

In Bronfenbrenner's developmental model, growth is observed between microsystems and mesosystems, which I would argue occurs beyond just physical spaces. However, a blended approach recognizes all these systems and the power you have in shaping your digital impact and the environment around you. To simplify this for student affairs practice, we begin at the center of the model: self, recognizing and navigating the systems around you, and using tools to amplify your online presence and demonstrate digital leadership.

Strengthen Your Core

At the center of the Bronfenbrenner model is you, the emerging digital leader with multiple roles, identities, and audiences that shift within seconds throughout the day. In addition, you have a complex system of values and, I'm sure, even a great personality, all of which should be celebrated. Therefore, the focus on self within social media recognizes not only what you choose to post, where, and with whom but also awareness of both your core identity and values and your intentions and desired outcomes for being online.

Consider, then, that if you only approach digital identity and reputation with marketing and branding strategies, you miss the opportunity for real connection, vulnerability, and relationship building. Joe Sabado, chief information officer for student affairs at University of California–Santa Barbara, models this in the following:

> Authenticity, optimism, finding ways to add value to other people's lives are what drive my digital communication approach. I aim to understand others as human beings and not just folks with roles and/or objects. Because of

this mind-set, I am respectful, and I share my values/perspectives so folks I engage with feel like they're valued, and they get something positive from our interactions, even when our perspectives may differ.[29]

However, as I stated earlier, people with privileged identities have more affordances than others to express themselves online. Julie Payne-Kirchmeier, the associate vice president and chief of staff for student affairs at Northwestern University, stated,

> I am who I am, and I live that out loud both on campus and online. This allows me to connect in a real way with others and provides people in both arenas to get to know me both as a person and as a leader. There are challenges with being openly authentic in this way—I know there are places that will never hire me because of my lived values. However, at the end of the day, I have to live with myself, and I'd like to do that on my own terms.[30]

Like Payne-Kirchmeier, I believe that rooting your values and greater aims into your social media presence outweighs the risk of exposing yourself in digital communities. No longer is the question simply, "*Should* I connect with my students on Twitter?" (Yes, I think you should.) Instead, the question is more complicated: "*How* can I show up in different platforms in ways that honor my social identities in a variety of systems (work, family, personal) and are connected to the values and beliefs that fuel my life?"

As a student affairs educator, you need to do self-work: Ask yourself tough questions that ground your rationale for spending time and taking what may seem like risks to be online, and be real at that. This exercise will strengthen your core, build your confidence, and allow you to develop strategies for adopting platforms and impacting audiences.

Skills for Navigating Systems

Since you are situated between and within systems, you must recognize the influence they have on each other and even on you. Joy Hoffman, director of cross cultural centers at California State University–Fullerton, highlighted the importance of this:

> There is the reality that there's a power structure that we operate within; a hierarchy of systems that unfortunately includes some and excludes others . . . to make change, I've always navigated within the system, not outside of it. And for me, my choice has been to help make the change internally versus externally. So, I think it's figuring out what are those kind of key points for you internally as you're starting to navigate the field and then how that can translate to your digital identity.[31]

The easiest systems for you to navigate will likely be your microsystem, from a GroupMe chat with the students you advise to a small graduate school-cohort private Facebook group. You intimately know these audiences. They remain distinct from each other until a mesosystem enters the equation and identity context collapse results. For example, you post something on Facebook, and people from different microsystems interact with it, from your mother-in-law to a colleague you just met at the Social Justice Training Institute. Because they don't know each other, a disconnect may result, possibly a heated exchange in what is a very public forum. To navigate these heightened interactions, return to the first strategy: post with a value-purpose, owning and standing behind every piece of content you put out there even if it results in conflict. Do this because there are systems that need to be publicly pushed and posted about.

In a broader social media context, you might express your digital identity by contributing to a globally trending hashtag on Twitter, which means you'll interact with not only your everyday contacts but also contacts outside of your close circles. These interactions can be entertaining and lively, like the awards show hashtag #Oscars, or they may be fueled by injustices, like the statement hashtag #takeaknee. Every post on Twitter connects you to different users and systems; therefore, you'll interact with and need to be able to make meaning of macrosystems that infiltrate social media.

How we interact online through civil discourse matters. Instead of fearing eyes being on us and remaining silent, we need to embrace the privilege we have to make an impact, utilize these platforms, and connect with people on them. Our students especially need us to be active coaches (not just referees) on digital identity. In my work with students, I have discovered that they make many assumptions about the reality of being a working professional in social spaces. Have open conversations with students about evolving their digital identity within these systems during and after college and approaches you have taken to thrive online, including the stumbles and strengths.

Listen to Your Heartware

Being a digital leader is not as simple as saying, "be active on Twitter," "join a student affairs related Facebook group," or "start blogging," nor is it checking off items in a Tech competency bulleted list. Digital identity and social media use are complicated: Your identity evolves, platforms change, systems flux, audiences vary and merge. They may rise in a symphony of joy or descend into discord.

Creating a blended identity on social media celebrates individuality, ethics, and values at the same time as awareness and navigation of the systems in our society that are both within and outside of our control. Strengthening your core and developing an awareness of systems positions you for a bigger call than just a blended digital identity. Digital leadership amplifies the "heartware" of tech, "connecting software and hardware innovations to relationships and community building."[32] As technology continues to rapidly change, remain grounded in a values-based approach that embodies and connects our communities with genuine heart and soul, not just the emoji kind.

Discussion Questions

1. What systems exist in your life that give affordances and place restrictions on how you use social media?
2. What are core components of your identity that can be found in social media spaces? What about sharing and living out your values on social platforms? Which of them feel more natural or privileged to share than others?
3. For whom could you be a digital role model, based on just how you post, as well as the people you interact with intentionally both online and on campus?

Notes

1. Hodgins, P. (2016, November 13). Simon Rattle returns, older and wiser. *The Orange County Register.* Retrieved from https://www.ocregister.com/2016/11/13/simon-rattle-returns-older-and-wiser/
2. Margetts, H., John, P., Hale, S., & Yasseri, T. (2015). *Political turbulence: How social media shape collective action.* Princeton, NJ: Princeton University Press, p. 5.
3. Greenwood, S., Perrin, A., & Duggan, M. (2016, November 11). *Social media update 2016.* Washington DC: Pew Research Center. Retrieved from http.//www.pewinternet.org/2016/11/11/social-media-update-2016/
4. Here's how many people are on Facebook, Instagram, Twitter and other big social networks. (2016, April 4). *Adweek.* Retrieved from http://www.adweek.com/digital/heres-how-many-people-are-on-facebook-instagram-twitter-other-big-social-networks/
5. Greenwood et al., *Social media update 2016.*
6. Ibid.
7. Ibid.
8. Number of monthly active Twitter users worldwide from 1st quarter 2010 to 4th quarter 2017 (in millions)." (2018). *Statista.* Retrieved from https://www.statista.com/statistics/282087/number-of-monthly-active-twitter-users

9. Greenwood et al., *Social media update 2016*.

10. Ibid.

11. Ahlquist, J. *Digital leadership in higher education*. Sterling, VA: Stylus. Forthcoming.

12. Barrett, W. (2000). Technology and student affairs: An unlikely pair. *Student Affairs On-Line, 1*(1). Retrieved from https://www.academia.edu/33186302/Technology_and_Student_Affairs_An_Unlikely_Pair_Separating_the_media_from_the_message

13. College Student Educators International (ACPA), & Student Affairs Professionals in Higher Education (NASPA). (2015). *Professional competency areas for student affairs educators*. Retrieved from http://www.naspa.org/images/uploads/main/ACPA_NASPA_Professional_ Competencies_FINAL.pdf

14. ACPA & NASPA, *Professional competency areas for student affairs educators*.

15. Ibid.

16. Ibid.

17. S. Ardoin, personal communication, July 15, 2017.

18. Duggan, M. (2017, July 11). *Online harassment 2017*. Washington DC: Pew Research Center. Retrieved from http://www.pewinternet.org/2017/07/11/online-harassment-2017/

19. Dordick, E. (2017, July 8). I'm "wary of White gays," "women," says new LGBTQ director. *Claremont Independent*. Retrieved from http://claremontindependent.com/im-wary-white-gays-women-says-new-lgbtq-director/

20. Bauer-Wolf, J. (2017, July 11). Social media storm. *Inside Higher Ed*. Retrieved from https://www.insidehighered.com/news/2017/07/11/after-news-reports-tweets-queer-advocate-fired-claremont-colleges

21. Demby, C., Logsdon, C., Johnson, N. J., Venable, C. J., Tyson, K., Gibson, S. R., . . . & Peterson, P. (n.d.). In defense of Dr. Jonathan Higgins. Retrieved from http://claremontindependent.com/wp-content/uploads/2017/07/Open-Letter-Defense.pdf

22. F. Smith, personal communication, July 1, 2017.

23. J. Bhatt, personal communication, July 15, 2017.

24. P. Konwerski, personal communication, August 1, 2017.

25. Ahlquist, *Developing digital student leaders*.

26. Eaton, P. W. (2014, May 11). Viewing digital space(s) through Bronfenbrenner's ecological model. Retrieved from https://profpeaton.com/2014/05/11/viewing-digital-spaces-through-bronfenbrenners-ecological-model/

27. Brown, P. G. (2014, June 23). Applying Bronfenbrenner's student development theory to college students & social media. Retrieved from https://paulgordonbrown.com/2014/06/23/applying-bronfenbrenners-student-development-theory-to-college-students-social-media/

28. N. J. Evans, D. S. Forney, F. M. Guido, L. D. Patton, & K. A. Renn (Eds.). (2016). *Student development in college: Theory research, and practice* (2nd ed), p. 163. San Francisco, CA: Jossey-Bass.

29. J. Sabado, personal communication, August 1, 2017.

30. J. Payne-Kirchmeier, personal communication, July 16, 2017.

31. Josie the Podcast interview, October 19, 2017. Retrieved from http://www.josieahlquist.com/podcast/digleadthroughcampus/

32. Ahlquist, *Developing digital student leaders.*

Speaking Up: How Student Affairs Professionals of Color Navigate Social Media With Authenticity

Julia R. Golden

In 2016, the Nielson Company wrote, "Usage of mobile devices (particularly smartphones) among African-Americans, especially African-American Millennials, is bringing a heightened awareness to social issues, brand affinity and even pop culture commentary via social media."[1] If African American and Black individuals are using social media to talk about their lived experiences, we must allow those voices to show up without expecting those same voices to code-switch for White colleagues' comfort. Ahlquist used Bronfenbrenner's development model to talk about the microsystem we are faced with as "digital leader[s] with multiple roles, identities, and audiences that shift within seconds throughout the day."[2] The question we should ask is, "Who has more ability to be their authentic self online and the luxury of facing fewer consequences for doing so?" As Ahlquist states, "People with privileged identities have more affordances than others to express themselves online" and suggests we consider, "how can I show up in different platforms in ways that honor my social identities in a variety of systems (work, family, personal) and are connected to the values and beliefs that fuel my life?"[3] However, when one of the risks is a personal identity you cannot hide, such as race, others already make the decision on how you can show up due to unconscious bias. Since online discrimination persists, how do we moderate social networking spaces (e.g., Twitter) that allow student affairs educators to authentically engage with, learn from, and challenge one another, when participation is characterized by differential risks and safety needs?

Online Discrimination

People of color and queer people of color who share their thoughts or values through social media often become the targets of racial discrimination. *Online racial discrimination* is defined as denigrating or excluding an individual on the basis of race through the use of symbols, voice, video, images, text, and graphic representations. It occurs in social networking sites, chat rooms, discussion boards, through text messaging, web pages, online videos, music, and online games.[4]

As Ahlquist argued, the Student Affairs Professionals Facebook group can be a place where colleagues discuss current events in the field and beyond. However, the response and reaction to those discussions can differ based on the poster's identities.

Career Risks for Queer and Transgender People of Color

Ahlquist explains,

> Working in higher education, you maneuver even more complicated layers of privileged professionalism, serving in public positions where your employment could be at risk based upon not only factors outside of your control, like budgets, but also your personal actions, like something you tweet.[5]

Ahlquist is referring to Jonathan Higgins but does not mention his personal identities and how they played a role in his dismissal. In June of 2017, Pomona College hired Higgins to serve as the director of the resource center for queer students. One month later, students discovered Higgins's tweets from the past year on police brutality and oppression from White LGBTQ+ people and "well-meaning White women." *College Fix*, a conservative student-reported news website, interviewed students who felt uneasy with Higgins: "The students said they are concerned his apparently anti-White, antipolice views will carry over into misguided teachings and unequal treatment at the Queer Resource Center."[6] Discussions regarding social justice and White supremacy were naturally going to occur because of his work responsibilities. His identities as an African American and queer man could have potentially led to conversations on not only how lesbian, gay, bisexual, transgender, or queer plus (LGBTQ+) students could be supported but also how LGBTQ+ students can recognize the additional resources queer and transgender students of color may need to thrive. Pomona addressed their community, stating, "We recognize that [Higgins] brings an important voice to the support of lesbian, gay bisexual, transgender, queer, intersex, or allies (LGBTQIA) students, and especially Queer and Trans People of Color students, and that he approaches his work with passion and concern."[7]

In this example, how can we delineate the difference between passion for social justice and raising awareness of social justice work? Are we allowing for queer, transgender People of Color (QTPOC) professionals to be their authentic selves online and at work?

However, not all professionals who post controversial content on social media find themselves out of a job. Ann Marie Klotz, vice president for student affairs at Radford College, recently wrote a blog post about how one may use social media as a branding tool. Klotz claimed the Facebook group for student affairs professionals was "a place for unhappy, broken, people to showcase their brokenness. . . . It is our job to role model how to engage in online spaces so that students can learn about respectful dialogue and how to have tough conversations. Instead, it has often become a place where folks are sharing their pain in destructive ways."[8]

Student affairs professionals of color had many concerns regarding the blog post. Colleagues within the Facebook group did not understand how Klotz—or other educators—could determine who is "broken" and who is not, especially through social media.[9] Klotz initially only responded to comments within the Facebook group that supported her blog piece and eventually deleted her post.

One observer, Patton Davis, a well-known higher education scholar who studies African Americans in postsecondary context, critical race theory, and campus climates, wrote a statement on Facebook indicating that she had received an e-mail after she retweeted another professional's opinion regarding the blog post. The e-mail was from a White, male, senior student affairs officer who was also a mentor of Klotz's defending Klotz's blog. The implicit bias in the e-mail assumed Patton Davis and people of color did not see Klotz's well-meaning intentions.

Protecting Whiteness

When our White colleagues say offensive things on social media, it does not necessarily result in them losing their job. However, as evidenced by the Higgins case, that same philosophy does not extend to individuals from marginalized communities. This is largely due to a need to protect Whiteness within campus communities. In 2012, Bondi wrote in "Students and Institutions Protecting Whiteness as Property: A Critical Race Theory Analysis of Student Affairs Preparation," that "while the demographics of the United States are changing to include more racial diversity in higher education, scholars continue to report unwelcoming and hostile climates for racially minoritized persons and groups on predominantly White campuses."[10] Bondi continued, "racially minoritized people may feel out of place within student affairs programs through the discounting of their experiences."[11]

The climate discussed by Bondi is true for faculty, staff, and students. It is also important to note that the climates on campus for professionals of color are not always so overt. Exclusion within institutions can occur through not only blatantly racist interactions but also the allowance of microaggressions, "which are subtle, often nonverbal interactions that devalue people and have a significant cumulative effect after continual abuse."[12]

Higgins and Klotz can be viewed as educators who lead through authenticity but may face different consequences in using social media. While Klotz's post talks about being "positive" and "whole" in order to effectively contribute to student affairs, how can we expect our colleagues of color to feel this way when student affairs educators critique their approach to the profession and censor how they state their experiences?

Resiliency Online and Offline

How can student affairs professionals of color remain authentic online while navigating institutional politics? The American College Personnel Association (ACPA) and NASPA competencies state that two foundational skills are to "raise social consciousness" and "articulate one's identities and intersectionality."[13] However, when people of color talk about their personal experiences and what they have endured in academia, they are punished, silenced, and potentially blackballed.

As a new or younger educator, it is crucial to learn about campus climate and campus politics, especially when job searching. Observe the social media of potential colleagues and see if their account consists of personal or professional content or both. The interviews and hiring process can be key in asking questions about what the policies are about social media usage. If you are a person of color in diversity and multicultural affairs, you most likely have social media to explore and share articles on social justice. On conservative campuses, sharing an opinion can be perceived as unprofessional. The choice is for educators to decide what type of campus climate will allow them to professionally thrive.

Ask yourself if you want students to view your social media content and how can one benefit from students viewing one's content. Ahlquist states that technology rapidly changes and digital reputation is others' perception of your digital identity. Our students are often at the forefront of technology, and as a new social media platform is introduced, marketing teams and departments that directly work with students will want to try to use these applications immediately. As a new professional, it is important to take your time in understanding how the new technology works and who can view your content. Unfortunately, as we noted in the Higgins case, students can take social media out of context or use one's words against them.

What should you do if you post something you later regret? Understand that even if the post is deleted, people can always take a screenshot of the social media content or archive the content. Listen to your followers as to why they believe you made a misstep. If they feel you went off-brand, reexamine your content. If they feel you were offensive, know that there is a time to apologize, but there is also a time to challenge your readers. Offer educational resources, academic literature, or tangible examples that support your claim, but most importantly explain your passion for writing your content. One piece I personally wrote was a letter to Kevin Kruger, president of NASPA, in response to Pomona firing Higgins. I questioned how student affairs professionals of color could do their work if no one protects their freedom of speech. I wrote with passion, but I also included action steps that allowed Kruger to consider how he could help create a solution. This allowed for readers, advocates, and allies to get involved and think about how they can create an inclusive space in higher education.

In addition, allies to student professionals of color can learn about how their roles play into the hierarchy of systems. Consider learning about critical race theory or best practices in creating inclusive spaces. Know the difference when another professional critiques someone's digital identity and what someone is saying versus that person's actual identity or who that professional is. If you feel you read social media content in a difference perspective, offer your perspective.

In closing, we must be careful when labeling someone as a person who is not upholding an institutional value because we may not know the context in which that individual was hired. Perhaps the university hired the individual to create change, for his or her differing opinions, or to show up for students with marginalized identities. For student affairs professionals of color, many are no longer interested in having their expertise used without being seen and valued. Lorde reminds us, "The master's tools will never dismantle the master's house."[14] We must continue to question our privileges and think about where we oppress others and how we silence others, especially in digital media where our work can be indefinitely archived.

Discussion Questions

1. What values and parts of your identity are you not willing to compromise?
2. Who are your mentors or colleagues that can provide feedback on your social media content?
3. As an ally, how will you encourage a hard conversation beyond social media, in the classroom, or work environment?

Notes

1. African American millennials are tech savvy leaders in digital advancement. (2016, October 26). *Nielsen.com*. Retrieved from http://www.nielsen.com/us/en/insights/news/2016/african-american-millennials-are-tech-savvy-leaders-in-digital-advancement.html

2. Ahlquist, J., this volume, p. 420.

3. Ibid., p. 420.

4. Tynes, B. M., Umana-Taylor, A. J., Rose, C. A., Lin, J., & Anderson, C. J. (2012). Online racial discrimination and the protective function of ethnic identity and self-esteem for African American adolescents. *Developmental Psychology*, *48*(2), 343–355, p. 343.

5. Ahlquist, J., this volume, p. 417.

6. Dordick, E. (2017). Black LGBTQ campus director says he's wary of white gays, white women, police and heterosexuals. *The College Fix*. Retrieved from https://www.thecollegefix.com/post/34257/.

7. Ibid.

8. Messmore, N. (2016, November 30). *An open letter to the open letter* [web log post]. Retrieved from https://danceswithdissonance.wordpress.com/2016/11/30/an-open-letter-to-the-open-letter/

9. Ibid.

10. Bondi, S. (2012). Students and institutions protecting whiteness as property: A critical race theory analysis of student affairs preparation. *Journal of Student Affairs Research and Practice*, *49*(4), 397–414, p. 397.

11. Ibid., p. 406.

12. Ibid., p. 397.

13. ACPA/NASPA Professional Competency Rubrics (2016). Retrieved from https://www.naspa.org/images/uploads/main/ACPA_NASPA_Professional_Competency_Rubrics_Full.pdf

14. Lorde, A. (2007). The master's tools will never dismantle the master's house. *Sister Outsider: Essays and Speeches*. Berkeley, CA: Crossing Press, pp. 110–114.

23

What Does It Mean for Student Affairs Educators to Maintain Self-Care in Turbulent Times?

Practicing Self-Care Is a Radical Notion in Student Affairs and It Shouldn't Be

Tiffany J. Davis

"**C**aring for myself is not self-indulgence, it is self-preservation, and that is an act of political warfare."[1] Audre Lorde's words have become a contemporary mantra for those engaging in self-care practices.[2] This quote is especially appropriate to begin dialogue around the question, "What does it mean for student affairs professionals to maintain self-care in turbulent times?" Student affairs educators have long been responsible for caring for the whole of students' lives,[3] called upon to support and advocate for students' academic, physical, mental, and emotional well-being. Yet, our current role in supporting students is complex and shifting, due in part to what some have called the nation's "new civil rights movement"[4] emerging in our communities and on campuses. The broad social justice agenda for this movement considers issues such as police brutality; the criminal justice system; immigration reform; lesbian, gay, bisexual, transgender (LGBT) rights; and race, gender, and class inequalities. Within the context of the local, national, and global turbulence associated with the new movement, student affairs professionals strive to foster inclusive and safe environments while also helping students to identify, navigate, and resist oppressive systems

433

in their personal and academic lives. This work is often nuanced and deeply personal; subsequently, it is stressful and overwhelming. But as the popular saying goes, "you cannot pour from an empty cup."

Throughout my career, nearly all of my professional pursuits have centered on socializing students within the field of higher education and student affairs. Work-life balance and professional boundaries have been two topics discussed ad nauseam at conferences and professional development sessions, yet student affairs professionals still do a better job of taking care of students than themselves. This has important implications for professionals, their institutions, and, ultimately, students they serve (e.g., role strain, job satisfaction, and field attrition). As the cultural climates of our campuses and nation continue to shift, practicing self-care must become a focal point as a way of mitigating the effects of compassion fatigue and cultural taxation often experienced by professionals. In this essay, I focus on four questions to make sense of this issue: What is self-care? Why is self-care important? Where do we learn self-care? How do we engage in self-care?

What Is Self-Care?

Self-care is the act of consciously tending to your own well-being. The concept is historically linked to the field of medicine, as doctors discussed patients' abilities to treat themselves by engaging in healthy habits.[5] I do not conflate the notion of self-care with concepts of work-life balance and professional boundaries. Work-life balance focuses on the prioritization between work and personal life;[6] one's career is viewed as distinct from one's personal life (e.g., friendships, hobbies) and should be kept separate. However, "today the boundaries between one's professional and personal life are constantly blurring."[7] As a result, employees may begin to implement professional boundaries in an effort to "balance the scales," such as not responding to work e-mails outside of work hours, adhering to faith traditions regardless of work responsibilities, and not sharing their personal cell phone number with colleagues and/or students. Thus, implementing professional boundaries is often an attempt to achieve work-life balance, which is not the goal of self-care. Self-care is a holistic process toward strengthening our overall well-being, which the Centers for Disease Control suggests "includes the presence of positive emotions and moods (e.g., contentment, happiness), the absence of negative emotions (e.g., depression, anxiety), satisfaction with life, fulfillment, and positive functioning."[8] Rath and Harter[9] contend achieving well-being allows for living more effectively and thriving, which remains a key hallmark of a college educated person that student affairs professionals should model for students.

Why Is Self-Care Important?

Student affairs educators often experience, but are unable to name, compassion fatigue. Well known in the fields of psychology and traumatology, *compassion fatigue* is the "cost of caring," in that helpers experience secondary stress and trauma because of their role in and strong identification with helping those who are emotionally distressed, marginalized, or traumatized.[10] The term was coined by researchers in the 1990s studying nurse reactions to handling continual emergencies. Student affairs professionals often work with students facing homelessness, mental illness, sexual assault, addiction, and other crises. Thus, it is understandable student affairs educators shoulder the trauma of these incidents.

However, the current political and social climate—inclusive of such issues as unstable protections afforded by the Deferred Action for Childhood Arrivals policy, the #BlackLivesMatter movement, and the escalation of White nationalism—have produced additional stressors that students, faculty, and staff feel in very real ways. Campus demonstrations such as the "I, Too, Am" campaign[11] highlight students' experiences with racially based microaggressions. Student protests across the country around issues such as police brutality,[12] immigration suppression,[13] rape,[14] and racial bigotry[15] center the marginalized voices of students who face trauma in their everyday lives. Students are not only expecting administrators to listen and help them unpack their lived experiences but also looking for staff to become allies in these movements as students engage in organized, collective action. Encountering these students and their stories day after day fosters the types of chronic stress and emotional challenges that characterize compassion fatigue.[16] This fatigue is experienced by professionals across levels, including graduate students. As a faculty member, I continually ask students, "How are you processing your personal emotions and experience in this role?" and "How are you engaging in self-care?"

Compassion fatigue affects many dimensions of well-being, as evidenced in the nature of symptoms that manifest themselves in both personal and professional lives: bottled-up emotions, poor self-care practices, difficulty concentrating, physical and mental exhaustion, being critical of others, frustration, anxiety, and preoccupation.[17] According to the Compassion Fatigue Awareness Project,[18] some organizational symptoms of compassion fatigue include high absenteeism, professional errors, constant changes among coworker relationships, negativism toward management, inability for teams to work together, and inability of staff to believe improvement is possible. Individually and collectively, these symptoms present real threats to student affairs educators' job satisfaction and retention, as well as organizational performance and effectiveness, which ultimately influences student success.

Cultural Taxation

Coping with compassion fatigue and developing sustainable self-care practices are critical tasks for all student affairs professionals. However, self-care can be particularly challenging for student affairs educators of Color,[19] given the multiple institutional and student demands placed on these professionals. In the academy, *cultural taxation* describes the unique burden placed upon faculty of Color related to the expectation to address diversity-related issues[20] and often results in emotional and invisible labor by faculty of Color. Emotional labor is the expectation that certain professionals, namely People of Color and White women, shoulder the burden for caring, empathy, and validation within the work environment, yet regulate and suppress their emotions during these interactions.

Invisible labor is unpaid work that is done related to these diversity-related expectations and includes higher advising loads, more committee service, and increased expectation to serve as departmental (and sometimes institutional) experts on diversity issues.[21] Cultural taxation is not exclusive to faculty of Color; student affairs educators of Color also experience this in their daily work. As a Black woman who has worked as a student affairs administrator and now as a faculty member, I know this to be true. Given the psychological and physical toll associated with fostering inclusive and safe campus environments, it is important *all* student affairs educators attend to their own well-being. However, the toll student affairs professionals of Color experience may be amplified by their own social location, especially within predominantly White and hegemonic spaces, as they work to navigate organizational politics and negotiate their social identities on a daily basis.

One way that workers have negotiated their identities within the workplace is through the practice of "calling in Black," which began when YouTuber Evelyn From The Internets posted a video advocating the need for a mental health day following the national outrage related to highly publicized police brutality cases. The idea has been discussed in various media outlets.[22] As *For Harriet* writer Danielle Rene explains,

> Evelyn's comedic reenactment takes us through the standard process of calling out of work for an illness. But rather than physical sickness, we're calling in because the constant exposure to trauma in the Black community, day after day, is taking an emotional toll.[23]

Imagine how this emotional toll may be intensified knowing that, in addition to processing your own trauma to attempt to make sense of what's happening, you must also hold space for the students and colleagues who will ask, and sometimes demand, you help them to do the same or explain why and how the institution should respond. This is what professionals of Color are asked to do. Sometimes professionals of Color need to say, "I won't be that person for you today. I cannot engage in conversations on the murdering of Black men today." "Calling in Black" may be an alternative mechanism for professionals, who are expected to engage in emotional labor, to protect their energy and model self-care in the face of uncertain political implications of disengaging with students and colleagues.

While I draw specific attention to the experiences of educators of Color, I acknowledge other minoritized administrators also deal with cultural taxation, invisible labor, and emotional labor related to their social identities. For example, LGBT professionals carried the burden of labor following the Pulse Nightclub shootings and for the #TransLivesMatter movement. Muslim colleagues are compelled to continually defend themselves and their faith against accusations of extremism given recent acts of terrorism, and our Deferred Action for Childhood Arrivals (DACA) colleagues are faced with emotional and invisible labor amid legislative uncertainty.

Why is self-care important? The answer is clear when considering the adverse effects of compassion fatigue, cultural taxation, invisible labor, and emotional labor among student affairs professionals. Developing authentic, sustainable, and proactive self-care practices can serve to inoculate professionals, which can result in greater personal and professional well-being.

Where Do We Learn Self-Care?

The changing national social climate has been strongly felt on our campuses and brought self-care to the forefront for students and staff. Displays of self-care only recently rose as a collective social practice in response to growing national stress levels.[24] But where do professionals learn how to engage in self-care practices? Student affairs professionals enter the field from diverse educational disciplines and paths; thus, understandably, it is difficult to pinpoint a specific context or experience in which professionals learn about self-care. However, I focus on graduate student socialization as this foundational training remains a primary path to the field, shaping professional attitudes, skills, and behaviors.

Moreover, according to the Bureau of Labor Statistics,[25] "the employment of postsecondary education administrators is projected to grow 10% from 2016 to 2026, faster than the average for all occupations" and typically requires a master's degree. Increasing numbers of students are likely to pursue higher education and student affairs degrees, and graduate preparation represents an ideal context to begin teaching the praxis of self-care that can help to disrupt the workaholic institutional cultures and expectations that I have seen perpetuated within the field.

Graduate Preparation and Training

Teaching self-care is an essential competency that should be embedded into student affairs graduate preparation programs as well as professional development curricula. Burke, Dye, and Hughey state,

> Preparing student affairs professionals to acquire personal growth opportunities through self-care practices and professional growth through mindfulness practices can potentially help with stress management and optimistically, prevent burnout which can be essential for enhancing work-life balance and decreasing attrition.[26]

While we have self-care training opportunities, I remain unconvinced that graduate programs fully take advantage of them in ways other helping professions do (e.g., counseling, nursing). For example, social workers have integrated competency-based approaches to teaching professional self-care into the graduate course curriculum.[27] Within their courses, social work faculty embed assignments that involve creating a self-care plan that integrates knowledge from research and practice about self-care with methods of prevention and intervention.[28] These curricular designs may offer promise to higher education and student affairs programs that want to use them as a benchmark.

The American College Personnel Association (ACPA) and NASPA's *Professional Competency Areas for Student Affairs Educators*[29] offers a nice starting point for graduate faculty seeking to promote self-care knowledge and practice among their students. The personal and ethical foundations competency area outcomes reference ideas related to wellness, healthy living, and work-life presence. However, I have discovered faculty (and supervisors) find it challenging to identify direct measures of these outcomes (particularly intermediate and advanced outcomes), decide how to evaluate students on these outcomes, and then utilize these results in meaningful ways. For example, competency outcomes include, "identify sources of dissonance and fulfillment in one's life and take appropriate steps in response" and "create and implement an individualized plan for healthy living." How do faculty members accurately and directly gather data regarding student achievement of these outcomes? Further, what are the consequences if a student "fails" to demonstrate these self-care practices? These are practical issues that may prevent faculty from engaging deeply in the education and training of self-care practices.

How Do We Engage in Self-Care?

"How do or should student affairs professionals engage in and maintain self-care?" There is no simple answer to this question. Regardless of educational background, professional level, or institutional context, there are several ways student affairs educators can effectively maintain self-care during turbulent times: practicing mindfulness, prioritizing their overall well-being, rethinking their relationship to social media, and building critical communities within digital and campus spaces. These strategies align well with the ABCs (awareness, balance, and connections) of compassion fatigue prevention advanced by Angelea Panos, a therapist specializing in trauma and grief.[30]

Awareness: Practicing Mindfulness

Awareness entails considering what types of situations contribute to a greater vulnerability to compassion fatigue. Student affairs professionals should identify triggering issues, events, even individuals, that produce an unusually strong emotional response. It is important professionals learn how to identify those experiences, so they can begin to seek balance, refocus, and/or realign. Most student affairs professionals have a deep desire to serve others. Often this translates into a lack of self-care practices because they have focused their lives and careers on helping others. Practicing mindfulness forces professionals to focus on themselves and has the added benefits of helping to reduce stress, manage anxiety, increase relaxation, and enhance one's individual capacity for attention and concentration.[31]

Often, the word *mindfulness* conjures pictures of meditation and yoga practice. According to mindful.org, "Mindfulness is the basic human ability to be fully present, aware of where we are and what we're doing, and not overly reactive or overwhelmed by what's going on around us."[32] At its core, mindfulness is about awareness, and is thus the foundation of self-care. "If I'm going to take care of myself, I need to be aware of myself and make choices about what I need."[33] Researchers of compassion fatigue found mindfulness training to be an effective buffer to job stress and burnout.[34] In fact, in a mixed methods study of mindfulness training in a student affairs graduate program,[35] all of the graduate student participants reported liking the mindfulness techniques and recognizing their benefits, noting positive changes in their personal and professional lives. Not every professional can or will participate in mindfulness training; however, there are additional strategies that we can all use to grow our capacity in developing this type of personal insight including therapy, journaling, support groups, yoga, and meditation.

Balance: Self-Care and Social Media

Getting and keeping your life in balance represents the next area of prevention, according to Panos. She argues that nurturing is important to proactive self-care practices: taking time off work, prioritizing activities you find joyful, and challenging negativity in your work life. Achieving balance might also entail seeking professional help through therapy or coaching to focus on the emotional and mental symptoms of compassion fatigue and cultural taxation.

Social media platforms (e.g., Facebook, Twitter, Tumblr) have become integral to daily living, both personally and professionally. Digital spaces offer a great opportunity for developing communities to create balance and challenge workplace negativity, yet they also have a shadow side that far too few people actively guard against. Individuals utilize these platforms, not only for social connection with friends, colleagues, and students but also as a source of news and outlet for activism and sociopolitical counterstorytelling. As a source of news, these platforms can bombard users with information, images, and perspectives—some inspiring and informative, others triggering and divisive—they would not ordinarily access in their daily lives. These inputs can become counterproductive to engaging in self-care, and professionals should seek balance, weighing social media's positive and negative influences. Therefore, I offer strategies for how professionals can rethink their relationship with social media, including curating your newsfeed, placing boundaries around social media use, and disengaging from social media.

Professionals should consider making explicit decisions about who or what to be exposed to by curating their newsfeed within the various platforms. As self-care practice begins first with mindfulness, it is important to become aware of the situations, events, or even people who detract from your sense of emotional, mental, and physical well-being. Consider the costs of maintaining a "friendship" or "connection" via social media against the possible benefit it provides.

Placing boundaries around social media is extremely helpful. For some, the use of social media is an important means of professionally connecting with students and colleagues and refraining from utilizing social media is not an option. For others, the personal use of social media is sustaining for them and offers connections and support. Whatever your purpose, it may be prudent to reflect on how much time you use on social media and in what contexts you are engaging. Make time to disconnect if you believe the emotional challenges outweigh the opportunities.

Lastly, disengaging from social media altogether is an option. Often Facebook users announce they are "engaging in a digital detox" and express an intention to refrain from checking any form of social media for a predetermined amount of time to tend to their mental or emotional health. The complex relationship that we have with digital spaces is an area that we must continually revisit when student affairs professionals think about work-life balance and its meaning for self-care.

Connections: Building Critical Communities

The last area of prevention is connections. It is important to identify personal networks of support[36] (e.g., family, civic organizations) both inside and outside work. A key factor should be that these connections do not fuel stress.

Developing safe and inclusive learning communities that promote belonging and mattering remains a core facet of student affairs work.[37] Communities help foster interdependence and can be a way of enacting social responsibility toward others.[38] We have seen increasing efforts to cultivate identity-based support and social communities on campus. Institutions are investing in retreats, conferences, and programming that seek to foster awareness, balance, and connections within specific minoritized student populations, such as students of Color, first-generation students, and LGBTQ students. However, these initiatives almost always exclude a specific focus on professionals who may want to engage in similar types of self-care programs. Institutional leaders should consider supporting programs that seek to foster dialogue, support, and community among faculty and staff.

The connection dimension of self-care also highlights the importance of having healthy relationships with supervisors and colleagues with whom you can confidentially and safely discuss the distress and tensions that may be present for you within the organization. This is not always an easy task, especially in supervisory relationships across social identities, where cultural humility and emotional intelligence are critical skills to ensure positive interactions. Professionals desire and need these spaces collectively and within supervisory dyads to aid in the praxis of self-care.

In the digital space, Facebook groups (LatinX in Student Affairs, Queer and Trans People of Color [QTPOC] Student Affairs Professionals, and Black Student Affairs Professionals) have served as surrogate communities, bringing professionals together to discuss their career journeys, offer resources, and provide support. These groups transcend digital spaces to host meetups and coordinate opportunities for mentorship and connection at national, regional, and local conferences. However, Silvia Cristina Bettez prompts us to move beyond simply belonging in communities, calling instead for critical communities that recognize the multiple socially constructed realities and lived experiences that are shaped by issues of power.[39] Critical communities are "interconnected, porously ordered, shifting webs of people who through dialogue, active listening, and critical question posing, assist each other in critically thinking through issues of power, oppression, and privilege."[40]

Openness, active listening, and commitment coupled with accountability are implicit in Bettez's definition of *critical communities*. Building critical communities should be a goal for student affairs professionals and can represent an intersectional approach to enhancing self-care practice and sustaining social justice efforts. These communities offer a place to prompt professionals to engage in authentic dialogue around issues of compassion fatigue, cultural taxation, and labor, while naming specific aspects of culture and climate that contribute to these feelings. Critical communities have the potential to contribute to overall well-being by providing and allowing professional spaces to unpack and process tensions within their work and workplace.

Conclusion

For student affairs educators to maintain self-care in turbulent times, they must ensure that "self-care" does not become empty rhetoric like the well-worn phrase "work-life balance." Instead, critical conversations are important and necessary to address how we encourage self-care among colleagues through professional and organizational transformation and enact self-care through practicing mindfulness, building critical communities, and rethinking our relationship to social media. Given the important role graduate preparation programs play in professional socialization, more dialogue is necessary to illuminate ways that faculty and supervisors can not only engage students in these conversations in both curricular and experiential methods but also model self-care.

Discussion Questions

1. How can supervisors intentionally support minoritized professionals across identities who often face inequitable expectations and labor around issues of diversity, equity, and inclusion?
2. What are the roles of graduate preparation faculty and assistantship supervisors in equipping and socializing students around the need for and practice of self-care?
3. What institutional policies and practices could support better help-seeking and active self-care practices for student affairs professionals across all levels?

4. How can student affairs professional associations better encourage and support sustainable and proactive self-care practices?

Notes

1. Lorde, A. (1988). *A burst of light*. Ithaca, NY: Firebrand Books.

2. Harris, A. (2017, April 5). A history of self-care: From its radical roots to its yuppie-driven middle age to its election-inspired resurgence. *Slate Magazine*. Retrieved from http://www.slate.com/articles/arts/culturebox/2017/04/the_history_of_self_care.html

3. American Council on Education. (1937). *The student personnel point of view*. Washington DC: Author.

4. Denby, G. (2014, December 31). The birth of a new civil rights movement. *Politico Magazine*. Retrieved from https://www.politico.com/magazine/story/2014/12/ferguson-new-civil-rights-movement-113906

5. Harris, A history of self-care.

6. Sathyanarayana Rao, T. S., & India, V. (2010). Work, family, or personal life: Why not all three? *Indian Journal of Psychiatry, 52*(4), 295–297.

7. Dresdale, R. (2016, December 18). Work-life balance vs. work-life integration, is there really a difference? *Forbes*. Retrieved from https://www.forbes.com/sites/rachelritlop/2016/12/18/work-life-balance-vs-work-life-integration-is-there-really-a-difference/-49318c853727

8. Centers for Disease Control (CDC). (2017). Health-related quality of life (HRQOL). In *Well-being concepts* (para. 6). Retrieved from https://www.cdc.gov/hrqol/well-being.htm#three

9. Rath, T., & Harter, J. (2010). *Wellbeing: The five essential elements*. Washington DC: Gallup Press.

10. Figley, C. R. (2002). *Treating compassion fatigue*. New York, NY: Taylor & Francis.

11. Butler (2014, March 5). "I, Too, Am Harvard": Black students show they belong. *The Washington Post*. Retrieved from https://www.washingtonpost.com/blogs/she-the-people/wp/2014/03/05/i-too-am-harvard-black-students-show-they-belong/?utm_term=.eb1a61d0b7ce

12. Shimsock, R. (2017, March 25). "It's life or death for us": Students protest racism, police brutality at college. *Daily Caller*. Retrieved from http://dailycaller.com/2017/05/25/its-life-or-death-for-us-students-protest-racism-police-brutality-at-college-video/

13. Tran, D. (2016, November 17). #Sanctuarycampus: NYU protests Trump's immigration policies. *Fresh U*. Retrieved from https://nyu.freshu.io/deanna-tran/marginalized-students-and-allies-stand-together-for-a-sanctuarycampus

14. Flaherty, C. (2017, October 11). Classroom, interrupted. *Inside Higher Education*. Retrieved from https://www.insidehighered.com/news/2017/10/11/students-storm-class-columbia-protest-universitys-handling-rape-cases

15. Pearson, M. (2015, November 15). A timeline of the University of Missouri protests. *CNN*. Retrieved from http://www.cnn.com/2015/11/09/us/missouri -protest-timeline/index.html

16. Jackson, K. (2014, May/June). Social worker self-care: The overlooked core competency. *Social Work Today*. Retrieved from http://www.socialworktoday .com/archive/051214p14.shtml

17. Jackson, K. (2003, March 23). Compassion fatigue: The heavy heart. *Social Work Today*, 20–23.

18. Compassion Fatigue Awareness Project (CFAP). (2017). Recognizing compassion fatigue. Retrieved from http://www.compassionfatigue.org/pages/ symptoms.html

19. As articulated by the *Journal of College Student Development (JCSD)* editorial staff, "The decision to capitalize terms is not a neutral one, especially when clarifying the racial identity of people. Capitalization matters and denotes power and legitimacy. Capitalization can also denote solidarity and representation of collective identities." Therefore, I have chosen to capitalize terms related to People of Color within this chapter not only to highlight their power and collective experience but also to support the intentional focus of this volume on equity and inclusion.; ACPA: College Student Educators International. (2018). *JCSD Supplemental Style Guide for Bias-Free Writing*. Washington DC: Author.

20. Joseph, T. D., & Hirschfield, L. E. "Why don't you get somebody new to do it?": Race and cultural taxation in the academy. *Ethnic and Racial Studies, 34*(1), 121–141; Padilla, A. M. (1994). Ethnic minority scholars, research, and mentoring: Current and future issues. *Educational Researcher, 23*(4), 24–27.

21. Joseph & Hirschfield, "Why don't you get somebody new to do it?"

22. Scotti, V. (2016, July 15). When you want to call in Black to work, try this. *Huffington Post*. Retrieved from https://www.huffingtonpost.com/entry/when-you-want-to-call-in-black-to-work-try-this_us_578f6f7ae4b06fcf086d6d09;Edit ors. (2015, July 29). "Calling in Black"—The break you need from the toll of racism in the news. *Everyday Feminism Magazine*. Retrieved from https://everydayfeminism .com/2015/07/calling-in-black/; O'Brien, S. A. (2016, July 7). Some Silicon Valley tech workers are calling in "Black" to work. *CNN*. Retrieved from http://money.cnn .com/2016/07/07/technology/philando-castile-tech-workers-calling-in-black/index .html; Rene, D. (2017). The case for "calling in Black": Why we must take time to tend to our racial trauma [web log post]. Retrieved from http://www.forharriet .com/2016/07/the-case-for-calling-in-black-why-we.html#ixzz4uEL25WwL

23. Rene, The case for "calling in Black," para. 8.

24. Kisner, J. (2017, March 14). The politics of conspicuous displays of self-care. *The New Yorker*. Retrieved from https://www.newyorker.com/culture/culture-desk/the-politics-of-selfcare

25. Bureau of Labor Statistics. (2017). *Postsecondary education administrators: Occupational outlook handbook*. Retrieved from https://www.bls.gov/ooh/ management/postsecondary-education-administrators.htm#tab-1

26. Burke, M. G., Dye, L., & Hughey, A. W. (2016). Teaching mindfulness for the self-care and well-being of student affairs professionals. *College Student Affairs Journal, 34*(3), 93–107, p. 104.

27. Newell, J. M., & Nelson-Gardell, D. (2014), A competency-based approach to teaching professional self-care: An ethical consideration for social work educators. *Journal of Social Work Education, 50*(3), 427–439.

28. Ibid.

29. ACPA & NASPA. (2015). *Professional competency areas for student affairs educators.* Washington DC: Authors.

30. Panos, A. (2007). Understanding and preventing compassion fatigue: A handout for professionals. *Gift from Within.* Retrieved from http://www.giftfromwithin.org/html/prvntcf.html

31. Burke et al., Teaching mindfulness for the self-care and well-being of student affairs professionals.

32. Mindful.org. (2014, October 8). What is mindfulness? Retrieved from https://www.mindful.org/what-is-mindfulness/

33. Smyth, N. J. (2014). Self-care in the digital age [web log post]. Retrieved from https://njsmyth.wordpress.com/2014/03/09/self-care-in-the-digital-age/

34. Jackson, Compassion fatigue.

35. Burke et al., Teaching mindfulness for the self-care and well-being of student affairs professionals.

36. Panos, Understanding and preventing compassion fatigue.

37. Museus, S. D., Yi, V., & Saelua, N. (2017). How culturally engaging campus environments influence sense of belonging in college: An examination of differences between White students and students of Color. *Journal of Diversity in Higher Education.* Retrieved from http://psycnet.apa.org/record/2017-42955-001

38. Bettez, S. C. (2011). Building critical communities: Beyond belonging. *Educational Foundations, 25*(3–4), 3–19.

39. Ibid.

40. Ibid., p. 10.

More Than Consumption: Creating Space for Self-Care in Higher Education

Shamika N. Karikari

avis asserts practicing self-care should not be a radical notion in student affairs. Although I agree with this perspective, I argue that genuine self-care will never be a priority of higher education institutions because they were not created to care for student affairs professionals, especially ones with multiple marginalized identities. Caring for oneself while navigating oppression and mounting pressure[1] to be twice as good as colleagues from dominant identities is indeed radical. Once professionals accept that self-care is not an institutional priority, identifying self-care strategies beyond institutional support becomes both easier and an imperative.

In this essay, I argue that an expansion of the way self-care is understood and performed is necessary for student affairs professionals to practice self-care unapologetically. I highlight points of connection and divergence with Davis's perspective and also introduce new possibilities for student affairs professional self-care. I close by discussing the political implications of self-care and provide discussion questions for professionals to reflect upon as they consider what self-care will look like in their lives.

Self-Care Expanded

In the preceding essay, Davis describes self-care and why it is important, explains where we learn self-care, and discusses how we engage in self-care. This approach to self-care is helpful and gives readers a path to reflect on their own self-care practices. Davis defines *self-care* as, "the act of consciously tending to your own well-being."[2] The crux of self-care is that it is your individual responsibility to cultivate this care. You cannot wait for someone to do this for you. It is important for early career student affairs professionals to reflect on the self-care strategies they find most helpful and then intentionally incorporate these practices into daily routines.

Although Davis lays the groundwork for understanding self-care, there is a need to expand the self-care conversation, because our current understanding is limited. Self-care conversations currently center on the assumption that others must create space to practice self-care and that self-care is a function of consumption.[3] I challenge these notions and offer two expanded versions of self-care as well as discuss the political implications of attending to one's well-being.

Self-Care Is Individual and the Responsibility of Self

Self-care is rooted in the self. It is tending to your own well-being. Diminished public funding coupled with rising costs have challenged colleges and universities to do more with fewer resources.[4] As budgets are cut, student affairs educators are asked to expand their workload, often without additional compensation. In order to survive and thrive in this exhausting work environment, self-care must become a priority, and professionals must determine the strategies of self-care that match their unique needs. Extroverts may find their well-being is enhanced by spending time with others. Conversely, for introverts, carving out solitary time to enjoy a book might be the right way to practice self-care. One approach is not better than the other; instead, everyone must decide what is best for them. Student affairs professionals must also remain open to the possibility that their approach to self-care may change as life circumstances shift. For example, caring for children, recovering from an illness, starting a new job, or assuming elder care responsibilities are life changes that are likely to alter self-care opportunities. However, individuals who find ways to incorporate self-care practices into existing routines will find it easier to attend to their own well-being. For example, I utilize my work commute to practice self-care, setting aside this time to listen to podcasts instead of calling family or friends. Listening to podcasts enhances my well-being by allowing me the space to escape into compelling stories about topics that interest me. It is an opportunity for me to nourish my mind for the sake of my own mental and emotional well-being, not for the purpose of education or to benefit someone else. Those 90 minutes in the car are sometimes the only alone time I have in a day where no one else is my responsibility, so making the most of the time is important.

Along with recognizing the individual nature of self-care preferences, it is also critical to assume personal responsibility for practicing self-care. Student affairs educators are asked to do a lot, give a lot, and be a lot to those around them. The demanding nature of the job is taxing. It is important to make self-care a priority[5] and advocate for what one needs. Throughout my career, I have learned to identify my needs and then speak up for them. These needs may include ensuring I get comp time when I've worked well over my hours, having a quiet space to work when doing a big project, or saying "no" to additional responsibilities such as serving on a campus committee or engaging with professional organizations. I learned that I know best what I need, and it is up to me to be vocal about that in order to care for myself.

Self-Care Is More Than Consumption

In addition to assuming personal responsibility for self-care, I encourage student affairs professionals to question the consumption-oriented nature of common self-care practices. For many, self-care has become a commodity to buy and a way to further capitalism.[6] Getting a manicure or pedicure, going shopping, taking a trip, or indulging in ice cream are a few common examples of consumer-oriented self-care strategies.[7] These activities are not bad; however, they perpetuate the notion that you must consume stuff,[8] food, or services in order to care for yourself. This is a dangerous proposition.

Many student affairs educators cannot afford to participate in these consumption activities on a regular basis, given the modest salaries of entry and midlevel professionals.[9] While these costly self-care suggestions sound appealing, if they are fiscally unattainable, their contribution to advancing one's well-being will not be realized. Second, and more important, when we view self-care from the lens of consumption, we assume that in order to practice self-care we must attain more. More stuff. More food. More. More. More. This mentality is harmful because more is not always better. Doing less might actually be a better approach to practicing self-care. Occasionally saying "no" to requests for one's time and energy and saving coins instead of spending them are underappreciated and underpracticed forms of self-care. Viewing self-care as more than consumption may be a bridge to fewer headaches and more wholeness.

Political Implications of Self-Care

As Brownn[10] points out, "Rest and self-care are so important. When you take time to replenish your spirit, it allows you to serve others from the overflow. You cannot serve from an empty vessel." This quote exemplifies the necessity of self-care and the reality that we cannot serve others when we have not first served ourselves. We cannot give what we do not have. We must prioritize caring for ourselves, and this decision often comes with a cost. It is important to acknowledge the differential costs of self-care associated with diverse social identities. As a Black woman, I experience the "cultural taxation" that Joseph and Hirschfield[11] describe as the burden that people of color carry regarding the expectation to deal with issues related to diversity. I wish I had a quarter for every time I have been asked to be the spokesperson for Black people or to educate my colleagues about diversity related issues, because I would be rich. Because of who I am, I feel an additional burden for other Black people in the spaces I occupy. I volunteer to be a mentor, show up to events hosted by students, and put in extra time to support those who look like me. This extra work costs my mind, body, and soul as I give pieces of it away daily.

Since I cannot give what I do not have, I must find ways to replenish. This becomes challenging when I am expected to be twice as good, given my race. And if my colleagues do not understand the burden I am carrying, they will not understand my need to step away and practice self-care. In that sense, self-care becomes political when we reflect on who has the power to practice self-care in a way that is genuine to them, whose definition of *self-care* is privileged, and who is encouraged to practice self-care. For example, there may be consequences for practicing self-care. If a professional chooses to say no to a supervisor's request to assume additional responsibilities, the individual might not be encouraged to move up in the organization. If a staff member takes lunch daily and leaves work on time, colleagues may make assumptions about the individual's dedication to the office. Although it is a personal responsibility to advocate for the self-care one needs to be success-ful, self-advocacy becomes difficult when supervisors and colleagues inflict consequences for attending to one's well-being.

Reflecting on and developing strategies to navigate the professional and political consequences of self-care is imperative. One approach to mitigating these consequences is to communicate the rationale behind self-care decisions. The more supervisors and colleagues understand the motivations driving self-care strategies, the more they can support these efforts. Additionally, it might be necessary to document how one's self-care practices align with institutional policy. For example, if part of an individual's compensation package includes paid vacation days, referencing the policy may be wise if requests for time off are met with hostility. Additionally, if an individual experiences retaliation for practicing self-care, providing documentation of permission granted for time off or pointing to an institutional policy (e.g., rules regarding lunch breaks) may be useful. It is important to remember that no one will care about your self-care more than you do. Finding ways to practice self-care at work and in your personal life is necessary for living a whole life.

Conclusion

Self-care is imperative for student affairs professionals, given the contempo-rary sociopolitical climate, expanding nature of student concerns and needs, and the politics of higher education institutions. If we keep waiting on our places of employment to support our self-care, we will be waiting forever. Institutions are not the answer to our self-care woes and the quicker we accept this, the better off we will be.

Self-care is not just consuming more stuff, but instead is an opportunity to fill one's soul with a source of energy that is lasting. Doing this in a productive manner can lead to sustained improvement in professionals that benefits themselves and the students they serve. Self-care is an individual responsibility, self-care is more than consumption, and self-care has political implications. Embracing these perspectives will likely expand the possibility of experiencing sustained self-care.

Discussion Questions

1. How might you determine what self-care means to you? How can you identify appropriate self-care strategies?
2. In what ways have you viewed self-care from a consumption standpoint, and how can you expand the possibilities of what it means to practice self-care?
3. How can you mitigate the political implications associated with self-care?

Notes

1. Pate, S. (2014, April 22). The radical politics of self-love and self-care. *The Feminist Wire*. Retrieved from http://www.thefeministwire.com/2014/04/self-love-and-self-care/

2. Davis, T. J., this volume, p. 434.

3. Reynolds, M. (2017, August 01). When self-care is a mask for conspicuous consumption. *The Billfold*. Retrieved from https://www.thebillfold.com/2017/02/when-self-care-is-a-mask-for-conspicuous-consumption/

4. Manning, K. (2018). *Organizational theory in higher education* (2nd ed.). New York, NY: Routledge.

5. Burke, M. G., Dye, L., & Hughey, A. W. (2016). Teaching mindfulness for the self-care and well-being of student affairs professionals. *College Student Affairs Journal, 34*(3), 93–107.

6. Myers, L. (2014, May 23). The self-help industry helps itself to billions of dollars [web log post]. Retrieved from http://brainblogger.com/2014/05/23/the-self-help-industry-helps-itself-to-billions-of-dollars/

7. Silva, C. (2017, June 4). The millennial obsession with self-care. *NPR*. Retrieved from https://www.npr.org/2017/06/04/531051473/the-millennial-obsession-with-self-care

8. Hatmaker, J. (2012). *An experimental mutiny against excess: Clothes, shopping, waste, food, possessions, media, stress.* Nashville, TN: B & H Publishing.

9. Marshall, S. M., Gardner, M. M., Hughes, C., & Lowery, U. (2016). Attrition from student affairs: Perspectives from those who exited the profession. *Journal of Student Affairs Research and Practice, 53*(2), 146–159.

10. Brownn, E. (n.d.). Self care isn't selfish. You cannot serve from an empty vessel [web log post]. Retrieved from http://www.eleanorbrownn.com/

11. Joseph, T. D., & Hirschfield, L. E. (2010). "Why don't you get somebody new to do it?": Race and cultural taxation in the academy. *Ethnic and Racial Studies, 34*(1), 121–141; Padilla, A. M. (1994). Ethnic minority scholars, research, and mentoring: Current and future issues. *Educational Researcher, 23*(4), 24–27.

Part Four

Epilogue

24

What Is the Promise/Potential of the Student Affairs Profession to Foster Inclusive Environments for Learning?

Putting Potential to Work

Susan R. Jones

In considering the question "What is the promise/potential of the student affairs profession to foster inclusive environments for learning?" I am reminded of James Baldwin's often cited and persistently relevant words that "not everything that is faced can be changed. But nothing can be changed until it is faced."[1] Why is it that a profession that was founded upon the values of equity, inclusion, and education of the whole student;[2] that has been termed the moral compass of the campus;[3] and that has consistently identified multicultural competence as core to what we do,[4] been unable to *face* the realities of the structures and practices that prevent us from fostering truly inclusive learning environments? It is not for lack of trying, it is not for dedicated staff and resources to lead certain initiatives, and it is not for the absence of scholarship that documents the positive outcomes associated with doing so.

As discussed in chapter 1, this is hard work and we don't have it right yet. Hardly a day goes by that we don't see examples of how institutions struggle with their stated goals of developing and sustaining inclusive learning environments.[5] The terms *microaggressions* and *hostility* have become as much a part of our lexicon (and campus reality) as *diversity* and *inclusion*.

Despite years of rhetoric and well-intentioned efforts, we struggle. For example, in 1998, Levine and Cureton wrote, "multiculturalism remains the most unresolved issue on campus today."[6] Fast forward to a 2016 volume of *New Directions for Student Services* titled "Angst and Hope: Current Issues in Student Affairs Leadership" and Roper and Whitt identify diversity and inclusion as an example of "what keeps you up at night."[7] They elaborate, suggesting that student affairs leaders bear the brunt of responsibility for diversity and inclusion on the campus, yet we tend to "express commitment to diversity, while continuing to function in ways that perpetuate inequality, as well as demonstrating little understanding of the dimensions of diversity among students."[8] Given what could be perceived as a dim outlook on our capacity to change so that we are actually fostering inclusive learning environments for all students, what does the profession of student affairs have going for us? Is there any hope we might get this right? In this essay, I highlight several key elements that situate student affairs as uniquely well-equipped for this work and which illuminate the potential of the student affairs profession to lead the way in cultivating and sustaining inclusive environments for learning. Yet, I also suggest that resting on our laurels (history, philosophy, stated commitments, desired competencies, research findings) will not be enough. Moving forward and actually realizing all this potential, *putting this potential to work,* will take moral courage and willingness on the part of all student affairs educators to *act* on these commitments, what Dugan referred to as moving individuals from actors to agents.[9]

Philosophy, Competencies, and Research Outcomes

As student affairs professionals consider what drives our stated commitments to cultivating and sustaining inclusive learning environments, there is much upon which to draw. Central among these elements that undergird this interest are the philosophical foundations of the field, what have been identified as key competencies for effective professional practice in student affairs, and consistent results from empirical research that document the positive outcomes associated with fostering inclusive environments for learning. In other words, working to create and sustain inclusive learning environments is integral to the professional values we purport to hold, what it means to be a good professional in student affairs, and consistent with research outcomes that should guide professional practice.

Philosophical Foundations

Significantly related to the promise and potential of the student affairs profession to foster inclusive learning environments is the historical and philosophical foundation of the field. The profession of student affairs is built upon a philosophy that foregrounds the education of the whole student, the values of respect and equity, and innovative practice. In a statement published on the occasion of the 50th anniversary of *The Student Personnel Point of View*, intended to communicate "what the higher education community can expect from student affairs,"[10] the core assumptions of student affairs practice were made explicit. These include: Each student is unique, each person has worth and dignity, bigotry cannot be tolerated, feelings affect thinking and learning, and a supportive and friendly community life helps students learn. In these assumptions, designed to frame student affairs work at the time of the writing of the original statements in 1937 and 1949, we see the present-day values of respect, inclusion, and welcoming campus climates, which should serve as the anchors of professional practice in student affairs. In a review of 13 documents written between 1937 and 1999 that articulate the philosophical foundations and values guiding the student affairs profession, Evans and Reason concluded that "although the field's knowledge base has increased and the language used to describe its mission may have changed, its overarching goals remain constant and provide a clear and critical direction."[11] These enduring goals and values center around four guiding principles: placing students at the center of student affairs work, recognizing the influence of the college environment, grounding practice in empirical research, and understanding student affairs work in relation to our responsibilities to society.[12]

These values and commitments are evident in contemporary documents that present core competencies and professional obligations to ensure that promoting student learning and development, cultivating campus environments that are welcoming and in which all students feel they belong, and ensuring student success are central to our work as student affairs educators. Articulation of core competencies for effective professional practice should reflect the values of the profession; that is, becoming *competent* means that a professional is effectively putting values to work in their day to day practice.

Professional Competencies

Professional competencies "define professional knowledge, skills, and dispositions (attitudes, beliefs, and values) expected of student affairs professionals regardless of their area of specialization."[13] In 2015, the American College Personnel Association (ACPA) and NASPA published a revised *Professional Competency Areas for Student Affairs Educators* that identifies core competencies student affairs professionals ought to possess. Included among the 10 competency areas are social justice and inclusion. As described in this document, at a minimum (what the authors describe as foundational outcomes as opposed to intermediate and advanced outcomes), student affairs educators ought to be able to *do* (exhibit competence) in the following:

- Identify systems of socialization that influence one's multiple identities and sociopolitical perspectives and how they impact one's lived experiences.
- Understand how one is affected by and participates in maintaining systems of oppression, privilege, and power.
- Engage in critical reflection in order to identify one's own prejudices and biases.
- Participate in activities that assess and complicate one's understanding of inclusion, oppression, privilege, and power.
- Integrate knowledge of social justice, inclusion, oppression, privilege, and power into one's practice.
- Connect and build meaningful relationships with others while recognizing the multiple, intersecting identities, perspectives, and developmental differences people hold.
- Articulate a foundational understanding of social justice and inclusion within the context of higher education.
- Advocate on issues of social justice, oppression, privilege, and power that impact people based on local, national, and global interconnections.[14]

This competency area is also addressed as a standard (equity and access; diversity) by the Council for the Advancement of Standards (CAS) in Higher Education.[15] This list of social justice and inclusion competencies and CAS standards are not intended to be aspirational. Instead, their utility comes only in the actions taken by student affairs educators to ensure their own competence in these areas and in the design of campus environments that support the development of these competencies.

For example, we know a lot about what it means to be multiculturally competent[16] and how to effectively create multicultural change on campuses.[17] In the model developed by Pope, Reynolds, and Mueller, multicultural competence is not pulled out as a stand-alone competency but instead, and importantly, is integrated across the major domains of professional practice (e.g., administration, ethics, advising, teaching, assessment). In addition, multicultural change requires student affairs practitioners to examine the multicultural issues that emerge every day on campuses at personal and professional levels.[18] Taken together, these guiding documents and scholarship demonstrate a long-standing and a contemporary commitment to fostering inclusive learning environments for all students. This commitment is an integral part of who we are as a profession, and it also conveys a profile of what is means to be a *professional* in the field of student affairs.

In 1954, Esther Lloyd-Jones and Margaret Smith framed the purpose of student affairs work as *deeper teaching* and student affairs practitioners as innovative and visionary leaders who knew better than others in the university about how to develop students who were committed to social change and the betterment of society.[19] Student affairs educators have consistently led the way as champions of diversity and inclusion though "carrying a heavier responsibility regarding diversity and inclusion than other institutional leaders."[20] Indeed, even if student affairs were doing its job well in creating inclusive learning environments, the classroom context is the site of many microaggressions[21] and not necessarily the purview of student affairs.

Emphasizing the critical role student affairs educators play in supporting diversity and promoting inclusive environments for learning, Griffin suggested that

> student affairs professionals are perhaps in closest proximity as students engage with those who embrace different social identities and come from different backgrounds. Consequently, they are well positioned to help students make meaning of these experiences, facilitating the link between engagement across difference and learning. Further, as key parts of the established structure and leadership of the institution, student affairs professionals are in positions to support and encourage (or silence and further marginalize) those who are lacking power.[22]

However, proximity, positioning, and leadership position within an institution do not assure that student affairs professionals will actively engage with the work required to promote equity and inclusion. Further, very real political realities exist, both outside and within our institutions, that highlight how becoming competent is much more than possessing a toolbox from which one can pull out strategies, programs, and practices and be guaranteed success. Becoming competent means not waiting for "urgent conditions" to engage in conversations about diversity and inclusion[23] and translating our knowledge about social justice and inclusion competencies into meaningful action.[24]

Research Evidence

Another significant element the student affairs profession has going for it to support the potential and promise to foster inclusive learning environments is empirical evidence that documents positive outcomes associated with inclusive environments for learning. A robust body of scholarship provides a compelling rationale for embracing this work. A comprehensive way in which to consider the research evidence and applications to student affairs practice is to draw upon the multicontextual model for diverse learning environments advanced by Hurtado, Alvarez, Guillermo-Wann, and Arellano[25] which builds upon an earlier model of campus racial climate developed by Hurtado, Milem, Clayton-Pederson, and Allen.[26] Based upon a comprehensive review of research on underrepresented students in higher education, this framework highlights the importance of key external and internal forces in developing and sustaining campus climates that foster diverse learning environments. External forces include governmental policies and legislative mandates as well as the sociohistorical context in which institutions exist. Central internal forces include the institution's historical legacy of inclusion or exclusion, structural diversity, psychological climate (e.g., perceptions of racial tension, discrimination) and behavioral climate, which capture the degree of cross-racial interactions, classroom diversity, and social interactions across groups. The multicontextual model places students and their social identities at the center of the model and allows for understanding students' interactions and experiences in the classroom and cocurricular contexts. The model also adopts an ecological approach in connecting educational outcomes with micro and macro spheres of influence.

While the multicontextual model provides an overarching framework of key elements to consider and assess in developing and sustaining diverse learning environments and their relationship to key student learning outcomes, results from research provide more specific guidance. In their review of published research on campus racial climates spanning 15 years (1992–2007), Harper and Hurtado synthesized findings into the following categories: (a) differential perceptions of campus climate by race, (b) racial/ethnic minority student reports of prejudicial treatment and racist campus environments, and (c) benefits associated with campus climates that facilitate cross-racial engagement.[27] More recent research substantiates these claims. For example, we know that different groups of students perceive and experience the campus environment differently.[28] And we know that if students perceive their campus environment as hostile and unwelcoming, then there are negative consequences relative to a range of outcomes including learning, social, personal, and overall persistence.[29] The research on cross-racial interactions on campuses points to the importance of structural diversity (numerical representation), propinquity (proximity of students from different groups to one another), and homophily (students' preferences for same-race friends) and how students' experiences on campus differentially impact different racial/ethnic groups.[30] For example, in a longitudinal study comparing and contrasting predictors of cross-racial interaction and interracial friendship among a diverse group of undergraduate students at 28 institutions, researchers found that structural diversity was the strongest predictor of cross-racial interaction for White students (as students of color necessarily interact across racial groups as part of daily life), and that participation in ethnic student organizations promotes cross-racial interaction for students of color (rather than serving as spaces of self-segregation as many assume).[31] Applying the results of their research to implications for practice, Bowman and Park conclude by suggesting that:

> Clearly, focusing on a single mechanism will probably not be as effective in accomplishing this goal as leveraging multiple mechanisms. Campuses should seek not only to improve the availability of different-race peers (e.g., through recruitment, admissions, and retention practices that maintain a diverse student body), but also to facilitate the propinquity of different-race peers (e.g., through residence hall assignments and student organizations that enable interracial contact) and to reduce students' tendencies toward homophily (e.g., through diversity-related courses and workshops).[32]

These research findings provide important and useful scaffolding for the efforts of student affairs educators in designing and sustaining inclusive learning environments for all students. Although numerous studies of students from underrepresented groups point to campus experiences punctuated by hostility, disrespect, microaggressions, and disregard, these outcomes should elevate the concerns of student affairs educators at the institutional level, as they speak to the campus climates students are encountering. While pointing educators in the direction of more effective practice, research applications also highlight the complexities of fostering inclusive learning environments and that one strategy does not fit all contexts or situations.

The Problematics of Potential and What to Do About It

The origin of the word *promise* emphasizes the existence of a vow and a pledge; similarly, the word *potential* means that which is possible, but it also comes from the word *potens*, which means *powerful*. To think about the potential and promise of something suggests that we feel strongly enough about this something that we pledge to get something done, to make a difference. Herein lies the problematics of potential. Potential and promise are not enough if we do not act on our pledges and vows—or in more contemporary language, on our stated commitments and values; and on what we know about what it means to be a competent professional who uses research to guide practice. The challenges campuses are facing today with incivility, hate, and oppression (e.g., the White supremacist rally in Charlottesville and the

University of Virginia; Milo Yiannopoulos and "Free Speech Week" at the University of California, Berkeley; a Facebook group called U PC BREAUX at Pomona College; and #BlackLivesMatter protests on many campuses) all present difficulties for "competent" student affairs administrators. Having suggested in this essay thus far that the profession of student affairs has great potential and is well situated to foster inclusive learning environments because of who we are as a profession—our philosophical foundations and values; because of the competencies identified as central to effective practice; and because of what we know from empirical research about the benefits of inclusion, and the negative consequences when diverse learning environments are absent or not experienced—I now take up the the consideration of what the problem actually is and how we can more successfully put our potential to work.

First, our good intentions are never enough. We cannot rest solely on our past but must look to the future; and in looking to the future, we must recognize that we need to do our work differently because we don't have the work of diversity and inclusion right yet. As a profession, and as individuals within the profession, we need to stop behaving as though we have this right and start acknowledging, publicly, that we do not. Several scholars point to the importance of vulnerability and humility in this work. Freire suggested that dialogue cannot occur without critical thinking and humility,[33] and hooks emphasized that as educators we must be willing to exhibit the same vulnerability we expect of our students if change is to happen and inclusive learning environments fostered.[34] However, as Osei-Kofi points out, without self-reflexivity, vulnerability will be self-serving if we "steal the pain of others" by viewing ourselves "as understanding the pain of others by being a compassionate witness, in no way implicated in the situation."[35] As educators, we know of promising practices and we have lots of potential that comes both from who we are as individuals as well as from a long-standing foundation anchored in principles of respect, inclusion, and valuing the whole student. However, in order to put our potential to good work we need to scrutinize the realities of our daily lives and professional practices and act on our values, convictions, and professional commitments. We need to ask ourselves how we are contributing to the problem. And we have "to talk about what's really going on and what it has to do with us."[36] Because if we can't *face* these realities, then we can't do anything about them.

Second, in addition to scrutinizing our individual commitments, an institutional analysis is also integral to success. Indeed, as Smith poignantly suggests, very few of us have actually worked at the institutions we envision relative to diversity and inclusion.[37] In her many years of studying higher education's capacity for diversity, Smith discusses the importance of "interrupting the usual" and highlights three critical areas institutions must address: identifying and retaining talent (Smith focuses on faculty diversity but the same case may be made for hiring in student affairs), working with and across differences (intergroup relations), and promoting student learning and success (drawing upon what we know about student success; e.g., the importance of involvement, sense of belonging, high expectations for all students, faculty-student interactions).[38] Educators in higher education and student affairs can interrupt the usual by examining who is in leadership roles. For example, if the vice president for student affairs states a commitment to diversity, who is in that person's inner circle? Who does that person hires? (The same question should be raised for the college or university president.) How can student affairs initiatives, programs, and activities be designed with intergroup relations in mind? These programs need not (and should not) be housed only in multicultural centers but instead in areas where we know outcomes associated with intergroup interaction occur, such as service-learning programs, residence life initiatives, and problem-based learning projects in classrooms. As educators, we need to hold our institutions accountable for what they declare to be important learning outcomes for all students.

Third, it is important to recognize that the costs associated with acting on one's values and convictions are greater for individuals with minoritized identities than for White professionals. For example, Patton introduces to an analysis of institutional policy "the politics of respectability," which not only enables a form of resistance for those with minoritized identities by bolstering self-esteem and self-definition but also reinforces "hegemonic standards of what it means to be respectable."[39] To fit into a system that is experienced as racist and broken (e.g., the ever-apparent disconnect between the rhetoric of diversity and inclusion and the realities of campus life) requires for some individuals inauthentic ways of being. For others from dominant groups, the system is serving them and functioning well. Ahmed's research on diversity work in higher education bolsters this point. She found that transforming institutions requires practitioners who come up against their institutions, who

> become conscious of "the brick wall," as that which keeps its place even when an official commitment to diversity has been given. Only the practical labor of "coming up against" the institution *allows this wall to become apparent.* To those who do not come up against it, the wall does not appear—the institution is lived and experienced as being open, committed, and diverse.[40]

Imagine if higher education, and student affairs in particular, were organized, not around those who never come up against the brick wall, but those who do. This idea is similar to the "trickle-up" approach advanced by Nicolazzo that focuses "on creating inclusive learning environments for the most marginalized student populations on campus, which would invariably mean equity would 'trickle-up' to all other student populations."[41] These examples provide guidance for putting our potential to work. We first need to reflect on the brick wall and understand our individual and collective role(s) in sustaining this wall that may not be obvious to us. Then we need to work to unveil the brick wall so that we can come up against it in order to foster inclusive learning environments. This practice means scrutinizing our taken-for-granted policies and programs to center the perspectives and experiences of those from underrepresented groups. For example, if a student leadership educator planning a program were first to reflect on their own biases and assumptions about which students make "good" leaders, next to ensure that program planning included a diverse group of students (those involved and those not, as well as diverse along dimensions of social identities), and then created an infrastructure and resources to support programs that promoted intergroup contact, leadership development might begin to look different. For student affairs educators, building coalitions among others across the campus who seek to foster diverse learning environments and are willing to come up against the wall to do so is another strategy that provides support and encouragement for these educators, and is also a collective voice with which to advocate at the institutional level.

In the end, change in order to truly facilitate the development of inclusive environments for learning requires both individual and institutional transformation. After all, institutions are not inanimate objects but are made up of individuals. And individuals carry with them their own commitments, values, assumptions, institutional positioning, and prior experiences—all of which may or may not lead them to actively work toward dismantling barriers and working toward inclusion. Institutions, in contrast, through institutional leaders, policies, climates, and politics can do a lot to either constrain or advance individual and collective efforts toward fostering inclusive learning environments.

Conclusion

There is much promise and potential in the student affairs profession to foster inclusive learning environments. This potential rests on long-standing values and commitments to the power in educating the whole student and cultivating and sustaining welcoming campus environments that enable all students to thrive and succeed. But we must also face the reality that there is much work that remain and this work must be actively engaged by *us*. This requires moral courage, utilizing what we know to advocate for changes that will bring about the conditions for inclusive learning environments, and scrutinizing the details of our everyday lives for ways in which we are implicated in larger structures of inequality and fall short in delivering on our espoused values, goals, and commitments. If we can *face* these realities of contemporary student affairs practice, as well as our own complicity in maintaining the brick wall, then the potential for productive change is great.

Discussion Questions

1. Examine the realities of your everyday practice on campus. How are you *facing* (or not) the barriers to fostering inclusive learning environments? Can you think of situations when you have expressed commitment to diversity and inclusion yet functioned in ways that perpetuated inequality?

2. Using the ACPA/NASPA competencies for social justice and inclusion as a guide, conduct an honest self-assessment of how competent you are on these measures. How do you know? Identify specific steps you could take to advance your competency in this area.

3. Consider your division of student affairs organized around the interests of those most marginalized. How would programs, policies, and practices be different?

Notes

1. Baldwin, J. (1962, January 14). As much as one can bear. *New York Times Book Review*, p. BR11.

2. American Council on Education. (1937). *The student personnel point of view.* Washington DC: Author.

3. Canon, H. J. (1985). Ethical problems in daily practice. In H. J. Canon & R. D. Brown (Eds.), *How to think about professional ethics* (New Directions for Student Services, no. 30, pp. 5–15). San Francisco, CA: Jossey-Bass.

4. Pope, R. L., Reynolds, A. L., & Mueller, J. A. (2014). *Creating multicultural change on campus.* San Francisco, CA: Jossey-Bass.

5. Griffin, K. A. (2017). Campus climate and diversity. In J. H. Schuh, S. R. Jones, & V. Torres (Eds.), *Student services: A Handbook for the profession* (6th ed., pp. 73–88). San Francisco, CA: Jossey-Bass.

6. Levine, A., & Cureton, J. S. (1998). *When hope and fear collide: A portrait of today's college student.* San Francisco, CA: Jossey-Bass, p. 91.

7. Roper, L. D., & Whitt, E. J. (2016). What troubles you? What keeps you up at night? In E. J. Whitt, L. D. Roper, K. T. Porterfield, & J. E. Carnaghi (Eds.), *Angst and hope: Current issues in student affairs leadership* (New Directions for Student Services, no. 153, pp. 19–38). San Francisco, CA: Jossey-Bass, p. 19.

8. Ibid., p. 26.

9. Dugan, J. P. (2011). What would student affairs organizational structures look like if they supported inclusive, learning-centered practices? In P. M. Magolda & M. B. Baxter Magolda (Eds.), *Contested issues in student affairs* (pp. 394–406). Sterling, VA: Stylus.

10. NASPA. (1989). *Points of view.* Washington DC: Authors, p. 5.

11. Evans, N. J., & Reason, R. D. (2001). Guiding principles: A review and analysis of student affairs philosophical statements. *Journal of College Student Development, 42,* 359–377, p. 374.

12. Reason, R. D., & Broido, E. M. (2017). Philosophy and values. In J. H. Schuh, S. R. Jones, & V. Torres (Eds.), *Student services: A Handbook for the profession* (6th ed., pp. 39–55). San Francisco, CA: Jossey-Bass.

13. Arminio, J., & Ortiz, A. M. (2017). Professionalism. In J. H. Schuh, S. R. Jones, & V. Torres (Eds.), *Student services: A Handbook for the profession* (6th ed., pp. 377–391). San Francisco, CA: Jossey-Bass, p. 379.

14. American College Personnel Association-College Student Educators International (ACPA) and Student Affairs Administrators in Higher Education (NASPA). (2015). *Professional competency areas for student affairs educators.* Washington DC: Authors, p. 30.

15. Council for the Advancement of Standards in Higher Education (CAS). (2015). *CAS professional standards for higher education* (9th ed.). Washington DC: Author.

16. Pope, R. L., Reynolds, A. L., & Mueller, J. A. (2004). *Multicultural competence in student affairs.* San Francisco, CA: Jossey-Bass.

17. Pope, R. L., Reynolds, A. L., & Mueller, J. A. (2014). *Creating multicultural change on campus.* San Francisco, CA: Jossey-Bass.

18. Pope, R. L., & Mueller, J. A. (2017). Multicultural competence and change on campus. In J. H. Schuh, S. R. Jones, & V. Torres (Eds.), *Student services: A Handbook for the profession* (6th ed., pp. 392–407). San Francisco, CA: Jossey-Bass.

19. Lloyd-Jones, E., & Smith, M. R. (1954). *Student personnel work as deeper teaching.* New York, NY: Harper & Brothers.

20. Roper & Whitt, What troubles you? p. 26.

21. Suarez-Orozco, C., Casanova, S., Martin, M., Katsiaficas, D., Cuellar, V., Smith, N. A., & Dias, S. I. (2015). Toxic rain in class: Classroom interpersonal microaggressions. *Educational Researcher, 44*(3), 151–160.

22. Griffin, K. A. (2017). Campus climate and diversity. In J. H. Schuh, S. R. Jones, & V. Torres (Eds.), *Student services: A Handbook for the profession* (6th ed., pp. 73–88). San Francisco: Jossey-Bass, p. 82.

23. Roper & Whitt, What troubles you? p. 25.

24. Osei-Kofi, N. (2011). Beyond awareness: Student affairs educators as social justice advocates. In P. M. Magolda & M. B. Baxter Magolda (Eds.), *Contested issues in student affairs* (pp. 387–392). Sterling, VA: Stylus, p. 388.

25. Hurtado, S., Alvarez, C. L., Guillermo-Wann, C., & Arellano, L. (2012). A model for diverse learning environments. In J. C. Smart & M. B. Paulsen (Eds.), *Higher Education: Handbook of theory and research* (pp. 41–122). New York: Springer.

26. Hurtado, S., Milem, J. F., Clayton-Pederson, A. R., & Allen, W. R. (1999). Enacting diverse learning environments: Improving the campus climate for racial/ethnic diversity in higher education. *ASHE-ERIC Higher Education Reports Series, 26*(8). San Francisco, CA: Jossey-Bass.

27. Harper, S. R., & Hurtado, S. (2007). Nine themes in campus racial climates and implications for institutional transformation. In S. R. Harper & L. D. Patton (Eds.), *Responding to the realities of race on campus* (New Directions for Student Services, no. 120, pp. 7–24). San Francisco, CA: Jossey-Bass.

28. Hurtado, S., Griffin, K. A., Arellano, L., & Cuellar, M. (2008). Assessing the value of climate assessments: Progress and future directions. *Journal of Diversity in Higher Education, 1*(4), 204–221.

29. Chang, M. J., Eagin, M. K., Lin, M. H., & Hurtado, S. (2011). Considering the impact of racial stigmas and science identity: Persistence among biomedical and behavioral science aspirants. *Journal of Higher Education, 82*(5), 564–596; Hurtado, S., Griffin, K. A., Arellano, L., & Cuellar, M. (2008). Assessing the value of climate assessments: Progress and future directions. *Journal of Diversity in Higher Education, 1*(4), 204–221; Locks, A. M., Hurtado, S., Bowman, N. A., & Oseguera, L. (2008). Extending notions of campus climate and diversity to students' transition to college. *The Review of Higher Education, 31*(3), 257–285.

30. Bowman, N. A., & Park, J. (2014). Interracial contact on college campuses: Comparing and contrasting predictors of cross-racial interaction and interracial friendship. *The Journal of Higher Education, 85*(5), 660–690.

31. Ibid.

32. Ibid., p. 685.

33. Freire, P. (1993). *Pedagogy of the oppressed.* New York, NY: Continuum.

34. hooks, b. (1994). *Teaching to transgress: Education as the practice of freedom.* New York, NY: Routledge.

35. Osei-Kofi, N. (2011). Beyond awareness: Student affairs educators as social justice advocates. In P. M. Magolda & M. B. Baxter Magolda (Eds.), *Contested issues in student affairs* (pp. 387–392). Sterling, VA: Stylus, p. 390.

36. Johnson, A. G. (2006). *Privilege, power, and difference* (2nd ed.). New York, NY: McGraw-Hill, p. 2.

37. Smith, D. G. (2015). *Diversity's promise for higher education: Making it work* (2nd ed.). Baltimore, MD: Johns Hopkins University Press.

38. Ibid.

39. Patton, L. D. (2014). Preserving respectability or blatant disrespect? A critical discourse analysis of the Morehouse Appropriate Attire Policy and implications

for intersectional approaches to examining campus policies. *International Journal of Qualitative Studies in Education, 27,* 724–746, p. 731.

40. Ahmed, S. (2012). *On being included: Racism and diversity in institutional life.* Durham, NC: Duke University Press, p. 174.

41. Nicolazzo, Z. (2016). "Just go in looking good": The resilience, resistance, and kinship-building of Trans* college students. *Journal of College Student Development, 57,* 538–556, p. 554.

It's the Means, Not the Ends: Incorporating Humanity Into Our Practice

Craig R. Berger

The course was named Talking Democracy, and the class session explored *symbolic interactionism*, defined as a theoretical perspective that examines how people make meaning of various social interactions and then act. Thirteen students and two instructors (one of them me) sat around a seminar table ready to explore the concept's role in their lives and its effect on our democracy. I asked students to think about a setting outside of our classroom in which they interact with other people or environments and challenged them to decipher what messages, stated in words or otherwise, those people or environments transmitted to them. My unusual phrasing of the question—even the fact that I asked a question instead of dictated a direction—confused the students, who responded with silence. "How do we want to move forward?" I tried again. After struggling to communicate with their newfound power, the students decided it would be best to divide into groups by counting off. Students processed their responses with each other. The class then discussed the meaning of me asking for direction, noted that it had violated their expectations, and explored why it led to the subsequent confusing moments. All of this served as a helpful foundation for our discussion of symbolic interactionism.

Like Jones, considering the question, "What is the promise/potential of the student affairs profession to foster inclusive environments for learning?" led me to the wise words of an intellectual from the past who thought a great deal about education, the learning process, and inclusivity. "The task of democracy is forever that of creation of a freer and more humane experience in which all share and to which all contribute," John Dewey wrote.[1] While Dewey wrote of "democracy" in the quote, his life's work was to examine the intersection of democracy and education. His use of the word "humane" is striking, and his background led me to approach the framing question a bit differently than Jones' treatment. Jones is correct—much of the basis of our profession centers on viewing students as whole people, the idea that out-of-class learning is just as critical as in-classroom learning, and that the entire institution plays a role in student learning. When I contemplate the answer to the apt question Jones articulates early in her essay—"Why is it that a profession that was founded upon the values of equity, inclusion, and education of the whole student [has] been unable to *face* the realities of the structures and practices that prevent us from fostering truly inclusive learning environments?"[2]—I do not see a problem with "ends"; I view our challenge as a "means" issue.

In my response, I contrast two of the foundational student affairs documents Jones referenced—the 1937 *Student Personnel Point of View's* call for a holistic approach and the 1949 *Student Personnel Point of View's* call for a specialized approach—that form the historical basis for our pedagogical difficulties regarding inclusivity. I also unpack the tension that exists between our *aspirations* of treating students as whole human beings and our common *practice* of designing programs and interventions in which we often do not expect *ourselves* to show up as whole people. After offering some initial thoughts on how we can take specific actions to approach our noble goals in a more inclusive, vulnerable, and human way, I conclude with remarks on the political considerations at work as we confront the discrepancies between our vision of creating inclusive and equitable learning environments and strengthen our efforts to manifest them through our practice.

Historical and Philosophical Considerations

As Jones asserts, inclusion, equity, and education of the whole student form the heart of the student affairs profession going back to the 1937 publication of the *Student Personnel Point of View*—a foundational document for the field. Roberts summarizes the statement, noting that "viewing students holistically, believing in the potential of all students, and relying on rich experiences, both in and out of classrooms were proposed as . . . essential principles."[3]

This late-1930s description of student affairs work may ring familiar to early-twenty-first century student affairs educators; however, the profession experienced an important shift reflected in a revisionary statement issued twelve years later. The 1949 statement included prescriptions that reflected post-World War II thinking about production and efficiency.[4] The authors called on student personnel administrators to organize its work "with the customary definiteness found in instructional departments and colleges," asserting "trained personnel staff members" should perform "specialized functions."[5] This shift in approach, captured in the 1949 *Student Personnel Point of View*, is responsible for Jones having to ask why a profession such as ours, valuing equity, inclusion, and liberal education, has been unable to overcome the barriers disrupting our efforts to cultivate inclusive learning environments. The changes in the 1949 statement continue to challenge our profession today in our struggles to build whole institutions to educate whole students.[6] Jones notes that our aspirations are much the same now as they were nearly a century ago. In other words, it is not an ends issue. It is a means problem.

Examining a Foundational Tension

In my experience, student affairs educators do not spend enough time thinking about how the actions that we take—the ways we apply high-impact practices—affect the nature and the quality of the experiences themselves. We preoccupy ourselves with outcomes in this age of accountability and expend significant energy and time writing and assessing achievement of learning outcomes so that we can communicate our work to various audiences (e.g., students, their families, accreditation commissions, state legislators). Yet we often do not study how the actions we take—and the way we take them—affect the message we ultimately transmit to students.

When we as student affairs educators are not human and vulnerable in the spaces we share with students, we miss opportunities to nurture the inclusivity of the learning process. With good intention, we might construct a sound program that transmits messages supporting inclusion; yet *even if it proceeds according to plan* students may (a) experience student affairs educators reducing their humanity to data points; (b) internalize a message that says they can be prepared for life after college by attending episodic, scripted workshops; and (c) if the interventions they experience are siloed from the university, learn the lesson that these efforts are marginal at the university and lack significance.

In our Talking Democracy course, my coinstructor and I wanted the environment of each class session to embody the messages we hoped to convey. We sought opportunities to give students power in the course by encouraging the class to "get meta," to interrupt the goings-on of the class and go "off script" to point out an interesting undercurrent in the room. Continual analysis of in-the-moment dynamics made for vivid discussion and an opportunity to unpack those dynamics together. Furthermore, the transgression of sacrosanct educational norms (e.g., interruption, spontaneity, emphasis of instructors' humanity and vulnerability) gave students space and authority to name challenges with over- and underparticipation they experienced.

Building on Our Promise and Potential

What does an affirmative vision of an inclusive environment look like, and what steps might we take to get there? Here are some possibilities.

Student Affairs Educators Can Create or Participate in a Larger, Long-Term Strategy to Foster Cultural Practices That Bind Divisions and Departments and Foster Inclusive Learning Environments Across Campus

People learn from their whole environments and every interaction, not just from courses and programs predesigned to educate. If we wish for students to be proficient in navigating the complex world outside of our institution's borders and understanding how systemic forces work to shape our society, students must learn everywhere in their college experience to develop agency—not just in political science courses, service-learning experiences, or student organizations—but in all settings.

We need to broaden our scope from thinking about our work as a collection of disparate programs and initiatives to viewing our work as contributing to a campus ecosystem—a web of experiences that students encounter everywhere. A deeper, more holistic approach would foreground relationship building and deemphasize organizational boundaries. A student affairs educator working in civic engagement could identify people and initiatives already aligned with their work at the institution, develop relationships with them, and then convene those new partners and spotlight and link the work together. The ostensible goal for this coalition might take the form of something like a yearlong initiative tying together disparate programs, but the boundary-busting partnerships forged in this process would remain, laying the groundwork for additional interdivisional, interdisciplinary work touching campus programs, research, and teaching.

Student Affairs Educators Can Espouse and Model the Perspective That College Is Life, Not Merely Preparation for Life

What happens on college campuses is real. The relationships, institutional structures, and organizations on a college campus are affected by, contain, and reproduce the systems at work in our society. When we validate the incorrect notion that our campuses are "bubbles" disconnected from reality, we discourage students from viewing the campus as a learning forum packed with opportunities to experiment and a shared community in which they can authentically engage.

Paolo Freire called on educators to nurture students' innate desire for existential freedom, what Freire called their "ontological vocation to be more fully human."[7] When we emphasize that our institutions are real places where students experience real learning, meet real people, and complete real accomplishments, we help students achieve this freedom, as they experience themselves as uniquely capable of learning and working individually and collectively to enrich our common life. As they witness their own contributions, students internalize the message that they are present in an environment that they were able to shape.

Student Affairs Educators Can Intentionally Diminish the Prevalence of "Scripts," or the Roles Students Play That We Have Defined for Them, In Our Work

We often see students in "scripted" moments, experiences in which students navigate collegiate life as actors—filling roles ascribed to, or designed for, them—rather than agents—exercising their agency to create new knowledge or contribute to the institution in a new, unique way. These instances might range from a student experiencing a disengaging course with little practical application to moments when students offer an idea to improve campus life but encounter faculty or staff members who reject their idea out of hand based on their role in the campus community. One study of this phenomenon described designed activities as a culprit to blame for these agency-diminishing experiences. Students participating in the study suggested that the preplanned nature of activities and interventions felt like simulations and discouraged students from recognizing the opportunities as real opportunities for learning and engagement.[8]

Designed activities are useful and unavoidable in higher education. While banishing preplanned efforts is not feasible, we as student affairs educators *can* find ways to emphasize students' agency in the learning process.[9] We can make students' experiences more real by sacrificing control of every moment of the education experience and, instead, focus on creating spaces that students can fill themselves.

While leadership retreats are necessarily preplanned, leadership educators can fill the experience with empowering messages (e.g., each student's individual voice matters, spontaneity is welcome, and the staff who facilitate the retreat are not masters of content but are people who have experienced many of the same situations and feelings the students navigate). These efforts will fall short, though, if educators communicate these messages verbally but do not enact them; traditional authority figures reflecting vulnerability, humanity, and spontaneity in these experiences disrupt familiar scripts and create a new reality with students.[10]

Political Implications

An obvious political challenge to enhancing learners' agency is the demanding era of accountability. How can we measure learning in amorphous experiences while also being mindful of how that assessment affects the essence and quality of the learning experience itself? Developing real relationships and learning opportunities are slow endeavors. Can we invest significant time in these strategies while also satisfying our stakeholders' immediate expectations? In a world in which "learning opportunities" can explode into viral embarrassing material, sacrificing what control educators do possess sounds laughable. Additionally, any coalition-building approach must reconcile its priorities with organizational realities, like hierarchy, and budgets. Each of these considerations is challenging, and I do not have complete answers to any of them.

I do know this: For several decades we have asked ourselves why a profession with ideals as humane and inclusive as ours struggles so significantly to ensure that *everyone* is seen and included in our environments. Scholars celebrate our devotion to inclusivity and student learning, we design learning experiences in which we expect our students to authentically engage as whole people (often without including our own humanity and vulnerability), and we continuously align assessment tools with learning outcomes. Our wheels have spun and continue to spin.

It is time we delve deeper into *how* we do our work. If we want to tap the promise of our student affairs profession, we must examine the most sacrosanct, untouchable aspects of our rituals as educators to identify the messages we send students unintentionally and unconsciously. When we live these values by learning as a profession how to engage in organizing work, inject our work with humanity and vulnerability, and help students view the college experience as the real world it is, we begin to liberate ourselves to work together with students, faculty, and administrators to create the inclusive learning environments we seek.

Discussion Questions

1. Reflect on the planning process behind the interventions and programs with which you presently work. What "scripts" operate subconsciously? Do you allow space for students to learn spontaneously?
2. Are there programs or initiatives for which your division or department is responsible that communicates one message through its content and another, conflicting message in the design of the activity?

3. How can you infuse more of your humanity and vulnerability in your work with students?

Notes

1. Dewey, J. (1988). Creative democracy: The task before us. In J. Boydston (Ed.), *John Dewey: The later works, 1925–1953* (Vol. 14, pp. 225–231). Carbondale, IL: Southern Illinois University Press.

2. Jones, S. R., this volume, p. 455.

3. Roberts, D. C. (1998). Student learning was always supposed to be the core of our work. *About Campus, 3(3),* 18–22, p. 19.

4. Ibid.

5. National Association of Student Personnel Administrators (1949). *The student personnel point of view.* Washington DC: Authors, p. 30.

6. Ibid.

7. Freire, P. (1970). *Pedagogy of the oppressed.* New York, NY: Bloomsbury, p. 74.

8. Hoffman, D. (2015). Fostering civic agency by making education (and ourselves) "real." In H. Boyte (Ed.), *Democracy's education: Public work, citizenship, and the future of colleges and universities* (pp. 154–160). Nashville, TN: Vanderbilt University Press.

9. Ibid.

10. Ibid.

CONTRIBUTORS

Josie Ahlquist is a digital engagement and leadership speaker, consultant, and coach. She is a research associate and online instructor with Florida State University Leadership Learning Research Center. Her research agenda focuses on teens' and young adults' digital experiences, senior executives' online leadership practices, and digital leadership pedagogy.

Rafael E. Alvarado is a doctoral candidate in higher education at the Pennsylvania State University. He is a graduate research assistant at the Center for the Study of Higher Education. He earned his bachelor's degree at Washington University in St. Louis, his master's degree in student affairs in higher education at Miami University of Ohio, and his law degree at Penn State Law.

Sonja Ardoin is a learner, educator, facilitator, author, scholar-practitioner and assistant professor of student affairs administration at Appalachian State University. Ardoin's research focuses on social class identity, college access and success for first-generation college students and students from rural areas, student and women's leadership, and professional preparation and career pathways in higher education and student affairs.

Cassie L. Barnhardt is associate professor of higher education and student affairs at the University of Iowa. She received her doctorate in higher education and two bachelor's degrees from the University of Michigan and a master's degree in student affairs from Michigan State University. Barnhardt's research focuses on civic and public engagement, including the ways college students learn about and enact social responsibility and the ways that universities, as organizations, contribute to democracy and civic life.

Marcia B. Baxter Magolda is distinguished professor emerita (Miami University). She received her master's degree and doctorate in higher education from The Ohio State University. Her 32-year longitudinal study of young adult development portrays the evolution of self-authorship and learning partnerships that promote developmental complexity.

Craig R. Berger is assistant director of community engaged learning at Kent State University. He previously held positions at the University of Maryland, Baltimore County and Penn State Erie, The Behrend College, and his areas of interest include civic learning, democratic engagement, and democratic pedagogy. Berger earned his bachelor's degree at Allegheny College and his master's degree at Miami University.

Nicholas A. Bowman is professor of higher education and student affairs and director of the Center for Research on Undergraduate Education at the University of Iowa. His research uses a social psychological lens to explore key issues in higher education, including diversity, student success, admissions, rankings, and quantitative methodology.

Jeannie Brown Leonard is dean of student academic affairs—advising, retention, and transitions at George Mason University, where previously she was a faculty member and director of an interdisciplinary adult degree-completion program. Brown Leonard earned a PhD in college student personnel from the University of Maryland, College Park, a MEd in higher education and student affairs from the University of Vermont, and a BA from Mount Holyoke College.

Hoa Bui is a resident director at Miami University in Ohio where she earned her master of science in student affairs in higher education. Bui holds a bachelor of arts in educational studies from Colgate University. She is interested in interrogating and exploring the higher education landscape through the lens of cultural studies, transnational studies, and postcolonial feminist studies.

Taran Cardone is director of the Office for Learning Partnerships and oversees the Thrive living-learning community at Virginia Tech. She earned her master's degree in student affairs in higher education from Miami University and is a doctoral student in the Leadership and Change program at Antioch University. Her work focuses on designing empowering learning-centered environments and integrating student affairs work through a personal learning design approach.

Rozana Carducci is associate professor and director of the master of arts in higher education program at Elon University. She earned her master's degree in college student personnel from Miami University and her doctorate in higher education and organizational change from the University of California, Los Angeles. Her research and teaching interests include higher education leadership, student affairs administration, qualitative methodology, and the politics of inquiry.

D. Chase J. Catalano is an assistant professor in college student personnel at Western Illinois University. He earned his master's degree in higher education administration and a doctorate of education in social justice education from the University of Massachusetts at Amherst. His research involves exploring the experiences of college students and their trans*ness, masculinities, and the inclusion of students with marginalized genders and sexualities in higher education.

Angela Cook is the assistant director of the MBA program at the University of Cincinnati, having previously worked in residence life, academic advising, training and development, and diversity education. Cook participated for three years in Teach for America in the Mississippi Delta. She earned her MEd in elementary education from Delta State University and MS in student affairs and higher education from Miami University.

Tiffany J. Davis is clinical assistant professor and program director of the higher education master's programs at the University of Houston. Her scholarship addresses the pipeline to and socialization within the higher education profession, Black contingent faculty within the academy, the experiences of Black students in higher education, and student and professionals' experiences at equity-oriented institutions. She earned her master's degree at Bowling Green State University and her doctorate at the University of Georgia.

Jill Dunlap is director for equity, inclusion, and violence prevention at NASPA. She received her PhD in political science from Northern Illinois University and has 14 years of administrative experience in student affairs at three different institutions. Her research focuses on prevention of and response to sexual and relationship violence on campus in addition to issues of equity and inclusion.

Michelle M. Espino, a first-generation college student, earned her master's degree in college student personnel at Bowling Green State University and her doctorate in higher education at the University of Arizona. She is associate professor of higher education, student affairs, and international education policy at the University of Maryland, College Park. Her research addresses individual, organizational, and community factors that affect educational attainment and career advancement for racial/ethnic minorities, particularly for Latinas/os/x.

Julia R. Golden is assistant dean of diversity inclusion, student affairs at Massachusetts College of Pharmacy and Health Sciences University. She earned her master's of education from Springfield College. She serves on the NASPA Region I regional advisory board and conference committee, where she created and directs the Ubuntu Institute for student affairs professionals of color.

Jessica Gunzburger promotes student learning, fosters staff development, and works toward justice in Housing & Residential Life at the University of Minnesota–Twin Cities. She earned her PhD from Miami University, MS from Western Illinois University, and BS from Iowa State University. Her dissertation research addressed cross-racial supervision of professionals in student affairs and how racism influences those supervision relationships.

Molly Reas Hall is associate director of assessment and evaluation at Virginia Tech. She previously held positions at Santa Clara University, Tufts University School of Medicine, and Radford University. She earned her master's degree in college student personnel from Miami University and her doctorate in educational research and evaluation from Virginia Tech.

Jessica C. Harris is assistant professor of higher education and organizational change at the University of California, Los Angeles. She earned her master's degree in college student affairs from the Pennsylvania State University and her doctorate in higher education from Indiana University. Her research addresses multiraciality in higher education, women of color and campus sexual violence, and the possibilities of using critical race theory to explore postsecondary contexts.

Gavin W. Henning is professor and program director of higher education at New England College. Henning is president of the Council for the Advancement of Standards in Higher Education (CAS) and has extensive experience in assessment. He has a PhD in educational policy and leadership studies, an MA in sociology from the University of New Hampshire, an MA in college and university administration, and a BS from Michigan State University.

Stephanie Hernandez Rivera is a doctoral student at the University of Missouri in the educational leadership and policy analysis program. She has previously worked in student affairs doing equity and inclusion work. Her primary research interest is the experiences of students who navigate with multiple marginalized identities.

Mei-Yen Ireland is executive director of Holistic Student Support at Achieving the Dream. Her scholarship addressed Deferred Action for Childhood Arrivals (DACA) college students' educational access and identity development. She earned her bachelor's degree from Lewis & Clark College, her master's degree from the University of Maryland College Park, and her doctorate from The Ohio State University.

Kathryn S. Jaekel is assistant professor of adult and higher education at Northern Illinois University. She earned her PhD from Iowa State University. Her research examines how lesbian, gay, bisexual, queer, and trans* students experience curriculum and classrooms in postsecondary contexts as well as the uses of critical pedagogy in college teaching.

R. Bradley Johnson is clinical associate professor of higher education at the University of North Carolina (UNC), Greensboro. He earned his master's degree in counselor education from Wake Forest University and his doctorate in curriculum and teaching from UNC Greensboro. His research interests include lesbian, gay, bisexual, transgender, queer plus (LGBTQ+) issues in higher education and students' experiences in residence hall environments.

Matthew R. Johnson is associate professor of educational leadership at Central Michigan University. He earned his master's degree from Miami University and doctorate from the University of Maryland, both in college student personnel. His research explores the intersections of leadership, civic engagement, and social justice.

Susan R. Jones is professor of higher education and student affairs at The Ohio State University. She earned her MA at the University of Vermont and her PhD at the University of Maryland. She held several positions in student affairs, including dean of students, prior to becoming a faculty member. Her research focuses on college student development, social identities, intersectionality, and qualitative methodologies.

Shamika N. Karikari is associate director in the Office of Residence Life at Miami University. She earned her MS from Miami University and her BA from Bowling Green State University. She is currently a PhD candidate at Miami University, and her primary research interest is Black women's leadership approaches.

Bridget Turner Kelly is associate professor of student affairs at the University of Maryland, College Park. She received her master's degree and doctorate in social foundations of education from the University of Maryland, College Park. Her scholarship focuses on the experiences of women, students, and faculty of color in higher education from a critical race and feminist lens.

Chris Linder is assistant professor of higher education at the University of Utah. Previously Linder worked as a student affairs educator for 10 years, primarily as director of a campus-based women's center, supporting survivors of sexual violence. Linder's research examines power and equity in higher education, with specific foci on sexual violence and student activism.

Cynthia H. Love is the CEO of Out for Undergrad (O4U) and former executive director of American College Personnel Association (ACPA)–College Student Educators International. Love is a content expert for the Center for Global Inclusion. She earned her bachelor's degree at Abilene Christian University, her master's degree from Louisiana Tech, and her doctorate of education from Texas Tech University.

Peter M. Magolda was professor emeritus (Miami University). He received a BA from LaSalle College, an MA from The Ohio State University, and a PhD from Indiana University. His scholarship focuses on ethnographic studies of college subcultures and critical issues in qualitative research. In 2016, he wrote *The Lives of Campus Custodians: Insights Into Corporatization and Civic Disengagement in the Academy* (Stylus Publishing).

Kelly E. Maxwell is assistant dean for undergraduate education at the University of Michigan and board chair of the Difficult Dialogues National Resource Center. Previously, she served as faculty codirector of the Program on Intergroup Relations at the University of Michigan. She earned her doctorate from Arizona State University, her master's degree from Florida State University, and her bachelor's degree from Baldwin Wallace University. Maxwell trains and conducts research on intergroup dialogue, social identity, facilitation training, and social justice education.

Jonathan A. McElderry is assistant dean of students and director of the Intercultural Center at Wake Forest University. He earned his bachelor's degree from George Mason University, his master's degree from Ohio University, and his doctorate from the University of Missouri. His experience in higher education has focused on enhancing diversity, equity, and inclusion on college campuses.

Susana M. Muñoz is assistant professor and codirector of higher education leadership in the School of Education at Colorado State University—Fort Collins. Muñoz employs critical race theories to examine activism and identity development, educational policies and equity, campus climate and college persistence for minoritized communities in higher education, specifically undocumented Latinx students. She earned her PhD in educational leadership and policy studies from Iowa State University.

Samuel D. Museus is professor of education studies at the University of California, San Diego, and director of the National Institute for Transformation and Equity (NITE). He previously held positions at the University of Massachusetts Boston, University of Hawaii at Manoa, University of

Denver, and Indiana University. His work advances knowledge about how institutions of higher education can cultivate more inclusive and equitable systems that allow diverse populations to thrive.

Ajay Nair is president of Arcadia University. He is a nationally recognized expert in student affairs issues and an accomplished social justice, race, and ethnicity scholar. He has delivered dozens of influential keynote speeches and penned more than 20 op-eds, book chapters, journal articles, and other publications that have influenced the landscape of higher education.

Z Nicolazzo is assistant professor of trans* studies of education in the Center for the Study of Higher Education and a member of the Trans* Studies Initiative at the University of Arizona. Nicolazzo earned a PhD in Student Affairs and Higher Education from Miami University in Ohio. Nicolazzo's research focuses on tracing discourses of gender in postsecondary education, with a specific focus on affirmative and resilience-based research alongside transgender college students.

Amelia Parnell is vice president for research and policy at NASPA and directs the Research and Policy Institute (RPI). Her research portfolio includes studies on leadership attributes of college presidents and vice presidents, documenting and assessing cocurricular learning, and assessment and evaluation in student affairs. Parnell holds a doctorate in higher education from Florida State University and master's and bachelor's degrees in business administration from Florida A&M University.

David Pérez II is associate professor of educational leadership at Miami University in Ohio. He received his PhD from Pennsylvania State University. His research integrates asset-based theories to understand and duplicate conditions that increase the success of undergraduate men of color and to prepare student affairs educators who serve underrepresented student populations.

Rosemary J. Perez is assistant professor of higher education and student affairs in the Iowa State University School of Education. She earned her BS from Carnegie Mellon University, her MEd from the University of Vermont, and her PhD from the University of Michigan. Her research explores college student learning and development, and she is particularly interested in graduate education, professional socialization, and the holistic development of graduate students.

Nick Rathbone earned his MEd in student affairs counseling at Northern Arizona University, where he is a career development specialist and program coordinator for student employment. In addition to building student-focused programs and coaching students toward their goals, Rathbone's talents include playing board games, writing haikus on-demand, and enacting racial justice.

Brian D. Reed is associate dean for student academic support services and dean of undergraduate students at Dartmouth College. Reed earned his PhD in higher education from the University of Virginia's Curry School of Education. His scholarly work focuses on first-generation and low-income student postsecondary access and completion.

P. Jesse Rine is clinical associate professor and director of the MS program in higher education administration at Duquesne University. He previously directed the research programs of the Council of Independent Colleges and the Council for Christian Colleges and Universities, and he also served as assistant provost at Grove City College, his undergraduate alma mater. He earned his MAT in Latin from Washington University in St. Louis and his PhD in higher education from the University of Virginia.

Sandra Rodríguez is director of the Associated Students of the University of Nevada Center for Student Engagement at the University of Nevada, Reno. She has 27 years of experience engaging students in civic learning and democratic engagement. Her focus is the strong ties between student engagement, civic literacy, civic agency, and equity and inclusion in creating just, democratic learning communities. She is a PhD candidate in higher education administration at University of Nevada, Reno.

Penny Rue is vice president for campus life and professor of counseling at Wake Forest University. She previously was vice chancellor for student affairs at the University of California, San Diego and dean of students at the University of Virginia. She earned her AB from Duke University, her MA from The Ohio State University, and her PhD in counseling and psychological services from the University of Maryland. She is board chair-elect for the NASPA.

Maria Sanchez Luna is a second year master's student of geography at Miami University (Ohio) and earned her bachelor's degree at The Ohio State University. She is a 2018 Hispanic Scholarship Fund scholar. She has worked and advocated for education equity and access to higher education for undocumented students in the state of Ohio. She has been an ambassador during national campaigns for educational equity and at her home universities.

Benjamin S. Selznick is assistant professor and coordinator of the postsecondary analysis and leadership concentration in the School of Strategic

Leadership Studies at James Madison University. He holds an MA and a PhD in higher education from New York University and a BA in religion from Dartmouth College. His research primarily focuses on how innovative educational practices and organizational cultures affect college student learning and development in the twenty-first century.

Tricia R. Shalka is assistant professor in the higher education program in the Warner School of Education and Human Development at the University of Rochester. She holds a BA from Dartmouth College, an MA from the University of Maryland, and a PhD from The Ohio State University. Her primary research area concerns the impacts of traumatic experience(s) on college students, particularly in terms of developmental outcomes.

Frank Shushok Jr. is senior associate vice president for student affairs and associate professor of higher education at Virginia Tech. He served as executive editor of *About Campus* since 2013. Shushok's scholarship focuses on student learning, positive psychology, and educational interventions that build community and strengthen friendship. He holds degrees from Baylor University; The Ohio State University; and the University of Maryland, College Park.

Naomi Daradar Sigg is director of multicultural affairs at Case Western Reserve University. She oversees initiatives that focus on equity, justice, and dialogue for undergraduate and graduate students. She earned both her bachelor's degree in political science and master's degree in college student personnel at Miami University (Ohio).

Laura Elizabeth Smithers is an assistant professor of higher education at Old Dominion University. She has decades of experience working in student athlete academic services at several Division I universities. Her research focuses on the possible futures created and foreclosed by assessment regimes in undergraduate education. She holds a PhD in critical and sociocultural studies in education from the University of Oregon.

Dafina-Lazarus (D-L) Stewart is professor in the School of Education and cochair of student affairs in higher education at Colorado State University. He earned his bachelor's degree from Kalamazoo College and master's and doctoral degrees from The Ohio State University. His research focuses on minoritized populations and issues of equity and justice in postsecondary education.

Monita C. Thompson is student life codirector of the Program on Intergroup Relations at the University of Michigan—Ann Arbor. Her work in intergroup relations focuses on the training, development, and support of peer educators in skills and techniques of intergroup dialogue facilitation, conflict management, and on becoming a social change agent. She is a graduate of Tennessee State University and Western Kentucky University.

Abby C. Trout is curriculum coordinator in the College of Liberal Arts career services at the University of Minnesota. Trout earned her master's degree in student affairs in higher education from Miami University and has worked in career services and academic advising for over a decade. In addition to assessment, she is also passionate about adoption, equity and diversity, and student development theory.

JoNes R. VanHecke is vice president for student life and dean of students at Gustavus Adolphus College. She earned her PhD in higher education at the University of Michigan and was on the Wabash National Study research team. She holds a master's degree from Indiana University and a bachelor's degree from Gustavus Adolphus College. Her scholar/practitioner research interests include college student development, liberal arts education, and citizenship/civic engagement.

Julie A. Manley White is senior vice president of student engagement and learning support at Onondaga Community College. She provides leadership and support for residence life, academic support services, enrollment management, academic advising, accessibility resources, student life and leadership, athletics, registration and records, and student support services. She received her bachelor's degree from Miami University, her master's degree from Xavier University, and her PhD from the University of Rochester.

Kelli D. Zaytoun is professor and graduate studies director in the department of English at Wright State University, where she was previously the director of women's studies and the women's center. Her work focuses on multiethnic American literature, identity and narrative (particularly the narration of self-concept and social consciousness), and the work of Gloria E. Anzaldúa.

(*Continued from following page*)

graduate students how to think about the future, but is also useful as a guide for the new professional in their first or second job who is thinking, 'What is next and how do I get there?!'"—*Robert A. Schwartz, Professor of Higher Education and Chair, Department of Educational Leadership and Policy Studies, Florida State University*

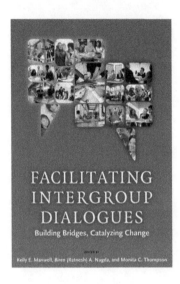

Facilitating Intergroup Dialogues

Building Bridges, Catalyzing Change

Edited by Kelly E. Maxwell, Biren Ratnesh Nagda, and Monita C. Thompson

Foreword by Patricia Gurin

"This is an invaluable resource for college administrators and faculty. As today's elected leaders and media shout past one another, our next generation needs to learn how to talk and work together across our political and social differences to address critical global concerns. This scholarly book provides the research and necessary practical, hands-on experience of how to facilitate constructive intergroup dialogues with students from different backgrounds."—*David Schoem, Director, Michigan Community Scholars Program, University of Michigan; Co-Editor of Intergroup Dialogue: Deliberative Democracy in School, College, Community and Workplace*

22883 Quicksilver Drive
Sterling, VA 20166-2019   Subscribe to our e-mail alerts: www.Styluspub.com

(Continued from following page)

Authoring Your Life

Developing Your INTERNAL VOICE to Navigate Life's Challenges

Marcia B. Baxter Magolda

Illustrated by Matthew Henry Hall

Foreword by Sharon Daloz Parks

"This book should be considered an essential addition to the library for the young professional just entering a career in academic advising. The emphasis placed on developing the skills to become a more independent thinker is essential to understanding the needs of college and university students who are in the early stages of understanding the complexities of becoming successful contributors to society as a whole."—*NACADA Journal (National Academic Advising Association)*

The Strategic Guide to Shaping Your Student Affairs Career

Sonja Ardoin

Foreword by Marcia B. Baxter Magolda

"This book fills a huge hole in the field of student affairs—namely, helping graduate students and new professionals chart a path for their career. By taking a strategic approach to identifying career goals and planning a deliberate approach to one's own professional development, Dr. Ardoin's book is a clear and useful guide to the profession. It will be very useful in teaching

(Continues on preceding page)

Also available from Stylus

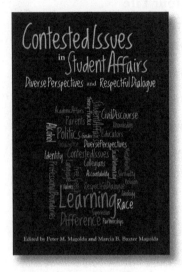

Contested Issues in Student Affairs

Diverse Perspectives and Respectful Dialogue

Edited by Peter M. Magolda and Marcia B. Baxter Magolda

Contested Issues in Student Affairs augments traditional introductory handbooks that focus on functional areas (e.g., residence life, career services) and organizational issues. It fills a void by addressing the social, educational and moral concepts and concerns of student affairs work that transcend content areas and administrative units, such as the tensions between theory and practice, academic affairs and student affairs, risk taking and failure; and issues of race, ethnicity, sexual orientation, and spirituality. It places learning and social justice at the epicenter of student affairs practice.

"It is not often that we witness our profession challenging, broadening, and clarifying questions in such an honest fashion . . . the smooth flow of the writing and format, the variety of perspectives presented, and the currency of the contested issues all offer a very thought-provoking and subsequently worthwhile read for graduate students in their preparation. This book will offer a sense of realities of student affairs practice. For that reason, professionals will also find this book useful as excellent fodder for professional development dialogue and reflection."—*Journal of College Student Development*

(Continues on preceding page)